PMP® Project Management Professional Study Guide, Third Edition

Joseph Phillips

New York   Chicago   San Francisco   Lisbon   London   Madrid
Mexico City   Milan   New Delhi   San Juan   Seoul   Singapore   Sydney   Toronto

The McGraw·Hill Companies

Cataloging-in-Publication Data is on file with the Library of Congress

McGraw-Hill books are available at special quantity discounts to use as premiums and sales promotions, or for use in corporate training programs. To contact a representative, please e-mail us at bulksales@mcgraw-hill.com.

PMP® Project Management Professional Study Guide, Third Edition

1 2 3 4 5 6 7 8 9 0   DOC DOC   0 1 9

ISBN: Book p/n 978-0-07-162670-5 and CD p/n 978-0-07-162671-2
of set 978-0-07-162673-6

MHID: Book p/n 0-07-162670-0 and CD p/n 0-07-162671-9
of set 0-07-162673-5

Sponsoring Editor Timothy Green	**Technical Editor** Peter Carr	**Composition** International Typesetting and Composition
Editorial Supervisor Jody McKenzie	**Copy Editor** Lisa McCoy	**Illustration** International Typesetting and Composition
Project Manager Madhu Bhardwaj, International Typesetting and Composition	**Proofreader** Laura Bowman **Indexer** Jack Lewis	**Art Director, Cover** Jeff Weeks
Acquisitions Coordinator Meghan Riley	**Production Supervisor** James Kussow	**Cover Series Design** Peter Grame

To my son, Kyle

About the Author

Joseph Phillips, PMP, CBAP, Project+, is the Director of Education for Project Seminars. He has managed and consulted on projects for industries including technical, pharmaceutical, manufacturing, and architectural, among others. Phillips has served as a project management consultant for organizations creating project offices, maturity models, and best-practice standardization.

As a leader in adult education, Phillips has taught organizations how to successfully implement project management methodologies, information technology project management, risk management, and other courses. Phillips has taught for Columbia College, University of Chicago, and Ball State University, among others. He is a Certified Technical Trainer and has taught more than 10,000 professionals. Phillips has contributed as an author or editor to more than 35 books on technology, careers, and project management.

Phillips is a member of the Project Management Institute and is active in local project management chapters. He has spoken on project management, project management certifications, and project methodologies at numerous trade shows, PMI chapter meetings, and employee conferences in the United States and in Europe. When not writing, teaching, or consulting, Phillips can be found behind a camera or on the working end of a fly rod. You can contact Phillips through www.projectseminars.com.

About the Technical Editor

Peter Carr, Ph.D., is the Director of the Masters in Management Sciences at the University of Waterloo in Canada. Peter has been involved in project management for the past 20 years as a consultant and professor. He managed internal consultancy for British Alcan Aluminum in their 20 UK plants, focusing on the implementation of large-scale manufacturing, supply chain, and information technology projects. He has consulted widely with organizations in the private and public sectors on project management, lean operations, and supply chain. He lives in Toronto, Canada.

Peter has also worked in university-level online education for the past 15 years and has wide experience in the development and management of online degree programs, especially at the master's level for working professionals. The Masters in Management Sciences at the University of Waterloo is a fully online master's program delivered to students globally. Peter is also Director of the University of Waterloo Certificate in Project Leadership, which he authored. The certificate program prepares students for the Project Management Professional examination and includes a strong focus on leadership and human and organizational aspects of project management. Students work with each other and their professor intensively online and gain a strong applied knowledge in project management and leadership. For more information please visit http://projectleadership.uwaterloo.ca. Peter has also authored courses at the bachelor's and master's levels in project management, including a master's-level project management course that has students working in virtual teams on projects involving technology-based third-world development with the world's major aid organizations.

CONTENTS AT A GLANCE

<u>Part III</u>
Appendices

CONTENTS

Part I
Project Initiation

Part II
PMP Exam Essentials

ACKNOWLEDGMENTS

Books, like projects, are never done alone.

Thank you to Peter Carr for keeping me on track and focused on the PMP exam objectives. Peter has been a great resource for ideas, practical application, and direction on the book's content. Thank you, as well, to my friend and editor Tim Green for his guidance on this book and others. Thanks, Tim, for the phone calls, encouragement, and willingness to let me bounce ideas off you—I'm lucky to count you among my friends. Thank you, Meghan, for keeping me on track and this book organized through the updates. Kudos, Riley! Lisa McCoy, thank you for helping me be a better writer. Thanks also to the production teams at McGraw-Hill Professional and International Typesetting & Composition for your hard work in making this book a success.

I would also like to thank the hundreds of folks that have attended my PMP Boot Camps over the past couple of years. Your questions, conversations, and recommendations have helped me write a better book. A big thank you to my friends Fred and Carin McBroom, Martha Thieme, Mike and Kelly Favory, John and Cara Konzelmann, and Greg and Mary Huebner. Finally, thanks to my parents, Don and Virginia Phillips, and my old, old brothers Steve, Mark, Sam, and Ben.

This book is organized in such a way as to serve as an in-depth review for the PMP® Project Management Professional exam for those with a strong foundation in project management, as well as for those who are new PMP candidates. Each chapter covers a major aspect of the exam, with an emphasis on the "why" as well as the "how to" of project management.

On the CD

For more information on the CD-ROM, please see the Appendix A "About the CD" at the back of the book.

Exam Readiness Checklist

At the end of the Introduction, you will find an Exam Readiness Checklist. This table has been constructed to allow you to cross-reference the official exam objectives with the objectives as they are presented and covered in this book. The checklist also allows you to gauge your level of expertise on each objective at the outset of your studies. This should allow you to check your progress and make sure you spend the time you need on more difficult or unfamiliar sections. References have been provided for the objective exactly as the Project Management Institute presents it, the section of the study guide that covers that objective, and a chapter and page reference.

In Every Chapter

We've created a set of chapter components that call your attention to important items, reinforce important points, and provide helpful exam-taking hints. Take a look at what you'll find in every chapter.

■ Every chapter begins with **Certification Objectives**—what you need to know in order to pass the section on the exam dealing with the chapter topic. The objective headings identify the objectives within the chapter, so you'll always know an objective when you see it!

■ **Exam Watch** notes call attention to information about, and potential pitfalls in, the exam. These helpful hints are written by the author, who has taken the exams and received his certification—who better to tell you what to worry about? He knows what you're about to go through!

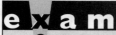

Don't forget that resources are more than just people. Equipment, facilities, and materials are resources, and these can affect the project duration too.

■ **On the Job** notes describe the issues that come up most often in real-world settings. They provide a valuable perspective on certification and product-related topics. They point out common mistakes and address questions that have arisen from on-the-job discussions and experience.

■ **Inside the Exam** sidebars highlight some of the most common and confusing problems that students encounter when taking a live exam. Designed to anticipate what the exam will emphasize, getting inside the exam will help ensure you know what you need to know to pass it. You can get a leg up on how to respond to those difficult-to-understand questions by focusing extra attention on these sidebars.

■ The **PMP Coach** is there to encourage you. It's the author's way of saying, "Keep going and don't give up!"

■ The **Certification Summary** is a succinct review of the chapter and a restatement of salient points regarding the exam.

- The **Key Terms** you will need to know for the exam, as well as their definitions, are listed after each Certification Summary.

- The **Two-Minute Drill** at the end of every chapter is a checklist of the main points of the chapter. It can be used for last-minute review.

Q&A
- The **Self Test** offers questions similar to those found on the certification exams. The answers to these questions, as well as explanations of the answers, can be found at the end of each chapter. By taking the Self Test after completing each chapter, you'll reinforce what you've learned from that chapter while becoming familiar with the structure of the exam questions.

Some Pointers

Once you've finished reading this book, set aside some time to do a thorough review. You might want to return to the book several times and make use of all the methods it offers for reviewing the material.

1. **Re-read all the Two-Minute Drills, or have someone quiz you.** You also can use the drills as a way to do a quick cram before the exam. You might want to make some flashcards out of 3 × 5 index cards that have the Two-Minute Drill material on them.

2. **Re-read all the Exam Watch notes and Inside the Exam elements.** Remember that these notes are written by authors who have taken the exam and passed. They know what you should expect—and what you should be on the lookout for.

3. **Re-take the Self Tests.** Taking the tests right after you've read the chapter is a good idea, because the questions help reinforce what you've just learned. However, it's an even better idea to go back later and do all the questions in the book in one sitting. Pretend that you're taking the live exam. When you go through the questions the first time, you should mark your answers on a separate piece of paper. That way, you can run through the questions as many times as you need to until you feel comfortable with the material.

INTRODUCTION

This book is divided into two major sections. The first section, which consists of Chapters 1, 2, and 3, discusses the broad overview of project management and how it pertains to the PMP examination. Section two contains Chapters 4 through 13, which detail each of the nine knowledge areas and the PMI Code of Ethics and Professional Conduct.

If you are just beginning your PMP quest, you should read the first section immediately, as it'll help you build a strong foundation for the PMP exam. If you find, however, that you've already a strong foundation in project management and need specific information on the knowledge areas, move on to the second section. PMP candidates who have years of project management experience can move on to the second section.

The book is designed so that you can read the chapters in any order you'd like. However, if you examine the *Guide to the Project Management Body of Knowledge*, you'll notice that the order of information presented is the same as the order of information in this book. In other words, you can read a chapter of the *PMBOK* and then read a more detailed explanation in this book. This book is a guide to the guide. In addition, practically every question in this book stems directly from the *PMBOK Guide* for additional information—so it's a good idea to have the *PMBOK* handy as you read.

Exam Readiness Checklist

Exam Domain and Exam Percentage	Chapter #
Initiating the Project......11%	
Conduct Project Selection Methods	1, 3, 4
Define Scope	1, 3, 4, 5
Document Project Risks, Assumptions, and Constraints	1, 3, 5, 11
Identify and Perform Stakeholder Analysis	1, 2, 3, 4, 5, 10
Develop Project Charter	1, 3, 4
Obtain Project Charter Approval	1, 3, 4
Planning the Project......23%	
Define and Record Requirements, Constraints, and Assumptions	1, 2, 3, 5, 6, 7
Identify Project Team and Define Roles and Responsibilities	1,3, 9
Create the WBS	1, 5
Develop Change Management Plan	5
Identify Risks and Define Risk Strategies	11
Obtain Plan Approval	1, 4
Conduct Kick-off Meeting	4, 5
Executing the Project......27%	
Execute Tasks Defined in Project Plan	1, 4, 5, 6, 7
Ensure Common Understanding and Set Expectations	1, 4, 5, 8
Implement the Procurement of Project Resources	1, 4, 5, 6, 7, 12
Manage Resource Allocation	5, 6, 7, 9, 12
Implement Quality Management Plan	4, 5, 8
Implement Approved Changes	4, 5, 6, 7, 8, 10, 11, 12
Implement Approved Actions and Workarounds	4, 5, 6, 7, 8, 11
Improve Team Performance	4, 9
Monitoring and Controlling the Project......21%	
Measure Project Performance	5, 6, 7, 8, 10, 11
Verify and Manage Changes to the Project	4, 5, 6, 7, 8, 9, 10, 11, 12

Exam Readiness Checklist

Exam Domain and Exam Percentage	Chapter #
Ensure Project Deliverables Conform to Quality Standards	4, 5, 8
Monitor All Risks	4, 5, 11
Closing the Project......9%	
Obtain Final Acceptance for the Project	4, 5, 10
Obtain Financial, Legal, and Administrative Closure	4, 5, 7, 10
Release Project Resources	3, 4, 5, 9
Identify, Document, and Communicate Lessons Learned	4, 5, 6, 7, 8, 9, 10
Create and Distribute Final Project Report	4, 5, 10
Archive and Retain Project Records	10
Measure Customer Satisfaction	1, 3, 4, 8, 9, 10
Professional and Social Responsibility......9%	
Ensure Individual Integrity	9, 13
Contribute to the Project Management Knowledge Base	13
Enhance Personal Professional Competence	9, 13
Promote Interaction Among Stakeholders	4, 5, 10, 13

Part I

Project Initiation

1

Introducing Project Management

Your PMP examination is based on your experience, your ability to problem-solve, and a strong foundation in project management. This chapter aims to explain how both this book and *PMI's Guide to the Project Management Body of Knowledge* can help you grasp what you must know to pass the exam. From now on, references to *PMI's A Guide to the Project Management Body of Knowledge* will be called the *PMBOK Guide* – fourth edition (pronounced pim-bok).

Besides learning about the *PMBOK Guide* and the exam, we'll dive into what a project is, how project management works, the process itself, and knowledge areas regarding both project management and how project offices operate. We've lots to do, so let's go!

CERTIFICATION OBJECTIVE 1.01

The *PMBOK Guide*, This Book, and the PMP Exam

If you've ever sat down to read the *PMBOK Guide*, you've obviously had a lot of time on your hands, you were really curious about it, or someone told you it was required reading for passing the Project Management Professional (PMP) examination. Here's the truth about the *PMBOK Guide*: It's boring. My apologies to all my friends at Project Management Institute (PMI), but it's true. The *PMBOK Guide* is, however, concise, organized, and an excellent reference manual. I use it all the time. But it's not written to be a thriller.

The fourth edition of the *PMBOK Guide* will be referenced throughout this book. Why? Well, your PMP exam is largely based on the facts, figures, and subtleties of the *PMBOK Guide*. The good news is that unlike the *PMBOK Guide*—fine book that it is—the book you have in your hands is written in plain language. This book, unlike the *PMBOK Guide*, focuses on how to pass the PMP exam. It will also help you be a better project manager and explain some mysterious formulas and concepts, but its main goal is to get you over the hump toward those three glorious letters: PMP.

All About the *PMBOK Guide*

The *PMBOK Guide* is, as its abbreviated name suggests, a guide, not the end-all-be-all of project management. It's based on what's generally recognized as good practice on most projects most of the time. It's not specific to IT, construction, manufacturing, or any other discipline, being applicable to any industry, any project, and any project manager.

For the most part, if you follow the *PMBOK Guide*, you'll increase your odds of project success. That means you'll be more likely to complete the project scope, reach the cost objectives of your project's budget, and achieve those schedule commitments your project must adhere to. But there's no guarantee.

PMP Coach

*Throughout this book, you'll see little tips like this one. These tips are here to cheer you on, get you moving, and remind you that you can do this. Create a strategy to study this book and the **PMBOK Guide**, and keep working towards your goal of earning the PMP.*

ON THE CD

See the video Earning the PMP.

The *PMBOK Guide* readily admits that not everything in it should be applied to every conceivable project. That just wouldn't make sense. Consider a small project to swap out all of the workstation lights in an office building versus that of building a skyscraper. Guess which one needs more detail and will likely implement more of the practices the *PMBOK Guide* defines. The skyscraper project, of course.

All About This Book

Your PMP examination is based largely on the *PMBOK Guide*. As mentioned, the *PMBOK Guide* is not a study guide. But this book is. The following explains what this book will do for you:

- Cover all of the objectives as set by PMI for the PMP examination
- Focus only on exam objectives
- Prep you to pass the PMP exam, not just take it
- Encapsulate exam essentials for each exam objective
- Offer 925 PMP total practice questions
- Serve as a handy project management reference guide
- Not be boring

Every chapter in this book correlates to a chapter in the *PMBOK Guide*. If you have a copy of the *PMBOK Guide*, blow the dust off it and flip through its 12 chapters. Now flip through this book, and you'll see that it covers the same 12 chapters in the same order. And there's a magical Chapter 13. Okay, it's not magical, but it explains in detail the Code of Ethics and Professional Conduct, which is a major exam objective. Chapter 13 covers leadership, motivation, and how to balance stakeholder interests. Chapter 13 also introduces the concept of project priorities and dealing with cultural issues.

Each chapter is full of exciting, action-packed, and riveting information. Well, that's true if you find the PMP exam exciting, action-packed, and riveting. Anyway, each chapter covers a specific topic relevant to the PMP exam. The first three chapters of this book offer a big-picture view of project management, while the remaining 10 chapters are the ones most specific to the PMP exam.

In each chapter, you'll find an Inside the Exam sidebar. This is what I considered to be the most important message from the chapter. At the end of the chapter, you'll find a quick summary, key terms, and a two-minute drill that recaps all the major points of the chapter. Then you'll be given a 25-question exam that's specific to just that chapter.

e x a m

w a t c h

The questions in this book will give you some idea of what to expect on the actual PMP exam. Those contained here, though not the actual exam questions, are styled similarly to what you'll eventually run into. Focus on understanding why your answer to a question was right or wrong. The questions are part of the learning process. I have, I believe, written the questions in this book and on its accompanying CD to be tricky, pesky questions. My logic is that if you can make it through my exams, you should be able to get through the PMP, too.

All About the PMP Exam

Not everyone can take the PMP exam—you have to qualify to take it. And this is good. The project management community should want the PMP exam to be tough, the application process to be rigorous, and the audits to be thorough. All of this will help elevate the status of the PMP and ensure it doesn't fall prey to the "paper certifications" other professions have seen.

Here are the major details of the 2009 PMP examination:

- As of this writing, a score of 61 percent is required to pass the exam. The exam has 200 questions, 25 of which don't actually count towards your passing score. These 25 questions are scattered throughout your exam and are used to collect statistics regarding student responses to see if they should be incorporated into future examinations. So this means you'll actually have to answer 106 correct questions out of 175 live questions.

- Clear and factual evidence of project management experience must be shown in each process group. On your PMP exam application, you'll have to provide specifics on tasks you've completed in a process group. (See Table 1-1 for specific examples from PMI.)

- Each application is given an extended review period. If your application needs an audit, you'll be notified via e-mail.

- Applicants must provide contact information for supervisors on all projects listed on their PMP exam application. In the past, applicants did not have to provide project contact information unless their application was audited. Now each applicant must give project contact information as part of the exam application.

- Once the application has been approved, candidates have one year to pass the exam. If you procrastinate in taking the exam by more than a year, you'll have to start the process over.

- PMP candidates are limited to three exam attempts within one year. If they fail each time during that period, they'll have to wait one year before resubmitting their exam application.

PMP
Coach

Always check the exam details through the PMI website: www.pmi.org. They can change this information whenever they like.

The PMP exam will test you on your experience and knowledge in six different areas, as Table 1-1 shows. You'll have to provide specifics on tasks completed in each knowledge area of your PMP examination application. The following domain specifics and their related exam percentages are taken directly from PMI's website regarding the PMP examination. While this information is correct as of this writing, always hop out to www.pmi.org and check their site for any updates as you prepare to pass the PMP exam.

TABLE I-I	Exam Domain	Domain Tasks	Percentage of Exam
The Six Domains of Experience Needed to Pass the PMP Exam	Initiating the Project		11.59 percent
		Conduct Project Selection Methods	
		Define Scope	
		Document Project Risks, Assumptions, and Constraints	
		Identify and Perform Stakeholder Analysis	
		Develop Project Charter	
		Obtain Project Charter Approval	
	Planning the Project		22.7 percent
		Define and Record Requirements, Constraints, and Assumptions	
		Identify the Project Team and Define Roles and Responsibilities	
		Create the Work Breakdown Structure (WBS)	
		Develop a Change Management Plan	
		Identify Risks and Define Risk Strategies	
		Obtain Plan Approval	
		Conduct Kick-off Meeting	
	Executing the Project		27.5 percent
		Execute Tasks Defined in Project Plan	
		Ensure Common Understanding and Set Expectations	
		Implement the Procurement of Project Resources	
		Manage Resource Allocation	
		Implement a Quality Management Plan	
		Implement Approved Changes	

TABLE 1-1	Exam Domain	Domain Tasks	Percentage of Exam
The Six Domains of Experience Needed to Pass the PMP Exam *(continued)*		Implement Approved Actions and Workarounds	
		Improve Team Performance	
	Monitoring and Controlling the Project		21.03 percent
		Measure Project Performance	
		Verify and Manage Changes to the Project	
		Ensure Project Deliverables Conform to Quality Standards	
		Monitor All Risks	
	Closing the Project		8.57 percent
		Obtain Final Acceptance for the Project	
		Obtain Financial, Legal, and Administrative Closure	
		Release Project Resources	
		Identify, Document, and Communicate Lessons Learned	
		Create and Distribute Final Project Report	
		Archive and Retain Project Records	
		Measure Customer Satisfaction	
	Professional and Social Responsibility		8.61 percent
		Ensure Individual Integrity	
		Contribute to the Project Management Knowledge Base	
		Enhance Personal Professional Competence	
		Promote Interaction Among Stakeholders	
	TOTAL		100.00 percent

CERTIFICATION OBJECTIVE 1.02

Defining What a Project Is—and Is Not

Projects are endeavors. Projects are temporary. A project creates something, provides a service, or brings about a result. I know, I know, it sounds like some marriages.

To define a project, you only have to think of some work that has a deadline associated with it, involves resources besides you, has a budget to satisfy the scope of the project work, and you can state what the end result of the project should be. So, projects are temporary work assignments, with a budget, that require some amount of resources, some amount of time to complete, and create a definite deliverable, service, or environment.

Let's look at project characteristics in more detail.

Projects Are Temporary

Regardless of what some projects may feel like, they are usually temporary. Like a good story, projects have a beginning, a middle, and an end. Projects end when the scope of the project has been met—usually. Sometimes projects end when the project runs out of time or cash or when it becomes clear that the project won't be able to complete the scope objectives, so it's scrapped.

The goal of a project will vary based on what the project's deliverable is, but typically, the result is to create something that'll be around longer than the process it took to create it. For example, if you're managing a project to create a skyscraper, you expect the skyscraper to be around much longer than the time it took to build it.

So *temporary* usually means that the *project* is temporary, *not* the deliverable. Notice the word *usually*? You can have a project to host a giant picnic for your entire organization and its customers. The project's logistics, invitations, and coordination of chefs may take months to complete, but the picnic will only last for a few hours. However, you could argue that although the picnic event was temporary, the memories and goodwill your picnic created could last a lifetime. (That had better be one good picnic!)

Sometimes *temporary* describes the market window. We've all seen fads come and go over the past years: pet rocks, the dot.com boom, streaking, and more. Projects can often be created that capitalize on fads, which means projects have to deliver fast before the fad fades away and the next craze begins. Fads and opportunities are temporary; projects that feed off these are temporary as well.

When's the last time you managed a project where the entire project team stuck with the project through the entire duration? It probably doesn't happen often. Project teams are often more temporary than the project itself, but typically, project teams only last as long as the project does. Once the project is complete, the team disbands and the project team members move on to other projects within the organization.

Projects Create Unique Products, Services, or Results

This one isn't tough to figure out. Projects have to create a thing, invent a service, or change an environment. The deliverable of the project—a successful project, that is—satisfies the scope that was created way, way back when the project got moving. Projects create the following:

- **Things**   Projects can create a thing such as a skyscraper, which is the end of the project. Or projects can create components that contribute to other projects or things, such as a project to install all of the glass windows in a skyscraper.
- **Services**   A project creating a service could establish a new call center, an order fulfillment process, or a faster way to complete inventory audits.
- **Results**   Projects can be research-driven. Consider a research-and-development project with a pharmaceutical company to find a cure for the common cold.

Projects are unique. This means that every project you ever do is different from all the other projects you've done in the past. Even if it's the same basic approach to get to the same end result, there are unique factors within each project, such as the time it takes, the stakeholders involved, the environment the project takes place in, and on and on the uniqueness goes. Basically, all projects are unique, even if your company does the same type of project repeatedly. Lucky you.

Progressive Elaboration

All projects begin as a concept. A project concept to create a new product or service typically includes a broad vision of what the end result of the project will be. The temporary project results in the unique product or service through progressive elaboration. Progressive elaboration is simply developing in steps and continuing by increments. For example, you'd take the project scope, decompose it to the work breakdown structure (WBS), then make an activity list, and so on. This is just one example of progressive elaboration.

As a project moves closer to completion, the identified needs that launched the project are revisited and monitored. Complete understanding of the needs—and the ability to fulfill those needs—comes from progressive elaboration. Progressive elaboration is an iterative process designed to correctly and completely fulfill the project objectives. This is evident in how the planning and execution processes each contribute to one another. A similar example can be seen in the process to create a WBS. The WBS begins with the project vision, which is then elaborated upon to create the project scope, and then expanded again into the WBS, and so on.

Consider a concept to construct a new building that would handle the manufacturing and shipping of blue jeans. The headlines of this project would be planning and then the construction, with materials delivered, assembly equipment, and the outward-bound shipping bays.

As the project team continues to research the needs and expectations of the project, the project vision would be refined, honed, and polished to a detailed outline of what the project would deliver. As you can see in Figure 1-1, through incremental steps, the project plan is developed and the unique project deliverables are created.

FIGURE 1-1

Progressive elaboration is the refinement that project components pass through to reach their final state, such as a project plan.

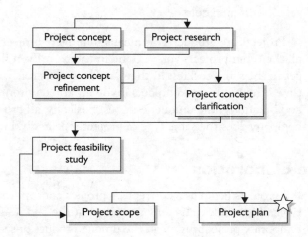

Projects vs. Operations

Meet Jane. Jane is a project manager for her organization. Vice presidents, directors, and managers with requests to investigate or to launch potential projects approach her daily—or so it seems to Jane. Just this morning, the sales manager met with Jane because he wants to implement a new direct-mail campaign to all of the customers in the sales database. He wants this direct-mail campaign to invite customers to visit the company website to see the new line of products. Part of the project also requires that the company website be updated so that it's in sync with the mailing. Sounds like a project, but is it really? Could this actually be just a facet of an ongoing operation?

In some organizations, everything is a project. In other organizations, projects are rare exercises in change. There's a fine line between projects and operations, and often, these separate entities overlap in function. Consider the following points shared by projects and operations:

- Both involve employees
- Both typically have limited resources: people, money, or both
- Both are hopefully designed, executed, and managed by someone in charge

In the preceding example, Jane has been asked to manage a direct-mail campaign to all of the customers in the sales database. Could this be a project? Sure—if this company has never completed a similar task and there are no internal departments that do this type of work as part of their regular activities. Often, projects are confused with general business duties: marketing, sales, manufacturing, and so on. The tell-tale sign of a project is that it has an end date and that it's unique from other activities within the organization. Some examples of projects include

- Designing a new product or service
- Converting from one computer application to another
- Building a new warehouse
- Moving from one building to another
- Organizing a political campaign
- Designing and building a new airplane

The end results of projects can result in operations. For example, imagine a company creating a new airplane. This new airplane will be a small personal plane (like one of those bubble cars from *The Jetsons*) that would allow people to fly to different destinations with the same freedom they use in driving their car. The project team will have to design an airplane from scratch that'd be similar to a car so consumers could easily adapt and fly to Sheboygan at a moment's notice. The project to create a personal plane is temporary, but not necessarily short-term. It may take years to go from concept to completion—but the project does have an end date. A project of this magnitude may require hundreds of prototypes before a working model is ready for the marketplace. In addition, there are countless regulations, safety issues, and quality control concerns that must be pacified before completion.

Once the initial plane is designed, built, and approved, the end result of the project is business operations. As the company creates a new vehicle, they would follow through with the design by manufacturing, marketing, selling, supporting, and improving the product. The initial design of the airplane is the project—the business of manufacturing it, supporting sold units, and marketing the product constitutes the ongoing operations part of business.

Operations are the day-to-day work that goes on in the organization. A manufacturer manufactures things, scientists complete research and development, and businesses provide goods and services. Operations are the heart of organizations. Projects, on the other hand, are short-term endeavors that fall outside of the normal day-to-day operations an organization offers.

on the job

Let's be realistic. In some companies, everything's a project. This is probably true if you work in an organization that completes projects for other companies. That's fine and acceptable, however, since you're participating in management by projects.

Once the project is complete, the project team moves along to other projects and activities. The people who are actually building the airplanes on the assembly line, however, have no end date in sight and will continue to create airplanes as long as there's a demand for the product.

exam Watch

The customer is the most important person in the project. He is the one the project is for.

Projects and Strategic Planning

Sometimes, if not always, projects are weird. I say weird because projects often don't fit into the normal day-to-day operations of an organization. Maybe weird isn't the best word after all. How about unique? They're unique because they don't fit into the regular operations of a company and there's been some special reason why the project has been created. Work and deliverables that don't fit into the normal day-to-day operations but still have merit for the organization are logical opportunities for a project.

INSIDE THE EXAM

The PMP exam is not for rookies. The application process alone can filter out the unqualified and the merely curious. You've purchased this book to find more information on how to pass the exam, what the exam entails, and to prep for your exam—a wise decision. Now, make another wise decision: Begin completing your PMP exam application. The application process can be lengthy, since you'll have to track down past information relating to projects you've completed.

By starting sooner rather than later in completing your exam application, you'll be focusing more on completing your exam studies than on completing the exam application. In addition, response time from the Project Management Institute (PMI) to accept and approve your application can vary from a few days to weeks. Start now and you'll be on your way.

You will be presented with scenario-based questions that will test your project management abilities. The chapter exams and the exams on the CD have been written to be tricky, tough, and to make you think. Practice these exams repeatedly, and they'll help you prepare to pass your PMP exam.

Besides answering practice questions, you'll want to focus on how the project manager should react in different scenarios. Specifically, you'll need to know how the project manager works through the project processes.

You should be familiar with the project management process groups, what a project deliverable is, and the requirements of a project scope.

All projects are bound by the Triple Constraints of Project Management: time, cost, and scope. Quality is affected by the balance of these three components. The Triple Constraints model is also known as the Iron Triangle, as shown in the following illustration. If any one angle of the triangle changes, the other two should change as well—if not, quality will suffer.

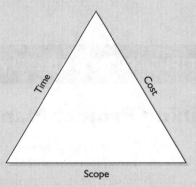

Know that the project moves through phases to reach completion. The project manager oversees the project work as it moves through phases, but the project customer must approve the work. Specifically, the results of phases must pass through scope verification, which is the formal acceptance of the project work.

Consider the reasons why a project is created:

■ **Opportunity**   Your company is growing so quickly that a project is launched to create a sales- and order-fulfillment application.

■ **Problems**   All of the computers are older than Moses, so a project is launched to replace all of the computers and standardize office applications.

■ **Customers**   Many organizations, such as IT integrators, construction companies, architects, and dozens more, complete projects for other people. Customers drive new projects.

■ **Technology**   Technology changes so quickly that there are constantly new technical projects within an organization.

■ **Lawyers**   Laws can cause a new project to launch. Consider the recent Sarbanes-Oxley requirements, for example. This new law spurred many projects to adhere to the new privacy requirements. Laws and regulations within different industries can also spur new projects—consider pharmaceutical, insurance, health care, and on and on. Regulations are required, but standards are guidelines.

CERTIFICATION OBJECTIVE 1.03

Defining Project Management

Project management is the supervision and control of the work required to complete the project vision. The project team carries out the work needed to complete the project, while the project manager schedules, monitors, and controls the various project tasks. Projects, being the temporary and unique things that they are, require the project manager to be actively involved with the project implementation. They are not self-propelled.

Project management is comprised of the following nine knowledge areas. Chapters 4 through 12 will explore these knowledge sections in detail.

■ **Project integration management**   This knowledge area focuses on creating the project charter, the project scope statement, and a viable project plan. Once the project is in motion, project integration management is all about monitoring and controlling the work. If changes happen, and we know they will, you have to determine how that change may affect all of the other knowledge areas.

- **Project scope management** This knowledge area deals with the planning, creation, protection, and fulfillment of the project scope. One of the most important activities in all of project management happens in this knowledge area: creation of the work breakdown structure. Oh, joy!

- **Project time management** Time management is crucial to project success. This knowledge area covers activities, their characteristics, and how they fit into the project schedule. This is where you and the project team will define the activities, plot out their sequence, and calculate how long the project duration will actually take.

- **Project cost management** Cost is always a constraint in project management. This knowledge area is concerned with the planning, estimating, budgeting, and control of costs. Cost management is tied to time and quality management—screw either of these up and the project costs will increase.

- **Project quality management** What good is a project that's done on time if the scope isn't complete, the work is faulty, or the deliverable is horrible? Well, it's no good. This knowledge area centers on quality planning, assurance, and control.

- **Project human resource management** This knowledge area focuses on organizational planning, staff acquisition, and team development. You have to somehow acquire your project team, develop this team, and then lead them to the project results.

- **Project communications management** Ninety percent of a project manager's time is spent communicating. This knowledge area details how communication happens, outlines stakeholder management, and shows how to plan for communications within any project.

- **Project risk management** Every project has risks. This knowledge area focuses on risk planning, analysis, monitoring, and control. You'll have to complete qualitative analysis and then quantitative analysis in order to adequately prepare for project risks. Once the project moves forward, you'll need to monitor and react to identified risks as planned.

- **Project procurement management** Projects often need things and services in order to reach closing. This knowledge area covers the business of project procurement, the processes to acquire and select vendors, and contract negotiation. The contract between the vendor and the project manager's organization will guide all interaction between the project manager and the vendor.

Project Management Application Areas

Project management application areas are projects that fit into different disciplines, but the approach to project management is similar. For example, an application area is construction. Another application area is information technology management. Another is manufacturing. Each application has specific approaches, disciplines, and characteristics that are totally different from any other application in the world.

Now, within each application area, you have a project management approach. In terms of the PMP exam, the project management approach is basically the same. The project work itself, however, is unique. In other words, and these are good words, you won't have to know much about application areas to pass your PMP exam. You will, however, need to know all about project management to pass the exam.

The following are some examples of application areas:

- Sales, law, manufacturing, marketing, and any other functional disciplines you'd find in just about any company
- Technical disciplines, such as mechanical engineering, architectural design, software development, and more
- Management categories, such as consulting, research and development, and community development

Management by Projects

In today's competitive, tight-margin business world, organizations have to move and respond quickly to opportunities. Many companies have moved from a functional environment—that is, organization by function—to an organization, or management, by projects. A company that organizes itself by job activity, such as sales, accounting, information technology, and other departmental entities, is a functional environment. A company that manages itself by projects may be called a projectized company.

An organization that uses projects to move the company forward is using the *Management by Projects* approach. These project-centric entities could manage any level of their work as a project. These organizations, however, apply general business skills to each project to determine its value, efficiency, and, ultimately, the return on investment. As you can imagine, some projects are more valuable, more efficient, or more profitable than others.

There are many examples of organizations that use this approach. Consider any business that completes projects for their clients, such as architectural, graphic design, consulting, or other service industries. These service-oriented businesses typically complete projects as their business.

The following are some other examples of management by projects:

- Training employees for a new application or business method
- Marketing campaigns
- The entire sales cycle from product or service introduction, proposal, and sales close
- Work completed for a client outside of the organization
- Work completed internally for an organization

Understanding the Project Environment

The project environment is more than where the project work will take place—though that should also be considered. The project environment is a term to describe the impact the project will have, good or bad, on the cultural, political, and physical environments. The project manager must examine the project environment and consider the influence of each environment on the project's success—and vice versa. Consider the influence and impact of each of the following:

- **Physical environment**   Before a project begins, the project manager should ensure that project team members or consultants evaluate the effect of the project on the physical environment where the project will take place—and how the physical environment will affect the project's success. The ecology, geographical makeup, and the health of the environment must be considered as part of the project planning processes.
- **Cultural and social environment**   This one isn't pleasant. Every project manager should examine how the project might affect the cultural and social environment, and how the cultural and social environment might affect the project. Consider a technical project that will move all of an organization's

computer operating systems to a standard operating system (OS). What if the majority of the employees don't like the OS that's been selected? There'll be complaints, work slowdown, a decline in morale, and challenges throughout the project implementation. In addition, the project manager (PM) must understand the autonomy he or she has within an organization and the affect the level of power will have on the project's success.

- **International and political environment** Projects that span multiple countries require knowledge of the laws and customs of each environment the project influences. Project managers must also consider the political consideration of international projects. Finally, the environment also includes time zone differences, holidays, travel logistics, face-to-face and teleconference meetings, currency exchanges, and language barriers.

on the job

A nice way to term a "cultural issue" is to call it cultural achievability. It's a way to describe the unhappiness and unrest that often accompany an unpopular or unpleasant project. It means it's difficult to gain consensus and buy-in on the project's value in an organization.

The environment that affects the ability of a project to operate is something every project manager must consider when a new project is launched. The specific conditions of the environment are called enterprise environmental factors. You'll see this term often throughout this book and probably on your PMP exam. The term *enterprise environmental factors* is just a nice way of describing the conditions, rules, policies, and culture that the project must operate within. Some enterprise environmental factors can constrain the project manager, while other factors can be a boon to the project.

Relying on General Management Skills

You cannot be an effective project manager without some abilities as a manager. Makes sense, right? Get this: Management is focused on results. So, to get your project team, vendors, and stakeholders to create project results, you should rely on the following:

- Planning for project strategy, tactics to achieve objectives, and operational planning
- Accounting and cash flow management

- Sales and marketing (within your organization and to stakeholders outside of the project)
- Procurement processes, including contracting procedures
- Logistics for travel, schedule, supply chain, and order fulfillment
- Human resource practices and procedures, including working within organizational structures; managing team personnel, compensation, and benefits; and helping project team members reach their career goals
- Industry-specific health and safety practices
- Working with information technology

Relying on Interpersonal Skills

Having interpersonal skills doesn't mean you're the "nice guy" everyone takes advantage of. Interpersonal skills are your abilities as a project manager to get along with stakeholders, be somewhat likeable, and work with others to reach an outcome on disagreements, problems, and challenges within the project. Interpersonal skills include the following:

- **Problem solving**   Part of being a good project manager is the ability to problem-solve. Even the PMP exam is a good example of problem solving.
- **Motivating**   You need to have the ability to motivate your project team to move forward with the project and their work and to energize your project team to excel.
- **Communicating**   Communication is a huge part of the project manager's job, so you'll have to be able to communicate effectively with your project team and stakeholders.
- **Influencing the organization**   You know there are undercurrents of politics, procedures, and other influences that affect your project's ability to move forward. The ability to influence the organization is how you operate within stated and implied confines to get things done.
- **Leadership**   A good project manager is a good leader. Leadership involves motivating and inspiring the project team and stakeholders to move forward.
- **Negotiations**   It's not unusual for conflicts to arise within a project. The project manager must be able to negotiate, solve conflicts, and keep the project moving forward.

Examining Related Areas of Project Management

Project management is the administration of activities to change the current state of an organization into a desired future state. It is a complex organization of decision-making, planning, implementation, control, and documentation of the experience from start to finish. In addition to traditional project management, there are related areas you may encounter, have encountered, or are actively participating in. These related aspects often are superior to individual project management, are part of project management, or equate to less than the management of any given project.

In this section, we'll dissect the related areas of project management and see how they tie together to change a current state to a desired future state.

Program Management

Program management is the management of multiple projects all working in unison toward a common goal. Consider all of the work that goes into building a skyscraper. Within the overall work, several projects may lead to the result, as demonstrated in Figure 1-2. You could have a project for the planning and design of the building. Another project could manage the legal, regulatory, and project inspections

FIGURE 1-2

Programs consist of multiple projects working together toward a common goal.

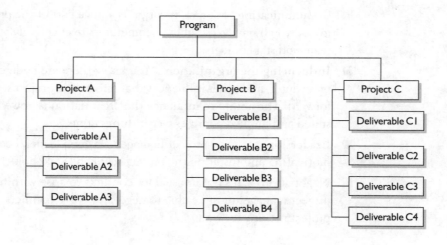

that would be required for the work to continue. Another project could be the physical construction of the building, while other projects might entail electrical wiring, elevators, plumbing, interior design, and more. Could one project manager effectively manage all of these areas of expertise? Possibly, but probably not.

A better solution could be to create a program that is comprised of multiple projects. Project managers would manage each of the projects within the program and report to the program manager. The program manager would ensure that all of the integrated projects work together on schedule, on budget, and ultimately towards the completion of the program.

In other instances, the program is an ongoing effort that really does not have an end in sight. Consider the publication of a newspaper, newsletter, website, or magazine. Essentially, the workers of these publications do the same activities for each issue, but each issue is unique and different from the last.

Another example is NASA's space program. It's an organization developed to explore space, and it is comprised of individual projects within that program. Each project under the program has its own goals, initiatives, and objectives that are in alignment with the overall mission of the space program. Programs are a collection of individual projects working in alignment towards a common end.

Project Portfolio Management

Often, projects are lumped into a portfolio rather than into a program. A program is a collection of projects that work together for a common cause. For example, a program could be a collection of projects to build a skyscraper. A portfolio describes the collection of investments in the form of projects and programs in which the organization invests capital. The project manager and, if applicable, the program manager report to a portfolio review board on the performance of the projects and programs. The portfolio review board may also direct the selection of projects and programs.

Portfolio projects could be interdependent, but they don't have to be. A portfolio is not the same as a program, but it is a collection of projects. The projects in a portfolio could be within one line of business, based on the strategies within an organization, or follow the guidance of one director within an organization.

 on the job

Project selections may pass through a project selection committee, where these executives will look at the return on investment, the value of the project, risks associated with taking on the project, and other attributes of the project. This is all part of project portfolio management.

Subproject Implementation

Subprojects are an alternative to programs. Some projects may not be wieldy enough to require the creation of a full-blown program, yet they may still be large enough that some of the work can be delegated to a subproject. A subproject exists under the parent project, but it follows its own schedule to completion. Subprojects may be outsourced, assigned to other project managers, or managed by the parent project manager but with a different project team. The following illustration shows a project containing multiple subprojects.

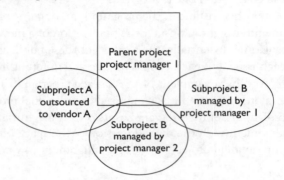

Subprojects are often areas of a project that are outsourced to vendors. For example, if you were managing a project to create a new sound system for home theaters, a subproject could be the development of the user manual included with the sound system. You would thus hire writers and graphic designers to work with your project team. The writers and designers would learn all about the sound system and then retreat to their own space to create the user manual according to their project methodology. The deliverable of their subproject would be included in your overall project plan, but the actual work done to complete the manual would not be in your plan. You'd simply allot the funds and time required by the writers and graphic designers to create the manual.

Subprojects do, however, follow the same quality guidelines and expectations of the overall project. The project manager has to work with the subproject team regarding scheduling, value, and cost to ensure the deliverables and activities of the subproject integrate smoothly with the "master" project.

Working with a Project Management Office

A project management office (PMO) organizes and manages control over all projects within an organization. A PMO is also known as a program management office, project office, or simply the program office. (And I'm sure some project managers have other names for them that won't be on the PMP exam.)

PMOs usually coordinate all aspects, methodology, and nomenclature for project processes, templates, software, and resource assignment. Ideally, a PMO creates a uniform approach within an organization so that all projects, regardless of their discipline, technology, or purpose, are managed with the same approach.

Besides creating a uniform approach to project management within an organization, a PMO provides support to the project managers. The support they give will vary, of course, from organization to organization. Typically, project managers that act within a PMO can expect training, software, templates, standardized project management approaches, and mentoring for project managers.

PMOs have an advantage over decentralized project management: risk and communication centralization. All projects have risks, and a PMO can centrally track and monitor all risks within all projects and take advantage and prepare for risks that may, or may not, come to fruition. Thus, a PMO can create a risk database to track pending and past risks and plan accordingly.

On the communications front, a PMO can centralize communication among project managers, project sponsors, managers, and other stakeholders. A centralized communication center can alleviate the demand on project managers to communicate with stakeholders, as all communications can flow through the PMO rather than the individual project manager.

CERTIFICATION SUMMARY

This chapter covered the fundamentals of project management and the expectations for the PMP examination. The *PMBOK Guide* is an excellent book that documents the ideal processes and procedures for project management. The PMP exam is based on the *PMBOK Guide*, and this book (the one you're reading now) focuses on the key exam essentials to help you pass your PMP exam.

We discussed what a project is and is not. Projects are temporary endeavors to create a unique thing, product, or service. An operation, on the other hand, is a series of activities that go on and on, like manufacturing a car, writing a newspaper column, or running a business. Many businesses complete projects for other people or organizations, and those are their operations.

The PMP exam will focus on the function of the project manager, which covers the nine knowledge areas of project management: integration management, time, cost, scope, quality, human resources, communications, risk, and procurement.

Each of these knowledge areas will be discussed in detail in Chapters 4 through 12 in this book. We'll also cover the PMP Code of Ethics and Professional Conduct.

Finally, we discussed how projects may exist within large entities called programs and PMOs. Recall that programs are a collection of projects working toward a common goal, whereas a PMO coordinates projects within an organization. Programs are led by a program manager that the project manager reports to. PMOs may be led by a chief project officer.

KEY TERMS

To pass the PMP exam, you will need to memorize the following terms and their definitions. For maximum value, create your own flashcards based on these definitions and review them daily.

application areas   The areas of discipline that a project may center upon. Consider technology, law, sales, marketing, and construction, among many others.

deliverable   A thing that a project creates; projects generally create many deliverables as part of the project work.

Iron Triangle   A term used to describe the three constraints of every project: time, cost, and scope. The sides of the Iron Triangle must be kept in balance or the quality of the project will suffer.

Management by Projects   An organization that uses projects to move the company forward is using the Management by Projects approach. These project-centric entities could manage any level of their work as a project.

operations   The ongoing work of the business. Operations are a generic way to describe the activities that support the core functions of a business entity.

PMBOK Guide   The abbreviated definition for PMI's *A Guide to the Project Management Body of Knowledge.*

PMP   Your goal. A PMP is certified by the Project Management Institute as a Project Management Professional.

programs   A collection of projects working in unison to realize benefits that could not be achieved by managing each project independently of one another.

progressive elaboration   The process of starting with a large idea and, through incremental analysis, actions, and planning, making the idea more and more specific. Progressive elaboration is the generally accepted planning process for project management, wherein the project management team starts with a broad scope and works towards a specific, detailed plan.

project   An undertaking outside of normal operations to create a unique product, service, condition, or result. Projects are temporary, while operations are ongoing.

project communications management   One of the nine project management knowledge areas; it is the planning and management of communication among project stakeholders. (See Chapter 10 for more information on this topic.)

project cost management   One of the nine project management knowledge areas; it is the estimating, budgeting, and controlling of the project expenses. (See Chapter 7.)

project human resource management   One of the nine project management knowledge areas; projects are completed by people, and the project manager generally oversees the management of the human resources on the project team. (See Chapter 9.)

project integration management   One of the nine project management knowledge areas; this knowledge area coordinates the activities and completeness of the other eight knowledge areas. (See Chapter 4.)

project management   The management of the projects within an organization. It is the initiation, planning, executing, monitoring and controlling, and closing of the temporary endeavor of the project.

project management office (PMO)   Organizes and manages control over all projects within an organization. A PMO also may be known as a program management office, project office, or simply the program office. Coordinates all aspects, methodology, and nomenclature for project processes, templates, software, and resource assignment.

project manager   The individual who manages the project's activities for an organization.

project portfolio management   A management process to select the projects that should be invested in. Specifically, it is the selection process based on the need, profitability, and affordability of the proposed projects.

project procurement management   One of the nine project management knowledge areas; this knowledge area oversees the purchasing and contract administration for a project. (See Chapter 12.)

project quality management   One of the nine project management knowledge areas; this knowledge area defines quality assurance, quality control, and the quality policy for the project. (See Chapter 8.)

project risk management   One of the nine project management knowledge areas; project risk management defines the risk identification, analysis, responses, and control of risk events. (See Chapter 11.)

project scope management   One of the nine project management knowledge areas; this knowledge area defines the project requirements, scope creation, and control. (See Chapter 5.)

project time management   One of the nine project management knowledge areas; this knowledge area defines the approach to time estimating, scheduling, and control of the project activities. (See Chapter 6.)

subprojects   A subproject exists under a parent project, but follows its own schedule to completion. Subprojects may be outsourced, assigned to other project managers, or managed by the parent project manager but with a different project team.

Triple Constraints of Project Management   Describes the required balance of time, cost, and scope for a project. The Triple Constraints of Project Management is also defined by the Iron Triangle of Project Management.

work breakdown structure   The visual decomposition of the project scope. It represents all of the deliverables the project promises to create.

✓ TWO-MINUTE DRILL

The *PMBOK Guide*, This Book, and the PMP Exam

- ❏ The PMP Exam is based on your experience and the fourth edition of PMI's book A *Guide to the Project Management Body of Knowledge*.
- ❏ This book, the one you're reading now, explains project management in plain language and helps you prepare to pass the PMP exam.
- ❏ Not everyone can take the PMP exam—you have to qualify for the test first.

Defining What a Project Is—and Is Not

- ❏ Projects are temporary, unique, and create a product or service.
- ❏ Projects move from concept to completion through progressive elaboration.
- ❏ Not all projects get selected. The decisions to choose one project over another may vary from organization to organization. The process, however, may be called project portfolio management.
- ❏ Projects have a definite beginning, middle, and ending; operations do not.
- ❏ Project management offices standardize the project management approach within an organization.

Defining Project Management

- ❏ Within the project management framework are nine knowledge areas, which span the project management life cycle.
- ❏ The focus of project integration management is managing all of the interactions of project components, processes, and knowledge areas.
- ❏ The focus of project scope management is on protecting, fulfilling, and delivering the project scope.
- ❏ The focus of project time management is on scheduling activities, monitoring the project schedule, and working with the project team and stakeholders to ensure the project completes on time.
- ❏ The focus of project cost management is on estimating and maintaining project costs.

❑ The focus of project quality management is on setting the quality expectations and then delivering the project product with the expected level of quality.

❑ The focus of project human resources management is on developing the project team to work together to deliver the project as expected.

❑ The focus of project communications management is on delivering needed information to the correct parties at the correct time. Much of project communications is on keeping the stakeholder informed of the project issues, risk, progress, and overall performance.

❑ The focus of project risk management is on identifying, mitigating, and managing project risks.

❑ The focus of project procurement management is soliciting, selecting, and managing vendors to complete project work or supply project materials.

Examining Related Areas of Project Management

❑ Projects often operate under the auspices of a PMO or a program. A program is a collection of projects working together for a common goal.

❑ A project manager must have multiple skills to be successful, including the ability to communicate, manage a budget, be organized, negotiate, and provide leadership for the project.

❑ Project managers in different sectors of business and nonprofit entities will encounter situations unique to their area of expertise. For example, a project manager of a construction project will have different issues and concerns than a project manager of a manufacturing project.

❑ Project managers require organization, problem solving, communication, and leadership skills and management abilities.

SELF TEST

1. Which one of the following is not an attribute of a project?
   A. Definite starting date
   B. Has no definite end date
   C. Creates a product, service, or result
   D. Requires resources

2. You are a project manager for Johnson Keyboards, Inc. Your organization has adapted the *PMBOK Guide* as a standard tool for how projects should operate, and you are involved in shaping the standardization for all future projects. In light of this information, what is the recommended course of action for the processes and procedures in the *PMBOK Guide*?
   A. Not all processes and procedures in the *PMBOK Guide* are actually required on all projects.
   B. All processes and procedures are to be followed as defined in the *PMBOK Guide*.
   C. Not all processes and procedures are needed, unless the *PMBOK Guide* states the process or procedure is a requirement for the project type.
   D. All processes and procedures are to be followed as identified in the *PMBOK Guide*; otherwise, the PMP is in violation of the PMP Code of Ethics and Professional Conduct.

3. Nancy is the project manager of the INCORP1 Project. She and the stakeholders created a scope two months ago, but since then, the scope has evolved and now provides much more detail about the project. The process of the scope evolving is also known as which one of the following terms?
   A. Decomposition
   B. Scope verification
   C. Scope creep
   D. Progressive elaboration

4. You are explaining to a junior engineer the difference between a project and operations. Which one of the following is true only of operations?
   A. They are performed by people.
   B. They are constrained by limited resources.
   C. They are ongoing.
   D. They are planned, executed, and controlled.

5. You are the project manager for your company, Mark Manufacturers. Your company has a large client that has requested a special component be created for one of their test engines. Your organization agrees and creates a standard contract with the customer, and your manager assigns you to manage this project. The project was launched because of which one of the following?

   A. A customer request

   B. A change in the technology your customer is creating

   C. A legal requirement (contractual)

   D. An organizational need

6. Project managers are not responsible for which one of the following in most organizations?

   A. Identifying the project requirements

   B. Selecting the projects to be initiated

   C. Balancing demands for time, cost, scope, and quality

   D. Establishing clear and achievable project objectives

7. You and William, a project stakeholder, are discussing risks within your project. Which one of the following best describes risk?

   A. Any event that can cause your project to fail

   B. Any event that may have a positive or negative effect on your project's team

   C. An uncertain event that may have a positive or negative effect on your project

   D. An event that will cause time and cost constraints to be broken

8. You are the project manager for a large software development project. You have concerns that one of the components of the Iron Triangle is slipping. Your project sponsor, Jim Bob, is not familiar with the Iron Triangle, so you explain the concept to him. What will be affected if any angle of the Iron Triangle is not kept in balance?

   A. Cost

   B. Quality

   C. Time

   D. Scope

9. Which knowledge area includes the creation of the project charter?

   A. Project scope management

   B. Project cost management

   C. Project integration management

   D. Project communications management

10. You and your project team are located in Des Moines, Iowa, but your project execution will take place in Mexico. You have valid concerns about the interactions with the stakeholders; time zone differences; language barriers; the different laws that could affect your project; and

the logistics of travel, face-to-face meetings, and even teleconferencing. Which of the following project environments are you concerned with most?

- A. Cultural and social
- B. International and political
- C. Physical
- D. Organizational structure

11. Which one of the following is not a general management skill?

- A. Motivating the project team
- B. Purchasing and procurement
- C. Sales and marketing
- D. Contracts and commercial law

12. Smith Construction has won a contract to build a 77-story condominium building in downtown Chicago. The building will have 650 condos, a parking garage, indoor and outdoor pools, two floors for retail, two floors of offices, and several shared community rooms. Mary Anne Kedzie has elected to create a program for the creation of the building. Which one of the following best describes a program?

- A. A standardized approach to project management within an organization
- B. A standardized approach to project management with multiple projects coordinated together
- C. A collection of related projects managed in coordination to gain control that would not necessarily be available if the projects were managed independently
- D. A collection of related projects all contributing to one deliverable

13. You are the project manager for an architectural design company. Your company consistently completes projects for other companies. Within your organization, the project managers have the highest level of authority on a project. You are likely operating within what type of company?

- A. A company using a functional structure
- B. A company using a matrix structure
- C. A company using Management by Projects
- D. A company using an ISO 9000 program

14. Who is usually responsible for portfolio management within an organization?

- A. Project managers
- B. Project sponsors
- C. Stakeholders
- D. Senior management

15. You are the project manager of a large project to install 1,900 kiosks throughout college campuses in North America. The kiosk will collect applications for credit cards, phone services, and other services marketable to college students. The bulk of your project is focused on the information technology integration, the wide area network (WAN) connections from each kiosk, security of the data transferred, and the database of the information gathered. For ease of management, you have hired local contractors to install the kiosks that you will ship to each campus. The contractors on each campus will be responsible for the WAN connection, the electrical connection, the security of the kiosk, and all testing. The local contracted work could be called what?
    A. Risk mitigation
    B. Operations
    C. Subprojects
    D. Management by Projects

16. Where can a project manager expect software, templates, and standardized policies?
    A. A project management office
    B. With the stakeholders
    C. Human resources
    D. The project budget

17. Which of the following is likely to be part of an operation?
    A. Providing electricity to a community
    B. Designing an electrical grid for a new community
    C. Building a new dam as a source for electricity
    D. Informing the public about changes at the electrical company

18. Of the following, which one is not part of project integration management?
    A. The creation of the project plan
    B. The interaction between project teams
    C. The execution of the project plan
    D. The documentation of changes to the project plan

19. Which one of the following describes the physical environment for a construction project?
    A. The terrain where the construction will take place
    B. The approval of the blueprints for the building
    C. The demographics of the community where the construction will take place
    D. The laws that govern where the building may take place

20. Which document will guide the interaction between the project manager and a selected vendor on a project?
    A. The project plan
    B. The statement of work (SOW)
    C. The procurement management plan
    D. The contract

21. What is the difference between a standard and a regulation?
    A. Standards and regulations are the same.
    B. Standards are regulated by specific industries; regulations are laws.
    C. Standards are optional; regulations are required.
    D. Standards are required; regulations are laws.

22. The project manager typically devotes the most amount of time to which of the following tasks?
    A. Communications
    B. Budget management
    C. Project organization
    D. Management of team negotiations

23. You have an excellent idea for a new project that can increase productivity by 20 percent in your organization. Management, however, declines to approve the proposed project because too many resources are already devoted to other projects. You have just experienced what?
    A. Parametric modeling
    B. Management by exception
    C. Project portfolio management
    D. Management reserve

24. Which one of the following is an interpersonal skill a project manager must have to be successful?
    A. Sales and marketing
    B. Leadership
    C. Health and safety practices
    D. Information technology experience

25. Of the following, which is the most important stakeholder involved with a project?
    A. The project manager
    B. The project sponsor
    C. The chief executive officer (CEO)
    D. The customer

SELF TEST ANSWERS

1. Which one of the following is not an attribute of a project?
    A. Definite starting date
    B. Has no definite end date
    C. Creates a product, service, or result
    D. Requires resources

    ☑ **B.** A project does have a definite end date; operations do not.
    ☒ **A, C,** and **D** are all incorrect choices because projects do have a definite starting date; they do create a unique product, service, or changes to an environment; and all projects require resources.

2. You are a project manager for Johnson Keyboards, Inc. Your organization has adapted the *PMBOK Guide* as a standard tool for how projects should operate, and you are involved in shaping the standardization for all future projects. In light of this information, what is the recommended course of action for the processes and procedures in the *PMBOK Guide*?
    A. Not all processes and procedures in the *PMBOK Guide* are actually required on all projects.
    B. All processes and procedures are to be followed as defined in the *PMBOK Guide*.
    C. Not all processes and procedures are needed, unless the *PMBOK Guide* states the process or procedure is a requirement for the project type.
    D. All processes and procedures are to be followed as identified in the *PMBOK Guide*; otherwise, the PMP is in violation of the PMP Code of Ethics and Professional Conduct.

    ☑ **A.** Not all information in the *PMBOK Guide* should be applied uniformly to all projects. It is the responsibility of the project management team to determine what practices are appropriate for each project.
    ☒ **B, C,** and **D** are all false statements regarding the implementation of the *PMBOK Guide*.

3. Nancy is the project manager of the INCORP1 Project. She and the stakeholders created a scope two months ago, but since then the scope has evolved and now provides much more detail about the project. The process of the scope evolving is also known as which one of the following terms?
    A. Decomposition
    B. Scope verification
    C. Scope creep
    D. Progress elaboration

☑ **D.** Progress elaboration is a term used to describe the development that happens in incremental steps. The project scope is the most common example of progress elaboration, but the WBS, product description, and even the project plan can pass through progressive elaboration.
☒ **A** is incorrect, as decomposition is the term used to describe the creation of the work breakdown structure. **B,** scope verification, is incorrect, as this term describes the process to verify that the deliverable matches what the scope promised to create. **C,** scope creep, is a term to describe small, unauthorized changes to the project scope.

4. You are explaining to a junior engineer the difference between a project and operations. Which one of the following is true only of operations?
   A. They are performed by people.
   B. They are constrained by limited resources.
   C. They are ongoing.
   D. They are planned, executed, and controlled.

   ☑ **C.** Projects are temporary; they do not go on forever.
   ☒ **A, B,** and **D** are all incorrect, as projects and operations are performed by people; are constrained by limited resources; and are planned, executed, and controlled.

5. You are the project manager for your company, Mark Manufacturers. Your company has a large client that has requested a special component be created for one of their test engines. Your organization agrees and creates a standard contract with the customer, and your manager assigns you to manage this project. The project was launched because of which one of the following?
   A. A customer request
   B. A change in the technology your customer is creating
   C. A legal requirement (contractual)
   D. An organizational need

   ☑ **A.** This project was launched because the customer requested the new component.
   ☒ **B** is incorrect because the project is not a response to a change in technology, but a customer request. **C,** a legal requirement, is not correct because this actually refers to a law or mandated regulation that has been created. **D,** an organizational need, typically refers to a project to behoove the performance of the organization.

6. Project managers are not responsible for which one of the following in most organizations?

A. Identifying the project requirements

B. Selecting the projects to be initiated

C. Balancing demands for time, cost, scope, and quality

D. Establishing clear and achievable project objectives

☑ **B.** Project managers typically do not select which projects are to be initiated. The project selection committee, customers, or project sponsors are typically responsible for this.

☒ **A, C,** and **D** are all incorrect choices because the project manager is responsible for these activities.

7. You and William, a project stakeholder, are discussing risks within your project. Which one of the following best describes risk?

A. Any event that can cause your project to fail

B. Any event that may have a positive or negative effect on your project's team

C. An uncertain event that may have a positive or negative effect on your project

D. An event that will cause time and cost constraints to be broken

☑ **C.** Risk is an uncertain event that can have positive or negative effects on your project.

☒ **A, B,** and **D** are characteristics of risk, but the best choice is **C** because risk is uncertain and may have a positive or negative effect on the project.

8. You are the project manager for a large software development project. You have concerns that one of the components of the Iron Triangle is slipping. Your project sponsor, Jim Bob, is not familiar with the Iron Triangle, so you explain the concept to him. What will be affected if any angle of the Iron Triangle is not kept in balance?

A. Cost

B. Quality

C. Time

D. Scope

☑ **B.** If any angle of the Iron Triangle is changed, the quality of the project will suffer.

☒ **A, C,** and **D** are incorrect choices, as these are the three sides of the Iron Triangle. These three sides must be kept in balance or quality will suffer.

9. Which knowledge area includes the creation of the project charter?
    A. Project scope management
    B. Project cost management
    C. Project integration management
    D. Project communications management

> ☑   **C.** Project integration management, which focuses on the coordination of all components of project management, includes the development of the project charter.
>
> ☒   **A** is incorrect, as project scope management focuses on the creation and control of the project scope. **B,** project cost management, is incorrect, as its role is to manage, control, and respond to the financial concerns within the project. **D,** project communications management, focuses on who needs what information, when is it needed, and in what modality.

10. You and your project team are located in Des Moines, Iowa, but your project execution will take place in Mexico. You have valid concerns about the interactions with the stakeholders; time zone differences; language barriers; the different laws that could affect your project; and the logistics of travel, face-to-face meetings, and even teleconferencing. Which of the following project environments are you concerned with most?
    A. Cultural and social
    B. International and political
    C. Physical
    D. Organizational structure

> ☑   **B.** All of the concerns listed fall into the international and political environment.
>
> ☒   Cultural and social, choice **A,** describes the demographic, educational, and ethical environment. **C,** physical, is concerned with the ecology and geography affected by the project. **D,** organizational structure, is not a project environment.

11. Which one of the following is not a general management skill?
    A. Motivating the project team
    B. Purchasing and procurement
    C. Sales and marketing
    D. Contracts and commercial law

☑ **A.** Motivation is actually an interpersonal skill that the project manager must have to inspire and energize the project team.

☒ **B, C,** and **D** are all incorrect choices, as these are general management skills the project manager must have in order to successfully manage a project. Management skills are always about getting the project work done. Interpersonal skills, sometimes called soft skills, are about inspiring, leading, and directing the project team and people to do what's required of them.

12. Smith Construction has won a contract to build a 77-story condominium building in downtown Chicago. The building will have 650 condos, a parking garage, indoor and outdoor pools, two floors for retail, two floors of offices, and several shared community rooms. Mary Anne Kedzie has elected to create a program for the creation of the building. Which one of the following best describes a program?

A. A standardized approach to project management within an organization

B. A standardized approach to project management with multiple projects coordinated together

C. A collection of related projects managed in coordination to gain control that would not necessarily be available if the projects were managed independently

D. A collection of related projects, all contributing to one deliverable

☑ **C.** A program is a collection of related projects managed and coordinated to gain a higher level of control.

☒ **A, B,** and **D** do not accurately describe a program. Note that **D** is not the best choice because programs typically create many deliverables and benefits—rarely just one deliverable.

13. You are the project manager for an architectural design company. Your company consistently completes projects for other companies. Within your organization, the project managers have the highest level of authority on a project. You are likely operating within what type of company?

A. A company using a functional structure

B. A company using a matrix structure

C. A company using Management by Projects

D. A company using an ISO 9000 program

☑ **C.** Your company is likely using Management by Projects. Management by Projects may also be called a projectized organization.

☒ **A** is incorrect since functional describes an organization that is arranged by function, such as sales, marketing, finance, and IT. **B** is incorrect because a matrix-structured organization uses resources from around the organization and the project manager has a low level of authority. **D** is incorrect because ISO programs describe a certified method of completing work the same exact way over and over.

14. Who is usually responsible for portfolio management within an organization?

 A. Project managers
 B. Project sponsors
 C. Stakeholders
 D. Senior management

☑ **D.** Senior management is responsible for portfolio management.

☒ **A** is incorrect because project managers are responsible for a project's success, but not for the portfolio. **B,** project sponsors, authorize projects. **C,** stakeholders, is an incorrect choice, as stakeholders is too vague of an answer to be acceptable.

15. You are the project manager of a large project to install 1,900 kiosks throughout college campuses in North America. The kiosk will collect applications for credit cards, phone services, and other services marketable to college students. The bulk of your project is focused on the information technology integration, the wide area network (WAN) connections from each kiosk, security of the data transferred, and the database of the information gathered. For ease of management, you have hired local contractors to install the kiosks that you will ship to each campus. The contractors on each campus will be responsible for the WAN connection, the electrical connection, the security of the kiosk, and all testing. The local contracted work could be called what?

 A. Risk mitigation
 B. Operations
 C. Subprojects
 D. Management by Projects

☑ **C** is the best choice because work that is subcontracted out for ease of management, as in this situation, becomes subprojects.

☒ **A** is incorrect, as risk mitigation describes when a project manager takes measures to reduce or eliminate risks. The scenario did not give enough information to determine what risks would have been mitigated. **B,** operations, is incorrect since it does not describe this scenario at all. **D,** Management by Projects, is incorrect, as this term describes a company that operates through projects. There is no indication that this is true with the scenario presented.

16. Where can a project manager expect software, templates, and standardized policies?
  A. A project management office
  B. With the stakeholders
  C. Human resources
  D. The project budget

☑ **A.** The project management office (PMO) supports the project manager through templates, standardized policies, and software.
☒ **B, C,** and **D** do not fully answer the question, so these answers are incorrect.

17. Which of the following is likely to be part of an operation?
  A. Providing electricity to a community
  B. Designing an electrical grid for a new community
  C. Building a new dam as a source for electricity
  D. Informing the public about changes at the electrical company

☑ **A.** An electrical company's primary operation is to provide electricity.
☒ **B** and **C** are projects. While **D,** providing information, could potentially be part of an ongoing operation, choice **A** is still the best answer presented.

18. Of the following, which one is not part of project integration management?
  A. The creation of the project plan
  B. The interaction between project teams
  C. The execution of the project plan
  D. The documentation of changes to the project plan

☑ **B.** Project integration management focuses on the project plan and its implementation.
☒ While **B** could, in some instances, be considered accurate if the project plan had some interaction with other project teams, the assumption cannot be made in this question. **A, C,** and **D** are all part of project integration management, so they are not valid answers.

19. Which one of the following describes the physical environment for a construction project?
  A. The terrain where the construction will take place
  B. The approval of the blueprints for the building
  C. The demographics of the community where the construction will take place
  D. The laws that govern where the building may take place

☑ **A.** The physical environment describes the effects on and by the ecology and geography of the area where the project will take place.

☒ **B** describes the requirements and technical documents for the project plan. **C** describes the cultural and social environment of the project. **D** describes the international and political environment of where the project will take place.

20. Which document will guide the interaction between the project manager and a selected vendor on a project?
   A. The project plan
   B. The SOW
   C. The procurement management plan
   D. The contract

☑ **D.** The contract between the organization and the vendor supersedes all other work-related documents.

☒ The project plan will guide the project manager and the project team to completion, but it will not supersede contracts. The SOW (statement of work), while needed and necessary, is not as important as a contract. The procurement management plan explains how project procurement takes place.

21. What is the difference between a standard and a regulation?
   A. Standards and regulations are the same.
   B. Standards are regulated by specific industries; regulations are laws.
   C. Standards are optional; regulations are required.
   D. Standards are required; regulations are laws.

☑ **C.** Standards are optional and may sometimes be called guidelines. Regulations are not optional and are typically enforced by laws.

☒ **A, B,** and **D** are all incorrect because they do not accurately describe standards and regulations.

22. The project manager typically devotes the most amount of time to which of the following tasks?
   A. Communications
   B. Budget management
   C. Project organization
   D. Management of team negotiations

> ☑ **A.** It's been said that project managers spend 90 percent of their time communicating.
> ☒ **B, C,** and **D** are all incorrect because these do not accurately describe a project manager's time.

23. You have an excellent idea for a new project that can increase productivity by 20 percent in your organization. Management, however, declines to approve the proposed project because too many resources are already devoted to other projects. You have just experienced what?

A. Parametric modeling
B. Management by exception
C. Project portfolio management
D. Management reserve

> ☑ **C.** Project portfolio management is the process of choosing and prioritizing projects within an organization. An excellent project idea can still be denied if there aren't enough resources to complete the project work.
> ☒ **A** is incorrect, as it is a model to estimate costs, such as cost per ton or cost per hour. **B** is incorrect because this is a management theory to manage people and problems. **D** is incorrect, as it is an amount of time and money reserved for projects running late or over budget.

24. Which one of the following is an interpersonal skill a project manager must have to be successful?

A. Sales and marketing
B. Leadership
C. Health and safety practices
D. Information technology experience

> ☑ **B.** Leadership is the only interpersonal skill listed.
> ☒ **A, C,** and **D** are incorrect, as these are general management skills and not interpersonal skills.

25. Of the following, which is the most important stakeholder involved with a project?

A. The project manager
B. The project sponsor
C. The CEO
D. The customer

> ☑ **D.** Customers, internal or external, are the most important stakeholders in a project.
> ☒ **A** is incorrect because the project manager manages the project for the customer. **B** is incorrect, since the project sponsor authorizes the project. **C** is incorrect because the CEO may not even know about the project—and even then he would be interested in the success of the project for the customer.

2

Examining the Project Life Cycle and the Organization

Project management, the ability to get things done, must support the higher vision of the organization that the project management activities are occurring in. Projects must be in alignment with the organization's vision, strategy, tactics, and goals. Projects that are not in alignment with the higher vision of the organization won't be around long—or, at best, they are doomed to fail.

Project managers must realize and accept that their projects should be components that support the vision of the organization where the project is being completed. It occasionally happens that projects are chartered and initiated that are not in alignment with the company strategy. Unless the company strategy changes, these projects can face political and organizational cultural challenges.

At the launch of a project, the project manager must have inherited the vision of the project. This person must understand why the project is being created and what its purpose in the organization is. It's beneficial to also know the priority of the project and its effect on the organization. A project to install pencil sharpeners throughout the company's shop floor may be important, but not as significant as the project to install new manufacturing equipment on the shop floor.

In this chapter, we'll cover how the life of a project, the interest of stakeholders, and the organization's environment influence the success and completion of projects.

CERTIFICATION OBJECTIVE 2.01

Revving Through Project Life Cycles

Consider any project, and you'll also have to consider any *phases* within the project. Construction projects have definite phases. IT projects have definite phases. Marketing, sales, and internal projects all have definite phases. Projects—all projects—are comprised of phases. The sum of a project's phases equates to the project's life cycle.

In regard to the PMP exam, it's rather tough for the PMI to ask questions about specific project life cycles. Why? Because every organization may identify different phases within all the different projects that exist. Bob may come from a construction background and Susan from IT, each one being familiar with totally different disciplines and totally different life cycles within their projects. However, all PMP candidates should recognize that every project has a life cycle—and all life cycles are comprised of phases.

a t c h *Phases are unique to each project. Phases are not the same as initiating, planning, executing, monitoring and controlling, and closing. These are the process groups, and are universal to all projects.*

Because every project life cycle is comprised of phases, it's safe to assume that each phase has a specific type of work that allows the project to move towards the next phase in the project. In a simple construction example, this is easy to see:

- Phase 1: Planning and pre-build
- Phase 2: Permits and filings
- Phase 3: Prep and excavation
- Phase 4: Basement and foundation
- Phase 5: Framing
- Phase 6: Interior
- Phase 7: Exterior

Typically, one phase is completed before the next phase begins, but sometimes project managers allow phases to overlap because of time constraints. When time's an issue and a project manager allows one phase to begin before the last phase is completed, it's called fast tracking. Fast tracking, as handy as it is, increases the risk within a project, however.

A project is an uncertain business—the larger the project, the more uncertainty. It's for this reason, among others, that projects are broken down into smaller, more manageable phases. A project phase allows a project manager to see the project as a whole and yet still focus on completing the project one phase at a time.

Working with Project Life Cycles

Projects are like snowflakes: No two are alike. Sure, sure, some may be similar, but when you get down to it—each project has its own unique attributes, activities, and requirements from stakeholders. Within each project, one attribute that typically varies from project to project is the project life cycle. As the name implies, the project life cycle determines not only the start of the project, but also when the project should be completed. All that stuff packed in between starting and ending? Those are the different phases of the project.

In other words, the launch, a series of phases, and project completion comprise the project life cycle. Each project will have similar project management activities, but the characteristics of the project life cycle will vary from project to project.

The PMP exam will test your knowledge on the outcome of project phases rather than the idealistic outputs of a project phase. Know that each phase **creates a deliverable and allows the project to move forward if the deliverables meet preset metrics.**

Project feasibility studies can be a separate project.

Completing a Project Feasibility Study

The project's feasibility is part of the initiating process. Once the need has been identified, a feasibility study is called for to determine if the need can realistically be met.

So how does a project get to be a project? In some organizations, it's pure luck. In most organizations, however, projects may begin with a feasibility study. Feasibility studies can be, and often are, part of the initiation process of a project. In some instances, however, a feasibility study may be treated as a stand-alone project. Let's assume that the feasibility of Project ABC is part of the project initiation phase. The outcome of the feasibility study may tell management several things.

- Whether the concept should be mapped into a project
- If the project concept is worth moving forward with
- The expected cost and time needed to complete the concept
- The benefits and costs to implement the project concept
- A report on the needs of the organization and how the project concept can satisfy these needs

Examining the Project Life Cycle

By now, you're more than familiar with the concept of a project life cycle. You also know each project is different and that some attributes are common across all project life cycles. For example, the concept of breaking the project apart into manageable phases to move toward completion is typical across most projects. As we've discussed, at the completion of a project phase, an inspection or audit is usually completed. This inspection confirms the project is in alignment with the requirements and expectations of the customer. If the results of the audit or briefing are not in alignment, rework can happen, new expectations may be formulated, or the project may be killed.

See the video Project Life Cycle.

Working Through a Project Life Cycle

Project life cycles, comprised of phases, move the project along. They allow a project manager to determine several things about the project, such as:

- What work will be completed in each phase of the project?
- What resources, people, equipment, and facilities will be needed within each phase?
- What are the expected deliverables of each phase?
- What is the expected cost to complete a project phase?
- Which phases contain the highest amount of risk?

Armed with the appropriate information for each project phase, the project manager can plan for cost, schedules, resource availability, risk management, and other project management activities to ensure that the project progresses successfully.

While projects differ, there are other common traits from project to project. The following lists a few examples:

- Phases are generally sequential, as the completion of one phase allows the next phase to begin.
- Cost and resource requirements are lower at the beginning of a project, but grow as the project progresses. Projects spend the bulk of their budget and use the most resources during the executing process. Once the project moves into the final closing process, costs and resource requirements taper off dramatically.

■ Projects fail at the beginning, not at the end. In other words, the odds of completing are low at launch and high at completion. It also means that decisions made at the beginning of a project live with the project throughout and that a poor decision in the early phases can cause failure in the later phases.

■ The further the project is from completing, the higher the risk and uncertainty. Risk and doubt decrease as the project moves closer to fulfilling the project vision.

■ Changes are easier and more likely at the early phases of the project life cycle than at the completion. Stakeholders can have a greater influence on the outcome of the project deliverables in the early phases, but in the final phases of the project life cycle, their influence on change diminishes. Thankfully changes at the beginning of the project generally cost less and have lower risk than changes at the end of a project.

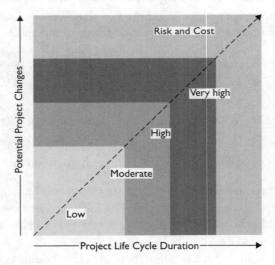

Project Life Cycles vs. Product Life Cycles

There is some distinction between the project life cycle and the product life cycle. We've covered the project life cycle—the accumulation of phases from start to completion within a project, but what is a product life cycle?

A product life cycle is the parent of projects. Consider a company that wants to sell a new type of lemon soft drink. One of the projects the company may undertake to sell its new lemon soft drink is to create television commercials showing how tasty the beverage is. The creation of the television commercial may be considered one project in support of the product creation.

Many other projects may fall under the creation of the lemon soft drink: research, creation and testing, packaging, and more. Each project, however, needs to support the ultimate product: the tasty, lemon soft drink. Thus, the product life cycle oversees the smaller projects within the process. As a general rule, the product life cycle is the cradle-to-grave ongoing work of the product. Projects affecting the product are just blips on the radar screen of the whole product life cycle. Consider all of the projects that may happen to a home. The home is the product, while all the projects are just things that make the product better or sustain the existing product.

The Project Life Cycle in Action

You're the project manager for HollyWorks Productions. Your company would like to create a new video camera that allows consumers to make video productions that can be transferred to different media types, such as VHS, DVDs, and PCs. The video camera must be small, light, and affordable. This project life cycle has several phases from concept to completion (see Figure 2-1). Remember, the project life

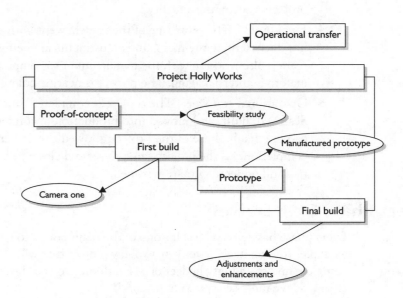

FIGURE 2-1

The project life cycle for Project HollyWorks

cycle is unique to each project, so don't assume the phases within this sample will automatically map to any project you may be undertaking.

1. **Proof-of-concept**   In this phase, you'll work with business analysts, electrical engineers, customers, and manufacturing experts to confirm that such a camera is feasible to make. You'll examine the projected costs and resources required to make such a camera. If things go well, management may even front you some cash to build a prototype.

2. **First build**   Management loves the positive information you've discovered in the proof-of-concept phase—they've set a budget for your project to continue into development. Now you'll lead your project team through the process of designing and building a video camera according to the specifications from the stakeholders and management. Once the camera is built, your team will test, document, and adjust your camera for usability and feature-support.

3. **Prototype manufacturing**   Things are going remarkably well with your video camera project. The project stakeholders loved the first build and have made some refinements to the design. Your project team builds a working model, thereby moving into prototyping the video camera's manufacture and testing its cost-effectiveness and ease of mass production. The vision of the project is becoming a reality.

4. **Final build**   The prototype of the camera went fairly well. The project team has documented any flaws, and adjustments are being made. The project team is also working with the manufacturer to complete the requirements for materials and packaging. The project is nearing completion.

5. **Operational transfer**   The project is complete. Your team has successfully designed, built, and moved into production a wonderful, affordable video camera. Each phase of the project allowed the camera to move toward completion. As the project came closer and closer to moving into operations, risk and project fluctuation waned.

Project Phase Deliverables

Every phase has deliverables. It's one of the main points to having phases. For example, your manager gives you a wieldy project that will require four years to complete and has a hefty budget of $16 million. Do you think management is going to say, "Have fun—see you in four years"?

Oh, if only they would, right?

Of course, in most organizations, that's not going to happen. Management wants to see proof of progress, evidence of work completed, and good news of how well the project is moving. Phases are an ideal method of keeping management informed of the project progression. The following illustration depicts a project moving from conception to completion. At the end of each phase there is some deliverable that the project manager can show to management and customers.

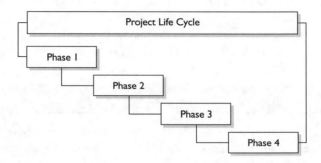

Project Advancement

Once a phase concludes, how does the project manager know it's safe to continue? Based on the size and type of the project, some form of scope verification must take place. Management and customers will want to see if the deliverable you have completed to date is in alignment with what they've expected.

Project governance defines the rules for a project, and it's up to the project manager to enforce the project governance to ensure the project's ability to reach its objectives. The project management plan defines the project governance and how the project manager, the project team, and the organization will all follow the rules and policies within the project. Project governance can be seen as a constraint, but it really defines the boundaries and expectations of the project.

Let's go back to that juicy project with the $16 million budget. We know management is not going to set us loose for four years. They'll want a schedule of when we'll be spending their money and what they'll be getting in return. And when will this fun happen? At the end of a project phase. The project manager will be accountable for several things at the end of a project phase.

- The performance of the project to date
- The performance of the project team to date
- Proof of deliverables in the project phase
- Verification of deliverables in alignment with the project scope

The verification of the performance and the project deliverables are key to management determining if the project (cross your fingers) should continue or not. Imagine that your project with a $16 million budget has produced a lousy deliverable, outside of the project scope, and you've blown a few hundred thousand *more* than what you said it would take to get to this point in the project. Hmmm... Do you think the project will continue? An analysis by management will determine if the project should be killed or allowed to go on. The idea of killing a project at phases is why phase completion is also called a kill point. Uh, kill point for the project, not the project manager—hopefully. Who's to blame or why the project should be killed can be debated on a scenario-by-scenario basis.

e x a m
ⓦatch

Money already spent on a project is called sunk costs and should not be taken into consideration when determining if a project should continue.

Instead, the cost of the work to complete is one of the elements that should be taken into consideration when deciding whether to kill a project.

Usually, phases are completely done before the next phase can begin—it's called a sequential relationship between phases. Each phase of a project relies on the phase before it. However, if you've ever driven past a large construction project, you might have seen something different at work. For example, I lived in Indianapolis during the construction of the new stadium for the Indianapolis Colts. During construction, we could see the foundation for one side of the stadium well underway and loads of construction happening. On the other side of the stadium it was muddy and construction was just barely starting on the foundation.

The construction company chose to allow phases of the construction to overlap as it worked. Rather than completing all of the foundation for this giant stadium, the next phase of the project was started as soon as possible—even if not all of the first phase was completed. Smart, huh? This approach to scheduling is called an overlapping relationship, and you might also know it as fast tracking. Fast tracking allows phases to overlap in order to compress the schedule and finish the job faster. Fast tracking does, however, add some risk to the project, as errors that go undetected in the prior phases could affect the current phase of the project work.

Finally, project managers can use an iterative relationship to manage project phases. Iterative relationships are wild and are great for projects like research.

The idea is that the next phase of the project is not planned until the current phase of the project is underway. The direction of the project can change based on the current work in the project, the market conditions, or as more information is discovered. I say that's a wild approach because it's next to impossible to do any reliable long-term planning.

Stage Gates

Project phase completions are also known as stage gates. Stage gates are used often in manufacturing and product development, and they allow a project to continue after a performance and deliverable review against a set of predefined metrics. If the deliverables of the phase, or stage, meet the predefined metrics, the project is allowed to continue. Should the deliverables not meet the metrics, the project may not be allowed to pass through the gate to move forward. In these unfortunate cases, the project may be terminated or sent through revisions to meet the predetermined metrics. The following illustration shows the advancement of the project through phases.

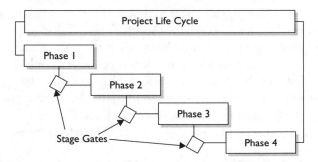

As a project manager, you should identify the requirements as close to the project launch as possible. With the expectations and requirements, the project manager can know what the exit criteria for a phase may be and can plan accordingly. There are few things more frustrating than to get to the end of a project phase only to learn the exit criteria you had in mind is different from what the customer was expecting.

The completion of a phase may also be known as a phase exit. A phase exit requires that the project deliverables meet some predetermined exit criteria. Exit criteria are typically inspection-specific and are scheduled events in the project schedule. Exit criteria can include many different activities, such as:

- Sign-offs from the customer
- Regulatory inspections and audits

■ Quality metrics

■ Performance metrics

■ Security audits

■ The end of a project phase

Meeting the Project Stakeholders

Stakeholders are those fine folks and organizations who are actively involved in the project or who will be affected by its outcome—in other words, people, groups, businesses, customers, and communities that have a vested interest in the project.

Stakeholders may like, love, or hate your project. Consider an organization that is hosting a project to move all their workers to a common word-processing application. Everyone within this organization must now use the same word-processing application. Your job, as the project manager, is to see that it happens.

Now, within your project, you've got stakeholders that like the project, being in favor of the project deliverable. Other stakeholders love the project—they cannot wait for the entire organization to use the same application for word processing. And, sigh, there are those stakeholders who are diehard fans of the application your project will take away from them. These folks hate your project.

on the job

In high-profile projects, where stakeholders will be in conflict over the project purpose, deliverables, cost, and schedule, the project manager may want to use the Delphi Technique to gain anonymous consensus among stakeholders. The Delphi Technique allows stakeholders to offer opinions and input without fear of retribution from management. More on this in Chapter 11.

Stakeholders, especially those not in favor of the project deliverable, may try to influence the project itself. This can be attempted in many ways, such as through:

■ Political capital leveraged to change the project deliverable

■ Change requests to alter the project deliverable

■ Scope addendums to add to the project deliverable

■ Sabotage, through physical acts or rumors, gossip, and negative influence

Your role as the project manager is to identify, align, and ascertain stakeholders and their expectations of the project. Stakeholder identification is not always as clear-cut as in the preceding example. Because stakeholders are identified as people that are affected by the outcome of your project, external customers may be stakeholders in your project, too.

Consider a company that is implementing a frequent customer discount project. External customers will use a card that tracks their purchases and gives them discounts on certain items they may buy. Is the customer in this instance a stakeholder? What if the customer doesn't want to use the card? Is she still a stakeholder?

INSIDE THE EXAM

Projects don't last forever. Though projects may sometimes seem to last forever, they fortunately do not. Operations, however, go on and on. Projects pass through logical phases to reach their completion, while operations may be influenced, or even created, by the outcome of a project.

The phases within a project create deliverables. The deliverables typically allow the project to move forward to the next phase—or allow the project to be terminated based on the quality, outcome, or condition of the phase deliverable. Some projects may use stage gates. Recall that stage gates allow a project to continue (after performance and deliverable review) against a set of predefined metrics. Other projects may use kill points. Kill points, like phase gates, are preset times placed in the project when it may, based on conditions and discovery within the phase, be "killed."

The project life cycle is different from the project management life cycle. The project management life cycle is comprised of the five project management processes (initiation, planning, execution, control, and closure).

The project life cycle, meanwhile, is comprised of the logical phases within the project itself.

The project life cycle is affected by the project stakeholders. Project stakeholders have a vested interest in the outcome of the project. Stakeholders include the project manager, project team, management, customers, communities, and anyone affected by the project outcome. Project managers should scan the project outcome in order to identify all of the stakeholders and collect and record their expectations, concerns, and input regarding the project processes.

The project manager's power is relative to the organization structure he is operating within. A project manager in a functional organization will have relatively low authority. A project manager in a matrix environment can have low, balanced, or high authority over the project. A project manager in a projectized organization, on the other hand, will have a high level of authority on the project. Essentially, the project manager's authority is typically inverse to the authority of the functional manager.

Mystery Stakeholders

Stakeholders can go by many different names: internal and external customers, project owners, financiers, contractors, family members, government regulatory agencies, communities, cities, citizens, and more. The classification of stakeholders into categories is not as important as realizing and understanding their concerns and expectations. The identification and classification of stakeholders, however, does allow the project manager to deliver effective and timely communications to the appropriate stakeholders.

Key Project Stakeholders

Beyond those stakeholders affected by the project deliverable, there are key stakeholders on every project. Let's meet them.

- **Project manager**   The project manager is the person—ahem, you—that is accountable for managing the project. She guides the team through the project phases to completion.

- **Program manager**   The program manager coordinates the efforts of multiple projects working together in the program. Programs are comprised of projects, so it makes sense that the program manager would be a stakeholder in each of the projects within the program, right?

- **Portfolio management review board**   Organizations only have so much capital to invest in projects. The portfolio management review board is a collection of the decision makers, usually executives, that review proposed projects and programs for their value and return on investment for the organization.

- **Functional managers** Most organizations are chopped up by functions or disciplines, such as information technology, sales, marketing, and finance. Functional managers are the managers of the permanent staff in each of these functions. Project managers and functional managers interact on project decisions that affect functions, projects, and operations.

- **Project customer** The customer is the person or group that will use the project deliverable. In some instances, a project may have many different customers. Consider a book publisher for children. The bookstores distribute the children's book. The adults pay for the book. The children read the book. There is also some consideration given to the user versus the customer. The user uses the product; the customer pays for it. A stakeholder can be both a user and a customer.

- **Operations management** The core business of an organization is supported primarily by operations management. Operations managers deal directly with the income-generating products or services the company provides. Projects often affect the core business, so these managers are stakeholders in the project. Project deliverables that affect the core business usually include an operational transfer plan that defines support, training, and maintenance on the project deliverables.

- **Project team** The project team is the collection of individuals that will, hopefully, work together to ensure the success of the project. The project manager works with the project team to guide, schedule, and oversee the project work. The project team completes the project work.

- **Project management team** These are the folks on the project team who are involved with managing the project.

- **Project sponsor** The sponsor authorizes the project. This person or group ensures that the project manager has the necessary resources, including monies, to get the work done. The project sponsor is someone within the performing organization who has the power to authorize and sanction the project work, and is ultimately accountable for the project's success.

- **Sellers and business partners** Organizations often rely on vendors, contractors, and business partners to help projects achieve their objectives. These business partners can affect the project's success, and they are considered stakeholders in the project.

- **The project management office** If a PMO exists for the organization, it's considered a stakeholder of the project because it supports the project managers and is responsible for the project's success. PMOs typically provide administrative support, training for the project managers, resource management for the project team and project staffing, and centralized communication.

PMP Coach *There are loads of terms and special vocabulary you'll need to know for this exam. Don't let the terms scare you away—you can do this! Do yourself a favor and grab a stack of index cards. As you go through this fascinating material, jot down every term that's new or interesting to you. Once you've read the chapter, you can create some fast flashcards. If you start now, you'll have a nice stack of cards by the time you reach the end of the book. Keep going—I have confidence in you.*

Managing Stakeholder Expectations

Ever had an experience that didn't live up to your expectations? Not much fun, is it? With project management and a large number of stakeholders, it's easy to see how some stakeholders' expectations won't be realistic due to cost, schedule, or feasibility. A project manager must find solutions to create win-win scenarios between stakeholders.

exam
watch *When it comes to stakeholder expectations, nothing beats documentation! Get stakeholder expectations in writing as soon as possible.*

Managing Expectations in Action

Consider a project to implement new customer relationship management software. In this project, there are three primary stakeholders, with differing expectations.

- The sales director primarily wants a technical solution that will ensure fast output of order placements, proposals, and customer contact information—regardless of the cost.

- The marketing director primarily wants a technical solution that can track call volume, customer sales history, and trends with the least cost to implement.

- The IT director wants a technical solution that will fan into the existing network topology and have considerable ease of use and reliability—without costing more than 20 percent of his budget for ongoing support.

In this scenario, the project manager will have to work with each of the stakeholders to determine a winning solution that satisfies all of the project requirements while appeasing the stakeholders' demands. Specifically, the solution for the conflict of stakeholders is to satisfy the needs of the customer first. Customer needs, or the business need of why the project was initiated, should guide the project through the project life cycle. Once the project scope is aligned with the customer's needs, the project manager may work to satisfy the differing expectations of the stakeholders.

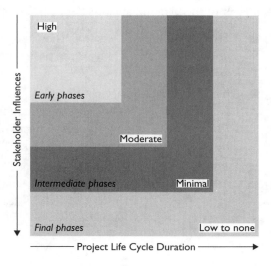

Identifying Organizational Models and Attributes

Projects are not islands. They are components of larger entities that work to create a unique product or service. The larger entities, organizations, companies, or communities will have direct influence over the project itself. Consider the values, maturity, business model, culture, and traditions at work in any organization. All of these variables can influence the progress and outcome of the project.

Project managers must also consider the legal requirements and influences over their projects. In the United States, this includes laws and regulations such as Sarbanes-Oxley, Health Insurance Portability and Accountability Act (HIPAA), Occupational Safety and Health Act (OSHA), and others. Projects can also be influenced by communities, other companies (when joint ventures exist), and professional associations. As a rule, the larger the project scope, the more influencers the project manager can expect.

Project managers must recognize the role of the project as a component within an organization. The role of the project, as a component, is to support the business model of the organization as a whole—not replace it. You can see in Figure 2-2 the major layers and purpose of the components within most organizations. Note that each layer of the pyramid answers a specific question in relation to the project.

■ The Executive Layer sets the vision and strategy of the organization. The Business Layer asks, "Why is the project important to our organization? Our vision? Our strategy?"

■ The Functional Management Layer of the pyramid must support the Executive Layer's objectives. Specifically, the Functional Management Layer is concerned with tactics to accomplish the vision and strategy as set by upper management. The Functional Management Layer asks, "What is the project purpose? What business processes are affected?"

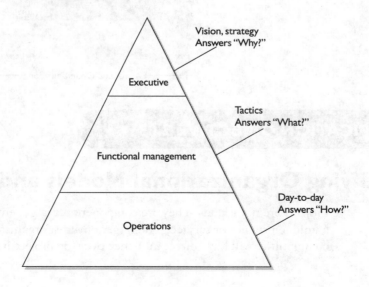

FIGURE 2-2

Each layer of an organization supports the layer above it.

- The Operational Layer of the pyramid supports the Executive and Functional Management Layers. This layer is concerned with the specifics of getting the work done. The Operational Layer asks, "How can the work be accomplished? How can we reach the desired future state with these requirements?"

Considering Organizational Systems

What kind of an organization are you in? Does your organization complete projects for other entities? Does your organization treat every process of an operation as an operation? Or does your organization not know what to do with people like you: project managers?

When it comes to project management, organizations fall into one of three models.

- **Completing projects for others**   These entities swoop into other organizations and complete the project work based on specifications, details, and specification documents. Classical examples of these types of organizations include consultants, architectural firms, technology integration companies, and advertising agencies.

- **Completing projects internally through a system**   These entities have adopted Management by Projects (discussed in Chapter 1). Recall that organizations using Management by Projects have accounting, time, and management systems in place to account for the time, cost, and worth of each project.

- **Completing projects as needed**   These nonproject–centric entities can complete projects successfully, but may not have the project systems in place to efficiently support projects. The lack of a project support system can cause the project to succumb to additional risks, lack of organization, and reporting difficulties. Some organizations may have special internal business units to support the projects in motion that are separate from the accounting, time, and management systems used by the rest of the organization.

Know that customers can be internal or external, but they all have the same theme: Customers pay for, or use, *the product deliverables. In some instances, they'll pay for and use the deliverables.*

Considering Organizational Culture

Imagine what it would be like to work as a project manager within a bank in downtown London versus working as a project manager in a web development company in Las Vegas. Can you picture a clear difference in the expected cultures within these two entities? The organizational culture of an entity will have a direct influence on the success of a project. Organizational culture includes:

- Polices and procedures for managing projects in the organization
- Values, beliefs, and expectations
- Views of authority, management, labor, and workers
- Work ethic
- Expectations on hours worked and contributions made

exam

watch   *The unique style and culture within each organization is called the cultural norm. It's just a way to describe the expectations of behavior within an organization. You won't find the same cultural norm in my company as you would in a Wall Street firm.*

As you can imagine, projects with more risk (and expected reward) may be welcome in an organization that readily accepts entrepreneurial ventures rather than in an organization that is less willing to accept chance and risk. Project formality is typically in alignment with the culture of an organization.

Another influence on the progress of a project is the management style of an organization. A project manager who is autocratic in nature will face challenges and opposition in organizations that allow and encourage self-led teams. A project manager must take cues from management as to how the management style of a project should operate. In other words, a project manager emulates the management style of the operating organization.

Completing Projects in Different Organizational Structures

Organizations are structured into one of six models, the organizational structure of which will affect the project in some aspect. In particular, the organizational structure will set the level of authority, the level of autonomy, and the reporting structure that the project manager can expect to have within the project. Figure 2-3 shows the level of authority in each of the organizational structures for the project

The organizational structure affects the project manager's authority.

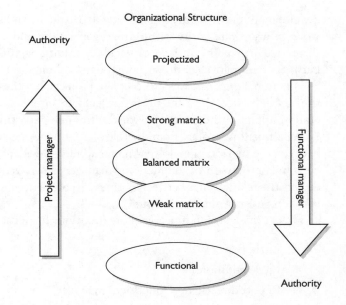

manager and the functional manager. The organizational structures we'll discuss include:

- Functional
- Weak matrix
- Balanced matrix
- Strong matrix
- Projectized
- Composite

Being able to recognize your organizational structure in regard to project management will allow you to leverage and position your role as a project manager effectively.

Functional Organizations

Functional organizations are entities that have a clear division regarding business units and their associated responsibilities. For example, a functional organization may have an accounting department, a manufacturing department, a research and development department, a marketing department, and so on. Each department works as a separate entity within the organization, and each employee works in a separate department. In these classical organizations, there is a clear distinction between an employee and a specific functional manager.

Functional organizations do complete projects, but these projects are specific to the function of the department the project falls into. For example, the IT department could implement new software for the finance department. The role of the IT department is separate from the role of the finance department, but the coordination between the two functional departments would be evident. Communication between departments flows through functional managers down to the project team. Figure 2-4 depicts the relationships between business departments and the flow of communication between projects and departments.

Project managers in functional organizations have the following attributes:

- Little power
- Little autonomy
- Report directly to a functional manager
- May be known as project coordinators or team leaders
- Have a part-time role (the project team will also be part-time as a result)
- May have little or no administrative staff to expedite the project management activities

FIGURE 2-4

Projects in functional organizations route communications through the functional managers.

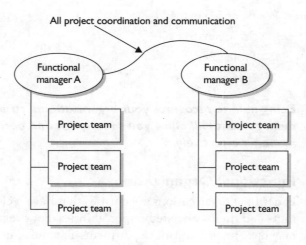

Matrix Structures

Matrix structures are organizations that use employees that perform a blend of departmental and project duties. This type of structure allows for project team members to be from multiple departments, yet all work toward the project completion. In these instances, the project team members have more than one boss. Depending on the number of projects a team member is participating in, he may have to report to multiple project managers as well as to his functional manager.

Weak Matrix

Weak matrix structures map closely to a functional organization. The project team may come from different departments, but the project manager reports directly to a specific functional manager. In weak matrix organizations, the project manager has the following attributes:

- Limited authority
- Management of a part-time project team
- Project role is part-time
- May be known as a project coordinator or team leader
- May have part-time administrative staff to help expedite the project

Balanced Matrix

A balanced matrix structure has many of the same attributes as a weak matrix, but the project manager has more time and power regarding the project. A balanced matrix still has time-accountability issues for all of the project team members, since their functional managers will want reports on their time spent on the project. Attributes of a project manager in a balanced matrix are:

- Reasonable authority
- Management of a part-time project team
- Full-time role as a project manager
- May have part-time administrative staff to help expedite the project

Strong Matrix

A strong matrix equates to a strong project manager. In a strong matrix organization, many of the same attributes for the project team exist, but the project manager gains power and time when it comes to project work. The project team may also have more time available for the project even though they may come from multiple departments within the organization. Attributes of a project manager in a strong matrix include:

- A reasonable to high level of power
- Management of a part-time to nearly full-time project team
- A full-time role as a project manager
- A full-time administrative staff to help expedite the project

Projectized Structure

At the pinnacle of project management structures is the projectized structure. These organizational types group employees, collocated or not, by activities on a particular project. The project manager in a projectized structure may have complete, or very close to complete, power over the project team. Project managers in a projectized structure enjoy a high level of autonomy over their projects, but they also have a higher level of responsibility regarding the project's success.

Project managers in a projectized structure have the following attributes:

- High to complete authority over the project team
- Work full-time on the project with their team (though there may be some slight variation)
- A full-time administrative staff to help expedite the project

Composite Organizations

On paper, all of these organizational structures look great. In reality, there are very few companies that map to only one of these structures all of the time. For example, a company using the functional model may create a special project consisting of talent from many different departments. Such project teams report directly to a project manager and will work on a high-priority project for its duration. These entities are called composite organizations, in that they may be a blend of multiple organizational types. Figure 2-5 shows a sample of a composite structure. While the AQQ Organization, in the figure, operates as a traditional functional structure, they've created a special projectized project where each department has contributed resources to the project team.

Table 2-1 outlines the benefits and drawbacks of various organizational types.

FIGURE 2-5

Composite
structures
are a blend
of traditional
organizational
structures.

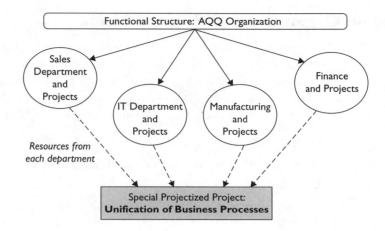

TABLE 2-1 Benefits and Drawbacks of Various Organizational Types

Organizational Type	Pros	Cons
Projectized	The project manager has autonomy of control of the project decisions. Improves communication as teams focus on current project work.	Project teams may compete for or stockpile resources. The project team may also lose focus towards the end of the project since they are uncertain about their next assignment.
Strong matrix	Project team may be assigned to a project for 50 to 90 percent of its duration. The project manager has a high level of authority. This model also provides good communication.	Competition over resources still exists. Overall costs may also increase due to redundant administrative staff among projects.
Balanced matrix	The project manager has balanced project authority with management. This model allows efficient use of functional resources.	The functional manager and the project manager may battle for project team members' time. The project team may feel they are reporting to multiple bosses.
Weak matrix	The project manager has little project authority and acts as a project coordinator.	The project is more a part of the functional department operations than a separate activity. Project team resources may be divided among too many projects at once.
Functional	Ideal for organizations with recurring projects, such as manufacturing. Everyone on the project knows who is in charge: the functional manager.	The project manager has little, if any, project authority and may be known as a project expeditor.

Relying on Organizational Process Assets

Organizational process assets is a nice way of referring to all of the stuff within an organization that can be used, leveraged, researched, or interviewed to make a project successful. This means past projects, risk databases, procedures, plans, processes, and methods of operations. Of course, organizational assets will vary from industry to industry, but for the PMP exam, consider all of the following:

- Standards, policies, and organizational procedures
- Standardized guidelines and performance measurements
- Templates
- Guidelines for adapting project management processes to the current project—remember, not every process needs to be completed on every project
- Communication requirements within your organization, such as standard forms, procedures, and reports that you must use as a project manager in your organization
- Processes for project activities, such as closing, communications, financial controls, and risk control procedures

Ideally, your organization has a method to catalogue, archive, and retrieve information from past projects and work. The PMBOK calls this the corporate knowledge base. This can be a fancy electronic data storage and retrieval system, or it might just be a hallway closet full of past project files. Things the corporate knowledge base should provide include:

- Process measurement for project performance
- Project files
- Historical information from past projects
- Issue and defect databases
- Configuration management databases
- Financial databases

Throughout this book, you'll see the term *organizational process assets* for different processes and inputs for processes. It simply means that you'll rely on information that has been created to help you, the project manager, complete your current job. It's templates, software, and historical information that you can use on your current project. A template, by the way, doesn't always mean a shell of a document like you might use in Microsoft Word. Templates in project management can be past project plans, scope statements, and just about any other document that you adapt for your current project. There is no reason to reinvent the wheel—project management is tedious enough.

The Project Management Office

In the last several years, there has been a surge in the popularity of the project office. The project office is the central source for project management support within an organization. So what can a project manager expect from the project office? How about:

- Project management software
- Training and mentoring
- HR and project manager support
- Guidance
- Templates
- Administrative help
- Project oversight
- Access to knowledge repository

CERTIFICATION OBJECTIVE 2.04

Defining Key General Management Skills

There is more to project management than just getting the work done. Inherent to the process of project management are general management skills that allow the project manager to complete the project with some level of efficiency and control. In some respects, managing a project is similar to running a business: There are risks and rewards, finance and accounting activities, human resource issues, time management, stress management, and a purpose for the project to exist.

The effective project manager will have experience, or guidance, in the general management skills we'll discuss in this section. These general management skills are needed in just about every project type—from architectural design to manufacturing.

Other management skills are more specialized in nature, such as OSHA conformance in a manufacturing environment, and aren't needed in every project.

Leading the Project Team

Project managers manage things but lead people. What's the difference? Management is the process of getting the results that are expected by project stakeholders. Leadership is the ability to motivate and inspire individuals to work towards those expected results.

Ever work for a project manager who wasn't motivating or inspiring? A good project manager can motivate and inspire the project team to see the vision and value of the project. The project manager as a leader can inspire the project team to find a solution to overcome the perceived obstacles to get the work done. Motivation is a constant process that the project manager must have to help the team move towards completion—with passion and a profound reason to complete the work. Finally, motivation and inspiration must be real; a personal relationship with the project team to help them achieve their goals is mandatory.

Communicating Project Information

Project communication can be summed up as "who needs what information and when." Project managers spend the bulk of their time communicating information—not doing other activities. Therefore, they must be good communicators, promoting a clear, unambiguous exchange of information. Communication is a two-way street; it requires a sender and a receiver.

A key part of communication is *active listening*. This is the process by which the receiver restates what the sender has said in order to clarify and confirm the message. For example, a project team member tells the project manager that a work package will be done in seven days. The project manager clarifies and confirms by stating the work package will be done a week from today. This gives the project team member the opportunity to clarify that the work package will actually be done nine days from today because of the upcoming weekend.

There are several communication avenues.

- Listening and speaking
- Written and oral
- Internal to the project, such as project team member to team member
- External to the project, such as the project manager to an external customer
- Formal communications, such as reports and presentations
- Informal communications, such as e-mails and "hallway" meetings
- Vertical communications, which follow the organizational flow chart
- Horizontal communications, such as director to director within the organizational flow chart

Within management communication skills, there are also variables and elements unique to the flow of communication. While we'll discuss communications in full in Chapter 10, here are some key facts for now.

- **Sender-receiver models**   Communication requires a sender and a receiver. Within this model, there may be multiple avenues to complete the flow of communication, but there may also be barriers to effective communication. Other variables within this model include recipient feedback, surveys, checklists, and confirmation of the sent message.
- **Media selection**   There are multiple choices when it comes to sending a message. Which one is appropriate? Based on the audience and the message being sent, the media should be in alignment. In other words, an ad-hoc hallway meeting is probably not the best communication avenue to explain a large variance in the project schedule.
- **Style**   The tone, structure, and formality of the message being sent should be in alignment with the audience and the content of the message.
- **Presentation**   When it comes to formal presentations, the presenter's oral and body language, visual aids, and handouts all influence the message being delivered.

■ **Meeting management** Meetings are forms of communication. How the meeting is led, managed, and controlled all influence the message being delivered. Agendas, minutes, and order are mandatory for effective communications within a meeting.

Negotiating Project Terms and Conditions

Project managers must negotiate for the good of the project. In any project, the project manager, the project sponsor, and the project team will have to negotiate with stakeholders, vendors, and customers to reach a level of agreement acceptable to all parties involved in the negotiation process. In some instances, typically in less-than-pleasant circumstances, negotiations may have to proceed with assistance. Specifically, mediation and arbitration are examples of assisted negotiations. Negotiation proceedings typically center on:

■ Priorities
■ Technical approach
■ Project scope
■ Schedule
■ Cost
■ Changes to the project scope, schedule, or budget

■ Vendor terms and conditions
■ Project team member assignments and schedules
■ Resource constraints, such as facilities, travel issues, and team members with highly specialized skills

exam
ⓦatch *The purpose of negotiations is to reach a fair agreement among both parties.*

Active Problem Solving

Like riddles, puzzles, and cryptology? If so, you'll love this area of project management. Problem solving is the ability to understand the heart of a problem, look for a viable solution, and then make a decision to implement that solution. In any project, there are countless problems requiring viable solutions. And like any good puzzle, the solution to one portion of the problem may create more problems elsewhere.

The premise for problem solving is problem definition. Problem definition is the ability to discern between the cause and effect of the problem. This centers on root-cause analysis. If a project manager treats only the symptoms of a problem rather than its cause, the symptoms will perpetuate and continue throughout the project's life. Root-cause analysis looks beyond the immediate symptoms to the cause of the symptoms—which then affords opportunities for solutions.

e x a m
w a t c h
Completing the PMP exam is an example of problem-solving skills. Even though you may argue that things described in this book don't work this way in your environment, know that the exam is not based on your environment. Learn the PMI method for passing the exam and allow that to influence your "real-world" implementations.

Once the root of a problem has been identified, a decision must be made to effectively address the problem. Solutions can be presented from vendors, the project team, the project manager, or various stakeholders. A viable solution focuses on more than just the problem. It looks at the cause and effect of the solution itself. In addition, a timely decision is needed, or the window of opportunity may pass and then a new decision will be needed to address the problem. As in most cases, the worst thing you can do is nothing.

Influencing the Organization

Project management is about getting things done. Every organization is different in its policies, modes of operations, and underlying culture. There are political alliances, differing motivations, conflicting interests, and power struggles within every organization. So where does project management fit into this rowdy scheme? Right smack in the middle.

e x a m
w a t c h
These exam questions are shallow. Don't read too much into the questions as far as political aspirations and influences go. Take each question at face value and assume all of the information given in the question is correct.

A project manager must understand all of the unspoken influences at work within an organization—as well as the formal channels that exist. A balance between the implied and the explicit will allow the project manager to take the project from launch to completion. We all reference politics in organizations with disdain. However, politics aren't always a bad thing.

Politics can be used as leverage to align and direct people to accomplish activities—with motivation and purpose.

Managing Social, Economic, and Environmental Project Influences

Social, economic, and environmental influences can cause a project to falter, stall, or fail completely. Awareness of potential influences outside of traditional management practices will help the project finish. The acknowledgement of such influences, from internal or external sources, allows the project manager and the project team to plan how to react to these influences in order for the project to succeed.

For example, consider a construction project that may reduce traffic flow to one lane over a bridge. Obviously, stakeholders in this instance are the commuters that travel over the bridge. Social influences are the people who are frustrated by the construction project, the people who live in the vicinity of the project, and even individuals or groups that believe their need for road repairs is more pressing than the need to repair the bridge. These issues must all be addressed, on some level, for the project team to quickly and efficiently complete the project work.

The economic conditions in any organization are always present. The cost of a project must be weighed against the project's benefits and perceived worth. Projects may succumb to budget cuts, project priority, or their own failure based on the performance to date. Economic factors inside the organization may also hinder a project from moving forward. In other words, if the company sponsoring the project is not making money, projects may get axed in an effort to curb costs.

Finally, environmental influence on, and created by, the project must be considered. Let's revisit the construction project on the bridge. The project must consider the river below the bridge and how construction may affect the water and wildlife. Consideration must be given not only to short-term effects that arise during the bridge's construction but also to long-term effects that the construction may have on the environment.

In most projects, the social, economic, and environmental concerns must be evaluated, documented, and addressed within the project plan. Project managers can't have a come-what-may approach to these issues and expect to be successful.

Dealing with Standards and Regulations

Standards and regulations within any industry can affect a project's success. But what's the difference between a standard and a regulation? Standards are accepted practices that are not necessarily mandatory, while regulations are rules that must be followed—otherwise, fines, penalties, or even criminal charges may result.

For example, within information technology, there are standard sizes for CDs, DVDs, and floppy disks. Manufacturers generally map to these sizes for usability purposes. However, manufacturers can, and have, created other media that are slightly different in size and function from the standard. Consider the disposable mini-CDs that hold short movies or advertisements for consumers. Some of these CDs come shaped like stars, footballs, and baseballs. Such products aren't exactly standard regarding format, but they don't break any regulations either. After a time, though, standards can indeed become de facto regulations. They may begin as guidelines and then, due to marketplace circumstances, grow into an informal regulation.

An example of a regulation is a set rule or law. For example, the food packaging industry has some particular regulations related to the packaging and delivery of food items. Violations of the regulations will result in fines or even more severe punishment. Regulations are more than suggestions—they are project requirements.

 on the job *Every industry has some standards and regulations. Knowing which ones affect your project before you begin your work will not only help the project to unfold smoothly, but will also allow for effective risk analysis. In some instances, the requirements of regulations can afford the project manager additional time and monies to complete a project.*

Considering International Influences

If a project spans the globe, how will the project manager effectively manage and lead the project team? How will teams in Paris communicate with teams in Sydney? What about the language barriers, time zone differences, currency differences, regulations, laws, and social influences? All of these concerns must be taken into consideration early in the project. Tools can include teleconferences, travel, face-to-face meetings, team leaders, and subprojects.

As companies and projects span the globe to offer goods and services, the completion of those projects will rely more and more on individuals from varying educational backgrounds, social influences, and values. The project manager must create a plan that takes these issues into account.

Cultural Influences

Project plans must deal with many cultural influences: geographical, political, organizational, even relationships between individual team members. Projects in Dallas, Texas, have different cultural influences than projects taking place in Dublin, Ireland. Culture consists of the values, beliefs, political ties, religion, art, aspirations, and purpose of being. A project manager must take into consideration these various cultural influences and how they may affect the project's completion, schedule, scope, and cost.

CERTIFICATION SUMMARY

This chapter detailed the framework of projects. Project managers operate within the framework of a project to coordinate all of the parts and to move the project toward completion. A project achieves momentum by completing project phases. Project phases comprise the project life cycle. The project life cycle corresponds to the project management framework and provides several benefits.

- Each phase results in some type of deliverable.
- Phase completion shows accomplishment and progression.
- Phase completion allows time for review to determine if the project should move forward.
- Phases allow the project to be progressively elaborated.

Projects must operate within the organizational structure. Organizational structures control how the project manager can obtain resources, the level of authority the project manager can expect, and the participation of the project team. There are five organizational structures: functional, weak matrix, balanced matrix, strong matrix, and projectized.

KEY TERMS

To pass the PMP exam, you will need to memorize these terms and their definitions. For maximum value, create your own flashcards based on these definitions and review them daily.

composite structure   An organizational structure that uses a blend of the functional, matrix, and projectized organizations to operate and manage projects.

cultural norm   The accepted practices, culture, ideas, vision, and nature of an organization.

fast tracking   A schedule-compression technique that allows phases to overlap in order to compress the schedule and finish the job faster. Fast tracking does increase project risk.

functional managers   The managers of the permanent staff in each organizational department, line of business, or function such as sales, finance, and technology. Project managers and functional managers interact on project decisions that affect functions, projects, and operations.

functional organizations   Entities that have a clear division regarding business units and their associated responsibilities. Project managers in functional organizations have little power and report to the functional managers. This is an organization that groups staff according to their expertise—for example, sales, marketing, finance, and information technology. Project managers in functional structures report to functional managers, and the project team exists within one department.

iterative relationships of project phases   Ideal for projects like research. The next phase of the project is not planned until the current phase of the project is underway. The direction of the project can change based on the current work in the project, market conditions, or as more information is discovered.

kill point   An opportunity to halt the project based on project performance in the previous phase. Kill points typically come at the end of a project phase and are also known as phase gates.

matrix structure   An organization that groups staff by function but openly shares resources on project teams throughout the organization. Project managers in a matrix structure share the power with functional management. There are three types of matrix structures: weak, balanced, and strong to describe the amount of authority for the project manager.

operations management   Operations managers deal directly with the income-generating products or services the company provides. Projects often affect the core business, so these managers are stakeholders in the project.

overlapping relationship of phases   Allows project phases to overlap to compress the project duration. This is also known as fast tracking.

portfolio management review board   A collection of organizational decision makers, usually executives, that review proposed projects and programs for their value and return on investment for the organization.

product life cycle   The unique life, duration, and support of the thing a project creates. A product life cycle is separate from the project life cycle.

program manager   Coordinates the efforts of multiple projects working together in the program. Programs are comprised of projects, so it makes sense that the program manager would be a stakeholder in each of the projects within the program, right?

project customer/end user   The person or group that will use the project deliverable. In some instances, a project may have many different customers.

project governance   Defines the rules for a project; it's up to the project manager to enforce the project governance to ensure the project's ability to reach its objectives. The project management plan defines the project governance and how the project manager, the project team, and the organization will follow the rules and policies within the project.

project life cycle   Unique to each project and comprised of phases of work. Project life cycles typically create a milestone and allow subsequent phases to begin.

project management office (PMO)   A stakeholder of the project because it supports the project managers and is responsible for the project's success. PMOs typically provide administrative support, training for the project managers, resource management for the project team and project staffing, and centralized communication.

project management team   People on the project team that are involved with managing the project.

project manager   The person accountable for managing the project and guiding the team through the project phases to completion.

project sponsor   Authorizes the project. This person or group ensures that the project manager has the necessary resources, including monies, to get the work done. The project sponsor is someone within the performing organization who has the power to authorize and sanction the project work and who is ultimately accountable for the project's success.

project team   The collection of individuals that will work together to ensure the success of the project. The project manager works with the project team to guide, schedule, and oversee the project work. The project team completes the project work.

projectized structure   Grouping employees, collocated or not, by activities on a particular project. The project manager in a projectized structure may have complete, or very close to complete, power over the project team.

sellers and business partners   Vendors, contractors, and business partners that help projects achieve their objectives. These business partners can affect the project's success and are considered stakeholders in the project.

sequential relationship of phases   Each phase of a project relies on the completion of the previous phase before it can begin.

✓ TWO-MINUTE DRILL

Revving Through Project Life Cycles

❑ Projects follow a logical sequence of phases to completion. Phases are typically different from project to project, since the project work will differ from one project to the next. The point of segmenting projects into phases is to allow for smaller, manageable sections and to provide deliverables in support of the ongoing operations.

❑ The collection of the project phases, as a whole, is known as the project life cycle.

❑ Project life cycles define the beginning, middle, and end of a project. Projects have a greater risk and uncertainty in the early phases of the project life cycle than near their end. The project is also most susceptible to change, failure, and stakeholder influences at the beginning of the life cycle than near its end.

❑ In tandem, project costs and demand for resources are generally low at the beginning of the project, have a tendency to peak near the end of the project work, and then diminish.

Meeting the Project Stakeholders

❑ Project stakeholders are individuals, businesses, or communities that have a vested interest in the project's outcome. Typically, project stakeholders are involved in the project process, and their expectations drive the project requirements.

❑ It is essential to scan for hidden stakeholders early in the project life cycle to eliminate the need for change when addressing stakeholder needs later in the project.

❑ There are several key stakeholders that have direct influence over the project. They are:

   ❑ **Project manager**   Manages the project

   ❑ **Customer**   Pays for the project; uses the project deliverable

   ❑ **Performing organization**   The organization hosting the project

   ❑ **Project team**   The collection of individuals completing the project work

❑ **Project management team**   The collection of individuals that contribute to the management of a project

❑ **Project sponsor**   Authorizes the project work and budget

❑ **Influencers**   People who can influence the project for better or worse

❑ **PMO**   May have direct responsibility for the project's success

Identifying Organizational Models and Attributes

❑ Organizational structures have direct influence over the project. Organizational structures determine the procedures that the project manager must follow and the amount of authority the project manager possesses. A project office may oversee project management activities and provide additional support in any of the organizational structures. The organizational types and the level of authority a project manager can expect are shown in the following table.

Organizational Structure	Level of Power
Functional	Low to none
Weak matrix	Low
Balanced matrix	Low to moderate
Strong matrix	Moderate to high
Projectized	High to complete
Composite	Varies

❑ Beyond the concept of getting the work done, project managers must also consider the social, economic, and environmental influences that may sway a project. Specifically, the project manager must evaluate the project to see its social, economic, and environmental impact—as well as note the project's surroundings. The project manager may have some external guidance in these areas in the form of standards and regulations.

❑ Standards are guidelines that are generally followed but not enforced or mandated. Regulations come in the form of laws and industry demands, which are enforced by various governing bodies.

Defining Key General Management Skills

❏ Management is all about key results. It is about the project team getting things done in the project.

❏ Leadership is about motivating, inspiring, and directing people to accomplish the project objectives and personal goals.

❏ Project managers spend the bulk of their time communicating information—not doing other activities. Therefore, they must be good communicators, promoting a clear, unambiguous exchange of information. Communication is a two-way street; it requires a sender and a receiver.

❏ Project managers must negotiate for the good of the project. In any project, the project manager, the project sponsor, and the project team will have to negotiate with stakeholders, vendors, and customers to reach a level of agreement acceptable to all parties involved in the negotiation process.

❏ Project managers have to work with stakeholders to influence the decisions within the project. This includes politics; tradeoffs; and managing requirements, changes, and issues within the project.

SELF TEST

1. The project life cycle is comprised of which of the following?
   A. Phases
   B. Milestones
   C. Estimates
   D. Activities

2. Marcy, the project manager for the ERP Project, is about to complete the project phase review. The completion of a project phase is also known as which of the following?
   A. A lesson learned
   B. A kill point
   C. Earned value management
   D. Conditional advancement

3. Which of the following is not a key stakeholder in a project that creates a service internal to an organization?
   A. The project manager
   B. External customers
   C. Project vendors
   D. Project team members

4. Of the following management skills, which will a project manager use most?
   A. Leading
   B. Communicating
   C. Influencing the organization
   D. Negotiating

5. Managing a project is best described as which one of the following?
   A. Establishing direction
   B. Functional controls over the project team and stakeholders
   C. Consistently producing key results expected by stakeholders
   D. Motivating and inspiring the project team to produce results that are expected by project stakeholders

6. When will stakeholders have the most influence over a project's product?
   A. At the end of the project
   B. During scope verification

    C. At the start of a project

    D. At the start of each phase

7. Which of the following is an example of negotiation?

    A. Arbitration

    B. Formal communications

    C. Conferring

    D. Scope creep

8. You are the project manager for your organization. Influencing your organization requires which of the following?

    A. An understanding of the organizational budget

    B. Research and documentation of proven business cases

    C. An understanding of formal and informal organizational structures

    D. Positional power

9. Your global project is sabotaged by rumors and gossip about the project deliverable. This is an example of:

    A. Cultural achievability

    B. Cultural influences within the project team

    C. Project team mutiny

    D. Ineffective planning

10. What is the difference between a standard and a regulation?

    A. Standards are mandatory; regulations are not.

    B. Standards are optional; regulations are not.

    C. Regulations and standards are essentially the same.

    D. Regulations are usually mandatory; standards may be seen as guidelines.

11. All of the following are examples of stakeholders that have a positive influence on a project except for which one?

    A. Business leaders in a community affected by a commercial development project

    B. Team members that will receive a bonus if the project is successful

    C. Employees that prefer the older version of the software that a project is replacing

    D. Functional managers that want your project to complete so their employees can move onto other projects

12. Which of the following is an example of a deliverable at the end of the requirements-gathering phase in a software design project?

    A. Responsibility matrix creation

    B. Detail design document

    C. Business needs

    D. Project team assembled

13. You are the project manager for the ERP Project. Your organization uses a PMO. The primary purpose of a project office is to:

    A. Support the project managers

    B. Support the project sponsor

    C. Support the project team

    D. Identify the stakeholders

14. Which of the following best describes a project deliverable?

    A. The resources used by the project to complete the necessary work

    B. The resources exported from the project as a result of the project work

    C. The end result of a project planning session

    D. The tangible good or service created by the project team

15. At what point in a project would a kill point be acceptable?

    A. When a project team member is not performing as planned

    B. When a project reaches the end of a project phase

    C. When a project reaches the end of its budget

    D. When a project manager determines the project team cannot continue

16. Of the following, which is not an exit criterion?

    A. Customer sign-offs

    B. Quality metrics

    C. Stakeholder analysis

    D. Regulatory inspections

17. The compilation of all the phases within a project equates to _____.

    A. The project life cycle

    B. The product life cycle

    C. Project completion

    D. Project processes

18. Management has asked Nancy to determine if a project concept is valid and can be completed using a reasonable amount of time and finances. Management is asking for which of the following?

A. Kill points

B. Cost and time estimates

C. A project case study

D. A feasibility study

19. Henry, the project manager of the MHB Project, has allowed a subsequent project phase to begin before the predecessor phase is complete. This is an example of which of the following?

A. Crashing

B. Fast tracking

C. Risk management

D. Tandem scheduling

20. Which of the following describes the early stages of a project?

A. High costs and high demand for resources

B. A high demand for change

C. A high demand for project team time

D. Low costs and low demand for resources

21. At which point is the risk of failure the least but the consequence of failure the highest?

A. During the early stages

B. During the middle stages

C. During the final stages

D. Risk of failure is even across all project phases

22. Tracey is the project manager of the KHG Project. Her organization is a classic functional environment. Her level of authority as a project manager can be best described as which of the following?

A. Low

B. Moderate

C. Balanced

D. High

23. Project team members are most likely to work full-time on a project in which of the following organizational structures?

   A. Functional

   B. Weak matrix

   C. Strong matrix

   D. Projectized

24. A project with much risk and reward is most likely to be accepted in which of the following?

   A. An entrepreneurial company

   B. A heavily regulated company

   C. A nonprofit organization

   D. A community

25. Where can a project manager expect to receive templates?

   A. Commercial databases

   B. The project office

   C. The project sponsor

   D. Project Management Information System (PMIS)

SELF TEST ANSWERS

1. The project life cycle is comprised of which of the following?
   A. Phases
   B. Milestones
   C. Estimates
   D. Activities

   ☑ **A.** The project life cycle is comprised of phases.
   ☒ **B** is incorrect, since milestones may exist within the project plan, but they do not comprise the project life cycle. **C** is wrong because estimates are not directly related to the project life cycle. Choice **D,** activities, comprise the phases within the project life cycle, but not the project life cycle itself.

2. Marcy, the project manager for the ERP Project, is about to complete the project phase review. The completion of a project phase is also known as which of the following?
   A. A lesson learned
   B. A kill point
   C. Earned value management
   D. Conditional advancement

   ☑ **B.** The completion of a project phase may also be known as a kill point.
   ☒ Lessons learned is a collection of information and knowledge gained through an experience, typically a phase, within the project, so **A** is wrong. EVM, earned value management, can happen at different times throughout the project, not just at the end of a project phase; therefore, **C** is wrong. Choice **D,** conditional advancement, is a term used to describe the conditions that must be present for the work to continue on a project. Conditional advancement, however, does not have to happen only at the end of a project phase.

3. Which of the following is not a key stakeholder in a project that creates a service internal to an organization?
   A. The project manager
   B. External customers
   C. Project vendors
   D. Project team members

☑ **B.** External customers are not key stakeholders in this instance, as they are not actively involved in an internal project.

☒ **A** and **D** are actively involved in the project processes. Choice **C,** project vendors, is most likely a key stakeholder before an external customer, since their ability to perform services and deliver goods may affect project schedule, budget, and completion.

4. Of the following management skills, which will a project manager use most?
   A. Leading
   B. Communicating
   C. Influencing the organization
   D. Negotiating

   ☑ **B.** Communication is the key general management skill a project manager will use the most.

   ☒ Choices **A, C,** and **D** are necessary, but communication accounts for the majority of a project manager's time.

5. Managing a project is best described as which one of the following?
   A. Establishing direction
   B. Functional controls over the project team and stakeholders
   C. Consistently producing key results expected by stakeholders
   D. Motivating and inspiring the project team to produce results that are expected by project stakeholders

   ☑ **C.** Managing has to do with consistently producing key results that are expected by stakeholders.

   ☒ Choices **A** and **D** describe the leadership processes a project manager must possess; therefore, they are wrong. Choice **B** is incorrect, as it describes the functional management position over project team members.

6. When will stakeholders have the most influence over a project's product?
   A. At the end of the project
   B. During scope verification
   C. At the start of a project
   D. At the start of each phase

> ☑ **C.** Of all the choices presented, answer **C** is correct. Stakeholders have the most influence over a project's deliverable at the start of the project.
>
> ☒ Choices **A, B,** and **D** are incorrect because the project is "in motion" and change requests will likely drive the project costs and schedule duration.

7. Which of the following is an example of negotiation?
   A. Arbitration
   B. Formal communications
   C. Conferring
   D. Scope creep

> ☑ **A.** Arbitration is a form of negotiation. Technically, it is a form of assisted negotiation.
>
> ☒ **B** is not a negotiation technique. Choice **C,** conferring, is not negotiating, but a process to seek consensus on a decision. **D** is incorrect, as scope creep is the process of allowing additional activities into the project scope.

8. You are the project manager for your organization. Influencing your organization requires which of the following?
   A. An understanding of the organizational budget
   B. Research and documentation of proven business cases
   C. An understanding of formal and informal organizational structures
   D. Positional power

> ☑ **C.** To influence an organization (in order to get things done), a project manager must understand the explicit and implied organizational structures within an organization.
>
> ☒ Choice **A** is incorrect, since the project manager may not even have access to an organizational budget. **B** is incorrect because a proven business case may not map to every scenario when influencing an organization. Finally, **D** is incorrect because positional power may relate to only a small portion of an organization, not to multiple facets of influence.

9. Your global project is sabotaged by rumors and gossip about the project deliverable. This is an example of:
   A. Cultural achievability
   B. Cultural influences within the project team
   C. Project team mutiny
   D. Ineffective planning

☑ **A.** Rumors and gossip can sabotage a project. This is an example of cultural achievability.

☒ **B** and **C** are incorrect, since rumors and gossip may happen internally and externally to the project team. **D** may be tempting, but the rumors and gossip could happen outside of the effective planning completed by the project manager and the project team.

10. What is the difference between a standard and a regulation?
    A. Standards are mandatory; regulations are not.
    B. Standards are optional; regulations are not.
    C. Regulations and standards are essentially the same.
    D. Regulations are usually mandatory; standards may be seen as guidelines.

☑ **B.** Of all the choices presented, **B** is the best answer, since regulations are mandatory requirements.

☒ Choice **A** is incorrect because it does not accurately describe regulations and standards. **C** is incorrect—standards and regulations are not the same. Choice **D** is incorrect since regulations are always mandatory.

11. All of the following are examples of stakeholders that have a positive influence on a project except for which one?
    A. Business leaders in a community affected by a commercial development project
    B. Team members that will receive a bonus if the project is successful
    C. Employees that prefer the older version of the software that a project is replacing
    D. Functional managers that want your project to complete so their employees can move onto other projects

☑ **C.** The employees that do not want the deliverable of a project are negative stakeholders.

☒ Choices **A, B,** and **D** are all greatly affected by the success of the project; these are positive stakeholders.

12. Which of the following is an example of a deliverable at the end of the requirements-gathering phase in a software design project?
    A. Responsibility matrix creation
    B. Detail design document
    C. Business needs
    D. Project team assembled

☑ **B.** The detail design document is an output of the design phase.
☒ Choice **A** is incorrect because the responsibility matrix creation is a process, not an output of itself. **C** is incorrect because business needs may prompt the project to begin; they are not an output of a phase. **D** is also wrong because the project team assembled is part of the project process; it is not an output.

13. You are the project manager for the ERP Project. Your organization uses a PMO. The primary purpose of a project office is to:
- A. Support the project managers
- B. Support the project sponsor
- C. Support the project team
- D. Identify the stakeholders

☑ **A.** The PMO supports the project manager.
☒ **B** and **C** are incorrect because the project office does not support the project sponsor and project team. Choice **D** is incorrect because stakeholder objectives may vary from stakeholder to stakeholder.

14. Which of the following best describes a project deliverable?
- A. The resources used by the project to complete the necessary work
- B. The resources exported from the project as a result of the project work
- C. The end result of a project planning session
- D. The tangible good or service created by the project team

☑ **D.** Recall that projects are temporary endeavors to create a unique product or service.
☒ **A** is incorrect because resources devoted to the project do not constitute a project deliverable. **B** and **C** are incorrect, since project work is not a deliverable and there will be multiple planning sessions on most projects. The work of a project often will result in a deliverable, not resources or a work product.

15. At what point in a project would a kill point be acceptable?
- A. When a project team member is not performing as planned
- B. When a project reaches the end of a project phase
- C. When a project reaches the end of its budget
- D. When a project manager determines the project team cannot continue

☑ **B.** Kill points are typically executed at the end of a project phase. A kill point does not mean the project is killed, just that the potential for termination exists.

☒ Choices **A, C,** and **D** may appear to be correct, but they do not adequately describe a kill point.

16. Of the following, which is not an exit criterion?

   A. Customer sign-offs

   B. Quality metrics

   C. Stakeholder analysis

   D. Regulatory inspections

☑ **C.** Exit criterion are activities or evidence that allow a project to move forward. Stakeholder expectations are universal to the entire project, not just to one project phase.

☒ Choices **A, B,** and **D** are all examples of activities that can be considered exit criteria.

17. The compilation of all the phases within a project equates to _____.

   A. The project life cycle

   B. The product life cycle

   C. Project completion

   D. Project processes

☑ **A.** The project life cycle is comprised of all of the project phases within a project.

☒ **B** describes the life of many projects that create a unique product or service. **C** and **D** are incorrect, since they do not accurately describe the project life cycle.

18. Management has asked Nancy to determine if a project concept is valid and can be completed using a reasonable amount of time and finances. Management is asking for which of the following?

   A. Kill points

   B. Cost and time estimates

   C. A project case study

   D. A feasibility study

☑ **D.** Management is looking for a feasibility study to determine if it is practicable for a project to exist.

☒ Choice **A** is incorrect, since kill points are within a project and typically don't prove project feasibility. Cost and time estimates, answer **B,** are not the elements Nancy or management needs at this juncture. Choice **C,** project case study, may seem correct, but **D** is a superior answer, since it is the formal name for the report documenting the project's feasibility.

19. Henry, the project manager of the MHB Project, has allowed a subsequent project phase to begin before the predecessor phase is complete. This is an example of which of the following?

    A. Crashing

    B. Fast tracking

    C. Risk management

    D. Tandem scheduling

    ☑ **B.** Fast tracking is the process of allowing successor phases (or activities) to begin before predecessor phases (or activities) are complete.

    ☒ **A** is incorrect because crashing is the process of adding more resources to the project in an attempt to complete the project sooner. **C,** risk management, happens throughout the project; therefore, it is wrong. **D** is also wrong because tandem scheduling is not a relevant term in this instance.

20. Which of the following describes the early stages of a project?

    A. High costs and high demand for resources

    B. A high demand for change

    C. A high demand for project team time

    D. Low costs and low demand for resources

    ☑ **D.** Projects typically have low costs and low demand for resources early in their life cycle.

    ☒ Choices **A, B,** and **C** are incorrect statements in regard to projects.

21. At which point is the risk of failure the least but the consequence of failure the highest?

    A. During the early stages

    B. During the middle stages

    C. During the final stages

    D. Risk of failure is even across all project phases

☑ **C.** As the project moves closer to completion, the likelihood of risk diminishes.

☒ Choices **A, B,** and **D** are incorrect in regard to risk assessment in a project.

22. Tracey is the project manager of the KHG Project. Her organization is a classic functional environment. Her level of authority as a project manager can be best described as which of the following?

    A. Low

    B. Moderate

    C. Balanced

    D. High

☑ **A.** Tracey will most likely have a low amount of authority in a functional organizational structure.

☒ Choices **B** and **C** are incorrect because they describe the matrix structures. Choice **D** is incorrect, since it is relevant to a projectized structure.

23. Project team members are most likely to work full-time on a project in which of the following organizational structures?

    A. Functional

    B. Weak matrix

    C. Strong matrix

    D. Projectized

☑ **D.** Projectized structures often have project team members assigned to the project on a full-time basis.

☒ Choices **A, B,** and **C** are incorrect, since these structures have part-time project teams.

24. A project with much risk and reward is most likely to be accepted in which of the following?

    A. An entrepreneurial company

    B. A heavily regulated company

    C. A nonprofit organization

    D. A community

☑ **A.** Projects with much risk and reward are most likely to be accepted within an entrepreneurial organization.

☒ Choices **B, C,** and **D** are typically more adverse to risk and likely wouldn't accept a project with a large amount of risk.

25. Where can a project manager expect to receive templates?
   A. Commercial databases
   B. The project office
   C. The project sponsor
   D. PMIS

☑ **B.** The project office is the best choice, since its role is to support the project manager.

☒ Choice **A,** commercial databases, may be feasible, but it is not the best choice presented. Project sponsors, choice **C,** are not typically going to provide the project manager with templates. Choice **D,** project management information systems, may have project templates available, but the project office is the best choice presented.

3

Adapting the Project Management Processes

Did you ever have one of those Junior Scientist Chemistry Kits when you were a kid? These kits had recipes for different reactions, formulas, and experiments. You could make smoke, sparks, smells, and iridescent colors if you followed the step-by-step directions. Of course, if you were a "real scientist," you'd experiment and things could go haywire. One small change, an uncalculated variable, or a mistaken catalyst could cause your whole experiment to literally blow up in your face.

Sounds like project management, doesn't it?

All of the different elements in project management are integrated. The cost, time, scope, cultural achievability, technical achievability, and more are all related and interdependent. A small change, delay, decision (or lack thereof) can amplify into serious problems further down the project timeline.

The work of project management is full of processes—42 of 'em in fact. There are logical groupings of these processes: initiating, planning, executing, monitoring, controlling, and, finally, closing. Of course, for your PMP exam, you'll want to be familiar with all of these process groups and all of the activities that happen in each group. But more importantly (yes, even more important than your PMP exam), you'll need to know how to apply these processes to your job out in the real world.

Just because there are loads of processes available doesn't uniformly mean that a project manager can—or should—complete every project management process in every project. You do not have to follow every process on every project—only use the processes that are most appropriate. The project manager along with the project team should determine which processes are needed in order to successfully complete the project. Just to be clear, project managers don't have to use every process on every project. As a whole, for projects to be successful, you'll need four things:

- The application of the most appropriate project management processes to complete the project
- A solid plan and execution of this solid plan to meet project and product requirements
- A method to satisfy stakeholder expectations and requirements
- An approach to keep the project's time, cost, quality, scope, resources, and risk in balance

Project management, unlike those Junior Scientist Chemistry Kits, doesn't come with exact step-by-step directions. It is a fluid process with general guidelines, stakeholder requirements, and you leading the project to achieve the customer's requirements. In this chapter, we'll talk about how all of the different parts of a project are interrelated. Specifically, we'll discuss the project processes and their interactions, the ability to customize the project processes, and how all of this business works towards your current project of passing the PMP examination.

CERTIFICATION OBJECTIVE 3.01

Learning the Project Processes

All projects, from technology to architecture, are composed of processes. Recall that phases are unique to each project and that the goal of the phase is to conclude with a specific, desired result. The completion of phases is the end of the project, culminating in the creation of a unique product, service, or result. Processes are a series of actions with a common, parent goal to create a result, such as the one Figure 3-1 reflects. Processes within project management monitor and move the phases along.

In your organization, you may treat equipment as a true resource. For example, manufacturing equipment, printing equipment, or even transactions may be treated as resources whose time is billable to project customers.

FIGURE 3-1

Projects are completed through project processes.

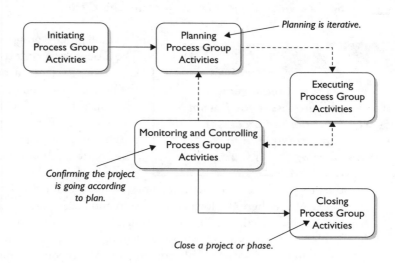

People perform processes. It may be tempting to say that a piece of equipment, such as a manufacturing device, a computer, or a bulldozer, completes the process, but it is technically, for your exam, a person or group of people that complete the process. Think of the processes within a project you've worked on. Know that the processes are not the individual activities, but the control of individual activities to complete a project phase.

Identifying the Project Management Process Groups

The following are the five project management process groups and what occurs under each:

- **Initiating** The project or project phase is authorized.
- **Planning** Project objectives are determined, as well as how to reach those objectives with the identified constraints, project scope, schedule, costs, quality demands, and risks.
- **Executing** The project is executed utilizing acquired resources.
- **Monitoring and controlling** Project performance is monitored and measured to ensure the project plan is being implemented to design specifications and requirements.
- **Closing** The project, its phases, and contracts are brought to a formal end.

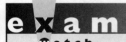 *See the video Project Management Life Cycle.*

Project management processes are the processes you'll want to study. Product-oriented processes, on the other hand, are unique to the organization creating the product.

These process groups are not solo activities. The groups are a collection of activities that contribute to the control and implementation of the project management life cycle. The output of one process group will act as input for another process group. For example, one of the outputs of the initiating process is the project charter. The charter is thus input for the planning processes, being that it authorizes and sanctions the project, the project manager, and the resources required to complete the project work. While there is a logical succession and order to the flow of the processes, process groups will overlap other groups (as shown in Figure 3-2).

Not only will process groups overlap, but some process groups may be repeated based on the activities within the project. When you're managing a multiphase, large project, you'll even repeat initiating and closing. Most projects, because of

FIGURE 3-2

Process groups may overlap other process groups.

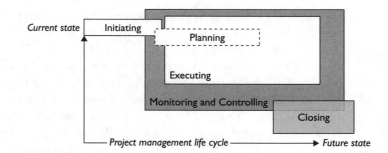

the cyclic nature of the project management work, will at least repeat planning, monitoring and controlling, and executing processes throughout the project, as Figure 3-3 demonstrates.

For example, within a project designed to create a new piece of software, there will be logical project phases: design, build, test, implement, and so on. Within each of the phases, project processes can also exist. Each phase of the project has processes unique to the logical activities within that phase. The closing processes

FIGURE 3-3

Processes may be iterative throughout the project.

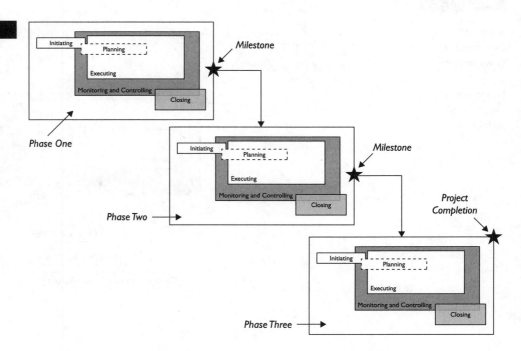

happen at the end of each project phase and at the end of the project. With that thought, know that the closing process of a project phase can serve as input for the next phase within the project.

There's more than one correct way to manage a project. It's a project manager's role to follow the method for project management that his organization subscribes to—or, in many instances, it's the project manager's role to find the best approach to reach a successful project conclusion. Every organization can have a slightly different approach to project management. Regardless of the project management approach, however, the project management processes within project management are always the same: integrative and interdependent.

Project management does, to some extent, follow W. Edwards Deming's quality approach of "Plan-Do-Check-Act," as shown in Figure 3-4. Project management is full of iterations, repetitive work, and constant controlling and monitoring. The primary difference between Deming's model and PMI's model is that a project will end with the closing process group, whereas Deming's quality approach is continuously repeated.

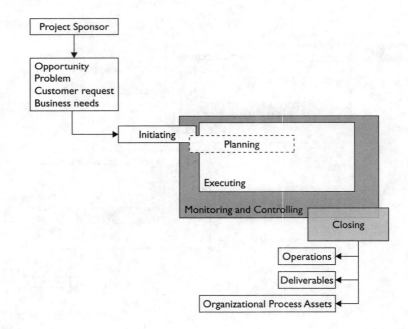

FIGURE 3-4

A project's management flows through project boundaries and iterations of processes.

CERTIFICATION OBJECTIVE 3.02

Identifying the Initiating Process Group

This process group launches the project or phase and allows the project manager to have authority over the project. Project initiation, while simple on the surface, admits that there is some problem that a solution should solve. As a solution is considered, a level of authority is transferred from senior management to the project manager to lead the organization to the desired future state.

In most organizations, much of the work of the initiation process group happens outside of the project manager's control and sometimes doesn't even involve this person. This is one of those "chicken-or-the-egg" scenarios. Many PMP candidates ask, "If a project manager isn't identified until the charter is formed, what's initiation got to do with the project manager?" Let's be realistic for a moment: The project manager is involved with the initiation process group because her input, guidance, and participation are needed. Sure, sure, the project isn't official until the charter is signed, but everyone usually knows who the project manager is going to be.

Identifying Needs

A project is generally called upon to provide a solution to a problem or to take advantage of an opportunity. The needs of the current state are then answered by the deliverables of the proposed project. These needs might have to do with:

- Reducing costs
- Increasing revenues
- Eliminating waste
- Increasing productivity and efficiency
- Solving a business or functional problem
- Taking advantage of market opportunities

This is just a short list. Countless other needs can be addressed through project plans.

Business reasons for why a project is created depend on your business objectives. If you're pitching a project to management, address the most prevalent business needs first. So first, from a business perspective, answer the following question: "Why is this important to my organization?"

Creating a Feasibility Study

A feasibility study is conducted to prove a problem actually exists, document the opportunities at hand, and then determine if a project can be created to resolve the problem or take advantage of the opportunity cited. A feasibility study may also look at the cost of the solution in relation to the possible rewards gained by its implementation.

Identifying the Business Needs

The business needs will examine the problem, opportunity, and solution to see how the potential project and its expected outcome fit within the realm of the business vision and goals. Recall the organizational pyramid in the following illustration? The business level of an organization asks, "Why is this important?" The focus of the business level is vision and strategy, so the results of the project must support that level. Projects must align with the strategy of the organization.

Creating a Product Description

The initial product description will describe what the expected outcome of the project is to be. This may be a service, a product, or even a description of the desired future state. The initial product description does not have to be an exact specification document of what the project will create, though in some instances it may. Typically, the product description describes the high-level solution or realized opportunity that the project will accomplish.

Creating a Project Charter

The project charter authorizes the project, officially naming the project manager and authorizing the project work. Yes, it's true that the project manager and the project management team may write the project charter, but the charter's approval and funding are outside the project's boundaries. In others words, the project charter should be approved and funded by an individual within the organization who has the proper authority to approve the project manager, the needed funds, and the resources that will be utilized within the project work.

on the **job**

Project charters authorize. When you think of the project charter, think authority for the project manager.

The project manager is officially named in the project charter, but the involvement of the project manager will likely come early on in this process group. The project manager will need to know the expectations of his role in the type of organizational structure he is participating in (functional, matrix, projectized, or composite). The organizational structure recognition is important, since it will determine the level of authority and power that the project manager can expect within a project.

The project charter should also reflect the initial scope, the needed resources to complete the project, and any identified assumptions and constraints. Constraints such as a preset budget or mandatory project deadline must be identified in the project charter, as this sets the tempo and immediate expectations for the project's success.

In order to create a project charter, the project management team requires the following:

- A contract, if the project is being completed for another entity
- Business case defining the project purpose to capture an opportunity, solve a problem, or other reason why the project is authorized
- A project statement of work identifying the project's goals
- Enterprise environmental factors, such as the organization's structure, culture, and relevant regulations and standards
- Organizational process assets, including policies, standard project management forms, templates, and organizational procedures that affect the project work

Identify the Project Stakeholders

Stakeholders are the people, groups, and organizations that are affected by the project's existence and outcome. Stakeholders have varying roles in the project, such as contributing project information, paying for the project, working on the project, or receiving and using the project deliverables. Stakeholders' roles, interest, participation, and contact information should all be recorded in the stakeholder registry.

Some stakeholders will be happy your project exists and will want your project to succeed. These are your favorite people, and they're considered positive stakeholders. Those pesky, gloomy people who don't like your project and want your project to fail are, as you might have guessed, negative stakeholders. A stakeholder management strategy is needed, as you'll want to communicate accurately, timely, and effectively with both positive and negative stakeholders. The stakeholder management strategy is directly linked to the project communications management.

CERTIFICATION OBJECTIVE 3.03

Identifying the Planning Process Group

The planning processes are iterative in nature; a project manager does not complete the planning processes and then move on to other activities within the project, never to return. Throughout the project, the project manager and the project team will be returning to the planning processes as often as needed. Changes to the project scope, new risks, challenges, and issues all can send the project back to planning. It's not a bad thing—it's supposed to work this way.

<table>
<tr>
<td>

watch   *Perhaps the most important reason to include stakeholders is that they can contribute to the project management plan. Stakeholders know things that the project team doesn't; thus, you should use the stakeholders to help plan the project and to help it succeed.*

</td>
</tr>
</table>

The project manager should include the stakeholders in the planning processes as much as possible to obtain buy-in of the project deliverables. Including the project stakeholders not only accomplishes buy-in, but also provides shared ownership of the project. This is important because shared ownership allows the customer to recognize the value and intensity of the project work and process. In addition, the project manager should include stakeholders to ensure the project deliverables are in alignment with what the stakeholders and the project team are expecting to receive.

Collect and Document Project Requirements

As part of planning, the stakeholders' expectations and requirements must be analyzed. The stakeholders' expectations must be documented, prioritized, and balanced between competing objectives. Managing stakeholders' expectations is crucial to a project's success, so having a complete understanding of their expectations is mandatory. Business analysts can help the project manager identify and elicit project requirements. It's paramount to have a clear vision of the project's deliverables to save time and frustration and to promote accuracy within project planning.

Stakeholder analysis allows the project manager and the project team to determine the expectations of the customer. If the customer doesn't know what their expectations are, the project manager cannot decide for them. The project manager and the customer must be in agreement with what the project should create before the creation begins.

Within large or highly technical projects, planning can also be known as rolling wave planning. Rolling wave planning focuses detailed planning on the immediate activities of the project rather than on remote, future activities that may be affected by the outcome of the direct project results. The issues further downstream are addressed in rolling wave planning, but in high-level detail, rather than the specifics the pressing focus is on. This is an example of progressive elaboration.

on the job

Rolling wave planning is an acceptable planning solution for long projects whose later planned activities in the project schedule are unknown or will be determined based on the results of early project phases.

Creating the Project Scope

Project managers must have a scope management plan that defines how the project scope will be defined, what changes will be allowed, and how the scope can be controlled. The scope management plan also defines the approach to create the work breakdown structure.

The scope statement is a document that describes the work, and only the required work, necessary to meet the project objectives. It is based on the project charter, identified requirements, and organizational process assets. The scope statement establishes a common vision among the project stakeholders to establish the point and purpose of the project work. It is used as a baseline against which all future project decisions are made in order to determine if proposed changes or work results are aligned with expectations. The scope statement may, with adequate reason, be updated to reflect changes in the project work.

The project manager and the project team should create a change management plan that specifies how the project scope may be changed, what the procedure to change the scope is, and what the requirements are to make a change. On large or high-profile projects, the project manager may be working with a change control board (CCB) to determine if changes should be approved and factored into a project scope.

Creating the Work Breakdown Structure

The work breakdown structure (WBS) is an organized collection of the project-deliverable components to be created by project work. The project manager cannot complete this activity alone. The input and guidance of the project team is required, as they are the individuals closest to the work and will be completing the actual activities within the project phases. The WBS is not a list of activities—it's a deliverables-oriented decomposition of the project. The activity list is based on the identified deliverables within the WBS.

Along with the WBS, the project team will create a WBS dictionary. The WBS dictionary is a companion document to the WBS. It defines all of the elements of the WBS and their project attributes, such as time, cost, quality, and risk. When (and if) the project scope is changed, the WBS and the WBS dictionary are also changed to reflect the scope updates.

Creating the Activity List

The activity list, as I mentioned, is based on the WBS. The project manager and the project team will decompose the project scope statement into deliverables in the form of a WBS. The smallest item in the WBS is called a work package. Each work package is related to an activity or set of activities that will create the deliverables. The sum of all of the activities will create all the work packages, which in turn satisfies the project scope. In other words, if your project team completes all of the project activities on the activity list, they will have created all of the work packages. When all of the work packages are created, the project scope is fulfilled.

This planning process also documents the attributes of each activity in the activity list. The project team should document any risks, issues, or concerns about the nature of the activity to prevent problems during project execution. The project manager and the project management team will also identify the project milestones with the activity list. A milestone is a timeless event that signals project progress. By identifying the milestones with the activity list, it is clear which activities will contribute to the milestone. It's also useful, as milestones are typically created by the completion of a project phase. Now the project manager and team can see the work required in each phase of the project.

Creating the Network Diagram

Once the activity list has been created, the project team can sequence the activities in the order in which the work should be completed. The network diagram, also called the project network diagram (PND), illustrates the flow of activities to complete the project and/or the project phase. It identifies the sequencing of activities noted within the WBS and determines which activities may be scheduled sequentially versus in tandem.

PMP
Coach

You'll create a plan for your projects, so you ought to create a plan for your PMP exam preparation. Define what areas you need to work on, how you'll study, and when you'll study. And like all plans—it's largely up to the execution to complete the project objectives. Work smart and knock this exam out!

Estimating Project Resources

Resources are people, equipment, facilities, and materials that are needed in order to complete the project activities. You'll need to know what resources are needed in order to do accurate time and cost estimates later in planning. The project manager can rely on the project team for much of the project resource estimating, as they're closest to the project work, but you can also rely on historical information, expert judgment, and supporting detail.

It's at this point in the project planning that a resource calendar should be created, if one does not exist within the organization already. A resource calendar helps the project manager identify when resources are available and complete scheduling of the needed resources. Consider people, meeting rooms, and equipment when you think of the resource calendar—it's more than just the project team members you'll utilize on the project work.

Developing the Project Schedule

The project schedule is dependent on the creation of the WBS, the PND, and the availability of the resources. Based on when the resources, the project team, and other required resources, such as equipment and facilities, are available, the schedule can be determined. In many instances, the project must be scheduled according to time constraints. Using the constraint of a deadline on the project, all activities must be scheduled, from the project's start to its completion, to ensure the project can finish on time.

The critical path is the chain of activities within the PND that cannot be delayed without delaying the project end date. There can be more than one critical path,

FIGURE 3-5

Project network
diagrams illustrate
a project's
workflow.

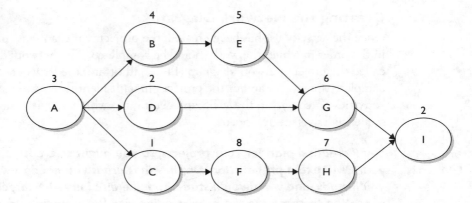

and it is possible for the critical path to change. The other paths within the PND
have float or slack. Float or slack means these paths may be delayed to a point
without delaying the end result of the project. Figure 3-5 shows a typical project
network diagram.

Completing Estimates

Time and cost estimates are completed within the planning process. Time estimates
reflect the amount of time to complete each activity within the WBS. Once the
estimates are mapped to the PND, an accurate estimate of how long the project will
take to complete may be created.

Cost estimates can be calculated a number of different ways, such as through
top-down estimates, bottom-up estimates, or the dreaded informal "hallway
estimates." All estimates should identify a range of variance reflective of the degree
of confidence of the estimate, the assumption the estimate is based on, and how long
the estimate is valid.

Planning for Project Financials

The project manager and the project team need to create a cost estimate for the
project work. Cost estimates should include a qualifier, such as +/– 10 percent and
the reasoning behind the qualifier.

The project budget is the cost of the project, cash flow projections, and how the
monies will be spent. The project budget should cover the cost of the team's time,
facilities, and all foreseeable expenses. Cash flow projections are needed to alert
management as to when monies must be available for the project to continue.
Figure 3-6 demonstrates a project with expected cash flow expenses.

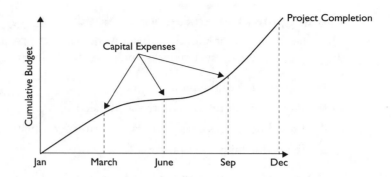

FIGURE 3-6

Cash flow projections allow an organization to plan for project expenses.

Creating a Quality Management Plan

The quality management plan details how the project will map to the organizational quality policy—for example, ISO 9000 or Six Sigma specific actions. The plan will provide specifics on how the project team will meet the quality expectations of the organizational quality assurance (QA) program. The quality management plan also sets the guidelines for how the project will adhere to quality control (QC) mechanisms and ongoing quality improvement. The following illustration demonstrates how QC fits within QA.

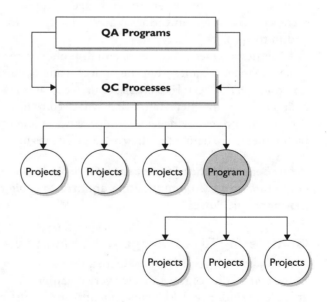

Planning for Human Resource Needs

The project team completes the project work, while the project manager relies on the project team to do several tasks, including the following:

- Completion of the project work
- Providing information on the work needed to complete the project scope
- Providing the necessary accuracy in project estimating
- Reporting on project progress

The project manager must use human resource and leadership skills to guide and lead the project team to project completion. The human resource plan will document planning decisions made about the project resources. In some organizations, the project team may be assigned to the project, while in other organizations, the project manager may have the luxury of handpicking the project team members.

Creating a Communications Management Plan

The communications management plan determines who needs what information, how they need it, and when it will be delivered. The plan specifies team meetings, reports, expectations for reports, and expectations of communication among team members. The communications plan must account for all needed communications within the project.

Consider a project manager of a high-profile project called Project XYZ. The project manager requires that the project team members report their progress on Project XYZ every Tuesday at the project status meeting. In addition to team members reporting their status, they will need to update their work electronically through the project management information system (PMIS). These communication requirements are defined in the communications management plan.

It has been said that 90 percent of a project manager's time is spent communicating. Communicating equates to a big chunk of project management duties.

Completing Risk Management Planning

Risk can be both good and bad. Generally, risk is a perceived threat (or opportunity) to the completion of the project. Every organization has a different approach and attitude towards risk. Risk management planning defines the project manager's obligations to acknowledge, document, research, and plan for risks within the project. Many organizations use a predefined risk management plan that all project managers must adhere to.

Identifying Project Risks

The initial risk assessment allows the project manager and the project team to determine what high-level risks may influence the feasibility, resources, and requirements needed to complete the project. The initial risk assessment may also steer the project toward a different solution. Risk assessment is an ongoing, active project management process. All identified risks and their characteristics, responses, and analysis results are recorded in the project risk register.

Completing Qualitative and Quantitative Risk Analyses

Risk assessment is an in-depth analysis of the project risks through qualitative and quantitative analyses. Qualitative risk analysis calls for a probability and impact matrix. Risks are typically categorized as high, medium, and low. Quantitative risk analysis is a more in-depth study of the identified risks. This technique calls for a risk matrix based on probability and impact. Quantitative analysis also uses simulations and decision tree models.

Completing Risk Response Planning

The risks are analyzed for both positive and negative impacts, entered through a risk matrix, and then planned for accordingly. Risks may be accepted, avoided, mitigated, countered, or planned for through contingency. Risks are also assigned to risk owners, who will monitor thresholds and triggers.

Planning for Project Procurement

Chances are that a project will need to purchase materials and services and hire contractors to complete the project work. The purchase of a thing or service requires the project manager to follow the organizational policies and procedures for procurement. This can include finding qualified vendors, requesting quotes or proposals, and reviewing those proposals for the best vendor. The procurement management plan will guide the project manager through the processes of selecting vendors, the appropriate procurement documents, and contract selection and administration.

Officially Launching the Project Work

Planning is an iterative process. The result of planning is to allow the project work to begin. Once the project has reached a collective state of agreement between the project manager, management, the project team, and the customer, the project execution is officially allowed to begin. Bear in mind that planning does not have to be 100 percent complete for project execution to begin. Planning can move through iterations, as appropriate, based on the project work, conditions, and demands of the organization.

CERTIFICATION OBJECTIVE 3.04

Managing the Executing Processes

The executing processes allow the project team to perform the project work. It is the execution of the project plan, the execution of the vendor management, and the management of the project implementation. The project manager works closely with the project team in this process to ensure that the work is being completed and that the work results are of quality. The project manager also works with vendors to ensure that their procured work is complete, of quality, and meets the obligations of the agreed-upon contracts.

Variances are the difference between what was planned and what was experienced. Common variances are time and cost estimates, risk impacts, risks that were not identified but came into planning, and the availability of project resources. Some variances can spur change requests that will cause the project management plan to be changed, the scope to be broadened or reduced, or, in some situations, cause the project to be rebaselined.

Directing and Managing Project Execution

This is the business of getting the project done. The project team executes the work as defined in project management plan, and the project manager manages the work. This also includes the management of the organizational and technical interfaces the project manager must interact with to ensure that project work flows smoothly and as planned. The bulk of the project time and budget are consumed during project execution.

A work authorization system is a method that allows work to begin according to schedule and circumstance. It provides for the verification of predecessor activities and the permission to begin successor activities. When changes have been approved, the project management plan is updated, baselines are rebaselined to reflect the changes, and the changes are, according to the plan, executed into being.

Mapping to Quality Assurance

As the project work continues, the project team and the project manager will need to verify that the project work results are mapping to the organization's quality assurance program as described in the quality management plan. Failure to adhere to

INSIDE THE EXAM

What, in this chapter, must you focus on for your PMP exam? Hmm ... could it be processes? Processes are activities that are completed by people, not things. On the exam, you won't need to know facts like which process is the most important, but rather which activity should the project manager complete next. Just substitute "activity" for the appropriate process, and you're on your way.

Focus on the project management processes. Know the five process groups and how the processes among those groups are interrelated. It will behoove you to know, if not memorize, all 42 project management processes (shown later in this chapter). If you want to pass your exam, and I know you do, know which processes happen in which knowledge area.

Create some witty acrostic to memorize the knowledge areas and the processes within each process group. Here are a few other key exam tips to take from this chapter:

- Larger projects require more detail than smaller projects.
- Projects fail at the beginning, not at the end.
- The processes may be customized to meet the demands or conditions of the project.
- Planning is iterative.
- Planning, executing, and controlling are tightly integrated.

the quality assurance program may result in penalties, project delays, and work that needs to be redone, as shown in the following illustration.

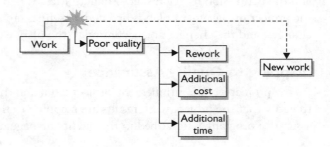

Acquiring and Developing the Project Team

There needs to be a project team in order for the project to be completed. Based on the organizational structure, the project manager will recruit the project team or the project team will be assigned to the project manager. In some organizations, such as with a functional structure, the project team will already be assembled. The project plan will dictate what roles and responsibilities are needed for the project, while the staffing management plan will guide how human resources, the project manager, and the project team members interact.

The project team members will be assigned work to complete, while the project manager oversees and manages the work the project team members do. One challenge for all project managers is the availability of project team members. It's not much fun for project managers or project team members when multiple projects create various demands simultaneously. This happens far too much in matrix structures, where project team members are likely to work on multiple projects. That's why, once again, the reliance of a resource calendar is needed to identify when resources are available and to reserve resources for your project.

on the **job**

Competition for resources is common. It's not unusual for some less-than-bright project managers to hoard resources. For example, I once consulted on a project where a developer was assigned to a project that lasted 18 months. The developer was only needed for about 200 hours for the entire project duration. He surfed the Web, read books, and nearly died of boredom because his time was reserved for the project. It was a total waste of time and talent.

The project manager must work with the project team members to ensure that their level of proficiency is in line with their obligations on the project. This may involve classroom learning, shadowing among project team members, or on-the-job training.

The success of the project work is dependent on the project team's ability. Should the team or team members be lagging in required knowledge to complete the project work, additional education and development are necessary.

As project team members complete their work, the staffing management plan will be referenced by the project manager on how to complete project team member assessments. In particular, reward and recognition systems should be documented and followed. Project team members, just like project managers, like to be rewarded for a job well done.

Managing the Project Team

The project team completes the work, and the project manager ensures that they do so according to the plan. Team management is limited to the authority the project manager has over the project team. In any organizational structure, however, the project manager should evaluate the project team performance and seek methods to improve all team performance to improve the project deliverables. The outcome of managing the project team includes the following:

- Change requests
- Corrective actions
- Preventive actions
- Project management plan updates

At some point in the project, based on the organizational structure, team members will be reassigned to new projects. Reassigning project team members is of utmost importance in a projectized organization, where project team members are with a project full-time through completion. As the project in a projectized organization nears completion, the project team may be anxious about their next assignment. In a functional matrix environment, the project team may fluctuate at phases or milestones as they complete their assignments and then move on to other activities within the organization.

Dispersing Project Information

Information must be disseminated according to the communications plan. Stakeholders will need to be kept abreast of the project status. Management may want milestone reports, variance reports, and status reports, and customers will have specific communications requirements. All of these demands, from any stakeholder, should be documented within the communications plan—and then followed through in the execution process.

Manage Stakeholder Expectations

When it comes to managing stakeholder expectations, it's really about communicating with the project stakeholders. The project manager needs to address the stakeholders' concerns, needs, and perceived threats about the project. This execution process is somewhat reliant on the stakeholder management strategy identified earlier in the project. Issues, risks, and changes are all things that the project manager needs to address directly with stakeholders to keep the project moving.

Managing Procurement Activities

In most projects, vendors are involved at some point. Part of the executing process is to find the best vendors to be involved with the project. Adequate timing is required for the procurement process to allow the vendors to provide adequate, appropriate information for the project—and to allow the project manager to make an educated decision on which vendors should be selected. Procurement includes obtaining quotations, bids, and proposals for the services or goods to be purchased for the project's completion.

This part of procurement involves making a decision as to which identified vendor will be the source of the service or good being procured. Source selection is based upon the selection criteria determined by the performing organization.

Once a vendor has been selected, procurement involves administering the contracts between the buyer and the seller. The contract must be fair and legal. The contract typically is a document that represents the offer and acceptance of both parties. Some organizations may utilize centralized contracting or a contracting office to manage all project contracts.

CERTIFICATION OBJECTIVE 3.05

Monitoring and Controlling the Project

The monitoring and controlling processes are the activities that ensure the project goes according to plan and identifies the actions that need to be implemented when evidence proves the project isn't going according to plan. Specifically, the controlling processes verify project work and the response to that work. In addition, the project manager must work to control the predicted cost and schedule of the project. Variances to the cost and schedule will affect the project's success.

At the heart of this process group is simply controlling and monitoring the project work. This means the project manager and the project team actively collect and measure the project's performance, risk, time, cost, and scope. Then, based on the collection of project performance, performance reports, and the project management plan, the project manager can react to performance to improve the project and to forecast project performance based on trend analysis.

Managing Integrated Change Control

Integration management is the control of the project's components and how each part of a project may affect its other parts. For example, a proposed change to the project scope may affect the project schedule, time, cost, quality, risk, communications, human resources, and even procurement issues.

Integrated change control is the process of examining change requests, changes, preventive actions, corrective actions, and defect repairs to see how these issues affect the remaining portions of the project. The outcome of integrated change control includes updates to the project management plan and project scope, but also approved or declined change requests, approved corrective and preventative actions, and validated defect repair. The ultimate result of integrated change control is the project deliverable.

Providing Scope Verification

Scope verification is the process of verifying that the work results are within the expectations of the scope. It is typically done at project phase completion, where the customer formally accepts the product of the project work. Should scope verification fail, corrective actions are generally needed to bring the work results back into alignment with the expectations of the project scope. If the scope has not been met, the project may be halted, reworked, or delayed during a decision-making process by the customer.

Scope verification is a control process. However, at the end of the project, the scope must be verified for final acceptance. This process is completed with the project manager and the key stakeholders. Scope verification is the process of inspecting, touring, and "taking a walkthrough" of the project deliverables to confirm that the requirements of the project have been met. Scope verification may happen at different intervals throughout the project, such as at key milestones or phase completions. Scope verification at the end of a project may require a formal sign-off from the customer that the project is complete and to their satisfaction.

Implementing Scope Change Control

The project manager must follow the change management plan to ensure inappropriate changes to the project scope do not occur. This includes scope creep that the project team may be creating on its own accord—for example, the project team members may be making additional adjustments to the equipment they are installing in a project, even through the project scope does not call for the additional adjustments. Scope change control ensures that the documented procedures to permit changes to the scope are followed.

Enforcing Schedule Control

Schedule control requires constant monitoring of the project's progress, approval of phase deliverables, and task completion. Slippage must be analyzed early in the project to determine the root cause of the problem. Activities that slip may indicate inaccurate estimates, hidden work, or a poor WBS. Quality issues can also throw off the project schedule when the time to redo project activities is taken into consideration, as shown in the following illustration. Finally, the project manager must also consider outside influences and their effect on the project—for example, weather, market conditions, cultural issues, and so on.

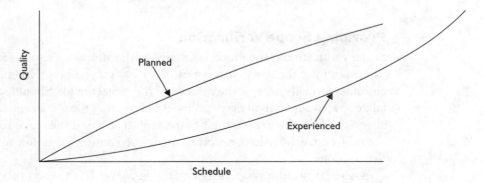

Managing Cost Control

Controlling the project's cost requires accurate estimates and then a check and balance against those estimates. Procurement management, cash flow, and fundamental accounting practices are required. Though cost control is dependent on project expenses, it also hinges on hidden and fluctuating expenses, such as shipping, exchange rates for international projects, travel, and incidentals. Thus, accurate and thorough record keeping is imperative.

Ensuring Quality Control

Quality control (QC) measures work results to determine if they are in alignment with quality standards. If the work results are not of quality, QC uses methods to determine why the results are inadequate and how to eliminate the causes of the quality deficiencies. QC is inspection-driven and strives to keep mistakes away from the project customer.

Ensuring Performance Reporting

The project manager and the project team must work together to report and record accurate completions of work. Performance reporting stems from accurate measurement by the project team, proof of work completion, and factual estimates. The project manager then churns the reported projects through earned value management, schedule baselines, cost baselines, and milestone targets. The status reports to management are reflective of where the project has been, where it stands now, and where it's heading.

Completing Performance Reporting

It's been said that if an organization doesn't measure itself, it cannot improve. As the project moves towards completion, the project manager and the project team must measure the project performance. Performance reporting includes the following:

- Status reports
- Progress measurement
- Forecasting
- Performance reports
- Recommended corrective actions

Monitoring and Controlling Project Risks

Risk management requires risk ownership and monitoring by the project team members. As activities in the project network diagram (PND) are completed, the project manager and the risk owners must pay special attention to the possible risks and the mitigation plans that may come into play. Risk responses, should they be acted on, may cause secondary risks, cost increases, and schedule delays. Risk response must be rapid and thorough—and their outcomes well documented for historical reference for downstream activities and other projects.

on the
job *Risk response may also include risk impact statements that detail project risk, its possible impact on the project, and its probability. The project manager and management sign the risk impact statement for each identified risk beyond a predetermined score.*

Administering Project Procurement

Based on the procurement documents, the project contracts, and the performance of the contracted work, the project manager will administer the project contracts. This means the project manager and the vendor work together to ensure that both parties are adhering to the terms and conditions of the contract. This process is also about fostering relationships with the vendors, clients, and subcontractors. Much of this process can be linked to project communications and documented expectations.

CERTIFICATION OBJECTIVE 3.06

Closing the Project

Closing a project is a wonderful feeling. Project closure has many requirements for it to be successful, however. Project closure requires a final, complete effort by the project manager, the project team, the project stakeholders, and management to officially close the project and move on to other opportunities. The activities in this process are typically associated with the end of a project, but most may also be completed within project phases.

Closing Vendor Contracts

At the completion of a project or project phase, the vendor contracts must be closed out. Confirmation that vendor invoices and purchase orders have been fulfilled, met, and paid is needed to complete the vendor closeout process. Closing out vendor contracts may also require proof of delivery of the goods or services purchased, and vendor contracts may be audited to confirm that vendor responsibilities have been met.

Closing Administrative Duties

When the project is completed, the project manager must finalize all reports, document the project experience, and provide evidence of customer acceptance.

The project manager will create a final report reflecting the project's success or its failure. The project manager will also provide information reflective of the project product and how it met the project requirements, and then will complete the lessons-learned documentation.

on the **Job**

At project completion, a celebration to thank and reward the project team for their hard work and dedication to the project is needed. Celebrations are also a good time to reflect on the work completed, the challenges of the project, and to come back together as a team before moving on to other projects and opportunities within the organization.

How Process Groups Interact

Imagine any project: building a new house, creating a new service, deploying a technology solution. Within any of these projects there will be a logical approach from start to finish. Within project management, and in particular for your PMP exam, the flow of activities must be documented from initiation to closure. The five process groups don't necessarily allow the work to progress—they serve more as a mechanism to identify and oversee the flow of actions within the project.

Each process has unique activities, as you've seen already in this chapter, but each of these activities contributes to and coincides with the project work. The activities guide the project work from concept to completion. Specifically, the parts of the processes are the gears to the "project machine." The processes allow for a specific, manageable, and expected outcome of the project. Within each process, there are three common components:

- **Inputs** Documented conditions, values, and expectations that start the given process
- **Tools and techniques** The actions to evaluate and act upon the inputs to create the outputs
- **Outputs** The documented results of a process that may serve as an input to another process

These three components are fundamental through all five process groups. Typically, plans, documented evidence of problems, or documented outcomes of activities are inputs to a project process—for example, resource planning requires the WBS. The WBS is an input to resource planning, but it's also an output of the planning process group. The tools and techniques used to plan for resources include expert judgment, alternative identification, and your nifty project management software.

Customizing Process Interactions

The processes discussed in the previous section are the mainstream, generally accepted order of operations. You can count on these processes existing and progressing in the preceding order. However, having said that, you can also count on these processes to be flexible and customized to work in any order that the project demands. Project processes are made not of stone but of flexible steel.

The following are some general guidelines about customizing project processes:

■ Projects that are resource-dependent may define roles and responsibilities prior to scope creation. This is because the scope of the project may be limited by the availability of the resources to complete the scope.

■ The processes may be governed by a project constraint. Consider a predetermined deadline, budget, or project scope. The project constraint, such as a deadline, will determine the activity sequencing, the need for resources, risk management, and other processes.

■ Larger projects require more detail. Remember that projects fail at the beginning, not at the end.

■ Subprojects and smaller projects have more flexibility, with the processes based on the usefulness of the process. For example, a project with a relatively small team may not benefit from an in-depth communications plan the same way that a large project with 35 project team members might.

Plotting the Processes

The first three chapters of this book have focused on the project management endeavor, the project management context, and the project management processes. Chapters 4 through 12 will focus on the project management knowledge areas. In those chapters, we'll zoom in on the processes we've identified and break down the topics into exam-specific information. You know that there are five process groups—that's been the thrust of this chapter. There are also, however, nine knowledge areas:

■ **Project integration management**   How all of the project knowledge areas and processes work together

■ **Project scope management**   Defining, executing, and managing the project scope

■ **Project time management**   Creating and controlling the project schedule

- **Project cost management**   Defining and controlling all things financial
- **Project quality management**   Defining and adhering to a project quality policy
- **Project human resources management**   Managing the people on the project team
- **Project communications management**   Communicating the most appropriate information in the best way at the right time in the project
- **Project risk management**   Identifying, analyzing, responding to, and controlling risks within the project
- **Project procurement management**   Purchasing the contracted resources the project needs in order to be successful

While the information covered in this chapter is important, it is more of an umbrella of the nine knowledge areas that you'll want to focus on for your PMP exam. You'll see all of the 42 project management processes in detail in the upcoming chapters. At the beginning of each chapter, I'll highlight the processes the knowledge area deals with. As a quick recap, here's a breakdown of the 42 processes as you've learned about them in this broad chapter.

Initiating the Project

There are just two processes to know for project initiation.

- Create the project charter
- Identify the project stakeholder

Planning the Project

There are 20 processes to know for project planning.

- Create the project management plan
- Gather project requirements
- Create the project scope
- Build the work breakdown structure
- Define the project activities
- Sequence the project activities
- Estimate the project resources

- Estimate the project schedule duration
- Develop the project schedule
- Estimate the project costs
- Establish the project budget
- Create the quality management plan
- Write the human resources plan
- Create the project communications management plan
- Create the project risk management plan
- Identify the project risks
- Complete qualitative risk analysis
- Complete quantitative risk analysis
- Create risk responses
- Create the procurement management plan

Executing the Project

There are eight executing processes.

- Execute the project plan
- Do quality assurance
- Obtain the project team
- Perform team development
- Manage your project team
- Perform information distribution
- Administer stakeholder expectations
- Execute the procurement management plan

Monitoring and Controlling the Project

There are 10 monitoring and controlling processes.

- Monitor and control the project
- Administer integrated change control
- Complete scope verification
- Control the project scope

- Perform schedule control
- Perform cost control
- Administer quality control activities
- Report on the project performance
- Control the project risks according to the risk management plan
- Control and monitor procurement activities

Closing the Project

There are just two closing processes.

- Close out the project or the project phase
- Close out procurement according to the procurement management plan

CERTIFICATION SUMMARY

There are 5 process groups and 42 processes within a project. You'll want to know what activity happens within each of these groups. Projects start in the initiating process group, where projects get authorized. From here, the project moves into the planning process group. Planning is an iterative process and allows the project objectives to be determined, as well as how the project will achieve those objectives. The project plan is executed in the executing process group. The monitoring and controlling process group is where project performance is monitored, measured, and controlled. Finally, the project is completed and the contracts are completed in the closing process group.

You should know that a project can move between planning, monitoring and controlling, and executing as conditions change—for example, a new risk may be identified. This risk is analyzed and then a risk response is created in the planning processes group. The project work moves on, but the risk management is implemented during the executing processes. The response to the risk is monitored in the controlling process group. Should the risk change, the project can revisit the planning processes. Don't subscribe to the theory that the project work stops as the project moves back into planning. Other project activities may continue to operate as the project planning processes group is revisited.

The project moves along according to the project schedule and the project network diagram. Activities on the critical path are actively monitored for slippage, while noncritical path activities are periodically checked for slippage. This is important, as activities on the critical path have no tolerance for delays, while noncritical path activities can be delayed as long as they do not delay the project's completion.

As the project progresses, the project manager must monitor and communicate the project performance. Work results that are below an accepted level of performance must be adjusted with corrective actions to bring the project back into alignment with the cost, schedule, and scope baselines. Communication of the project performance is one of the key elements for successful project management—and for passing the PMP exam.

KEY TERMS

To pass the PMP exam, you will need to memorize these terms and their definitions. For maximum value, create your own flashcards based on these definitions and review them daily.

closing   The fifth of five project management process groups. It contains the processes responsible for closing a project, a project phase, or the procurement relationships.

executing   The project management process group that carries out the project management plan to create the project deliverables.

initiating   The start and authorization of the project; the project manager is identified, the project is authorized through the charter, and the stakeholders are identified.

knowledge areas   There are nine knowledge areas within project management; each knowledge area is a specific portion of the project, and all nine project management knowledge areas are interrelated.

monitoring and controlling   The project management process group responsible for ensuring that the project execution is completed according to the project management plan and expectations.

planning   The iterative process group where the intention of the project is determined and documented in the project management plan.

project charter   The first project document that authorizes the project, identifies the project manager, and creates the high-level objectives for the project.

project communications management   A project management knowledge area that carries out the directions of the project's communication management plan.

project cost management   A project management knowledge area that defines cost estimating, cost budgeting, and cost control.

project human resource management   A project management knowledge area that creates the human resource plan, acquires the project team, develops the project team, and manages the project team.

project integration management   A project management knowledge area that coordinates all of the effort of the project's initiation, planning, executing, monitoring and controlling, and closing.

project procurement management   A project management knowledge area that plans what needs to be procured, procures the project needs, administers the procurement process, and closes procurement according to the project terms and the procurement management plan.

project quality management   A project management knowledge area that coordinates the quality planning, quality assurance, and quality control of the project.

project risk management   A project management knowledge area that creates the risk management plan, performs qualitative and quantitative risk analysis, plans risk responses, and monitors and controls the project risks.

project scope management   A project management knowledge area responsible for collecting project requirements, defining the project scope, creating the WBS, performing scope verification, and controlling the project scope.

project time management   A project management knowledge area that defines the project activities, sequences project work, estimates resources and activity durations, and develops the project schedule. This knowledge area is also responsible for control of the project schedule.

✓ TWO-MINUTE DRILL

Learning the Project Processes

❑ Projects are comprised of processes. People, not things, complete processes; processes move the project or phase to completion.

❑ Process groups comprise the actions within a project. These five process groups have sets of actions that move the project forward towards completion. There are five groups of processes in the project management life cycle:

❑ Initiating

❑ Planning

❑ Executing

❑ Monitoring and controlling

❑ Closing

❑ Just because a process was not completed does not mean it was not needed. A project manager, however, doesn't always have to complete every process within each process group—just those processes that are needed for the project to be successful.

❑ Projects are created to provide a solution for a problem or to take advantage of an opportunity. They can be created to reduce costs, reduce waste, increase revenue, increase productivity and efficiency, or produce other results. The project manager should know why the project is created in order to aim towards the project purpose.

❑ Some projects require a feasibility study to prove that the problem exists or to conduct root-cause analysis to find the root of a given problem. Feasibility studies also determine the capability of the project to solve the identified problem for a reasonable cost and within a reasonable amount of time.

❑ The product description describes the expected outcome of the project. The product description should define what the project is creating. If the project is solving a problem, the product description should describe how the organization will perform without the problem in existence. If the project is seizing a market opportunity, it should describe the organization once the opportunity is seized. Basically, product descriptions describe life after a successful project.

Identifying the Initiating Process Group

❑ This process group launches the project or phase and allows the project manager to have the authority over the project.

❑ The project charter authorizes the project, officially naming the project manager and authorizing the project work.

❑ Stakeholders are the people, groups, and organizations that are affected by the project's existence and outcome.

Identifying the Planning Process Group

❑ Throughout the project, the project manager and the project team will be returning to the planning processes as often as needed. Changes to the project scope, new risks, challenges, and issues all can send the project back to planning.

❑ The stakeholders' expectations must be documented, prioritized, and balanced between competing objectives. Managing stakeholders' expectations is crucial to a project's success, so having a complete understanding of their expectations is mandatory.

❑ Rolling wave planning focuses detailed planning on the immediate activities of the project rather than on remote, future activities that may be affected by the outcome of the direct project results.

Managing the Executing Processes

❑ The executing processes allow the project team to perform the project work. It is the execution of the project plan, the execution of the vendor management, and the management of the project implementation.

❑ Variances are the difference between what was planned and what was experienced.

❑ A work authorization system is a method that allows work to begin according to schedule and circumstance.

Monitoring and Controlling the Project

❑ Integration management is the control of the project's components and how each part of a project may affect its other parts.

❑ Scope verification is the process of verifying that the work results are within the expectations of the scope. It is typically done at project phase completion, where the customer formally accepts the product of the project work.

❑ Quality control (QC) measures work results to determine if they are in alignment with quality standards.

Closing the Project

❑ At the completion of a project or project phase, the vendor contracts must be closed out. Confirmation that vendor invoices and purchase orders have been fulfilled, met, and paid is needed to complete the vendor closeout process.

❑ When the project is completed, the project manager must finalize all reports, document the project experience, and provide evidence of customer acceptance. The project manager will create a final report reflecting the project's success or its failure.

SELF TEST

1. What is a project process?
   A. The creation of a product or service
   B. The progressive elaboration resulting in a product
   C. A series of actions that brings about a result
   D. A series of actions that allows the project to move from concept to deliverable

2. Within a project, there are two distinct types of processes. Which of the following processes is unique to the project?
   A. EVM processes
   B. Project management planning
   C. IPECC
   D. A product-oriented process

3. There are five project management processes that allow projects to move from start to completion. Which one of the following is not one of the project management process groups?
   A. Initiating
   B. Planning
   C. Communicating
   D. Closing

4. Of the following, which is the logical order of the project management processes?
   A. Initiating, planning, monitoring and controlling, executing
   B. Planning, initiating, monitoring and controlling, executing, closing
   C. Initiating, planning, executing, monitoring and controlling, closing
   D. Planning, initiating, executing, closing

5. Which of the project management processes is progressively elaborated?
   A. Planning
   B. Communicating
   C. Contract administration
   D. Closing

6. The ongoing process of project planning is also known as _____.
   A. Constant integration planning
   B. Rolling wave planning
   C. Continuous planning
   D. Phase gates

7. You are the project manager for the AQA Project. You would like to include several of the customers in the project planning sessions, but your project leader would like to know why the stakeholders should be involved since your project team will be determining the best method to reach the project objectives. You explain to the project leader that the stakeholders should be included because _____.
   A. It generates goodwill between the project team and the stakeholders.
   B. It allows the stakeholders to see the project manager as the authority of the project.
   C. It allows the project team to meet the stakeholders and express their concerns regarding project constraints.
   D. It allows the stakeholders to realize the shared ownership of the project.

8. You have requested that several of the stakeholders participate in the different phases of the project. Why is this important?
   A. It prevents scope creep.
   B. It allows for scope constraints.
   C. It improves the probability of satisfying the customer requirements.
   D. It allows for effective communications.

9. The information from the planning phase is input into which of the following processes?
   A. Initiating
   B. Monitoring and controlling
   C. Executing
   D. Closing

10. The information from the initiating phase is input into which of the following processes?
    A. Planning
    B. Executing
    C. Controlling
    D. All of the project phases

11. Which process represents an ongoing effort throughout the project?
    A. Lessons learned
    B. Planning
    C. Closing
    D. EVM

12. Which of the following processes happen in the correct order?

   A. Activity definition, scope planning, activity duration estimating, cost budgeting

   B. Scope planning, resource planning, activity duration estimating, activity sequencing

   C. Scope definition, scope planning, activity definition, activity sequencing

   D. Define scope, define activities, plan quality

13. Which of the following processes happens in the closing process?

   A. Activity definition

   B. Cost budgeting

   C. Quality planning

   D. Close procurement

14. Which of the following planning processes is concerned with reporting relationships?

   A. Organizational planning

   B. Human resource planning

   C. Scope planning

   D. Activity definition

15. Of the following, which process is most concerned with mitigation?

   A. Quality planning

   B. Risk response planning

   C. Procurement planning

   D. Risk identification

16. You are the project manager for the FTG Project. This project will affect several lines of business, and controversy on the project deliverables already abounds. You have 45 key stakeholders on this project representing internal customers from all areas of your organization. With this many stakeholders, what challenge will be the most difficult for the project's success?

   A. Communication

   B. Managing stakeholder expectations

   C. Managing scope creep

   D. Coordinating communications between the project manager, project team, and the project stakeholders

17. Which of the following is representative of a project constraint?

   A. A project that must be finished by year's end

   B. That 45 stakeholders exist on a long-term project

   C. The requirement to complete EVM

   D. The requirement to produce a new product

18. You are a project manager of a large construction project. There are many different stakeholders involved in the project, and each has their own opinion as to what the project should create. To maintain communication, set objectives, and document all decisions, you can say that larger projects generally require _____.

   A. A larger budget

   B. More detail

   C. Phase gate estimating

   D. A large project team

19. In order to create a network diagram, the project manager needs which of the following?

   A. Activity sequencing

   B. Project sponsor approval of the WBS

   C. The WBS dictionary

   D. A cost baseline

20. All of the following are processes that happen within the project cost management knowledge area except for which one?

   A. Cost estimating

   B. Control cost

   C. Determine the project budget

   D. Establishing the resource estimates

21. Which of the following is considered an output of risk management planning?

   A. Activity lists

   B. WBS

   C. The risk management plan

   D. The scope management plan

22. Which project management knowledge area coordinates the efforts of the five process groups?

   A. Project integration management

   B. Project planning

   C. Project management plan creation process

   D. Monitoring and controlling

23. Frances is the project manager of the JHG Project. This project is similar to a recent project she completed for another customer. Which planning process will Frances need to finish first to ensure the project is completed successfully?

   A. Contract planning

   B. Scope definition

   C. Activity sequencing

   D. Quality planning

24. You are the project manager for the BKL Project. This type of project has never been attempted before by your organization. The stakeholders already have high requirements for the project deliverables, and you need to create a change control system. This system should be controlled by which of the following?

   A. A formal change control form

   B. It should be completed by the team.

   C. The change control board

   D. It is specific to the organizational structure.

25. Complete this statement: Projects fail _____.

   A. At the beginning, not at the end

   B. During initiating, not closing

   C. Because of inadequate project managers

   D. Because of the project manager

SELF TEST ANSWERS

1. What is a project process?
   A. The creation of a product or service
   B. The progressive elaboration resulting in a product
   C. A series of actions that brings about a result
   D. A series of actions that allows the project to move from concept to deliverable

   ☑ **C.** A process is a series of actions bringing about a result. Recall that processes exist in projects and in project phases.

   ☒ **A** is incorrect, since this describes the project as a whole. **B** is incorrect, since it also somewhat describes a phase or project as a whole. **D** is incorrect, as it describes the series of processes moving through the project.

2. Within a project, there are two distinct types of processes. Which of the following processes is unique to the project?
   A. EVM processes
   B. Project management planning
   C. IPECC
   D. A product-oriented process

   ☑ **D.** Product-orientated processes are unique to the product the project is creating.

   ☒ EVM processes, choice **A**, are part of project performance measurement. **B**, project management planning, is universal to project management. **C**, IPECC, is the acrostic for the five process groups: initiation, planning, executing, controlling, and closing.

3. There are five project management processes that allow projects to move from start to completion. Which one of the following is not one of the project management process groups?
   A. Initiating
   B. Planning
   C. Communicating
   D. Closing

   ☑ **C.** Communications is an activity that will consume much of the project manager's time, but it is not one of the five process groups.

   ☒ **A, B,** and **D** are incorrect choices, as initiating, planning, and closing are three of the five process groups.

4. Of the following, which is the logical order of the project management processes?
   A. Initiating, planning, monitoring and controlling, executing
   B. Planning, initiating, monitoring and controlling, executing, closing
   C. Initiating, planning, executing, monitoring and controlling, closing
   D. Planning, initiating, executing, closing

☑ **C.** Initiating, planning, executing, monitoring and controlling, and closing is the correct order of the processes presented.
☒ **A** is incorrect, since it is not the correct order of the processes. While **A** does list all five of the process groups, it does not list them in the correct order. **B** and **D** are incorrect, since they do not list the processes in the proper order (or, with **D**, in their entirety). Remember on the PMP exam you will need to choose the answer that is most correct according to the question presented.

5. Which of the project management processes is progressively elaborated?
   A. Planning
   B. Communicating
   C. Contract administration
   D. Closing

☑ **A.** Planning is an iterative process, which is also progressively elaborated. Throughout the project, the project team and the project manager will revisit the planning processes to consider, update, and react to conditions and circumstances within the project.
☒ **B** is incorrect, since communicating is not one of the process groups. **C** is incorrect, as contract administration is not a process group. **D** is incorrect, since closing is not an iterative process, but a concluding process.

6. The ongoing process of project planning is also known as _____.
   A. Constant integration planning
   B. Rolling wave planning
   C. Continuous planning
   D. Phase gates

☑ **B.** Rolling wave planning is a description of the planning process in most large projects. It requires the project manager and the project team to revisit the planning process to address the next phase, implementation, or piece of the project.

☒ **A** is incorrect, since the planning process is not constant but iterative. **C** is incorrect, since there is some pause to the planning processes. **D** is incorrect because phase gates are conditions that allow the projects to move from phase to phase.

7. You are the project manager for the AQA Project. You would like to include several of the customers in the project planning sessions, but your project leader would like to know why the stakeholders should be involved since your project team will be determining the best method to reach the project objectives. You explain to the project leader that the stakeholders should be included because _____.
   A. It generates goodwill between the project team and the stakeholders.
   B. It allows the stakeholders to see the project manager as the authority of the project.
   C. It allows the project team to meet the stakeholders and express their concerns regarding project constraints.
   D. It allows the stakeholders to realize the shared ownership of the project.

   ☑ **D.** Involving the stakeholders in the planning processes allows for shared ownership of the project.
   ☒ **A** is incorrect because although it may generate goodwill between the project team and the stakeholders, this is not the predominant goal of stakeholder involvement. **B** is incorrect because the project charter and the project manager reputation will establish authority more than stakeholder involvement. **C** is incorrect because while the stakeholders may express their concerns regarding the project constraints, such concerns should be addressed as part of the planning processes, not in addition to them.

8. You have requested that several of the stakeholders participate in the different phases of the project. Why is this important?
   A. It prevents scope creep.
   B. It allows for scope constraints.
   C. It improves the probability of satisfying the customer requirements.
   D. It allows for effective communications.

   ☑ **C.** By involving the stakeholders at different aspects of the project, their requirements are more likely to be met. Specifically, scope verification ensures that the stakeholders are seeing that phase deliverables, project progress, quality, and expectations are being met.
   ☒ **A** is incorrect because the untimely introduction of stakeholders can actually increase scope creep. **B** is incorrect because scope constraints will be evident early in the project, rather than during the implementation of the project work. **D** is incorrect, since stakeholder presence does not ensure effective communications. Effective communications will stem from the project manager and the requirements identified and documented in the communications management plan.

9. The information from the planning phase is input into which of the following processes?
  A. Initiating
  B. Monitoring and controlling
  C. Executing
  D. Closing

  ☑ **C.** The outputs of the planning phase are a direct input to the executing processes.
  ☒ **A** is incorrect, since initiating processes precede planning processes. **B** is incorrect, since conditions in the controlling processes are inputs to the planning processes, not the reverse. **D** is incorrect because planning processes do not serve as a direct input to the closing processes.

10. The information from the initiating phase is input into which of the following processes?
  A. Planning
  B. Executing
  C. Controlling
  D. All of the project phases

  ☑ **A.** The initiating processes serve as a direct input to the planning processes.
  ☒ **B, C,** and **D** are incorrect because initiating processes do not directly serve as an input to the executing, controlling, and closing processes.

11. Which process represents an ongoing effort throughout the project?
  A. Lessons learned
  B. Planning
  C. Closing
  D. EVM

  ☑ **B.** Planning is the iterative process evident throughout the project.
  ☒ **A** is incorrect, since lessons learned is not a process group. Closing, **C,** may be evident at the end of project phases and at the end of the project, but it is not an ongoing effort like the planning process. **D,** EVM, is not an ongoing process.

12. Which of the following processes happen in the correct order?
  A. Activity definition, scope planning, activity duration estimating, cost budgeting
  B. Scope planning, resource planning, activity duration estimating, activity sequencing
  C. Scope definition, scope planning, activity definition, activity sequencing
  D. Define scope, define activities, plan quality

☑ **D.** The correct order is scope definition, activity definition, and then plan quality.
☒ Choices **A**, **B**, and **C** do not show the processes in the correct order.

13. Which of the following processes happens in the closing process?
    A. Activity definition
    B. Cost budgeting
    C. Resource planning
    D. Close procurement

☑ **D.** Close procurement is the only process that happens during the closing process group.
☒ **A** is incorrect, since activity definition happens during planning. **B** is incorrect, since cost budgeting is also a planning process. **C,** resource planning, is also a planning process so it, too, is not a correct answer.

14. Which of the following planning processes is concerned with reporting relationships?
    A. Organizational planning
    B. Human resource planning
    C. Scope planning
    D. Activity definition

☑ **B.** Human resource planning is the facilitating planning process that defines roles and responsibilities—and the reporting structure within the project.
☒ **A** is incorrect because organizational planning is not a valid term for this question. **C** is incorrect, since it is the determination of what the project will and will not do. **D** is incorrect, since activity definition is the definition of the required activities to complete the project work.

15. Of the following, which process is most concerned with mitigation?
    A. Quality planning
    B. Risk response planning
    C. Procurement planning
    D. Risk identification

☑ **B.** Mitigation is a response to risk.
☒ **A,** quality planning, is incorrect, since it focuses on QA and the enforcement of QC. **C** is concerned with procurement management. **D** is incorrect because the identification of risk does not guarantee, or in some instances warrant, mitigation.

16. You are the project manager for the FTG Project. This project will affect several lines of business, and controversy on the project deliverables already abounds. You have 45 key stakeholders on this project representing internal customers from all areas of your organization. With this many stakeholders, what challenge will be the most difficult for the project's success?
    A. Communication
    B. Managing stakeholder expectations
    C. Managing scope creep
    D. Coordinating communications between the project manager, project team, and the project stakeholders

☑ **B.** On a project with 45 key stakeholders, the project manager must work to manage stakeholder expectations. Given the impact of the project and the identified controversy, the project manager will need to proceed with caution to ensure the project deliverables meet the required expectations of the stakeholders.

☒ **A** is incorrect because while communication may be the most time-consuming activity for the project, it is not the most difficult to manage. **C** is incorrect because managing scope creep can be controlled through an effective change control system. Scope creep may be an issue, but it is likely not the largest issue with this number of key stakeholders. **D** is incorrect, since the communication between the project manager, the project team, and the stakeholders will be governed by the communications management plan.

17. Which of the following is representative of a project constraint?
    A. A project that must be finished by year's end
    B. That 45 stakeholders exist on a long-term project
    C. The requirement to complete EVM
    D. The requirement to produce a new product

☑ **A** is the best choice, since it is a time constraint.

☒ Choice **B** is not a constraint but a project attribute. **C** is incorrect, since it describes a project requirement, not a project constraint. **D** is incorrect, since the requirement to produce a new product may be the project itself, not the constraint.

18. You are a project manager of a large construction project. There are many different stakeholders involved in the project, and each has their own opinion as to what the project should create. To maintain communication, set objectives, and document all decisions, you can say that larger projects generally require _____.
    A. A larger budget
    B. More detail

C. Phase gate estimating

D. A large project team

☑ **B.** Larger projects require more detail.

☒ **A** is incorrect, since larger projects don't always require a larger budget; consider an add/move/change project to replace a piece of equipment. The project work is shallow, but the piece of equipment may be expensive. **C** is incorrect because not all large projects will implement phase gate estimating. **D** is incorrect because a large project does not always mandate a large project team; consider a large project with very few resources available to complete the project work.

19. In order to create a network diagram, the project manager needs which of the following?

A. Activity sequencing

B. Project sponsor approval of the WBS

C. The WBS dictionary

D. A cost baseline

☑ **A.** The network diagram illustrates the sequence of events within the project.

☒ **B** is incorrect, as the project sponsor may not approve, or need to approve, the WBS in all projects. **C** is incorrect because the WBS dictionary is not needed to create a network diagram. **D** is also incorrect, since the cost baseline is not necessary to create a network diagram.

20. All of the following are processes that happen within the project cost management knowledge area except for which one?

A. Cost estimating

B. Control cost

C. Determine the project budget

D. Establishing the resource estimates

☑ **D.** Establishing the resource estimates happens during project time management.

☒ **A, B,** and **C** are incorrect because the three processes that happen within the cost knowledge area are cost estimating, cost control, and determining the project budget.

21. Which of the following is considered an output of risk management planning?
- **A.** Activity lists
- **B.** WBS
- **C.** The risk management plan
- **D.** The scope management plan

☑ **C.** The risk management plan is the output of the risk management planning process.
☒ Answers **A** and **B**, activity lists and the WBS, are incorrect because they are neither inputs nor outputs of the risk management planning process. Choice **D**, the scope management plan, is incorrect, since it is not an output of the risk management planning process.

22. Which project management knowledge area coordinates the efforts of the five process groups?
- **A.** Project integration management
- **B.** Project planning
- **C.** Project management plan creation process
- **D.** Monitoring and controlling

☑ **A.** The project integration management knowledge area coordinates the activities of the project's initiation, planning, executing, monitoring and controlling, and closing.
☒ **B.** Project planning is not a project management knowledge area; it is a process group. Choice **C** is incorrect, since the project management plan creation is a process, not a knowledge area. **D** is incorrect because monitoring and controlling is a process group that ensures the project execution is going according to project plan.

23. Frances is the project manager of the JHG Project. This project is similar to a recent project she completed for another customer. Which planning process will Frances need to finish first to ensure the project is completed successfully?
- **A.** Contract planning
- **B.** Scope definition
- **C.** Activity sequencing
- **D.** Quality planning

☑ **B.** Even though the projects are similar, Frances must still define the project scope.
☒ **A** is incorrect, since not all projects will need procurement. **C** and **D** are incorrect because scope definition must precede activity sequencing and quality planning.

24. You are the project manager for the BKL Project. This type of project has never been attempted before by your organization. The stakeholders already have high requirements for the project deliverables, and you need to create a change control system. This system should be controlled by which of the following?
    A. A formal change control form
    B. It should be completed by the team.
    C. The change control board
    D. It is specific to the organizational structure.

    ☑ **C.** A change control board (CCB) will review and approve changes to the project scope. Due to the high requirements of the stakeholders, a CCB can help fend off unneeded changes and allow the project manager to focus on the project management activities, rather than the potential flood of change requests.
    ☒ **A and D,** while correct in theory, are incorrect, since they do not answer the question as fully as choice **C** does. Choice **B** is incorrect because the project team should not review and approve changes in this scenario.

25. Complete this statement: Projects fail _____.
    A. At the beginning, not at the end
    B. During initiating, not closing
    C. Because of inadequate project managers
    D. Because of the project manager

    ☑ **A.** Projects fail at the beginning, not at the end. A poor requirements document, inadequate needs assessments, unfulfilled planning, and earlier processes can contribute to project failure.
    ☒ **B, C,** and **D** are not correct choices. Choice **A** is the best answer.

Part II

PMP Exam Essentials

4

Implementing Project Integration Management

What the heck is *project integration management?* Project integration management is the heart of project management and is made up of the day-to-day processes the project manager relies on to ensure that all of the parts of the project work together.

Put simply, project integration management is the way the gears of the project work together.

Within any project there are many moving parts: time management, cost management, schedule conflicts, human resource issues, iterative planning, and much, much more. Project integration management is the art and science of ensuring that your project moves forward and that your plan is fully developed and properly implemented. Project integration management requires that your project—regardless of its size and impact—meshes with the existing operations of your organization.

Project integration management requires finesse. You, as the project manager, will have to negotiate with stakeholders to resolve competing project objectives. This requires organization, since you'll have to develop, coordinate, and record your project plan. It requires the ability to accomplish your project plan. It requires leadership, record keeping, and political savvy, given you'll have to deal with potential changes throughout your project implementation. And, perhaps most importantly, it requires flexibility and adaptability throughout the project plan execution.

In this chapter, I'll cover the big topics you have to master to pass your PMP exam, as well as the skills necessary to successfully implement projects out in the real world. These topics include the following:

- Developing the project charter
- Developing the project plan
- Directing and managing the project execution
- Monitoring and controlling the project
- Managing integrated change control
- Closing the project or the project phase

As you've learned already, all projects need a project plan—it's up to the project manager and the project team to create one. Then the project manager must work with the project team to ensure the work is being completed as planned. Finally, the project manager must work throughout the project to control changes across all facets of the project. Figure 4-1 shows the complete picture of project integration management.

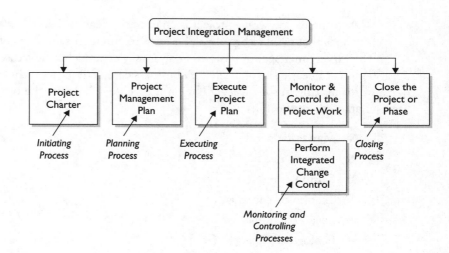

FIGURE 4-1

Project integration management coordinates the project from launch to close.

Developing the Project Charter

Let's not linger. You know what the project charter is and what it does: It authorizes the project and allows the project manager to assign resources to the project work. It's all about power. The project manager is officially identified in the project charter, though the project manager should be selected as early as possible during the project—hopefully while the charter is being developed.

The project manager, however, doesn't issue the project charter. Nope. The project charter, which the PMBOK may call the project initiator, comes from outside of the project. Specifically, the project charter should be issued outside the confines of the project by any of the following:

- An enterprise
- A government agency
- A company
- A program organization
- A portfolio organization

And the reason why a project is chartered? It can be because of opportunities, problems that need to be solved, business requirements, and lots of other reasons. The project manager or business analyst may create a business case that defines why a project needs to be chartered. A business case determines if the investment is worth making in the project. The business case will define the project purpose and characteristics, such as:

■ Market demand
■ Business need
■ Customer request
■ Technological advance
■ Legal requirements
■ Ecological impacts
■ Social need

Creating the Project Charter

The point of the charter, other than authorizing the project and the project manager, is to officially launch the project and allow the project manager to go about the business of getting the project work planned and then finished. The project charter needs to clearly communicate all of the following directly or through references to other documents:

■ **Project requirements for satisfaction**   The charter must identify what it'll take to complete the project—in other words, it should identify the metrics for success.

- **Project approval requirements**   The project charter needs to clearly state what it takes for the project to be successful and who signs off on project deliverables, project decisions, and project completion.

- **Project manager**   The project charter defines who the project manager is and what level of power the project manager has in the project.

- **Project sponsor**   The project charter defines who the project sponsor is; if the project sponsor is not the person signing the project charter, it should define who is authorizing the project (it's almost always the project sponsor who signs the charter).

- **The big picture**   The charter should identify the high-level purpose of the project, the business need the project aims to accomplish, and/or the product requirements the project will create.

- **Project purpose**   The charter needs to answer why the project is being launched and why it's important to the organization.

- **Milestone schedule**   Milestones are timeless events that show the progress within a project.

- **Stakeholder influences**   The charter needs to identify the stakeholders who will influence the project.

- **Risks**   Any of the known risks should be referenced in the project charter.

- **Functional organizations**   Functional organizations, such as departments, communities, agencies, and other stakeholders, should be identified and their expected level of participation should be addressed.

- **Summary budget**   The charter should have a summary budget.

- **Contract**   If the project is being completed for another entity that is an external customer, a contract is also needed. I'll discuss contracting in detail in Chapter 12. Until then, curb your excitement.

exam watch

Assumptions should be documented whenever they are used. This includes estimates, planning, scheduling, and so on. Assumptions can be considered risks because false assumptions can alter the entire project.

Relying on the Project Statement of Work

The statement of work (SOW) is a summary of what the project will provide and is an input to creating the project charter. For organizations completing an internal project, the SOW provides the business needs of the project, the product the project must create, or the service the project will create. For organizations that complete projects for external customers, the SOW is typically provided by the customer to the vendor. The vendor then responds with a proposal, quote, or bid—depending on what the customer asked for. In either case, the SOW includes the following:

■ The business need for the project
■ The product scope description
■ How the project fits within the strategic plan

Considering Enterprise Environmental Factors

Project managers know there are many things that influence a project's success; it's not all planning, execution, and good luck. Projects take place within organizations, and there are many components of any organization that can, and will, affect a project's success. These are enterprise environmental factors that have to be considered throughout the project and that should be identified in the project charter. Enterprise environmental factors include the following:

■ Organizational cultures and structures
■ Government and industry standards
■ Organizational infrastructures, such as facilities and equipment (or the lack thereof)
■ The availability of human resources and their competencies
■ Personnel administration
■ A work authorization system
■ Marketplace conditions
■ Stakeholder risk tolerances
■ Standardized cost estimating databases
■ Project management information system (PMIS)

Examining the Project Selection Criteria

Project selection methods are about resolving the unknown, predicting the likelihood of project success, and determining the expected value of that project's success—or the cost of its failure. The process of selecting those projects to keep and those to discard is based on the following two methods:

- Benefit measurement methods
- Constrained optimization methods

Benefit measurement methods are the most common approaches to project selection. Benefit measurement methods are tools that allow management and key stakeholders to examine the benefits of a project and how the project completion will contribute to the organization. Constrained optimization methods are also tools for selecting projects, but their approach is much more scientific and math-driven. Don't worry. You won't need to know much, if anything, about constrained optimization on the PMP exam. I'll examine both selection types later in this chapter.

on the Job

Project selection is also known as Go/No Go decision making. Projects with many variables are excellent candidates for phase gates. The project is allowed a Go decision to the end of the first phase. Another Go/No Go decision happens at the end of each phase based on the performance and deliverables.

Meet Tracy. Tracy has a great project she'd like to see authorized. She has to "sell" the project to management in order to have it authorized. She needs to determine what's so great about her project and why management should buy into it. She is looking for project selection criteria—reasons why her project should be authorized. Possible considerations Tracy can include might be the following:

- Return on investment
- Realized opportunities
- Market share
- Customer perspective
- Demand for the product
- Social needs
- Increased revenues
- Reduced costs

Historical Information

Has anyone ever done something like this before? Historical information is an organizational process asset that resource project managers can use to make decisions about their current projects. Historical information provides proven documentation of the success or failure of performance, and can be referenced for project selection criteria. For instance: Has management squelched similar projects for specific reasons? Historical information can be referenced for comparable projects and how they performed through to execution, as well as how the deliverables of the project performed according to prediction.

In addition, historical information is one of the key elements in determining if an existing project should move forward into the next project phase. If the completed project phase has proven successful and provided some merit or value, it's likely to move forward. Projects that don't prove valuable—based on the performance of the phase or less-than-desirable phase results—will likely be axed.

Examining Benefit Measurement Methods

There are several different benefit measurement methods. These methods are all about comparing values of one project against the values of another. As you might expect, the projects with higher, positive values typically get selected over projects with low values. The following sections describe some common benefit measurement methods you may encounter.

Murder Boards

Murder boards are committees full of folks that ask every conceivable negative question about the proposed project. Their goal is to expose strengths and weaknesses of the project—and kill the project if it's deemed worthless for the organization to commit to. Not a pleasant decision-making process.

Scoring Models

Scoring models (sometimes called weighted scoring models) are models that use a common set of values for all of the projects up for selection. For example, values can be profitability, complexity, customer demand, and so on. Each of these values has a weight assigned to it—values of high importance have a high weight, while values of lesser importance have a lesser weight. The projects are measured against these values and assigned scores by how well they match the predefined values. The projects with high scores take priority over projects will lesser scores. Figure 4-2 demonstrates the scoring model.

Benefit/Cost Ratios

Just like they sound, benefit/cost ratio (BCR) models examine the cost-to-benefit ratio. For example, a typical measurement is the cost to complete the project plus the cost of ongoing operations of the project product compared against the expected benefits of the project. For example, consider a project that will use $575,000 to create a new product, market the product, and provide ongoing support for the product for one year. The expected gross return on the product, however, is $980,000 in year one. The benefit of completing the project is greater than the cost to create the product.

The Payback Period

How long does it take the project to "pay back" its costs? For example, the AXZ Project will cost the organization $500,000 to create over five years. The expected cash inflow (income) on the project deliverable, however, is $40,000 per quarter. From here, it's simple math: $500,000 divided by $40,000 is 12.5 quarters, or a little over three years to recoup the expenses.

FIGURE 4-2 The weighted model bases project selection on predefined values.

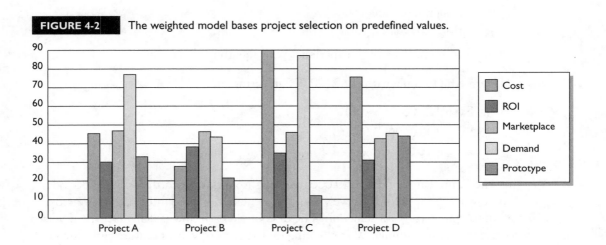

This selection method, while one of the simplest, is also the weakest. Why? The cash inflows are not discounted against the time it takes to begin creating the cash. This is the time value of money. The $40,000-per-quarter five years from now is worth less than $40,000-in-your-pocket today. Remember when sodas were a quarter? It's the same idea. The soda hasn't gotten better. The nickel is just worth less today than it was way back then.

PMP Coach *I originally said that sodas were a nickel and my editor corrected me. Who ever remembers soda being a nickel? Gee-whiz, do I feel like an old man. The lesson learned, however, is that time does change the value, or the perceived value, of the project's worth. And I'm not an old man, I was just thinking from my brother's perspective.*

See the video Future Value and Present Value.

Considering the Discounted Cash Flow

Discounted cash flow accounts for the time value of money. If you were to borrow $100,000 from your uncle for five years, you'd be paying interest on the money, yes? (If not, you've got a great uncle.) If the $100,000 were invested for five years and managed to earn a whopping sixpercent interest per year, compounded annually, it'd be worth $133,822.60 at the end of five years. This is the future value of the money in today's terms.

The magic formula for future value is $FV = PV (1 + i)^n$, where:

- FV is future value
- PV is present value
- i is the interest rate
- n is the number of time periods (years, quarters, and so on)

Here's the formula with the $100,000 in action:

1. $FV = 100,000(1 + .06)^5$
2. $FV = 100,000(1.338226)$
3. $FV = 133,822.60$

The future value of the $100,000 five years from now is worth $133,822.60 today. So how does that help? Now we've got to calculate the discounted cash flow across all of the projects up for selection. The discounted cash flow is really just the inverse of the preceding formula. We're looking for the present value of future cash flows: $PV = FV \div (1 + i)^n$.

In other words, if a project says it'll be earning the organization $160,000 per year in five years, that's great. But what's $160,000 five years from now really worth today? This puts the amount of the cash flow in perspective with what the projections are in today's money. Let's plug it into the formula and find out (assuming the interest rate is still six percent):

1. $PV = FV \div (1 + i)^n$
2. $PV = 160,000 \div (1.338226)$
3. $PV = \$119,561$

So… $160,000 in five years is really only worth $119,561 today. If we had four different projects with various times to completion, costs, and expected project cash inflows at completion, we'd calculate the present value and choose the project with the best PV, since it'll likely be the best investment for the organization.

Calculating the Net Present Value

The net present value (NPV) is a somewhat complicated formula, but allows a more precise prediction of project value than the lump-sum approach found with the PV formula. NPV evaluates the monies returned on a project for each time period the project lasts. In other words, a project may last five years, but there may be a return on investment in each of the five years the project is in existence, not just at the end of the project.

For example, a retail company may be upgrading the facilities at each of their stores to make shopping and purchasing easier for their customers. The company has 1,000 stores. As each store makes the conversion to the new facility design, the project deliverables will begin, hopefully generating cash flow as a result of the project deliverables. (Uh, we specifically want cash inflow from the new stores, not cash outflow. That's some nerdy accounting humor.) The project can begin earning money when the first store is completed with the conversion to the new facilities. The faster the project can be completed, the sooner the organization will see a complete return on their investment. In this example, an interest rate of six percent per year is assumed.

The following outlines how the NPV formula works:

1. Calculate the project's cash flow per time unit (typically quarters or years).
2. Calculate each time unit total into the present value.
3. Sum the present value of each time unit.

4. Subtract the investment for the project.

5. Take two aspirins.

6. Examine the NPV value. An NPV greater than zero is good and the project should be approved. An NPV less than zero is bad and the project should be rejected.

When comparing two projects, the project with the greater NPV is typically better, though projects with high returns (PV) early in the project are better than those with low returns early in the project. The following is an example of an NPV calculation:

Time Period	Cash Flow	Present Value
1	$15,000.00	$14,150.94
2	$25,000.00	$22,249.91
3	$17,000.00	$14,273.53
4	$25,000.00	$19,802.34
5	$18,000.00	$13,450.65
Totals	$100,000.00	$83,927.37
Investment		$78,000.00
NPV		$5,927.37

PMP
Coach

I bet you're wishing you could try some of these out for yourself, right? You're in luck. On the CD you'll find a Microsoft Excel file called "Time Value of Money" with a few exercises and all of the formulas to test your work. Enjoy!

Considering the Internal Rate of Return

The last benefit measurement method is the internal rate of return (IRR). The IRR is a complex formula to calculate when the present value of the cash inflow equals the original investment. Don't get too lost in this formula—it's a tricky business, and you won't need to know how to calculate the IRR for the exam. You will need to know, however, that when comparing multiple projects' IRRs, projects with high IRRs are better choices than projects with low IRRs. This makes sense. Would you like an investment with a high rate of return or a lower rate of return?

Examining Constrained Optimization Methods

Constrained optimization methods are complex mathematical formulas and algorithms that are used to predict the success of projects, the variables within projects, and tendencies to move forward with selected project investments. For the exam, thankfully, all you need to know about these selection methods is that they are not typically used for most projects, being instead utilized for multiphase, complex projects. The following are the major constrained optimization methods:

- Linear programming
- Nonlinear programming
- Integer algorithms
- Dynamic programming
- Multiobjective programming

Adopting a Project Plan Methodology

A project plan methodology is a structured approach to developing the project plan. Methodologies can be simple or complex and based on the project type, the requirements of the performing organization, or multiple inputs. Organizations can use hard or soft tools to lead the project plan methodology. In its choice of hard tools, one organization may require that the project team create a project plan based on a checklist of plan requirements, while another organization may require that project teams complete a computer-based project template.

Soft tools include project meetings, business analysts to investigate and research all facets of the problem or opportunity, and subject matter experts' interviews of stakeholders and project team members. A methodology used in creating the project plan can include the following:

- Project templates
- Paper and electronic forms
- Monte Carlo simulations for risk management
- Project simulations for expected results
- The design of experiments
- Project startup meetings
- Interviews

Employing a Project Management Information System (PMIS)

A PMIS is typically a computer-driven system (though it can be paper-based) to aid a project manager in the development of the project. It is a tool for, not a replacement of, the project manager. A PMIS can calculate schedules, costs, expectations, and likely results. It cannot, however, replace the expert judgment of the project manager and the project team. The goal of the system is to automate, organize, and provide control of the project management processes. A typical PMIS software system has:

- Work breakdown structure creation tools
- Calendaring features
- Scheduling abilities
- Work authorization tools
- Earned value management controls
- Quality control charts, program evaluation and review technique (PERT) charts, Gantt charts, and other charting features
- Calculations for the critical path, EVM, target dates based on the project schedule, and more
- Resource tracking and leveling
- Reporting functionality

Relying on Expert Judgment

Have you ever heard the expression "To be successful, surround yourself with smarter people than yourself"? That's the idea of expert judgment. When it comes to project selection, another tool that management (and the project manager throughout the project) can rely on is expert judgment. Expert judgment is referenced over and over as a tool and technique in the PMBOK. So, what is it? Expert judgment is a technique to rely on the experts within your organization, consultants, stakeholders (including the project customers), professional associations, or industry groups for advice. These experts can contribute to the project selection method by offering their opinion, research, and experience.

CERTIFICATION OBJECTIVE 4.02

Developing the Project Plan

The project plan is not a museum piece. You'll use, wrinkle, update, and depend on your project plan like a Super Bowl coach depends on the playbook. The project plan is developed with the project team, stakeholders, and management. It is the guide to how the project should flow and how the project will be managed, and it reflects the values, priorities, and conditions influencing the project.

Project plan development requires an iterative process of progressive elaboration. The project manager will revise and update the plan as research and planning reveal more information and as the project develops. For example, an initial project plan may describe a broad overview of what the project entails, what the desired future state should be, and the general methods used to achieve the goals of the plan. Then, after research, careful planning, and discovery, the project plan will develop into a concise document that details the work involved in, and the expectations

e x a m
watch *The project plan guides the project manager through the execution and monitor and control process groups. The project plan is designed to control the* *project. As a whole, the point of the project plan is to communicate to the project team, stakeholders, and management how the project will be managed and controlled.*

of, the project; how the project will be controlled, measured, and managed; and how the project should move. In addition, the project plan will contain all of the supporting details, specify the project organization, and allow for growth in the plan through a disciplined change control process.

Understanding the Project Plan's Purpose

The project plan is more than a playbook to determine what work needs to be accomplished. The project plan is a fluid document that will control several elements.

- **Provide structure** The project plan is developed to provide a structure that advances the project toward completion. It is a thorough but concise collection of documents that will serve as a point of reference through the project execution, monitoring and controlling, and project or phase closing.

- **Provide documentation** "Noggin plans"—the kind between your ears—are not good. A documented project plan is needed for truly successful projects. They provide a historical reference and the reasoning for why decisions were made. A project plan must provide documentation of the assumptions and constraints influencing the project plan development.

- **Provide communication** Project plans are documents that provide the information, explanations, and reasoning underlying the decisions made for the project. The project plan serves as a source of communication among stakeholders, the project team, and management on how the project plan will be controlled.

- **Provide baselines** A project plan contains several baselines. As the project moves toward completion, management, stakeholders, and the project manager can use the project plan to see what was predicted as far as costs, scheduling, quality, and scope—and then see how these predictions compare with what is being experienced.

Preparing to Develop the Project Plan

To effectively develop the project plan, the project manager and the stakeholders must be in agreement with the project objectives. For this agreement to exist, the project manager works with the stakeholders to negotiate a balance of expectations and required objectives. Competing objectives is a recurring theme in project management (and on the PMP exam). Project managers must be able to negotiate among stakeholders for the best solution to the problem or opportunity. The project plan is created based on the organization's project management methodology, the nature of the work to be implemented, and the overall scope of the project.

on the **Job** *The triple constraints of project management provide an excellent negotiation tool. No side of the equilateral triangle can change without affecting the other sides. The goal is for all sides of the triangle to remain even. Want to change the project end date to something sooner rather than later? Okay, but you'll have to add more resources to get it done—which means a bigger budget. Don't have enough cash in the old budget to complete the work? Okay, then just reduce the project scope. This type of triangle is sometimes called the "Iron Triangle."*

Applying Tools and Techniques for Project Plan Development

All the planning is done, right? Of course not. The planning processes are iterative and allow the project manager and the project team to revisit them as needed. But at what point do we push back from the planning buffet and move on with a working, feasible plan? Every project is different when it comes to planning, but a project team will continue in the planning stage until it is knowledgeable about the project work and has a clear vision of what needs to be done.

Figure 4-3 depicts the evolution of the planning to action process for a typical technology project. Once the business and the functional requirements have been

FIGURE 4-3

The planning processes require documentation and a logical, systematic approach.

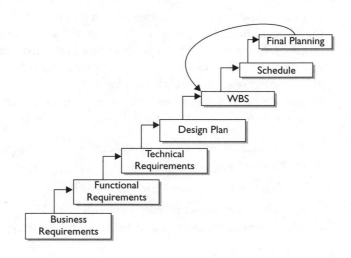

established, the planning processes move into the specifics. Recall that the business requirements establish the project vision and that the functional requirements establish the goals for the project. The technical requirements and the design plan shift the focus onto the specifics the project will accomplish.

All of the inputs to the project plan should be readily available for the project manager, because he or she may need to rely on this information for additional planning. With all of the "stuff" the project manager has to work with, it should be a snap to create the actual project plan, right? Well, not exactly. The project manager, the project team, stakeholders, and management will work together to finalize the project plan. The contributions from each include the following:

- **Project manager**   Leadership, facilitation, organization, direction, and expert judgment
- **Project team members**   Knowledge of the project work and time estimates; they also influence the schedule, provide advice and opinions on risk, as well as expert judgment
- **Customer**   Objectives, quality requirements, expert judgment, and have some influence over budget and schedule
- **Management**   Influence budget, resources, project management methodology, quality requirements, and project plan approval

Using a Project Management Information System

The PMBOK will repeatedly recommend using a project management information system (PMIS). Here's the scoop: It's an automated system to quickly create, manage, and streamline the project management processes. In the development portion of the project, the PMIS can be used to help the project management team create the schedule, estimates, and risk assessments, and to gather feedback from stakeholders.

The PMIS also includes a configuration management system. Configuration management is an approach for tracking all approved changes, versions of project plans, blueprints, software numbering, and sequencing. A configuration management system aims to manage all of the following:

- Functional and physical characteristics of the project deliverables
- Control, track, and manage any changes to the project deliverables
- Track any changes within the project
- Allow the project management team to audit the project deliverables to confirm conformance to defined criteria for acceptance

The configuration management system also includes the change control system. The change control system defines all of the rules and procedures for how a change may enter the project, or be declined, and how each proposed changed is documented.

Let's say that, for the moment, the project manager and the project team have finished their project plan. Before the project team can set about implementing it, the plan must be approved. Let's hear that again: The project plan is a formal, documented plan that must be approved by management. Once management has signed off on the project plan, the work is truly authorized to begin.

Examining the Typical Project Plan

The project plan is actually a bunch of plans and documents. Which ones, you ask? Well, let's take a peek.

The Project Scope Management Plan

The scope management plan details how the project scope should be maintained and protected from change, as well as how a change in scope may be allowed. The plan also provides information on how likely it is that the project scope will change, and if changes do occur, how drastic those changes may be. I'll discuss scope management and change control in Chapter 5.

The Project Change Management Plan

The change management plan works in tandem with the scope management plan. When changes are approved for a project, including time, cost, scope, or contract, there needs to be a plan on how the project team will manage these new changes within the project. I'll discuss scope management and change control in Chapters 5, 6, 7, and 12.

The Schedule Management Plan

The project plan details the scheduled work, milestones, and target completion dates for the project phases and the project itself. The schedule management plan, on the other hand, identifies circumstances that may change the project schedule, such as the completion of project phases or the reliance on other projects and outside resources. The schedule management plan identifies the likelihood that the schedule will change and the impact of such changes, should they occur. Finally, the schedule management plan details the approval and accountability process for changes within the project. Along with the schedule management plan, the project manager creates the schedule baseline. I'll discuss the schedule management and schedule baseline in Chapter 6.

The Cost Management Plan

The project plan includes the project budget, the cash flow forecast, and procedures for procurement and contract administration. The subsidiary cost management plan explains how variances to the costs of the project will be managed. The plan may be based on a range of acceptable variances and the expected response to variances over a given threshold. The project plan also includes a cost performance baseline to measure accuracy of estimates and budgeting. Variances are revealed by comparing the actual project costs to the original cost performance baseline. I'll cover cost management in Chapter 7.

The Quality Management Plan

The quality management plan describes how the project will operate and meet its quality expectations. It details the quality improvement and quality controls, and how the project will map to the quality assurance program of the performing organization. The quality management plan provides information on the required resources and time to meet the quality expectations. I'll discuss quality management in Chapter 8.

The Process Improvement Plan

No project is perfect, but the process improvement plan strives to find ways to make the project better. It identifies methods to track and eliminate waste and non-value-added activities in order to reduce the work and deliverables that don't contribute to the project value. I'll discuss this plan in Chapter 8.

Human Resources Plan

The project plan includes information on the resources needed to complete the project work. The human resources plan, however, provides details on how the project team members will be brought onto the project and released from the project. For example, a project may have a need for an electrical engineer for three months during a ten-month project. The human resources plan will then determine how the engineer's time is accounted for on the project and how the employees can be released when they're no longer needed on the project. I'll discuss staffing management in Chapter 9.

The Communication Management Plan

It's been said that project managers spend 90 percent of their time communicating. When you consider all of the different requirements and communications of a project, it's easy to believe that statistic. The communication management plan describes the required communications and how they will be fulfilled. It also explains the methods used for gathering, storing, and dispersing information to appropriate parties.

In addition, the communication management plan maps out the schedule of when the expected communication needs will be met. For example, milestone reports, timely status reports, project meetings, and other expected communication events are included in the communications management plan. The communication schedule also will include accepted procedures to update, access, and revise communications between scheduled communication events. I'll discuss communications in Chapter 10.

The Risk Management Plan

The risk management plan details the identified risks within the project, the risks associated with the constraints and project assumptions, and how the project team will monitor, react, or avoid the risks. The risk management plan, and the processes to create it, will be detailed in Chapter 11.

The Procurement Management Plan

If the project includes vendors, the project plan needs a procurement management plan. This plan describes the procurement process from solicitation to source selection. The plan may also include the requirements for selection as set by the organization. The selected offers, proposals, and bids from vendor(s) should be incorporated into the procurement management plan. I'll discuss procurement processes in Chapter 12.

PMP Coach

There are loads of project plans and documents covered in this chapter. I highly recommend that you know all of the project plans and documents. Knowing these documents will help you in all of the other knowledge areas, too, as you'll see these plans there. Keep at it—if it were easy, everyone would do it.

Project Documents and Files

Besides the compilation of project management subsidiary plans, there are also many project documents that you'll rely on to help plan and execute the project. These are not officially part of the project plan, but you should be familiar with them for your PMP exam.

- **Project charter**   Every project needs a charter. Charters authorize the project and give the project manager power over the project resources.
- **Milestone list**   A listing of the project milestones and anticipated completion dates.
- **Forecasts**   Throughout the project, the project manager will create forecasts about the expected project completion date and projected project costs.
- **Activity list**   A shopping list of all the activities the project team must complete in order to satisfy the project. This list is an input to the project network diagram.
- **Activity attributes**   Activities with special conditions, requirements, risks, and other conditions should be documented.
- **Activity cost estimates**   The cost of resources, including materials, services, and, when warranted, labor should be estimated.
- **Project funding requirements**   In larger projects, this document identifies the timeline of when capital is required for the project to move forward. This document defines the amount of funds a project needs in order to reach its objectives and when the project funds are needed.
- **Duration estimates**   The prediction of how long the project work will take to complete.
- **Supporting detail for estimates**   The project manager should document how time and cost estimates were created.
- **Resource calendars**   You'll need to know when people and facilities are available or scheduled to work on the project.
- **Resource requirements**   The identification of what resources are needed to complete the project work is required as a supporting document for planning. This includes people, materials, equipment, facilities, and services.
- **Resource breakdown structure**   This chart identifies the resources utilized in the project in each section of the WBS.
- **Responsibility assignment matrix**   This is a table that maps roles to responsibilities in the project.

- **Roles and responsibilities**   This maps project roles, such as carpenter, to project activities, such as framing the house.

- **Teaming agreement**   A contractual agreement that defines the roles, responsibilities, considerations, and partnerships of two or more organizations that work together in a project. It's not unlike a partnership or subcontractor relationship.

- **Sellers list**   A listing of the vendors an organization does business with. You might know this document as a preferred vendors list in your company.

- **Source selection criteria**   A predefined listing of the criteria to determine how a vendor will be selected— for example, cost, experience, certifications, and the like.

- **Statement of work**   Defines the work that a vendor is to complete for the buyer. Statement of work documents accompany procurement documents so vendors can bid, quote, or create proposals for the project work. Internally, statement of work documents define the requirements of the project.

- **Requirements traceability matrix**   A table that identifies all of the project requirements, when the requirements are due, when the requirements are created, and any other pertinent information about the requirements.

- **Procurement documents**   All of the documents for purchasing, such as request for quotes, invitation to bid, request for proposal, and the responses, are stored as part of the project documentation.

- **Proposals**   Proposals are an exposé on ideas, suggestions, recommendations, and solutions to an opportunity provided by a vendor for a seller. Proposals include a price for the work and document how the vendor would provide the service to the buyer.

- **Contracts**   A legally binding agreement between the buyer(s) and seller(s) that defines the roles and responsibilities of all parties in the agreement.

- **Assumption log**   A document that clearly identifies and tracks assumptions that are made in the project. All assumptions need to be tested for their validity, and the outcome of the test should be recorded.

- **Issue log**   Issues are decisions that are usually in disagreement among two or more parties. They are recorded in the issue log, along with an issue owner designation, an issue date for resolution, and the eventual outcome of the issue.

■ **Risk register**   A risk is an uncertain event or condition that can have a positive or negative effect on the project. All risks, regardless of their probability or impact, are recorded in the issue log, and their status is kept current.

■ **Change log**   As changes to the project time, cost, or scope enter the project, they should be recorded in the change log for future reference.

■ **Performance reports**   These formal reports define how the project is performing on time, cost, scope, quality, and any other relevant information.

■ **Work performance information**   The current status of the project work. This includes the results of activities, corrective and preventive action status, forecasts for activity completion, and other relevant information. You might know this information as a status report.

■ **Work performance measurements**   These are predefined metrics for measuring project performance, such as cost variances, schedule variances, and estimate to complete.

■ **Quality control measurements**   Quality control is an inspection-driven process; quality control measurements are predefined values that signal problems with quality within the project deliverables. These can vary, based on the discipline the project centers on, for example, manufacturing or information technology.

■ **Quality metrics**   Predefined values that the results of project work should match in order to be acceptable for the project deliverables and project performance.

■ **Quality checklists**   These are ideal for repetitive activities to ensure that each activity is done identically to the other activities in the project. They are also ideal for safety procedures.

■ **Project organizational structure**   This document defines the reporting relationships within and without the project. This is especially useful for large virtual project teams.

■ **Stakeholder analysis**   The examination and documentation of the project stakeholders and their requirements for the project deliverables.

■ **Stakeholder registry**   All stakeholders, their position towards the project, contact information, and other characteristics are recorded in this document.

- **Stakeholder requirements** As a result of stakeholder analysis, the stakeholder requirements are identified. These can be project deliverables, approval requirements, and communication demands.
- **Stakeholder management strategy** Larger projects will generally have more stakeholders than smaller projects. The attitude and position of the project stakeholders will affect how the project manager communicates and manages the project stakeholders.
- **Team performance assessments** Often at the end of project phases and the end of the project, the project manager reviews the project team members performance and contribution to the project's success or failure.

CERTIFICATION OBJECTIVE 4.03

Executing the Project Plan

So you've got a project plan—great! Now the work of executing the project plan begins. The project manager and the project team will go about completing the promises made in the project plan to deliver, document, measure, and complete the project work. The project plan will communicate to the project team, the stakeholders, management, and even vendors what work happens next, how it begins, and how it will be measured for quality and performance.

The product of the project is created during these execution processes. The largest percentage of the project budget will be spent during the project execution processes. The project manager and the project team must work together to orchestrate the timings and integration of all the project's moving parts. A flaw in one area of the execution can have ramifications in cost and additional risk, and can cause additional flaws in other areas of the project.

As the project work is implemented, the project manager refers to the project plan to ensure that the work is meeting the documented expectations, requirements, quality demands, target dates, and more. The completion of the work is measured and then compared against the cost, schedule, and scope baselines as documented in the project plan. Should there be—GASP!—discrepancies between the project work and the baselines, prompt and accurate reactions are needed to adjust the slipping components of the project.

Executing the project plan includes the following:

- Doing the work to satisfy the project objectives
- Spending funds to satisfy the project objectives
- Managing, training, and leading the project team
- Completing procurement requirements
- Acquiring, managing, and using resources such as materials, tools, facilities, and equipment to get the project work completed
- Managing risks
- Fleshing approved changes into the project
- Managing communications
- Collecting project data on schedules, costs, quality, and overall project progress—and then reporting on these components
- Completing lessons-learned documentation

Applying Corrective Action

Things go awry. Corrective actions are methods the project manager and the project team can take to bring the project back into alignment with the project plan—for example, a delay in the project work has now shifted the project schedule by a month. The project manager, the project team, and even the stakeholders can examine the project schedule to see what possible alternatives can be taken in the schedule to complete the project on time. Solutions may include additional resources, fast-tracking, changing the order of work packages, and so on. Corrective actions bring the project performance back in line with the project plan. In addition to communicating, project managers spend a great deal of their time applying corrective actions.

Considering Preventive Actions

Do you wear your seat belt? Take an umbrella when there's a chance of rain? These are preventive actions against some risk. In project management, preventive actions are steps the project manager and the project team can take to prevent the negative outcome of possible risk events. Preventive actions are documented methods to avoid risks and keep them from influencing the project success in a negative way. Preventive actions take risk events out of play.

Managing Change Requests

As the project team completes the work, the project manager will be faced, challenged, or even bombarded with change requests. Part of project execution is to evaluate the worthiness of the proposed change, feed the change through the change control system, and then act on the approval or denial of the change request. All change requests are documented for future reference, while approved changes are incorporated into the project plan.

Managing Defect Repair

Sometimes the project team will screw up. Defect repair is the action to fix the problem and to fix it correctly. The project manager will need to ensure that the actions taken to fix the problem have indeed corrected the defect and allowed the project to move forward as planned. Sometimes when a project team member faces a defect, he will rush through the defect repair, causing errors and waste again. The project manager must work with the project team to ensure that the defect is fixed efficiently and properly.

Implementing Tools and Techniques for Project Execution

You have completed a workable, approved project plan. Now it's time to implement the thing. This is the heart of project management: taking your project plan and putting it into action. You'll act, do, adjust, and repeat. The project manager will use several tools and techniques to execute the project plan.

Project Management Methodology

Every performing organization has rules and regulations that are specific to the industry it operates within. In addition, the performing organization will likely have standard operating procedures that determine the order, approach, and autonomy of the project manager and the project team.

For example, an organization operating within the construction industry must operate according to the laws and regulations of the country, state (or province), and city. In addition, the performing organization may require its construction crew to adhere to its safety standards, quality inspections, and other company rules that are not mandated by a government agency. The project manager must work within not only the law, but also the additional constraints the organization has added to the project.

on the **job** *Collaborative PMIS packages can also serve as a work authorization system—if they are configured and used properly. Any PMIS, electronic or paper-based, is only as good as the person (or persons) keeping the information up-to-date.*

Examining the Outputs of Project Plan Execution

The project is being completed; there is visible evidence that it is moving towards the desired future state. Inspections by the project manager and scope verification by the customer also prove the project team is completing their work as planned. Status meetings provide opportunity for the project team to report their work and evaluate it against the WBS and the network diagram. Things are moving along smoothly.

And then it happens. The project team begins to slip on the quality of the project work. Team members begin to take longer than what was planned to complete their project work. The scope verification with the clients takes longer—and their satisfaction with the project work begins to wane. What's a project manager to do?

This scenario is typical of project plan execution. The team completes the work, and then the project manager reviews the work and makes adjustments to bring the project back into alignment with the baselines created in the project plan. There are several major components of project plan execution that happen throughout project execution, not just at the end.

- Project deliverables
- Change requests
- Project management plan updates for approved change requests
- Work performance information
- Project document updates

Examining the Project Work Results

The team completes their work based on the project plan. The end result of the work should be measured against the quality metrics, scope requirements, and expected outcomes of the work as defined in the project plan. In addition, the project manager must examine the time and cost required to reach the work results and compare them against the baselines recorded in the project plan. Any difference between what was experienced and what was planned is a variance.

Work results are not always physical, tangible things: the creation of a service, the completion of a training class, the completion of a certification process—these, too, can be measured as work results.

Examining Change Requests

How many times have stakeholders begged, pleaded, or demanded a change in the project scope? Probably more times than you can count, right? Change requests are any requested deviation from, or addition to, the project scope, schedule, budget, quality, or staffing. Change requests will predominantly trickle (or flood) to the project manager during project plan execution. Change requests almost always affect one of four facets of a project.

- **Schedule** This is a desire to shorten or lengthen the project duration—for example, a key stakeholder would like the project to be completed before a particular business cycle begins. If the project can't be completed by that time, the project will be delayed until the business cycle has completed, so the project won't interfere with the business operations.

- **Cost** This is a reduction or increase in the project's budget. For example, the project's priority has been reduced in the organization, so the budget may, unfortunately, be reduced as well. Budgets can also be increased: A functional manager may want to spend the entire remaining departmental budget at the end of the fiscal year so that next year's budget may meet or exceed the current year's budget. In this questionable instance, additional funds, new features, and more resources, needed or not, are added to a project's budget to "help" the functional manager spend the budget.

- **Scope** This is the most common instance of change. Stakeholders may request additional features, different features, or small changes to the project product. Each change must be evaluated against the project plan, the project scope, and supporting details to determine the cost, time, and risks implied.

- **Combination** This is a change made to the schedule, cost, or scope that may affect more than one facet of the project. This goes back to the idea of the Triple Constraints of Project Management. For example, a change to finish the schedule faster may be reasonable if more resources are applied to the project to complete the work faster. More resources, in turn, mean more money.

Updating the Project Documents

Change is expected in projects, though not always welcome. When changes are approved, the project management plan should be updated to reflect the approved changes. This means that the project management scope baseline, schedule baseline, and the cost baseline should all be updated to reflect the new project deliverables. You'll also need to update the project activities lists to reflect the new activities the project changes will require, and, in turn, you'll update the project network diagram. Finally, changes can cause a ripple effect into the project management subsidiary plans and the project documents that all need to be updated to reflect the changes in the project.

CERTIFICATION OBJECTIVE 4.04

Monitoring and Controlling the Project Work

Sure, sure, it'd be nice to have a project plan and a team that follows orders and to have all the work requests completed on budget and on time every time—but this isn't fiction. One of the key activities for the project manager is to monitor the project team and control the work that they complete as part of the project. This is the hands-on portion of the project management career.

The project manager, with the project management plan in hand, will examine what was promised in the plan and what's been executed by the project team. This means the project manager needs work information—work results—to inspect in order to ensure that the project is being completed as planned.

Using Monitoring and Controlling Tools and Techniques

Recall that the product scope is the vision of what the customer expects, while the project scope is the work completed by the project team to create the product scope. This means that if the project team is completing activities outside of the project scope, they are not contributing to the project scope, which in turn means they're creating a product scope that's different from what the customer is expecting. Not a good thing. This leads to waste, frustration, delays, and unhappy customers—and unhappy project managers. We don't want this. We want control and accuracy.

Using a Methodology

A project management methodology is more than just a philosophy for project management. It's an approach to project management that follows a documented, proven model for completing projects. Many organizations have a project management methodology that requires the project manager to complete checklists, follow standards, and report on the accuracy of the project completion. The goal of the project management methodology is to assist all project managers within an organization to accurately execute the project management plan.

Another tool that complements the project management plan is a project management information system (PMIS). A PMIS can automate some of the procedures, questions, and prompts to assist all project managers within an organization to ask the right questions in order to retrieve answers, status, and information on task completion. A PMIS does not replace the project manager—it only assists the project manager.

Relying on Earned Value Management

Earned value management (EVM) is a set of formulas that help a project manager determine the overall success and performance of a project. I'll discuss this in detail in Chapter 7. For now, know that EVM is a set of tools to measure project performance from initiation to project closure. It's loads of fun.

Relying on Expert Judgment

Project managers should use expert judgment. Expert judgment is simply relying on a resource that's smarter in one or more areas than the project manager to help the project manager make the best decision. Expert judgment can come from many different sources.

- Third-party consultants
- Subject matter experts
- Project team members
- Stakeholders
- Individuals within the organization that may not be directly affected by the project

Examining the Results of Project Work

As a project moves towards completion and the project manager monitors and controls the project, there will be evidence of the project's success, failures or, at a minimum, some results of the work as performed by the project team. Here's the business you can expect to be tested on when it comes to the PMP exam.

- **Requested changes**   Yep, change requests can come out of monitoring and controlling. I'll talk more about change control in Chapter 5, but for now, know that change requests usually mean that the project scope will widen—although in some instances, the project scope may be trimmed due to lack of funds, time, or other possibilities.

- **Recommended corrective actions**   Corrective actions are actions that must be followed to bring future project results into alignment with expected project performance. These require documented change requests to implement.

- **Recommended preventive actions**   These are actions to ensure that mistakes don't get repeated within a project. For example, if a piece of equipment fails if it gets too hot, the project manager and the project team will take action to ensure that the equipment doesn't overheat and delay the project work. These require documented change requests to implement.

- **Recommended defect repair**   Quality control is an inspection-driven process to find mistakes or errors with the project work results before the customer does. When a defect is found, the project manager should document the defect and then, usually, require the project team to fix the problem. Defects require documented change requests to implement.

- **Forecasts**   Forecasts are harbingers of things to come. They provide information based on current and past project performance to predict when a project may finish and what the estimate at completion (the project's final costs) and the estimate to complete (how much more the project will cost) the project will be. EVM is an example of a tool that can provide forecasts.

- **Project document updates**   When project work changes, the project manager has to update the corresponding project documents and project plans. This is a recurring theme throughout project management, so you can bet dollars to donuts you'll see this concept on your PMP exam.

Reacting to Change

When changes are proposed to the project, the project manager must route the proposed changes through a change control system (CCS). The CCS may also include the review of proposed changes through a change control board (CCB). Changes may be discarded or approved on the basis of different criteria, such as benefit/cost ratios (BCRs), value-added changes, risk, and political capital.

When changes are approved, the project manager must then update the project baselines, as changes will likely affect a combination of scope, cost, and time. The updated baselines allow the project to continue with the new changes fleshed in and provide for accurate measurement of the performance of the project as changed.

This is an important concept: *Update the project baselines.* Consider a project to which work has been added but for which the schedule baseline has not been updated: The project's end date will thus be sooner than what is possible, because the project baseline does not reflect the additional work that should extend that date. In addition, a failure to revise the project baseline could skew reporting, variances, future project decisions, and even future projects.

Consider a project manager who does not update the project baseline after a change. The completion of the project goes into the archives and can serve as historical information for future projects. In such cases, the historical information would be skewed, since it doesn't accurately account for the added work and the projected end date or budget.

Changes, small or large, must be accounted for throughout the project plan. Notice how the integrated change control processes influence the communications of the change, including the change approval or denial. That's the whole point: to integrate proposed changes into the project processes. Figure 4-4 details integrated change control.

Implementing Tools and Techniques for Integrated Change Control

Given that changes, or requests for change, are likely to happen in the project, what tools are available to squelch, evaluate, and approve the proposed changes? And how can the project manager organize change requests in an orderly system so he or she is not constantly evaluating change requests instead of focusing on project completion? And how do change requests get approved, worked into the project plan, and accounted for in costs, schedule, and risk?

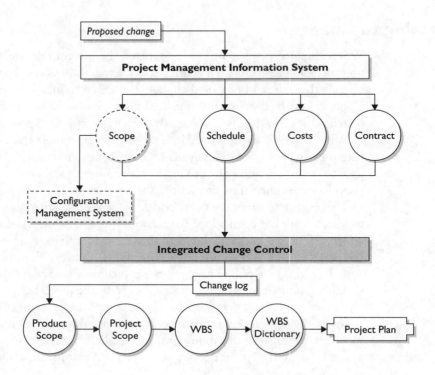

FIGURE 4-4

All change
requests must
pass through
integrated
change control.

Many tools can be applied to requests for change: consistency, scope comparison, benefit/cost ratios, risk analysis, and the estimate of the time and cost to incorporate the change, among others. The tools will guide the project manager, the project team, and the stakeholders through the process of approving and declining changes. The best approach for integrated change control is a constant, purposeful process of reviewing, considering, and evaluating, followed by a decision as to whether the change is needed.

Relying on a Change Control System

A change control system is a formal process of documenting and reviewing proposed changes. It establishes the flow of change from proposal to decision. The change control system is a process that describes how project performance will be monitored, how changes may occur, and then how the project plan may be revised and sent through versioning when the changes are approved.

A change control system is a collection of documented activities, factors for decisions, and performance measurements—not a computer program. While many

INSIDE THE EXAM

What must you know from this chapter to pass the exam? Know the purpose of the project plan: to guide the project manager through the execution and control groups. The project plan is also in place to provide communication to the project team, stakeholders, and management. Additionally, it will guide all future project decisions.

You should know all of the components of the project plan. Know what each of the subsidiary project plans are used for, how they can be updated, and what their objectives are. Remember, the point of planning is to create the project plan. The project plan, then, is to provide leadership and direction for the project execution and control processes. It is a formal, management-approved document—and once approved, work can begin.

Remember the WBS? It's a major piece of the PMP exam. Know the attributes of the WBS: It serves as an input to the planning process and execution, and it requires input from the project manager and the project team. The WBS is an input to seven planning processes.

- Develop the project management plan
- Define the project activities
- Estimate the project costs
- Determine the project budget
- Plan the project quality
- Identify the project risks
- Complete procurement planning

After the WBS, historical information is another big factor on the exam.

Why? Historical information is proof from other project managers. It allows the project manager to rely on what has been proven, what has been accomplished, and what has been archived for reference. And remember: The current project plan will become a future historical reference.

Assumptions and constraints are present on every project. Assumptions are beliefs held to be true but not *proven* to be true. They should be documented in the project plan, while constraints are restrictions the project must operate within. The Triple Constraint of Project Management—time, cost, and scope—will visit you on exam day, as will other internal and external constraints.

To begin the project, a project charter is needed. Project charters come from a manager external to the project. Once the charter is present, the project manager is named. The project manager then assembles the project team and begins the planning processes. The primary output of any planning is a project plan, and its execution cannot begin until management approves the plan. All work described in the project plan must pass through a work authorization system, either formal on a larger project or informal on smaller projects.

Integrated change control requires the evaluation of change requests to determine their worthiness for approval—or lack thereof for denial. Change requests can be written or verbal, internal or external. They can stem from stakeholders or external sources such as government agencies, laws, or industry mandates.

electronic project management information systems offer a change control system, know that a change control system is a documented approach to change, not an automated approval structure.

Some organizations may have a change control system that is used across all projects and maps to common guidelines within the organization. If the performing organization does not have a change control system, it is the responsibility of the project manager and the project team to create one. A change control system is mandatory for effective project management.

Within a change control system there may be a collection of management, key stakeholders, and project team members that review the changes for approval or denial. This board is defined in the project plan, and its roles and responsibilities are defined prior to project plan execution. Common names for the board include the following:

- Change control board (CCB)
- Schedule change control board
- Technical review board (TRB)
- Technical assessment board (TAB)
- Engineering review board (ERB)

Implementing Configuration Management

Configuration management focuses on controlling the characteristics of a product or service. It is a documented process of controlling the features, attributes, and technical configuration of any product or service. When it comes to project management, configuration management has a focus on the project deliverables. In some organizations, configuration management is a part of the change control system, while in some industries, such as manufacturing, configuration management refers to the control of existing operations. In a general sense, configuration management consists of the following:

- **Configuration identification** The documentation and labeling of the features, characteristics, and functions of a product or service
- **Configuration status accounting** The management and coordination of efforts to change the product or service. This includes status of proposed changes, both pending and implemented
- **Configuration verification and audit** The process of documenting any changes to the product or service. It is the ongoing auditing of products and services to ensure their conformance to documented requirements, including tracking approved changes to the product's features and functions

Applying Performance Measurement

The end result of project plan execution must be measured to see if the implementation of the plan meets the expected results of the project plan. The most common measurement of project plan execution is earned value. Earned value is a collection of formulas to measure the project worth, performance, and likelihood of the project completing on time and on budget.

Revisiting Planning Processes

Planning is iterative. As project plans rarely, if ever, happen exactly the way the project team and project manager planned them, the project freely moves between the controlling, executing, and planning processes. This is most evident when changes enter the project scene. The project manager and the project team must evaluate the proposed changes for additional cost, time, and risk concerns.

If the project work slips from the expected performance, quality, or schedule, adjustments are needed. These adjustments will require the consideration of project activities, the critical path, resources, cost, sequence of activities, and other refinements to the project plan.

Evaluating the Outputs of Integrated Change Control

As the project follows the project plan and changes are presented, the project manager will implement integrated change control. Some changes will be denied, documented, and archived for reference if needed. Other changes will be approved and factored into the project scope and have their time, cost, and risks documented and accounted for. The process of integrated change control is ongoing until project closure. Integrated change control can spur the following:

- Approved change requests
- Rejected change requests
- Project plan updates
- Project scope statement updates
- Approved corrective actions
- Approved preventive actions
- Approved defect repair
- Project deliverables

CERTIFICATION OBJECTIVE 4.05

Closing the Project or Phase

The project management plan defines what the project or phase is, how the project or phase will be completed, and finally—the good part—how the project or phase will be closed. The close project processes are those activities that the project manager, the project management team, vendors, and the organization's management will undertake to close out the project work. If a project has multiple phases, as most projects do, the closing processes will be implemented at the end of each phase.

Preparing to Close the Project or Phase

The project manager must rely on several documents to prepare the close project processes. Specifically, the project manager relies on the project management plan to guide the required actions needed to close out the project. Of course, other components contribute to the start of the closing processes.

■ **Contract documentation**   When a project is being completed for another organization, the contract serves as a guide for how the project may be closed. The contract will define provisions for change, the criteria for acceptance, product description, and payment details.

■ **Enterprise environmental factors**   Recall that the organization's culture, project management approach, standards and regulations, human resource requirements, and tolerance for risk all affect how a project is initiated. These same factors also affect the procedures for project closure.

■ **Organizational process assets**   An organization may have procedures and processes that every project manager must follow to close a phase or project. These can include financial, reporting, and human resource obligations.

■ **Work performance information**   The success of the project is based on more than just a declaration of completion. The work performance information defines the schedule, costs, and deliverables that have been met as part of the project work.

■ **Deliverables**   The project has to create something, so it's no surprise that the deliverables serve as input to the project closing processes.

Formally closing the project or phase involves documenting and archiving all of the work necessary to formalize the closing process. This requires more than just the project manager, instead involving the project team, the project sponsor, key stakeholders, and vendors. Administrative closure includes all of the following activities:

- Collecting and assembling all project records
- Analyzing the project's success or failure
- Gathering lessons-learned documentation
- Archiving project information for future reference

PMP Coach *At the end of the project, project teams and the project manager are often rewarded. How will you reward yourself for finishing the project to pass your PMP exam? Set a reward for earning your PMP—you'll deserve it!*

Completing Contract Closure

If a contract has been involved with the project work, the project manager must work with the vendor or customer, depending on the scenario, to finalize the project or phase closure. The contract will serve as the guide for what constitutes the successful completion of the purchase. Contract closure includes the following:

- Product verification
- Early contract termination conditions
- Payment terms
- Formal acceptance documentation
- Project files
- Project closure documents
- Historical information

The terms of the contract define how the project work is to be executed, managed and controlled, and then finally closed. I'll discuss contracting and procurement details in Chapter 12. Something to look forward to!

CERTIFICATION SUMMARY

Project integration management is an ongoing process the project manager completes to ensure the project moves from start to completion. It is the gears, guts, and grind of project management—the day-in, day-out business of completing the project work. Project integration management takes your project plans; coordinates the activities, project resources, constraints, and assumptions; and massages them into a working model.

Of course, project integration management isn't an automatic process; it requires you, the project manager, to negotiate, finesse, and adapt to the project's circumstances. Project integration management relies on general business skills such as leadership, organizational skills, and communication to get all the parts of the project working together.

The process of project management can be broken down into three chunks.

- **Developing the project plan** Project plan development is an iterative process that requires input from the project manager, the project team, the project customers, and other stakeholders. It details how the project work will accomplish the project goals. The project plan provides communication.

- **Executing the project plan** Now that the plan has been created, it's time to execute it. The project execution processes authorize the work to begin, manage procurement and quality assurance, host project team meetings, and manage conflict between stakeholders. On top of all these moving parts, the project manager must actively work to develop the individuals on the project to work as a team for the good of the project.

- **Managing changes to the project** Changes can kill a project. Change requests must be documented and sent through a formal change control system to determine their worthiness for implementation. Integrated change control manages changes across the entire project. Change requests are evaluated and considered for impacts on risk, costs, schedule, and scope. Not all change requests are approved—but all change requests should be documented for future reference.

As the project moves from start to completion, the project manager and the project team must update the lessons-learned documentation. The lessons learned serve as future historical information to the current project and to other future projects within the organization. The project manager and project team should update the lessons learned at the end of project phases, when major deliverables are created, and at the project's completion.

Project Integration Management

Project integration management relies on project plan development, project plan execution, and integrated change control. Integrated change control manages all the moving parts of a project.

- Project integration management is a fancy way of saying that the project components need to work together—and the project manager sees to it that they do. Project integration management requires negotiation between competing objectives.

- Project integration management calls for general management skills, effective communications, organization, familiarity with the product, and more. It is the day-to-day operations of the project execution.

Planning the Project

On your exam, you'll need to know that planning is an iterative process and that the results of planning are inputs to the project plan. The project plan is a fluid document, authorized by management, and guides all future decisions on the project.

- The project plan is a fluid work in progress. Updates to the plan reflect changes to the project, discoveries made during the project plan execution, and conditions of the project. The project plan serves as a point of reference for all future project decisions, and it becomes future historical information to guide other project managers. When changes occur, the cost, schedule, and scope baselines in the project plan must be updated.

Project Constraints

Projects have at least one or more constraints: time, cost, and scope. These are known as the Triple Constraints of Project Management. Constraints are factors that can hinder project performance.

- Time constraints include project deadlines, availability of key personnel, and target milestone dates. Remember that all projects are temporary: They have a beginning and an end.
- Cost constraints are typically predetermined budgets for project completion. It's usually easier to get more time than more money.
- Scope constraints are requirements for the project deliverables, regardless of the cost or time to implement the requirements (safety regulations or industry mandates are examples).

Managing Change Control

Integrated change control is the process of documenting and controlling the features of a product, measuring and reacting to project conditions, and revisiting planning when needed.

- Projects need a change control system to determine how changes will be considered, reviewed, and approved or declined. A change control system is a documented approach to how a stakeholder may request a change and then what factors are considered when approving or declining the requested change.
- Configuration management is part of change control. It is the process of controlling how the characteristics of the product or service the project is creating are allowed to be changed.

KEY TERMS

If you're serious about passing the PMP exam, memorize these terms and their definitions. For maximum value, create your own flashcards based on these definitions and review them daily.

activity attributes   Activities that have special conditions, requirements, risks, and other conditions should be documented.

activity cost estimates   The cost of resources, including materials, services, and, when warranted, labor should be estimated.

activity list   A shopping list of all the activities the project team must complete in order to satisfy the project. This list is an input to the project network diagram.

assumption log   A document that clearly identifies and tracks assumptions that are made in the project. All assumptions need to be tested for their validity, and the outcome of the test should be recorded.

benefit measurement methods   Project selection methods that compare the benefits of projects to determine which project the organization should invest its funds into.

benefit/cost ratios   Shows the proportion of benefits to costs; for example 4:1 would equate to four benefits and just one cost.

change control board   A group of decision makers that review proposed project changes.

change control system   A predefined set of activities, forms, and procedures to entertain project change requests.

change log   As changes to the project time, cost, or scope enter the project, they should be recorded in the change log for future reference.

change management plan   When changes are approved for a project, including time, cost, scope, or contract, there needs to be a plan on how the project team will manage these new changes within the project.

communications management plan   Defines the required communications and how they will be fulfilled; explains the methods used for gathering, storing, and dispersing information to appropriate parties. In addition, the communications management plan maps out the schedule of when the expected communication needs will be met.

configuration management   The control and documentation of the project's product features and functions.

constrained optimization methods   Complex mathematical models to determine the likelihood of a project's success in order to determine if the organization should invest its funds into the project.

constraints Anything that limits the project manager's options; for example, time, cost, and scope are always project constraints.

contract A legally binding agreement between the buyer(s) and seller(s) that defines the roles and responsibilities of all parties in the agreement.

cost management plan Explains how variances to the costs of the project will be managed. The plan may be based on a range of acceptable variances and the expected response to variances over a given threshold.

duration estimates The prediction of how long the project work will take to complete.

earned value management A suite of formulas to measure the project's overall performance for time and costs.

forecast Throughout the project, the project manager will create forecasts about the expected project completion date and projected project costs.

future value A formula to predict the current amount of funds into a future amount of funds. The formula is Future Value = Present Value$(1+i)^n$, where i is the value of return and n is the number of time periods.

historical information Any information created in the past that can help the current project succeed.

human resources plan Details on how the project team members will be brought onto and released from the project.

internal rate of return A benefit measurement formula to calculate when the present value of the cash inflow equals the project's original investment.

issue log Issues are decisions that are usually in disagreement among two or more parties. Issues are recorded in the issue log, along with an issue owner designation, an issue date for resolution, and the eventual outcome of the issue.

lessons learned Ongoing collection of documentation about what has and has not worked in the project; the project manager and the project team participate in lessons-learned creation.

murder board A group of decision makers that may determine to "kill" a proposed project before it is officially launched, based on the board's findings on the likelihood of the project's success.

net present value   A benefit measurement formula that provides a precise measurement of the present value of each year the project generates a return on investment.

payback period   The duration of time it takes a project to earn back the original investment.

performance reports   These formal reports define how the project is performing on time, cost, scope, quality, and any other relevant information.

PMIS   A project management information system is typically a software system, such as Microsoft Project, to assist the project manager in managing the project.

present value   A benefit measurement formula to determine what a future amount of funds is worth today. The formula is Present Value = Future Value/$(1+i)^n$, where i is the value of the return and n is the number of time periods.

process improvement plan   Identifies methods to track and eliminate waste and non-value-added activities.

procurement documents   All of the documents for purchasing, such as request for quotes, invitation to bid, request for proposal, and the responses, are stored as part of the project documentation.

procurement management plan   Describes the procurement process from solicitation to source selection. The plan may also include the requirements for selection as set by the organization.

project baselines   Three baselines in a project are used to measure project performance: cost, schedule, and scope.

project charter   A document that authorizes the project, defines the high-level requirements, identifies the project manager and the project sponsor, and provides initial information about the project.

project funding requirements   In larger projects, this document identifies the timeline of when capital is required for the project to move forward. This document defines the amount of funds a project needs and when the project funds are needed in order to reach its objectives.

project integration management   One of nine knowledge areas that is responsible for coordinating the efforts of the other eight knowledge areas.

project plan   A comprehensive document comprised of several subsidiary plans that communicates the intent and direction of the project.

proposals   Proposals are an exposé on ideas, suggestions, recommendations, and solutions to an opportunity provided by a vendor for a seller. Proposals include a price for the work and document how the vendor would provide the service to the buyer.

quality management plan   Details the quality improvement, quality controls, and how the project will map to the quality assurance program of the performing organization.

requirements traceability matrix   A table that identifies all of the project requirements, when the requirements are due, when the requirements are created, and any other pertinent information about the requirements.

resource breakdown structure   This chart identifies the resources utilized in the project in each section of the WBS.

resource calendar   You'll need to know when people and facilities are available or scheduled to work on the project.

resource requirements   The identification of what resources are needed to complete the project work is needed as a supporting document for planning. This includes people, materials, equipment, facilities, and services.

responsibility assignment matrix   This is a table that maps roles to responsibilities in the project.

risk management plan   Details the identified risks within the project, the risks associated with the constraints and project assumptions, and how the project team will monitor, react, or avoid the risks.

risk register   A risk is an uncertain event or condition that can have a positive or negative effect on the project. All risks, regardless of their probability or impact, are recorded in the issue log and their status is kept current.

roles and responsibilities   Maps project roles to responsibilities within the project; roles are positions on the project team, and responsibilities are project activities.

schedule management plan   Identifies circumstances that may change the project schedule, such as the completion of project phases or the reliance on other projects and outside resources. The schedule management plan details the approval and accountability process for changes within the project.

scope management plan   Details how the project scope should be maintained and protected from change, as well as how a change in scope may be allowed.

scoring models   A project selection method that assigns categories and corresponding values to measure a project's worthiness of investment.

sellers list   A listing of the vendors an organization does business with. You might know this document as a preferred vendors list in your company.

source selection criteria   A predefined listing of the criteria to determine how a vendor will be selected—for example, cost, experience, certifications, and the like.

statement of work   A document that defines the project work that is to be completed internally or by a vendor.

supporting detail for estimates   The project manager should document how time and cost estimates were created.

teaming agreement   A contractual agreement that defines the roles, responsibilities, considerations, and partnerships of two or more organizations that work together in a project. It's not unlike a partnership or subcontractor relationship.

work performance information   The current status of the project work; includes the results of activities, corrective and preventive action status, forecasts for activity completion, and other relevant information.

work performance measurements   These are predefined metrics for measuring project performance, such as cost variances, schedule variances, and estimate to complete.

✔ TWO-MINUTE DRILL

Developing the Project Charter

❑ The project charter authorizes the project and names the project manager.

❑ It is not authorized by the project manager, but by a person or party that has the power to grant the project manager the authority over the project resources.

❑ The project charter defines the high-level requirements for the project and the conditions for success.

Developing the Project Plan

❑ The project plan is a collection of subsidiary project plans.

❑ The project plan communicates the intent of the project.

❑ Project planning is an iterative process that may require updates to the project plan and other project documents.

Executing the Project Plan

❑ The project team executes the project plan in order to create the requirements of the project.

❑ The majority of the project's time and budget are spent during project execution.

❑ Team development and team management are executing processes.

❑ Execution is also where the procurement requirements are completed.

Monitoring and Controlling the Project Work

❑ Monitoring and controlling processes happen in tandem with the project execution processes.

❑ Earned value management is a suite of formulas that can help the project management team monitor the project performance.

❑ Expert judgment is relying on someone with more experience to help the project manager make the best decision.

❑ Change requests include scope changes, recommended corrective actions, recommended preventive actions, and defect repair.

Closing the Project or Phase

❑ Closing the project or phase requires the project manager to follow the guidelines of the organization and the project plan.

❑ The project's contract documentation can help guide the procedures for closing a project or phase when the project is being completed by a vendor for a buyer.

❑ Project documentation should be archived as part of project closure.

SELF TEST

1. You are a project manager for your organization. Management has asked you to help them determine which projects should be selected for implementation. In a project selection model, which of the following is the most important factor?
   A. Business needs
   B. The type of constraints
   C. The budget
   D. The schedule

2. On any project, the lessons-learned document is created by which of the following?
   A. The customers
   B. The project sponsor
   C. The project team
   D. The stakeholders

3. Your project is moving ahead of schedule. Management elects to incorporate additional quality testing into the project to improve the quality and acceptability of the project deliverable. This is an example of which one of the following?
   A. Scope creep
   B. Change control
   C. Quality assurance
   D. Integrated change control

4. All of the following are true about change requests except:
   A. They happen while the project work is being done.
   B. They always require additional funding.
   C. They can be written or verbal.
   D. They can be requested by a stakeholder.

5. You are the project manager for a pharmaceutical company. You are currently working on a project for a new drug your company is creating. A recent change in a law governing drug testing will change your project scope. Since the project must be completed within two years, what's the first thing you should do as project manager?
   A. Create a documented change request.
   B. Proceed as planned, since the project will be grandfathered beyond the new change in the law.

C. Consult with the project sponsor and the stakeholders.

D. Stop all project work until the issue is resolved.

6. During project execution activities, a project sponsor's role in a functional organization can best be described as doing which one of the following?

A. Acting as a sounding board for the project stakeholders

B. Helping the project manager and stakeholders resolve any issues ASAP

C. Deflecting change requests for the project manager

D. Showing management the project progress and status reports

7. You are the project manager for the HALO Project. You and your project team are preparing the project plan. Of the following, which one is a project plan development constraint you and your team must consider?

A. The budget as assigned by management

B. Project plans from similar projects

C. Project plans from similar projects that have failed

D. Interviews with subject matter experts (SMEs) who have experience with the project work in your project plan

8. Which of the following is the primary purpose of the project management plan?

A. To define the work to be completed to reach the project end date

B. To define the work needed in each phase of the project life cycle

C. To prevent any changes to the scope

D. To define how the project is executed, monitored, controlled, and then closed

9. Of the following, which one is an input to project plan development?

A. The project scope statement

B. Project planning methodology

C. EVM

D. Business needs

10. What is the difference between a project baseline and a project plan?

A. Project plans change as needed, while baselines change only at milestones.

B. Project plans and baselines do not change—they are amended.

C. Project plans change as needed, while baselines are snapshots of the project plan.

D. Baselines are control tools, while project plans are execution tools.

11. Which one of the following is not beneficial to the project manager during the project plan development process?

    A. Gantt charts

    B. PMIS

    C. The project management methodology

    D. Stakeholder knowledge

12. Which one of the following represents the vast majority of a project's budget?

    A. Project planning

    B. Project plan execution

    C. Labor

    D. Cost of goods and services

13. The project plan provides a baseline for several things. Which one of the following does the project plan not provide a baseline for?

    A. Scope

    B. Cost

    C. Schedule

    D. Control

14. Which of the following can best help a project manager during project execution?

    A. Stakeholder analysis

    B. Change control boards

    C. PMIS

    D. Scope verification

15. You are the project manager for your organization. When it comes to integrated change control, you must ensure that which one of the following is present?

    A. Supporting detail for the change exists

    B. Approval of the change from the project team

    C. Approval of the change from an SME

    D. Risk assessment for each proposed change

16. The project plan provides what in regard to project changes?

    A. A methodology to approve or decline CCB changes

    B. A guide to all future project decisions

    C. A vision of the project deliverables

    D. A fluid document that may be updated as needed based on the CCB

17. You are the project manager for the DGF Project. This project is to design and implement a new application that will connect to a database server. Management of your company has requested that you create a method to document technical direction on the project and to document any changes or enhancements to the technical attributes of the project deliverable. Which one of the following would satisfy management's request?

A. Configuration management

B. Integrated change control

C. Scope control

D. The change management plan

18. Baseline variances, a documented plan to management variances, and a proven methodology to offer corrective actions to the project plan are all part of which process?

A. Change management

B. The change control system

C. The scope change control

D. Integrated change control

19. One of the requirements of project management in your organization is to describe your project management approach and methodology in the project plan. You can best accomplish this requirement through which one of the following actions?

A. Establishing a project office

B. Establishing a program office

C. Compiling the management plans from each of the knowledge areas

D. Creating a PMIS and documenting its inputs, tools and techniques, and outputs

20. You have just informed your project team that each team member will be contributing to the lessons-learned documentation. Your team does not understand this approach and wants to know what the documentation will be used for. Which one of the following best describes the purpose of the lessons-learned documentation?

A. Offers proof of concept for management

B. Offers historical information for future projects

C. Offers evidence of project progression as reported by the project team

D. Offers input to team member evaluations at the project conclusion

21. Which one of the following is a formal document to manage and control project execution?

   A. WBS

   B. The project management plan

   C. The organizational management plan

   D. The work authorization system

22. Configuration management is a process for applying technical and administrative direction and surveillance of the project implementation. Which activity is not included in configuration management?

   A. Controlling changes to the project deliverables

   B. Scope verification

   C. Automatic change request approvals

   D. Identification of the functional and physical attributes of the project deliverables

23. Which set contains parts of the project plan execution?

   A. PMIS, WBS, and EVM

   B. General management skills, status review meetings, and EVM

   C. Project management methodology and the PMIS

   D. General management skills, status review meetings, and interpersonal skills

24. EVM is used during the _____.

   A. Controlling processes

   B. Executing processes

   C. Closing processes

   D. Entire project

25. You are the project manager for your organization. Management would like you to use a tool that can help you plan, schedule, monitor, and report your findings on your project. This tool is which one of the following?

   A. PMIS

   B. EVM

   C. Status review meetings

   D. Project team knowledge and skill set

SELF TEST ANSWERS

1. You are a project manager for your organization. Management has asked you to help them determine which projects should be selected for implementation. In a project selection model, which of the following is the most important factor?
    A. Business needs
    B. The type of constraints
    C. The budget
    D. The schedule

    ☑ **A.** Projects are selected based on business needs first.
    ☒ **B** is incorrect. Project constraints are typically not an issue when a project is selected, but the feasibility of a project to operate within the project constraints may be. **C,** the project budget, is incorrect, as the project budget is a project constraint. **D** is incorrect, since the project schedule is also a constraint.

2. On any project, the lessons-learned document is created by which of the following?
    A. The customers
    B. The project sponsor
    C. The project team
    D. The stakeholders

    ☑ **C.** The project team contributes to the lessons-learned document. The project manager also contributes, if not leads, the creation, but this is not a choice in the question.
    ☒ **A** is incorrect, since the customers do not contribute to the lessons-learned document. **B** is incorrect, as the project sponsor does not contribute to the lessons-learned document. **D** is incorrect, since stakeholders, other than the project manager and the project team, do not contribute.

3. Your project is moving ahead of schedule. Management elects to incorporate additional quality testing into the project to improve the quality and acceptability of the project deliverable. This is an example of which one of the following?
    A. Scope creep
    B. Change control
    C. Quality assurance
    D. Integrated change control

☑ **D.** Additional quality testing will require additional time and resources for the project. This is an example of integrated change control.

☒ **A** is incorrect, since scope creep includes small, undocumented changes to the project execution. **B,** change control, is incorrect because change control falls within integrated change control. **C** is incorrect, since QA is an organization-wide program.

4. All of the following are true about change requests except:
   A. They happen while the project work is being done.
   B. They always require additional funding.
   C. They can be written or verbal.
   D. They can be requested by a stakeholder.

☑ **B.** Change requests do not always require more money. Approved changes may require more funds, but not always. The change request may be denied, so no additional funds are needed for the project.

☒ **A, C,** and **D** are all incorrect choices, since these are characteristics of change requests during a project. For more information, see Section 4.6 in the PMBOK.

5. You are the project manager for a pharmaceutical company. You are currently working on a project for a new drug your company is creating. A recent change in a law governing drug testing will change your project scope. Since the project must be completed within two years, what's the first thing you should do as project manager?
   A. Create a documented change request.
   B. Proceed as planned, since the project will be grandfathered beyond the new change in the law.
   C. Consult with the project sponsor and the stakeholders.
   D. Stop all project work until the issue is resolved.

☑ **A.** A formal, documented change request is the best course of action for a change request stemming from a law or regulation.

☒ **B** is incorrect, since the law or regulation will likely override any existing project implementation. **C** is incorrect because the project manager should first document the change through a change request. **D** is incorrect, since all project work shouldn't stop just because of a change request.

6. During project execution activities, a project sponsor's role in a functional organization can best be described as doing which one of the following?
   A. Acting as a sounding board for the project stakeholders
   B. Helping the project manager and stakeholders resolve any issues ASAP
   C. Deflecting change requests for the project manager
   D. Showing management the project progress and status reports

   ☑ **B.** The project sponsor can help the project manager and the stakeholders resolve issues during project execution.
   ☒ **A** is incorrect, as the project sponsor is going to have an active rather than passive role in the process of integration management. **C** is incorrect, as the project sponsor will guide changes through the change control system. **D** is not a valid choice, since the project sponsor is part of management and will do more than report the status to other management roles.

7. You are the project manager for the HALO Project. You and your project team are preparing the project plan. Of the following, which one is a project plan development constraint you and your team must consider?
   A. The budget as assigned by management
   B. Project plans from similar projects
   C. Project plans from similar projects that have failed
   D. Interviews with subject matter experts (SMEs) who have experience with the project work in your project plan

   ☑ **A.** If management has assigned the project the constraint of a fixed budget, the project manager and the project team must determine how the project can operate within that constraint.
   ☒ **B** describes historical information, not a project constraint. **C** also is historical information and not a project constraint, so it, too, is incorrect. **D** is a valuable tool to use as input into the project plan development, but it is not a constraint.

8. Which of the following is the primary purpose of the project management plan?
   A. To define the work to be completed to reach the project end date
   B. To define the work needed in each phase of the project life cycle
   C. To prevent any changes to the scope
   D. To define how the project is executed, monitored, controlled, and then closed

> ☑ **D.** Of all the choices presented, **D** is the best choice. Project management plans communicate to the project team, the project sponsor, and stakeholders how the entire project will operate.
>
> ☒ **A** and **B** are incorrect, since they do not define the primary purpose of the project plan. **C** is also incorrect, since the project plan is intended not to prevent changes but to communicate the project management life cycle.

9. Of the following, which one is an input to project plan development?

A. The project scope statement

B. Project planning methodology

C. EVM

D. Business needs

> ☑ **A.** Of the choices, project scope statement is the only input to the project plan development.
>
> ☒ **B** is incorrect, as it describes a tool and technique used to develop the project plan. **C** is also a tool and technique to develop the project plan, rather than serve as input to the plan. **D** is incorrect, since it is an input to the planning processes.

10. What is the difference between a project baseline and a project plan?

A. Project plans change as needed, while baselines change only at milestones.

B. Project plans and baselines do not change—they are amended.

C. Project plans change as needed, while baselines are snapshots of the project plan.

D. Baselines are control tools, while project plans are execution tools.

> ☑ **D.** A project baseline serves as a control tool. Project plan execution and work results are measured against the project baselines.
>
> ☒ **A** is incorrect, given that baselines are changed with the project plan. **B** is incorrect, since project plans and baselines do change. **C** is also incorrect because baselines are more than snapshots of the project plans—they are expectations of how the work should be performed.

11. Which one of the following is not beneficial to the project manager during the project plan development process?

A. Gantt charts

B. PMIS

C. The project management methodology

D. Stakeholder knowledge

☑ **A.** Gantt charts are excellent tools to measure and predict the project progress, but they are not needed during the project plan development process.

☒ Choices **B, C,** and **D** are needed, and expected, during the development of the project plan.

12. Which one of the following represents the vast majority of a project's budget?

A. Project planning

B. Project plan execution

C. Labor

D. Cost of goods and services

☑ **B.** The project plan execution represents the majority of the project budget.

☒ **A,** project planning, does not reflect the majority of the project budget, although it may contain the most project processes. Choice **C,** labor, does not reflect the biggest project expense in all projects. Choice **D,** cost of goods and services, is incorrect, as the procurement of the goods and services will fall within the project plan execution. In addition, not every project will procure goods and services.

13. The project plan provides a baseline for several things. Which one of the following does the project plan not provide a baseline for?

A. Scope

B. Cost

C. Schedule

D. Control

☑ **D.** Control is not a baseline.

☒ Choices **A, B,** and **C** describe the project baselines contained within the project plan. Incidentally, **A, B,** and **C** are also the attributes of the Triple Constraints of Project Management.

14. Which of the following can best help a project manager during project execution?

A. Stakeholder analysis

B. Change control boards

C. PMIS

D. Scope verification

☑ **C.** A PMIS can assist the project manager the most during project execution. It does not replace the role of the project manager.

☒ Choice **A** is incorrect, as stakeholder analysis should have been completed during the project planning processes. Choice **B** also is incorrect. CCBs can assist the project manager, but not as much as the control and assistance offered through a PMIS. **D** is incorrect. Scope verification is proof of the project work, not an assistant to the project manager.

15. You are the project manager for your organization. When it comes to integrated change control, you must ensure that which one of the following is present?

A. Supporting detail for the change exists

B. Approval of the change from the project team

C. Approval of the change from an SME

D. Risk assessment for each proposed change

☑ **A.** Integrated change control requires detail for implementing the change. Without evidence of the need for the change, there is no reason to implement it.

☒ Choice **B** is incorrect, as the project team's approval is not necessary for changes. **C** is incorrect, since a subject matter expert isn't always needed to determine the need for change. **D** is also incorrect. While risk assessment is needed for changes, some changes may be discarded based on reasons other than risk.

16. The project plan provides what in regard to project changes?

A. A methodology to approve or decline CCB changes

B. A guide to all future project decisions

C. A vision of the project deliverables

D. A fluid document that may be updated as needed based on the CCB

☑ **B.** The project plan serves as a guide to all future project decisions.

☒ **A** is incorrect. The project plan details more than how changes may be approved or denied—recall that the change control board (CCB) approves and declines changes. **C** is also incorrect. The project plan describes how to obtain the project vision, not just what the project vision may be. **D** does describe the project plan, but not as fully as choice **B**. In addition, the project plan can be updated without changing the project scope.

17. You are the project manager for the DGF Project. This project is to design and implement a new application that will connect to a database server. Management of your company has requested that you create a method to document technical direction on the project and to document any changes or enhancements to the technical attributes of the project deliverable. Which one of the following would satisfy management's request?

    A. Configuration management
    B. Integrated change control
    C. Scope control
    D. The change management plan

    ☑ **A,** configuration management, is the documentation of the project product, its attributes, and its changes to the product.
    ☒ **B** is incorrect, as integrated change control describes how to incorporate all of the project changes across the knowledge areas. **C** is incorrect, since scope control describes how to manage changes, or potential changes, to the project scope. **D** is also incorrect, since the change management plan does not describe the project product, its features, or changes to the product.

18. Baseline variances, a documented plan to management variances, and a proven methodology to offer corrective actions to the project plan are all part of which process?

    A. Change management
    B. The change control system
    C. The scope change control
    D. Integrated change control

    ☑ **D.** Integrated change control is a system to document changes, their impact, the response to those changes, and performance deficits.
    ☒ **A** is incorrect, since change management does not respond to performance deficits as integrated change control does. **B** is also incorrect, since the change control system is a documented procedure to manage change requests. **C** is incorrect because scope change control is the process of managing changes that only affect the work in the project scope.

19. One of the requirements of project management in your organization is to describe your project management approach and methodology in the project plan. You can best accomplish this requirement through which one of the following actions?

    A. Establishing a project office
    B. Establishing a program office

C. Compiling the management plans from each of the knowledge areas

D. Creating a PMIS and documenting its inputs, tools and techniques, and outputs

☑ **C.** The management approach is best described as a compilation of the individual plans in the project plan.

☒ **A** is incorrect, since a project office is not needed to describe the management approach. **B** is incorrect for the same reason as **A.** Choice **D** may be a good practice for project control, but it does not describe management approach and methodologies.

20. You have just informed your project team that each team member will be contributing to the lessons-learned documentation. Your team does not understand this approach and wants to know what the documentation will be used for. Which one of the following best describes the purpose of the lessons-learned documentation?

A. Offers proof of concept for management

B. Offers historical information for future projects

C. Offers evidence of project progression as reported by the project team

D. Offers input to team member evaluations at the project conclusion

☑ **B.** Lessons learned is a document that offers historical information.

☒ **A** is incorrect. Proof of concept likely comes early in the project's planning processes. **C** is also incorrect, as lessons learned may offer evidence of project progression, but it is not the purpose of the lessons-learned document. **D** is also incorrect, given that lessons learned offers historical information for future projects.

21. Which one of the following is a formal document to manage and control project execution?

A. WBS

B. The project management plan

C. The organizational management plan

D. The work authorization system

☑ **B.** The project management plan is the formal document used to manage and control project execution.

☒ **A** is incorrect—the WBS is an input to the project plan. **C** is incorrect, as the organizational management plan is part of the project plan. **D** is also incorrect because the work authorization system allows work to be approved and for new work to begin.

22. Configuration management is a process for applying technical and administrative direction and surveillance of the project implementation. Which activity is not included in configuration management?
    A. Controlling changes to the project deliverables
    B. Scope verification
    C. Automatic change request approvals
    D. Identification of the functional and physical attributes of the project deliverables

    ☑ **C.** Hopefully, in no project are there automatic change approvals. **C** is not a part of configuration management.
    ☒ **A, B,** and **D** all describe the attributes of configuration management.

23. Which set contains parts of the project plan execution?
    A. PMIS, WBS, and EVM
    B. General management skills, status review meetings, and EVM
    C. Project management methodology and the PMIS
    D. General management skills, status review meetings, and interpersonal skills

    ☑ **C.** Only the project management methodology and the PMIS are the tools and techniques used for project execution.
    ☒ **A** is incorrect, as EVM and the WBS are not part of the tools used in the project plan execution. **B** is incorrect, since it includes EVM. **D** is incorrect because it also includes EVM.

24. EVM is used during the _____.
    A. Controlling processes
    B. Executing processes
    C. Closing processes
    D. Entire project

    ☑ **D.** EVM, earned value management, is used throughout the project processes. It is a planning and control tool used to measure performance.
    ☒ Choices **A, B,** and **C** are correct in that EVM is used during these processes, but neither of them is as good a choice as **D.**

25. You are the project manager for your organization. Management would like you to use a tool that can help you plan, schedule, monitor, and report your findings on your project. This tool is which one of the following?

    A. PMIS
    B. EVM
    C. Status review meetings
    D. Project team knowledge and skill set

    ☑ **A.** The PMIS is the best answer, since it helps the project manager plan, schedule, monitor, and report findings.

    ☒ Choice **B** is incorrect, since EVM does not help the project manager schedule. Choice **C** is also incorrect. Status review meetings do not help the project manager schedule. Choice **D** is incorrect because the project team's knowledge and skills do not necessarily help the project manager plan, schedule, monitor, and report findings.

5

Managing the
Project Scope

CERTIFICATION OBJECTIVES

H ave you ever set out to clean your garage and ended up cleaning your attic? It usually starts by needing to move the car out of the garage so you can really dig in and clean. As you move your car, you realize the car could really use a cleaning, too.

So you clean out the car. You dust it down; clean the windows inside and out; and vacuum out pennies, old pens, and some green French fries. The vacuum, you discover, has something caught in the hose, so you have to fight to clear the blockage in order to finish cleaning out the car. Once the inside's spick and span, you think, "Might as well wash and wax the car, too."

This calls for the garden hose. The garden hose, you notice, is leaking water at the spigot by the house. Now you've got to replace the connector. This calls for a pair of channel-lock pliers. You run to the hardware store, get the pliers—and some new car wax. After fixing the garden hose, you finally wash and wax the car.

As you're putting the second coat of wax on, you see a few scratches on the car that could use some buffing. You have a great electric buffer, but can't recall where it is. Maybe it's in the attic? You check the attic only to realize how messy things are there, too. So you begin moving out old boxes of clothes, baby toys, and more interesting stuff.

Before you know it, the garage is full of boxes you've brought down from the attic. The attic is somewhat cleaner, but the garage is messier than when you started way back this morning. As you admire the mess, you realize it's starting to rain on your freshly waxed car, the garden hose is tangled across the lawn, and there are so many boxes in the garage you can't pull the car in out of the rain.

So what does this have to do with project management? Plenty! Project management requires focus, organization, and a laser-like concentration. In this chapter, we'll be covering project scope management: the ability to get the required work done—and only the required work—to complete the project. We'll look at how a project manager should create and follow a plan to complete the required work to satisfy the scope without wandering or embellishing on the project deliverables.

CERTIFICATION OBJECTIVE 5.01

Collecting and Eliciting Project Requirements

Projects don't exist without stakeholders. Sure, sure, sometimes they are a pain in the neck, but if it weren't for them, there would not be a reason to have projects—or project managers. Stakeholders and project managers need to work together as a team; it's the stakeholders that know what they want as the end result of your work, and it's the project manager and the project team that can make that end result a reality. It's the role of the project manager to elicit requirements from the stakeholders to create the best possible solution to satisfy the needs of the stakeholders, the organization, and the longevity of the solution.

In some places, such as the International Institute of Business Analysis (IIBA), the process of gathering requirements is not the responsibility of the project manager, but of a business analyst. The goal, whether it's the project manager leading the work or a business analyst, is the same: Find detailed specifications about exactly what the stakeholders want and expect from the project. Once the requirements have been identified, and I mean clearly identified, the project manager and team can work towards specific results. Loose, open-ended, foggy requirements waste time, monies, and effort. You'll be gathering two broad categories of requirements.

- **Functional requirements** These describe how the solution will work, what the solution will manage, and all the capabilities the solution will provide for the stakeholder. It's how your project deliverable will operate.
- **Non-functional requirements** These describe the conditions that the functional requirements must operate within. You might hear this also described as the quality requirements or environmental requirements, where the solution will operate at its ideal level or performance. You can recognize nonfunctional requirements when stakeholders talk about speed, capacity, security, user interfaces, or production.

The project is the first step in requirements gathering, as it paints the high-level objective of the project. Some project charters rely on a current state assessment and compare it to the desired future state assessment. This is basically a before and after of your project—your project deliverables create the future state. Other charters simply define the high-level goals of the project, and then it's up to you, your project team, and any other experts to figure out how to make it happen.

You'll also rely on the stakeholder registry to confirm that you're communicating, interviewing, and eliciting requirements from all of the stakeholders. Recall that some stakeholders won't want your project to succeed at all—those nasty, negative stakeholders. Just because they despise the project doesn't mean you get to ignore them. You'll need to work with both positive and negative stakeholders during requirements gathering and throughout the project.

Interview the Stakeholders

One of the most reliable requirements-gathering methods is interviewing. Interviewing is really a conversation between you and the project stakeholders about their needs, wants, and demands for the project. It's a learning process for you to absorb information from the project customer by asking them questions. You need and want the interviewee to talk to you, so you've got to ask questions. Let me rephrase that: You need to ask good questions.

The interviewer should go into the interview armed with questions that allow the stakeholder to ramble a bit, but also allow the stakeholder to be precise about the project deliverables. You probably aren't going to ask the stakeholder how to create the deliverable, but more likely how they'll be using the product that you'll be creating. You want to see how they'll be using the deliverable as part of their day-to-day lives. This is where you'll categorize the requirements as functional or nonfunctional.

Interviews are usually done one-on-one, but there's no reason why a project manager can't have several interviewers participate in the session. As a general rule, however, the more people you have participate in the interview, the more complex the elicitation process becomes. Smaller groups allow for a more conversational tone to the meeting. Sometimes, however, the project manager will need a subject matter expert to help the conversational along.

Leading a Focus Group

Focus groups are an opportunity for a group of stakeholders to interact with a project moderator about the requirements of the project, the current state of an organization, or how they'll see the project deliverables affecting the organization once the project is completed. Like an interviewer, the moderator is armed with questions, but he should be well versed on the topic to branch into new contributing discussions on the project requirements.

An ideal focus group has six to twelve people in one room, and the moderator should encourage open, conversational discussion. The moderator, often not the project manager, should be neutral to the project, have the ability to draw people into the conversation, and keep the session on track to the goals of the project. A scribe or recorder should document the discussion in the session so the project manager and team can review the results of the meeting and act accordingly.

Hosting a Requirements Workshop

Let's face facts: Sometimes stakeholders have agendas. And by sometimes, I mean they always do. When you're managing a project with stakeholders from across the organization, you'll be dealing with different departments, different functions, and different lines of business. The stakeholders from each of these groups may have different expectations and requirements from the project, and these expectations will often clash. A requirements workshop, sometimes called a facilitated workshop, aims to find commonality, consensus, and cohesion among the stakeholders for the project requirements.

If you're in software development work, you've probably participated in a joint application design (JAD) workshop. These strive to gather all the requirements and to create a well-rounded, balanced application for all the stakeholders. In manufacturing, project managers use a requirements workshop, sometimes called the voice of the customer (VOC), where the voice of the customer dictates what the project will create. You might also know VOC as quality function deployment (QFD). The idea is that quality is achieved by giving the customer exactly what they expect.

Using Group Creativity Techniques

Rarely will all of the requirements for a project be clearly defined when the project launches. I suppose there are some cases where projects that are repeated over and over, such as in manufacturing or construction, may be based on the same initial set of requirements, but usually the requirements for each project vary wildly, as each project is unique. When you're managing a large project, you need to work with groups of stakeholders to elicit their requirements for the project deliverables.

Sometimes stakeholders have a general idea of what they'd like you to create, but they aren't certain. Consider market opportunities; problems that need to be solved; and implementations of new materials, software, or organization-wide changes. The requirements in these instances can go in multiple directions and demand a good plan and uniformity to create a successful project and useable deliverable.

When there are multiple solutions for a project, or the stakeholders aren't entirely certain what the exact project requirements should be, group creativity techniques can be useful. Group creativity techniques are approaches the group of key stakeholders can use to generate ideas, solutions, and requirements for the project. Here are some examples you should know for your PMP exam.

■ **Brainstorming** Brainstorming is an anything-goes approach to idea generation. The group of participants "storm" about a topic and throw out as many ideas as possible to generate solutions and requirements.

- **Nominal group technique**   Like brainstorming, this approach generates ideas, but then the ideas are voted on by the stakeholders and ranked based on usefulness.

- **Mind mapping**   Mind maps link ideas, thoughts, requirements, and objectives to one another. You might use mind maps after a brainstorming or nominal group technique to organize possible solutions and requirements, and to show where differences are between the stakeholders (see Figure 5-1).

- **Affinity diagram**   This group creativity technique is often used for solutions, and groups ideas into clusters. Then each cluster can be broken down again to analyze each subset. It's basically a decomposition and organization of project ideas and requirements.

FIGURE 5-1

Mind maps visualize project requirements while they're being created.

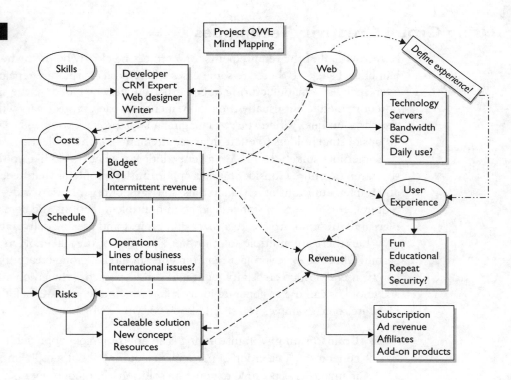

■ **Delphi Technique**   This approach uses rounds of anonymous surveys to foster consensus. Each round of surveys is based on answers from the past round so each participant can freely and anonymously comment on others' thoughts and inputs about the project requirements. The idea is that the comments will lead the group towards the most correct answer without the political attachment that may happen if the process were not anonymous.

o n   t h e   ○ o b   *If you're wondering why it's called the Delphi Technique, it's named after the Oracle at Delphi—the most important oracle from Greek mythology. It was first used in 1944 at the start of the Cold War to predict how technology may affect warfare.*

Using Group Decisions

When a project manager has many project stakeholders with loads of different competing objectives about the project deliverables, it's sometimes best to put the decision back on the project stakeholders. This approach generally allows the majority to vote on the project direction, but it doesn't always garner goodwill, cohesion, or buy-in from all the project stakeholders. There are four different models of group decisions you should be familiar with.

■ **Unanimity**   All of the stakeholders agree on the project requirements (and then rainbows appear, the sun shines, and bluebirds sing).

■ **Majority**   This is probably the most common group decision, where a vote is offered and the majority wins.

■ **Plurality**   Like a majority rule, this approach allows the biggest section of a group to win, even if a majority doesn't exist. You might experience this when there are three possible solutions for the project and the stakeholders vote their opinion for each solution in uneven thirds of 25 percent, 35 percent, and 40 percent. The group that represents the 40 percent would win, even though more people are opposed to the solution (60 percent!).

■ **Dictatorship**   The project manager, project sponsor, or the person with the most power forces the decision, even though the rest of the group may oppose the decision. No warm, fuzzy feelings here.

Relying on Surveys

Surveys are a fine approach to eliciting requirements from a large group of stakeholders in a relatively short amount of time. The challenge with surveys, however, is that they must be responded to and tabulated, and the survey questions must be well written to generate accurate responses. When the general requirements are known, closed-ended questions are ideal, but restrict the type of information the respondent may provide. Open-ended questions allow the respondent to write essays about a particular topic, but it takes more time to tabulate the responses.

Survey writers need to determine the best type of questions and they must consider the audience of the survey. You'll also want to consider how quickly you'd like respondents to complete the survey and how you'll collect and tabulate the results. Obviously, electronic surveys are ideal, as you can quickly sort the data, create charts, and track who has responded.

Observing Stakeholders

One of the best pieces of advice I ever received when it comes to learning a new skill was this: It's easier to watch someone peel a banana than describe how to peel a banana. It's true in requirements gathering, too. By observing someone do their work, you can see the processes, approaches, and challenges of their work more clearly than by just hearing about their work. Observing stakeholders, especially when your project is likely to affect their day-to-day work life, processes, and how they operate in your organization, is an excellent method to gather requirements.

As an observer, you shadow a person and watch how they do their work. You might complete the shadowing as a passive or invisible observer. In this role, you're quiet, out of the way, and just take notes on the processes you see. As an active or visible observer, you're stopping the person doing the work, asking loads of questions, and seeking to really understand how the person is completing his work.

Creating Prototypes

Have you ever seen a model of a skyscraper? Or what about a mockup for a new website, application, or even a brochure? These are prototypes that allow the stakeholder to see how the end result is going to function and help the project manager confirm that she understands the requirements the stakeholder expects from the deliverable. Some prototypes are considered throw-away, where they don't really work beyond communicating the idea of the deliverable. Other prototypes are considered functional or working, and evolve into the final deliverable of the project.

Managing the Project Requirements

The goal of eliciting the project requirements is to clearly identify and manage the requirements so the project scope can be created and the in-depth project planning can begin. It's ever-so-important for the project manager, the project team, and the key project stakeholders to be in agreement with the intent, direction, and requirements of the project before the project scope is created. There are three outputs of the collect project requirements process you should be familiar with.

- **Requirements documentation**   The clearly defined requirements must be measurable, complete, accurate, and signed-off by the project stakeholders. The requirements documentation may start broad and, through progressive elaboration, become more distinct, but the identification and agreement of what is required and demanded of the project is paramount. This includes definition of the functional and nonfunctional requirements, acceptance criteria, documentation of the impact of the deliverable on the organization, and any assumptions or constraints that have been identified.

- **Requirements management plan**   The requirements management plan defines how requirements will be managed throughout the phases of the project. This plan also defines how any changes to the requirements will be allowed, documented, and tracked through project execution. You'll also need to prioritize the project requirements and define what metrics will be used to measure requirement completion and acceptability.

- **Requirements traceability matrix (RTM)**   When you're managing loads of requirements, a requirements traceability matrix can help you track several characteristics for each requirement.
  - Requirement name
  - Requirements link to the business and project objectives
  - The function of each requirement
  - Any relevant data, coding, cost, or schedule about a requirement
  - The requirement's current status
  - Who the owner of the requirement is
  - Any comments or notes about the requirement

An RTM can help you ensure that every requirement in the project has been created to specification. This will help in quality control processes and in scope verification later in the project. Figure 5-2 is an example of a requirements traceability matrix.

FIGURE 5-2

A requirements traceability matrix can track elements and delivery of requirements.

Data and function

	Op1	Op2	Op3	Op4	Op5	Data	Status	Owner	Comments
REQ1	X		X	X	X	487	Fun	PM1	Currently functional
REQ2	X	X	X		X	7,321	Open	PM1	Open for review
REQ3	X	X		X		.99	Test	Pr2	Currently testing
REQ4		X	X			12.32	Prog	Pr2	Development
REQ5	X			X			Prog	BA3	Development
REQ6			X	X			Init	FM1	Initiating
REQ7	X			X		7.55	Test	IT1	Testing
REQ8			X		X		Fun	ITCIN	Currently functional
REQ9						475	Open	PS	Open for review

Requirements

CERTIFICATION OBJECTIVE 5.02

Defining Project Scope Management

Project scope management, according to the PMBOK, constitutes "the processes to ensure that the project includes all of the work required, and only the work required, to complete the project successfully." Project scope management has several purposes.

- It defines what work is needed to complete the project objectives.
- It determines what is included in the project.
- It serves as a guide to determine what work is not needed to complete the project objectives.
- It serves as a point of reference for what is not included in the project.

So what is a project scope statement? A project scope statement is a description of the work required to deliver the product of a project. The project scope statement defines what work will, and will not, be included in the project work. A project scope guides the project manager on decisions to add, change, or remove the work of the project.

Project Scope vs. Product Scope

Project scope and product scope are different entities. A project scope deals with the required work to create the project deliverables. For instance, a project to create a new barn would focus only on the required work to complete the barn with the specific attributes, features, and characteristics called for by the project plan. The scope of the project is specific to the work required to complete the project objectives.

Product scope, on the other hand, is the attributes and characteristics of the deliverables the project is creating. As in the preceding barn project, the product scope would define the features and attributes of the barn. In this instance, the project to create a barn would not include creating a flower garden, a wading pool, and the installation of a fence. There would be very specific requirements regarding the features and characteristics of the barn: the materials to be used, the dimensions of the different rooms and stalls, the expected weight the hayloft should carry, electrical requirements, and more.

The project scope and the product scope are bound to each other. The product scope constitutes the characteristics and features of the product that the project creates. The end result of the project is measured against the requirements for that product. The project scope is the required work to deliver the product. Throughout the project execution, the work is measured against the project plan to verify that the project is on track to fulfill the product scope. The product scope is measured against requirements, while the project scope is measured against the project plan.

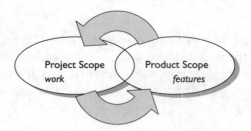

Planning the Project Scope

Planning the project scope involves progressive elaboration. The project scope begins broad and through refinement becomes focused on the required work to create the product of the project. The project manager and the project team must examine the product scope—what the customer expects the project to create—in order to plan on how to achieve that goal. Based on the project requirements documentation, the project scope can be created.

The scope planning process will rely on enterprise environmental factors, which is just a fancy way of saying the project manager will use the organization's culture, defined tools, human resources, and the policies of the organization to define how the project scope is created and then managed. Project managers will also rely on organizational process assets: the formal and informal policies and procedures that influence the way a project manager manages a project.

If you're a project manager, you do this already. Consider what work is like as a project manager in a bank versus being a project manager in a small, entrepreneurial company. The culture of both entities differs regarding how a project is initiated, planned, and then managed. Of course, the project charter, the requirements documentation, and organizational process assets will guide the scope planning process as well.

Using Scope Planning Tools and Techniques

The goal of scope planning is to create a project scope statement and the project scope management plan, two of the outputs of the scope planning process. The project manager and the project team must have a full understanding of the project requirements, the business need of the project, and stakeholder expectations to be successful in creating the scope statement and the scope management plan. Recall that there are two types of scope.

- **Product scope**   Features and functions of the product of the project
- **Project scope**   The work needed to create the product of the project

There are two tools that the project manager and the project team can rely on to plan the project scope. The first is expert judgment. Expert judgment is using someone smarter than the project team, the project manager, and even the key stakeholders to guide the scope planning process. Expert judgment can come from experts within the organization or third-party experts, such as consultants.

The second set of tools the project manager can rely on during scope planning is the templates, forms, and standards an organization may provide. Common templates and forms for projects include work breakdown structure templates, scope management plan templates, and project scope change control forms. Standards are guidelines that an organization has created to direct project teams in their scope planning endeavors.

Creating the Scope Management Plan

The scope management plan explains how the project scope will be managed and how scope changes will be factored into the project plan. Based on the conditions of the project, the project work, and the confidence of the exactness of the project scope, the scope management plan should also define the likelihood of changes to the scope, how often the scope may change, and how much the scope can change. The scope management plan also details the process of how changes to the project scope will be documented and classified throughout the project life cycle. Every scope management plan should define four things.

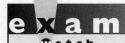

atch *Generally, you do not want the project scope to change. The implication of the scope management plan concerns how changes to the project scope will be permitted and what the justification is to allow the change.*

- The process to create a detailed project scope statement
- The process to create the WBS based on the project scope statement—and the methods for maintaining the WBS integrity and the process for WBS approval
- The process for formal acceptance of the project deliverables by the project customer
- The process for evaluating, and approving or declining, project change requests

CERTIFICATION OBJECTIVE 5.04

Defining the Project Scope Statement

The process of scope definition is all about breaking down the work into manageable chunks. If you had a desire to create a new house, you probably wouldn't stop by the lumberyard, pick up a truck of lumber, some cement, and nails, and set about building your dream house. You'd follow a logical approach to designing, planning, and then creating the house.

The same is true with project management. Your organization and stakeholders may have a general idea of where the project should end up, but a detailed, fully developed plan is needed to get you there. Scope definition is the process of taking the broad vision for the project and breaking it down into logical steps to reach its completion.

Examining the Inputs to Scope Definition

You should be very familiar with the inputs to scope definition; you've seen these several times already throughout the book. The following is a quick refresher of each and their role in this process:

- **The project charter** The project charter authorizes the project and the project manager.

- **Requirements documentation**   The project scope is founded on the requirements documentation, as this is what's expected of the project.
- **Organizational process assets**   The formal and informal guidelines, policies, and procedures that influence how a project scope is managed.

You'll also rely on the project's scope management plan, as it defines how the scope will be defined, managed, and controlled. Once your project is in motion, you can also expect change requests to influence the definition of your project scope.

Using Product Analysis

Product analysis is, as the name implies, analyzing the product the project will create. Specifically, it involves understanding all facets of the product, its purpose, how it works, and its characteristics. Product analysis can be accomplished through one or more of the following:

- **Product breakdown**   This method breaks down the product into components, examining each component individually and how it may work with other parts of the product. This approach can be used in chemical engineering to see how a product, such as a pharmaceutical, is created and how effective it is.
- **Systems engineering**   This process focuses on satisfying the customers' needs, cost requirements, and quality demands through the design and creation of the product. There is an entire science devoted to systems engineering in various industries.
- **Value engineering**   Deals with reducing costs and increasing profits, all while improving quality. Its focus is on solving problems, realizing opportunities, and maintaining quality improvement. Value engineering is also concerned with the customers' perception of the value of the different aspects of the product versus the project's cost to create the product's features and functions.
- **Value analysis**   Similar to value engineering, this focuses on the cost/quality ratio of the product. For example, your expected level of quality of a $100,000 automobile versus a $6,700 used car is likely relevant to the cost of each. Value analysis focuses on the expected quality against the acceptable cost.

■ **Function analysis**   Related to value engineering, this allows team input to the problem, institutes a search for a logical solution, and tests the functions of the product so the results can be graphed.

■ **Quality function deployment**   This is a philosophy and a practice to fully understand customer needs—both spoken and implied—without gold-plating the project deliverables.

Finding Alternatives

Project managers, project team members, and stakeholders must resist the temptation to fall in love with a solution too quickly. Alternative identification is any method of creating alternative solutions to the project's needs. This is typically accomplished through brainstorming and lateral thinking.

Performing Stakeholder Analysis

For a project to be successful, the project manager and the project team must know what the stakeholders of the project expect. This means communication between the project manager and the stakeholders. Business analysts may be involved or even facilitate this process of scope definition, but the end result is the same: The expectations of the project stakeholders must be identified, documented, and then prioritized.

This is also the time to define what constitutes project success. Unquantifiable metrics, such as customer satisfaction, "good," and "fast" don't cut it. The project manager and the stakeholders must agree on metrics that indicate a project's success or failure.

Examining the Scope Statement

The scope statement, an output of scope planning, is the guide for all future project decisions when it comes to change management. It is the key document to providing understanding of the project purpose. The scope statement provides justification for the project existence, lists the high-level deliverables, and quantifies the project objectives. The scope statement is a powerful document that the project manager and the project team will use as a point of reference for potential changes, added work, and any project decisions. The scope statement includes or references the following:

- **Product scope description**   Recall that the product scope description defines the characteristics and features of the thing or service the project is aiming to create. In most projects, the product scope will be vague early in the scope planning process, and then more details will become available as the product scope is progressively elaborated.

- **Product acceptance criteria**   The scope statement defines the requirements for acceptance. Product acceptance criteria establish what exactly qualifies a project's product as a success or failure.

- **Project deliverables**   The high-level deliverables of the project should be identified. These deliverables, when predefined metrics are met, signal that the project scope has been completed. When appropriate, the scope statement should also list what deliverables are excluded from the project deliverables. For example, a project to create a new food product may state that it is not including the packaging of the food product as part of the project. Items and features not listed as part of the project deliverables should be assumed to be excluded.

- **Project boundaries**   Every project has boundaries. The scope statement defines the boundaries of the project by defining what's included in the project scope and what's excluded. For example, a project to create a piece of software may include the created compilation of a master software image, but excludes the packaging and delivery of the software to each workstation within an organization. The project scope must clearly state what will be excluded from the project so there's no ambiguity as to what the stakeholders will receive as part of the product.

- **Project constraints**   A constraint is anything that restricts the project manager's options. Common constraints include predefined budgets and schedules. Constraints may also include resource limitations, material availability, and contractual restrictions.

- **Project assumptions**   An assumption is anything held to be true but not proven to be true. For example, weather, travel delays, the availability of key resources, and access to facilities can all be assumptions.

- **Project requirements**   The scope statement must define the requirements that the project must adhere to in order for the project to be deemed successful. This includes the prioritization of the stakeholders' needs, wants, and expectations.

Obviously, the project scope statement is a hefty document that aims to create the confines of the project and the expectations of the project manager, the project team, and the project customers. It defines what's in and what's out of the project scope. Overall, the project scope statement sets the tone of the project expectations and paints a picture of what the project will create and how long and how much it'll take to get there.

When the project scope is created, several documents and information should be established as early as possible in the project. While this information is not included directly in the project scope statement, it may be referenced as part of the support detail every project needs.

- **Initial project organization**   The project team members, the project manager, and the key stakeholders are identified and documented. The chain of command within the project is also documented.

- **Initial defined risks**   The scope statement should document the known risks and what their expected probability and impact on the project may be.

- **Scheduled milestones**   The project customer may have identified milestones within the project and assigned deadlines using these milestones. The scope should thus identify these milestones, which are essentially schedule constraints.

- **Fund limits**   Most projects have a limitation on available funding. This limit should be identified in the project scope statement.

- **Cost estimate**   Just as organizations have a limited amount of funds to invest in a project, they have expectations for an estimate of what the project should cost to complete. This estimate usually includes some modifier, such as +/− a percentage or dollar amount.

- **Project configuration management requirements**   No project manager wants their project to be run amok with changes. This section of the scope statement identifies the level of change control and configuration management that can be expected within the project.

- **Project approval requirements**   The approval requirements for project documentation, processes, work, and project acceptance must be identified within the project scope statement.

During the scope statement creation, the project manager may also face, believe it or not, change requests from the project stakeholders. Change requests are managed through the integrated change control process, which basically means that any proposed change is reviewed and its impact on all areas of the project are considered. If a change is approved, the scope statement should be updated to reflect the approved change.

INSIDE THE EXAM

There are three big themes from this chapter that you'll encounter on the project exam: project scope management, the WBS, and scope verification.

There are two types of scope: project scope and product scope. Unless the exam is talking about features and characteristics of the project deliverables, it will be referring to the project scope. If you think this through, it makes sense: Think of all the billions of different product scopes that can exist … the exam will offer big hints if it's talking about product scope.

Project scope, on the other hand, focuses on the work that has to be done in order to create the product. Recall that the project scope is concerned with the work required—and only the work required—to complete the project.

Your favorite project management tool, the WBS, is the most important tool in your project management toolbox. It is used as input to seven planning processes.

- Develop the project management plan
- Define the project activities
- Estimate the project costs
- Determine the project budget
- Plan the project quality
- Identify the project risks
- Complete procurement planning

Here's a nifty hint: WBS templates come from previous projects and/or the project management office, if the organization has one. WBS work packages are defined in the WBS dictionary.

Scope verification is all about the project customer accepting the project deliverables. Scope verification uses inspection as the tool to complete the process, which makes perfect sense. After all, how else will the customer know if the deliverable meets the project requirements unless they examine it?

CERTIFICATION OBJECTIVE 5.05

Creating the Work Breakdown Structure

As you hopefully know by now, the WBS is a deliverables-orientated collection of project components. Work that doesn't fit into the WBS does not fit within the project. The point of the WBS is to organize and define the project scope. As you can see in Figure 5-3, each level of the WBS becomes more detailed.

The WBS is more than a shopping list of activities—it is a visual representation of the high-level deliverables broken down into manageable components. A WBS is not a chart of the activities to complete the work—it is a breakdown of the deliverables. The smallest element in the WBS is called the work package. The components in the WBS are typically mapped against a code of accounts, which is a tool to number and identify the elements within the WBS. For example, a project manager and a stakeholder could reference work package 7.3.2.1, and both would be able to find the exact element in the WBS.

The components in the WBS should be included in a WBS dictionary. A WBS dictionary is a reference tool to explain the WBS components, the nature of the work package, the assigned resources, and the time and billing estimates for each element. The WBS also identifies the relationship between work packages. Finally, the WBS should be updated to reflect changes to the project scope.

The following are some essential elements you must know about the WBS:

- It serves as a major component of the project scope baseline.
- It's one of the most important project management tools.

FIGURE 5-3

A sample structure for a technology project

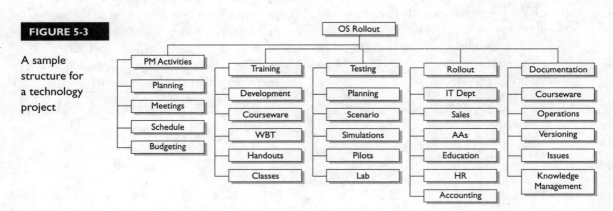

- The WBS serves as the foundation for planning, estimating, and project control.
- It visualizes the entire project.
- Work not included in the WBS is not part of the project.
- It builds team consensus and buy-in to the project.
- The WBS serves as a control mechanism to keep the project on track.
- It allows for accurate cost and time estimates.
- It serves as a deterrent to scope change.

As you can tell, the WBS is pretty darn important. If you're wondering where exactly the WBS fits into the project as a whole, it is an input to the following seven processes:

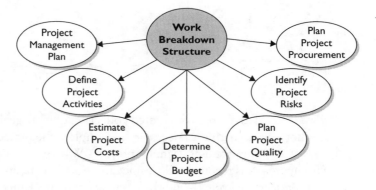

- Developing the project management plan
- Defining the project activities
- Estimating the project costs
- Determining the project budget
- Planning for project quality
- Identifying the project risks
- Planning the project procurement needs

Using a Work Breakdown Structure Template

One of the tools you can use in scope definition is a WBS template. This chapter details how a WBS gets created from scratch in a moment. A WBS breaks down

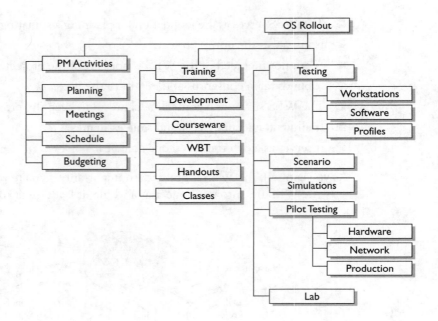

work into a deliverables-orientated collection of manageable pieces (see Figure 5-4).
It is not a list of activities necessary to complete the project.

A WBS template uses a similar project's WBS as a guide for the current work.
This approach is recommended, since most projects in an organization are similar in
their project life cycles—and the approach can be adapted to fit a given project.

Depending on the organization and its structure, an entity may have a common
WBS template that all projects follow. The WBS template may have common
activities included in the form, a common lexicon for the project in the organization,
and a standard approach to the level of detail required for the project type.

Decomposing the Project Deliverables

Decomposition is the process of breaking down the major project deliverables into
smaller, manageable components. So what's a manageable component? It's a unit
of the project deliverable that can be assigned resources, measured, executed, and
controlled. So, how does one decompose the project deliverables? It's done this way:

1. The major deliverables of the project are identified. This includes the project
   management activities. A logical approach includes identifying the phases of
   the project life cycle or the major deliverables of the project.

2. Determine if adequate cost and time estimates can be applied to the lowest level of the decomposed work. Adequate is subjective to the demands of the project work. Deliverables that won't be realized until later portions of the project may be difficult to decompose, since there are many variables between now and when the deliverable is created. The smallest component of the WBS is the work package. A simple heuristic of decomposition is the 8/80 rule: no work package smaller than 8 hours and none larger than 80.

3. Identify the deliverable's constituent components. This is a fancy way of asking whether the project deliverable can be measured at this particular point of decomposition. For example, the decomposition of a user manual may have the constituent components of assembling the book, confirming that the book is complete, shrink-wrapping the book, and shipping it to the customer. Each component of the work can be measured, and may take varying amounts of time to complete, but it all must be done to complete the requirement.

4. Verify the decomposition. The lower-level items must be evaluated to ensure they are complete and accurate. Each item within the decomposition must be clearly defined and deliverable-orientated. Finally, each item should be decomposed to the point that it can be scheduled, budgeted, and assigned to a resource.

5. Other approaches include breaking it out by geography or functional area, or even breaking the work down by in-house and contracted work.

Updating the Scope Statement

The second output of scope definition is scope updates. During the decomposition of the project deliverables, the project manager and the project team may discover elements that were not included in the scope statement but should be. Or the project manager and the team may discover superfluous activities in the scope statement that should be removed. For whatever reason, when updating the scope statement, the appropriate stakeholders must be notified of the change and given the justification for why the change is being made.

exam
watch   *Whenever a change enters the project that causes the project requirements to change, you also have to change the project scope baseline. The*   *project scope baseline is comprised of the project scope statement, the WBS, and the WBS dictionary.*

Verifying the Project Scope

Imagine a project to create a full-color, slick catalog for an electronics manufacturer. The project manager has completed the initiation processes, moved through planning, and is now executing the project work. The only trouble is that the project manager and the experts on the project team aren't sharing their work progress with the customer. Plus, the work they're completing isn't in alignment with the product description or the customer's requirements.

The project team has created a trendy 1950s-style catalog with funky green and orange colors, lots of beehive hairdo models, horn-rimmed glasses, and tongue-in-cheek jokes about "the future" of electronics. The manufacturer wants to demonstrate a professional, accessible, current look for its publications. What do you think will happen if the project manager presents the catalog with his spin rather than following the request of the customer?

Scope verification is the process of the project customer accepting the project deliverables. Scope verification happens at the end of each project phase, or as major deliverables are created. Scope verification is ensuring that the deliverables the project creates are in alignment with the project scope. It is concerned with the acceptance of the work. A related activity, quality control, is concerned with the correctness of the work. Scope verification and quality control happen in tandem, as the quality of the work contributes to scope verification. Poor quality will typically result in scope verification failure.

PMP Coach *You'll be doing some scope verification when you pass the PMP examination. Your project is to pass the exam, and once you do, you'll have verified that you've completed your project scope. Study smart, work hard, and keep after it. If you've made it this far, you can go just a bit farther. You can do it!*

Should a project get cancelled before it has completed the scope, scope verification is measured against the deliverables up to the point of the project's cancellation. In other words, scope verification measures the completeness of the work up to cancellation, not the work that was to be completed after project termination.

Examining the Inputs to Scope Verification

To verify the project scope, which is accomplished through inspection, there must be something to inspect—namely, work results. The work results are compared against the project plan to check for their completeness and against the quality control measure to check the correctness of the work.

One of the biggest inputs of scope verification is the requirements documentation you created as part of the collect requirements process. This information describes the requirements and expectations of the product, its features, and attributes. The product documentation may go by many different names, depending on the industry. A few project documentation names are:

- Plans
- Specifications
- Technical documentation
- Drawings
- Blueprints

As you know, the WBS is a collection of deliverables-orientated components. This collection of components can be used to ensure that the defined project work has been completed. The WBS allows the project manager, the project team, and the customer to verify that the necessary work was completed to create the deliverable.

The scope statement and the project plan serve as input to the project plan since they provide details on the project work, the product, and the expectations of the customer. A reference to these documents may be needed to clarify any issues during scope verification.

Inspecting the Project Work

To complete scope verification, the work must be inspected. This may require measuring, examining, and testing the product to prove it meets customer requirements. Inspection usually involves the project manager and the customer inspecting the project work for verification, which in turn results in acceptance. Depending on the industry, inspections may also be known as:

- Reviews
- Product reviews
- Audits
- Walkthroughs

Formally Accepting the Project Deliverables

Assuming the scope has been verified, the customer accepts the deliverable. This is a formal process that requires signed documentation of the acceptance by the sponsor or customer. Scope verification can also happen at the end of each project phase or at major deliverables within the project. In these instances, scope verification may be conditional, based on the work results. When the scope is not verified, the project may undergo one of several actions. It may be cancelled and deemed a failure, sent through corrective actions, or put on hold while a decision is made based on the project or phase results.

CERTIFICATION OBJECTIVE 5.07

Protecting the Project Scope from Change

When it comes to project management, the one constant thing is change. Changes happen, or try to happen, all the time in projects. The project manager must have a reliable system to track, monitor, manage, and review changes to the project scope. Change control focuses on three things.

- ■ It facilitates scope changes to determine that changes are agreed upon.
- ■ It determines if a scope change has happened.
- ■ It manages the scope changes when, and if, they happen.

Examining the Inputs to Scope Change Control

Throughout a project's life, the need and desire for change will come from project team members, the sponsor, management, customers, and other stakeholders. All of these change requests must be coupled with supporting evidence to determine the need of the change; the change's impact on the project scope (and usually on other processes as well); and the required planning, schedule, and budget to account for the changes.

See the video Managing Scope Changes.

Using the Project Management Plan

The project management plan does offer some specific direction on how changes are allowed into the project. While most project managers are resistant to change once the scope has been created and agreed upon, there are instances when changes are valid. You'll rely on the change management plan as a general direction of the flow of decisions to determine if a change is valid for your project. I'm assuming, of course, that you, the project manager, have control over change management decisions.

You'll also rely on the configuration management plan to determine how change is allowed specifically to the project scope. Configuration management is the control and documentation of the features and functions of the project's product. It's important to communicate the impact of change on the product to all of the stakeholders as part of the change control review.

Finally, you'll rely on your favorite project management tool, the scope baseline. The scope baseline represents the sum of the components, and ultimately the project work, that make up the project scope. The change requests may be for additional components in the project deliverables, changes to product attributes, or changes to different procedures to create the product. The WBS and WBS dictionary are referenced to determine which work packages would be affected by the change and which may be added or removed as a result of the change.

Evaluating Performance Reports

The communications management plan, which we'll cover in Chapter 10, includes specific requirements on the need for performance reports. Performance reports indicate how the project is going—good or bad. Performance reports can lead to change requests. How? When a project is going bad, operating beyond its budget, or off schedule, changes may be made to reduce the project scope, add corrective actions, or add quality activities to ensure the product is correct.

Considering Change Requests

Some project managers despise change requests. Change requests can mean additional work, adjustments to the project, or a reduction in scope. They mean additional planning for the project manager and time for consideration, and they can be seen as a distraction from the project execution and control. Change requests, however, are a very real and expected part of project management.

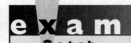

Change requests are more than just changes to the project scope. They include preventive action, corrective action, and defect repairs.

Why do change requests happen? Which ones are most likely to be approved? Most change requests are a result of:

- **Value-added** The change will reduce costs (this is often due to technological advances since the time the project scope was created)
- **External events** These could be such things as new laws or industry requirements.
- **Errors or omissions** Ever hear this one: "Oops! We forgot to include this feature in the product description and WBS!" Errors and omissions can happen to both the project scope (the work to complete the project) and the product scope, and typically constitute an overlooked feature or requirement.
- **Risk response** A risk has been identified and changes to the scope are needed to mitigate the risk.

Relying on the Scope Management Plan

Remember this plan earlier in the chapter? It's an output of scope planning and controls how the project scope can be changed. The scope management plan also defines the likelihood of the scope to change, how often the scope may change, and how much it may change. You don't have to be a mind reader to determine how often the project scope may change and by how much; you just have to rely on your level of confidence in the scope, the variables within the project, and the conditions the project must operate under. The scope management plan also details the process of how changes to the project scope will be documented and classified throughout the project life cycle.

Implementing a Change Control System

The most prominent tool applied with scope change control is the change control system. Because changes are likely to happen within any project, there must be a way to process, document, and manage the changes. The change control system is the answer. This system includes the following:

- Cataloging the documented requests and paperwork
- Tracking the requests through the system
- Determining the required approval levels for varying changes
- Supporting the integrated change control policies of the project
- In instances when the project is performed through a contractual relationship, the scope change control system must map to the requirements of the contract.

Revisiting Performance Measurement

Performance reports are inputs to scope change control—the contents of these reports, the actual measurements of the project are evaluated to determine what the needed changes may be. The reports are not meant to expose variances as much as they're meant to drive root-cause analyses of the variances. Project variances happen for a reason: The correct actions required to eliminate the variances may require changes to the project scope.

There is a distinct difference between performance reports and performance measurement, as shown in Table 5-1.

Completing Additional Planning

Planning is iterative. As change requests are presented, evidence of change exists, or corrective actions are needed within the project, the project manager and the project team will need to revisit the planning processes. Change within the project may require alternative identification, study of the change impact, analysis of risks introduced by the change, and solutions to problems within the project execution.

TABLE 5-1	Performance Reports	Performance Measurement
Performance Reports versus Performance Measurement	Signal an inconsistency	Evaluates the degree of inconsistency
	Serve as an output of performance reporting	Defines expected and experienced performance levels
	Serve as an input to change control	Measures current performance against what was planned

Changes made as part of this planning could cause the project plan, WBS, and baselines to be revised.

Updating the Project Scope

When changes to the project scope have been approved, the documented project scope must be updated to reflect these new changes. The stakeholders affected by the scope changes must be notified. The WBS must also be updated to reflect the components added or removed from the project. Scope changes can include cost updates, schedule updates, quality updates, or changes to the project deliverables.

When the project scope is to be changed, the new requirements must pass through the planning processes. The changes must be evaluated for cost and time estimates, risk, work considerations, product specification, and technical specification.

Correcting the Project

Often, the reason for change is due to faulty deliverables, quality problems, or poor performance of the project deliverables. Corrective actions are activities that will make an effort to bring the project back in line with the project plan. Errors and omissions in the product specifications are scope changes, not corrective action changes.

Updating the Lessons Learned

The lessons-learned documentation should be updated as an output of scope change control. The project manager should document reasons why changes were approved, corrective actions were taken, and components were added or removed from the scope, and she should also document the reasoning behind these decisions. Lessons learned will serve as future historical information to help guide other project managers.

Adjusting the Project Baselines

When changes are made, the project baselines will need to be adjusted to reflect these changes. Such changes can affect time, cost, schedule, and scope. The changes that affect the appropriate baseline should be updated to reflect the new project scope. The new baselines serve as a point of reference for the remainder of the project (assuming there are no additional changes). Should other changes occur, the baseline should be updated—enabling the project to continue.

CERTIFICATION SUMMARY

Projects exist in order to satisfy the project requirements. Project requirements are discovered through interviews, focus groups, workshops, and other elicitation techniques to help the stakeholders and the project team clearly understand what the project should create. The requirements documentation, the requirements management plan, and a requirements traceability matrix all help the project stay focused on expected deliverables and serve as input to the project scope.

Project scope management is the ability to complete all of the project's required work—and only the required work. This means no extras, no favors, and no cutting corners. The project scope is the focus of the project—or rather, the necessary work to complete the project. Project scope management is a tool the project manager uses to determine what work is in the project and what work is extraneous.

Projects, big or small, fit within the confines of the performing operation's strategic plans. Projects don't meander, at least not often, outside of the business focus of the organization. You won't find too many car manufacturers creating projects to make chocolate pies. Projects fit within the vision and function of the organization they operate within.

In order to determine what the project scope actually is, there's plenty of scope planning. The project manager and the project team must have a clear vision of the project, the business need for the project, the requirements, and the stakeholder expectations for the project. The end result of the scope planning processes is the scope statement. The scope statement says, in no uncertain terms, what is within the project and what is without.

For your PMP exam, focus on protecting the project scope. This includes finding the real purpose of the project so the scope is in alignment with identified needs. Once the scope has been created, the project team, the stakeholders, the project sponsor, and even the project manager should not change the scope—unless there is overwhelming evidence of why the scope needs to be changed.

KEY TERMS

To pass the PMP exam, you'll need to memorize these terms and their definitions. For maximum value, create your own flashcards based on these definitions and review them daily. The definitions can be found within this chapter and in the glossary.

affinity diagram   Clusters similar ideas together and allows for decomposition of ideas to compare and contrast project requirements.

brainstorming   A group creativity technique to express as many ideas as possible about project requirements.

decomposition   The breakdown of the project scope statement into the project's work breakdown structure. The smallest item of the project's decomposition into the WBS is called the work package.

Delphi Technique   A consensus-building group creativity technique that uses rounds of anonymous surveys during requirements elicitation. The Delphi Technique may also be used during risk assessment.

dictatorship   A group decision process where the person with the most power forces the decision, even though the rest of the group may oppose the decision.

facilitated workshop   A collection of stakeholders from around the organization that come together to analyze, discuss, and determine the project requirements.

focus group   A conversation of stakeholders led by a moderator to elicit project requirements.

function analysis   Related to value engineering, this allows team input to the problem, institutes a search for a logical solution, and tests the functions of the product so the results can be graphed.

interviews   A requirements elicitation process to collect requirements from the project stakeholders.

majority   A group decision process where a vote is offered and the majority wins.

mind mapping   A visual representation of like and opposing ideas, thoughts, and project requirements.

nominal group technique   A group creativity technique that follows the brainstorming model but ranks each brainstorm idea.

observation   A requirements elicitation process where the observer shadows a person to understand how she completes a process. An observer may be a participant observer or an invisible observer.

plurality   A group decision process approach that allows the biggest section of a group to win even if a majority doesn't exist.

product scope   The attributes and characteristics of the deliverables the project is creating.

project scope statement   The definition of what the project will create for the project stakeholders. The project scope statement includes the product scope description, product acceptance criteria, project deliverables, project exclusions, project assumptions, and project constraints.

prototype   A mockup of the project deliverable to confirm, adapt, or develop the project requirements.

quality function   A philosophy and a practice to fully understand customer needs—both spoken and implied—without gold-plating the project deliverables.

requirements documentation   A clearly defined explanation of the project requirements. The requirements must be measurable, complete, accurate, and signed off by the project stakeholders.

requirements management plan   Defines how requirements will be managed throughout the phases of the project. This plan also defines how any changes to the requirements will be allowed, documented, and tracked through project execution.

requirements traceability matrix   A table that helps the project team identify the characteristics and delivery of each requirement in the project scope.

scope baseline   Comprised of the project scope statement, the work breakdown structure, and the WBS dictionary.

scope management plan   Explains how the project scope will be managed and how scope changes will be factored into the project plan. Based on the conditions of the project, the project work, and the confidence of the project scope, the scope management plan should also define the likelihood of changes to the scope, how often the scope may change, and how much the scope can change.

scope verification An inspection-driven process led by the project customer to determine the exactness of the project deliverables. Scope verification is a process that leads to customer acceptance of the project deliverables.

systems engineering Focuses on satisfying the customers' needs, cost requirements, and quality demands through the design and creation of the product. There is an entire science devoted to systems engineering in various industries.

unanimity A group decision process where all participants are in agreement.

value analysis Similar to value engineering, this focuses on the cost/quality ratio of the product. Value analysis focuses on the expected quality against the acceptable cost.

value engineering Deals with reducing costs and increasing profits, all while improving quality. Its focus is on solving problems, realizing opportunities, and maintaining quality improvement.

voice of the customer The initial collection of customer requirements that serves as part of quality function deployment in a facilitated workshop.

work breakdown structure A decomposition of the project scope statement into work packages. The WBS is an input to seven project management processes: developing the project management plan, defining the project activities, estimating the project costs, determining the project budget, planning the project quality, identifying the project risks, and planning the project procurement needs.

work breakdown structure dictionary A companion to the WBS, this document defines all of the characteristics of each element of the WBS.

work breakdown structure templates Based on historical information, this is a WBS from a past project that has been adapted to the current project.

TWO-MINUTE DRILL

Collecting and Eliciting Project Requirements

❑ Collecting the project requirements is the process of eliciting the requirements from the project stakeholders so that the project manager and the project team may create the project deliverables. The project manager, the project team, and/or a business analyst elicit requirements from the stakeholders.

❑ There are eight tools and techniques that can be used to collect requirements: interviews, focus groups, facilitated workshops, group creativity techniques, group decision making, surveys, observations, and prototypes.

❑ A requirements traceability matrix is a table that maps all of the project requirements, their characteristics, related data, expected delivery date, and any comments or notes about each requirement. The requirements traceability matrix helps the project manager, the project team, and the stakeholders confirm that all of the requirements have been included in the project and have been created as expected.

Defining Project Scope Management

❑ Project scope management is part of any project's good foundation. By accurately defining the project scope, communicating how the scope will be managed, and then working with project stakeholders to control changes to the scope, time and cost objectives are easier to maintain.

❑ Project scope management is concerned with what the project will include for the project stakeholders, but it's also concerned with what won't be in the project. By establishing and communicating boundaries for the project, the project manager and the project team can focus on creating the agreed-upon project requirements.

❑ The project scope is based on the product scope. If the definition of the product scope changes, so, too, should the project scope. The fulfillment of the project scope will create the anticipated product scope. Configuration management links the features and functions of the product scope to the project scope.

Planning the Project Scope

❑ Progressive elaboration is the process of allowing the project scope to start broad and through iterations of analysis, development, and refinement, the project scope becomes specific.

❑ The scope management plan communicates how the project scope will be managed and how scope changes will be allowed. It defines how the scope statement is created, how the WBS is created, the scope verification process, and the project's change control system.

❑ All change requests should be written and entered into the project's change control system. Changes to the project scope may affect all of the project's knowledge areas: time, cost, quality, human resources, communication, risk, and procurement. The knowledge area of project integration management evaluates the project change and its impact on the entire project.

Defining the Project Scope Statement

❑ Project scope planning aims to define what work is needed to complete the project objectives. The project scope statement defines what's in—and out of—scope and then serves as a guide to determine what work may be contributing to elements outside of the project scope.

❑ The project scope builds the product scope. If the project scope contains work that's not needed, the product scope has changed from what the project customer is expecting. The product scope and the project scope support each other.

❑ Projects move through product-oriented processes to create the project's product. These processes are typically marked by phases unique to the project work—for example, foundation, framing, roofing, finishing, and so on. Project management processes are the activities universal to all projects.

❑ There are two scopes: the project scope and the product scope. The project scope is the work to be completed to create the product. The product scope describes the features of the product and its characteristics.

Creating the Work Breakdown Structure

❑ The WBS is a deliverables-oriented decomposition of the project scope. It is not the activity list, but the predecessor to creating the activity list. The WBS reflects, in detail, the elements and components that contribute to the project scope.

❑ The smallest item in the WBS is called the work package. The work package should follow the 8/80 rule, which means it should not take fewer than 8 hours and no more than 80 hours of labor to create the work package item. Don't worry; this is just a heuristic. There may be small items that you want to account for in your WBS that don't follow this guideline.

❑ A WBS dictionary is a reference tool to explain the WBS components, the nature of the work package, the assigned resources, and the time and billing estimates for each element. The WBS also identifies the relationship between work packages.

Verifying the Project Scope

❑ At the end of the project or project phase—or even at major deliverables within the project—scope verification happens. Scope verification is the process of formally accepting the project work as defined in the product documentation, in the project scope, or in the contractual agreement, if relevant. Formal acceptance requires sign-off for acceptance of the product.

❑ Scope verification has just one technique: inspection. It's completed by the project stakeholders to determine if the project has delivered on its promises. The goal of scope verification is for the project customer to sign off on the project deliverables.

Protecting the Project Scope from Change

❑ Scope management is the process that follows the scope management plan. It ensures that the scope includes all of the required work—and only the required work—to complete the project. It documents how changes may enter into the scope and how frequently the scope is expected to change.

❑ Should a change occur to the project scope, configuration management must be enacted. Configuration management documents and controls changes to the features and function of the project's product. Configuration management strives for consistency between the project scope and the product scope.

❑ Scope creep is a loose term to describe the small, seemingly innocent changes the project team may allow into the project execution that can rob the project of time and costs. Scope creep can also be known as project poison, and it is an unapproved scope change.

SELF TEST

1. You are the project manager of the OQH Project and are working with the project stakeholders to determine the project requirements. You and the stakeholders are discussing as many solutions to the project as possible. A recorder documents all of the solutions on a white board so everyone can see the ideas and how they may be related. After the solutions have been documented, you lead the group through a voting process to discuss and rank each idea and requirement that has been proposed. What is this requirements gathering called?

   A. Brainstorming
   B. Nominal group technique
   C. Affinity diagram creations
   D. Mind mapping

2. You are the project manager for the HGD Project and will need as many inputs to the scope planning as possible. Of the following, which one is not an organizational process asset?

   A. Organizational procedures
   B. Organizational policies
   C. WBS
   D. Historical information

3. You are a project manager for your organization. Sarah, a project manager in training, wants to know which project documents can stem from templates? Your answer should be what?

   A. Risk policies
   B. Organizational policies
   C. Scope management plans
   D. Historical information

4. You are the project manager for a technical project. The project product is the complete installation of a new operating system on 4,500 workstations. You have, in your project cost and time estimates, told the customer that the estimates provided will be accurate if the workstations meet the hardware requirements of the new operating system. This is an example of which of the following?

   A. Risk
   B. Assumption
   C. Constraint
   D. Order of magnitude

5. You are the project manager for the NBG Project. This project must be completed within six months. This is an example of which of the following?

A. Schedule

B. Assumption

C. Constraint

D. Planning process

6. Which of the following best describes the project scope statement?

A. The description of the project deliverables

B. The authorizing document that allows the project manager to move forward with the project and to assign resources to the tasks

C. The process of managing all of the required work—and only the required work—to create the project's deliverables

D. The process of planning and executing all of the required work in order to deliver the project to the customer

7. During the planning phase of your project, your project team has discovered another method to complete a portion of the project scope. This method is safer for the project team, but may cost more for the customer. This is an example of:

A. Risk assessment

B. Alternative identification

C. Alternative selection

D. Product analysis

8. You are the project manager of a large software development project. There are hundreds of requirements that need to be documented, annotated, and communicated to the project stakeholders. Management would also like to you report when the requirements should be created and when they're actually created by the project team. What document can help you monitor all of the characteristics of each requirement?

A. Project management plan

B. Configuration management plan

C. Requirements traceability matrix

D. Project communications management plan

9. You are the project manager for the JHN Project. Mike, a project manager you are mentoring, does not know which plan he should reference for guarding the project scope. Which of the following plans does Mike need?

   A. The scope management plan
   B. The scope change control system
   C. The scope verification
   D. The scope charter

10. You are the project manager for the JKL Project. This project has more than 45 key stakeholders and will span the globe when implemented. Management has deemed that the project's completion should not cost more than $34 million. Because of the global concerns, the final budget must be in U.S. dollars. This is an example of which of the following?

    A. Internationalization
    B. Budget constraint
    C. Management constraint
    D. Hard logic

11. You are the project manager for your organization. You need to ensure the customer formally accepts the deliverables of each project phase. This process is known as _____.

    A. Earned value management
    B. Scope verification
    C. Quality control
    D. Quality assurance

12. Which of the following is an output of scope verification?

    A. WBS template
    B. Rework
    C. Formal acceptance
    D. SOW acceptance

13. Where can the project manager find work package information such as the code of an account identifier, a statement of work, information on the responsible organization, quality requirements, and information on the required resources?

    A. Project plan
    B. WBS
    C. WBS dictionary
    D. Project management plan

14. You are a project manager for a large manufacturer. Your current project is to create a new manufacturing assembly line that will allow your organization to create its products with less downtime and faster turnaround time for its clients. A stakeholder has presented a change request for your project, which will likely increase the cost and time needed to complete the project. All of the following components are not part of the change control system except for which one?

A. Adding more team members to the project to get the project work done faster

B. Outsourcing portions of the project execution to transfer risk

C. Tracking systems for the proposed change

D. Documenting the project and how the manufacturing assembly should work

15. A project team member has, on his own initiative, added extra vents to an attic to increase air circulation. The project plan did not call for these extra vents, but the team member decided they were needed based on the geographic location of the house. The project team's experts concur with this decision. This is an example of:

A. Cost control

B. Ineffective change control

C. Self-led teams

D. Value-added change

16. Which of the following is an output of scope control?

A. Workarounds

B. Recommended corrective action

C. Transference

D. Risk assessment

17. You are the project manager for the JHG Project. Your project is to create a new product for your industry. You have recently learned your competitor is also working on a similar project, but their offering will include a computer-aided program and web-based tools, which your project does not offer. You have implemented a change request to update your project. This is an example of which of the following?

A. A change due to an error or omission in the initiation phase

B. A change due to an external event

C. A change due to an error or omission in the planning phase

D. A change due to a legal issue

18. You are the project manager for a pharmaceutical company. A new government regulation will change your project scope. For the project to move forward and be in accordance with the new regulation, your next action should be?

A. Prepare a new baseline to reflect the government changes

B. Notify management

C. Present the change to the CCB

D. Create a feasibility study

19. You have finished the project scope according to plan. For the customer to accept the project, what must happen next?

A. Nothing. The plan is complete, so the project is complete.

B. Scope verification should be conducted.

C. Lessons learned should be finalized.

D. Proof-of-concept should be implemented.

20. You are the project manager for an airplane manufacturer. Your project concerns the development of lighter, stronger material for commercial jets. As the project moves towards completion, different material composition is considered for the deliverable. This is an example of which of the following?

A. Program management

B. Alternatives identification

C. Quality assurance

D. Regulatory guidelines

21. You are the project manager of a large project. Your project sponsor and management have approved you to outsource portions of the project plan. The _____ must document project scope management decisions.

A. Project sponsor

B. Organization's management

C. Vendor(s)

D. Project management team

22. A project team member has asked you what project scope management is. Which of the following is a characteristic of project scope management?

A. It defines the baseline for project acceptance.

B. It defines the requirements for each project within the organization.

C. It defines the processes to ensure that the project includes all the work required—and only the work required—to complete the project successfully.

D. It defines the functional managers assigned to the project.

23. One of the stakeholders of the project you are managing asks why you consider the scope statement so important in your project management methodology. You answer her question with which of the following?

A. It is mandatory to consult the plan before authorizing any change.

B. Project managers must document any changes before approving or declining them.

C. The project scope statement serves as a reference for all change requests to determine if the change is in or out of scope.

D. The project plan and EVM work together to assess the risk involved with proposed changes.

24. A WBS serves as an input to many of the project management processes. Of the following, which is not true?

A. WBS serves as an input to activity sequencing.

B. WBS serves as an input to activity definition.

C. WBS serves as an input to resource planning.

D. WBS serves as an input to cost budgeting.

25. You are the project manager of the WIFI Project. You would like to meet with a stakeholder for scope verification. Which of the following is typical of scope verification?

A. Reviewing changes to the project scope with the stakeholders

B. Reviewing the performance of the project deliverables

C. Reviewing the performance of the project team to date

D. Reviewing the EVM results of the project to date

SELF TEST ANSWERS

1. You are the project manager of the OQH Project and are working with the project stakeholders to determine the project requirements. You and the stakeholders are discussing as many solutions to the project as possible. A recorder documents all of the solutions on a white board so everyone can see the ideas and how they may be related. After the solutions have been documented, you lead the group through a voting process to discuss and rank each idea and requirement that has been proposed. What is this requirements gathering called?

   A. Brainstorming
   B. Nominal group technique
   C. Affinity diagram creations
   D. Mind mapping

   ☑ **B.** This is an example of the nominal group technique. This approach asks for as many ideas and solutions as possible, but includes a ranking of the concepts to better guide the requirements development.

   ☒ **A,** brainstorming, is incorrect; brainstorming is similar to this concept, but it does not include the ranking of the concepts identified. **C** is incorrect, as affinity diagrams cluster ideas into similar groups for further analysis. **D** is also incorrect, as mind mapping shows the relation of ideas but it does not rank them.

2. You are the project manager for the HGD Project and will need as many inputs to the scope planning as possible. Of the following, which one is not an organizational process asset?

   A. Organizational procedures
   B. Organizational policies
   C. WBS
   D. Historical information

   ☑ **C.** The WBS is not an organizational process asset.

   ☒ **A, B,** and **D** are incorrect choices because these responses are examples of organizational process assets.

3. You are a project manager for your organization. Sarah, a project manager in training, wants to know which project documents can stem from templates? Your answer should be what?

   A. Risk policies
   B. Organizational policies

C. Scope management plans

D. Historical information

☑ **C.** Scope management plans can be based on templates. For the record, so can the WBS and project scope change control forms.

☒ Choices **A, B,** and **D** are incorrect because these documents do not stem from templates.

4. You are the project manager for a technical project. The project product is the complete installation of a new operating system on 4,500 workstations. You have, in your project cost and time estimates, told the customer that the estimates provided will be accurate if the workstations meet the hardware requirements of the new operating system. This is an example of which of the following?

A. Risk

B. Assumption

C. Constraint

D. Order of magnitude

☑ **B.** This is an example of an assumption, since the workstations must meet the hardware requirements.

☒ **A** and **C** are incorrect because the scenario did not describe a risk or constraint. **D** is incorrect because the order of magnitude refers to the level of confidence in an estimate.

5. You are the project manager for the NBG Project. This project must be completed within six months. This is an example of which of the following?

A. Schedule

B. Assumption

C. Constraint

D. Planning process

☑ **C.** A project that must be completed by a deadline is dealing with time constraints.

☒ **A** is incorrect, since the condition does not offer a schedule, but a "must finish no later than" constraint. **B** is incorrect because the condition is not an assumption. **D** is also incorrect because this is not a planning process.

6. Which of the following best describes the project scope statement?
   A. The description of the project deliverables
   B. The authorizing document that allows the project manager to move forward with the project and to assign resources to the tasks
   C. The process of managing all of the required work—and only the required work—to create the project's deliverables
   D. The process of planning and executing all of the required work in order to deliver the project to the customer

   ☑ C. A project scope statement focuses on completing all of the required work, and only the required work, to create the project's deliverables.
   ☒ Choice A is a product description, not a scope. B is incorrect because this choice describes the charter. D is incorrect because it does not define the project scope as completely as choice C.

7. During the planning phase of your project, your project team has discovered another method to complete a portion of the project scope. This method is safer for the project team, but may cost more for the customer. This is an example of:
   A. Risk assessment
   B. Alternative identification
   C. Alternative selection
   D. Product analysis

   ☑ B. Alternative identification is a planning process to find alternatives to completing the project scope.
   ☒ A is incorrect because this is not a risk assessment activity. C is incorrect because the team has identified the alternative, but has not selected it. D is incorrect because this is not product analysis.

8. You are the project manager of a large software development project. There are hundreds of requirements that need to be documented, annotated, and communicated to the project stakeholders. Management would also like you to report when the requirements should be created and when they're actually created by the project team. What document can help you monitor all of the characteristics of each requirement?
   A. Project management plan
   B. Configuration management plan
   C. Requirements traceability matrix
   D. Project communications management plan

☑ **C.** The requirements traceability matrix can help the project manager track and monitor all of the characteristics of each project requirement. It helps to communicate the requirement's status and completion, and it records any notes or comments about each requirement.

☒ **A,** the project management plan, does define how all of the components of the project will be planned, executed, and monitored, but it does not answer the question as completely as choice **C. B,** the configuration management plan, defines how changes to the product scope will be allowed, controlled, and documented. **D,** the project communications management plan, defines who needs what information, when the information is needed, and the expected modality.

9. You are the project manager for the JHN Project. Mike, a project manager you are mentoring, does not know which plan he should reference for guarding the project scope. Which of the following plans does Mike need?
   A. The scope management plan
   B. The scope change control system
   C. The scope verification
   D. The scope charter

☑ **A.** The scope management plan provides details about how the project scope may be changed.

☒ **B** is not a valid choice because it refers to the scope change control system, not the plan to guard the scope from changes. **C** is incorrect because scope verification is the process of formally accepting the product. **D** is also incorrect because the charter does not define how changes to the project may happen.

10. You are the project manager for the JKL Project. This project has more than 45 key stakeholders and will span the globe when implemented. Management has deemed that the project's completion should not cost more than $34 million. Because of the global concerns, the final budget must be in U.S. dollars. This is an example of which of the following?
    A. Internationalization
    B. Budget constraint
    C. Management constraint
    D. Hard logic

☑ **B.** This is an example of a budget constraint. The budget must not exceed $34 million. In addition, the metric for the values to be in U.S. dollars can affect the budget if most of the product is to be purchased in a foreign country.

☒ **A** is incorrect because this does not define a constraint. Internationalization focuses on time zones, languages, cultural differences, and so on. **C** is incorrect because this is not an adequate answer; a management constraint describes a management decision such as resources, risk policies, or control over the project budget. **D** is also incorrect because hard logic describes the most logical or required method for events or conditions to happen.

11. You are the project manager for your organization. You need to ensure the customer formally accepts the deliverables of each project phase. This process is known as _____.
    A. Earned value management
    B. Scope verification
    C. Quality control
    D. Quality assurance

    ☑ **B.** Scope verification is the process of formally accepting the deliverable of a project or phase.
    ☒ **A** is incorrect because earned value management measures project performance. **C** is incorrect because quality control is concerned with the correctness of the work, not the acceptance of the work. **D,** quality assurance, is incorrect because this describes the quality program for the organization as a whole.

12. Which of the following is an output of scope verification?
    A. WBS template
    B. Rework
    C. Formal acceptance
    D. SOW acceptance

    ☑ **C.** Scope verification results in one thing: formal acceptance.
    ☒ **A** is incorrect because WBS templates come from past projects or the PMO. **B** is incorrect because rework does not come from verification. **D** is incorrect because SOW (statement of work) acceptance is not the best choice.

13. Where can the project manager find work package information such as the code of an account identifier, a statement of work, information on the responsible organization, quality requirements, and information on the required resources?
    A. Project plan
    B. WBS
    C. WBS dictionary
    D. Project management plan

☑ **C.** The WBS dictionary provides all of this information—along with information on milestones and contract information—and then cross-references each work package with related work package information.

☒ Choice **A,** the project plan, is technically not an accurate term for the project management plan. This also does not define the question as accurately as the WBS dictionary. **B,** the WBS, is incorrect because the WBS does not define the work to the extent the WBS dictionary does. **D** is incorrect because the project management plan communicates the project intent. The subsidiary plans, which are part of the project management plan, communicate information on specific knowledge areas

14. You are a project manager for a large manufacturer. Your current project is to create a new manufacturing assembly line that will allow your organization to create its products with less downtime and faster turnaround time for its clients. A stakeholder has presented a change request for your project, which will likely increase the cost and time needed to complete the project. All of the following components are not part of the change control system except for which one?

    A. Adding more team members to the project to get the project work done faster
    B. Outsourcing portions of the project execution to transfer risk
    C. Tracking systems for the proposed change
    D. Documenting the project and how the manufacturing assembly should work

    ☑ **C.** The only answer that describes a component of the change control system is the tracking system for the proposed change.

    ☒ **A** is incorrect because this describes crashing. **B** is incorrect because transference is not a value-added change. **D** is incorrect because this process should be part of the product description already included in the project plan.

15. A project team member has, on his own initiative, added extra vents to an attic to increase air circulation. The project plan did not call for these extra vents, but the team member decided they were needed based on the geographic location of the house. The project team's experts concur with this decision. This is an example of:

    A. Cost control
    B. Ineffective change control
    C. Self-led teams
    D. Value-added change

☑   **B.** The project team member did not follow the change management plan's method of incorporating changes into the scope.

☒   **A** is incorrect because this scenario describes change control, although the decision may lead to additional expenses. **C** is incorrect because self-led teams are not described in this scenario. **D** is also incorrect because the added vents do not apparently reduce cost in this example.

16. Which of the following is an output of scope control?

A.   Workarounds

B.   Recommended corrective action

C.   Transference

D.   Risk assessment

☑   **B.** Recommended corrective actions are outputs of change control. Poor performance leads to corrective actions to bring the project back in alignment with the project plan. Recall that a corrective action is a change request.

☒   **A** is incorrect because a workaround is a reaction to an identified risk or issue. **C** and **D** are also incorrect because transference is the process of transferring the risk. Risk assessment is the process of identifying and analyzing risk within the project or phase.

17. You are the project manager for the JHG Project. Your project is to create a new product for your industry. You have recently learned your competitor is also working on a similar project, but their offering will include a computer-aided program and web-based tools, which your project does not offer. You have implemented a change request to update your project. This is an example of which of the following?

A.   A change due to an error or omission in the initiation phase

B.   A change due to an external event

C.   A change due to an error or omission in the planning phase

D.   A change due to a legal issue

☑   **B.** The change is requested to remain competitive with the competition—an external event. Change is inevitable and requires a change control process to manage.

☒   **A, C,** and **D** are all incorrect choices based on the conditions of the change request.

18. You are the project manager for a pharmaceutical company. A new government regulation will change your project scope. For the project to move forward and be in accordance with the new regulation, your next action should be?

A.   Prepare a new baseline to reflect the government changes

B.   Notify management

C. Present the change to the CCB

D. Create a feasibility study

☑ **C.** Presenting the change to the change control board is the best choice.

☒ **A** is incorrect because the change has not been approved—the project could be stopped based on the required change. **B** is incorrect, though tempting. It is wrong for two primary reasons: The project manager should never contact management with a problem, and no solution is offered for the problem. It is also incorrect because **C** more fully answers the question, since management is likely part of the group of appropriate stakeholders. **D** is incorrect because it is not appropriate for the conditions surrounding the change.

19. You have finished the project scope according to plan. For the customer to accept the project, what must happen next?

A. Nothing. The plan is complete, so the project is complete.

B. Scope verification should be conducted.

C. Lessons learned should be finalized.

D. Proof-of-concept should be implemented.

☑ **B.** Scope verification concerns itself with the formal acceptance of the product.

☒ Choice **A** is incorrect because acceptance must happen for closure. **C** is incorrect—lessons learned do not close out the project. **D** is incorrect because it is not relevant to the issue.

20. You are the project manager for an airplane manufacturer. Your project concerns the development of lighter, stronger material for commercial jets. As the project moves towards completion, different material composition is considered for the deliverable. This is an example of which of the following?

A. Program management

B. Alternatives identification

C. Quality assurance

D. Regulatory guidelines

☑ **B.** Alternatives identification is the technique to consider different approaches, materials, and solutions for the project work.

☒ **A** is incorrect—program management is not relevant. **C** is incorrect because QA describes the quality system of an organization. **D** is incorrect because regulatory guidelines do not refine the project scope.

21. You are the project manager of a large project. Your project sponsor and management have approved you to outsource portions of the project plan. The _____ must document project scope management decisions.

    A. Project sponsor

    B. Organization's management

    C. Vendor(s)

    D. Project management team

    ☑ **D.** The responsibility to ensure project scope management decisions rests with the project management team.

    ☒ **A, B,** and **C** are all incorrect because these stakeholders do not have the responsibility of the project manager in this scenario.

22. A project team member has asked you what project scope management is. Which of the following is a characteristic of project scope management?

    A. It defines the baseline for project acceptance.

    B. It defines the requirements for each project within the organization.

    C. It defines the processes to ensure that the project includes all the work required—and only the work required—to complete the project successfully.

    D. It defines the functional managers assigned to the project.

    ☑ **C.** Project scope management defines the processes to ensure that the project includes all the work required—and only the work required—to complete the project successfully.

    ☒ **A** is incorrect because the scope statement provides information on the project product acceptance. **B** is incorrect because a scope statement does not address all projects within an organization. **D** is also incorrect because functional managers are not addressed in the scope statement.

23. One of the stakeholders of the project you are managing asks why you consider the scope statement so important in your project management methodology. You answer her question with which of the following?

    A. It is mandatory to consult the plan before authorizing any change.

    B. Project managers must document any changes before approving or declining them.

    C. The project scope statement serves as a reference for all change requests to determine if the change is in or out of scope.

    D. The project plan and EVM work together to assess the risk involved with proposed changes.

☑ **C.** The scope statement serves as a point of reference when considering if change requests are in or out of scope.

☒ **A** is incorrect because it is too vague. **B** is incorrect because some changes may come orally and be declined immediately based on historical information or other factors. **D** is incorrect because EVM is not an issue in this scenario.

24. A WBS serves as an input to many of the project management processes. Of the following, which is not true?
    A. WBS serves as an input to activity sequencing.
    B. WBS serves as an input to activity definition.
    C. WBS serves as an input to resource planning.
    D. WBS serves as an input to cost budgeting.

☑ **A.** The WBS does not directly serve as an input to activity sequencing.

☒ **B, C,** and **D** are incorrect choices because the WBS does serve as an input to these processes. Incidentally, the WBS also serves as input to the cost estimating and risk management planning processes.

25. You are the project manager of the WIFI Project. You would like to meet with a stakeholder for scope verification. Which of the following is typical of scope verification?
    A. Reviewing changes to the project scope with the stakeholders
    B. Reviewing the performance of the project deliverables
    C. Reviewing the performance of the project team to date
    D. Reviewing the EVM results of the project to date

☑ **B.** When it comes to scope verification, the customer is concerned with the performance of the product.

☒ Choice **A** may seem correct, but the stakeholder should already know about the changes prior to scope verification. **C** and **D** are incorrect because these reviews are not relevant to scope verification.

6

Introducing Project Time Management

T here's an old joke when it comes to project management time: "The first 90 percent of a project schedule takes 90 percent of the time. The last 10 percent takes the other 90 percent of the time."

And isn't that the way it goes? You always hope it won't, but far too often that's precisely what happens. Projects, especially projects that are running behind schedule, fail at the beginning, not at the end. The importance of planning a project is never more evident than when you reach the rush to completion. The final actions to complete a project are dependent on the plans and motivations set during the project planning processes.

Effective project management requires adequate time for planning and—based on the results of that planning—adequate time for the implementation of those plans. In this chapter, we'll discuss how project activities are decomposed and then how the work packages are sequenced, calculated, and accounted for. We'll also discuss the art and science of estimating the time for work packages in new and familiar projects. Once the work's been decomposed, we'll create and visualize the network diagram.

Time management is an essential element on the PMP exam. You'll need a solid understanding of the activities and methods to predict and account for project time. Time management is crucial to not only passing the PMP exam, but also to successful project management.

CERTIFICATION OBJECTIVE 6.01

Defining the Project Activities

Projects are temporary undertakings to create a unique product or service. The idea of time is inherent to the very definition of a project in that all projects are temporary. Even though they may seem to last forever, sooner or later they must end. Adequate planning of the temporary project can predict when a project will end. Within this short, limited time, the project manager must create something: a product or a service. The creation is about change—and change, as you may have guessed, takes time. Figure 6-1 shows the components of project time management.

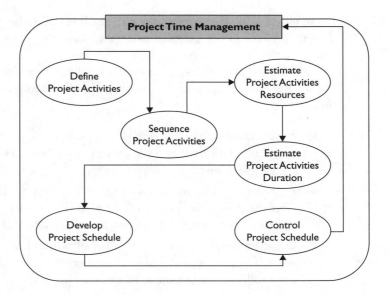

FIGURE 6-1

Time management relies on several inputs to monitor and control the project schedule.

Creation of the product or service comes about due to the work the project team completes. The sum of the time of the work equates to when the project is completed. In addition to the duration of activities, there are other factors of time to consider, such as the following:

- Project management activities
- Planning processes
- The sequence of activities
- Procurement
- Reliance on internal and external events
- Known and unknown events affecting the project

Project time management is based predominantly on planning. The rest is about control and execution. Planning for project schedules may stem from deadlines, customer demands, hard and soft logic, and a bit of prediction.

Getting to Work: Defining the Activities

The activity list is an output of activity definition, and includes all of the activities to be performed within the project. The list must be in line with the project scope. Remember the project scope? It's a description of all the required work, and only the required work, to complete the project. In a sense, the activity list is a further definition of the project scope, since it includes only those actions needed to complete the project scope.

Creating the activity list relies on knowledge, actions, and several completed documents. The creation of the activity list uses the following as inputs to the process:

- **Scope baseline**   Recall that the scope baseline is comprised of the WBS, the WBS dictionary, and the project scope statement. You'll need these three elements to define the project activities.

- **Enterprise environmental factors**   This is all the stuff an organization can offer the project manager to assist with the activity definition. In particular, it's the project management information system and scheduling software.

- **Organizational process assets**   Organizations have a way of getting things done. The process assets are the methods and procedures an organization must follow to create the activity list. This also includes historical information from past projects that can help the project team define activities on the current project.

Decomposing the Project Work Packages

The WBS, the collection of deliverable-orientated components, must now be broken into activities. Specifically, the work packages within the WBS must be decomposed into manageable work elements. What's the difference between decomposing the project deliverables and the project work? The elements in the WBS are deliverables; this process is concerned with the actions needed to create the deliverables.

It's quite possible to create the WBS and the activity list in tandem. Don't get too caught up in the timing of the activity list definition and the WBS. Simply put, the WBS describes the components of the deliverables; the activity list defines the actions to create the deliverables. Typically, the project manager and the project team work together to decompose the work

The creation of the WBS and the activity list is not a solo activity. The WBS and the activity list are created with the project team.

packages. In some instances, it's ideal to use expert judgment to help with the decomposition.

Using Rolling Wave Planning

Have you ever stood in the ocean? Wave after wave keeps knocking up against you. In fact, way out in the distance, you can see a crest of water that glides along the surface until it crashes at your knees. In project management, the concept of a rolling wave plan is similar to your ocean visit.

Work that is imminent is planned in detail, while work that is way off in the future is planned at a high level. As the work in the future approaches, more detail is allotted to planning this work. Rolling wave planning allows the project team to focus planning on pressing matters as the project moves towards completion. This is a form of progressive elaboration.

Relying on Templates

Why reinvent the wheel? If similar projects have been completed in the past, rely on the WBS and activity lists from this historical information to serve as a template for the current project. Even if a portion of a project is similar, a project manager can use the activity list and focus on the similarities of the current project.

A template can include several elements to make a project manager's life easier and the new project more successful.

- Required actions to complete the project scope
- Required resources and skills
- Required hours of duration for activities
- Known risks
- Outputs of the work
- Descriptions of the work packages
- Supporting details

Using Planning Components

Sometimes there just isn't enough detail in the project scope to decompose everything down to the smallest level: the work package level in the WBS. This isn't a problem, but it has to be acknowledged during planning. For example, a project to build a home may have defined the room dimensions, lighting needs, and windows, but the specifics on paint color, flooring choices, and exact light fixtures haven't been defined. You can still plan for these elements with a to-be-determined-later characteristic.

When there isn't enough information in the project scope to decompose the work to the work packages, the project team can use two planning components.

■ **Control account** A management control account is a marker that indicates there's additional decisions and planning for the work below the control account in the WBS. All work and effort for the associated deliverables is documented through a control account plan.

■ **Planning packages** Planning packages allow the project team to position planning activities below the control account but still above the work packages. A planning package is the planning time and activities to determine what should exist within the control account. You could say that the planning package is a visual marker of planning that's yet to come. This acknowledges the need for future planning while not delaying immediate work on the project.

Compiling the Activity List

Ta-dah! The primary output of decomposing the work is the activity list, which is a collection of all the work elements required to complete the project. The activity list is actually an extension of the WBS, and will serve as a fundamental tool in creating the project schedule. The activity list is needed to ensure that all of the deliverables of the WBS are accounted for and that the necessary work is mapped to each, as shown in Figure 6-2.

The activity list also ensures that there is no extra work included in the project. Extra work costs time and money—and defeats the project scope. The WBS is

FIGURE 6-2

The activity list comes after the creation of the WBS.

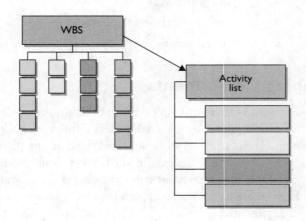

comprised of all of the components the project will create, while the activity list is made up of all the work required to create the components within the WBS.

In addition, the work on the activity list includes attributes of each identified activity. This accomplishes three things.

- It ensures the team members are in agreement on what the work package accomplishes.
- It ensures the work supports and creates the WBS deliverables.
- It ensures the work is within the project scope.

Documenting the Activity Attributes

You'll need to do more than create a shopping list of activities for the project in order to effectively plan, execute, and control the project work. By documenting the activity attributes, you're communicating the intent of the project work, the supporting detail of the project decisions, and more. As information becomes available, the activity attributes should be updated to include:

- **Activity name and description**   Each activity should have its name and description recorded.
- **Activity ID**   This is a unique number for each activity in the activity list. It's especially useful when there are repetitions in the project work, similar activities, or similar activities throughout the project lifecycle.
- **WBS identifier**   Each activity is linked to a corresponding WBS package through the WBS code of accounts. This helps link the work to a specific project deliverable.
- **Relationships**   The predecessor and successor tasks of each activity may be identified to help with planning and monitoring and controlling processes.
- **Leads and lags**   If any leads or lags have been added to the activity, this information should be documented as part of the activity attributes.
- **Resource requirements**   The people, materials, facilities, tools, equipment, and any other resources required to complete the activity should be documented for each activity.
- **Imposed dates**   Any constraints, such as must start on, or other deadlines attached to the project activities, should be documented.

■ **Constraints and assumptions**   All activity-based constraints and assumptions should be documented.

■ **Additional information**   There may be additional information that's unique to the discipline and application area of the project for the project activities.

CERTIFICATION OBJECTIVE 6.02

Sequencing Project Activities

Now that the activity list has been created, the activities must be arranged in a logical sequence. This process calls on the project manager and the project team to identify the logical relationships between activities and the preferred relationship between those activities. This can be accomplished in a few different ways.

■ **Computer-driven**   Many different scheduling and project management software packages are available. These programs can help the project manager and the project team determine which actions need to happen in what order.

■ **Manual process**   On smaller projects, and on larger projects in the early phases, manual sequencing may be preferred. An advantage of manual sequencing is that it's easier to move around dependencies and activities than in some programs.

■ **Blended approach**   A combination of manual and computer-driven scheduling methods is fine. It's important to determine the finality of the activity sequence, however. Sometimes a blended approach can be more complex than relying on just one or another.

on the job *"Sticky notes" can help sequence events. Put your activities on sticky notes and then plot them out on a white board. Draw arrows to show the relationship between activities. Want to make a change? It's easy to rearrange the notes and the relationships.*

Considering the Inputs to Activity Sequencing

There are many approaches to completing the activity sequencing. Perhaps the best, however, is that activity sequencing is done with the project team, not as a solo activity.

The project manager must rely on the project team and the inputs to activity sequencing.

- **The activity list** As just mentioned, this is the list of actions needed to complete the project deliverables.

- **Activity attributes** Each scheduled activity has attributes that need to be documented. For example, the successor and predecessor of each activity, the lead and lag information, and the person responsible for completing the activity should all be documented. This information is important when it comes to schedule development and project control.

- **Milestone list** Milestones must be considered and evaluated when sequencing events to ensure all of the work needed to complete the milestones is included.

- **The project scope statement** The scope statement is needed, since it may influence the sequence of events. For example, in construction, technology, or community planning (among other project types), the scope statement may include requirements, constraints, and assumptions that will logically affect the planning of activity sequencing.

- **Organizational process assets** When you consider how most organizations repeat the same type of projects, it's easy to see why project managers rely on historical information as much as they do. After all, historical information is proven information that can be adapted to the current project. It is part of your organizational process assets.

Creating Network Diagrams

Network diagrams visualize the project work. A network diagram shows the relationship of the work activities and how they will progress from start to completion. Network diagrams can be extremely complex or easy to create and configure. Most network diagrams in today's project management environment use an approach called "activity-on-node" to illustrate the activities and the relationship between those activities. Older network diagramming methods used "activity-on-arrows" to represent the activities and their relationships.

Using the Precedence Diagramming Method

The precedence diagramming method (PDM) is the most common method of arranging the project work visually. The PDM puts the activities in boxes, called nodes, and connects the boxes with arrows. The arrows represent the relationship and the dependencies of the work packages. The following illustration shows a simple network diagram using PDM.

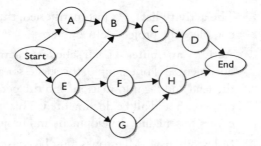

PDM is also known as AON—activity-on-node. It's the most common approach to network diagramming, since it's used by most project management information systems, but it can also be done manually.

Relationships between activities in a PDM constitute one of four different types (as shown in Figure 6-3).

- **Finish-to-start (FS)**   This relationship means Task A must be completed before Task B can begin. This is the most common relationship. For example, the foundation must be set before the framing can begin.
- **Start-to-start (SS)**   This relationship means Task A must start before Task B can start. This relationship allows both activities to happen in tandem. For example, a crew of painters is painting a house. Task A is to scrape the flecking paint off the house and Task B is to prime the house. The workers

FIGURE 6-3

Task relationships
can vary, but
finish-to-start
is the most
common.

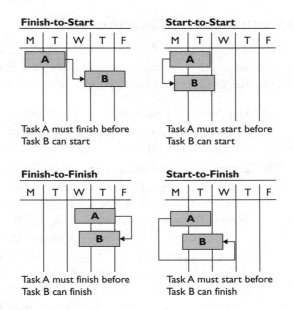

scraping the house must start before the other workers can begin priming the
house. All of the scraping doesn't have to be completed before the priming
can start, just some of it.

■ **Finish-to-finish (FF)** This relationship means Task A must complete before
Task B does. Ideally, two tasks must finish at exactly the same time, but this
is not always the case. For example, two teams of electricians may be working
together to install new telephone cables throughout a building by Monday
morning. Team A is pulling the cable to each office. Team B, meanwhile, is
connecting the cables to wall jacks and connecting the telephones. Team A
must pull the cable to the office so Team B can complete their activity. The
activities need to complete at nearly the same time, by Monday morning, so
the new phones are functional.

■ **Start-to-finish (SF)** This relationship is unusual and is rarely used. It
requires that Task A start so that Task B may finish. Such relationships may
be encountered in construction and manufacturing. It is also known as just-
in-time (JIT) scheduling. An example is a construction of a shoe store. The
end of the construction is soon, but an exact date is not known. The owner of
the shoe store doesn't want to order the shoe inventory until the construction
is nearly complete. The start of the construction tasks dictates when the
inventory of the shoes is ordered.

Determining the Activity Dependencies

The progression of the project is built on the sequence of activities. Activities are dependent on their predecessor activities completing before successor activities may begin. The following are the dependencies you should know for your PMP exam:

- **Mandatory dependencies**   These dependencies are the natural order of activities. For example, you can't begin building your house until your foundation is in place. These relationships are called hard logic.

- **Discretionary dependencies**   These dependencies are the preferred order of activities. Project managers should use these relationships at their "discretion" and document the logic behind the decision. Discretionary dependencies allow activities to happen in a preferred order because of best practices, conditions unique to the project work, or external events. For example, a painting project typically allows the primer and the paint to be applied within hours of each other. Due to the expected high humidity during the project, however, all of the building will be completely primed before the paint can be applied. These relationships are also known as soft logic, preferred logic, or preferential logic.

- **External dependencies**   As its name implies, these are dependencies outside of the project's control. Examples include the delivery of equipment from a vendor; the deliverable of another project; or the decision of a committee, lawsuit, or expected new law.

Considering Leads and Lags

Leads and lags are values added to work packages to slightly alter the relationship between two or more work packages. For example, a finish-to-start relationship may exist between applying primer to a warehouse and applying the paint. The project manager in this scenario has decided to add one day of lead time to the work package for painting the warehouse. Now the painting can begin one day before the priming is scheduled to end. Lead time is considered a negative value because time is subtracted from the downstream activity to bring successor activities closer to the start of the project.

Lag time is waiting time. Imagine a project to install wood floors in an office building. Currently, there is a finish-to-start relationship between staining the floors and adding a layer of shellac to seal the wood floors. The project manager has elected, because of the humidity in the building, to add two days of lag time to the downstream activity of sealing the floors. Now the shellac cannot be applied immediately after the stain, but must wait two additional days. Lag is considered a positive value, since time is added to the project schedule.

PMP Coach

How is your lead time? You should be thinking about scheduling your PMP exam soon (if you've not already). You'll need lead time to complete the application, get PMI's approval, and find an open slot at the testing center. You don't want to complete all of your studying and then schedule to pass your exam. Be a good project manager and look for opportunities to save time by completing activities in tandem.

The following illustration shows the difference between lead and lag. Leads and lags must be considered in the project schedule, since an abundance of lag time can increase the project duration. An abundance of lead time, while decreasing duration, may increase risks.

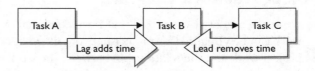

Utilizing Network Templates

Just as a project manager can rely on WBS templates, network templates may be available to streamline the planning process or to conform to a predetermined standard. Network templates can represent an entire project, if appropriate, though portions of a network template, such as the required project management activities, are common.

The portions of a network template are also known as subnets or fragnets. Subnets are often associated with repetitive actions within a network diagram. For example, each floor in a high-rise apartment building may undergo the same or similar actions during construction. Rather than complete the network diagram for each floor, a subnet can be implemented.

CERTIFICATION OBJECTIVE 6.03

Examining the Sequencing Outputs

There are many approaches to using activity sequencing: a project manager and the project team can use software programs, the approach can be done manually, or the team can manually do the scheduling and then transfer the schedule into a PMIS. Whichever method is selected, the project manager must remember four things.

- Only the required work should be scheduled.
- Finish-to-start relationships are the most common and preferred.
- Activity sequencing is not the same as a schedule.
- Scheduling comes after activity sequencing.

Using a Project Network Diagram

Once the activity list has been put into sequential order, the flow of the project work can be visualized. A project network diagram (PND) illustrates the flow of the project work and the relationship between the work packages. PNDs are typically "activity on node" (AON), and most PMIS packages use the PDM method. The following illustration is a typical example of a network diagram.

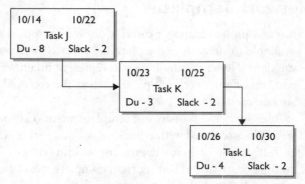

Network diagrams may also include summary activities, also known as hammock activities. Accompanying the network diagram, there should be an explanation of the workflow, why decisions were made, and details on any preferred logic the project manager may have used. A network diagram is really just a flow chart, as it shows how the project work should flow from its launch to its conclusion. Should changes enter the project scope, the WBS will need to be updated. The WBS update will likely cause the activity list to be updated, which will, in turn, cause the network diagram to be updated to reflect the new project requirements.

Risks in the project can affect the project schedule, too. Rushed work, unrealistic deadlines, and a lack of *resources are all common risks that affect the project completion.*

Updating the Work Breakdown Structure

When creating the activity list, the project team and the project manager may discover discrepancies or inadequacies in the existing WBS. Updates to the WBS allow the project manager to ensure that all of the needed project deliverables are included in the WBS and then map the discovered deliverables to the identified work in the activity list.

In addition, the elements within the WBS may not be defined fully or correctly. During the decomposition of the work, elements of the WBS may need to be updated to reflect the proper description of the WBS elements. The description of the WBS should be complete and full—and leave no room for ambiguity or misinterpretation. Finally, updates to the WBS may also include cost estimates of the discovered deliverables.

Updates to the WBS are called refinements. As the project moves towards completion, refinements ensure *that all of the deliverables are accounted for within the WBS. They may also indirectly call for updates to the activity list.*

CERTIFICATION OBJECTIVE 6.04

Considering the Resource Requirements

The identified resource requirements will affect the project schedule. Remember the difference between duration and effort? Duration is how long the activity will take, while effort is the labor applied to the task. For example, painting a building may take 80 hours to complete with two workers assigned to the job. Add two more workers, and now the work will take only 40 hours.

The duration to complete the painting in the preceding example is 40 hours, but there will still be 160 hours of effort expended on the activity. At some point in the work, the "duration to effort ratio" becomes saturated and adding laborers will actually become counterproductive. This is the law of diminishing returns. The following illustration demonstrates the previous example.

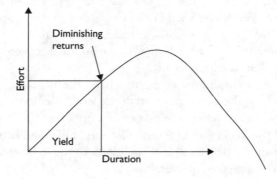

Don't forget that resources are more than just people. Equipment, *facilities, and materials are resources, and these can affect the project duration too.*

Considering Resource Availability

In a perfect world, all of the needed resources for a project would be available whenever the project manager says so. In the real world, however (and on your PMP exam), the availability of project resources fluctuates due to the demands of other projects, the demands of ongoing operations, personal lives, vacations, sick days, and more. Organizational process assets and enterprise environmental factors can also guide the project manager and project team as to when certain resources may be needed, or allowed, in a project.

The availability of the project pool must be evaluated. If certain activities require a worker with a highly specialized skill, these activities are resource-dependent. Should the worker not be available for the time frame of the required activity, one of several things must happen.

- The project manager must negotiate to make the resource available for the activity in the project schedule.
- The activity must be moved in the schedule for when the resource is available.
- The activity, and possibly the project, must wait for the resource to become available.
- The project may incur additional costs by finding other resources to complete the scheduled work.

Resources mean more than just people. The project manager must also consider things such as equipment, facilities, software, and other materials. With each non-human resource, the project manager must consider the cost and procurement procedures needed to acquire it. We'll discuss procurement in more detail in Chapter 12.

Considering the Calendars

Two calendar types will affect the project.

- **The project calendar**   This calendar shows when work is allowed on the project. For example, a project may require the project team to work nights and weekends so as not to disturb the ongoing operations of the organization during working hours. In addition, the project calendar accounts for holidays, working hours, and work shifts that the project will cover.

- **The resource calendar**   The resource calendar controls when resources such as project team members, consultants, and SMEs are available to work on the project. It takes into account vacations; other commitments within the organization; or restrictions on contracted work, overtime issues, and so on.

The consideration of the project calendar and the resource calendar is mandatory to predict when a project may realistically begin and end. Figure 6-4 shows the project calendar setting from Microsoft Project. Keep in mind that the PMP exam is not concerned with which PMIS system is used, only that you understand the role of the PMIS.

FIGURE 6-4

Project calendars determine when the project work may take place.

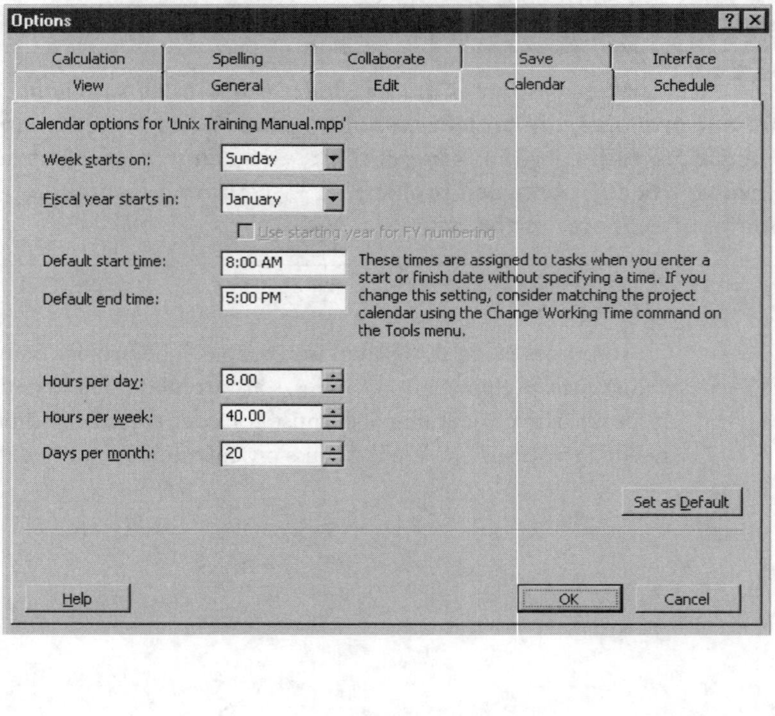

Creating a Resource Breakdown Structure

A resource breakdown structure, like the work breakdown structure, is a decomposition of the utilization of the project resources by category, phases, or types of resources. It's a visual mapping of the types of resources the project requires, organized by logical groupings. In a construction project, the project manager might create a resource breakdown structure using the construction phases, whereas in an IT project, the project manager might use hardware, software, network, and data as the categories. In either instance, the project manager would include all resources needed—both people and things.

Updating the Activity Lists

During the creation of the network diagram, assumptions about the activity sequence may reveal missing activities in the activity list. Just as the creation of the activity list may prompt the project team and the project manager to update the WBS, the creation of the network diagram may prompt the project team to update the activity lists.

While this may seem redundant—updating the activity list illustrated in the project network diagram—it is essential documentation. A reflection of the WBS, the activity list and the network diagram should both support the project scope. A key stakeholder should thus be able to follow the logic of the WBS to the activity list, and from the activity list, find all the activities mapped in order.

CERTIFICATION OBJECTIVE 6.05

Estimating Activity Durations

Ready for a loaded question? "Now how long will all of this take?" Project managers hear this one all the time, right? And maybe right after that: "How much will all of this cost?" We'll talk about cost estimates in Chapter 7. For now, let's talk about time.

The answer to the question "How long will it take?" depends on the accuracy of the estimates, the consistency of the work, and other variables within the project. The best a project manager can do is create honest estimates based on the information he's been provided. Until the schedule is finalized, no one will know the duration of the project.

The tasks are first identified, the sequencing of the activities takes place, resources are defined, and then durations are estimated. These activities are required to complete the project schedule and the estimated project duration. These four activities are iterated as more information becomes available. If the proposed schedule is acceptable, the project can move forward. If the proposed schedule takes too long, the scheduler can use a few strategies to compress the project. We'll discuss the art of scheduling in a few moments.

Activity duration estimates, like the activity list and the WBS, don't come from the project manager—they come from the people completing the work. They may also undergo progressive elaboration. In this section, we'll examine the approach to completing activity duration estimates, the basis of estimates, and the allowance for activity list updates.

Considering the Activity Duration Estimates Inputs

The importance of accurate estimates is paramount. The activity estimates will be used to create the project schedule and predict when the project should end. Inaccurate estimates could cost the performing organization thousands of dollars in fines, lost opportunities, lost customers, or worse. To create accurate estimates, the project manager and the project team will rely on several inputs.

- **Activity lists** You know this, right? Activity lists are the work elements necessary to create the deliverables.

- **The project scope statement** Identification of the project constraints and assumptions is needed, since they may influence the estimates. The project scope statement provides this information.

- **Activity resource requirements** Activity resource requirements define the resources that are needed to complete a particular activity. For example, a project to build a home will require lots of different resources: plumbers, electricians, architects, framers, and landscapers. The project manager would not, however, assign all of the different resources to every task, but only to the tasks that the resource was qualified to complete. Remember that resources also include equipment and materials, so those are identified as part of the activity resource requirements as well.

- **Activity attributes** Effort is the amount of labor applied to a task. Duration, on the other hand, is how long the task is expected to take with the given amount of labor. For example, a task to unload a freight truck may take eight hours with two people assigned to the task. If the effort is increased by adding more labor to the task (in this instance, more people), then the duration of the task is decreased. Some activities, however, have a fixed duration and are not affected by the amount of labor assigned to the task. For example, installing a piece of software on a computer will take the same amount of time if one computer administrator is completing the work or if two computer administrators are doing it.

■ **Resource capabilities**   The abilities of the project team members must be taken into consideration. Consider a task in an architectural firm. Reason says that if a senior architect is assigned to the task, she will be able to complete it faster than if a junior architect were assigned to the same job. Material resources can also influence activity time. Consider predrilled cabinets versus cabinets that require the carpenter to drill each cabinet as it's installed. The predrilled cabinets allow the job to be completed faster.

■ **Organizational process assets**   Okay, the big one here is historical information. Historical information is always an excellent source for information on activity duration estimates. It can come from several sources, such as the following:

   ■ Historical information can come from project files of other projects within the organization.

   ■ Commercial duration estimating databases can offer information on how long industry-specific activities should take. These databases should take into consideration the materials and the experience of the resources, and define the assumptions the predicted work duration is based upon.

   ■ Project team members may recollect information regarding the expected duration of activities. While these inputs are valuable, they are generally less valuable than documented sources such as other project files or the commercial databases.

The project manager and the project team should evaluate the project risks when it comes to project duration. I'll discuss risk in detail in Chapter 11. Risks, good or bad, can influence the estimated duration of activities. The risks on each activity should be identified, analyzed, and then predicted as to their probability and impact. If risk mitigation tasks are added to the schedule, the mitigation activities will need their duration estimated and then sequenced into the schedule in the proper order. The project activity cost estimates, if they exist yet, should also be referenced during activity duration estimates to determine the most cost-effective amount of labor or resources to apply to any given activity.

Applying Expert Judgment

The project manager and the project team should utilize expert judgment, if possible, to predict the duration of project activities. Expert judgment can come from subject matter experts, project team members, and other resources, internal or external to the performing organization, who are familiar with the activities the project demands.

Estimating durations is not easy, as many variables can influence an activity's duration. Consider the amount of resources that can be applied to the activities, the experience of the resources completing this type of work, and their competence with the work packages.

A big dose of reality is also needed with activity duration estimates. Imagine an activity that has been estimated to take 40 hours. While on paper that looks like a typical workweek, it's pretty unlikely the task will be completed within one week. Why? Consider all the phone calls, impromptu meetings, e-mail, and other interruptions throughout the day. These slivers of time chip away at the actual productive hours within a workday. The project manager should find a base of actual productive hours per day based on typical interruptions, meetings, and so on—for example, six productive hours out of eight working hours is typical. Based on this assumption (that six hours out of a day are productive), this means a task slated to last 40 hours will actually take nearly seven working days to complete.

Creating an Analogy

Analogous estimating relies on historical information to predict what current activity durations should be. Analogous estimating is also known as top-down estimating and is a form of expert judgment. To use analogous estimating, the activities from the historical project are similar in nature and are used to predict what similar activities in the current project will require.

A project manager must consider if the work has ever been done before and, if so, what help the historical information will provide. The project manager must consider the resources, project team members, and equipment that completed the activities in the previous project compared to the resources available for the current project. Ideally, the activities should be more than similar; they should be identical. And the resources that completed the work in the past should be the same resources used in completing the current work.

When the only source of activity duration estimates is the project team members instead of expert judgment and historical information, your estimates will be uncertain and inherently risky.

Applying Parametric Estimates

Quantitatively based durations use mathematical formulas to predict how long an activity will take based on the "quantities" of work to be completed. For example, a commercial printer needs to print 100,000 brochures. The workers include two pressmen and two bindery experts to fold and package the brochures. Notice how the duration is how long the activity will take to complete, while the effort is the total number of hours (labor) invested because of the resources involved. The decomposed work, with quantitative factors, is shown in Table 6-1.

TABLE 6-1	Workers	Units per Hour	Duration for 100,000	Effort
Decomposed Work with Quantitative Factors	Pressman (two)	5,000	20 hours	40 hours
	Bindery (two)	4,000	25 hours	50 hours
	Totals		45 hours	90 hours

Creating a Three-Point Estimate

How confident can a project manager be when it comes to estimating? If the project work has been done before in past projects, the level of confidence in the duration estimate is probably high. But if the work has never been done before, there are lots of unknowns—and with that comes risk. To mitigate the risk, the project manager can use a three-point estimate. A three-point estimate requires that for each activity, optimistic, most likely, and pessimistic time estimates be created. Based on these three time estimates, an average can be created to predict how long the activity should take (see Figure 6-5).

If you're thinking this sounds really similar to the program evaluation and review technique (PERT), you're correct. The formula for PERT is similar to a three-point estimate, *but differs slightly: (Optimistic time + (4 × Most likely time) + Pessimistic time)/6. It's six instead of three because you're using six factors in the numerator.*

Factoring in Reserve Time

Parkinson's Law states: "Work expands so as to fill the time available for its completion." This little nugget of wisdom is oh-so-true. Consider a project team member who knows an activity should last 24 hours. The team member decides, in his own wisdom, to say the activity will last 32 hours. This extra eight hours, he

FIGURE 6-5

Three-point estimates rely on averages to predict duration.

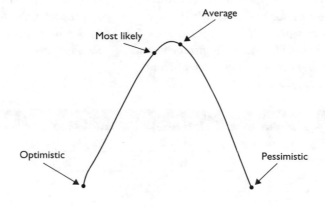

figures, will allow plenty of time for the work to be completed should any unforeseen incidents pop up. The trouble is, however, that the task will magically expand to require the complete 32 hours. Why does this happen? Consider the following:

- **Hidden time**   Hidden time, the time factored in by the project team member, is secret. No one, especially the project manager, knows why the extra time has been factored into the activity. The team member can then "enjoy" the extra time to complete the task at leisure.

- **Procrastination**   Most people put off starting a task until the last possible minute. The trouble with bloated, hidden time is people may wait through the additional time they've secretly factored into the activity. Unfortunately, if something does go awry in completing the activity, the work result is later than predicted.

- **Demands**   Project team members may be assigned to multiple projects with multiple demands. The requirement to move from project to project can shift focus, result in a loss of concentration, and require additional ramp-up time as workers shift from activity to activity. The demand for multitasking allows project team members to take advantage of hidden time.

- **On schedule**   Activities are typically completed on schedule or late, but rarely early. Users that have bloated the activity duration estimates may finish their task ahead of what they promised, but they have a tendency to hold onto those results until the activity's due date. This is because workers aren't usually rewarded for completing work early. In addition, workers don't want to reveal the inaccuracies in their time estimates. Workers may believe future estimates may be based on actual work durations, rather than estimates, so they'll "sandbag" the results to protect themselves—and finish "on schedule."

So what's a project manager to do? First off, the project manager should strive to incorporate historical information and expert judgment to predicate accurate estimates. Second, the project manager should stress a genuine need for accurate duration estimates. Finally, the project manager can incorporate a reserve time.

A reserve time is a percentage of the project duration or a preset number of work periods and is usually added to the end of the project schedule. Reserve time may also be added to individual activity durations based on risk or uncertainty in the activity duration. When activities are completed late, the additional time for the activity is subtracted from the reserve time. As the project moves forward, the reserve time can be reduced or eliminated as the project manager sees fit. Reserve time decisions should be documented.

Evaluating the Estimates

The end result of estimating activities provides the following three things:

- **Activity duration estimates** Activity duration estimates reflect how long each work package will take to complete. Duration estimates should include an acknowledgement of the range of variance. For example, an activity whose duration is expected to be one week may have a range of variance of one week ± three days. This means the work can take up to eight days or as little as two days. This is assuming a week is five days.

INSIDE THE EXAM

There's a ton of information in this chapter— all of it important—but there are some key things you must know to pass the PMP exam. For starters, you should understand how activity estimates are created.

Analogous estimates use historical information to predict how long current project activities will last. These estimates are considered top-down estimates and are part of expert judgment. Quantifiable estimates, on the other hand, use a quantity to predict how long activities will take. Consider any unit, such as square feet painted per hour or the number of units created per day.

Lag is positive time added to a task to indicate waiting. Lead is negative time added to a task to "hurry up." Fast-tracking arranges activities to happen in tandem rather than in succession, which increases risk. Crashing adds more resources to activities to decrease their duration, which typically adds cost.

Monte Carlo analysis is a computer program typically used to estimate the many possible variables within a project schedule. Monte Carlo simulations predict probable end dates, not an exact end date. Another tool the project manager can use is *resource leveling*. Resource leveling smoothes out the project schedule so resources are not overallocated. A result of this is that projects are often scheduled to last longer than initial estimates.

The critical path in a project has zero float; it is the path with the longest duration to completion. There can be more than one critical path in a network diagram. Should delays happen on noncritical paths and consume all float, the critical path may change.

The project schedule is a calendar-based system used to predict when the project, and work, will start and end. Gantt charts map activities against a calendar and may show the relationship between activities. Milestone charts show when key deliverables are expected; they do not show the relationship between activities.

■ **Basis of estimates**   Any assumptions made during the activity estimating process should be identified. In addition, any historical information, subject matter experts, or commercial estimating databases that were used should also be documented for future reference.

■ **Activity list updates**   During the estimating process, missing activities within the activity list may be discovered. The project manager should confirm that the new work packages are reflected in the activity list for the project.

CERTIFICATION OBJECTIVE 6.06

Developing the Project Schedule

Now that the estimates for the activities are completed, it's time to work some magic and see how long the entire project will take. The project manager specifically pursues the start date and, more importantly, the completion date. Projects that don't provide realistic schedules aren't likely to get approved. Or worse, the projects will get approved, but they will most likely fail, as the project team will not be able to meet the unrealistic schedule.

The creation of the project schedule is iterative. It's rare for a schedule to get created, approved, and implemented without some iterative examination, arrangement, and management input—though on smaller projects it may be possible. When activity list updates, constraints, assumptions, and other inputs are considered, it's easy to see why scheduling can become complex.

Revisiting the Project Network Diagram

The PND illustrates the project. Recall that the PND shows the sequence of activities and the relationship between activities. It is important during schedule creation because it allows the project manager and the project team to evaluate the decisions, constraints, and assumptions that were made earlier in the process to determine why certain activities must occur in a particular order.

Hard logic and soft logic must be evaluated to confirm that the decisions and logic are feasible, accurate, and fit within the expected completion of the project. The following illustration is a simple PND for a small project.

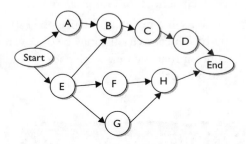

Relying on Activity Duration Estimates

Another key input to schedule creation is the activity duration estimates. Makes sense, right? The project manager needs to know how long the whole project will take, so the activity duration estimates will help calculate that number. Recall, however, the range of variances for each activity—these possible variances need to be accounted for in the actual project schedule creation. We'll discuss the schedule creation in a few moments.

Evaluating the Project Constraints

Constraints will restrict when and how the project may be implemented. They are added to a project for a purpose, not just to rush the work to completion. It's important to understand why the constraint has been imposed. The following offers a few common examples as to why constraints exist:

- To take advantage of an opportunity to profit from a market window for a product or service
- To work within the parameters of expected weather conditions (for seasonal or outdoor projects)
- To adhere to government requirements
- To adhere to industry regulations, best practices, or guidelines
- To work within time frames that incorporate the expected delivery of materials from vendors or other projects

Perhaps one of the biggest constraints is the predetermined project deadline. Imagine a company creating a product to take to a tradeshow. If the creation of the product is running late, the tradeshow isn't going to move its date back so the product has enough time to be completed for the show. There are four time constraints to consider.

- **Start no earlier than (SNET)**   This constraint requires that the project or activity not start earlier than the predetermined date. Consider an activity to add software to an existing network server in a technology project. The project manager adds a "start no earlier than" constraint to the activity to ensure the activity begins on a Saturday when the server is not in use by the organization. The activity can begin any time after the preset date, but not before it.

- **Start no later than (SNLT)**   This constraint requires the activity to begin by a predetermined date. For example, the creation of a community flower garden must "start no later than" May 15. The creation of the garden may, weather permitting, begin earlier than the preset date, but it must start by that date.

- **Finish no later than (FNLT)**   This constraint requires the project or activity to finish by a predetermined date. For example, the installation of flooring tile in a restaurant must be finished by October 25 so the kitchen equipment can be installed. The constraint "finish no later than" is tied to the date of October 25. The activity can end sooner than October 25, but not after it.

- **Finish no earlier than (FNET)**   This somewhat unusual constraint requires the activity to be in motion up until the predetermined date. Consider a project to create a special blend of wine. The wine must be aged a specific amount of time before the winemaking process can continue. Thus, the process requires a set amount of time so it may "finish no earlier than" the determined time. The activity can end any time after the preset date, but not before it.

Project constraints can also include milestones. The project sponsor may request, for example, a milestone for a deliverable within the project on April 28. Based on this milestone, all of the work needed to create a deliverable must be scheduled against the expected due date. In addition, once these milestones are set, it's pretty darn tough to change them.

Milestone constraints can also be tied to activities outside of the project. Consider a scheduled walkthrough with a customer on a construction project. Or consider the demands of a project to create a product or service by a scheduled milestone that another project within the performing organization is expecting.

Reevaluating the Assumptions

Assumptions are beliefs held to be true but that may not necessarily be so. Assumptions, such as being able to have access to a building 24 hours a day, seven days a week, can wreak havoc on the project schedule if they are proved false. Consider a schedule that plans on working three shifts during the remodeling of an office building only to discover late in the project planning that the customer will not allow the work to happen during daytime hours. Assumptions factored into the project should be documented and accounted for.

Evaluating the Risk Management Plan

We'll discuss risk and risk management completely in Chapter 11. For now, know that risks can alter the project schedule—for better or for worse. This isn't difficult to see. A risk in the project may be identified as delays from the vendor for the equipment needed to complete the project. The response to this risk, should it happen, may be to secure an alternate vendor that charges slightly more for the same equipment but has it in stock. The delay of the equipment with the original vendor may throw the project off schedule, and the additional time to find, purchase, and ship the needed equipment could also add extra time to the project.

Examining the Activity Attributes

The activity attributes can have a direct impact on the project schedule. Some activities are effort-driven, which means more effort can reduce the duration. Other activities are of fixed duration—that is, additional effort does nothing to reduce their expected duration. Activity attributes are the characteristics of the work to be completed, including:

- The person(s) responsible for completing each work package
- Where the work will take place (building, city, outdoors)
- The type of activity (electrical, technical, supervised, and so on)
- When the activity must take place (business hours, off-hours, more unusual times)

CERTIFICATION OBJECTIVE 6.07

Defining the Project Timeline

The project manager, the project team, and possibly even the key stakeholders will examine the inputs previously discussed and apply the techniques discussed in this section to create a feasible schedule for the project. The point of the project schedule is to complete the project scope in the shortest amount of time possible without incurring exceptional costs, risks, or a loss of quality.

Creating the project schedule is part of the planning process group. It is calendar based and relies on both the project network diagram and the accuracy of time estimates.

ON THE CD

See the video Calculating Project Float.

Performing Schedule Network Analysis

Schedule network analysis is the process of factoring theoretical early and late start dates and theoretical early and late finish dates for each activity within the PND. The early and late dates are not the expected schedule, but rather a potential schedule based on the project constraints, the likelihood of success, the availability of resources, and other constraints.

The most common approach to calculating when a project may finish is by using the critical path method. It uses a "forward" and "backward" pass to reveal which activities are considered critical. Activities on the critical path may not be delayed;

otherwise, the project end date will be delayed. The critical path is the path with the longest duration to completion. Activities not on the critical path have some float (also called slack) that allows some amount of delay without delaying the project end date. The following illustration is an example of the critical path.

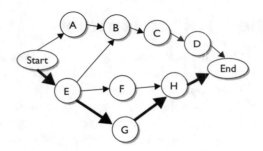

Calculating Float in a PND

Float, or slack, is the amount of time a task can be delayed without delaying the project's completion. Technically, there are three different types of float.

- **Free float** This is the total time a single activity can be delayed without delaying the early start of any successor activities.
- **Total slack** This is the total time an activity can be delayed without delaying project completion.
- **Project slack** This is the total time the project can be delayed without passing the customer-expected completion date.

Most project management software will automatically calculate float. On the PMP exam, however, candidates will be expected to calculate float manually. Don't worry, it's not too tough. Here goes:

Examine the PND and find the critical path. The critical path is typically the path with the longest duration and will always have zero float. The critical path is technically found once you complete the forward and backward pass. Start with the forward pass. After the backward pass, you can identify the critical and near critical paths, as well as float.

1. The early start (ES) and early finish (EF) dates are calculated first by completing the "forward pass." The ES of the first task is one. The EF for the first task is its ES, plus the task duration, minus one. Don't let the "minus one value" throw you. If Task A is scheduled to last one day, it would only take one day to complete, right? The ES would be 1, the duration is 1, and the EF would also be 1 because the activity would finish within one day, not two days. The following illustration shows the start of the forward pass.

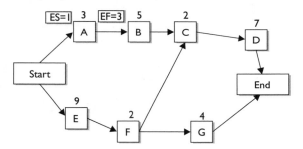

2. The ES of the next task(s) will be the EF for the previous activity, plus one. In other words, if Task A finishes on day eight, Task B will begin on day nine.

3. The EF for the next task(s) equals its ES, plus the task duration, minus one. Sound familiar?

4. Now each task moves forward with the forward pass. Use caution when there are predecessor activities; the EF with the largest value is carried forward. The following illustration shows the completed forward pass.

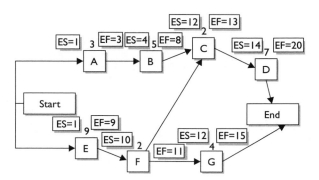

5. After the forward pass is completed, the backward pass starts at the end of the PND. The backward pass is concerned with the late finish (LF) and the late start (LS) of each activity. The LF for the last activity in the PND equals its EF value. The LS is calculated by subtracting the duration of the activity from its LF, plus one. The one is added to accommodate the full day's work; it's just the opposite of subtracting the one day in the forward pass. Here's a tip: The last activity is on the critical path, so its LS will equal its ES.

6. The next predecessor activity's LF equals the LS of the successor activity, minus one. In other words, if Task Z has an LS of 107, Task Y will have an LF of 106. The following illustration shows the process of the backward pass.

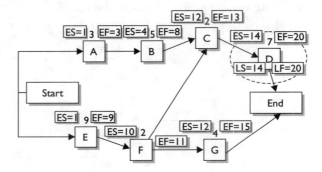

7. The LS is again calculated by subtracting the task's duration from the task's LF, plus one. The following shows the completed backward pass.

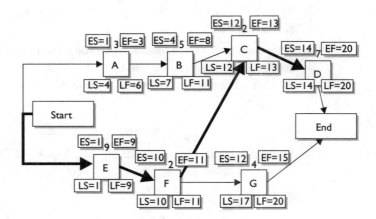

8. To officially calculate float, the LS is subtracted from the ES and the LF is subtracted from the EF. Recall the total float is the amount of time a task can be delayed without delaying the project completion date. The next illustration shows the completed PND with the float exposed.

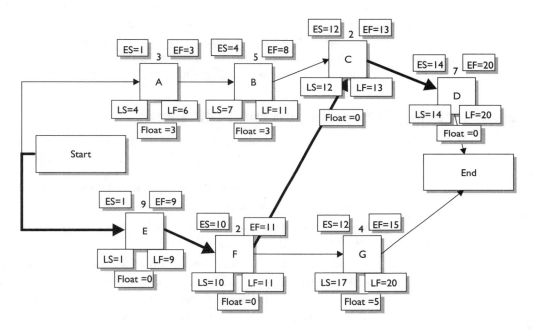

Using the Critical Chain Method

The critical chain method aims to eliminate Parkinson's Law by eliminating bottlenecks that hold up project progression, and it examines the availability of project resources. In the critical chain method (CCM), deadlines associated with individual tasks are removed and the only date that matters is the promised due date of the project deliverable. CCM works to modify the project schedule based on the availability of project resources rather than the pure sequence of events, as in the critical path method.

CCM first requires the discovery of the critical path but then applies available resources to determine the true resource-limited schedule. Based on the availability of resources to complete the project work, the critical path is often different than what it would have been using the pure CPM approach.

CCM scheduling evaluates each activity's latest possible start and finish dates. This allows project managers to manage the buffer activity duration—that is, the activities that are not on the critical path—but their completion contributes to the start of critical path activities. In other words, the focus is on completing each activity in order to complete the entire project by the promised end date.

Encountering Scheduling on the PMP Exam

You'll encounter float, scheduling, and critical path activities on the PMP exam. You should count these questions as "gimmies" if you remember a few important rules.

- Always draw out the network diagram presented on your scratch paper. It may be used in several questions.

- Know how to calculate float. (The complete process was shown earlier in the "Calculating Float in a PND" section.)

- You may encounter questions that ask on what day of the week a project will end if no weekends or holidays are worked. No problem. Add up the critical path, divide by five (Monday through Friday), and then figure out which day of the week the activity will end on.

- You may see something like Figure 6-6 when it comes to scheduling. When three numbers are presented, think three-point estimate. Optimistic is the smallest number, pessimistic is the largest, so most likely it's somewhere between the two. When a number is positioned directly over the tasks, it is the task duration. When a number is positioned to the upper-right corner of a task, this represents the early finish date.

Applying Duration Compression

Duration compression is also a mathematical approach to scheduling. The trick with duration compression, as its name implies, is calculating ways the project can get done sooner than expected. Consider a construction project. The project may be slated to last eight months, but due to the expected cold and nasty weather typical

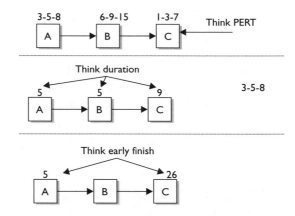

FIGURE 6-6

Scheduling
follows many
rules to arrive
at project
completion.

of month seven, the project manager needs to rearrange activities where possible to end the project as soon as possible.

In some instances, the relationship between activities cannot be changed due to hard or soft logic. The relationships must remain as scheduled. Now consider the same construction company that is promised a bonus if they can complete the work by the end of month seven. Now there's incentive to complete the work, but there's also the fixed relationship between activities.

To apply duration compression, the performing organization can rely on two different methods. These methods can be used independently or together, and are applied to activities or the entire project based on need, risk, and cost. The methods are:

- **Crashing**   This approach adds more resources to activities on the critical path to complete the project earlier. When crashing a project, costs are added as the labor expenses increase. Crashing doesn't always work. Consider activities that have a fixed duration and won't finish faster with additional resources. The project manager must also consider the expenses in relation to the gains of completing on time. For example, a construction company may have been promised a bonus to complete the work by a preset date, but the cost incurred to hit the targeted date is more than what the bonus offers.

- **Fast-tracking**   This method changes the relationship of activities. With fast-tracking, activities that would normally be done in sequence are allowed to be done in parallel or with some overlap. Fast-tracking can be accomplished by changing the relationship of activities from FS to SS or by adding lead time to downstream activities. For example, a construction company could change the relationship between painting the rooms and installing the carpet by adding lead time to the carpet installation task. Before the change, all of the rooms had to be painted before the carpet installers could begin. With the added lead time, the carpet can be installed hours after a room is painted. Fast-tracking increases risk and may cause rework in the project. Can't you just imagine those workers getting fresh paint on the new carpet? However, it's often ideal to fast-track the project. When it's done properly and with qualified resources, it's a huge timesaver.

e x a m

w a t c h
It's easy to remember the difference between these two actions. Crashing and cost both begin with C— we're adding resources, and too many people will "crash" into each other. Fast-tracking is about speeding things up: Haste makes waste—risky.

Using a Project Simulation

Project simulations allow a project manager to examine the feasibility of the project schedule under different conditions, variables, and events. For example, the project manager can see what would happen to a project if activities were delayed, vendors missed shipment dates, and external events affected the project.

Simulations are often completed with the Monte Carlo analysis. The Monte Carlo analysis, named after the world-famous gambling city, predicts how scenarios may work out given any number of variables. The process doesn't actually churn out a specific answer, but a range of possible answers. When Monte Carlo is applied to a schedule, it can examine, for example, the optimistic completion date, the pessimistic completion date, and the most likely completion date for each activity in the project.

As you can imagine in a typical network diagram, there are likely thousands, if not millions, of combinations of tasks that complete early, late, or as expected. Monte Carlo analysis shuffles these combinations, usually through computer software, and offers a range of possible end dates coupled with an expected probability for achieving each end date.

In other words, Monte Carlo analysis is an odds-maker. The project manager chooses, or is at least influenced by, the end date with the highest odds of completion in ratio to the demands for completion by an expected time. The project manager can then predict with some certainty that the project has an 85 percent chance of completion by a specific date.

Simulations also provide time to factor in "what-if" questions, worst-case scenarios, and potential disasters. The end result of simulations is to create responses to the feasible situations. Then, should the situations come into play, the project team is ready with a planned response.

Using Resource-Leveling Heuristics

First off, a heuristic is a fancy way of saying "rule of thumb." A resource-leveling heuristic is a method to flatten the schedule when resources are overallocated. Resource leveling can be applied using different methods to accomplish different goals. One of the most common methods is to ensure that workers are not overextended on activities. Figure 6-7 is a screenshot from Microsoft Project where resource leveling has been applied.

FIGURE 6-7

Resource leveling flattens the project schedule and will likely extend the project duration.

Resource Leveling	? X

Leveling calculations

○ Automatic   ● Manual

Look for overallocations on a [Day by Day ▼] basis

☑ Clear leveling values before leveling

Leveling range for 'Unix Training Manual.mpp'

● Level entire project

○ Level   From: [Mon 10/31/05]

To: [Wed 1/18/06]

Resolving overallocations

Leveling order: [Standard ▼]

☐ Level only within available slack

☑ Leveling can adjust individual assignments on a task

☑ Leveling can create splits in remaining work

[Help]   [Clear Leveling...]   [Level Now]   [OK]   [Cancel]

For example, Sarah is assigned to Task C and Task H, which are planned to happen concurrently. Sarah cannot be in two places at once, so resource leveling changes the timing of the activities so Sarah can complete Task C and then move on to Task H. As expected, however, resource leveling often extends the project end date.

Another method for resource leveling is to take resources from noncritical path activities and apply them to critical path activities to ensure the project end date is met. This method takes advantage of available slack and balances the expected duration of the noncritical path with the expected duration of the critical path.

Resource leveling also provides for changing the project schedule to allow for long work hours to complete the project work—such as weekends, evenings, or even adding a second or third shift to bring the project back in alignment. Another approach, also part of resource leveling, is to change the resources, tools, or equipment used to complete the project work faster. For example, a project manager could request the printer to use a different, faster printing press to complete the printing activity than what was originally planned for. Of course, these approaches often increase cost.

Finally, some resources may be scarce to the project. Consider a highly skilled technician or consultant who is only available on a particular date to contribute to the project. These resources are scheduled from the project end date, rather than the start date. This is known as reverse resource allocation scheduling.

Using Project Management Software

When it comes to project management software, take your pick: The market is full of them. Project management applications are tools, not replacements, for the project management process. Many of the software titles today automate the processes of scheduling, activity sequencing, work authorization, and other activities. The performing organization must weigh the cost of the PMIS against the benefits the project managers will actually gain.

Relying on a Project Coding Structure

The coding structure identifies the work packages within the WBS and is then applied to the PND. This allows the project manager, the project team, experts, and even key stakeholders to extract areas of the project to examine, evaluate, and inspect. For example, a project to create a catalog for a parts distributor may follow multiple paths to completion. Each path to completion has its own "family" of numbers that relate to each activity on the path (see Table 6-2).

Path	Coding for Path	Typical Activities
Artwork	4.2	Concept (4.2.1) Logos (4.2.2) Font design (4.2.3)
Photography	4.3	Product models (4.3.1) Airbrushing (4.3.2) Selection (4.3.3)
Content	4.4	Message (4.4.1) Copywriting (4.4.2) Editing (4.4.3) Rewrites (4.4.4)
Print	4.5	Signatures (4.5.1) Plates (4.5.2) Four-color printing (4.5.3)
Bind	4.6	Assembly (4.6.1) Bindery (4.6.2) Trimming (4.6.3) Shrink-wrap (4.6.4)
Distribution	4.7	Packaging (4.7.1) Labeling (4.7.2) Shipping (4.7.3)

TABLE 6-2

Possible Paths in Creating a Catalog

Examining the Project Schedule

The project schedule includes, at a minimum, a date when the project begins and a date when the project is expected to end. The project schedule is considered proposed until the resources needed to complete the project work are ascertained. In addition to the schedule, the project manager should include all of the supporting details. Project schedules can be presented in many different formats, such as:

- **Project network diagram** Illustrates the flow of work, the relationship between activities, the critical path, and the expected project end date. PNDs, when used as the project schedule, should have dates associated with each project activity to show when the activity is expected to start and end.
- **Bar charts** These show the start and end dates for the project and the activity duration against a calendar. They are easy to read. Scheduling bar charts are also called Gantt charts.

- **Milestone charts** Plot out the high-level deliverables and external interfaces, such as a customer walkthrough, against a calendar. Milestone charts are similar to a Gantt chart, but with less detail regarding individual activities. The following is an example of a milestone chart.

Milestone	July	Aug	Sep	Oct	Nov	Dec
Customer	△▼					
Architect signature		△	▼			
Foundation				△		
Framing					△ ▼	
Roofing						△

Legend

△ Planned
▼ Actual

- **Schedule baseline** A schedule baseline is the agreed-upon project schedule based on your project network diagram. It's part of the project management plan, and your project progress is compared to the schedule baseline.
- **Schedule data** This is the supporting detail and relevant information for the project schedule. It includes details about the project milestones, project activities and their attributes, and relevant assumptions and constraints.

Utilizing the Schedule Management Plan

The schedule management plan is a subsidiary plan of the overall project plan. It is used to control changes to the schedule. A formal schedule management plan has procedures that control how changes to the project plan can be proposed, accounted for, and then implemented. An informal schedule management plan may consider changes on an instance-by-instance basis.

Updating the Resource Requirements

Due to resource leveling, additional resources may need to be added to the project. For example, a proposed leveling may extend the project beyond an acceptable completion date. To reach the project end date, the project manager elects to add additional resources to the critical path activities. The resources the project manager adds should be documented, and the associated costs should be accounted for and approved.

CERTIFICATION OBJECTIVE 6.08

Controlling the Project Schedule

Schedule control is part of integrated change management, as discussed in Chapter 4. Throughout a typical project, events will happen that may require updates to the project schedule. Schedule control is concerned with three processes.

■ The project manager works with the factors that can cause schedule change in an effort to confirm that the changes are needed, may have already happened, can't be avoided, and that the changes are agreed upon. Factors can include project team members, stakeholders, management, customers, and project conditions.

■ The project manager examines the work results and conditions to determine whether the schedule has changed.

■ The project manager manages the actual change in the schedule.

Managing the Inputs to Schedule Control

Schedule slippage can be caused by a number of things: scope creep, underestimating the project work, risks, decisions, and many more. The project manager needs to communicate with the resources and factors that can affect the project schedule often in the project. This is one area where the project manager can't assume that everything's going to work out just fine. Schedule control, the process of managing changes to the project schedule, is based on several inputs.

- The project management plan
- The schedule
- Performance reports
- Organizational process assets

Applying a Schedule Control System

A schedule control system is a formal approach to managing changes to the project schedule. It considers the conditions, reasons, requests, costs, and risks of making changes. It includes methods of tracking changes, approval levels based on thresholds, and the documentation of approved or declined changes. The schedule control system process is part of integrated change management.

Measuring Project Performance

Poor performance may result in schedule changes. Consider a project team that is completing its work on time but all of the work results are unacceptable. The project team may be rushing through their assignments to meet their deadline. To compensate for this, the project may be changed to allow for additional quality inspections and more time for activity completion. Project performance is often based on earned value management, which we'll discuss in Chapter 10.

Examining the Schedule Variance

The project manager must actively monitor the variances between when activities are scheduled to end and when they actually end. An accumulation of differences between scheduled and actual dates may result in a schedule variance.

The project manager must also pay attention to the completion of activities on paths with float, not just on the critical path. Consider a project that has eight different paths to completion. The project manager should first identify the critical path, but should also identify the float on each path. The paths should be arranged and monitored in a hierarchy from the path with the smallest float to the path with the largest float. As activities are completed, the float of each path should be monitored to identify any paths that may be slipping from the scheduled end dates.

Updating the Project Schedule

So what happens when a schedule change occurs? The project manager must ensure that the project schedule is updated to reflect the change, document the change, and follow the guidelines within the schedule management plan. Any formal processes, such as notifying stakeholders or management, should be followed.

Revisions are a special type of project schedule change, which cause the project start date and, more likely, the project end date to be changed. They typically stem from project scope changes. Because of the additional work the new scope requires, additional time is needed to complete the project.

Schedule delays, for whatever reason, may be so drastic that the entire project has to be rebaselined. Rebaselining is a worst-case scenario and should only be used when adjusting for drastic, long delays. When rebaselining happens, all of the historical information up to the point of the rebaseline is eliminated. Schedule revision is the preferred, and most common, approach to changing the project end date.

Applying Corrective Action

Corrective action is any method applied to bring the project schedule back into alignment with the original dates and goals for the project end date. Corrective actions are efforts to ensure future performance meets the expected performance levels. It includes the following:

- Extraordinary measures to ensure work packages complete as scheduled
- Extraordinary measures to ensure work packages complete with as little delay as possible
- Root-cause analysis of schedule variances
- Implementing measures to recover from schedule delays

Writing the Lessons Learned

Lessons learned on creating the schedule, changes to the project schedule, and responses to variances are needed as part of the project's historical information. Recall that lessons-learned documentation happens throughout the project plan, not just at the conclusion of the project.

CERTIFICATION SUMMARY

Projects cannot last forever—thankfully. To effectively finish and manage a project, a project manager must be able to effectively manage time. Within a project, many factors can affect the project length: activity duration, project calendars, resource calendars, vendors, activity sequencing, and more. Time management begins with the constraints of the product schedule, the project calendar, and the resource calendars, as well as the activities and their expected duration.

Many projects can rely on project templates that have worked before. Other projects, new and never-attempted technology, require that a project schedule be created from scratch. The WBS contributes to the activity list, which, in turn, allows the project manager and the project team to begin activity sequencing.

Activities to be sequenced must be estimated. The project manager and the project team must evaluate the required time to complete the work packages. The project manager can rely on a number of estimating methods to come to a predicted duration for activities. For example, a project manager may use analogous estimation of historical data to provide the needed estimate. Or, the project manager may use a parametric model to predict the amount of time for the activities. The importance of estimating is that each work package is considered and its duration calculated.

Within the process of activity sequencing there will be hard logic and soft logic. Hard logic is the mandatory relationships between activities: The foundation must be in place before the house framing can begin. Soft logic allows the relationship and order of activities to be determined based on conditions, preferences, or other factors. For example, the landscaping will happen before the house is painted so that dirt and dust won't get onto the fresh paint.

The relationships of activities are illustrated within a network diagram. Network diagrams show the path from start to completion and identify which activities are on the critical path. Of course, the critical path is the path with the longest duration and typically has zero slack or float. Activities on the noncritical paths may be delayed to the extent that they do not delay activities on the critical path.

Finally, project team members may have a tendency to bloat their duration estimates. Bloating the work to allow for "wiggle room" on assignments can cause durations to swell way beyond the practical completion of the project. In lieu of bloated estimates, project team members and the project manager should use a percentage of the project time as management reserve. Management reserve is a percentage of the overall project duration estimate, and it is set aside just for schedule slippage. When activities are late, the tardiness of the work is borrowed from management reserve rather than tacked on to the conclusion of the project.

KEY TERMS

To pass the PMP exam, you will need to memorize these terms and their definitions. For maximum value, create your own flashcards based on these definitions and review them daily. The definitions can be found within this chapter and in the glossary.

activity list   A listing of all of the project activities required to complete each project phase or the entire project.

activity on node   A network diagramming approach that places the activities on a node in the project network diagram.

activity sequencing   The process of mapping the project activities in the order in which the work should be completed.

analogous estimating   A duration-estimating technique that bases the current project duration estimate on historical information from similar projects.

crashing   A duration-compression technique that adds project resources to the project in an effort to reduce the amount of time allotted for effort-driven activities.

critical chain method   A network diagramming approach that considers the availability of project resources and the project's promised end date to determine the critical path(s) in the project.

critical path method   A network diagramming approach that identifies the project activities that cannot be delayed or the project completion date will be late.

discretionary dependencies   The order of the project activities do not have to be completed in a particular order. These tasks can be completed in the order of the project manager or at the project team's discretion.

fast-tracking   A duration-compression technique that allows entire phases of a project to overlap other phases.

finish-to-finish   A relationship between project activities where the predecessor activities must finish before successor activities may finish.

finish-to-start   A relationship between project activities where the predecessor activities must finish before the successor activities may start; this is the most common network diagramming relationship type.

float   A generic term to describe the amount of time an activity may be delayed without delaying any successor activities' start dates.

FNET   A project constraint that requires an activity to finish no earlier than a specific date.

fragnet   A portion of the project that is usually contracted to a vendor to complete, yet the project work is still represented in the project network diagram.

hard logic   The project activities must be completed in a particular order; this is also known as mandatory dependencies.

lag   Time added to a project activity to delay its start time; lag time is considered positive time, and it is sometimes called waiting time.

lead   Time added to an activity to allow its start time to begin earlier than scheduled; lead time is negative time, as it moves the activities closer to the project's start date.

mandatory dependencies   Project activities must happen in a particular order due to the nature of the work; also known as hard logic.

Monte Carlo analysis   A what-if scenario tool to determine how scenarios may work out, given any number of variables. The process doesn't actually create a specific answer, but a range of possible answers. When Monte Carlo is applied to a schedule, it can present, for example, the optimistic completion date, the pessimistic completion date, and the most likely completion date for each activity in the project.

network template   A network diagram based on previous similar projects that is adapted for the current project work.

parametric estimating   Ideal for projects with repetitive work where a parameter, such as five hours per unit, is used to estimate the project duration.

Parkinson's Law   Work expands to fill the amount of time allotted to it.

precedence diagramming method   The most common method of arranging the project work visually. The PDM puts the activities in boxes, called nodes, and connects the boxes with arrows. The arrows represent the relationship and the dependencies of the work packages.

project calendar   A calendar that defines the working times for the project. For example, a project may require the project team to work nights and weekends so as not to disturb the ongoing operations of the organization during working hours. In addition, the project calendar accounts for holidays, working hours, and work shifts the project will cover.

resource calendar   The resource calendar shows when resources, such as project team members, consultants, and SMEs, are available to work on the project. It takes into account vacations, other commitments within the organization, restrictions on contracted work, overtime issues, and so on.

resource-leveling heuristics   A method to flatten the schedule when resources are overallocated or allocated unevenly. Resource leveling can be applied in different methods to accomplish different goals. One of the most common methods is to ensure that workers are not overextended on activities.

schedule control   Part of integrated change management, schedule control is concerned with three processes: the project manager confirms that any schedule changes are agreed upon; the project manager examines the work results and conditions to know if the schedule has changed; and the project manager manages the actual change in the schedule.

schedule management plan   A subsidiary plan of the overall project plan. It is used to control changes to the schedule. A formal schedule management plan has procedures that control how changes to the project plan can be proposed, accounted for, and then implemented.

schedule variance   The difference between the planned work and the completed work.

SNET   A project constraint that demands that a project activity start no earlier than a specific date.

soft logic   The preferred order of activities. Project managers should use these relationships at their "discretion" and document the logic behind making soft logic decisions. Discretionary dependencies allow activities to happen in a preferred order because of best practices, conditions unique to the project work, or external events; also known as discretionary dependencies.

start-to-finish   A relationship that requires an activity to start so that a successor activity may finish; it is unusual and is rarely used.

start-to-start   A relationship structure that requires a task to start before a successor task activity may start. This relationship allows both activities to happen in tandem.

three-point estimate   An estimate that uses optimistic, most likely, and pessimistic values to determine the cost or duration of a project component.

TWO-MINUTE DRILL

Defining the Project Activities

❑ Based on the scope baseline, enterprise environmental factors, and organizational process assets, the project manager and the project team will define the activities that are required to be completed in order to create the project scope.

❑ Just as the project team decomposes the project scope into work packages, the work packages can be broken down into project activities. Decomposition is a project management tool that breaks down deliverables into activities to better execute the project.

❑ Rolling wave planning is a project management approach to progressive elaboration. Imminent work is planned in detail, while future work is only planned at a high level. Rolling wave planning is ideal for projects where the current work may shape future project requirements.

Sequencing Project Activities

❑ Projects are made up of sequential activities to create a product. The WBS and the activity list serve as key inputs to the sequencing of project activities. The science of arranging, calculating, and predicting how long the activities will take to complete allows the project manager to create a schedule and then predict when the project will end.

❑ Hard logic is the approach that requires activities to happen in a specific order due to the nature of the work—for example, configuring a computer workstation's operating systems before adding the software.

❑ Soft logic is a "preferred" method of arranging activities based on conditions, guidelines, or best practices—for example, the project manager preferring to have the photocopying of a user manual be completed before any bindery work on the manual begins.

Examining the Sequencing Outputs

❑ The sequence of activities is displayed in a project schedule network diagram. The network diagram illustrates the flow of activities and the relationship between activities. The precedent diagramming method is the most common approach to arranging activities visually.

❑ **Free float** This is the total time a single activity can be delayed without delaying the early start of any successor activities.

❑ **Total slack** This is the total time an activity can be delayed without delaying project completion.

❑ **Project slack** This is the total time the project can be delayed without passing the customer-expected completion date.

Considering Resource Requirements

❑ Resources can affect when a project is able to be completed. Effort-driven activities can allow more resources to be added to reduce their overall duration, but fixed-duration activities cannot be reduced by adding additional resources.

❑ Resources include materials, facilities, equipment, and other things and services besides people. The procurement of resources may also affect the project schedule.

❑ The calendar of the project is the time when the project work may take place. The project manager must consider access to the workplace, project schedule, organization holidays, and events that affect the project calendar.

❑ The resource calendar reflects when the project resources (project team members, consultants, and so on) are available to complete the project work.

Estimating Activity Durations

❑ Activity duration estimates are needed to calculate how long the project will take to complete. Estimates can come from project team members, commercial databases, expert judgment, and historical information.

❑ Analogous estimating relies on historical information to predict how long current project activities should last.

❑ Parametric estimates use a mathematical model to calculate how long activities should take based on units, duration, and effort.

Developing the Project Schedule

❑ The critical path is the longest path to completion in the network diagram. Activities on the critical path have no float or slack. Free float is the amount of time an activity can be delayed without affecting the next activity's scheduled start date. Total float is the amount of time an activity can be delayed without affecting the project end date.

❑ Duration compression is applied to reduce the length of the project or to account for project delays. Crashing adds resources to project activities and usually increases cost. Fast-tracking allows activities to happen in tandem and usually increases risk.

❑ The schedule management plan must be consulted when project schedule changes occur, are proposed, or are needed. The schedule control system implements the schedule management plan and is part of integration change management.

❑ The critical chain method relies on the availability of resources to determine when the project is most likely to finish. Activities are scheduled based on their latest possible start and finish dates.

Controlling the Project Schedule

❑ The project management plan, the project schedule, work performance information, and organizational process assets are all inputs to controlling the project schedule.

❑ Schedule compression is an approach to bring the project back into alignment with the project baseline. Crashing adds resources to the project work, which usually increases project costs. Fast-tracking allows entire phases of the project to overlap, which may increase risks.

❑ Updates to the project schedule may cause the schedule baseline, schedule management plan, and the cost baseline to be updated. All changes must flow through the schedule change control system and integrated change control.

SELF TEST

1. You are the project manager of the JHG Project. This project has 32 stakeholders and will require implementation activities in North and South America. You have been requested to provide a duration estimate for the project. Of the following, which will offer the best level of detail in your estimate?

    A. The resource calendar
    B. An order of magnitude
    C. A requirements document
    D. A stakeholder analysis

2. Michael is the project manager of the 78GH Project. This project requires several members of the project team to complete a certification class for another project the week of November 2. This class causes some of the project activities on Michael's activities to be delayed from his target schedule. This is an example of which of the following?

    A. Hard logic
    B. External dependencies
    C. Soft logic
    D. Conflict of interest

3. You are managing an interior decorating project. The walls are scheduled to be painted immediately after the primer. You have allowed 36 hours between the primer activity and the painting activity to ensure that the primer has cured. This is an example of which one of the following?

    A. Lead
    B. Lag
    C. Soft logic
    D. Finish-to-start relationship

4. As the project manager for the DFK Project, you are reviewing your project's network diagram (as shown in the following illustration).

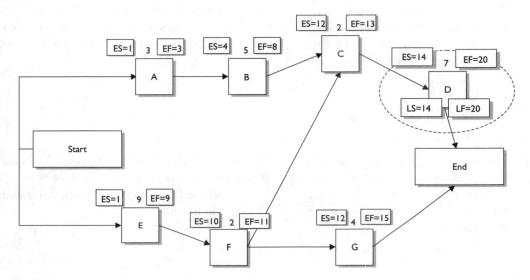

Given the diagram, what is the relationship between tasks F and G?

A. FS

B. SS

C. FF

D. SF

5. You are the project manager for the LLL Project. Steven, a project team member, is confused about network diagrams. Specifically, he wants to know what the critical path is in a network diagram. Your answer is which one of the following?

A. The critical path is the network that hosts the activities most critical to the project's success.

B. The critical path is the path with the longest duration.

C. The critical path is always one path that cannot be delayed or the entire project will be delayed.

D. The critical path is the path from start to completion with no deviation from the project plan.

6. What is the difference between PDM and ADM?

A. ADM places activities on arrows, while PDM places activities on nodes.

B. ADM is also known as AOA, while PDM is sometimes referred to as GERT.

C. ADM hosts activities on nodes, while PDM hosts activities on arrows.

D. PDM can have two types of relationships between tasks, while ADM can have only one type of relationship between tasks.

7. You are creating a schedule duration estimate for the activities in the PDR Project. You're working with your project and comparing the results of a past similar project to predict the time of the current project. What estimating approach are you using?

A. Organizational process assets

B. Parametric

C. Analogous

D. PERT

8. Where is a project manager most likely to experience a subnet?

A. WBS

B. Kill points

C. GERT charts

D. A network template

9. You are the project manager for the POL Project. This project will use a three-point estimate to calculate the estimates for activity duration. For Activity D, you have the following information: P = 9 weeks, O = 4 weeks, M = 5 weeks. What is the result of this estimate?

A. 18 weeks

B. 6 weeks

C. 33.33 days

D. 3 weeks

10. You are the project manager for the YKL Project. This project will affect several lines of business at completion. You have elected to schedule each milestone in the project to end so the work does not affect current business cycles. This is an example of which one of the following?

A. Constraint

B. Expert judgment

C. WBS scheduling

D. Soft logic

11. You are the project manager for the MNB Project. You and your project team are about to enter into the activity duration estimating process. Which of the following will not be helpful in your meeting?

A. Constraints

B. Assumptions

C. The project charter

D. Identified risks

12. You are the project manager for a new training program at your customer's site. This program will require each of the customer's employees to attend the half-day class and complete an assessment exam. You will be completing the training at the customer's facility and will need a trainer for the duration of the training, which is six months. This is an example of which of the following?

    A. Resource requirements

    B. Assumption

    C. Cost constraint

    D. A human resource issue

13. You are the project manager for a construction company. Your firm has been contracted to complete the drilling of a well for a new cabin in Arkansas. The specification of the well is documented, but your company has little experience in well drilling in Arkansas. The stakeholder is concerned your time estimates are not accurate, since the soil and rock in Arkansas are quite different from the soil in your home state. Which one of the following can you use to ensure your project estimates are accurate?

    A. An order of magnitude

    B. A commercial duration estimating database

    C. Local contractors

    D. Soil samplings from the Arkansas government

14. You are the project manager for your organization. You and your project team are in conflict on the amount of time allotted to complete certain activities. Several of the team members want to bloat the time associated with activities to ensure they will have enough time to complete their tasks should something go awry. The law of economics that these tasks may suffer from is which one of the following?

    A. Parkinson's Law

    B. The law of diminishing returns

    C. Hertzberg's theory of motivation

    D. Oligopoly

15. You are the project manager for your organization. You and your project team are in conflict on the amount of time allotted to complete certain activities. Several of the team members want to bloat the time associated with activities to ensure they will have enough time to complete their tasks should something go awry. Instead of overestimating their project activities, the project team should use which of the following?

    A. Capital reserve

    B. Contingency plans

    C. Contingency reserve

    D. Assumptions of plus or minus a percentage

16. Which of the following is not an output from the activity duration estimating process?
   A. WBS
   B. Activity list updates
   C. A basis of estimates
   D. Duration estimates

17. You are the project manager for the 987 Project. Should this project run over schedule, it will cost your organization $35,000 per day in lost sales. With four months to completion, you realize the project is running late. You decide, with management's approval, to add more project team members to the plan to complete the work on time. This is an example of which of the following?
   A. Crashing
   B. Fast-tracking
   C. Expert judgment
   D. Cost-benefit analysis

18. You are the project manager for the 987 Project. Should this project run over schedule, it will cost your organization $35,000 per day in lost sales. With four months to completion, you realize the project is running late. You decide, with management's approval, to change the relationship between several of the work packages so they begin in tandem rather than sequentially. This is an example of which one of the following?
   A. Crashing
   B. Fast-tracking
   C. Expert judgment
   D. Cost-benefit analysis

19. Chris, a project manager for his company, is explaining the difference between a Gantt chart and a milestone chart. Which of the following best describes a Gantt chart?
   A. A Gantt chart depicts what was planned against what actually occurred.
   B. A Gantt chart compares the work in the project against the work that has been completed.
   C. A Gantt chart depicts the work in the project against a calendar.
   D. A Gantt chart depicts the work in the project against each resource's calendar.

20. Which of the following is a correct attribute of the critical path?
   A. It determines the earliest completion date.
   B. It has the smallest amount of float.
   C. It has the most activities in the PND.
   D. It is the path with the most expensive project activities.

21. You are the project manager for a construction project. Your foreman informs you that, due to the humidity, the concrete will need to cure for an additional 24 hours before the framing can begin. To accommodate the requirement, you add _____ time to the framing activity.
    A. Lead
    B. Lag
    C. Delay
    D. Slack

22. Management has informed you that you must flatten your project through resource-leveling heuristics. What is likely to happen to your project schedule if your project team members are only allowed to contribute 30 hours per week?
    A. The project schedule will increase.
    B. The project schedule will decrease.
    C. The project critical path will change.
    D. The project manager will need to use the critical chain method.

23. You are the project manager for a project with the following network diagram. Studying the following diagram, which path is the critical path?

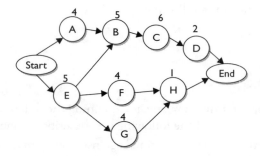

    A. ABCD
    B. EBCD
    C. EFH
    D. EGH

24. Bertha is the project manager for the HAR Project. The project is behind schedule, and Bertha has elected, with management's approval, to crash the critical path. This process adds more what? (Choose the best answer.)

    A. Cost
    B. Time
    C. Risk
    D. Documentation

25. Bertha is the project manager for the HAR Project. It's currently behind schedule, and Bertha has elected, with management's approval, to fast-track the critical path. This process adds more what? (Choose the best answer.)

    A. Cost
    B. Time
    C. Risk
    D. Documentation

SELF TEST ANSWERS

1. You are the project manager of the JHG Project. This project has 32 stakeholders and will require implementation activities in North and South America. You have been requested to provide a duration estimate for the project. Of the following, which will offer the best level of detail in your estimate?
   A. The resource calendar
   B. An order of magnitude
   C. A requirements document
   D. A stakeholder analysis

   ☑ **A.** The resource calendar is the best choice for this scenario, as it is the only activity duration estimating input listed.
   ☒ **B** is incorrect because the order of magnitude provides little information for accurate estimating. **C,** while tempting, is incorrect because the requirements document lists the high-level deliverable, while the WBS provides more detail. **D** is incorrect because stakeholder analysis does not provide enough information to accurately predict when the project will end.

2. Michael is the project manager of the 78GH Project. This project requires several members of the project team to complete a certification class for another project the week of November 2. This class causes some of the project activities on Michael's activities to be delayed from his target schedule. This is an example of which of the following?
   A. Hard logic
   B. External dependencies
   C. Soft logic
   D. Conflict of interest

   ☑ **B.** Before the work can begin, the certification class must be completed.
   ☒ **A** is incorrect; hard logic is the mandatory sequencing of particular events. **C** is incorrect because there is no preferential logic. **D** is incorrect because it does not apply to this scenario.

3. You are managing an interior decorating project. The walls are scheduled to be painted immediately after the primer. You have allowed 36 hours between the primer activity and the painting activity to ensure that the primer has cured. This is an example of which one of the following?
   A. Lead
   B. Lag

C. Soft logic

D. Finish-to-start relationship

☑ **B.** The time between the activities is lag time. The painting activity must wait 36 hours before it can begin.

☒ **A,** lead time, is when the activities are brought closer together or even overlap. **C,** soft logic, describes when activities are scheduled based on preferences, guidelines, or external conditions. **D** is incorrect because while this does describe a finish-to-start relationship, lag is a better choice because of the added waiting time.

4. As the project manager for the DFK Project, you are reviewing your project's network diagram (as shown in the following illustration):

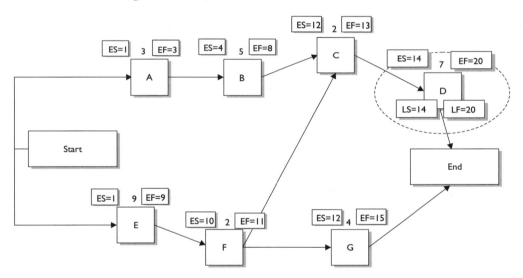

Given the diagram, what is the relationship between tasks F and G?

A. FS

B. SS

C. FF

D. SF

☑ **A.** G is slated to start immediately after F, so this is a finish-to-start relationship. In other words, F must finish so G may start.

☒ **B, C,** and **D** are all incorrect relationships.

5. You are the project manager for the LLL Project. Steven, a project team member, is confused about network diagrams. Specifically, he wants to know what the critical path is in a network diagram. Your answer is which one of the following?

   A. The critical path is the network that hosts the activities most critical to the project's success.
   B. The critical path is the path with the longest duration.
   C. The critical path is always one path that cannot be delayed, or the entire project will be delayed.
   D. The critical path is the path from start to completion with no deviation from the project plan.

   ☑ **B.** The critical path is always the path with the longest duration.
   ☒ **A** is incorrect because the critical path hosts the activities, not a network. **C** is a distracter and is incorrect because there can be more than one critical path in a network diagram. **D** is incorrect because it does not adequately describe the critical path.

6. What is the difference between PDM and ADM?

   A. ADM places activities on arrows, while PDM places activities on nodes.
   B. ADM is also known as AOA, while PDM is sometimes referred to as GERT.
   C. ADM hosts activities on nodes, while PDM hosts activities on arrows.
   D. PDM can have two types of relationships between tasks, while ADM can have only one type of relationship between tasks.

   ☑ **A.** ADM, the arrow diagramming method, is also known as "activity on arrow," while PDM, the precedence diagramming method, places activities on nodes. PDM is also known as "activity on nodes."
   ☒ **B** and **C** are incorrect because they do not accurately describe ADM and PDM. **D** is incorrect because PDM is allowed four different relationship types: FS, SF, FF, and SF.

7. You are creating a schedule duration estimate for the activities in the PDR Project. You're working with your project and comparing the results of a past similar project to predict the time of the current project. What estimating approach are you using?

   A. Organizational process assets
   B. Parametric
   C. Analogous
   D. PERT

☑ **C.** This is an example of an analogous estimate. You can remember this estimate approach by identifying the "analogy" between the two similar projects.

☒ **A** is incorrect because while the previous project data are part of organizational process assets, they are not an estimating approach. **B** is incorrect because parametric estimates use a parameter, such as five hours per unit. **D** is also incorrect because PERT uses an average of the optimistic, most likely, and pessimistic time estimates for each activity.

8. Where is a project manager most likely to experience a subnet?

    A. WBS

    B. Kill points

    C. GERT charts

    D. A network template

☑ **D.** Subnets are often included in network templates to summarize common activities in a project.

☒ **A, B,** and **C** do not use subnets.

9. You are the project manager for the POL Project. This project will use a three-point estimate to calculate the estimates for activity duration. For Activity D, you have the following information: P = 9, O = 4, M = 5. What is the result of this estimate?

    A. 18 weeks

    B. 6 weeks

    C. 33.33 days

    D. 3 weeks

☑ **B.** The formula is (P + 4M + O)/3. In this instance, the outcome is 6 weeks.

☒ **A, C,** and **D** are incorrect calculations, so they are incorrect.

10. You are the project manager for the YKL Project. This project will affect several lines of business at completion. You have elected to schedule each milestone in the project to end so the work does not affect current business cycles. This is an example of which one of the following?

    A. Constraint

    B. Expert judgment

    C. WBS scheduling

    D. Soft logic

☑   **D.** Soft logic allows the project manager to make decisions based on conditions outside of the project, best practices, or guidelines.
☒   **A** is incorrect because this is not an example of constraints, since the project manager is not required to use soft logic. **B** and **C** are incorrect; they do not describe the scenario fully.

11. You are the project manager for the MNB Project. You and your project team are about to enter into the activity duration estimating process. Which of the following will not be helpful in your meeting?
   A. Constraints
   B. Assumptions
   C. The project charter
   D. Identified risks

☑   **C.** The project charter is not an input to the activity duration estimating process.
☒   Choices **A, B,** and **D** are all correct choices because they are inputs to activity duration estimating.

12. You are the project manager for a new training program at your customer's site. This program will require each of the customer's employees to attend the half-day class and complete an assessment exam. You will be completing the training at the customer's facility and will need a trainer for the duration of the training, which is six months. This is an example of which of the following?
   A. Resource requirements
   B. Assumption
   C. Cost constraint
   D. A human resource issue

☑   **A.** The trainer is required for the project for six months.
☒   **B, C,** and **D** are incorrect because they do not describe the resource requirement of the trainer on the project.

13. You are the project manager for a construction company. Your firm has been contracted to complete the drilling of a well for a new cabin in Arkansas. The specification of the well is documented, but your company has little experience in well drilling in Arkansas. The stakeholder is concerned your time estimates are not accurate, since the soil and rock in Arkansas are quite different from the soil in your home state. Which one of the following can you use to ensure your project estimates are accurate?

A. An order of magnitude
B. A commercial duration estimating database
C. Local contractors
D. Soil samplings from the Arkansas government

☑ **B.** Commercial duration estimating databases are valid resources to confirm or base time estimates upon.
☒ **A** is incorrect because an order of magnitude offers very little detail on time estimates. **C** is incorrect because local contractors are not the best source for confirming time estimates; the question does not define if the contractors are local to Arkansas or to your home state. **D** is incorrect because commercial duration estimating databases are much more reliable in this scenario.

14. You are the project manager for your organization. You and your project team are in conflict on the amount of time allotted to complete certain activities. Several of the team members want to bloat the time associated with activities to ensure they will have enough time to complete their tasks should something go awry. The law of economics that these tasks may suffer from is which one of the following?
   A. Parkinson's Law
   B. The law of diminishing returns
   C. Hertzberg's theory of motivation
   D. Oligopoly

☑ **A.** Parkinson's Law states that work will expand to fulfill the time allotted to it.
☒ Bloated tasks will take all of the time allotted. Management reserve should be used instead. **B** is incorrect because this describes the relationship between effort, duration, and the maximum yield. **C** is incorrect because it describes personalities and worker motivation. **D** is incorrect because an oligopoly is a procurement issue where there are few vendors available to choose from. Plus, the vendors may seemingly have checks and balances with each other.

15. You are the project manager for your organization. You and your project team are in conflict on the amount of time allotted to complete certain activities. Several of the team members want to bloat the time associated with activities to ensure they will have enough time to complete their tasks should something go awry. Instead of overestimating their project activities, the project team should use which of the following?
   A. Capital reserve
   B. Contingency plans

C. Contingency reserve

D. Assumptions of plus or minus a percentage

☑ **C.** Rather than bloat activities, projects should use a contingency reserve. A contingency reserve is a portion of the project schedule allotted for time overruns on activities.

☒ **A** is incorrect because it does not describe the scenario. **B** is incorrect because contingency plans are a response to risk situations. **D** is incorrect because it describes a range of variance.

16. Which of the following is not an output from the activity duration estimating process?

A. WBS

B. Activity list updates

C. A basis of estimates

D. Duration estimates

☑ **A.** The WBS is not an output of activity duration estimating.

☒ Choices **B, C,** and **D** are incorrect because they are outputs of activity duration estimating.

17. You are the project manager for the 987 Project. Should this project run over schedule, it will cost your organization $35,000 per day in lost sales. With four months to completion, you realize the project is running late. You decide, with management's approval, to add more project team members to the plan to complete the work on time. This is an example of which of the following?

A. Crashing

B. Fast-tracking

C. Expert judgment

D. Cost-benefit analysis

☑ **A.** When more resources are added to a project to complete the work on time, this is called crashing.

☒ **B** is incorrect; fast-tracking is the process of changing the relationship between activities to allow tasks to overlap. **C** is incorrect because expert judgment is not used in this scenario. **D** is incorrect; cost-benefit analysis may be part of the process to decide the value of adding more workers to the schedule, but it is not the process described.

18. You are the project manager for the 987 Project. Should this project run over schedule, it will cost your organization $35,000 per day in lost sales. With four months to completion, you realize the project is running late. You decide, with management's approval, to change the relationship between several of the work packages so they begin in tandem rather than sequentially. This is an example of which one of the following?

    A. Crashing

    B. Fast-tracking

    C. Expert judgment

    D. Cost-benefit analysis

    ☑ **B.** Fast-tracking allows activities to operate in tandem with each other rather than sequentially.

    ☒ **A** is incorrect; when more resources are added to a project to complete the work on time, this is called crashing. **C** is incorrect, because expert judgment is not used in this scenario. **D** is incorrect; cost-benefit analysis may be part of the process to decide the value of fast-tracking the schedule, but it is not the process described.

19. Chris, a project manager for his company, is explaining the difference between a Gantt chart and a milestone chart. Which of the following best describes a Gantt chart?

    A. A Gantt chart depicts what was planned against what actually occurred.

    B. A Gantt chart compares the work in the project against the work that has been completed.

    C. A Gantt chart depicts the work in the project against a calendar.

    D. A Gantt chart depicts the work in the project against each resource's calendar.

    ☑ **C.** A Gantt chart is a bar chart that represents the duration of activities against a calendar. The length of the bars represents the length of activities, while the order of the bars represents the order of activities in the project.

    ☒ **A** and **B** are incorrect because this describes a tracking Gantt. **D** is incorrect because this does not describe a Gantt chart.

20. Which of the following is a correct attribute of the critical path?

    A. It determines the earliest completion date.

    B. It has the smallest amount of float.

    C. It has the most activities in the PND.

    D. It is the path with the most expensive project activities.

☑ **A.** Of all the choices presented, **A** is the best description of the critical path. The critical path is the path with the longest duration. There can be instances, however, when the project's expected end date is well beyond the duration of the scheduled work. In such cases, the critical path is considered the path with the least amount of float.

☒ Choices **B, C,** and **D** are incorrect because they are false descriptions of the critical path. The critical path has no float, has the longest duration, and does not necessarily have the most expensive activities.

21. You are the project manager for a construction project. Your foreman informs you that, due to the humidity, the concrete will need to cure for an additional 24 hours before the framing can begin. To accommodate the requirement, you add _____ time to the framing activity.

    A. Lead
    B. Lag
    C. Delay
    D. Slack

    ☑ **B.** You will add lag time to the framing activity. Lag is waiting time.
    ☒ **A** is incorrect; lead time allows activities to overlap. **C** is not the correct choice. **D** is also incorrect because slack is the amount of time a task can be delayed without delaying the scheduled start date of dependent activities.

22. Management has informed you that you must flatten your project through resource-leveling heuristics. What is likely to happen to your project schedule if your project team members are only allowed to contribute 30 hours per week?

    A. The project schedule will increase.
    B. The project schedule will decrease.
    C. The project critical path will change.
    D. The project manager will need to use the critical chain method.

    ☑ **A.** When the project schedule is flattened through resource leveling, the project duration will likely increase.
    ☒ **B, C,** and **D** are all incorrect; the project schedule will not decrease, and there's no evidence that the critical path will change. The project manager can use the critical chain method or not, and it will likely not affect the project duration.

23. You are the project manager for a project with the following network diagram. Studying the diagram, which path is the critical path?

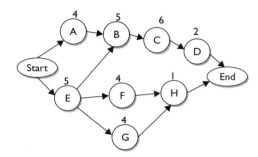

A. ABCD

B. EBCD

C. EFH

D. EGH

☑ **B** is the critical path because EBCD is the longest path to completion at 18 days.

☒ **A, C,** and **D** are incorrect because these paths have float.

24. Bertha is the project manager for the HAR Project. The project is behind schedule, and Bertha has elected, with management's approval, to crash the critical path. This process adds more what? (Choose the best answer.)

A. Cost

B. Time

C. Risk

D. Documentation

☑ **A.** Crashing involves adding resources, which typically increases cost.

☒ **B** is incorrect because crashing is an effort to reduce time, not add it. **C** may be correct, but it is not the best answer. **D** is incorrect.

25. Bertha is the project manager for the HAR Project. It's currently behind schedule, and Bertha has elected, with management's approval, to fast-track the critical path. This process adds more what? (Choose the best answer.)

    A. Cost
    B. Time
    C. Risk
    D. Documentation

    ☑ **C.** Fast-tracking adds risk because tasks are allowed to overlap.

    ☒ **A** may be correct in some instances, but it is not the best choice here. **B** is incorrect because Bertha wants to remove time, not add it. **D** is also incorrect.

7

Introducing Project Cost Management

Projects cost money. Ever worked with a client who had a huge vision for a project, but little capital to invest in that vision? Or worked with a client who gasped when you revealed how much it would cost to complete their desired scope of work? Or have you been fortunate and had a customer who accepted the costs for the project at face value, made certain the funds were available, and sent you on your way to complete the work? As a general rule, management and customers are always concerned with how much a project is going to cost in relation to how much a project is going to earn.

Most likely, there is more negotiating, questioning, and evaluating for larger projects than for smaller ones. The relationship between the project cost and the project scope should be direct: You get what you pay for. Think it's possible to buy a mansion at ranch home prices? Not likely. Think it's possible to run a worldwide marketing campaign at the cost of a postcard mailer? Not likely. A realistic expectation of what a project will cost will give great weight to the project's scope.

As the business need undergoes analysis, progressive elaboration and estimates are completed based on varying levels of detail, and eventually the cost of the project emerges. Often, however, predicted costs and actual costs vary. Poor planning, skewed assumptions, and overly optimistic estimates all contribute to this. A successful project manager must be able to plan, predict, budget, and control the costs of a project.

Costs associated with projects are not just the costs of goods procured to complete the project. The cost of the labor may be one of the biggest expenses of a project. The project manager must rely on time estimates to predict the cost of the labor to complete the project work. In addition, the cost of the equipment and materials needed to complete the project work must be factored into the project expenses. This chapter examines the management of project costs, how to predict them, account for them, and then, with plan in hand, to control them. We'll examine exactly how costs are planned for and taken into consideration by the performing organization and how the size of the project affects the cost estimating process.

CERTIFICATION OBJECTIVE 7.01

Estimating the Project Costs

Cost estimating is the process of calculating the costs of the identified resources needed to complete the project work. The person or group doing the estimating must consider the possible fluctuations, conditions, and other causes of variances that could affect the total cost of the estimate.

There is a distinct difference between cost estimating and pricing. A cost estimate is the cost of the resources required to complete the project work. Pricing, however, includes a profit margin. In other words, a company performing projects for other organizations may do a cost estimate to see how much the project is going to cost to complete. Then, with this cost information, they'll factor a profit into the project work, as shown.

More and more companies are requiring that the project manager calculate the project costs and then factor the ROI and other benefit models into the project product. The goal is to see the value of the project once its deliverables are in operation.

Considering the Cost Estimating Inputs

Cost estimating relies on several project components from the initiation and planning process groups. This process also relies on enterprise environmental factors, the processes and procedures unique to your organization, and the organizational process assets, such as historical information and forms and templates.

Using the Scope Baseline

You'll need the scope baseline, as it's the goal of the project team and the stakeholders: to create all of the elements in the project scope to satisfy the requirements of the project. The project scope statement pretty much follows the project manager around throughout the entire project, and it's useful to ensure that all of the requirements are being met.

At a deeper level, however, you'll want to rely on the WBS. Of course, the WBS is included—it's an input to seven major planning processes, all of which deal with costs.

- **Developing the project management plan**   This is the overarching project management plan that includes not only the cost management plan but also the information about how the project may be financed, contracted, and what the expectations in the organization are for cost management.

- **Defining the project activities** In some projects, the project has the cost of labor as part of its project expenses, but not in all projects. Any resources, such as equipment and material, will need to be paid for as part of the project budget.

- **Estimating the project costs** You'll use the WBS to help you identify how much each work package will cost, and this can help you create a definitive estimate (details coming up).

- **Determining the project budget** You can estimate all you want, but you never know how much a project costs until you're done. The project budget is the cost aggregation and cost reconciliation for each thing, service, and expense the project needs.

- **Planning the project quality** There is a cost associated with achieving the expected quality in a project. I'll discuss that more in Chapter 8.

- **Identifying the project risks** Risks often have a cost element associated with them, and the project manager and organization may create a contingency reserve to offset the risk exposure.

- **Planning the project procurement** When the project needs to procure materials, labor, or services, there is a cost element and purchasing process the project manager must follow.

Along with the WBS, you'll rely on the WBS dictionary as the third element of the scope baseline. The WBS dictionary provides information on each deliverable and the associated work needed to create the WBS component. In addition, the WBS may be referenced to an organization's code of accounts. The code of accounts is a coding system used by the performing organization's accounting system to account for the project work. Estimates within the project must be mapped to the correct code of accounts so that the organization's ledger reflects the actual work performed, the cost of the work performed, and any billing (internal or external) that was charged to the customer for the completed work.

Referencing the Project Schedule

Resources are more than just people—though people are a primary expense on most projects. The schedule management plan identifies what resources are needed, when they're needed, and the frequency of the need. Essentially, the schedule management plan is needed so that the project manager and the project team can estimate how much the resources will cost the project, when the funds will be used to employ or consume the resources, and the cost impact should the identified resources miss deadlines within the project.

Estimates of the duration of the activities, which predict the length of the project, are needed for decisions on financing the project. The length of the activities will help the performing organization calculate what the total cost of the project will be, including the finance charges. Recall the formula for present value? It's $PV = FV / (1 + i)^n$; PV is the present value, FV is the future value, i is the interest rate, and n is the number of time periods. The future value of the monies the project will earn may need to be measured against the present value to determine if the project is worth financing, as shown next.

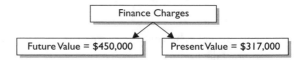

Calculations of the duration of activities are needed in order to extrapolate the total cost of the work packages. For example, if an activity is estimated to last 14 hours and Suzanne's cost per hour is $80, then the cost of the work package is $1,120. The duration shows management how long the project is expected to last and which activities will cost the most. It also provides the opportunity to resequence activities to shorten the project duration—which consequently shortens the finance period for the project.

on the **job**

Straight-line depreciation allows the organization to write off the same amount each year. The formula for straight-line depreciation is purchase value minus salvage value divided by number of years in use. For example, if the purchase price of a photocopier is $7,000 and the salvage value of the photocopier in five years is $2,000, the formula would read ($7,000 – $2,000)/ 5 = $1,000.

Resources can also cost the project if they miss deadlines with penalties, such as a schedule change in a union's contract, the cost of materials based on seasonal demand, and fines and penalties for failing to adhere to scheduled regulations.

Referencing the Human Resource Plan

The estimator has to know how much each resource costs, and the human resource plan may include this information, depending on the organizational policies, application area, and the type of project being completed. The cost should be in some unit of time or measure—such as cost per hour, cost per metric ton, or cost per use. If the rates of the resources are not known, the rates themselves may also have to be estimated. Of course, skewed rates on the estimates will result in a skewed estimate for the project. There are four categories of cost.

- **Direct costs**   These costs are attributed directly to the project work and cannot be shared among projects (airfare, hotels, long distance phone charges, and so on).

- **Indirect costs**   These costs are representative of more than one project (utilities for the performing organization, access to a training room, project management software license, and so on).

- **Variable costs**   These costs vary, depending on the conditions applied in the project (the number of meeting participants, the supply and demand of materials, and so on).

- **Fixed costs**   These costs remain constant throughout the project (the cost of a piece of rented equipment for the project, the cost of a consultant brought onto the project, and so on).

exam

ⓦatch   *Value engineering is a systematic approach to finding less costly ways to complete the same work. Project managers do this all the time: choosing the best resource to complete the work the fastest, with the highest quality, or with the appropriate materials while still keeping the overall project costs in check.*

Using the Risk Register

I've not said much about the risk register in the project. It's something that I'll discuss in detail in Chapter 11 on project risk management. However, due to the integrated nature of projects, this is one of those examples where I'll need to jump ahead just a bit. Risks, as you probably know from your project management experience, can have a positive or negative effect on the outcome of the project. All identified risks, their characteristics, status, and relevant notes are recorded in the risk register.

Most risks, especially the probable, high-impact, negative ones, need to pass through quantitative analysis to determine how much the risk may cost the project in time and cost. Based on risk analysis, the project manager creates a special budget just for the impact of project risks: the risk contingency reserve. You need the risk register here in cost estimating to determine how much cash you'll need to offset the risk events as part of your cost estimates.

Contingency reserves can also be allotted to deal with those pesky "unknown unknowns" that practically every project has to deal with. The "unknown unknowns" are essentially risks that are lurking within the project but that haven't been specifically identified by name, source, or probability.

Contingency reserves can be managed a number of different ways. The most common is to set aside an allotment of funds for the identified risks within the project. Another approach is to create a slush fund for the entire project for identified risks and "known unknowns." The final approach is an allotment of funds for categories of components based on the WBS and the project schedule. You'll see this again in much more detail later in this book. I hope you'll be able to sleep between now and Chapter 11.

Using Organizational Process Assets

One of the preferred organizational process assets is historical information. After all, if the project's been done before, why reinvent the wheel? Historical information is proven information and can come from several places:

- **Project files**   Past projects within the performing organization can be used as a reference to predict costs and time. Caution must be taken that the records referenced are accurate, somewhat current, and reflective of what was actually experienced in the historical project.

- **Commercial cost-estimating databases**   These databases provide estimates of what the project should cost based on the variables of the project, resources, and other conditions.

- **Team members**   Team members may have specific experience with the project costs or estimates. Recollections may be useful, but are highly unreliable when compared to documented results.

- **Lessons learned**   Lessons-learned documentation can help the project team estimate the current project if the lessons are from a similar project scope.

There are commercial estimating publications for different industries. These references can help the project estimator confirm and predict the accuracy of estimates. If a project manager elects to use one of these commercial databases, the estimate should include a pointer to this database for future reference and verification.

Estimating Project Costs

Management, customers, and certain stakeholders are all going to be interested in what the project is going to cost to complete. Several approaches to cost estimating exist, which we'll discuss in a moment. First, however, understand that cost estimates have a way of following the project manager around—especially the lowest initial cost estimate.

The estimates you'll want to know for the PMP exam, and for your career, are reflective of the accuracy of the information the estimate is based upon. The more accurate the information, the better the cost estimate will be. If you're steeped in experience in a particular industry, you'll probably have a good idea of what a project should cost based on your experience. Sometimes you may hire a consultant or rely on experts within your organization to help you predict the cost of a project. That's great! That's an example of expert judgment.

Using Analogous Estimating

Analogous estimating relies on historical information to predict the cost of the current project. It is also known as top-down estimating. The process of analogous estimating takes the actual cost of a historical project as a basis for the current project. The cost of the historical project is applied to the cost of the current project, taking into account the scope and size of the current project as well as other known variables.

Analogous estimating is a form of expert judgment. This estimating approach takes less time to complete than other estimating models, but is also less accurate. This top-down approach is good for fast estimates to get a general idea of what the project may cost.

The following is an example of analogous estimating: The Carlton Park Project was to grade and pave a sidewalk around a pond in the community park. The sidewalk of Carlton Park was 1,048 feet by 6 feet, had a textured surface, had some curves around trees, and cost $25,287 to complete. The current project, King Park, will have a similar surface and will cover 4,500 feet by 6 feet. The analogous estimate for this project, based on the work in Carlton Park, is $108,500. This is based on the price per foot of material at $4.02.

on the **!** **ⓙ o b** *As part of the planning process, the project manager must determine what resources are needed to complete the project. Resources include the people, equipment, and materials that will be utilized to complete the work. In addition, the project manager must identify the quantity of the needed resources and when the resources are needed for the project. The identification of the resources, the needed quantity, and the schedule of the resources are directly linked to the expected cost of the project work.*

Using Parametric Estimating

Parametric modeling uses a mathematical model based on known parameters to predict the cost of a project. The parameters in the model can vary based on the type of work being completed and can be measured by cost per cubic yard, cost per unit, and so on. A complex parameter can be cost per unit, with adjustment factors based on the conditions of the project. The adjustment factors may have additional modifying factors, depending on additional conditions. For example, parametric estimating could say that the cost per square foot of construction is $28 using standard materials, and then could charge additional fees if the client varies the materials.

To use parametric modeling, the factors the model is based on must be accurate. The factors within the model are quantifiable and don't vary much based on the effort applied to the activity. And finally, the model must be scalable between project sizes. The parametric model using a scalable cost-per-unit approach is depicted next.

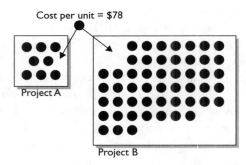

Cost per unit = $78

Project A

Project B

There are two types of parametric estimating.

■ **Regression analysis** This is a statistical approach to predict what future values may be, based on historical values. Regression analysis creates quantitative predictions based on variables within one value to predict variables in another. This form of estimating relies solely on pure statistical math to reveal relationships between variables and predict future values. In other words, it helps determine how much an organization needs to move backwards in order to go forwards. It also helps determine the cost of the regression and how long it may take to recoup the cost by the project's solution.

■ **Learning curve** This approach is simple: The cost per unit decreases the more units workers complete because workers learn as they complete the required work. The more an individual completes an activity, the easier it is to complete. The estimate is considered parametric, since the formula is based on repetitive activities, such as wiring telephone jacks, painting hotel rooms, or other activities that are completed over and over within a project. The cost per unit decreases as the experience increases because the time to complete the work is shortened.

Don't worry too much about regression analysis for the exam.

Learning curve is the topic you're more likely to have questions on.

Using Bottom-Up Estimating

Bottom-up estimating starts from zero, accounts for each component of the WBS, and arrives at a sum for the project. It is completed with the project team and can be one of the most time-consuming methods used to predict project costs. While this method is more expensive because of the time invested to create the estimate, it is also one of the most accurate. A fringe benefit of completing a bottom-up estimate is that the project team may buy into the project work since they see the cost and value of each cost within the project.

Creating a Three-Point Cost Estimate

It's risky to sometimes use just one cost estimate for a project's activity, especially when it's work that hasn't been completed before. And like any project work, you don't know how much it's really going to cost until you pay for it. Issues, errors, delays, and unknown risks can affect the project cost. A three-point cost estimate attempts to find the average of the cost of an activity using three factors.

- Optimistic cost estimate
- Most likely cost estimate
- Pessimistic cost estimate

You can then simply sum up the three cost estimate values and divide by three. Or you can use the PERT approach, which is slightly different. PERT is a weighted average to the most likely cost estimate value. The PERT formula is the optimistic cost estimate, plus four times the most likely cost estimate, plus the pessimistic cost estimate. That sum is then divided by six. Figure 7-1 shows the slight difference between a true average of the costs and the PERT approach.

In either approach, the basic average or PERT, you have to create three cost estimates for each activity. This can get tiresome and overwhelming, especially on a larger project. And if you elect to use an average estimate, be certain to document the approach you took and record the actual costs of the project activities for future historical information.

Using Computer Software

While the PMP examination is vendor-neutral, a general knowledge of how computer software can assist the project manager is needed. Several different

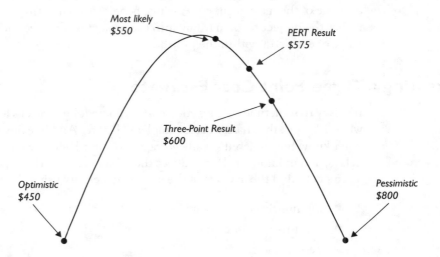

FIGURE 7-1

Costs can be averaged with PERT or three-point estimates.

Three-Point Estimate
Optimistic – $450
Most likely – $550
Pessimistic – $800
(450 + 550 + 800)/3 = $600

PERT Estimate
Optimistic – $450
Most likely – $550
Pessimistic – $800
(450 + (4 × 550) + 800)/6 = $575

Most likely
$550

PERT Result
$575

Three-Point Result
$600

Optimistic
$450

Pessimistic
$800

computer programs are available that can streamline project work estimates and increase their accuracy. These tools can include project management software, spreadsheet programs, and simulations.

Analyzing Vendor Bids

Sometimes it's just more cost-effective to hire someone else to do the work. Other times, the project manager has no choice because the needed skill set doesn't exist within the organization. In either condition, the vendors' bids need to be analyzed to determine which vendor should be selected based on their ability to satisfy the project scope, the expected quality, and the cost of their services. We'll talk all about procurement in Chapter 12.

CERTIFICATION OBJECTIVE 7.02

Analyzing Cost Estimating Results

The output of cost estimating is the actual cost estimates of the resources required to complete the project work. The estimate is typically quantitative and can be presented in detail against the WBS components or summarized in terms of a grand total according to various phases of the project or its major deliverables. Each resource in the project must be accounted for and assigned to a cost category. Categories include the following:

- Labor costs
- Material costs
- Travel costs
- Supplies costs
- Hardware costs
- Software costs
- Special categories (inflation, cost reserve, and so on)

The cost of the project is expressed in monetary terms, such as dollars, euros, or yen, so management can compare projects based on costs. It may be acceptable, depending on the demands of the performing organization, to provide estimates in staffing hours or days of work to complete the project along with the estimated costs.

As projects have risks, the cost of the risks should be identified along with the cost of the risk responses. The project manager should list the risks, their expected risk event value, and the response to the risk should it come into play. We'll cover risk management in detail in Chapter 11.

The project manager also has to consider changes to the project scope. Chances are that if the project scope increases in size, the project budget should reflect these changes. A failure to offset approved changes with an appropriate dollar amount will skew the project's cost baselines and show a false variance.

Refining the Cost Estimates

Cost estimates can also pass through progressive elaboration. As more details are acquired as the project progresses, the estimates are refined. Industry guidelines and organizational policies may define how the estimates are refined, but there are three generally accepted categories of estimating accuracy.

- **Rough order of magnitude** This estimate is "rough" and is used during the initiating processes and in top-down estimates. The range of variance for the estimate can be from –25 percent to +75 percent.

- **Budget estimate** This estimate is also somewhat broad and is used early in the planning processes and also in top-down estimates. The range of variance for the estimate can be from –10 percent to +25 percent.

- **Definitive estimates** This estimate type is one of the most accurate. It's used late in the planning processes and is associated with bottom-up estimating. The range of variance for the estimate can be from –5 percent to +10 percent.

Considering the Supporting Detail

Once the estimates have been completed, the basis of the estimates must be organized and documented to show how the estimates were created. This material, even the notes that contributed to the estimates, may provide valuable information later in the project. Specifically, the supporting detail includes the following:

- **Information on the project scope work** This may be provided by referencing the WBS.

- **Information on the approach used in developing the cost estimates** This can include how the estimate was accomplished and the parties involved with the estimate.

- **Information on the assumptions and constraints made while developing the cost estimates** Assumptions and constraints can be wrong and can change the entire cost estimate. The project manager must list what assumptions and constraints were made during the cost estimate in order to communicate with stakeholders how she arrived at the estimate.

- **Information on the range of variance in the estimate** For example, based on the estimating method used, the project cost may be $220,000 ± $15,000. This project cost may be as low as $205,000 or as high as $235,000.

Developing the Cost Management Plan

The cost management plan details how variances from the project costs will be managed. The performing organization may have policies and procedures on the expected reactions to cost variances within the project. For example, variances over a set dollar amount may prompt the project manager to create a variance report, meet with management, or even initiate an audit.

CERTIFICATION OBJECTIVE 7.03

Creating a Project Budget

Cost budgeting is the process of assigning a cost to an individual work package. The goal of this process is to assign costs to the work in the project so it can be measured for performance. This is the creation of the cost baseline, as shown.

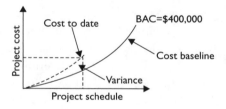

Cost budgeting and cost estimates may go hand in hand, but estimating should be completed before a budget is requested—or assigned. Cost budgeting applies the cost estimates over time. This results in a time-phased estimate for cost, allowing an organization to predict cash flow needs. The difference between cost estimates and cost budgeting is that cost estimates show costs by category, whereas a cost budget shows costs across time.

Developing the Project Budget

Many of the tools and techniques used to create the project cost estimates are also used to create the project budget. The following is a quick listing of the tools you can expect to see on the PMP exam:

- **Cost aggregation** Costs are parallel to each WBS work package. The costs of each work package are aggregated to their corresponding control accounts. Each control account then is aggregated to the sum of the project costs.

■ **Reserve analysis** You should be familiar with two reserves for your PMP exam. The first you've already learned about: the risk contingency reserve. The second cost reserve is for management reserve, and this chunk of cash is for unplanned changes to the project scope and cost. It's a buffer of cash for fluctuations for cost, errors, or other increases in project cost. These reserves are not part of the cost baseline, but are part of the project budget. In other words, you don't use these funds unless there's a problem in the project.

■ **Historical relationships** This approach uses a parametric model to extrapolate what costs will be for a project (for example, cost per hour and cost per unit). It can include variables and points based on conditions. This approach might also use a top-down estimate type based on historical information. A top-down estimate is also known as an analogous estimate type.

■ **Funding limit reconciliation** Organizations only have so much cash to allot to projects—and no, you can't have all the monies right now. Funding limit reconciliation is an organization's approach to managing cash flow against the project deliverables based on a schedule, milestone accomplishments, or data constraints. This helps an organization plan when monies will be devoted to a project rather than using all of the funds available at the start of a project. In other words, the monies for a project budget will become available based on dates and/or deliverables. If the project doesn't hit predetermined dates and products that were set as milestones, the additional funding becomes questionable.

Creating the Cost Baseline

A project's cost baseline shows what is expected to be spent on the project. It's usually shown in an S-curve, as in Figure 7-2. The idea of the cost baseline allows the project manager and management to predict when the project will be spending

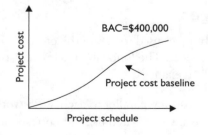

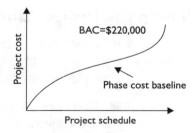

monies and over what time period. The purpose of the cost baseline is to measure and predict project performance.

Large projects that have multiple deliverables may have multiple cost baselines to illustrate the costs within each phase. In addition, larger projects may have cost baselines to predict spending plans, cash flows of the project, and overall project performance.

The purpose of a cost baseline is to measure performance, and a baseline will predict the expenses over the life of the project. Any discrepancies early on between the predicted baseline and the actual costs serve as a signal that the project is slipping.

Establishing Project Funding Requirements

The project's cost baseline can help the project manager and the organization determine when the project will need cash infusions. Based on phases, milestones, and capital expenses, the project funding requirements can be mapped to the project schedule and the organization can plan accordingly. This is where the concept of project step funding originates from. The curve of the project's timeline is funded in steps, where "step" is an amount of funds allotted to the project to reach the next milestone in the project.

<table>
<tr><td>

Recall from the project lifecycle that milestones are usually tied to the completion of project phases. Each phase creates a deliverable and usually

</td><td>

allows the project to move on to the next phase of project execution. The pause for review and determination of additional funds for the project is called a phase gate.

</td></tr>
</table>

CERTIFICATION OBJECTIVE 7.04

Implementing Cost Control

Cost control focuses on the ability of costs to change and on the ways of allowing or preventing cost changes from happening. When a change does occur, the project manager must document the change and the reason why the change occurred and, if necessary, create a variance report. Cost control is concerned with understanding why the cost variances, both good and bad, have occurred. The "why" behind the variances allows the project manager to make appropriate decisions on future project actions.

Ignoring the project cost variances may cause the project to suffer from budget shortages, additional risks, or scheduling problems. When cost variances happen, they must be examined, recorded, and investigated. Cost control allows the project manager to confront the problem, find a solution, and then act accordingly. Specifically, cost control focuses on the following activities:

- Controlling causes of change to ensure the changes are actually needed
- Controlling and documenting changes to the cost baseline as they happen
- Controlling changes in the project and their influence on cost
- Performing cost monitoring to recognize and understand cost variances
- Recording appropriate cost changes in the cost baseline
- Preventing unauthorized changes to the cost baseline
- Communicating the cost changes to the proper stakeholders
- Working to bring and maintain costs within an acceptable range

Considering Cost Control Inputs

To implement cost control, the project manager must rely on several documents and processes.

- **Cost performance baseline**   The cost performance baseline is the expected cost the project will incur. This time-phased budget reflects the amount that will be spent throughout the project. Recall that the cost performance baseline is a tool used to measure project performance. And yes, it's the same thing as the cost baseline.
- **Cost management plan**   The cost management plan dictates how cost variances will be managed.
- **Project funding requirements**   The funds for a project are not allotted all at once, but stair-stepped in alignment with project deliverables. Thus, as the project moves towards completion, additional funding is allotted. This allows for cash-flow forecasting. In other words, an organization doesn't need to have all of the project's budget allotted at the start of the project, but it

can predict, based on expected income, that all of the project's budget will be available in incremental steps.

- ■ **Performance reports**   These reports focus on project cost performance, project scope, and planned performance versus actual performance. The reports may vary according to stakeholder needs. We'll discuss performance reporting in detail in Chapter 10.

- ■ **Change requests**   When changes to the project scope are requested, an analysis of the associated costs to complete the proposed change is required. In some instances, such as removing a portion of the project deliverable, a change request may reduce the project cost.

Creating a Cost Change Control System

Sometimes a project manager must add or remove costs from a project. The cost change control system is part of the integrated change control system and documents the procedures to request, approve, and incorporate changes to project costs.

When a cost change enters the system, there is appropriate paperwork, a tracking system, and procedures the project manager must follow to obtain approval on the proposed change. Figure 7-3 demonstrates a typical workflow for cost change approval. If a change gets approved, the cost baseline is updated to reflect the approved changes. If a request gets denied, the denial must be documented for future potential reference.

FIGURE 7-3

A cost change control system tracks and documents cost changes.

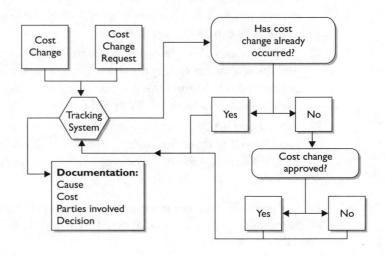

Measuring Project Performance

Earned value management (EVM) is the process of measuring the performance of project work against a plan to identify variances. It can also be useful in predicting future variances and the final costs at completion. It is a system of mathematical formulas that compares work performed against work planned and measures the actual cost of the work performed. EVM is an important part of cost control since it allows a project manager to predict future variances from the expenses to date within the project.

See the video Earned Value Management.

In regard to cost management, EVM is concerned with the relationships between three formulas that reflect project performance. Figure 7-4 demonstrates the connection between the following EVM values:

- **Planned value (PV)**   Planned value is the work scheduled and the budget authorized to accomplish that work. For example, if a project has a budget of $100,000 and month six represents 50 percent of the project work, the PV for month six is $50,000. The entire project's planned value—that is, what the project should be worth at completion—is known as the budget at completion. You might also see the sum of the planned value called the performance measurement baseline.

- **Earned value (EV)**   Earned value is the physical work completed to date and the authorized budget for that work. For example, if a project has a budget of $100,000 and the work completed to date represents 25 percent of the entire project work, its EV is $25,000.

- **Actual cost (AC)**   Actual cost is the actual amount of monies the project has required to date. For example, if a project has a budget of $100,000 and $35,000 has been spent on the project to date, the AC of the project would be $35,000.

These three values are key information about the worth of the project to date (EV), the cost of the project work to date (AC), and the planned value of the work to date (PV).

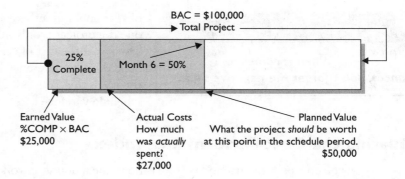

FIGURE 7-4

Earned value management measures project performance.

Finding the Variances

At the end of the project, will there be a budget variance (VAR)? Any variance at the end of the project is calculated by subtracting the actual costs (ACs) of the project work from the budget at completion (BAC). The term BAC refers to the estimated budget at completion—what you and the project customer agree the project will likely cost. Of course, you don't actually know how much the project will cost until it's completely finished. So throughout the project, a variance is any result that is different from what is planned or expected.

Cost Variances

The cost variance (CV) is the difference between the earned value and the actual costs (AC). For example, for a project that has a budget of $200,000 and has earned or completed 10 percent of the project value, the EV is $20,000. However, due to some unforeseen incidents, the project manager had to spend $25,000 to complete that $20,000 worth of work. The AC of the project, at this point, is $25,000 and the cost variance is –$5,000. Thus, the equation for cost variance is CV = EV – AC.

Schedule Variances

A schedule variance (SV) is the value that represents the difference between where the project was planned to be at a certain point in time and where the project actually is. For example, consider a project with a budget of $200,000 that's expected to last two years. At the end of year one, the project team has planned that the project be 60 percent complete. Thus, the planned value (PV) for 60 percent completion equates to $120,000—the expected worth of the project work at the end

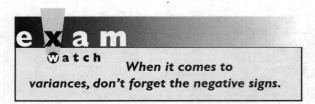

When it comes to variances, don't forget the negative signs.

of year one. But let's say that at the end of year one the project is only 40 percent complete. The EV at the end of year one is, therefore, $80,000. The difference between the PV and the EV is the SV: –$40,000. The equation for schedule variance is SV = EV – PV.

Calculating the Cost Performance Index

The cost performance index (CPI) shows the amount of work the project is completing per dollar spent on the project. In other words, a CPI of 0.93 means it is costing $1.00 for every 93 cents' worth of work. Or you could say the project is losing seven cents on every dollar spent on the project. Let's say a project has an EV of $25,000 and an AC of $27,000. The CPI for this project is thus 0.93. The closer the number is to 1, the better the project is doing. The equation for cost performance index is CPI = EV / AC.

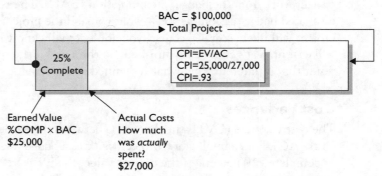

CPI is a value that shows how the project costs are performing to plan. It relates the work you've accomplished to the amount you've spent to accomplish it. A project with a CPI of 0.93 means you're spending 1.00 for every 0.93 worth of work accomplished. Therefore, a CPI under 1.00 means the project is performing poorly against the plan. However, a CPI over 1.00 does not necessarily mean that the project is performing well either. It could mean that estimates were inflated or that an expenditure for equipment is late or sitting in accounts payable and has not yet been entered into the project accounting cycle.

Finding the Schedule Performance Index

The schedule performance index (SPI) is similar to the CPI. The SPI, however, reveals how closely the project is on schedule. Again, as with the CPI, the closer the quotient is to 1, the better. The formula is EV divided by the PV. In our example, the EV is $20,000, and let's say the PV, where the project is supposed to be, is calculated as $30,000. The SPI for this project is then 0.67—way off target! The equation for schedule performance index is SPI = EV / PV.

Preparing for the Estimate at Completion

The estimate at completion (EAC) is a hypothesis of what the total cost of the project will be. Before the project begins, the project manager completes an estimate for the project deliverables based on the scope baseline. As the project progresses, there will be in most projects some variances between what the cost estimate was and what the actual cost is. The difference between these estimates is the variance for the deliverable.

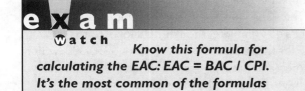

exam

@atch *Know this formula for calculating the EAC: EAC = BAC / CPI. It's the most common of the formulas presented.*

The estimate at completion (EAC) is a prediction of what the final project cost will be based on experiences in the project so far. There are several different formulas for calculating the EAC, as Figure 7-5 demonstrates. For now, and for the exam, here's the EAC formula you'll need to know: EAC = BAC / CPI. In our project, the BAC is $200,000. The CPI was calculated to be 0.80. The EAC for this project is $250,000.

Considering Project Performance

Another variation of the EAC is to consider the project performance beyond just the CPI. This approach looks at the project performance, good or bad, and considers

FIGURE 7-5			
There are many approaches to calculating the EAC.	$EAC = \dfrac{BAC}{CPI}$	$EAC = \dfrac{\$575,000}{.91}$	EAC = $631,868
	EAC = AC+ETC	EAC = $20,000+$175,000	EAC = $195,000
	EAC = AC+BAC–EV	EAC = $7,000+24,500–$2,450	EAC = $29,050
	$EAC = AC + \dfrac{(BAC-EV)}{CPI}$	$EAC = \$45,000 + \dfrac{(250,000-37,500)}{.83}$	EAC = $301,024

the actual costs of the project to date, the budget at completion, and the project's earned value. This EAC formula is: EAC = AC + BAC – EV.

For example, consider a project with a BAC of $350,000 that's 45 percent complete though it's supposed to be 60 percent complete. The earned value for this project is 45 percent of the $350,000, which is $157,500. In this scenario, the project has actually spent $185,000—considerably more than what the project should have spent. Let's plug in this EAC formula. EAC = $185,000 + $350,000 – $157,500. The EAC for this project using this formula would be $377,500.

Consider Project Variances

Sometimes a project may have some wild swings on the project cost variances and the project schedule variances, and you want to take these variances into consideration when predicting the project's estimate at completion. Usually, it's the project schedule that's affecting the project's ability to meet its cost obligations because the planned value continues to slip, which wrecks the SPI. Add to that the concept that the longer a project takes to complete, the more likely that the project costs will increase.

Here's this windy formula (get your slide rule out): EAC = AC + [(BAC – EV) / (CPI × SPI)]. I'll try this one using the same values as the last example. Consider a project with a BAC of $350,000 that's 45 complete, though it's supposed to be 60 percent complete. The earned value for this project is 45 percent of $350,000, which is $157,500. In this scenario, the project has actually spent $185,000—considerably more than what the project should have. Here are the parts of our formula:

Actual cost = $185,000

Planned value = $210,000

Budget at completion = $350,000

Earned value = $157,500

Cost performance index = 0.85

Schedule performance index = 0.75

I'll plug these values into the formula EAC = AC + [(BAC – EV) / (CPI × SPI)]:

EAC = $185,000 + [($350,000 – $157,500) / (0.85 × 0.75)]
EAC = $185,000 + (192,500 / 0.64)
EAC = $185,000 + 300,781.25
EAC = $485,781.25

Finding the Estimate to Complete

The estimate to complete (ETC) shows how much more money will be needed to complete the project. To calculate the ETC, you need to know another formula: the estimate at completion (EAC). Remember that the EAC is what you predict the project will cost based on current conditions. The estimate to complete is a pretty straightforward formula: EAC – AC. Let's say our EAC was calculated to be $250,000 and that our AC is currently $25,000; our ETC would then be $225,000.

Accounting for Flawed Estimates

Imagine a project to install a new operating system on 1,000 workstations. One of the assumptions the project team made was that each workstation had the correct hardware to install the operating system automatically. As it turns out, this assumption was wrong, and now the project team must change their approach to installing the operating system.

Because the assumption to install the operating system was flawed, a new estimate to complete the project is needed. This is the most accurate approach in estimating how much more the project will cost, but it's the hardest to do. This new estimate to complete the work is known as the estimate to complete (ETC). The ETC represents how much more money is needed to complete the project work, and its formula is simply a revised estimate of how much more the remaining work will cost to complete. Nothing tricky here.

Accounting for Anomalies

During a project, sometimes weird stuff happens. These anomalies, or weird stuff, can cause project costs to be skewed. For example, consider a project with a $10,000 budget to construct a wooden fence around a property line. One of the project team members makes a mistake while installing the wooden fence and reverses the face of the fencing material. In other words, the material for the outside of the fence faces the wrong direction.

The project now has to invest additional time to remove the fence material, correct the problem, and replace any wood that may have been damaged in the incorrect installation. The project, mistakes and all, is thus considered 20 percent done, so the earned value is $2,000. This anomaly likely won't happen again, but it will add costs to the project.

For these instances, when events happen but the project manager doesn't expect similar events to happen again, the following ETC formula should be used: ETC = (BAC – EV). Let's try this out with our fencing project. The project's EV is only

$2,000 since the project has barely started. The formula would read ETC = $10,000 − $2,000.

Accounting for Typical Variances

This last ETC formula is used when existing variances in the project are expected to be typical of the remaining variances in the project. For example, a project manager has overestimated the competence of the workers to complete the project work. Because the project team is not performing at the level the project manager expected, work is completed late and in a faulty manner. Rework has been a common theme for this project.

The formula for these instances is ETC = (BAC − EV) / CPI. In our example, let's say the AC is $45,000, the BAC is $250,000, the EV is $37,500, and our CPI is calculated to be 0.83. The ETC formula for this project is ETC = ($250,000 − $37,500) / 0.83. The result of the formula (following the order of operations) is thus $256,024.

Calculating the To-Complete Performance Index

Imagine a formula that would tell you if the project can meet the budget at completion based on current conditions. Or imagine a formula that can predict if the project can even achieve your new estimate at completion. Well, forget your imagination and just use the to-complete performance index (TCPI). This formula can forecast the likelihood of a project to achieve its goals based on what's happening in the project right now. There are two different flavors for the TCPI, depending on what you want to accomplish.

- If you want to see if your project can meet the budget at completion, you'll use this formula: TCPI = (BAC − EV) / (BAC − AC).

- If you want to see if your project can meet the newly created estimate at completion, you'll use this version of the formula: TCPI = (BAC − EV) / (EAC − AC).

Anything greater than 1 in either formula means that you'll have to be more efficient than you planned to achieve the BAC or the EAC, depending on whichever formula you've used. Basically, the greater the number is over 1, the less likely it is that you'll be able to meet your BAC or EAC. The lower the number is from 1, the more likely you are to reach your BAC or EAC (again, depending on which formula you've used).

Finding the Variance at Completion

Whenever you talk about variances, it's the difference between what was expected and what was experienced. The formula for the variance at completion (VAC) is VAC = BAC – EAC. In our example, the BAC was \$200,000 and the EAC was \$250,000, so the VAC is predicted to be \$50,000.

The Five EVM Formula Rules

For EVM formulas, the following five rules should be remembered:

1. Always start with EV.
2. Variance means subtraction.
3. Index means division.
4. Less than 1 is bad in an index.
5. Negative is bad in a variance.

The formulas for earned value analysis can be completed manually or through project management software. For the exam, you'll want to memorize these formulas. Table 7-1 shows a summary of all the formulas, as well as a sample, albeit goofy, mnemonic device.

PMP
Coach

These aren't much to memorize, I know, but you should. While you won't have an overwhelming amount of EVM questions on your exam, these are free points if you know the formulas and can do the math.

ON THE CD

On the CD, I have a present for you. It's a Microsoft Excel spreadsheet called "EVWorksheet." It has all of these formulas in action. I recommend you make up some numbers to test your ability to complete these formulas and then plug your values into Excel to confirm your math. Enjoy!

TABLE 7-1 A Summary of EVM Formulas

Name	Formula	Sample Mnemonic Device
Planned value	PV= percent complete of where the project should be	Please
Earned value	EV = percent complete × budget at completion	Eat
Cost variance	CV = EV – AC	Carl's
Schedule variance	SV = EV – PV	Sugar
Cost performance index	CPI = EV / AC	Candy
Schedule performance index	SPI = EV / PV	S (This and the following two spell "SEE")
Estimate at completion	EAC = BAC / CPI	E
Estimate to complete	ETC = EAC – AC	E
To-complete performance index (Using the BAC)	(BAC – EV) / (BAC – AC)	The
To-complete performance index (Using the EAC)	(BAC – EV) / (EAC – AC)	Taffy
Variance at completion	VAC = BAC – EAC	Violin

Additional Planning

Planning is an iterative process. Throughout the project, there will be demands for additional planning—and an output of cost control is one of those demands. Consider a project that must complete by a given date and that also has a set budget. The balance between the schedule and the cost must be kept. The project manager can't assign a large crew to complete the project work if the budget won't allow it. The project manager must, through planning, get as creative as possible to figure out an approach to accomplish the project without exceeding the budget.

The balance between cost and schedule is an ongoing battle. While it's usually easier to get more time than money, this isn't always the case. Consider deadlines that can't be moved; or perhaps the company faces fines and penalties; or a deadline that centers on a tradeshow, an expo, or the start of the school year.

Using Computers

It's hard to imagine a project, especially a large project, moving forward without the use of computers. Project managers can rely on project management software and spreadsheet programs to assist them in calculating actual costs, earned value, and planned value.

on the **J**ob

It's not hard to create a spreadsheet with the appropriate earned value formulas. Once the spreadsheet has been created, you can save it as a template and use it on multiple projects. If you want, and if your software allows it, you can tie in multiple earned value spreadsheets to a master file to track all of your projects at a glance.

CERTIFICATION OBJECTIVE 7.06

Considering the Cost Control Results

Cost control is an ongoing process throughout the project. The project manager must actively monitor the project for variances to costs. Specifically, the project manager should always do the following:

- Monitor cost variances and then understand why variances have occurred.
- Update the cost baseline as needed based on approved changes.
- Work with the conditions and stakeholders to prevent unnecessary changes to the cost baseline.
- Communicate to the appropriate stakeholders cost changes as they occur.
- Maintain costs within an acceptable and agreed-upon range.

Revising the Cost Estimates

As the project progresses and more detail becomes available, there may be a need to update the cost estimates. A revision to the cost estimates requires communication with the key stakeholders to share why the costs were revised. A revision to the cost estimates may have a ripple effect: Other parts of the project may need to be adjusted to account for the changes in cost, the sequence of events may need to be reordered, and resources may have to be changed. In some instances, the revision of the estimates may be expected, as with phased-gate estimating in a long project.

Updating the Budget

Updating the budget is slightly different from revising a cost estimate. Budget updates allow the cost baseline to be changed. The cost baseline is the "before project snapshot" of what the total project scope and the individual WBS components should cost. Should the project scope grow, as shown next, the cost will also likely change to be able to fulfill the new scope.

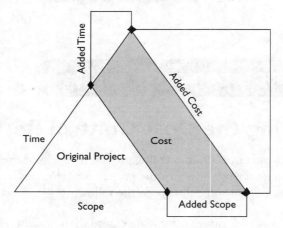

If a project undergoes drastic changes—due to large changes to the project scope, false assumptions, or new demands from the customer—it may be necessary to rebaseline the project cost. Rebaselining is done only in drastic changes, as it essentially resets the project.

Applying Corrective Actions

Throughout a project, the project manager will apply corrective actions. Corrective actions are any actions applied to project performance to bring the project back into alignment with the project plan. Corrective actions can be scheduling changes, a shift in resources, or a different approach to completing the project work—essentially any action, even nudges or shoves, designed to bring the project back to its expected level of performance.

Updating Lessons Learned

As part of cost control, the project manager should update the lessons-learned document to reflect the decisions behind the actions taken. For example, the project manager should identify the following:

- Any changes to the cost baseline and why they were approved
- Corrective actions and why they were implemented
- Cost control challenges and issues, and how they were resolved
- Other cost control information that may be beneficial for other projects

CERTIFICATION SUMMARY

There are several contributing factors to cost on any project: the expense of the labor to complete the project, the expense of materials needed to complete the project, and the expense of the equipment needed to complete a project. These expenses must be estimated, planned for, and monitored for a project to finish on budget.

Management and customers will want to know how much a project is going to cost so that they can determine if the project is worth doing, if the project deliverable will be worth the cost, and if the project will be profitable. The estimates for project costs can come in several forms.

- **Analogous estimating**   Uses similar historical information to predict the cost of the current project.
- **Top-down estimating**   Uses a similar project as a cost baseline and factors in current project conditions to predict costs. Note that analogous estimating is also top-down estimating.
- **Parametric estimating**   Uses a parameter, such as cost per metric ton, to predict project costs.
- **Bottom-up estimating**   Starts at zero and adds expenses from the bottom up.

The resources needed to complete a project may be one of the biggest expenses in the project's budget. The activities the resources complete must be worthy of the resources' time. In other words, the project manager does not want to assign a $125-per-hour engineer to perform filing that a $15-per-hour administrative assistant is qualified to do. Accurate assignment of project resources to project activities helps prevent waste.

Projects also have four different kinds of cost.

- **Direct costs** These costs are attributed directly to the project and cannot be shared with operations or other projects.
- **Indirect costs** These costs can be shared across multiple projects that use the same resources—such as for a training room or piece of equipment.
- **Variable costs** Costs that vary depending on the conditions within the project.
- **Fixed costs** Costs that remain the same throughout the project.

There is one last cost, called opportunity cost. This is a special cost because it really doesn't cost the organization anything out of pocket, but rather the cost of a lost opportunity. Opportunity costs are an expense that companies that complete projects for other organizations should realize. When an organization that completes projects for others must forgo one project in order to complete the other, the value of the forgone project is the opportunity cost. For example, let's say a company has two projects it can complete, but it must choose only one of them. Project A is worth $75,000, while Project B is worth $50,000. If the company chooses Project A, the opportunity cost is thus $50,000 because the company misses out on the opportunity.

KEY TERMS

If you're serious about passing the PMP exam, memorize these terms and their definitions. For maximum value, create your own flashcards based on these definitions and review them daily.

actual costs The amount of funds the project has spent to date. The difference between actual costs and the earned value will reveal the cost variance.

analogous estimating This relies on historical information to predict estimates for current projects. Analogous estimating is also known as top-down estimating and is a form of expert judgment.

bottom-up estimating A technique where an estimate for each component in the WBS is developed and then totaled for an overall project budget. This is the longest method to complete, but it provides the most accurate estimate.

budget at completion The predicted budget for the project; what the project should cost when it is completed. Budget at completion represents 100 percent of the planned value for the project's completion.

chart of accounts   A coding system used by the performing organization's accounting system to account for the project work.

cost baseline   This shows what the project is expected to spend. It's usually shown in an S-curve and allows the project manager and management to predict when the project will be spending monies and over what duration. The purpose of the cost baseline is to measure and predict project performance.

cost budgeting   A process of assigning a cost to an individual work package. This process shows costs over time. The cost budget results in an S-curve that becomes the cost baseline for the project.

cost change control   This is part of the integrated change control system and documents the procedures to request, approve, and incorporate changes to project costs.

cost control   An active process to control causes of cost change, to document cost changes, and to monitor cost fluctuations within the project. When changes occur, the cost baseline must be updated.

cost estimating   The process of calculating the costs, by category, of the identified resources to complete the project work.

cost management plan   A subsidiary plan of the overall project management plan that defines how costs will be estimated, budgeted, and controlled.

cost performance index   The process of calculating the costs, by category, of the identified resources to complete the project work.

cost variance   The difference between the earned value and the actual costs.

direct costs   These costs are attributed directly to the project and cannot be shared with operations or other projects.

earned value   The value of the work that has been completed and the budget for that work: $EV = \%\ \text{Complete} \times BAC$.

earned value management   Earned value management integrates scope, schedule, and cost to give an objective, scalable, point-in-time assessment of the project. EVM calculates the performance of the project and compares current performance against plan. EVM can also be a harbinger of things to come. Results early in the project can predict the likelihood of the project's success or failure.

estimate at completion   A hypothesis of what the total cost of the project will be. Before the project begins, the project manager completes an estimate for the project deliverables based on the WBS. As the project progresses, there will likely be some variances between what the cost estimate was and what the actual cost is. The EAC is calculated to predict what the new estimate at completion will be.

estimate to complete   Represents how much more money is needed to complete the project work: ETC = EAC – AC.

estimating publications   Typically, a commercial reference to help the project estimator confirm and predict the accuracy of estimates. If a project manager elects to use one of these commercial databases, the estimate should include a pointer to this document for future reference and verification.

fixed costs   Costs that remain the same throughout the project.

indirect costs   These costs can be shared across multiple projects that use the same resources—such as for a training room or piece of equipment.

parametric modeling   A mathematical model based on known parameters to predict the cost of a project. The parameters in the model can vary based on the type of work being done. A parameter can be cost per cubic yard, cost per unit, and so on.

planned value   The worth of the work that should be completed by a specific time in the project schedule.

risk   An uncertain event that can have a positive or negative influence on the project's success. It can affect the project costs, project schedule, and often both. All risks and their status should be recorded in the risk register.

schedule performance index   This reveals the efficiency of work. The closer the quotient is to 1, the better: SPI = EV / PV.

schedule variance   The difference between the planned work and the earned work.

to-complete performance index   An earned value management formula that can forecast the likelihood of a project to achieve its goals based on what's currently happening in the project.

top-down estimating   A technique that bases the current project's estimate on the total of a similar project. A percentage of the similar project's total cost may be added to or subtracted from the total, depending on the size of the current project.

variable costs   Costs that vary, depending on the conditions within the project.

variance   The time or cost difference between what was planned and what was actually experienced.

INSIDE THE EXAM

The PMP examination requires that the exam candidate know how to estimate, budget, and manage costs. The WBS is an input to estimating costs since it reflects the whole of the project. When creating the estimates, rely on documented historical information over team members' recollections. There are three estimating approaches.

- **Analogous** A top-down approach that is less costly and less accurate than others and that offers an idea of what the project will cost.

- **Bottom-up** Starts with zero and adds up all the expenses. This is more costly and takes longer, but gains team buy-in to the project.

- **Parametric modeling** Uses a parameter for labor and goods to calculate the cost of the project.

The accuracy of the estimates is based on available information. As the project manager and the project team progressively elaborate on the project plan, more details become available. The more details a project has, the more accurate the estimate. Know the following facts on estimating:

- **Rough order of magnitude** The accuracy of the estimate ranges from –25 percent to +75 percent, and is used in both the initiation process and in top-down estimating.

- **Budget estimate** The accuracy of the estimate ranges from –10 percent to +25 percent. This is used early in the planning process and also in top-down estimating.

- **Definitive estimate** The accuracy of the estimate ranges from –5 percent to +10 percent. This is used late in the planning process and in bottom-up estimating.

The resources on a project can include people, materials, and equipment. If the people on a project do not have the necessary skill set to complete the work, hire an SME to guide the project implementation, outsource the project work, or train the current people in the needed skills.

Earned value management is a tool to measure project performance. It is the budget at completion multiplied by the percentage of the project work that has been completed. The cost performance index shows how well the project is performing financially, and is calculated by dividing EV by the actual costs spent on the project. Use the most common formula for finding the estimate at completion: $EAC = BAC / CPI$.

TWO-MINUTE DRILL

Estimating the Project Costs

❑ The project manager must know what resources are needed to complete the project work. How will the project ever be completed without the resources? The project manager must know the people, the equipment, materials, and other resources needed to make the vision of the project a reality. Once the resources are identified, the costs of the resources can be calculated.

❑ The resources also must be known so the project manager can predict, monitor, and control what the project costs are expected to be. The relationship between the project vision and the needed resources can help the project manager work within the predicted costs.

❑ Resources to complete a project also include services, leases, real estate, and other components that contribute to the project work being completed.

Analyzing Cost Estimating Results

❑ **Rough order of magnitude estimate**   This estimate is "rough" and is used during the initiating processes and in top-down estimates. The range of variance for the estimate can be from −25 percent to +75 percent.

❑ **Budget estimate**   This estimate is also somewhat broad and is used early in the planning processes and in top-down estimates. The range of variance for the estimate can be from −10 percent to +25 percent.

❑ **Definitive estimate**   This estimate type is one of the most accurate. It's used late in the planning processes and is associated with bottom-up estimating. The range of variance for the estimate can be from −5 percent to +10 percent.

❑ Analogous estimating uses a similar project to predict what the costs of the current project should be. It is less accurate, but easier and faster to complete than other methods.

❑ Parametric estimating uses a parameter for units of goods and time to calculate what the project will cost, for example, cost per hour, cost per metric ton, or cost per cubic yard.

Creating a Project Budget

❑ Cost aggregation maps the overall costs to each WBS work package. The costs of each work package are aggregated to their corresponding control accounts. Each control account then is aggregated to the sum of the project costs.

❑ Funding limit reconciliation is an organization's approach to managing cash flow against the project deliverables based on a schedule, milestone accomplishment, or data constraints. This helps an organization plan when monies will be devoted to a project rather than using all of the funds available at the start of a project. In other words, the monies for a project budget will become available based on dates and/or deliverables.

Implementing Cost Control

❑ The cost management plan documents how the project manager will react to cost variances within the project. The performing organization will likely have policies and procedures on unacceptable variances.

❑ Variances that cross a given threshold may require the project manager to create a variance report to explain the variance, why it has happened, and what corrective action has been applied to prevent the variance from recurring.

❑ Cost control is the process of monitoring and documenting cost changes, whether they are allowed to occur or are prevented from occurring. The project manager studies the cost changes to understand why the change has happened and then makes corrective actions to the project if needed.

Measuring Project Performance

❑ Planned value is the work scheduled and the budget authorized to accomplish that work. The entire project's planned value—that is, what the project should be worth at completion—is known as the budget at completion. You might also see the sum of the planned value called the performance measurement baseline.

❑ Earned value is the physical work completed to date and the authorized budget for that work.

❑ Actual cost is the actual amount of monies the project has required to date.

❑ The cost variance is the difference between the earned value and the actual costs.

❑ A schedule variance (SV) is the value that represents the difference between where the project was planned to be at a certain point in time and where the project actually is.

❑ The cost performance index (CPI) shows the amount of work the project is completing per dollar spent on the project.

❑ The schedule performance index (SPI), however, reveals how closely the project is on schedule.

❑ The estimate at completion (EAC) is a hypothesis of what the total cost of the project will be.

❑ The estimate to complete (ETC) shows how much more money will be needed to complete the project.

❑ The to-complete performance index can forecast the likelihood of a project to achieve its goals based on what's happening in the project right now.

Considering the Cost Control Results

❑ Cost control can cause changes and updates within the project for the project scope, schedule, or overall costs. If the cost of material increases, there may be tradeoffs in the project scope to afford the existing materials. The stakeholders or project manager could elect to use a lower grade of material or remove the deliverable from scope, if that's feasible, to keep the costs in check. Either way, if the cost of materials increases, there'll be ripples throughout the project.

❑ Updating the budget is slightly different from revising a cost estimate. Budget updates allow the cost baseline to be changed. The cost baseline is the "before project snapshot" of what the total project scope and the individual WBS components should cost.

❑ Errors in the project can cause costs to increase. Corrective actions are an effort, technically a change request, to bring the project back into alignment with the cost baseline and what was planned.

SELF TEST

1. Which of the following best describes analogous estimating?
   A. Regression analysis
   B. Bottom-up estimating
   C. Less accurate
   D. More accurate

2. You are the project manager for the GHG Project. You are about to create the cost estimates for the project. Which input to this process will help you the most?
   A. Parametric modeling
   B. WBS
   C. Project scope
   D. Requirements document

3. You are the project manager for the JKH Project. You have elected to use parametric estimating in your cost estimating for the project. Which of the following is an example of parametric estimating?
   A. $750 per ton
   B. Historical information from a similar project
   C. Estimates built bottom-up based on the WBS
   D. Estimates based on top-down budgeting

4. You are the project manager for a new technology implementation project. Management has requested that your estimates be as exact as possible. Which one of the following methods of estimating will provide the most accurate estimate?
   A. Top-down estimating
   B. Top-down budgeting
   C. Bottom-up estimating
   D. Parametric estimating

5. Your company has been hired to install the tile in 1,000 hotel rooms. All rooms will be identical in nature and will require the same amount of materials. You calculate the time to install the tile in each hotel room at six hours. The cost of labor for each room is calculated at $700. Your project sponsor disagrees with your labor estimate. Why?
   A. You haven't completed one hotel room yet, so you don't know how long the work will actually take.
   B. You have not factored in all of the effort applied to the work.
   C. You have not considered the law of diminishing returns.
   D. You have not considered the learning curve.

6. You are the project manager for a construction project to build 17 cabins. All of the cabins will be identical in nature. The contract for the project is set at a fixed cost, the incentive being that the faster the project work is completed, the more profitable the job. Management has requested that you study the work method to determine a faster, less costly, and better method of completing the project. This is an example of which one of the following?

   A. Time constraint

   B. Schedule constraint

   C. Value engineering

   D. Learning curve

7. You are the project manager for a technical implementation project. The customer has requested that you factor in the after-the-project costs, such as maintenance and service. This is an example of which one of the following?

   A. Life-cycle costs

   B. Scope creep

   C. Project spin-off

   D. Operations

8. Which one of the following provides the least accuracy in estimating?

   A. Rough order of magnitude

   B. Budget estimate

   C. Definitive estimate

   D. WBS estimate

9. Which one of the following is true?

   A. The cost management plan controls how change management affects the BAC.

   B. The cost management plan controls how cost variances will be managed.

   C. The cost management plan controls how the project manager may update the cost estimates.

   D. The cost management plan controls how the BAC may be adjusted.

10. You have just started a project for a manufacturer. Project team members report they are 30 percent complete with the project. You have spent $25,000 out of the project's $250,000 budget. What is the earned value for this project?

    A. 10 percent

    B. $75,000

    C. $25,000

    D. Not enough information to know

11. You and your project team are about to enter a meeting to determine project costs. You have elected to use bottom-up estimating and will base your estimates on the WBS. Which one of the following is not an attribute of bottom-up estimating?

A. People doing the work create the estimates.

B. It creates a more accurate estimate.

C. It's more expensive to do than other methods.

D. It's less expensive to do than other methods.

12. What is the present value if an organization expects to make $100,000 four years from now and the annual interest rate is 6 percent?

A. $100,000

B. $79,000

C. $25,000

D. Zero

13. You are the project manager for the construction of a new hotel. Before you begin the cost budgeting process, what is needed?

A. Cost estimates and project schedule

B. Cost estimates and supporting detail

C. EAC and BAC

D. A parametric model to arrive at the costs submitted

14. You are the project manager of the MNJ Project. Your project is falling behind schedule, and you have already spent $130,000 of your $150,000 budget. What do you call the $130,000?

A. Planned value

B. Present value

C. Sunk costs

D. Capital expenditure

15. You are the project manager of the JHD Project. Your project will cost your organization $250,000 to complete over the next eight months. Once the project is completed, the deliverables will begin earning the company $3,500 per month. Which of the following represents the time to recover the costs of the project?

A. Not enough information to know

B. 8 months

C. 72 months

D. 5 years

16. You are the project manager for a consulting company. Your company has two possible projects to manage, but they can only choose one. Project KJH is worth $17,000, while Project ADS is worth $22,000. Management elects to choose Project ADS. The opportunity cost of this choice is which one of the following?

A. $5,000

B. $17,000

C. $22,000

D. Zero, as project ADS is worth more than Project KJH

17. You are the project manager for the CSR Training Project, and 21,000 customer service reps are invited to attend the training session. Attendance is optional. You have calculated the costs of the training facility, but the workbook expense depends on how many students register for the class. For every 5,000 workbooks created, the cost is reduced by a percentage of the original printing cost. The workbook expense is an example of which one of the following?

A. Fixed costs

B. Parametric costs

C. Variable costs

D. Indirect costs

18. You are the project manager of a construction project scheduled to last 24 months. You have elected to rent a piece of equipment for the duration of a project, even though you will need the equipment only periodically throughout the project. The costs of the equipment rental per month are $890. This is an example of which of the following?

A. Fixed costs

B. Parametric costs

C. Variable costs

D. Indirect costs

19. You are the project manager for the Hardware Inventory Project. You have a piece of equipment that was purchased recently for $10,000 and is expected to last five years in production. At the end of the five years, the expected worth of the equipment will be $1,000. Using straight-line depreciation, what is the amount that can be written off each year?

A. Zero

B. $1,000

C. $1,800

D. $2,000

20. You are the project manager of the LKG Project. The project has a budget of $290,000 and is expected to last three years. The project is now 10 percent complete and is on schedule. What is the BAC?

A. $29,000

B. $290,000

C. $96,666

D. $9,666

21. Your project has a budget of $130,000 and is expected to last ten months, with the work and budget spread evenly across all months. The project is now in month three, the work is on schedule, but you have spent $65,000 of the project budget. What is your variance?

A. $65,000

B. $39,000

C. $26,000

D. $64,999

22. You are the project manager of the Carpet Installation Project for a new building. Your BAC is $600,000. You are now 40 percent complete with the project, though your plan called for you to be 45 percent complete with the work by this time. What is your earned value?

A. $240,000

B. $270,000

C. $30,000

D. –$30,000

23. You are the project manager of the Carpet Installation Project for a new building. Your BAC is $600,000. You have spent $270,000 of your budget. You are now 40 percent done with the project, though your plan called for you to be 45 percent done with the work by this time. What is your CPI?

A. 100

B. 89

C. 0.89

D. 0.79

24. You are the project manager for the Facility Installation Project. The project calls for 1,500 units to be installed in a new baseball stadium. Your team wants to know why you have not assigned the same amount of time for the last 800 units as you had for the first 500 units. You tell them it is because of the learning curve. Which one of the following best describes this theory?

    A. Production increases as workers become more efficient with the installation procedure.

    B. Efficiency increases as workers become more familiar with the installation procedure.

    C. Costs decrease as workers complete more of the installation procedure.

    D. Time decreases as workers complete more of the installation procedure in the final phases of a project.

25. Of the following, which one is the most reliable source of information for estimating project costs?

    A. Historical information from a recently completed project

    B. An SME's opinion

    C. Recollections of team members that have worked on similar projects

    D. Vendors' whitepapers

SELF TEST ANSWERS

I. Which of the following best describes analogous estimating?
   A. Regression analysis
   B. Bottom-up estimating
   C. Less accurate
   D. More accurate

   ☑ **C.** Analogous estimating is less accurate than other estimating methods.
   ☒ **A** is incorrect, since regression analysis is a type of parametric modeling. **B** is incorrect, as bottom-up estimating starts with zero and adds up the project costs. **D** is incorrect, since analogous estimating is not more accurate.

2. You are the project manager for the GHG Project. You are about to create the cost estimates for the project. Which input to this process will help you the most?
   A. Parametric modeling
   B. WBS
   C. Project scope
   D. Requirements document

   ☑ **B.** The WBS is the input that can help you the most with the cost estimates.
   ☒ **A** is incorrect, as parametric modeling is a form of estimating, not an input. **C** is incorrect, as the project scope is not an input to the estimating process. **D** is incorrect, as the requirements document is also not an input to the estimating process.

3. You are the project manager for the JKH Project. You have elected to use parametric estimating in your cost estimating for the project. Which of the following is an example of parametric estimating?
   A. $750 per ton
   B. Historical information from a similar project
   C. Estimates built bottom-up based on the WBS
   D. Estimates based on top-down budgeting

   ☑ **A** is correct. $750 per ton is an example of parametric estimating.
   ☒ **B** is incorrect, since historical information is analogous, not parametric. **C** and **D** are incorrect, since these do not describe parametric modeling.

4. You are the project manager for a new technology implementation project. Management has requested that your estimates be as exact as possible. Which one of the following methods of estimating will provide the most accurate estimate?
    A. Top-down estimating
    B. Top-down budgeting
    C. Bottom-up estimating
    D. Parametric estimating

    ☑   **C.** Bottom-up estimating provides the most accurate estimates. The project manager starts at zero, the bottom, and accounts for each cost within the project.
    ☒   **A, B,** and **D** are all incorrect, since they do not reflect the most accurate method to create an estimate.

5. Your company has been hired to install the tile in 1,000 hotel rooms. All rooms will be identical in nature and will require the same amount of materials. You calculate the time to install the tile in each hotel room at six hours. The cost of labor for each room is calculated at $700. Your project sponsor disagrees with your labor estimate. Why?
    A. You haven't completed one hotel room yet, so you don't know how long the work will actually take.
    B. You have not factored in all of the effort applied to the work.
    C. You have not considered the law of diminishing returns.
    D. You have not considered the learning curve.

    ☑   **D** is the best choice. As the project team completes more and more units, the time to complete a hotel room should take less and less time.
    ☒   Choices **A, B,** and **C** are incorrect, since they do not answer the question as fully as answer **D.**

6. You are the project manager for a construction project to build 17 cabins. All of the cabins will be identical in nature. The contract for the project is set at a fixed cost, the incentive being that the faster the project work is completed, the more profitable the job. Management has requested that you study the work method to determine a faster, less costly, and better method of completing the project. This is an example of which one of the following?
    A. Time constraint
    B. Schedule constraint
    C. Value engineering
    D. Learning curve

☑ **C.** Value engineering is a systematic approach to finding less costly ways to complete the same work.

☒ **A** and **B** are not correct, since this situation does not describe a specific time or cost constraint. **D** is incorrect, since the learning curve happens as the project team completes the work. Value analysis is the study of a process in order to complete the work faster and more affordably.

7. You are the project manager for a technical implementation project. The customer has requested that you factor in the after-the-project costs, such as maintenance and service. This is an example of which one of the following?
   A. Life-cycle costs
   B. Scope creep
   C. Project spin-off
   D. Operations

☑ **A.** The after-project costs are known as the life-cycle costs.

☒ Though tempting, choices **B** and **C** are incorrect because they do not describe the process of calculating the ongoing expenses of the product the project is creating. **D** is incorrect. Operations do not fully describe the expenses unique to the product.

8. Which one of the following provides the least accuracy in estimating?
   A. Rough order of magnitude
   B. Budget estimate
   C. Definitive estimate
   D. WBS estimate

☑ **A.** The rough order of magnitude is the least accurate approach, since it may vary from –25 percent to +75 percent.

☒ Choices **B** and **C** are more accurate estimates than the rough order of magnitude. **D** is not a valid answer for this question.

9. Which one of the following is true?
   A. The cost management plan controls how change management affects the BAC.
   B. The cost management plan controls how cost variances will be managed.
   C. The cost management plan controls how the project manager may update the cost estimates.
   D. The cost management plan controls how the BAC may be adjusted.

    ☑ **B.** The cost management plan controls how cost variances will be managed.

    ☒ Choices **A, C,** and **D** are incorrect descriptions of the cost management plan.

10. You have just started a project for a manufacturer. Project team members report they are 30 percent complete with the project. You have spent $25,000 out of the project's $250,000 budget. What is the earned value for this project?

    A. 10 percent

    B. $75,000

    C. $25,000

    D. Not enough information to know

    ☑ **B.** The earned value is 30 percent of the project's budget.

    ☒ Choice **A** is not a valid answer for the question. **C** and **D** are incorrect responses, since they do not answer the question either.

11. You and your project team are about to enter a meeting to determine project costs. You have elected to use bottom-up estimating and will base your estimates on the WBS. Which one of the following is not an attribute of bottom-up estimating?

    A. People doing the work create the estimates.

    B. It creates a more accurate estimate.

    C. It's more expensive to do than other methods.

    D. It's less expensive to do than other methods.

    ☑ **D.** Using bottom-up estimating is not less expensive to do.

    ☒ **A, B,** and **C** are not correct choices, since these are attributes of a bottom-up estimating process.

12. What is the present value if an organization expects to make $100,000 four years from now and the annual interest rate is 6 percent?

    A. $100,000

    B. $79,000

    C. $25,000

    D. Zero

    ☑ **B.** The present value of $100,000 four years from now can be calculated by using this formula: present value = $FV / (1 + i)^n$. FV is the future value, i is the interest rate, and n is the number of time periods.

    ☒ Choices **A, C,** and **D** are all incorrect answers because they don't reflect the present value.

13. You are the project manager for the construction of a new hotel. Before you begin the cost budgeting process, what is needed?
    A. Cost estimates and project schedule
    B. Cost estimates and supporting detail
    C. EAC and BAC
    D. A parametric model used to arrive at the costs submitted

    ☑ **A.** Cost estimates and the project schedule are inputs to the cost budgeting process.
    ☒ Choices **B, C,** and **D** are all incorrect because they are not inputs to cost budgeting.

14. You are the project manager of the MNJ Project. Your project is falling behind schedule, and you have already spent $130,000 of your $150,000 budget. What do you call the $130,000?
    A. Planned value
    B. Present value
    C. Sunk costs
    D. Capital expenditure

    ☑ **C.** Sunk costs are monies that have been spent.
    ☒ **A** is incorrect because planned value is the amount the project should be worth at this point in the schedule. **B** is also incorrect; present value is the current value of future monies. **D** is incorrect because a capital expenditure is money spent to purchase a long-term asset, such as a building.

15. You are the project manager of the JHD Project. Your project will cost your organization $250,000 to complete over the next eight months. Once the project is completed, the deliverables will begin earning the company $3,500 per month. Which of the following represents the time to recover the costs of the project?
    A. Not enough information to know
    B. 8 months
    C. 72 months
    D. 5 years

    ☑ **C.** The time to recoup the monies from the project is 72 months. This is calculated by dividing the ROI of $3,500 per month into the project cost.
    ☒ **A** is an incorrect answer. **B** is incorrect; eight months is the amount of time left in the project schedule. **D,** five years, is also incorrect.

16. You are the project manager for a consulting company. Your company has two possible projects to manage, but they can only choose one. Project KJH is worth $17,000, while Project ADS is worth $22,000. Management elects to choose Project ADS. The opportunity cost of this choice is which one of the following?

    A. $5,000

    B. $17,000

    C. $22,000

    D. Zero, as project ADS is worth more than Project KJH

    ☑ **B.** The opportunity cost is the amount of the project that was not chosen.
    ☒ **A** is incorrect. $5,000 is the difference between the two projects. It is not the opportunity cost. **C** is incorrect, since $22,000 is the amount of the project that was selected. **D** is also an incorrect answer.

17. You are the project manager for the CSR Training Project, and 21,000 customer service reps are invited to attend the training session. Attendance is optional. You have calculated the costs of the training facility, but the workbook expense depends on how many students register for the class. For every 5,000 workbooks created, the cost is reduced by a percentage of the original printing cost. The workbook expense is an example of which one of the following?

    A. Fixed costs

    B. Parametric costs

    C. Variable costs

    D. Indirect costs

    ☑ **C.** This is an example of variable costs. The more students that register to take the class, the more the cost of the books will be.
    ☒ **A** is incorrect, since the cost of the book varies, depending on the number of students that register for the class. **B** is incorrect because the cost of each book diminishes as more books are created. A parametric cost would remain the same, regardless of how many books were created. **D** is not correct, since this is not an example of an indirect cost.

18. You are the project manager of a construction project scheduled to last 24 months. You have elected to rent a piece of equipment for the duration of a project, even though you will need the equipment only periodically throughout the project. The costs of the equipment rental per month are $890. This is an example of which of the following?

    A. Fixed costs

    B. Parametric costs

C. Variable costs

D. Indirect costs

> ☑ **A.** This is a fixed-cost expense of $890 per month—regardless of how often the piece of equipment is used.
> ☒ **B** is incorrect because a parametric cost is a value used to calculate cost per use, cost per metric ton, or cost per unit. While it may at first appear that **B** is the correct choice, there is no historical information mentioned upon which to base the parametric model. **C** is incorrect, since the cost does not vary within the project. **D** is also incorrect; this is a cost attributed directly to the project work.

19. You are the project manager for the Hardware Inventory Project. You have a piece of equipment that was purchased recently for $10,000 and is expected to last five years in production. At the end of the five years, the expected worth of the equipment will be $1,000. Using straight-line depreciation, what is the amount that can be written off each year?

 A. Zero

 B. $1,000

 C. $1,800

 D. $2,000

> ☑ **C.** The straight-line depreciation takes the purchase value of the item, minus the salvage price of the item, divided by the number of time periods. In this instance, it would be $10,000 minus $1,000, or $9,000. The $9,000 is divided by five years and equates to $1,800 per year.
> ☒ **A, C,** and **D** are all incorrect, since they do not reflect the correct calculation.

20. You are the project manager of the LKG Project. The project has a budget of $290,000 and is expected to last three years. The project is now 10 percent complete and is on schedule. What is the BAC?

 A. $29,000

 B. $290,000

 C. $96,666

 D. $9,666

> ☑ **B.** The BAC is the budget at completion, which is $290,000.
> ☒ **A** is incorrect because it describes the earned value for the project. **C** and **D** are both incorrect values.

21. Your project has a budget of $130,000 and is expected to last 10 months, with the work and budget spread evenly across all months. The project is now in month three, the work is on schedule, but you have spent $65,000 of the project budget. What is your variance?

A. $65,000

B. $39,000

C. $26,000

D. $64,999

☑ **C.** $26,000 is the variance. This is calculated by subtracting the actual costs of $65,000 from the earned value of $39,000. EV is calculated by taking the 30 percent completion of the project against the BAC. The project is considered to be 30 percent complete because it's slated for 10 months, is currently in month three, and is on schedule.

☒ **A, B,** and **D** are all incorrect calculations for the problem.

22. You are the project manager of the Carpet Installation Project for a new building. Your BAC is $600,000. You are now 40 percent complete with the project, though your plan called for you to be 45 percent complete with the work by this time. What is your earned value?

A. $240,000

B. $270,000

C. $30,000

D. –$30,000

☑ **A.** The earned value is calculated by multiplying the percentage of completion, 40 percent, by the BAC, which is $600,000, for a value of $240,000.

☒ **B, C,** and **D** are incorrect calculations of the earned value formula.

23. You are the project manager of the Carpet Installation Project for a new building. Your BAC is $600,000. You have spent $270,000 of your budget. You are now 40 percent done with the project, though your plan called for you to be 45 percent done with the work by this time. What is your CPI?

A. 100

B. 89

C. 0.89

D. 0.79

☑ **C** is the correct answer. The EV of $240,000 is divided by the AC of $270,000 for a value of 0.89.

☒ **A** and **D** are incorrect calculations. **B** is incorrect because the value needs a decimal.

24. You are the project manager for the Facility Installation Project. The project calls for 1,500 units to be installed in a new baseball stadium. Your team wants to know why you have not assigned the same amount of time for the last 800 units as you had for the first 500 units. You tell them it is because of the learning curve. Which one of the following best describes this theory?

A. Production increases as workers become more efficient with the installation procedure.
B. Efficiency increases as workers become more familiar with the installation procedure.
C. Costs decrease as workers complete more of the installation procedure.
D. Time decreases as workers complete more of the installation procedure in the final phases of a project.

☑ **B.** The learning curve allows the cost to decrease as a result of decreased installation time because workers will complete more of the installation procedure.

☒ Choices **A, C,** and **D** are all incorrect choices, since they do not correctly describe the learning curve in relation to time and cost.

25. Of the following, which one is the most reliable source of information for estimating project costs?

A. Historical information from a recently completed project
B. An SME's opinion
C. Recollections of team members that have worked on similar projects
D. Vendors' whitepapers

☑ **A.** Of the choices presented, historical information from a recently completed project is the most reliable source of information.

☒ **B,** while valuable, is not as proven as historical information. **C** is incorrect, since recollections are the least reliable source of information. **D** is also incorrect, though it may prove valuable in the planning process.

8

Introducing Project Quality Management

W hat is quality? Quality is the "totality of characteristics of an entity that bear on its ability to satisfy stated or implied needs." Every project has an anticipated level of quality for the project deliverables. Project quality management is the process to ensure that the project fulfills its obligations to satisfy the project needs. As projects vary, so, too, will the anticipated level of quality.

Picture this: It's late on a hot summer night and you're hungry. You pull onto a gravel road and see a diner with a neon "Open" sign. The sign, you notice, really says "Ope" since the "n" is burned out. Inside the diner, stale smoke drifts around like fog. Grease, onions, and garlic seep into your clothes. You opt for a booth only to find the table smeared with catsup, a little gravy, and, guessing by the stickiness, a glob of maple syrup.

Now picture this: You step off the elevator on the 43rd floor. A maitre d' welcomes you and guides you to a table next to a window offering a sweeping view of the city. A piano player massages a song into the evening. The waiter snaps open a napkin and drapes it across your lap. Another waiter pours you a glass of cold, crisp water and presents the menu. By the soft candlelight, everything looks, and feels, grand.

With these two contrasting scenarios, which one do you think will have the better quality? Or can they both have an *acceptable* level of quality? For the first scenario—the diner—you expect a certain level of quality when it comes to service, food, and atmosphere. With the second scenario—the fancy restaurant—you also have an expected level of quality regarding service, food, and atmosphere. Both experiences are measured by that expected level of quality.

In the diner, you might get one of the best bacon cheeseburger/milkshake combos you can find late at night in the middle of nowhere. Just what you'd expect from this kind of place. And the fancy downtown restaurant? A fancy meal cooked to perfection—also what you'd expect. The difference between the two restaurants is in their grade. The expected level of service, food, and atmosphere is the quality of the experience.

CERTIFICATION OBJECTIVE 8.01

The Big Quality Picture

Before we hop into the three different facets of project quality management, let's establish a few "PMI-isms" on quality. Because quality means so many different things to so many different people, it's important to confirm we're working with a common understanding of what quality is and what quality management hopes to accomplish from the PMI's point of view.

Accepting the Quality Management Approach

The details and specifications set out by the customer determine what the expected level of quality is. Project quality management, as far as your exam goes, is compatible with ISO 9000 and ISO 10000 quality standards and guidelines.

Project quality management also is concerned with both the management of the project and the product of the project. It's easy to focus on the product (the thing or service the project creates), but project managers must also provide quality for the project management activities. Aspects of the downside of focusing too much on the product include the following:

■ Overworking the project team in order to complete the project. This may result in unacceptable work, a decline in team morale, and the slow, steady destruction of the project team's willingness to work.

■ A hurry to complete the project work by speeding through quality inspections. This can result in unacceptable deliverables.

ISO 9000 is an international standard that helps organizations follow their own quality procedures. It is not a quality system, but a method of following procedures created internally to an organization. And for the curious, ISO means uniform in Greek and it's from the International Organization for Standardization.

See the video Project Quality Management.

Quality vs. Grade

Quality and grade are not the same.

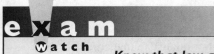

Quality is the sum of the characteristics of a product that allow it to meet the demands or expectations of the project. Quality is all about fulfilling requirements.

Grade, according to the PMBOK, "is a category or rank given to entities having the same functional use but different technical characteristics." For example, there are different grades of paint, different grades of metal, and even different grades of travel.

Implementing Quality Project Management

Quality management and project management have similar characteristics.

- **Customer satisfaction**   The project must satisfy the customer requirements by delivering what it promised in order to satisfy the needs of the customer. The PMBOK states it as "conformance to requirements" and "fitness for use."

- **Prevention**   Quality is planned into a project, not inspected in. It is always more cost-effective to prevent mistakes than to correct them.

- **Management responsibility**   The project team must work towards the quality goal, but management must provide the needed resources to deliver on the quality promises.

- **Plan-do-check-act**   Dr. W. Edwards Deming, arguably the world's leader in quality management theory thanks to his management methods implemented in Japan after World War II, set the bar with his "plan-do-check-act" approach to quality management. This approach is similar to the project management processes that every project passes through.

- **Kaizen technology**   Kaizen is a quality management philosophy of applying continuous small improvements to reduce costs and ensure consistency or project performance.

■ **Marginal analysis** Marginal analysis studies the cost of the incremental improvements to a process or product and compares it against the increase in revenue made from the improvements. For example, the price of the added feature may cost the company $7.50 per unit, but the amount of gained sales per year because of the improvement will meet or exceed the cost of the improvement.

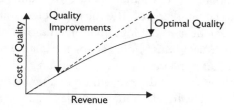

Preparing for Quality

Before a project manager can plan for quality, he must know what the quality expectations are. Specifically, what are the quality standards of the performing organization and which quality standards are applicable to the project? As part of the planning processes, the project manager and the project team must identify the requirements of planning, determine how the requirements may be met, and identify the costs and time demands to meet the identified requirements.

One of the key principles of project quality management is that quality is planned in, not inspected in. Planning for quality is more cost-effective than inspecting work results and doing the work over or correcting problems to adhere to quality demands.

The project manager must consider the cost of achieving the expected level of quality in contrast to the cost of nonconformance. The cost of quality includes training, safety measures, and action to prevent poor quality. The cost of nonconformance can far outweigh the cost of quality with its possible loss of customers, the rework needed, lost time, lost materials, and the danger to workers.

Determining the Quality Policy

Top management should define the quality policy; this is part of the organizational process assets. The quality policy of the organization may follow a formal approach, such as ISO 9000, Six Sigma, or quality function deployment, or it may have its own direction and approach to satisfying the demand for quality. There are loads of proprietary quality management methodologies, and you won't need to know much about any of them for your PMP exam. Out in the real world, however, you'll need to be familiar with the rules, policies, and procedures of whatever quality management methodology your organization subscribes to. Lucky you.

The project team should adapt the quality policy of the organization to guide the project implementation. This ensures that the management of the project and the deliverables of the project are in alignment with the performing organization's quality policy. In addition, the project manager should document how the project will fulfill the quality policy both in management and in the project deliverable.

But what if the performing organization doesn't have a quality policy? Or what if two different entities are working together on a project and they use differing quality policies? In these circumstances, the project management team should create the quality policy for the project. The quality policy, in these instances, will accomplish the same goals as a company's quality policy: to define quality requirements and determine how to adhere to them.

Regardless of where the quality policy comes from—management or the project team—the project stakeholders must be aware of the quality policy. This is important because the quality policy and associated quality methodology may require actions that could lengthen the project schedule—for example, quality audits, peer reviews, and other quality-centric activities. In addition to the required time to fulfill the quality requirements, other costs may be incurred.

Reviewing the Scope Baseline

Just as project quality management is focused on fulfilling the needs of the project, the project scope baseline is a key input to the quality planning process. I know you know that the scope baseline is comprised of the project scope statement, the WBS, and the WBS dictionary. Recall that the scope statement defines what will and will not be delivered as part of the project, as well as objectives regarding cost, schedule, and scope. The deliverables, and the expectations of the customers, will help guide the quality planning session to ensure the customer requirements are met in regard to quality.

While the project scope will define the initial product description, the product description may have supporting detail that the project manager and project team will need to review. Consider a project to create an apartment building. The requirements, specifications, and details of the building will need to be evaluated and reviewed since this information will, no doubt, affect the quality planning.

The WBS and WBS dictionary are needed during quality planning because they define the specific things that will satisfy the project requirements for deliverables. The WBS is like a catalogue of expectations the customer has of you. When you and your project team fulfill the elements of the WBS, you're meeting customer satisfaction, which maps to quality. The WBS dictionary tags along because it has the specific details of what each element of the WBS requires.

PMP
Coach
So what is quality in project management? Quality is the accurate completion of the project scope and the satisfaction of the stated and implied project needs. In your quest for your PMP certification, do you have quality? What is the scope of your certification goal and how will you reach it? Have quality in your studying, in your preparation, and in your mental mindset, and you'll find quality in the execution of your PMP test-taking.

Reviewing the Standards and Regulations

The standards and regulations of each industry will need to be reviewed to determine that both the project plan and the plan for quality are acceptable. For example, a project to wire a building for electricity will have certain regulations it must adhere to. The relevance of the regulations must be planned into the project to conform with requirements.

CERTIFICATION OBJECTIVE 8.03

Planning for Quality

Once the project manager has assembled the needed inputs and evaluated the product description and project scope, she can get to work creating a plan on how to satisfy the quality demands. She'll need to rely on the documentation created to date, her project team, and the project's key stakeholders for much of the input.

In addition, the project manager will use several different techniques to plan on meeting quality.

As planning is an iterative process, so, too, is quality planning. As events happen within the project, the project manager should evaluate the events and then apply corrective actions. This is a common PMI theme: plan, implement, measure, react—and document! Throughout the project implementation, things will go awry, team members may complete less-than-acceptable work, stakeholders will demand changes, and so on; all of these variables must be evaluated for their impact on project quality. What good is a project if it's "completed" on time, but the quality of the deliverable is unacceptable? Technically, if the product is unacceptable, the project is not finished since it failed to meet the project scope. Let's look at some tools and techniques the project manager will use to plan for quality.

Using a Benefit/Cost Analysis

Benefits should outweigh costs.

A benefit/cost analysis is a process of determining the pros and cons of any process, product, or activity. The straightforward approach when it comes to project management is concerned with the benefits of quality management activities versus the costs of the quality management activities. There are two major considerations with the benefit/cost analysis in quality management.

- **Benefit** Completing quality work increases productivity because shoddy work does not have to be redone. When work is completed correctly the first time as expected, the project does not have to spend additional funds to redo the work.

- **Costs** Completing quality work may cost more monies than the work is worth. To deliver a level of quality beyond what is demanded costs the project additional funds. The types of quality management activities that guarantee quality may not be needed for every project.

- **Gold plating** The customer does not need or want more than what was requested. Gold plating is the process of adding extra features that may drive up costs and alter schedules. The project team should strive to deliver what was expected.

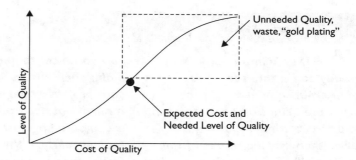

While quality is needed on every project, not every project has the same quality expenses based on the demands. For example, consider a project to create a temporary drainage ditch for a field. There are specifications for the ditch, but the project may not require the expense of a landscape architect to evaluate the slant and descent of the temporary ditch.

Another project, to create and secure an information technology department, may require the expense of a security consulting firm to evaluate, test, and certify the security of the software code, the network servers, and the physical security of the department. The cost of the quality requirements is in alignment with the demands of the project.

Applying Benchmarking Practices

Benchmarking, when it comes to quality project management, is all about comparing this project to another. It is a technique to take what the project manager has planned or experienced regarding quality and compare it to another project to see how things measure up. The current project can be measured against any other project—not just projects within the performing organization or within the same industry.

The goal of benchmarking is to evaluate the differences between the two projects and then to make corrective actions to the current project. For example, Project A may have better quality performance than Project B. When the project manager compares the two projects, he'll want to find out what the differences are between them. He'll look for what's missing in Project B or what activities the folks in Project A are doing that he's not.

Benchmarking allows the project manager and the project team to see what's possible and then strive toward that goal. Benchmarking can also be used as a measurement against industry standards, competitors' pricing, or competitors' level of performance.

Design of Experiments

The design of experiments approach relies on statistical what-if scenarios to determine what variables within a project will result in the best outcome. This type of approach is most often used on the product of the project rather than on the project itself. For example, a project team creating a new bicycle may experiment with the width of the tires, the weight of the frame, and the position of the handlebars in relation to the bike seat to determine the most comfortable ride at an acceptable cost to the consumer.

Although design of experiments is most often associated with product design, it can be applied to project management activities. For example, a project manager may evaluate the activities within a project and determine the time and cost of activities, depending on which employees are assigned to complete the work. A more experienced worker may cost the project more money on an hourly basis, but this individual is expected to complete the work in a third of the time that a less experienced worker would. This is design of experiments: experimenting with different variables to find the best solution at the best cost.

Design of experiments is also used as a method to identify which variables within a project or product are causing failures or unacceptable results. The goal of design of experiments is to isolate the root cause of an effect and then make adjustments to that cause to eliminate the unacceptable results.

Considering the Cost of Quality

The cost of quality considers the expense of all the activities within a project that are undertaken to ensure its quality. The cost of quality is divided into two major categories.

- **Cost of conformance to requirements** This approach is the cost of completing the project work to satisfy the project scope and the expected level of quality. Examples of this cost include training, safety measures, measurement, and quality management activities to ensure that quality is met.

- **Cost of nonconformance** This approach is the cost of completing the project work without quality. The biggest issue here is the money lost by having to redo the project work; it's always more cost-effective to do the work right the first time. Other nonconformance costs include loss of sales, loss of customers, downtime, and corrective actions to fix problems caused by incorrect work.

Creating the Quality Management Plan

The end result of quality planning is to find a method to implement the quality policy. Because planning is iterative, the quality planning sessions often require several revisits to the quality planning processes. On longer projects, there may be scheduled quality planning sessions to compare the performance of the project in relation to the quality that was planned.

One of the major outputs of quality planning is the quality management plan. This document describes how the project manager and the project team will fulfill the quality policy. In an ISO 9000 environment, the quality management plan is referred to as the "project quality system." The quality management plan addresses the following three things about the project and the project work:

- **Quality control** Work results are monitored to see if they meet relevant quality standards. If the results do not meet the quality standards, the project manager applies root-cause analysis to determine the cause of the poor performance and then eliminates the cause. Quality control is inspection-oriented.

- **Quality assurance** The overall performance is evaluated to ensure that the project meets the relevant quality standards. Quality assurance maps to an organization's quality policy and is typically a managerial process. Quality assurance is generally considered the work of applying the quality plan.

- **Quality improvement** The project performance is measured and evaluated, and corrective actions are applied to improve the product and the project. The improvements can be large or small, depending on the condition and the quality philosophy of the performing organization.

Identifying the Operational Definitions

Operational definitions, also known as metrics, are the quantifiable terms and values to measure a process, activity, or work result. An example of an operational definition could be an expected value for the required torque to tighten a bolt on a piece of equipment. By testing and measuring the torque, the operational definition would prove or disprove the quality of the product. Other examples can include hours of labor to complete a work package, required safety measures, cost per unit, and so on.

Operational definitions are clear, concise measurements. Designating that 95 percent of all customer service calls should be answered by a live person within 30 seconds is a metric. A statement that all calls should be answered in a timely manner is not.

Applying Checklists

Checklists are simple approaches to ensure that work is completed according to the quality policy. It's usually a list of activities that workers will check off to ensure that each task has been completed. Checklists can be quick instructions of what needs to be done to clean a piece of equipment, or questions that remind the employee to complete a task: "Did you turn off the printer before opening the cover?"

Creating the Process Improvement Plan

One of the goals of quality project management is continuous process improvement. The process improvement plan looks to improve the project, not just the end result of the project. Its aim is to identify and eliminate waste and non-value-added activity. Specifically, this plan aims to accomplish the following:

- Increase customer value by eliminating waste within the project
- Establish process boundaries
- Determine process configuration through a flow chart for evaluation and analysis in order to improve the project as a whole
- Create and manage process metrics within the project
- Establish targets for performance improvement

CERTIFICATION OBJECTIVE 8.04

Executing Quality Assurance

Quality assurance (QA) is an executing process. It is the sum of the planning and the implementations of the plans the project manager, the project team, and management applies to ensure the project meets the demands of quality. QA is not something that is done only at the end of the project, but before and during the project as well. Because QA is an executing process, you should link it to continuous process improvement, as it's work is to make the project better.

In some organizations, the quality assurance department or another entity will complete the QA activities. QA is interested in finding the defects and then fixing the problems. There are many different approaches to QA, depending on the quality system the organization or project team has adopted. There are two types.

- **Internal QA**   Assurance provided to management and the project team
- **External QA**   Assurance provided to the external customers of the project

Preparing for Quality Assurance

There are several inputs the project manager and the project team will need to prepare for QA.

- **The quality management plan**   This plan defines how the project team will implement and fulfill the quality policy of the performing organization.
- **Quality metrics**   Quality control tests will provide these measurements. The values must be quantifiable so results may be measured, compared, and analyzed. In other words, "pretty close to on track" is not adequate; "95 percent pass rate" is more acceptable.
- **The process improvement plan**   This plan aims to improve the project, not just the project's product.
- **Work performance information**   The results of the project work as needed—this includes technical performance measures, project status, information on what the project has created to date, corrective actions, and performance reports.
- **Results of quality control**   The measurements taken by the project manager and the project team to inspect the project deliverables' quality are fed back into the QA process.
- **Implemented actions**   Any change requests, defect repairs, corrective actions, or preventive actions that have been taken in the project should be documented and submitted to the QA process.

Applying Quality Assurance

The QA department, management, or, in some instances, even the project manager can complete the requirements for QA. QA can be accomplished using the following tools, the same tools used during quality planning:

- Benefit/cost analysis
- Benchmarking
- Flowcharting
- Design of experiments
- Cost of quality

Completing a Quality Audit

Quality audits are about learning. The idea of a quality audit is to identify the lessons learned on the current project to determine how to make things better for this project—and other projects within the organization. The idea is that Susan, the project manager, can learn from the implementations of Bob, the project manager, and vice versa.

Quality audits are formal reviews of what's been completed within a project, what worked, and what didn't work. The end result of the audit is to improve performance for the current project, other projects, or the entire organization.

Quality audits can be scheduled at key intervals within a project, or—surprise!— they can come without warning. The audit process can vary, depending on who is completing the audit: internal auditors or hired, third-party experts. The goal of a quality audit is to ensure that the project is adhering to the requirements of quality assurance. And the goal of quality assurance is to reduce the overall cost of quality. As you probably know from your experience, it's usually more cost-effective to do something right the first time than to do it right the second time. That's quality assurance—do the work according to plan, and it'll save time and monies.

Improving the Project

The primary output of QA? Quality improvement. But it's not just the quality of the project's deliverables, but also of the process to complete the project work. This is process analysis, and it follows the guidelines of the process improvement plan. Process analysis is completed through any or all of the following measures:

- An examination of problems and constraints
- An analysis of the project for non-value-added activities

■ Root-cause analysis

■ The creation of preventive actions for identified problems

Quality improvement requires action to improve the project's effectiveness. The actions to improve the effectiveness may have to be routed through the change control system, which means change requests, analysis of the costs and risks, and involvement from the change control board.

CERTIFICATION OBJECTIVE 8.05

Implementing Quality Control

Quality control (QC) requires the project manager, or another qualified party, to monitor and measure project results to determine that the results are up to the demands of the quality standards. If the results are unsatisfactory, root-cause analysis follows the quality control processes. Root-cause analysis is needed so the project manager can determine the cause and apply corrective actions. QC occurs throughout the life of a project, not just at its end.

QC is also not only concerned with the product the project is creating, but with the project management processes. QC measures performance, scheduling, and cost variances. The experience of the project should be of quality—not just the product the project creates. Consider a project manager that demands the project team work extreme hours to meet an unrealistic deadline; team morale suffers and likely so does the project work the team is completing.

The project team should do the following to ensure competency in quality control:

■ Conduct statistical quality control, such as sampling and probability.

■ Inspect the product to keep errors away from the customer.

■ Perform attribute sampling to measure conformance to quality on a per-unit basis.

■ Conduct variable sampling to measure the degree of conformance.

■ Study special causes to determine anomalies to quality.

■ Research random causes to determine expected variances of quality.

- Check the tolerance range to determine if the results are within or without an acceptable level of quality.
- Observe control limits to determine if the results are in or out of quality control.

Preparing for Quality Control

Quality control relies on several inputs, such as the following:

- **The quality management plan** The quality management plan defines how QA will be applied to the project, the expectations of quality control, and the organization's approach for continuous process improvement.
- **Work results** Execution brings about deliverables. The results of both the project processes and the product results are needed to measure the results of the project team's work and compare it to the quality standards. The expected results of the product and the project can be measured from the project plan.
- **Quality metrics** The operational definitions that define the metrics for the project are needed so QC can measure and react to the results of project performance.
- **Quality checklists** If the project is using checklists to ensure that project work is completed, a copy of the checklists will be needed as part of quality control. The checklists can then serve as an indicator of completed work and expected results.
- **Approved change requests** Approved change requests have an effect on how the project work is scheduled and performed, which may affect the project's overall quality.

Inspecting Results

Although quality is planned into a project, not inspected in, inspections are needed to prove conformance to requirements. An inspection can be done on the project as a whole, on a portion of the project work, on the project deliverable, or even on an individual activity. Inspections are also known as:

- Reviews
- Product reviews
- Audits
- Walkthroughs

Creating a Flow Chart

Technically, a flow chart is any diagram illustrating how components within a system are related. An organizational flow chart shows the bottom crew of operations up to the "little squirt" on top. A heating, ventilation, and air conditioning (HVAC) blueprint shows how the air flows through a building from the furnace to each room. Flow charts show the relationships between components, as well as help the project team determine where quality issues may be present and, once done, plan accordingly.

There are two types of flow charts you'll need to be concerned with for this exam.

- **Cause-and-effect diagrams**   These diagrams show the relationships between the variables within a process and how those relationships may contribute to inadequate quality. This diagram can help organize both the process and team opinions, as well as generate discussion on finding a solution to ensure quality. Figure 8-1 is an example of a cause-and-effect diagram. These diagrams are also known as Ishikawa diagrams and fishbone diagrams.

- **System or process flow charts**   These flowcharts illustrate the flow of a process through a system, such as a project change request through the change control system or work authorization through a quality control process. A process flow chart does not have to be limited to the project management activities. It could instead demonstrate how a manufacturer creates, packages, and ships the product to the customer, as seen in Figure 8-2.

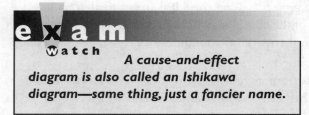

FIGURE 8-1

Cause-and-effect diagrams show the relationship of variables to a problem.

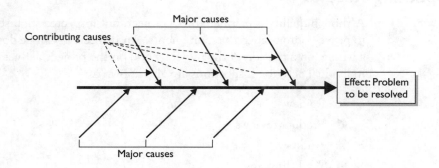

Major causes

Contributing causes

Effect: Problem to be resolved

Major causes

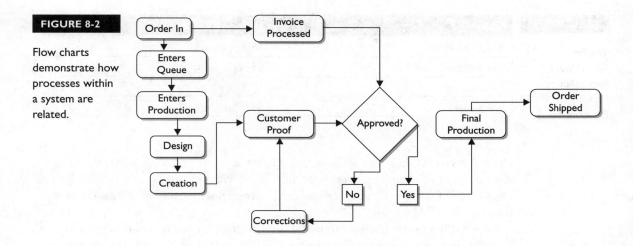

FIGURE 8-2

Flow charts demonstrate how processes within a system are related.

Creating a Control Chart

Ever feel like your project is out of control? A control chart can prove it.

Control charts illustrate the performance of a project over time. They map the results of inspections against a chart, as seen in Figure 8-3. Control charts are typically used in projects or operations where there are repetitive activities—such as for manufacturing, a testing series, or help desks.

The outer limits of a control chart are set by the customer requirements. Within the customer requirements are the upper control limits (UCLs) and the lower

FIGURE 8-3   Control charts demonstrate the results of inspections.

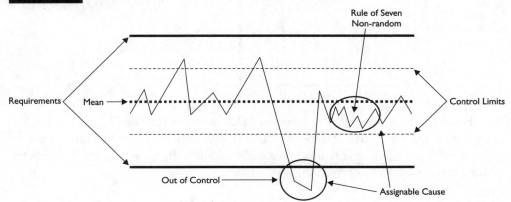

TABLE 8-1	Value	Percent Correct
	+/– 1 sigma	68.26 percent
The Four Sigma Values Representing Normal Distribution	+/– 2 sigma	95.46 percent
	+/– 3 sigma	99.73 percent
	+/– 6 sigma	99.99 percent

control limits (LCLs). The UCL is typically set at +3 or +6 sigma, while the LCL is set at –3 or –6 sigma. Sigma results show the degree of correctness. Table 8-1 outlines the four sigma values representing normal distribution. You'll need to know these for the PMP exam.

So what happened to sigma four and five? Nothing. They're still there; it's just that the difference between three sigma at 99.73 and six sigma at 99.99 are so small that statisticians just jump to six sigma. The mean in a control chart represents the expected result, while the sigma values represent the expected spread of results based on the inspection. A true six sigma allows only two defects per million opportunities, and the percentage to represent that value is 99.99985%. For the exam, you can go with the 99.99%.

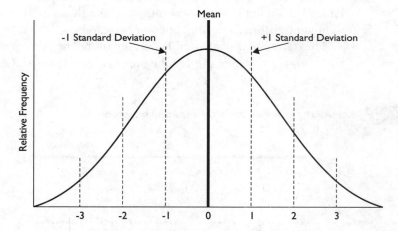

For example, if a manufacturer creates 1,000 units per hour and expects 50 units each hour to be defective, the mean would be 950 units. If the control limits were set at +/– three sigma, the results of testing would actually expect up to 953 correct units and down to 947 correct units.

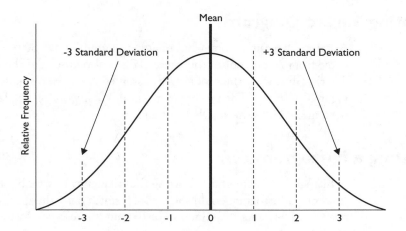

Over time, the results of testing are plotted in the control chart. Whenever a result of testing is plotted beyond the upper or lower control values, it is considered to be "out of control." When a value is out of control, there is a reason why—it's called an assignable cause. Something caused the results to change for better or for worse, and the result must be investigated to understand the why behind the occurrence.

Another assignable cause is "the Rule of Seven." The Rule of Seven states that whenever seven consecutive results are all on one side of the mean, this is an assignable cause. Thus, there's been some change that caused the results to shift to one side of the expected mean. Again, the cause must be investigated to determine why the change happened.

While control charts are easily associated with recurring activities, like manufacturing, they can also be applied to project management. Consider the number of expected change requests, delays within a project, and other recurring activities. A control chart can plot out these activities to measure performance, positive and negative results, and track corrective actions.

on the job

Some project managers may believe that there should be no variance at all in the results of testing—they expect it to be 100 percent correct all the time. In some instances, this is valid; consider hospitals, military scenarios, and other situations dealing with life and death. When a project manager demands 100 percent perfection, the cost of quality issues needs to be revisited. What is the cost of obtaining perfection versus the cost of obtaining 98 percent correctness?

Creating Pareto Diagrams

A Pareto diagram is somewhat related to Pareto's Law: 80 percent of the problems come from 20 percent of the issues. This is also known as the *80/20 rule*. A Pareto diagram illustrates the problems by assigned cause from smallest to largest, as Figure 8-4 shows. The project team should first work on the largest problems and then move on to the smaller problems.

Creating a Histogram

A histogram is a bar chart showing the frequency of variables within a project. For example, a histogram could show which states have the most customers. Within project management, a common histogram is a resource histogram that shows the frequency of resources used on project work. It's nothing more than a bar chart.

Creating a Run Chart

A run chart, as Figure 8-5 shows, is a line graph that shows the results of inspections in the order in which they've occurred. The goal of a run chart is to first demonstrate the results of a process over time and then use trend analysis to predict when certain trends may reemerge. Based on this information, an organization can work to prevent the negative trend or work to capitalize on an identified opportunity.

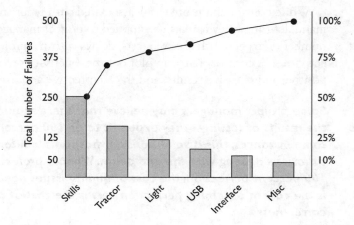

FIGURE 8-4

A Pareto diagram is a histogram that ranks the issues from largest to smallest.

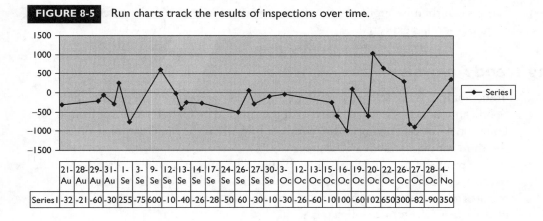

FIGURE 8-5   Run charts track the results of inspections over time.

Series1	21-Au	28-Au	29-Au	31-Au	1-Se	3-Se	9-Se	12-Se	13-Se	14-Se	17-Se	24-Se	26-Se	27-Se	30-Se	3-Oc	12-Oc	13-Oc	15-Oc	16-Oc	19-Oc	20-Oc	22-Oc	26-Oc	27-Oc	28-Oc	4-No
Series1	-32	-21	-60	-30	255	-75	600	-10	-40	-26	-28	-50	60	-30	-10	-30	-26	-60	-10	100	-60	102	650	300	-82	-90	350

Creating a Scatter Diagram

A scatter diagram is like a run chart, but it instead tracks the relationship between two variables. The two variables are considered related the closer they track against a diagonal line. For example, a project manager could track the performance of two team members, the time and cost, or even changes between functional managers and the project's schedule.

Completing a Statistical Sampling

Statistical sampling is the process of choosing a percentage of results at random. For example, a project creating a medical device may have 20 percent of all units randomly selected to check quality. This process must be completed on a consistent basis throughout the project, rather than on a sporadic schedule.

Statistical sampling can reduce the costs of quality control, but mixed results can follow if an adequate testing plan and schedule are not followed. The science of statistical sampling (and its requirements to be effective) is an involved process. There are many books, seminars, and professionals devoted to the process. For the PMP exam, know that statistical sampling uses a percentage of the results to test for quality. This process can reduce quality control cost.

Revisiting Flowcharting

Flowcharting uses charts to illustrate how the different parts of a system operate. Flowcharting is valuable in quality control because the process can be evaluated and tested to determine where in the process quality begins to break down. Corrective actions can then be applied to the system to ensure that quality continues as planned—and as expected.

Applying Trend Analysis

Trend analysis is the science of taking past results to predict future performance. Sports announcers use trend analysis all the time: "The Cubs have never won in St. Louis, on a Tuesday night, in the month of July, when the temperature at the top of the third inning was above 80 degrees."

The results of trend analysis allow the project manager to apply corrective action to intervene and prevent unacceptable outcomes. Trend analysis on a project requires adequate records to predict results and set current expectations. Trend analysis can monitor the following:

- **Technical performance** Trend analysis can ask, "How many errors have been experienced up to this point in the project schedule, and how many additional errors were encountered since the last testing of the technical performance?"

- **Cost and schedule performance** Trend analysis can ask, "How many activities were completed incorrectly, came in late, or had significant cost variances?"

The Results of Quality Control

Quality control should, first and foremost, result in quality improvement. The project manager and project team, based on the results of the tools and techniques to implement quality control, apply corrective actions to prevent unacceptable quality and improve the overall quality of the project management processes.

The corrective actions and the defect repairs that the project manager and the project team want to incorporate into the project may require change requests and management approval. The value and importance of the change should be evident so the improvement to quality is approved and folded into the project. In addition to quality improvement, there are other results of quality control.

- **Validated deliverables and changes** The work results are either accepted or rejected. Rejected items typically mean rework. When changes are approved and executed, these changes also need to be validated, as they're now part of the project scope baseline.

- **Rework**   Nonconformance to quality results in change requests for corrective action. Rework costs time and money, and it contributes to projects being late, over budget, or both. It is always more cost-effective to do the work right the first time than to do it correctly the second time.

- **Completed checklists**   If the project is using checklists to confirm the completion of work, the completed checklists should become part of the project records. Some project managers require the project team member completing the checklist to initial it as whole and complete.

- **Process adjustments**   When results of inspections indicate quality is out of control, process adjustments may be needed to make immediate corrective actions or planned preventative actions to ensure quality improves. Process adjustments, depending on the nature of the adjustment, may qualify for a change request and be funneled through the change control system as part of integration management.

- **Recommendations**   The project manager and the project team can also make recommendations for additional defect repairs, preventative actions, corrective actions, and even additional change requests.

INSIDE THE EXAM

Quality, in project management, has many different meanings. For the PMP exam, you should know the following four key facts:

- Customer satisfaction is the conformance of the requirements and fitness for use.
- Quality is distinct from grade.
- Quality is obtained by the project team doing what was promised at the start of the project.
- Quality is concerned with prevention over inspection.

Don't get flustered over the difference between QC and QA. QC focuses on monitoring the specific results of project work, while QA focuses on monitoring overall performance. If it helps for the exam, think of QC as being project-wide and QA as being organization-wide. Another aspect of QC is that the project team must be empowered to stop project work if quality is outside of the control limits set by the quality management plan.

The quality management plan spans all areas of project quality—not just the product the project is creating. The experience of the

(Continued)

project as led by the project manager should be of quality as well. There is a direct relationship between the project deliverables and the quality of project management.

Another area of quality is scheduling. A project manager must examine resources and how they are allocated, and pay attention to the cost of quality for the assigned resources. One scheduling technique, just-in-time (JIT) scheduling, demands higher quality. JIT does not order inventory, such as supplies and materials, until they are needed. This improves cash flow and reduces the cost of inventory not in use. However, a lack of quality in the project may cause defects. Because of the defects, the material in use is thus wasted and downtime occurs. This downtime results because there are no additional materials on hand and the project is waiting for new materials to arrive.

Finally, spend some time learning the values for the four sigmas shown in Table 8-1. You'll need them.

CERTIFICATION SUMMARY

What good is a project deliverable if it doesn't work, is unacceptable, or is faulty? Project quality management ensures that the deliverables that project teams create meet the expectations of the stakeholders. For your PMP examination, quality means delivering the project at the exact level of the design specifications and the project scope. No more, no less.

Quality and grade are two different things. Grade is the ranking assigned to different components that have the same functional purpose. For example, sheet metal may come in different grades based on what it is needed for. Another example is the grade of paper based on its thickness, ability to retain ink, and so on. Low quality is always a problem; low grade may not be.

Quality planning happens before project work begins—but also as work is completed. Quality planning can confirm the preexistence of quality or the need for quality improvements. Quality is planned into a project, not inspected in. However, quality control uses inspections to prove the existence of quality within a project deliverable.

There is a distinct difference between quality assurance and quality control. Quality assurance is a prevention-driven process. Management wants the project manager and the project team to do the work right the first time. Quality control, however, is an inspection-driven process—the project team, the project manager, and sometimes third-party inspectors examine the work to confirm that it is correct and of quality. Quality assurance is usually a program for the entire organization, or at least a line of business or department. In project management, quality control is specific to the actual project work.

The cost of quality is concerned with the monies invested in the project to ascertain the expected level of quality. Examples of this cost include training, safety measures, and quality management activities. The cost of nonconformance centers on the monies lost by not completing the project work correctly the first time. In addition, this cost includes the loss of sales, loss of customers, and downtime within the project.

Optimal quality is reached when the cost of the improvements equals the incremental costs to achieve quality. Marginal analysis is the study of when optimal quality is reached. The PMP candidate should know what marginal analysis is and why management is concerned with it. Ideally, the cost of quality is earned back because the deliverables of the project are better and more profitable than if the quality of deliverables was lacking.

KEY TERMS

If you're serious about passing the PMP exam, memorize these terms and their definitions. For maximum value, create your own flashcards based on these definitions and review daily.

benchmarking   A process of using prior projects internal or external to the performing organization to compare and set quality standards for processes and results.

benefit/cost analysis   The process of determining the pros and cons of any project, process, product, or activity.

checklists   A listing of activities that workers check to ensure the work has been completed consistently; used in quality control.

continuous process improvement   A goal of quality assurance to improve the project's processes and deliverables; meshes with the project's process improvement plan, which is to improve the processes of the project.

control charts   These illustrate the performance of a project over time. They map the results of inspections against a chart. Control charts are typically used in projects or operations that have repetitive activities, such as manufacturing, testing series, or help desk functions. Upper and lower control limits indicate if values are in control or out of control.

cost of conformance   The cost of completing the project work to satisfy the project scope and the expected level of quality. Examples include training, safety measures, and quality management activities. Also known as the cost of quality.

cost of nonconformance   The cost of not completing the project with quality, including wasted time for corrective actions, rework, and wasted materials. Could also mean loss of business, loss of sales, and lawsuits. Also known as the cost of poor quality.

design of experiments   This relies on statistical "what-if" scenarios to determine which variables within a project will result in the best outcome; it can also be used to eliminate a defect. The design of experiments approach is most often used on the product of the project, rather than on the project itself.

flow chart   A chart that illustrates how the parts of a system occur in sequence.

histogram   A bar chart; a Pareto diagram is an example of a histogram.

ISO 9000   An international standard that helps organizations follow their own quality procedures. ISO 9000 is not a quality system, but a method of following procedures created by an organization.

operational definitions   The quantifiable terms and values used to measure a process, activity, or work result. Operational definitions are also known as metrics.

Pareto diagrams   A Pareto diagram is related to Pareto's Law: 80 percent of the problems come from 20 percent of the issues (this is also known as the "80/20 rule"). A Pareto diagram illustrates problems by assigned cause, from smallest to largest.

process adjustments   When quality is lacking, process adjustments are needed for immediate corrective actions or for future preventive actions to ensure that quality improves. Process adjustments may qualify for a change request and be funneled through the change control system as part of integration management.

quality assurance   An executing process to ensure that the project is adhering to the quality expectations of the project customer and organization. QA is a prevention-driven process to perform the project work with quality to avoid errors, waste, and delays.

quality audits   A quality audit is a process to confirm that the quality processes are performing correctly on the current project. The quality audit determines how to make things better for the project and other projects within the organization. Quality audits measure the project's ability to maintain the expected level of quality.

quality control   A process in which the work results are monitored to see if they meet relevant quality standards.

quality management plan   This document describes how the project manager and the project team will fulfill the quality policy. In an ISO 9000 environment, the quality management plan is referred to as the "project quality system."

quality policy   The formal policy an organization follows to achieve a preset standard of quality. The project team should either adapt the quality policy of the organization to guide the project implementation or create its own policy if one does not exist within the performing organization.

run chart   Similar to a control chart, a run chart tracks trends over time and displays those trends in a graph with the plotted data mapped to a specific date.

scatter diagram   Tracks the relationship between two or more variables to determine if the one variable affects the other. It allows the project team, quality control team, or project manager to make adjustments to improve the overall results of the project.

statistical sampling   A process of choosing a percentage of results at random for inspection. Statistical sampling can reduce the costs of quality control.

trend analysis   Trend analysis is taking past results to predict future performance.

✔ TWO-MINUTE DRILL

The Big Quality Picture

❑ The project manager is responsible for the overall quality management of the project and must set quality expectations based on the requirements of the customers and stakeholders.

❑ The project manager must integrate the quality control of the project with the quality assurance program of the performing organization.

❑ Quality is planned into a project, not inspected in.

Preparing for Quality

❑ Quality doesn't happen by accident. Quality is satisfying the expectations of the project scope baseline.

❑ The project team members (the people actually completing the project work) are responsible for the quality of the deliverables.

❑ The project team, as guided by the project manager and the quality management plan, should be empowered to stop the project work when preset, quality thresholds are exceeded.

Planning for Quality

❑ Quality planning is an iterative process. As quality concerns creep into the project, the planning processes are revisited to ensure that actions—both preventive and corrective—are taken to ensure quality.

❑ The quality management plan is a subsidiary plan of the overall project management plan. It defines how the project will accomplish the quality expectations of the organization and how the project will adhere to the quality policy of the organization.

❑ The process improvement plan is a subsidiary plan of the overall project management plan. It defines how project processes will be analyzed and improved upon. The goal of this plan is to improve the value of the project by removing non-value-added activities.

❑ The cost of quality is the amount of monies the performing organization must spend to satisfy the quality standards. This can include training, safety measures, and additional activities implemented to prevent nonconformance.

❑ The cost of nonconformance to quality is the monies or events attributed to not satisfying the quality demands. These can include loss of business, downtime, wasted materials, rework, and cost and schedule variances.

Executing Quality Assurance

❑ Quality assurance aims to do the work properly and correctly the first time, according to plan.

❑ Quality assurance may use a QA program to set quality standards.

❑ Quality assurance represents the implementation of the quality plan.

❑ Quality management is the process to ensure the project is completed with no deviations from the requirements.

❑ Kaizen is used in an organization to apply small changes to products and processes in order to improve consistency, reduce costs, and provide overall quality improvements.

Implementing Quality Control

❑ Quality control monitors specific results within a project.

❑ A fishbone diagram is a cause-and-effect diagram that illustrates the factors that may be contributing to quality issues or problems. It is also known as an Ishikawa diagram.

❑ Pareto diagrams are histograms that are related to Pareto's 80/20 rule: "80 percent of the problems come from 20 percent of the issues." The diagram charts the problems, categories, and frequency. The project team should first solve the larger problems and then move on to smaller issues.

❑ A run chart is a line graph that shows the results of inspection in the order in which each inspection occurred. The goal of a run chart is to first demonstrate the results of a process over time and then use trend analysis to predict when certain trends may reemerge.

❑ Control charts plot out the results of inspections against a mean to examine performance against expected results. Upper and lower control limits are typically set to ± three or six sigma. Results that are beyond the control limit value are considered out of control.

SELF TEST

1. Which of the following is responsible for the quality of the project deliverables?
   A. The project champion
   B. The project team
   C. Stakeholders
   D. Customers

2. What type of chart is the following?

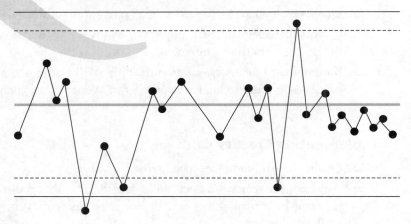

   A. Control
   B. Pareto
   C. Scatter
   D. Flow

3. You are the project manager for the BBB Project. Stacy, a project team member, is confused about what QA is. Which of the following best describes QA?
   A. QA is quality assurance for the overall project performance.
   B. QA is quality acceptance according to scope verification.
   C. QA is quality assurance for the project deliverable.
   D. QA is quality assurance for the project stakeholders.

4. You are the project manager for the Photo Scanning Project. This project is similar to another project you have completed. Your project is to electronically store thousands of historical photos for your city's historical society. Quality is paramount on this project. Management approaches you and asks why you have devoted so much of the project time for planning. Your response is which of the following?

A. This is a first-time, first-use project, so more time is needed for planning.

B. Planning for a project of this size, with this amount of quality, is mandatory.

C. Quality is planned into a project, not inspected in.

D. Quality audits are part of the planning time.

5. You are the project manager for the Floor Installation Project. Today, you plan to meet with your project team to ensure the project is completed with no deviations from the project requirements. This process is which of the following?

A. Quality planning

B. Quality management

C. Quality control

D. Quality assurance

6. You are the project manager for the ASE Project, which must map to industry standards in order to be accepted by the customer. You and your team have studied the requirements and have created a plan to implement the deliverables with the appropriate level of quality. What is this process called?

A. Quality planning

B. Quality management

C. Quality control

D. Quality assurance

7. Which of the following is an example of internal failure cost?

A. Rework

B. Quality audits

C. Random quality audits

D. Project team training

8. QC is typically a(n) _____ process.

A. Management

B. Project manager

C. Audit

D. Inspection

9. QA is typically a(n) _____ process.

A. Management

B. Project manager

C. Audit

D. Inspection

10. You are the project manager for a large manufacturer of wood furniture. Your new project is the Shop Table Project, which will involve the creation and manufacture of a new table for woodworkers to use in their wood shops. For this project, you have elected to use JIT for scheduling. Which of the following is an advantage to using JIT?
    A. It requires materials to be readily available.
    B. It allows the project team to have control over the materials.
    C. It decreases the inventory investment.
    D. It allows for a broad range of deviation compared to other inventory solutions.

11. Your company has elected to use ISO 9000 standards. What is an attribute of ISO 9000?
    A. It ensures that your company follows its own quality procedures.
    B. It ensures that your company follows the set phases in each project from initiation to closure.
    C. It ensures that your company maps its processes to a proven process within the program.
    D. It ensures that QA and QC are integrated into the product or service your organization offers.

12. You are the project manager of the Halogen Installation Project. As this project gets underway, you receive notice from the program manager that the organization will be moving to Kaizen technologies as part of its quality management program. What are Kaizen technologies?
    A. Small improvements for small results
    B. Small improvements for all projects
    C. Small process and product improvements that are carried out on a continuous basis
    D. Small process improvements that are made to shorten the project duration

13. A fishbone diagram is the same as a(n) _____ chart.
    A. Ishikawa
    B. Pareto
    C. Flow
    D. Control

14. Management has asked you to define the correlation between quality and the project scope. Which of the following is the best answer?
    A. The project scope will include metrics for quality.
    B. Quality metrics will be applied to the project scope.
    C. Quality is the process of completing the scope to meet stated or implied needs.
    D. Quality is the process of evaluating the project scope to ensure quality exists.

15. Which of the following is most true about quality?
    A. It will cost more money to build quality into the project.
    B. It will cost less money to build quality into the project process.
    C. Quality is inspection-driven.
    D. Quality is prevention-driven.

16. Which of the following can be described as a business philosophy to find methods that will continuously improve products, services, and business practices?
    A. TQM
    B. ASQ
    C. QA
    D. QC

17. In quality management, which of the following is not an attribute of the cost of nonconformance?
    A. Loss of customers
    B. Downtime
    C. Safety measures
    D. Rework

18. You are the project manager for the KOY Project, which requires quality that maps to federal guidelines. To ensure that you can meet these standards, you have elected to put the project team through training specific to the federal guidelines your project must adhere to. The costs of these classes can be assigned to which of the following?
    A. Cost of doing business
    B. Cost of quality
    C. Cost of adherence
    D. Cost of nonconformance

19. You are the project manager for the KOY Project, which requires quality that maps to federal guidelines. During a quality audit, you discover that a portion of the project work is faulty and must be done again. The requirement to correct the work is an example of which of the following?
    A. Cost of quality
    B. Cost of adherence
    C. Cost of nonconformance
    D. Cost of doing business

20. Optimal quality is reached at what point?

A. When the stakeholder accepts the project deliverable

B. When revenue from improvements equal the costs of conformance

C. When revenue from improvement equals the incremental costs to achieve the quality

D. When revenue from corrective actions equals the costs of the improvement

21. You are the project manager of the JKL Project, which currently has some production flaws. Which analysis tool will allow you to determine the cause and effect of the production faults?

A. A flow chart

B. A Pareto diagram

C. An Ishikawa diagram

D. A control chart

22. Linda is the project manager of a manufacturing project. She and her project team are using design of experiments to look for ways to improve quality. Which of the following best describes design of experiments?

A. It allows the project manager to move the relationship of activities to complete the project work with the best resources available.

B. It allows the project manager to experiment with the project design to determine what variables are causing the flaws.

C. It allows the project manager to experiment with variables to attempt to improve quality.

D. It allows the project manager to experiment with the project design document to become more productive and to provide higher quality.

23. You are the project manager of the Global Upgrade Project. Your project team consists of 75 project team members around the world. Each project team will be upgrading a piece of equipment in many different facilities. Which of the following could you implement to ensure that the project team members are completing all of the steps in the install procedure with quality?

A. Checklists

B. WBS

C. PND

D. The WBS dictionary

24. Mark is the project manager of the PMH Project. Quality audits of the deliverables show there are several problems. Management has asked Mark to create a chart showing the distribution of problems and their frequencies. Given this, management wants which of the following?

A. A control chart
B. An Ishikawa chart
C. A Pareto diagram
D. A flow chart

25. In the following graphic, what does the highlighted area represent?

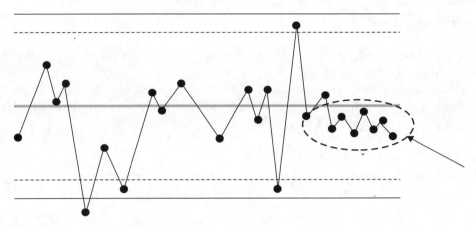

A. Out-of-control data points
B. In-control data points
C. The Rule of Seven
D. Standard deviation

SELF TEST ANSWERS

1. Which of the following is responsible for the quality of the project deliverables?
   A. The project champion
   B. The project team
   C. Stakeholders
   D. Customers

   ☑ **B.** The project team (the individuals completing the project work) is responsible for the quality of the project deliverables.
   ☒ **A** is incorrect. The project champion may review the work, but the responsibility of quality does not lie with this individual. **C** and **D** are also incorrect choices; the customer and other stakeholders are not responsible for the quality of the project.

2. What type of chart is the following?

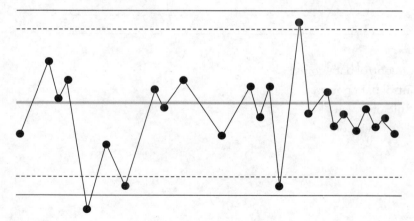

   A. Control
   B. Pareto
   C. Scatter
   D. Flow

   ☑ **A.** The chart shown is a control chart.
   ☒ **B** is incorrect, since a Pareto diagram maps categories of issues and their frequency. **C** is incorrect because a scatter chart compares common values across multiple categories. **D,** a flow chart, is also incorrect. Flow charts illustrate how a process moves through a system and how the components are interrelated.

3. You are the project manager for the BBB Project. Stacy, a project team member, is confused about what QA is. Which of the following best describes QA?

A. QA is quality assurance for the overall project performance.

B. QA is quality acceptance according to scope verification.

C. QA is quality assurance for the project deliverable.

D. QA is quality assurance for the project stakeholders.

   ☑ **A.** QA is concerned with overall project quality performance.

   ☒ **B, C,** and **D** are incorrect because they do not correctly explain quality assurance.

4. You are the project manager for the Photo Scanning Project. This project is similar to another project you have completed. Your project is to electronically store thousands of historical photos for your city's historical society. Quality is paramount on this project. Management approaches you and asks why you have devoted so much of the project time for planning. Your response is which of the following?

A. This is a first-time, first-use project, so more time is needed for planning.

B. Planning for a project of this size, with this amount of quality, is mandatory.

C. Quality is planned into a project, not inspected in.

D. Quality audits are part of the planning time.

   ☑ **C.** Of all the choices presented, this is the best answer. Quality is planned into the project and the planning requires time.

   ☒ **A** is incorrect because a project of this nature has been completed before. **B** is incorrect because there isn't enough information provided to determine what the quality demands of the project are. **D** is incorrect because quality audits are not part of the planning processes.

5. You are the project manager for the Floor Installation Project. Today, you plan to meet with your project team to ensure the project is completed with no deviations from the project requirements. This process is which of the following?

A. Quality planning

B. Quality management

C. Quality control

D. Quality assurance

   ☑ **A.** Quality planning should be completed prior to the work beginning—and should thereafter be revisited as needed.

   ☒ **B** is incorrect, since quality management is not an applicable answer to the scenario. **C** and **D** are incorrect because QA and QC are part of quality management.

6. You are the project manager for the ASE Project, which must map to industry standards in order to be accepted by the customer. You and your team have studied the requirements and have created a plan to implement the deliverables with the appropriate level of quality. What is this process called?

   A. Quality planning
   B. Quality management
   C. Quality control
   D. Quality assurance

   ☑   **A.** Quality planning is the process of creating a plan to meet the requirements of quality.
   ☒   **B, C,** and **D** are incorrect because they do not explain the process in the question's scenario.

7. Which of the following is an example of internal failure cost?

   A. Rework
   B. Quality audits
   C. Random quality audits
   D. Project team training

   ☑   **A.** Internal failure cost is attributed to failure that results in rework. It is an example of the cost of nonconformance to quality.
   ☒   **B** and **C** are incorrect. Quality audits are not a cost associated with nonconformance. **D** is incorrect because project team training is an example of the cost of conformance to quality.

8. QC is typically a(n) _____ process.

   A. Management
   B. Project manager
   C. Audit
   D. Inspection

   ☑   **D.** QC requires an inspection of the work results. While quality is planned into a project, inspections ensure it exists.
   ☒   **A** is incorrect because QA is a managerial function. **B** is incorrect because another department, team member, or SME can complete QC. **C** is incorrect; an audit is too broad an answer for this question. Audits can be financial-, schedule-, or quality-driven.

9. QA is typically a(n) _____ process.
   A. Management
   B. Project manager
   C. Audit
   D. Inspection

☑ **A.** QA is typically a management process.
☒ **B** is incorrect because another department, team member, or SME can complete QC. **C** is incorrect because an audit is too broad of an answer for this question. Audits can be financial-, schedule-, or quality-driven. **D** is wrong because QA is typically not an inspection process.

10. You are the project manager for a large manufacturer of wood furniture. Your new project is the Shop Table Project, which will involve the creation and manufacture of a new table for woodworkers to use in their wood shops. For this project, you have elected to use JIT for scheduling. Which of the following is an advantage to using JIT?
   A. It requires materials to be readily available.
   B. It allows the project team to have control over the materials.
   C. It decreases the inventory investment.
   D. It allows for a broad range of deviation compared to other inventory solutions.

☑ **C.** JIT (just-in-time) scheduling decreases the investment in inventory. However, mistakes with the materials can cause downtime if no additional materials are on hand.
☒ **A** is incorrect because materials are only available when they're needed. **B** is incorrect; the project team must use caution not to waste the materials. **D** is incorrect because JIT does not allow for a broad range of deviation.

11. Your company has elected to use ISO 9000 standards. What is an attribute of ISO 9000?
   A. It ensures that your company follows its own quality procedures.
   B. It ensures that your company follows the set phases in each project from initiation to closure.
   C. It ensures that your company maps its processes to a proven process within the program.
   D. It ensures that QA and QC are integrated into the product or service your organization offers.

☑ **A.** ISO 9000 is not a quality management system, but a system to ensure that an organization follows its own quality procedures.
☒ **B, C,** and **D** are all incorrect. These choices do not correctly describe ISO 9000.

12. You are the project manager of the Halogen Installation Project. As this project gets underway, you receive notice from the program manager that the organization will be moving to Kaizen technologies as part of its quality management program. What are Kaizen technologies?

A. Small improvements for small results

B. Small improvements for all projects

C. Small process and product improvements that are carried out on a continuous basis

D. Small process improvements that are made to shorten the project duration

☑ **C.** Kaizen technologies are small changes to processes and products on a steady, continuous basis to save costs and improve quality.

☒ **A** is incorrect. While Kaizen does implement small process changes, it does not aim for small results. **B** and **D** are also incorrect. Kaizen does not have to be implemented in all projects, though it often is. Kaizen is also not interested in necessarily reducing the project duration.

13. A fishbone diagram is the same as a(n) _____ diagram.

A. Ishikawa

B. Pareto

C. Flow

D. Control

☑ **A.** A fishbone diagram is the same as an Ishikawa diagram.

☒ **B, C,** and **D** are incorrect. These charts and diagrams accomplish goals other than the cause-and-effect of the Ishikawa.

14. Management has asked you to define the correlation between quality and the project scope. Which of the following is the best answer?

A. The project scope will include metrics for quality.

B. Quality metrics will be applied to the project scope.

C. Quality is the process of completing the scope to meet stated or implied needs.

D. Quality is the process of evaluating the project scope to ensure quality exists.

☑ **C.** Quality, in regard to the project scope, is about completing the work as promised and defined in the project scope. It is what the customer is expecting as part of the project deliverables.

☒ **A** is incorrect because though the project scope will have requirements for acceptance, it may not have metrics for quality defined. **B** and **D** are also incorrect.

15. Which of the following is most true about quality?
    A. It will cost more money to build quality into the project.
    B. It will cost less money to build quality into the project process.
    C. Quality is inspection-driven.
    D. Quality is prevention-driven.

    ☑ **D.** Quality is prevention-driven. Quality wants to complete the work correctly the first time in order to prevent poor results, a loss of time, and a loss of funds.
    ☒ **A** and **B** are incorrect. There is no guarantee that a project will cost more or less, depending on the amount of expected quality. Incidentally, lack of quality will likely cost more than quality planning because of the cost of nonconformance. **C** is incorrect because quality is planned into a project, not inspected in.

16. Which of the following can be described as a business philosophy to find methods that will continuously improve products, services, and business practices?
    A. TQM
    B. ASQ
    C. QA
    D. QC

    ☑ **A.** TQM, total quality management, is a business philosophy to find methods to continuously improve products, services, and business practices.
    ☒ **B,** ASQ (American Society of Quality), is not a business philosophy. **C** and **D** are attributes of TQM, but are not correct answers for this question.

17. In quality management, which of the following is not an attribute of the cost of nonconformance?
    A. Loss of customers
    B. Downtime
    C. Safety measures
    D. Rework

    ☑ **C.** A safety measure is not an attribute of the cost of nonconformance, but rather a cost of adhering to quality.
    ☒ **A, B,** and **D** are incorrect choices. These are all attributes of the cost of nonconformance.

18. You are the project manager for the KOY Project, which requires quality that maps to federal guidelines. To ensure you can meet these standards, you have elected to put the project team through training specific to the federal guidelines your project must adhere to. The costs of these classes can be assigned to which of the following?
    A. Cost of doing business
    B. Cost of quality
    C. Cost of adherence
    D. Cost of nonconformance

    ☑ **B.** Training to meet the quality expectations are attributed to the cost of quality.
    ☒ **A, C,** and **D** are incorrect because these choices do not describe training as a cost of quality.

19. You are the project manager for the KOY Project, which requires quality that maps to federal guidelines. During a quality audit, you discover that a portion of the project work is faulty and must be done again. The requirement to correct the work is an example of which of the following?
    A. Cost of quality
    B. Cost of adherence
    C. Cost of nonconformance
    D. Cost of doing business

    ☑ **C.** When project work results are faulty and must be done over, it is attributed to the cost of nonconformance to quality.
    ☒ **A, B,** and **D** are all incorrect. These values do not describe faulty work or the cost of non-conformance.

20. Optimal quality is reached at what point?
    A. When the stakeholder accepts the project deliverable
    B. When revenue from improvements equal the costs of conformance
    C. When revenue from improvement equals the incremental costs to achieve the quality
    D. When revenue from corrective actions equals the costs of the improvement

    ☑ **C.** Marginal analysis provides that optimal quality is reached when the cost of the improvements equals the incremental costs to achieve the quality.
    ☒ **A, B,** and **D** are incorrect. These answers do not describe marginal analysis.

21. You are the project manager of the JKL Project, which currently has some production flaws. Which analysis tool will allow you to determine the cause and effect of the production faults?

   A. A flow chart

   B. A Pareto diagram

   C. An Ishikawa diagram

   D. A control chart

> ☑ **C.** The key words "cause and effect" equate to the Ishikawa diagram.
>
> ☒ **A** is incorrect. A flow chart will show how a process moves through the system, but not the cause and effect of the problems involved. **B** is incorrect as well. A Pareto chart maps out the causes and frequency of problems. **D,** a control chart, plots out the results of sampling, but it doesn't show the cause and effect of problems.

22. Linda is the project manager of a manufacturing project. She and her project team are using design of experiments to look for ways to improve quality. Which of the following best describes design of experiments?

   A. It allows the project manager to move the relationship of activities to complete the project work with the best resources available.

   B. It allows the project manager to experiment with the project design to determine what variables are causing the flaws.

   C. It allows the project manager to experiment with variables to attempt to improve quality.

   D. It allows the project manager to experiment with the project design document to become more productive and to provide higher quality.

> ☑ **C.** Of all the choices presented, **C** is the best. Design of experiments uses experiments and "what-if" scenarios to determine what variables are affecting quality.
>
> ☒ **A** is incorrect because design of experiments, in regard to quality, is not interested in changing the relationship of activities to complete project work. **B** and **D** are also incorrect because design of experiments will not be changing project design to determine where flaws exist or to become more productive.

23. You are the project manager of the Global Upgrade Project. Your project team consists of 75 project team members around the world. Each project team will be upgrading a piece of equipment in many different facilities. Which of the following could you implement to ensure that the project team members are completing all of the steps in the install procedure with quality?

A. Checklists

B. WBS

C. PND

D. The WBS dictionary

☑ **A.** Checklists are simple but effective quality management tools that the project manager can use to ensure that the project team is completing the required work.

☒ **B, C,** and **D** are all incorrect. The WBS, PND, and WBS dictionary are not tools the project team can necessarily use to prove they've completed required work. Checklists are the best approach for this scenario.

24. Mark is the project manager of the PMH Project. Quality audits of the deliverables show there are several problems. Management has asked Mark to create a chart showing the distribution of problems and their frequencies. Given this, management wants which of the following?

A. A control chart

B. An Ishikawa chart

C. A Pareto diagram

D. A flow chart

☑ **C.** Management wants Mark to create a Pareto diagram. Recall that a Pareto diagram maps out the causes of defects and illustrates their frequency.

☒ **A** is incorrect because a control chart does not identify the problems, only the relationship of the results to the expected mean. **B** is incorrect because a cause-and-effect diagram does not map out the frequency of problems. **D** is also incorrect. Flow charts show how a process moves through a system and how the components are related.

25. In the following graphic, what does the highlighted area represent?

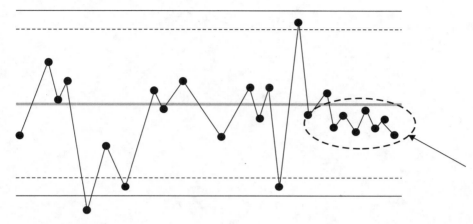

   A. Out-of-control data points

   B. In-control data points

   C. The Rule of Seven

   D. Standard deviation

☑ **C.** The highlighted area shows seven consecutive sampling results all on one side of the mean. This is known as the Rule of Seven and is an assignable cause.

☒ **A** is incorrect. These values are in control. **B** is correct, but it does not fully answer the question as choice **C** does. **D** is incorrect, since standard deviation is a predicted measure of the variance from the expected mean of a sampling.

9

Introducing Project Human Resource Management

Project human resource management is multifaceted. It is the ability to lead, direct, and orchestrate the project team, customers, project partners, contributors, and any other stakeholders to achieve the desired results for the project's purpose.

Project managers cannot, and must not, do everything. They must rely on the project team to complete the project work. Have you ever worked on a project where the project manager wanted to do the work? Or the project manager assigned the mundane tasks to the project team and did the most important activities himself? Or the project manager completed the activities with the highest exposure? Not good. Project managers must delegate activities.

Project human resource management relies on the general management skills we discussed in Chapter 2.

- Leading
- Communicating
- Negotiating
- Problem solving
- Influencing

Project managers must find ways to motivate the project team to complete the work. There is a tendency, in many projects, for the project team to be excited about the project at the start and then the excitement wanes as the project moves toward completion. The project manager must coach and mentor to develop the project team to ensure that the excitement, willingness, and dedication to the project work continue.

Throughout the project, the project manager will have to address project team retention, labor relations, performance appraisals, and, depending on the nature of the project work, health and safety issues. As most projects are new and temporary, so, too, are the relationships between the project team members and the project manager.

As the project progresses, the number of stakeholders in the project may change. The project manager and the project team will need to be aware of the coming influx of stakeholders and how this change may affect the dynamics of the project team and the project work. An approach to project human resources may work well in one phase of the project but not in another due to the stakeholders that have become involved.

Project human resource management may not be completely in the hands of the project manager. The performing organization's HR department may have control over the majority of the assignment and recruitment of the project team. It's important for the project manager to know his responsibility, power, and autonomy in order to comply with the organization's policies.

CERTIFICATION OBJECTIVE 9.01

Preparing for Human Resource Planning

Human resource planning is the process of mapping the project's roles, responsibilities, and reporting relationships to the appropriate people or groups of people. HR planning identifies the people involved with the project and determines what their role in the project is, whom they may report to—or receive a report from—and what their overall influence on the project work is.

Consider a project to create a community park. The project manager works for a commercial entity that will complete the project work. She identifies the people responsible for activities within her organization, the designers, engineers, installers, management, and so on. She will also have functional managers to coordinate employees' availability, financing to arrange procurement of resources needed for project completion, and senior management to report the status of the project work.

The project manager will also work and communicate with government officials for approval of the design, change requests, and overall schedule of the project. There'll be safety issues, landscaping questions, and other concerns that will come up as the project progresses.

Finally, the project manager will likely communicate with stakeholders that are not internal to her organization—for example, the people that live in the community and enjoy the park, and various government officials. These stakeholders will need to be involved in the planning and design of the park to ensure that it satisfies the community's needs.

As you can see, HR can involve both internal and external stakeholders. In most projects, organizational planning happens early in the project planning phase—but it should be reviewed and adjusted as the environment changes. Organizational planning is all about ensuring that the project performs properly in the environment it is working in. Much of organizational planning focuses on communications, which we'll cover in the next chapter.

Identifying the Project Interfaces

Project interfaces are the people and groups the project manager and the project team will work with to complete the project. There are five types of interfaces.

- **Organizational interfaces** These are the folks within the performing organization who the project team will work with to complete the project work. For example, a project to install a centralized, real-time database for customer orders and manufacturing will require the sales, finance, manufacturing, and information technology organizational units to be involved. The different organizational units may all be involved throughout the project life, or their level of involvement may fluctuate, depending on the project needs.

- **Technical interfaces** The technical interfaces describe the relationship between the project and the technical disciplines' input to the project. Consider a project to create a new building. The technical interfaces would include architects, mechanical engineers, structural engineers, and others. These interfaces would be involved throughout the project phases—and also between project phases for inspections, change requests, and so on.

- **Interpersonal interfaces** Interpersonal interfaces describe the reporting relationships among the people working on the project. Depending on the nature of the project and the information to be shared, the communication can be informal, such as a hallway meeting, or formal, such as a variance report. We'll discuss formal and informal communications in the next module.

- **Logistical interfaces** Project managers must consider the logistics of the project stakeholders. This means the project manager needs to know if they're collocated, what time zones may be in play, and even the countries of the stakeholders involved.

- **Political interfaces** Ah, there's always politics isn't there? The project manager must consider the individual goals of the stakeholders, their informal power with the organization, and whether formal or informal alliances exist.

Identifying the Resource Requirements

Every project needs people to complete the work. Resource requirements are the identified roles needed on a project to complete the assigned work. For example, a project to install a new telephone system throughout a campus would require a menagerie of workers with varying skill sets: hardware and software gurus, telephony

Sometimes project managers are influenced by the halo effect. This is when one attribute of a person influences a decision. For example, Bob is a great software developer, so he'd naturally *be a great project manager for software projects. In other words, there's no evidence that just because Bob's extremely skilled at software development that he'd also be a good project manager.*

experts, electricians, installers, and others. The identified staff would be pulled from the resource pool. Any skills gaps would need to be addressed through staff acquisition, additional training, or procurement.

Identifying the Project Constraints

Constraints limit. When it comes to human resource constraints, the project manager is dealing with any factors that limit options for project completion. This is where creativity comes into play: The project manager must find a way to creatively acquire, schedule, or train the needed resources to complete the project. Common constraints include the following:

■ **Organizational structure** Recall the organizational structures: functional, weak matrix, balanced matrix, strong matrix, and projectized. The project manager's authority in the organization is relevant to the organizational structure he is forced to work within.

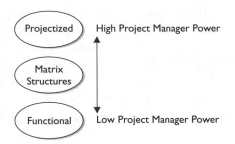

■ **Collective bargaining agreements** The contractual agreements between employee groups, unions, or other labor organizations may serve as a constraint on the project. In these instances, there may be additional reporting relationships regarding the project status, work, and performance of project team members.

structure of historical projects as a model for the current project. As a rule, current projects should emulate successful historical projects.

Applying Human Resource Practices

The performing organization will likely have policies and procedures for the project manager to follow. Enterprise environmental factors, usually through management or a human resources department, should specify:

- Job responsibilities
- Reporting structures
- The project manager's role and autonomy
- Policies regarding project team member discipline
- The definition for customized organizational terms, such as coach, mentor, or champion

Relating to Organizational Theories

There are many different organizational theories that a project manager can rely on to identify weakness and strengths, guide the project team, and move the project forward. The entire context of these theories is beyond the scope of this book; however, you should be familiar with several of these theories to pass the PMP exam.

ON THE CD

See the video Human Resource Theories.

Maslow's Hierarchy of Needs

According to Maslow, people work to take care of a hierarchy of needs. The pinnacle of their needs is self-actualization. People want to contribute, prove their work, and use their skills and abilities. Figure 9-1 shows the pyramid of needs that all people try to ascend by fulfilling each layer, one at a time.

Maslow's five layers of needs, from the bottom up, are:

- **Physiological**   The necessities to live: air, water, food, clothing, and shelter.
- **Safety**   People need safety and security; this can include stability in life, work, and culture.
- **Social**   People are social creatures and need love, approval, and friends.
- **Esteem**   People strive for the respect, appreciation, and approval of others.
- **Self-actualization**   At the pinnacle of needs, people seek personal growth, knowledge, and fulfillment.

FIGURE 9-1

Maslow says
people work for
self-actualization.

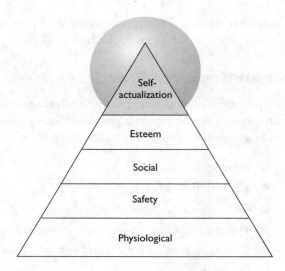

Herzberg's Theory of Motivation

According to Frederick Herzberg, a psychologist and authority on the motivation of work, there are two catalysts for success with people.

- **Hygiene agents**   These elements are the expectations all workers have: job security, a paycheck, clean and safe working conditions, a sense of belonging, civil working relationships, and other basic attributes associated with employment.

- **Motivating agents**   These are the elements that motivate people to excel. They include responsibility, appreciation of work, recognition, the chance to excel, education, and other opportunities associated with work other than just financial rewards.

This theory says the presence of hygiene factors will not motivate people to perform, as these are expected attributes. However, the absence of these elements will demotivate performance. For people to excel, the presence of motivating factors must exist. Figure 9-2 illustrates Herzberg's Theory of Motivation.

McGregor's Theory of X and Y

McGregor's theory states that management believes there are two types of workers, good and bad, as shown in Figure 9-3.

FIGURE 9-2

The absence of
hygiene factors
causes a worker's
performance
to suffer.

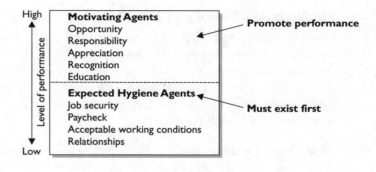

FIGURE 9-3

Management
believes "X"
people are bad
and "Y" people
are good.

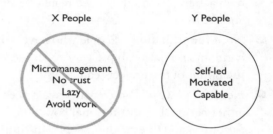

- X is bad. These people need to be watched all the time, micromanaged, and distrusted. X people avoid work, responsibility, and have no ability to achieve.

- Y is good. These people are self-led, motivated, and can accomplish new tasks proactively.

Ouchi's Theory Z

William Ouchi's Theory Z is based on the participative management style of the Japanese. This theory states that workers are motivated by a sense of commitment, opportunity, and advancement. Workers in an organization subscribing to Theory Z learn the business by moving up through the ranks of the company.

Ouchi's Theory Z also credits the idea of "lifetime employment." Workers will stay with one company until they retire because they are dedicated to the company that is in turn dedicated to them.

exam
watch *If you need a way to keep McGregor's X and Y and Ouchi's Z all separate in your mind, think of this: X is bad, Y is good, and Z is better.*

McClelland's Theory of Needs

David McClelland developed his acquired-needs theory based on his belief that a person's needs are acquired and develop over time. These needs are shaped by circumstance, conditions, and life experiences for each individual. McClelland's Theory of Needs is also known as the Three Needs Theory because there are just three-needs for each individual. Depending on the person's experiences, the order and magnitude of each need shifts.

- **Need for achievement**   These people need to achieve so they avoid both low-risk and high-risk situations. Achievers like to work alone or with other high achievers, and they need regular feedback to gauge their achievement and progress.
- **Need for affiliation**   People who have a driving need for affiliation look for harmonious relationships, want to feel accepted by people, and conform to the norms of the project team.
- **Need for power**   People who have a need for power are usually seeking either personal or institutional power. Personal power-seekers generally want to control and direct other people. Institutional power-seekers want to direct the efforts of others for the betterment of the organization.

McClelland developed the Thematic Apperception Test to determine what needs are driving individuals. The test is a series of pictures, and the test taker has to create a story about what's happening in the picture. Through the story telling, the test taker will reveal which need is driving his life at that time.

Expectancy Theory

Expectancy theory states that people will behave based on what they expect as a result of their behavior. In other words, people will work in relation to the expected reward of the work. If the attractiveness of the reward is desirable to the worker, she will work to receive the reward. In other words, people expect to be rewarded for their effort.

Management Styles

In addition to these fine theories, there are different approaches to managing the project team. Here's a quick rundown of the four major management styles:

- **Autocratic**   The project manager makes all of the decisions.
- **Democratic**   The project team is involved in the decision-making process.

- **Laissez faire**   The project manager has a hands-off policy, and the team is entirely self-led regarding the decision-making process.
- **Exceptional**   The project manager only pays attention to the top 10 percent and the bottom 10 percent of the project team performers.

Networking with Stakeholders

Networking and project management is all about meeting people in an organization, in a professional society, or within a business to find contacts, stakeholders, and influencers who may affect the project staffing. At the launch of a project, networking events, such as luncheons, conferences, and meetings, can help the project manager identify project stakeholders, learn about the project requirements, and influence project decisions.

Charting the Project Resources

There are several different charts the project manager can utilize to map the hierarchy of the project and the roles and responsibilities of the project team. The most common charts are:

- **Organizational charts**   These show how an organization, such as a company or large project team, is ordered, reporting structures, and the flow of information.
- **Organizational breakdown structure**   Though these charts are similar to the WBS, the breakdown is by department, by units, or by team.
- **Resource breakdown structure**   This type of chart breaks down the project by types of resources utilized on the project no matter where the resource is being utilized in the project.
- **Responsibility assignment matrix chart**   This chart type designates the roles and responsibilities of the project team.
- **RACI chart**   A RACI chart designates each team member against each project activity as Responsible, Accountable, Consult, or Inform (RACI). A RACI chart is technically a type of responsibility assignment matrix chart.

CERTIFICATION OBJECTIVE 9.03

Preparing for Project Team Management

Organizational planning is part of the overall planning process, so it, too, is iterative. The outputs of organizational planning should be reviewed periodically throughout the project to ensure completeness and accuracy. Should events, people, or stakeholders change throughout the project, the following outputs of organizational planning should be updated to reflect the changes.

Creating the Role and Responsibility Assignments

Some slick definitions for roles and responsibilities include the following:

- **Role**   Defines the accountable person by label or title
- **Authority**   Has the authority to assign project resources, make decisions, and sign off on project documents
- **Responsibility**   The work assigned to a project team member
- **Competency**   Determines what skill set is needed to complete an activity

The assignment of the roles and responsibilities determines what actions the project manager, project team member, or individual contributor will have in the project. Roles and responsibilities generally support the project scope, since this is the required work for the project.

An excellent tool that the project manager should create is the responsibility assignment matrix (RAM). A RAM can be high-level—for example, mapping project groups to the high-level components of a WBS, such as architecture, network, or software creation. A RAM can also be specific to the activities within the project work. Figure 9-4 is an example of a RAM.

Creating an Organizational Chart

An organizational chart can help the project manager and the project team identify the reporting relationships among the project team, management, and other key stakeholders. Figure 9-5 is an example of an organizational chart, or org chart. The org chart can help the project manager identify what communication protocols are

FIGURE 9-4

A responsibility assignment matrix (RAM) can map work to project team members.

WBS Component	Resource 1	Resource 2	Resource 3	Resource 4	Resource 5	Resource 6
Architectural	RS		R		A	
Foundation	A	R	I			
Framing	S		A		I	
Electrical	S			R		A
Interior	S	A			I	R

A = Accountable   R = Resource   I = Informed   S = Sign off

used in a large project. Org charts can also identify the relationship of team members and contributors in a smaller project.

An organizational breakdown structure (OBS) is also an organizational chart. This tool, however, identifies the organizational units or departments and what work packages they are responsible for within the project.

Creating a Staffing Management Plan

The staffing management plan, part of the human resource plan, details how project team members will be brought onto the project and excused from the project. This subsidiary plan documents the process the project manager is expected to complete to bring new project team members aboard based on the conditions of the project.

FIGURE 9-5

Organizational charts identify reporting relationships within the project.

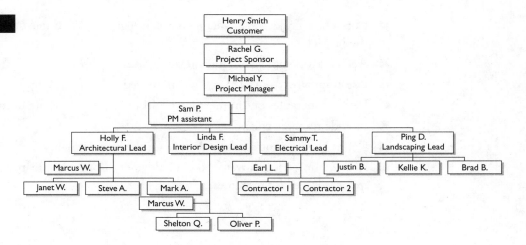

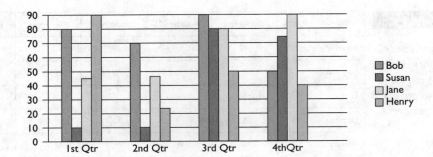

FIGURE 9-6

Resource histograms are bar charts that illustrate the utilization of labor.

For example, a project may require an application developer in the third phase of the project. The project manager may have to complete a job description of what the application developer will be responsible for, how her time will be used, and how long the role is needed on the project. HR or other functional managers may have to approve the request.

Management may also want to see a resource histogram, as Figure 9-6 illustrates, so they may plan employees' time and activities accordingly. Management may elect to hold off on the launch of a project based on the requirement for resources and the conflict with business cycles or other projects with higher priorities within the organization.

Each performing organization will likely have policies and procedures that should be documented and followed to bring resources onto the project team. In addition, the organization may have similar ways to excuse project team members from a project once their contribution has been completed.

The staffing management plan should do the following:

- Detail how project team members are brought onto and released from the project
- Account for employees' time on the project
- Use employees as needed and when needed
- Define timetables outlining when project team members are needed
- Provide resource calendars
- Define the training needs and plans for the project team
- Remove or reduce worries about employment by communicating the expected need for resources

- Define the project's reward and recognition system
- Define the project's compliance with government regulations, union contracts, and policies and procedures
- Include a staff release plan to define how project team members will be released from the project so labor costs are recorded accurately

exam

watch *Scheduling unneeded resources is a waste of time and money. Only schedule resources on a project when they are needed. Functional managers may want you, the project manager, to schedule resources on a project even though you don't need them. Not only is this outside of the staffing management plan, it is a violation of the project management Code of Ethics and Professional Conduct.*

Documenting the Supporting Detail

The details influencing project decisions should be documented. This supporting detail allows the project manager and management to reflect on why decisions were made. Supporting details may include the following:

- **Organizational impact** The project manager should identify the reasoning behind the decisions that were made. Specifically, if alternatives were identified, the project manager should explain why the alternatives were not selected in lieu of the plans that were created. This information can prove valuable later in the project if management needs to know the rationale behind the project manager's decisions.
- **Job descriptions** These position descriptions define the job requirements, responsibilities, authority, and other details about the positions within the project team.
- **Training needs** If the project team needs training in any area to complete the required work of the project scope, the project manager should identify and document the needs of the project team. Information on the type of training needed, the cost, the modality, and the reasoning why the training choice was selected should be included in this documentation.

CERTIFICATION OBJECTIVE 9.04

Acquiring the Project Human Resources

Have you ever managed a project where the resources you want on the project are not available? Or have you managed a project where the resources you've been assigned aren't the best resources to complete the project work? Staff acquisition is the process of getting the needed resources on the project team to complete the project work.

Staff acquisition focuses on working within the policies and procedures of the performing organization to obtain the needed resources to complete the project work. Negotiation, communication, and political savvy are the keys to getting the desired resources on the project team.

A project needs a project team. Actually, let me restate that. A project needs a *good, qualified, competent* project team. Their competency, experience, and availability will directly influence the success of the project. Armed with this notion, the project manager may rely on a few different tools and techniques to obtain the needed project team resources.

Referring to the Staffing Management Plan

The project manager will rely on the staffing management plan as an input to acquiring project team members. The staffing management plan details how project team members will be brought on to the project and excused from the project as conditions within the project demand. The staffing management plan is a subsidiary plan that documents the staffing requirements of the project.

Examining the Staffing Pool

In some organizations, the project manager has little or no say regarding project team assignments. Not fun. In other organizations, project managers have the ability to recruit, or at least influence, the project team assignments and should ask questions about the following:

- **Availability** Will the project team members desired for the project be available? Project managers should confer with functional managers on the availability of the potential team members.

- **Ability** What is the competency and proficiency of the available project team members?
- **Experience** What is the experience of the project team members? Have they done similar work in the past—and have they done it well?
- **Interest level** Are the project team members interested in working on this project?
- **Costs** How much will each individual team member cost the project?

Recruiting Project Team Members

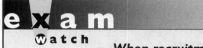

When recruitment policies or guidelines are in place within the performing organization, they act as a project constraint.

The project manager has to follow the rules of the organizations involved in the project. For example, an organization may forbid a project manager from approaching a worker directly to discuss her availability and desire to work on a project. The project manager may instead have to speak with the employee's functional manager to obtain the resource.

Working with Preassigned Staff

Project team members are often preassigned to a project for a number of reasons, such as:

- The availability of the individual
- They were promised as part of a competitive contract
- They were required as part of the project charter of an internal project
- It gives the staff member an opportunity to complete on-the-job training

Whatever the reasoning behind the assignment of the staff to the project, the project manager should evaluate the project team for skills gaps, the availability to complete the project work, and the expectations of the project team members. The project manager must address any discrepancies between the requirements of the project work and the project team's ability to complete the work.

Negotiating for Resources

Most projects require the project manager to negotiate for resources. The project manager will likely have to negotiate with functional managers to obtain the needed resources to complete the project work. The functional managers and the project manager may struggle over an employee's time due to demands in ongoing operations, other projects, and the effective utilization of resources. In other instances, functional managers may want to assign underutilized resources on projects to account for their employees' time.

Project managers may also have to negotiate with other project managers to share needed resources among projects. Scheduling the needed resources between the project teams will need to be coordinated so that both projects may complete successfully.

An organization's politics certainly come into play with staff acquisitions. Functional managers may want project managers to carry extra resources on the project in exchange for key personnel, added deliverables to the project, or other "favors" for the manager. In all instances, the project manager should follow the PMI Code of Ethics and Professional Conduct. We'll discuss this infamous code of conduct in Chapter 13.

Acquiring Staff

In some instances, the project manager may have no alternative but to procure the project team or individuals to complete the project work. Procurement will be discussed in detail in Chapter 12. In regard to project team procurement, reasons why the project manager can use this alternative include, but are not limited to:

- The performing organization lacks the internal resources with the needed skills to complete the project work.
- The work is more cost-effective to procure.
- The project team members are present within the organization, but they are not available for the current project due to their workload in their current job.
- The project team members are present within the organization, but they cannot complete the needed work due to other project assignments.

Working with Virtual Teams

Virtual teams are project teams that share a common goal—to complete the project work—but they are not collocated and may rarely, if ever, meet face-to-face with other project team members. The virtual team relies on e-mail, video, and telephone conferences to communicate on the project. Virtual teams allow the following:

- Teams composed of geographically dispersed individuals
- The ability to add experts to the project team that may not be in the same geographical area

- The inclusion of workers from home offices
- The ability to create project teams of individuals with varying working hours
- The inclusion of people with mobility handicaps
- The deletion or reduction of travel expenses

Assembling the Project Team

Congratulations! The project team has been recruited or assigned to the project. With the project team assembled, the project manager can continue planning, assigning activities, and managing the project's progression. Project team members can be assigned to the project on a full- or part-time basis, depending on the project conditions.

Once the project team is built, a project team directory should be assembled that includes the following:

- Project team members' names
- Phone numbers
- E-mail addresses
- Mailing addresses if noncollocated
- Contact information for key stakeholders
- Any other relevant contact information for each team member, such as photos, web addresses, and so on

CERTIFICATION OBJECTIVE 9.05

Developing the Project Team

Throughout the project, the project manager will have to work to develop the project team. The project manager may have to develop the abilities of the individual team members so that they can complete their assignments. The project manager will also have to work to develop the project team as a whole so that the team can work together to complete the project.

In matrix organizations, the project team members are accountable to the project manager and their functional managers. The development of the project team can prove challenging since the project team members may feel pulled between multiple bosses. The project manager must strive to involve and develop the project team members as individuals completing project work—and as team members completing the project objectives together.

Preparing to Develop the Project Team

The project manager will rely on several pieces of information to prepare for team development, such as:

- **Staff assignments**   The assignments of the project team members define the skills of the project team members, their need for development, and their ability to complete the project work as individuals and as part of the collective team.
- **Project management plan**   The project management plan, which contains the human resource plan, is needed, as it defines the training needs, the reward and recognition systems, and the process for disciplinary actions.
- **Resource calendars**   Project managers will use the resource calendar to determine when resources are needed and when they're available to participate in team development activities.

Leading Project Team Development

Due to the temporary and short-term nature of projects, it can be tough for a group of strangers to come together, form relationships, and immediately create a successful project. Team development is the guidance, direction, and leadership the project manager offers to influence a project team.

The project managers are the power on the project team. While there may be some resistance of the project team to cooperate with the project manager, complete assigned duties, or participate as requested, the project team should realize the project manager is the project authority. There are five types of powers that the project manager wields.

- **Expert**   The authority of the project manager comes from experience with the technology the project focuses on.
- **Reward**   The project manager has the authority to reward the project team.

- **Formal**   The project manager has been assigned by senior management and is in charge of the project. Also known as positional power.
- **Coercive**   The project manager has the authority to discipline the project team members. This is also known as "penalty power." When the team is afraid of the project manager, it's coercive. As you might guess, this is usually not an effective management style.
- **Referent**   The project team personally knows the project manager. Referent can also mean the project manager refers to the person who assigned him the position—for example, "The CEO assigned me to this position, so we'll do it this way." This power can also mean the project team wants to work on the project or with the project manager due to the high priority and impact of the project.

Creating Team-Building Activities

Team-building activities are approaches to develop the team through facilitated events. Events can include the following:

- Training the project team
- Team involvement during planning processes
- Defining rules for handling team disagreements
- Offsite activities
- Quick team-involvement activities
- Activities to improve interpersonal skills and form relationships

Naturally Developing Project Teams

There's a general belief that project teams actually go through their own natural development processes. These processes can shift, linger, and even stall based on the dynamics of the project team. This theory of team development was created by Dr. Bruce Tuckman in 1965. Here are the five phases of team development that project managers may face:

- **Forming**   The project team meets and learns about their roles and responsibilities on the project. Little interaction among the project team happens in this stage, as the team is learning about the project and project manager.

- **Storming**   The project team struggles for project positions, leadership, and project direction. The project team can become hostile towards the project leader, challenge ideas, and try to establish and claim positions about the project work. The amount of debate and fury can vary, depending on if the project team is willing to work together, the nature of the project, and the control of the project manager.

- **Norming**   Project team members go about getting the project work, begin to rely on one another, and generally complete their project assignments.

- **Performing**   If a project team can reach the performing stage of team development, they trust one another and work well together, and issues and problems get resolved quickly and effectively.

- **Adjourning**   Once the project is done, the team moves on to other assignments, either as a unit or the project team is disbanded and individual team members go on to other work.

on the job   *Tuckman originally used just the first four stages of team development, but added adjourning to the model in the 1970s.*

Relying on General Management Skills

A chunk of project management relies on general management skills. Specifically, the project manager relies on the following:

- **Leading**   Leading is the art of establishing direction, aligning people, and motivating the project team to complete the project work.

- **Communicating**   Good project managers are good communicators. Remember, half of communicating is listening.

- **Negotiating**   Project managers will likely negotiate for scope, cost, terms, assignment, and resources.

- **Problem solving**   Project managers must have the ability to confront and solve problems.

- **Influencing**   Project managers use their influence to get things done.

Rewarding the Project Team

A reward and recognition system encourages, emphasizes, and promotes good performance and behavior by the project team. The reward and recognition system should be a formal, achievable approach for the project team to perform and be rewarded for their outstanding performance.

The relationship between the requirements for the reward and the power to achieve should not be limited. In other words, if the project manager is rewarded for completing a project by a given date, she needs the autonomy to schedule resources and make decisions so the goal is achievable.

The project team should be rewarded for good work and not for bad. For example, a project team should not be rewarded for completing a crucial assignment on schedule if the work is unacceptable because of quality issues.

Finally, the culture where the project is taking place should also be considered. It may be inappropriate to reward individual team members over an entire group, or vice versa. The project manager should be aware of the cultural differences and operate within the customs and practices of the environment to reward the project team without causing offense.

Dealing with Team Locales

Collocated teams are teams that work geographically close together to improve team dynamics and team relations. On large projects, it may be particularly valuable to bring all of the project team members together to a central location to work collectively on the project. A project headquarters or war room may be ideal.

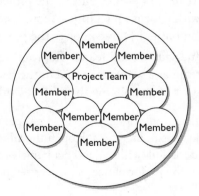

When collocation is not feasible, the project manager must make attempts to bring the project team together for team interaction, face-to-face meetings, and other avenues of communication to bolster relations.

Training the Project Team

The project team may require training to complete the project work, function as a project team, or participate in management skills such as finance or formal communications. Training can include such things as:

- Formal education
- Classroom training
- On-the-job training
- Cross training (shadowing)

Examining the Results of Team Development

Team development is an ongoing process. Optimum team performance doesn't happen on the first day of the project, but hopefully it does kick in well before the final day of the project. The primary goal of team development is to improve project team performance. Improvements can include the following:

- **Individuals**   Improvements to individual skill sets may allow the individual to complete his assigned work better, faster, or with more confidence.
- **Team**   Improvements to the project team may allow the team to perform with a focus on technical requirements, project work, and working together (in harmony) to complete the project work.
- **Individuals and team**   Improvements to either team members or the project team as a whole may lead to the better good of the project by finding better ways of completing the project work.

Another result of team development is the input to performance reviews of the project team members. Hopefully, all goes well and the project manager can report successful, willing, and cooperative team members. Honesty is paramount in reporting the performance of project team members.

CERTIFICATION OBJECTIVE 9.06

Managing the Project Team

Wouldn't it be great if the project team just did what was assigned to them and did it well? And the project manager could then just organize, document, and plan for future phases of the project? Sure, it would—but then project management would be way, way too easy. One of the trickiest parts of project management is managing the project team, which involves such things as:

- Tracking individual project team members' performance
- Providing feedback to the project team members about their performance and project work
- Finding solutions and facilitating conversations to find solutions for project issues
- Managing changes to the project and project processes to improve overall project performance
- Providing communications among the project team, project stakeholders, and in a matrix structure, communicating with functional managers

Communicating with the Project Team

We'll dive into communications in detail in the next chapter, but there are some obvious demands on the project manager to communicate with the project team members to manage them. Before talking, however, the project manager needs to observe the project team members. This means paying attention to the work, the work results, the attitude, project team accomplishments, and any interpersonal issues among team members. Knowing what to discuss with the project team is more important than just talking. Communication is a paramount factor in project team management.

Completing Project Performance Appraisals

Project team members need feedback. They need to know when they're doing a good job and a not-so-good job. But before the project manager can begin offering appraisals, organizational policies and procedures must determine the type of appraisals the project manager provides. The project manager should understand the organizational policies, labor contracting requirements, and whether the project even qualifies for formal appraisals. Smaller, lower-priority projects may not have a need for appraisals at all.

One popular approach for completing project team member appraisals is the 360-degree feedback approach. This method offers appraisals from more than just the project manager. They can also come from peers, supervisors, managers, and even project team members' subordinates.

Dealing with Team Disagreements

In most projects, there will be instances when the project team, management, and other stakeholders disagree on the progress, decisions, and proposed solutions within the project. It's essential for the project manager to keep calm, lead, and direct the parties to a sensible solution that's best for the project. The following are seven reasons for conflict, in order of most common to least common:

1. Schedules
2. Priorities
3. Resources
4. Technical beliefs
5. Administrative policies and procedures
6. Project costs
7. Personalities

So what's a project manager to do with all the potential for strife in a project? There are five different approaches to conflict resolution.

■ **Problem solving**   This approach confronts the problem head-on and is the preferred method of conflict resolution. You may see this approach as "confronting" rather than problem solving, however. Problem solving calls for additional research to find the best solution for the problem, and should be a win-win solution. It should be used if there is time to work through and resolve the issue. It also serves to build relationships and trust.

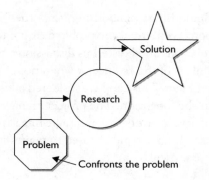

- **Forcing**   The person with the power makes the decision. The decision made may not be the best decision for the project, but it's fast. As expected, this autocratic approach does little for team development and is a win-lose solution. Used when the stakes are high and time is of the essence, or if relationships are not important.

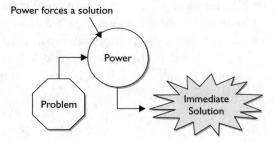

- **Compromising**   This approach requires that both parties give up something. The decision made is a blend of both sides of the argument. Because neither party really wins, it is considered a lose-lose solution. The project manager can thus use this approach when the relationships are equal and no one can truly "win." This approach can also be used to avoid a fight.

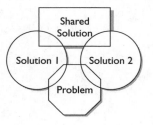

■ **Smoothing**   Smoothing "smoothes" out the conflict by minimizing the perceived size of the problem. It is a temporary solution, but can calm team relations and boisterous discussions. Smoothing may be acceptable when time is of the essence or when none of the proposed solutions will settle the problem. This can be considered a lose-lose situation since no one really wins in the long term. The project manager can use smoothing to emphasize areas of agreement between disagreeing stakeholders, thus minimizing areas of conflict. It's typically used to maintain relationships and when the issue is not critical.

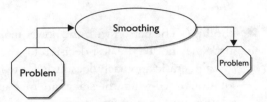

■ **Withdrawal**   This is the worst conflict resolution approach because one side of the argument essentially walks away from the problem, usually in disgust. The conflict is not resolved, and it is considered a yield-lose solution as the "loser" in the argument yields to the other person's point of view. The approach can be used, however, as a cooling off period or when the issue is not critical.

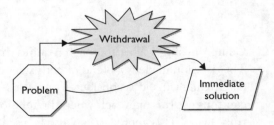

INSIDE THE EXAM

Most project managers taking the PMP exam can rely on their practical experience to ace these questions. But as reinforcement, let's examine some key issues you should know going into the examination.

Project human resource management questions on the exam center around four big points.

- **Role**   Defines the accountable person by label or title
- **Authority**   The authority to assign project resources, make decisions, and sign off on project documents
- **Responsibility**   The work assigned to a project team member
- **Competency**   Determines what skill set is needed to complete an activity

Because project managers are responsible for the success of the project, they have power, which they can exert over the project team.

Table 9-1 is a quick list of the powers that the project manager can have.

There are six organizational theories you may encounter on the exam.

- **Maslow's Hierarchy of Needs**   People don't work for money, but for self-actualization.
- **Herzberg's Theory of Motivation**   The presence of hygiene factors doesn't motivate people; the absence of hygiene factors, however, hinders people's performance.
- **McGregor's Theory of X and Y**   X people are lazy and do not want to work. Y people are self-led, motivated, and want to accomplish tasks.
- **Ouchi's Theory Z**   Workers and management cooperate for the good of the organization. Everyone wins!

| TABLE 9-1 | The Powers of the Project Manager |

Power	Definition
Expert	The project manager is an expert with the technology the project focuses on.
Reward	The project manager can reward the project team members.
Coercive	The project manager can punish the project team members.
Formal	The project manager is formally assigned to the role of project manager.
Referent	The project team knows the project manager. The project manager refers to the person who assigned him to the role of project manager.

(Continued)

INSIDE THE EXAM

- **McClelland's Theory of Needs**
  People have three needs: achievement, affiliation, and power. One of these needs drives the person's actions.

- **Expectancy Theory** People expect to be rewarded for their behavior.

There are many methods to resolving conflicts in a project. Table 9-2 lists various resolution methods you should know.

| TABLE 9-2 | Various Conflict Resolution Methods |

Conflict Resolution	Quick Example
Problem solving (confronting)	Let's put our heads together, research the problem, and find the best solution.
Forcing	Bob's got seniority here, so we'll go with his opinion on the solution.
Compromising	Let's take a little of both sides of the argument and create a blended solution.
Smoothing	Let's smooth this issue out. It's really not that big of a problem.
Withdrawal	I'm leaving. Do whatever solution works for you.

CERTIFICATION SUMMARY

Project human resources management requires the project manager to lead and direct the project team, customers, and other stakeholders in unison to complete the project scope. It requires working within the confines of the organizational policies, as well as the ability to relate to the concerns and expectations of the stakeholders. Perhaps most importantly, it is tightly integrated with project communications management.

There are several human resource theories the PMP candidate should be familiar with to successfully pass the PMP examination. Here's a quick listing of these theories and their core beliefs:

- **Maslow's Hierarchy of Needs**   People work for self-actualization.
- **Herzberg's Theory of Motivation**   Hygiene agents are expected by workers, and can only demotivate if they aren't present. Motivating agents include the opportunity to both exceed and advance, and to acquire rewards other than mere financial gain.
- **McGregor's Theory of X and Y**   This is a management theory that believes "X" people have to be micromanaged and distrusted. "Y" people are self-led and motivated.
- **Ouchi's Theory Z**   Workers are motivated by a sense of commitment, opportunity, and advancement. This theory centers on lifetime employment.
- **McClelland's Theory of Needs**   People have three needs: achievement, affiliation, and power. One of the needs drives the person's actions.
- **Expectancy Theory**   People behave based on what they expect as a result of their behavior.

Within a project there are roles and responsibilities. A role can be defined as "who does what," while a responsibility can be defined as "who decides what." A responsibility assignment matrix (RAM) can map project work to specific project team members. This matrix clarifies which project team member is responsible for what actions within the project.

The RAM can help the project manager determine which resources are needed for which activities, but can also ensure that the adequate amount of resources are assigned to the project work. The project manager must work to ensure that extra resources are not assigned to project activities. It is wasteful to add unneeded resources to project work.

The staffing management plan dictates how resources are brought on to the project—and taken off the project. The plan serves as an input to staff acquisition. Should functional managers want to add unneeded team members, the staffing management plan can restrict the functional manager. It should work with the operational policies of the performing organization.

KEY TERMS

If you're serious about passing the PMP exams, memorize these terms and their definitions. For maximum value, create your own flashcards based on these definitions and review them daily. You can find additional information on these terms in the project glossary.

360-degree appraisal   A performance review completed by a person's peers, managers, and subordinates. It's called a 360-degree appraisal because it's a circle of reviews by people at different levels of an organization.

adjourning   The final stage of team development; once the project is done, the team moves on to other assignments, either as a unit or the project team is disbanded and individual team members go on to other work.

autocratic   The project manager makes all of the decisions.

coercive power   The project manager uses fear and threats to manage the project team.

collective bargaining agreements   These are contractual agreements initiated by employee groups, unions, or other labor organizations; they may act as a constraint on the project.

compromising   A conflict resolution method; this approach requires both parties to give up something. The decision ultimately made is a blend of both sides of the argument. Because neither party completely wins, it is considered a lose-lose solution.

democratic   The project team is involved in the decision-making process.

exceptional   The project manager only pays attention to the top 10 percent and the bottom 10 percent of the project team performers.

Expectancy Theory   People will behave on the basis of what they expect as a result of their behavior. In other words, people will work in relation to the expected reward of the work.

expert power   A type of power where the authority of the project manager comes from experience with the area that the project focuses on.

forcing   A conflict resolution method where one person dominates or forces his point of view or solution to a conflict.

formal power   The type of power where the project manager has been assigned by senior management to be in charge of the project.

forming   The initial stage of team development; the project team meets and learns about their roles and responsibilities on the project.

halo effect   When one attribute of a person influences a decision.

Herzberg's Theory of Motivation   Posits that there are two catalysts for workers: hygiene agents and motivating agents. Hygiene agents do nothing to motivate, but their absence demotivates workers. Hygiene agents are the expectations all workers have: job security, paychecks, clean and safe working conditions, a sense of belonging, civil working relationships, and other basic attributes associated with employment. Motivating agents are components such as reward, recognition, promotion, and other values that encourage individuals to succeed.

human resource plan   Defines the management of the project human resources, timing of use, and enterprise environmental factors the project manager must adhere to in the organization.

laissez faire   The project manager has a hands-off policy, and the team is entirely self-led regarding the decision-making process.

Maslow's Hierarchy of Needs   A theory that states that there are five layers of needs for all humans: physiological, safety, social, esteem, and the crowning jewel, self-actualization.

McClelland's Theory of Needs   People have three needs: achievement, affiliation, and power. One of the needs drives the person's actions.

McGregor's Theory of X and Y   This theory states that "X" people are lazy, don't want to work, and need to be micromanaged. "Y" people are self-led, motivated, and strive to accomplish.

norming   Project team members go about getting the project work, begin to rely on one another, and generally complete their project assignments.

organizational breakdown structure   Though these charts are similar to the WBS, the breakdown is by department, unit, or team.

organizational charts   These show how an organization, such as a company or large project team, is ordered, its reporting structures, and the flow of information.

Ouchi's Theory Z   This theory posits that workers are motivated by a sense of commitment, opportunity, and advancement. Workers will work if they are challenged and motivated.

performing   If a project team can reach the performing stage of team development, they trust one another, they work well together, and issues and problems get resolved quickly and effectively.

problem solving   The ability to determine the best solution for a problem in a quick and efficient manner.

RACI chart   A chart designates each team member against each project activity as Responsible, Accountable, Consult, or Inform (RACI). A RACI chart is technically a type of responsibility assignment matrix chart.

referent power   Power that is present when the project team is attracted to or wants to work on the project or with the project manager. Referent power also exists when the project manager references another, more powerful person, such as the CEO.

resource breakdown structure   This type of chart breaks down the project by types of resources utilized on the project no matter where the resource is being utilized in the project.

resource histogram   A bar chart reflecting when individual employees, groups, or communities are involved in a project. Often used by management to see when employees are most or least active in a project.

responsibility   The person who decides what will happen in a project about a particular area.

responsibility assignment matrix chart   A chart type designating the roles and responsibilities of the project team.

reward power   The project manager's authority to reward the project team.

role   Who does what types of activities in a project.

smoothing   A conflict resolution method that "smoothes" out the conflict by minimizing the perceived size of the problem. It is a temporary solution, but it can calm team relations and reduce boisterousness of discussions. Smoothing may be acceptable when time is of the essence or when any of the proposed solutions would work.

staffing management plan   This subsidiary plan documents how project team members will be brought on to the project and excused from the project. This plan is contained in the human resources plan.

storming   The second stage of team development; the project team struggles for project positions, leadership, and project direction.

virtual teams   Project teams that are not collocated and that may rarely, if ever, meet face-to-face with other project team members. The virtual team relies on e-mail, video, and telephone conferences to communicate on the project.

war room   A centralized office or locale for the project manager and the project team to work on the project. It can house information on the project, including documentation and support materials. It allows the project team to work in close proximity.

withdrawal   A conflict resolution method that is used when the issue is not important or the project manager is out-ranked. The project manager pushes the issue aside for later resolution. It can also be used as a method for cooling down. The conflict is not resolved, and it is considered a yield-lose solution.

✓ TWO-MINUTE DRILL

Preparing for Project Human Resource Planning

- ❑ Project human resource management focuses on utilizing the people involved in the project in the most effective way. The people involved in the project are more than just the project team members, though they're the most obvious.

- ❑ The project manager can't forget to involve other stakeholders: customers, management, individual contributors, the project sponsor, and any other stakeholder unique to the project.

- ❑ Organizational planning calls on the project manager to identify the roles and responsibilities of the project and the reporting relationship within the organization.

- ❑ Organizational structures affect the amount of power a project manager has over project decisions. Project managers have the least amount of authority in a functional environment and the most amount in a projectized environment.

Completing Organizational Planning

- ❑ Because projects are often similar, the project manager can rely on templates to re-create the success of historical projects. Reporting structures, role and responsibility matrixes, and other human resource models can be replicated and adjusted between projects.

- ❑ Maslow's Hierarchy of Needs says that people work for five needs: physiological, safety, social, esteem, and self-actualization.

- ❑ Hertzberg's Theory of Motivation says that hygiene agents do not promote performance, but their absence can lower performance. Motivating agents, such as rewards and recognition, can improve performance.

- ❑ McClelland's Theory of Needs states that people are driven primarily by one of three needs: achievement, affiliation, or power.

Preparing for Project Team Management

- ❑ The staffing management plan describes the process that the project manager must follow to bring resources on to a project or to dismiss them from a project when the resources are no longer needed.

❑ The policies and procedures of the performing organization should be documented within the staffing management plan to ensure that the guidelines are followed as management intends.

❑ The staffing management plan will also detail the policies of how the project manager can recruit project team members. In addition, the plan may detail the procedure to procure resources for the project from vendors or consultants.

Acquiring the Project Human Resources

❑ The staffing management plan, part of the human resource management plan, defines how project team members may be brought on to and released from the project team. This plan is based on the project's resource requirements.

❑ The staffing management plan defines how members will be brought on to the project team and how the team members will be released from the project once their work has been completed. It's not cost-effective to keep project team members on the project once their work has been completed.

❑ Virtual teams are project teams that are not collocated and may rarely, if ever, meet face-to-face with other project team members. The virtual team relies on e-mail, video, and telephone conferences to communicate on the project. Communication demands increase when working with virtual teams.

Developing the Project Team

❑ Ideally, the project is collocated and has access to a war room to refer to project information, research, schedules, and other project team members.

❑ The goal of team development is outstanding performance for the good of the project. Through training, the project team may increase their ability to work together and individually, with a higher level of confidence, performance, and teamwork.

❑ A reward and recognition system can help the project manager motivate the project team to perform as hoped.

❑ Special care to involve the project team must be given when the team is scattered geographically. The project manager can rely on face-to-face meetings, videoconferences, or teleconferences to promote noncollocated teams.

❑ The result of team development is project performance improvements. The improvements should be noted in an honest appraisal of the project team members' efforts and contributions to the project.

Managing the Project Team

❑ Communicating is an important factor of managing the project team. The project manager must communicate the expectations, responsibilities, and performance of the project team members so they can work accordingly.

❑ Problem solving is a conflict resolution method where both parties work together to find a solution. This approach is also known as confronting.

❑ Forcing is a conflict resolution approach where the person with the power forces her decision.

❑ Compromising requires that both parties give up something they want to reach a resolution.

❑ Smoothing smoothes out the problem by minimizing the perceived size of the problem. It is a temporary solution, but can calm team relations and boisterous discussions. Smoothing may be acceptable when time is of the essence or when none of the proposed solutions will settle the problem.

❑ Withdrawal happens when one party retreats from the conflict and avoids the resolution.

SELF TEST

1. You are the project manager for the JHG Project. This project requires coordination with the directors of manufacturing, human resources, and the IT department, and the CIO. This is an example of what type of input to organizational planning?
   A. Organizational interfaces
   B. Technical interfaces
   C. Interpersonal interfaces
   D. Human resource coordination

2. Your project requires an electrician at month eight. This is an example of which of the following?
   A. Organizational interfaces
   B. Resource requirements
   C. Contractor requirements
   D. Resource constraints

3. You are the project manager of the PUY Project. This project requires a chemical engineer for seven months of the project, but there are no available chemical engineers within your department. This is an example of which of the following?
   A. Organizational interfaces
   B. Resource requirements
   C. Contractor requirements
   D. Resource constraints

4. You are the project manager in an organization with a weak matrix. Who will have the authority on your project?
   A. The project manager
   B. The customer
   C. Functional management
   D. The team leader

5. You are the project manager for the LMG Project. Your project will have several human resource issues that must be coordinated and approved by the union. Which of the following statements is correct about this scenario?
   A. The union is considered a resource constraint.
   B. The union is considered a management constraint.
   C. The union is considered a project stakeholder.
   D. The union is considered a project team member.

6. You are the project manager of the PLY Project. This project is similar to the ACT Project you completed earlier. What method can you use to expedite the process of organization planning?

A. Use the project plan of the ACT Project on the PLY Project.

B. Use the roles and responsibilities definitions of the ACT Project on the PLY Project.

C. Use the project team reward structure of the ACT Project on the PLY Project.

D. Use the project team of the ACT Project on the PLY Project.

7. In your organization, management is referred to as coaches. As a project manager, you are referred to as a project coach. A human resource document should be created to handle this scenario. What should it cover?

A. How coaches are separate from managers

B. How coaches are the same as managers

C. How a coach is to complete his job

D. How the project team is to work for a coach

8. Management has requested that you create a chart depicting all of the project resource needs and the associated activities. Management is looking for which type of chart?

A. A roles chart

B. A roles matrix

C. A roles and responsibilities matrix

D. A Gantt chart

9. Which of the following is an example of Theory X?

A. Self-led project teams

B. Micromanagement

C. Team members able to work on their own accord

D. EVM

10. You are the project manager of the PLN Project. The team members are somewhat "afraid" of you as project manager because they see you as management. They know that a negative review from you about their project work will affect their yearly bonus. This is an example of which of the following?

A. Formal power

B. Coercive power

C. Expert power

D. Referent power

11. You are the project manager of the MMB Project. The president of the company has spoken to the project team and told them the confidence and respect he has in you to lead the project to a successful completion. The project manager has what type of power on this project?

    A. Formal power

    B. Coercive power

    C. Expert power

    D. Halo power

12. Management has approached Tyler, one of your project team members. Tyler is a database administrator and developer whose work is always on time, accurate, and of quality. He also has a reputation of being a "good guy" and is well liked. Because of this, management has decided to move Tyler into the role of a project manager for a new database administration project. This is an example of which of the following?

    A. Management by exception

    B. The halo effect

    C. Management by objectives

    D. McGregor's Theory of X and Y

13. Susan is the project manager for the PMG Project. She makes all decisions on the project team, regardless of the project team's objections. This is an example of which of the following management styles?

    A. Autocratic

    B. Democratic

    C. Laissez faire

    D. Exceptional

14. Which problem-solving technique is the best for most project management situations?

    A. Confronting

    B. Compromising

    C. Forcing

    D. Avoidance

15. Harold is an outspoken project team member. All of the project team members respect Harold for his experience with the technology, but things usually have to be done as Harold sees fit; otherwise, things don't go well. During a discussion on a solution, a project team member throws up her arms and says, "Fine, Harold, do it your way." This is an example of which of the following?

    A. A win-win solution

    B. A leave-lose solution

    C. A lose-lose solution

    D. A yield-lose solution

16. You are the project manager for the GBK Project. This project affects a line of business, and the customer is anxious about the success of the project. Which of the following is likely not a top concern for the customer?

    A. Project priorities

    B. Schedule

    C. Cost

    D. Personality conflicts

17. Which theory believes that workers need to be involved with the management process?

    A. McGregor's Theory of X and Y

    B. Ouchi's Theory Z

    C. Herzberg's Theory of Motivation

    D. The Expectancy Theory

18. Which of the following states that as long as workers are rewarded they will remain productive?

    A. McGregor's Theory of X and Y

    B. Ouchi's Theory Z

    C. Herzberg's Theory of Motivation

    D. The Expectancy Theory

19. You are the project manager for the Industrial Lights Project. You have been hired by your organization specifically because of your vast experience with the technology and with projects of this nature. The project team is aware of your experience. You likely have what type of power on this project?

    A. Formal power

    B. Coercive power

    C. Expert power

    D. Referent power

20. You are the project manager for the GHB Project. You have served as a project manager for your organization for the past 10 years. Practically all of your projects come in on time and on budget. The project team has worked with you in the past, and they consider you to be an expert project manager. They also like working with you. Given all of this, you likely have what type of power on this project?

    A. Formal power

    B. Coercive power

C. Expert power

D. Referent power

21. Which of the following is an example of coercive power?

A. A project manager that has lunch with the project team every Thursday

B. A project manager that will openly punish any team member who is late with an activity

C. A project manager that has worked with the technology on the project for several years

D. A project manager that is friends with all of the project team members

22. Charles is the project manager for the WAC Project. The customer and a project team member are in conflict over the level of quality needed on a sampling. Charles decides to split the difference between what the two stakeholders want. This is an example of which of the following?

A. A win-win solution

B. A win-lose solution

C. A lose-lose solution

D. A leave-lose solution

23. Mike is the project manager for a project with a very tight schedule. The project is running late, and Mike feels that he does not have time to consider all the possible solutions that two team members are in disagreement over. Mike quickly decides to go with the team member with the largest amount of seniority. This is an example of which of the following?

A. Problem solving

B. Compromising

C. Forcing

D. Withdrawal

24. You are a project manager in a projectized organization. Your job as a project manager can be described best by which of the following?

A. Full-time

B. Part-time

C. Expeditor

D. Coordinator

25. What is the benefit of using a collocated team?

A. The project team is dispersed, so the team is self-led.

B. The project team is dispersed, so communication increases.

C. The project team is in the same physical location, so their ability to work as a team is enhanced.

D. The project team is in the same physical location, so project costs are greatly reduced.

SELF TEST ANSWERS

1. You are the project manager for the JHG Project. This project requires coordination with the directors of manufacturing, human resources, and the IT department, and the CIO. This is an example of what type of input to organizational planning?
   A. Organizational interfaces
   B. Technical interfaces
   C. Interpersonal interfaces
   D. Human resource coordination

   ☑ **A.** The reporting interfaces for this project—the directors of manufacturing, human resources, and the IT department, as well as the CIO—are examples of the organizational interfaces.
   ☒ **B** is incorrect. Technical interfaces are the technical gurus for the project, such as the engineers and designers. **C,** the interpersonal interfaces, is not the best choice, since this relationship describes the different individuals working on the project. **D,** human resource coordination, is also incorrect.

2. Your project requires an electrician at month eight. This is an example of which of the following?
   A. Organizational interfaces
   B. Resource requirements
   C. Contractor requirements
   D. Resource constraints

   ☑ **B.** Because the project requires the electrician, a project role, this is a resource requirement.
   ☒ **A** is incorrect because it does not accurately describe the situation. **C** is incorrect. Contractor requirements would specify the procurement issues, the minimum qualifications for the electrician, and so on. **D** is incorrect because a resource constraint, while a tempting choice, deals more with the availability of the resource or the requirement to use the resource.

3. You are the project manager of the PUY Project. This project requires a chemical engineer for seven months of the project, but there are no available chemical engineers within your department. This is an example of which of the following?
   A. Organizational interfaces
   B. Resource requirements

C. Contractor requirements

D. Resource constraints

☑ **B.** The project needs the resource of the chemical engineer to be successful. When the project needs a resource, it is a staffing requirement.

☒ **A, C,** and **D** are all incorrect. This is not a situation describing an organizational interface or contractor requirements. Resource constraints might include a requirement to use a particular resource or that a resource must be available when certain project activities are happening.

4. You are the project manager in an organization with a weak matrix. Who will have the authority on your project?

A. The project manager

B. The customer

C. Functional management

D. The team leader

☑ **C.** In a weak matrix structure, functional management will have more authority than the project manager.

☒ **A, B,** and **D** are all incorrect, since they do not have as much authority on a project in a weak matrix environment as functional management will have.

5. You are the project manager for the LMG Project. Your project will have several human resource issues that must be coordinated and approved by the union. Which of the following statements is correct about this scenario?

A. The union is considered a resource constraint.

B. The union is considered a management constraint.

C. The union is considered a project stakeholder.

D. The union is considered a project team member.

☑ **C.** In this instance, the union is considered a project stakeholder, since it has a vested interest in the project's outcome.

☒ **A** is incorrect because the union is not a resource constraint—they are interested in the project management methodology and the project human resource management. **B** is incorrect. The union is the counterweight to the management of the organization—not to the project itself. **D** is also incorrect. The union is not a project team member.

6. You are the project manager of the PLY Project. This project is similar to the ACT Project you completed earlier. What method can you use to expedite the process of organization planning?
   A. Use the project plan of the ACT Project on the PLY Project.
   B. Use the roles and responsibilities definitions of the ACT Project on the PLY Project.
   C. Use the project team reward structure of the ACT Project on the PLY Project.
   D. Use the project team of the ACT Project on the PLY Project.

   ☑ **B.** When projects are similar in nature, the project manager can use the roles and responsibilities definitions of the historical project to guide the current project.
   ☒ **A** is incorrect. The entire project plan of the ACT Project isn't needed. Even the roles and responsibilities matrix of the historical project may not be an exact fit for the current project. **C** is also incorrect because copying the project team reward structure is not the best choice of all the answers presented. **D** is incorrect as well because using the same project team may not be feasible at all.

7. In your organization, management is referred to as coaches. As a project manager, you are referred to as a project coach. A human resource document should be created to handle this scenario. What should it cover?
   A. How coaches are separate from managers
   B. How coaches are the same as managers
   C. How a coach is to complete his job
   D. How the project team is to work for a coach

   ☑ **C.** When project managers, or managers in general, are referred to as different terms, a job description is needed so the project manager can successfully complete the required obligations.
   ☒ **A** and **B** are incorrect choices. The project manager must know what the specific responsibilities are, not the similarities and differences, between the current role and management. **D** is also incorrect. By the project manager knowing how to complete his job, the role of the project team should be evident.

8. Management has requested that you create a chart depicting all of the project resource needs and the associated activities. Management is looking for which type of chart?
   A. A roles chart
   B. A roles matrix
   C. A roles and responsibilities matrix
   D. A Gantt chart

☑ **C.** Management is looking for a roles and responsibility matrix. This chart lists the roles and responsibilities, and depicts the intersection of the two.

☒ **A** and **B** are incorrect. Management is looking for more than a listing of the roles and the associated responsibilities. **D** is not an acceptable answer for the scenario presented.

9. Which of the following is an example of Theory X?
   A. Self-led project teams
   B. Micromanagement
   C. Team members able to work on their own accord
   D. EVM

☑ **B.** Theory X believes workers have an inherent dislike of work and will avoid it if possible. Micromanagement is a method in regard to Theory X to make certain workers complete their work.

☒ **A** and **C** are actually examples of McGregor's Theory of X and Y. **D** is incorrect because EVM is not directly related to McGregor's Theory of X and Y.

10. You are the project manager of the PLN Project. The team members are somewhat "afraid" of you as project manager because they see you as management. They know that a negative review from you about their project work will affect their yearly bonus. This is an example of which of the following?
    A. Formal power
    B. Coercive power
    C. Expert power
    D. Referent power

☑ **B.** When the project team is afraid of the power the project manager yields, this is called coercive power.

☒ **A, C,** and **D** are incorrect, since these describe assigned, referential, and technical power over the project.

11. You are the project manager of the MMB Project. The president of the company has spoken to the project team and told them the confidence and respect he has in you to lead the project to a successful completion. The project manager has what type of power on this project?
    A. Formal power
    B. Coercive power

    C. Expert power

    D. Halo power

    ☑   **A.** The company president has assigned you to the position of the project manager, so you have formal power.

    ☒   **B** is incorrect because coercive power is the associated fear of the project manager. **C** is incorrect because expert power is derived from the project manager's experience with the technology being implemented. **D** is also incorrect. Halo power is not a viable answer to the question.

12. Management has approached Tyler, one of your project team members. Tyler is a database administrator and developer whose work is always on time, accurate, and of quality. He also has a reputation of being a "good guy" and is well liked. Because of this, management has decided to move Tyler into the role of a project manager for a new database administration project. This is an example of which of the following?

    A. Management by exception

    B. The halo effect

    C. Management by objectives

    D. McGregor's Theory of X and Y

    ☑   **B.** The halo effect is the assumption that because a person is good at a certain technology, she will also be good at managing a project dealing with said technology.

    ☒   **A, C,** and **D** are all incorrect, since these do not describe the halo effect.

13. Susan is the project manager for the PMG Project. She makes all the decisions on the project team, regardless of the project team's objections. This is an example of which of the following management styles?

    A. Autocratic

    B. Democratic

    C. Laissez faire

    D. Exceptional

    ☑   **A.** Susan is an autocratic decision maker.

    ☒   **B** is incorrect because a democracy counts each project team member's opinion. **C** is incorrect as well because laissez faire allows the project team to make all the decisions. **D** is also incorrect. This is not exceptional project management.

14. Which problem-solving technique is the best for most project management situations?
    A. Confronting
    B. Compromising
    C. Forcing
    D. Avoidance

    ☑ **A.** Confronting is the best problem-solving technique, since it meets the problem directly.
    ☒ **B** is incorrect. Compromising requires both sides on an argument to give up something.
    C is incorrect. Forcing requires the project manager to force a decision based on external inputs, such as seniority, experience, and so on. **D** is also incorrect. Avoidance ignores the problem and does not solve it.

15. Harold is an outspoken project team member. All of the project team members respect Harold for his experience with the technology, but things usually have to be done as Harold sees fit; otherwise, things don't go well. During a discussion on a solution, a project team member throws up her arms and says, "Fine, Harold, do it your way." This is an example of which of the following?
    A. A win-win solution
    B. A leave-lose solution
    C. A lose-lose solution
    D. A yield-lose solution

    ☑ **D.** When Harold always has to win an argument and team members begin to give in to Harold's demands simply to avoid arguments rather than to find an accurate solution, this is a yield-lose situation.
    ☒ **A** is incorrect, since both parties do not win. **B** is incorrect because the project team member did not leave the conversation, but rather ended it. **C** is also incorrect. A lose-lose solution is a compromise where both parties give up something.

16. You are the project manager for the GBK Project. This project affects a line of business, and the customer is anxious about the success of the project. Which of the following is likely not a top concern for the customer?
    A. Project priorities
    B. Schedule
    C. Cost
    D. Personality conflicts

☑ **D.** Personality conflicts are likely a concern for the customer, but are not as important as project priorities, schedule, and cost. The customer hired your company to solve the technical issues.

☒ Choices **A, B,** and **C** are all incorrect, since these are most likely the top issues for a company in a project of this magnitude.

17. Which theory believes that workers need to be involved with the management process?
    A. McGregor's Theory of X and Y
    B. Ouchi's Theory Z
    C. Herzberg's Theory of Motivation
    D. The Expectancy Theory

    ☑ **B.** Ouchi's Theory Z states that workers need to be involved with the management process.

    ☒ **A** is incorrect. McGregor's Theory of X and Y believes X workers don't want to work and need constant supervision. Y workers will work if the work is challenging, satisfying, and rewarding. **C** is also incorrect because Herzberg's Theory of Motivation describes the type of people and what excites them to work. **D,** the Expectancy Theory, describes how people will work based on what they expect because of the work they do.

18. Which of the following states that as long as workers are rewarded they will remain productive?
    A. McGregor's Theory of X and Y
    B. Ouchi's Theory Z
    C. Herzberg's Theory of Motivation
    D. The Expectancy Theory

    ☑ **D.** The Expectancy Theory describes how people will work based on what they expect because of the work they do. If people are rewarded because of the work they complete and they like the reward (payment), they will continue to work.

    ☒ **A, B,** and **C** are all incorrect, since these theories do not accurately describe the scenario presented.

19. You are the project manager for the Industrial Lights Project. You have been hired by your organization specifically because of your vast experience with the technology and with projects of this nature. The project team is aware of your experience. You likely have what type of power on this project?
    A. Formal power
    B. Coercive power

C. Expert power

D. Referent power

☑ **C.** You, the project manager, have expert power on this project because of your experience with the technology and with projects that are similar in nature.

☒ **A, B,** and **D** are all incorrect. These project management powers do not accurately describe the scenario. Formal power is appointed power. Coercive power describes fear of the project manager. Referent power describes power by association and personal knowledge.

20.   You are the project manager for the GHB Project. You have served as a project manager for your organization for the past 10 years. Practically all of your projects come in on time and on budget. The project team has worked with you in the past, and they consider you to be an expert project manager. They also like working with you. Given all of this, you likely have what type of power on this project?

A.   Formal power

B.   Coercive power

C.   Expert power

D.   Referent power

☑ **D.** This is referent power because the project team knows the project manager personally.

☒ **A** and **B** are incorrect choices. These do not describe the scenario. **C** is incorrect because expert power does not deal with the ability to lead and complete a project, but instead focuses on being an expert with the technology that the project deals with.

21.   Which of the following is an example of coercive power?

A.   A project manager that has lunch with the project team every Thursday

B.   A project manager that will openly punish any team member who is late with an activity

C.   A project manager that has worked with the technology on the project for several years

D.   A project manager that is friends with all of the project team members

☑ **B.** Coercive power is the power a project manager yields over the project team, which is essentially formal authority.

☒ **A** is incorrect. Only referent power may come through lunch meetings. **C** is incorrect because experience is expert power. **D** is incorrect because interpersonal relationships are examples of referent power.

22. Charles is the project manager for the WAC Project. The customer and a project team member are in conflict over the level of quality needed on a sampling. Charles decides to split the difference between what the two stakeholders want. This is an example of which of the following?

    A. A win-win solution

    B. A win-lose solution

    C. A lose-lose solution

    D. A leave-lose solution

    ☑ **C.** When both parties give up something, it is a compromise. A compromise is an example of a lose-lose solution.

    ☒ **A** is incorrect. Win-win is accomplished through confrontation. **B** is incorrect because win-lose allows only one party to get what they want from the scenario. **D** is incorrect because a leave-lose solution is when one party walks away from the problem.

23. Mike is the project manager for a project with a very tight schedule. The project is running late, and Mike feels that he does not have time to consider all the possible solutions that two team members are in disagreement over. Mike quickly decides to go with the team member with the largest amount of seniority. This is an example of which of the following?

    A. Problem solving

    B. Compromising

    C. Forcing

    D. Withdrawal

    ☑ **C.** Forcing happens when the project manager makes a decision based on factors not relevant to the problem. Just because a team member has more seniority does not mean this individual is correct.

    ☒ **A, B,** and **D** are incorrect choices. Problem solving is not described in the scenario. **B,** compromising, happens when both parties agree to give up something. **D,** withdrawal, happens when a party leaves the argument.

24. You are a project manager in a projectized organization. Your job as a project manager can be described best by which of the following?

    A. Full-time

    B. Part-time

    C. Expeditor

    D. Coordinator

☑ **A.** Project managers are typically assigned to a project on a full-time basis in a projectized organization.

☒ **B, C,** and **D** do not accurately describe the work schedule of a project manager in a projectized environment.

25. What is the benefit of using a collocated team?
  A. The project team is dispersed, so the team is self-led.
  B. The project team is dispersed, so communication increases.
  C. The project team is in the same physical location, so their ability to work as a team is enhanced.
  D. The project team is in the same physical location, so project costs are greatly reduced.

☑ **C.** When a project team is collocated, all of the project team members are in the same physical location in order to increase their ability to work as a team.

☒ **A** and **B** are incorrect. Collocated teams are not dispersed. **D** is incorrect because a collocated team does not ensure that costs are reduced. In some situations, costs may be increased due to travel in order to bring all the team members together to complete the project.

10

Introducing Project Communications Management

What's the most important skill a project manager has?

Communication.

Project managers spend about 90 percent of their time communicating. Think about it: meetings, phone calls, memos, e-mails, reports, presentations—the list goes on and on. Project managers spend the bulk of their day communicating news, ideas, and knowledge. They are communicators.

Project communications management centers on determining who needs what information and when—and then producing a plan to provide that needed information. It includes generating, collecting, disseminating, and storing communication. Successful projects require successful communication—thus, communication is the key link between people, ideas, and information.

Project communications management includes five processes, which may overlap each other and other knowledge areas. The five processes include the following:

- **Identify stakeholders**   The project stakeholders must be identified and categorized, and their needs, perceived threats, and objectives documented.

- **Communication planning**   The project manager needs to identify the stakeholders and their communication needs and determine how to fulfill their requirements.

- **Information distribution**   The project manager needs to get the correct information on the correct schedule to the appropriate stakeholders.

- **Performance reporting**   The project manager relies on EVM and other performance measurements to create status reports, measure performance, and forecast project conditions.

- **Managing stakeholders**   Stakeholder management isn't easy, but it's vital to a project's success. As the project moves forward, the project manager needs to communicate project successes and setbacks—and resolve issues with stakeholders.

CERTIFICATION OBJECTIVE 10.01

Identifying Project Stakeholders

Before the project manager can begin project management communications, she needs someone to communicate with. This is where project stakeholders come into play. Stakeholders are the people and organizations that are affected by the project. It's essential for planning and for communications to identify the project stakeholders as early as possible in the project. Things can get ugly pretty fast when the project manager realizes that she may have overlooked a group of stakeholders that need to contribute to the project.

Stakeholder identification helps the project manager and the project team plan for the activities, resources, and deliverables of the project. The project manager and the project team may lead the stakeholder identification process, or a business analyst may help identify the stakeholders. In either case, it's ideal to group stakeholders by their overall influence over project decisions, their involvement in the project work, and their interest in the project outcome. This categorization can help streamline communication.

Contracts are the most formal of all communications, as they are legally binding agreements between two or more parties. If the project is a result of a contract, then everyone mentioned in the contract is considered a key stakeholder to the project. The organization's procurement management processes, part of enterprise environmental factors, may affect how stakeholder identification and management happen when contracts are involved.

Performing Stakeholder Analysis

Stakeholder analysis is a process that considers and ranks project stakeholders based on their influence, interests, and expectations of the project. This process uses a systematic approach to identify all of the project stakeholders, ranking the stakeholders by varying factors, and then addressing stakeholders' needs, requirements, and expectations. Stakeholder analysis follows three logical steps.

1. Identify the project stakeholders and their interest, influence, project contributions, contact information, and expectations of the project. You can complete this through interviews, determining the project decision makers and champions of the project objectives.

2. Prioritize the identified stakeholders based on their power, influence, or impact on the project decisions. Project managers can use a grid system to rank stakeholder attributes from low to high.

3. Anticipate and plan how stakeholders will respond in different project scenarios. This anticipation helps the project manager influence the stakeholders and prepare them for project news, actions, and risk management.

Creating a Stakeholder Register

Stakeholder identification should help the project manager to create a stakeholder register. This document defines the stakeholders and their contact information for the project. The stakeholder register is a directory of all the stakeholders and should include the following:

- Stakeholder name and contact information
- Geographic location
- Project role and contribution
- Project requirements and expectations
- Project influence
- Phase of the project the stakeholder is most concerned with
- Details on the role of the stakeholder; for example, internal or external, supporter of the project, negative stakeholder, or neutral

The stakeholder registry can help the project management team create a stakeholder management strategy. This strategy is an effort to manage stakeholder expectations and create synergy and buy-in from the stakeholders. A stakeholder analysis matrix can help define the stakeholders' interest, assessment of project impact, and any potential responses to the anticipated stakeholder results.

CERTIFICATION OBJECTIVE 10.02

Communications Planning

Because project managers spend so much of their time communicating, it's essential for them to provide adequate planning for communication. Such planning focuses on who needs what information and when they need it. A project manager must identify the stakeholders' requirements for communication, determine what information is actually needed, and then plan to deliver the needed information on a preset schedule or based on project conditions.

Communications planning is typically completed early in the project. As part of this planning, the modality of the communications is documented. Some stakeholders may prefer a hard copy document rather than an e-mail. Later in the project, these needs can change. Throughout the project, the needs of the stakeholders, the type of information requested, and the modality of the information should be reviewed for accuracy—and updated if needed.

Leveraging Project Inputs

Project managers should first consider their enterprise environmental factors when planning project communications. As a reminder, the following are the basic enterprise environmental factors that need to be considered for communications planning:

- Organizational culture and structure
- Relevant standards and regulations
- Organizational infrastructure
- Human resources
- Marketplace conditions
- Risk tolerances
- Project management information systems

These factors can help the project management team determine what needs to be communicated and to whom. The project manager can also rely on organizational process assets (covered in Chapter 4). The two that the project manager should pay most attention to during communications planning are lessons learned and historical information. The project manager can use this proven information from the past to make decisions about the present project.

Of course, the project manager will rely on the project scope statement as part of communications planning. Why? Because the scope statement ensures that everyone involved in the project understands the project's goals, and it provides a common point of reference for all stakeholders. This will come in handy when the project manager is managing the project stakeholders.

Evaluating the Project Constraints and Assumptions

Every project has constraints and assumptions. Recall that constraints are any force that limits the project's options. A project constraint, such as contractual obligations, may require extensive communications. The requirements of the contract should be evaluated against the demands of the project staff to determine if extra resources will be needed to handle the communications. Constraints the project manager should consider when it comes to communications include such things as:

- The project team members' geographical locales
- The compatibility of communications software
- Technical capabilities
- Language barriers
- Telephone and videoconferencing abilities

Assumptions will no doubt vary from project to project. Thus, the project manager and the project team should attempt to identify the assumptions made in the project that may hinder successful project communications.

Consider a project operating under the assumption that communications with management can happen only through e-mail. Management, however, expects the project manager to provide formal status reports and daily updates via memos, and also needs staffing updates from each of the project team members. This false assumption can impose time demands that the project manager doesn't expect.

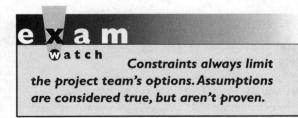

Constraints always limit the project team's options. Assumptions are considered true, but aren't proven.

Identifying Communication Requirements

Stakeholders will need different types of information, depending on their interest in the project and the priority of the project. The project manager will need to complete an analysis of the identified stakeholders to determine what information they actually need and how often the information is needed.

There is no value in expending resources on generating information, reports, and analyses for stakeholders who have no interest in the information. An accurate assessment of stakeholders' needs for information is required early in the project-planning processes. As a rule of thumb, provide information when its presence contributes to success or when a lack of information can contribute to failure.

ON THE CD

See the video Project Communications Management.

The project manager and the project team can identify the demand for communications using the following:

- Organization charts
- The project structure within the performing organization
- Stakeholder responsibility relationships
- Departments and disciplines involved with the project work
- The number of individuals involved in the project and their locales
- Internal and external information needs
- Stakeholder information

On the PMP exam, and in the real world, the project manager will need to identify the number of communication channels within a project. Here's a magic formula to calculate the number of communication channels: $N (N - 1) / 2$, where N represents the number of identified stakeholders. For example, if a project has 10 stakeholders, the formula would read $10 (10 - 1) / 2$ for a total of 45 communication channels. Figure 10-1 illustrates the formula.

FIGURE 10-1

Communication channels must be identified.

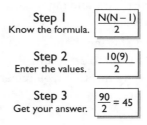

Step 1
Know the formula. $\dfrac{N(N-1)}{2}$

Step 2
Enter the values. $\dfrac{10(9)}{2}$

Step 3
Get your answer. $\dfrac{90}{2} = 45$

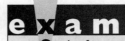

Exploring Communication Technologies

Let's face it: There are many different avenues a project manager and a project team can take to communicate. Project teams can effectively communicate through hallway meetings or formal project status meetings. Information can be transferred from stakeholder to stakeholder through written notes to complex online databases and tracking systems.

As part of the communications planning, the project manager should identify all of the required and approved methods of communicating. Some projects may be sensitive and contain classified information that not all stakeholders are privy to, while other projects may contain information that's open for anyone to explore. Whatever the case, the project manager should identify what requirements exist, if any, for the communication modalities.

Communication modalities can also include meetings, reports, memos, e-mails, and so on. The project manager should identify the preferred methods of communicating based on the conditions of the message to be communicated. Consider the following, which may have an effect on the communication plan:

- **Urgency of the information** When the information is communicated can often be as important as what's being communicated. For some projects, information should be readily available, while for other projects, information needs are less demanding.

- **Technology** Because of the demands of the project, technology changes may be needed to fulfill the project request. For example, the project may require an internal website that details project progress. If such a website does not exist, time and monies will need to be invested into this communication requirement.

- **Project staffing** The project manager should evaluate the abilities of the project team to determine if appropriate levels of competency exist to fulfill the communication requirements or if training will be required for the project team.

- **Project length**   The length of the project can have an influence on the project technology. Advances in technology may replace a long-term project's communication model. A short-term project may not have the same technology requirements as a long-term project, but could nevertheless benefit from the successful model a larger project uses.

- **Project environment**   How a team communicates often depends on its structure. Consider a collocated team versus a virtual team. Each type can be effective, but there will be differing communication demands for each type of team.

CERTIFICATION OBJECTIVE 10.03

Creating the Communications Plan

Based on stakeholder analysis, the project manager and the project team can determine what communications are needed. There's no advantage to supplying stakeholders with information that isn't needed or desired, and the time spent creating and delivering such information is a waste of resources.

A communications management plan can organize and document the process, types, and expectations of communications. It provides the following:

- The stakeholder communications requirements in order to communicate the appropriate information as demanded by the stakeholders.

- Information on what is to be communicated. This includes the expected format, content, and detail—think project reports versus quick e-mail updates.

- Details on how needed information flows through the project to the correct individuals. The communication structure documents where the information will originate, to whom the information will be sent, and in what modality the information is acceptable.

- Appropriate methods for communicating include e-mails, memos, reports, and even press releases.

- Schedules of when the various types of communication should occur. Some communication, such as status meetings, should happen on a regular schedule, while other communications may be prompted by conditions within the project.

- Escalation processes and time frames for moving issues upwards in the organization when they can't be solved at lower levels
- Methods to retrieve information as needed
- Instructions on how the communications management plan can be updated as the project progresses
- A project glossary

CERTIFICATION OBJECTIVE 10.04

Preparing for Information Distribution

Information distribution is the process of ensuring that the proper stakeholders get the appropriate information when and how they need it. Essentially, it's the implementation of the communications management plan. The communications management plan details how the information is to be created and dispersed—and also how the dispersed information is archived.

Three elements serve as inputs to information distribution.

- **Work results** Work results, good or bad, serve as inputs to communication because they show progress (or lack of progress), quality issues, and other relevant information.
- **The communications management plan** This plan serves as the guide for communicating project issues within the performing organization.
- **The project plan** The comprehensive project may have information, requirements, or described conditions that are integrated with communications.

Examining Communication Skills

Here's a news flash: Communication skills are used to send and receive information. Sounds easy, right? If communication is so easy, then why are there so many problems on projects stemming from misunderstandings, miscommunications, failures to communicate, and similar communication failings?

Figure 10-2 demonstrates a few different communication models. All models, regardless of the technology involved, have a sender, a message, and a recipient. Depending on the communication model, several additional elements can be included. Here's a summary of all the different parts of communication models:

- **Sender** The person or group sending the message to the receiver
- **Encoder** The device or technology that encodes the message to travel over the medium. For example, a telephone encodes the sender's voice to travel over the medium, the telephone wires.
- **Medium** This is the path the message takes from the sender to the receiver. This is the modality in which the communication travels and typically refers to an electronic model, such as e-mail or telephone.
- **Decoder** This is the inverse of the encoder. If a message is encoded, a decoder translates it back to a usable format. For example, the sender's message is encoded to travel the telephone wires, and the receiver's phone system translates the message back to a usable format.
- **Receiver** This is, of course, the recipient of the message.
- **Noise** This includes anything that disrupts the transfer of the message
- **Acknowledgement** Verbal and/or nonverbal signs that the message has been received. Just because a message has been received doesn't mean the receiver necessarily aggress with the message.

FIGURE 10-2

Sender models can vary based on the modality of the message.

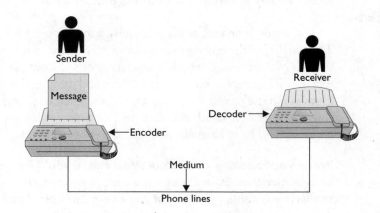

Creating Successful Communications

The most common type of communication between a sender and a receiver is verbal communication. When verbal communications are involved, the project manager should remember that half of communication is listening. This means the project manager must confirm that the receiver understands the message being sent. The confirmation of the sent message can be seen in the recipients' body language, feedback, and verbal confirmation of the sent message. Five terms are used to describe the process of communicating.

- **Paralingual**   The pitch, tone, and inflections in the sender's voice affect the message being sent. `
- **Feedback**   The sender confirms that the receiver understands the message by directly asking for a response, questions for clarification, or other confirmation of the sent message.
- **Active listening**   The receiver confirms the message is being received through feedback, questions, prompts for clarity, and other signs of confirmation.
- **Effective listening**   The receiver is involved in the listening experience by paying attention to visual clues from the speaker and paralingual characteristics, and by asking relevant questions.
- **Nonverbal**   Approximately 55 percent of communication is nonverbal. Facial expressions, hand gestures, and body language contribute to the message.

o n   t h e
j o b

How you say something is as important as what you say.

The words in an oral message actually only account for 7 percent of the message. The tonality of the message accounts for 38 percent of the message. The remaining 55 percent of the message is body language. A classic example involves a person talking to a dog. If the person has a friendly voice and posture, the dog will likely be receptive. However, if the person has a mean voice and guarded posture, the dog may feel threatened and on guard. When project managers talk with stakeholders, they must be aware of their body language and posture—not just the words they are communicating.

PMP
Coach

When you're taking the actual PMP exam, you'll be participating in nonverbal communication. Even though the text is written, there are still clues as to what the writer is telling you about the exam answers. Look for plurals, subject-verb agreements that would best answer the question, and determine what the question is really asking you. On long questions, it sometimes helps to skip the back story and get right to the interrogative.

The medium in communication can help or hinder the message. For example, when a project manager talks to a stakeholder in person, the stakeholder has the advantage not only of hearing the message and tone but also of seeing the body language. Remove body language from a conversation, and the message is interpreted by just the words and tonality. Always be aware of the downsides of various nondirect communication modalities: e-mail, reports, memos, and letters.

Electronic communications are more prevalent now than ever before: e-mail, texting, chats, collaborative software, and web meetings. All of these forms of communications are evolving daily, and the rules of how you communicate with these tools change just as quickly. It's important for the project manager and the project team to establish ground rules for communication when it comes to electronic communication. The project type may dictate what type of communication is appropriate or official, and when to use electronic communication versus face-to-face communication.

Creating Information Retrieval Systems

What good is information if no one can find it? An information retrieval system allows for fast and accurate access to project information. It can be a simple manual filing system, an advanced database of information storage, or a robust project management software suite. Whatever the approach, the information must be accessible, organized, and secure.

The project team, the project manager, the customer, and other stakeholders may need access to design specs, blueprints, plans, and other project information. A good information retrieval system is reliable and easy to navigate, and is updated as new information becomes available.

Creating Lessons Learned

Do you ever wish you could travel back in time? With lessons learned, you almost can. The whole point of lessons learned is to improve future projects by sharing what was learned during the current project.

A lessons-learned session is completed with the project manager, the project team, and key stakeholders to identify lessons they've learned in the technical, managerial, and project processes. Think of it: You're helping other project managers way off in the future by documenting what works and what doesn't in your project.

Lessons learned should happen throughout the project—not just at the project's conclusion. As a project moves through phases, project managers can use a lessons-learned session as a good team-building exercise. This means documenting and learning from what worked and what didn't within the project.

Distributing Information

Throughout the project, the project manager, the project sponsor, the project team, and other stakeholders are going to need information from and supply information to one another. The methods for distributing information can vary, but the best modality is the one that's most appropriate to the information being conveyed. In other words, an e-mail may not be the correct format in which to share variance information regarding project costs.

Information can be distributed through some of the following methods, given project demands and available technology:

- Project meetings
- Hard-copy documentation
- Databases
- Faxes
- E-mail
- Telephone calls
- Videoconferences
- A project website

Examining the Results of Information Distribution

Information distribution results in the following:

- **Lessons learned**   When lessons-learned sessions are completed, they're available to be used and applied. They are now part of the organization's process assets.
- **Project records**   All the business of the project communications are also part of the organizational process assets. This includes e-mails, memos, letters, and faxes. In some instances, the project team can also contribute by keeping their records in a project notebook.
- **Project reports**   Reports are formal communications on project activities, their status, and conditions. Management, customers, and policies within the performing organization may have differing requirements for when reports are needed.

- **Project presentations** Presentations are useful in providing information to customers, management, the project team, and other stakeholders. The delivery and degree of formality of the presentation should be appropriate for the conditions and information being delivered within the project.
- **Feedback from stakeholders** Stakeholders are usually happy to offer their feedback on the project performance. Project managers should then document this feedback and apply it to improve the project's performance.
- **Stakeholder notifications** No doubt as the project rolls along there will be notifications to the stakeholders about resolved issues, approved changes, and the overall health of the project. This information should be kept for future reference.

CERTIFICATION OBJECTIVE 10.05

Managing Stakeholder Expectations

In project management, it seems that someone always wants something from the project manager: updates; status reports; quick questions; and queries on issues, risks, and other demands. Managing stakeholder expectations is a proactive process to organize, prioritize, and anticipate stakeholder communication needs before they happen and as they happen. This can go somewhat smoothly if the project manager has done adequate stakeholder analysis to document what stakeholders will want from the project. If poor stakeholder analysis has been done, you can expect a maelstrom of issues, problems, phone calls, and reactionary management. Not good.

The odds of project success increase when stakeholder expectations are managed effectively because issues are resolved faster, time is spent actually managing the project rather than in response mode, and issue management can happen proactively rather than reactively. Issue management, a huge time suck on the project manager and project team, is part of managing stakeholder expectations. When the project manager and team have time to evaluate and respond to identified issues, the issues can be resolved before they become risks and disrupt the project even more. The message? Effective stakeholder identification and planning lead to better stakeholder management.

Preparing for Stakeholder Expectations Management

The responsibility of stakeholder expectations management lies squarely on the shoulders of the project manager. With this responsibility, the project manager needs to quickly gather information, create an approach to deal with stakeholders' expectations, and then take consistent action to keep stakeholders informed and up-to-date on the project status and issues. The project manager will rely on six things for stakeholder expectation management.

■ **Stakeholder register**   The project manager must know what stakeholders expect, their project information, their project influence, and other relevant project information.

■ **Stakeholder management strategy**   If the project manager understands the goals and objections of each stakeholder, he can address stakeholder expectations based on what each stakeholder finds most important in the project.

■ **Project management plan**   The project management plan contains the communications management plan. This plan, as you may recall, defines who needs what information, when they need the information, and what the expected modality is of the information. Executing this project management plan can help with the management of stakeholder expectations.

■ **Issue log**   Recall that the issue log documents all issues, their status, and their ultimate resolution. The issue log is needed to communicate project status, update the stakeholders about certain issues, and foster stakeholder relationships.

■ **Change log**   Changes will happen within projects, and this log tracks the proposed changes, their approval status, and their effect on the project as a whole. Changes must be communicated to stakeholders so they can know what changes are occurring in the project and the effect that the change may have on the project requirements.

■ **Organization process assets**   Communication requirements, issue management rules and procedures, change control rules, and historical information can all affect how the project manager manages stakeholder expectations.

This is an iterative process that should be done on a consistent basis throughout the project. Stakeholders will become frustrated with the project manager if communication is irregular and does not follow the promises of the project's communication management plan.

Performing Stakeholder Expectations Management

The best approach, frankly, for performing stakeholder expectations management is to communicate with the stakeholders. These people want to know what's happening with the project, and they want news about issues, deliverables, and project status. The stakeholder management plan will help the project manager communicate in the most accurate method possible for each stakeholder. Not every stakeholder and not every instance demands formal project communications.

The project manager should use interpersonal skills and management skills to manage stakeholder expectations. This means the project manager works to build trust with the stakeholders, resolve conflicts, and influence the stakeholders for the betterment of the project. On the management side of the equation, the project manager uses presentation skills, writing skills, and likely public speaking skills to convey the news of the project.

Managing stakeholder expectations may result in change requests, something not all project managers are going to be thrilled with. As stakeholders develop a deeper understanding of what's happening in the project, they may respond to project scenarios with requests for fewer, or more, scope requirements. All change requests, whether it be scope, time, cost, or even corrective actions, should be documented and follow the change control processes.

The project manager may also need to update the project management plan based on the outcome of stakeholder expectations management. Specifically, new communication requirements may cause the communications management plan to be updated to reflect what the stakeholders are now expecting. The issues log may also need to be updated if the status of an issue changes or if new issues have been identified. Finally, the stakeholder register may also need to be updated if new stakeholders are identified or if contact information for stakeholders changes.

Managing Project Stakeholders

The project manager is responsible for managing stakeholders, who often require, or demand, attention from the project manager. Therefore, the project manager must make time to answer questions, get the stakeholders involved in the project, and, at a minimum, communicate the project status. Stakeholder management is vital to a project's success for several reasons.

- It leads to resolving stakeholder issues.
- It promotes synergy.
- It limits disruptions during the project.
- It promotes project buy-in.

Stakeholder management relies on the communication management plan to direct what needs to be communicated and when. The communications management plan will also define the goals and expectations of the stakeholders, which in turn will guide conversations between the project manager and the project stakeholders.

Communicating with Stakeholders

What's the best way to communicate when resolving stakeholder issues? Face-to-face. Sure, sure, sometimes an e-mail or phone call is quicker and more appropriate for what's being communicated—but when it comes to resolving issues with stakeholders, a project manager can't go wrong with face-to-face meetings.

As a result of stakeholder communications and management, the project manager will document project issues in an issue log. Issue logs acknowledge the problem and the importance of the issue to the project manager and the project stakeholders. Many times, an owner is assigned to the issue, and a date for the issue to be resolved by is likewise assigned.

But what happens if these issues don't get addressed, documented, or assigned to an owner? The project manager can expect conflict, project delays, and unhappy stakeholders. Ideally, the issues in the issue log are resolved, and documentation on how the issue was resolved is included.

CERTIFICATION OBJECTIVE 10.06

Reporting Project Performance

Throughout the project, customers and other stakeholders are going to need updates on the project performance. The work performance information, the status of what's been completed and what's left to do, is always at the heart of performance reporting. Stakeholders want to be kept abreast of how the project is performing.

Performance reporting is the process of collecting, organizing, and disseminating information on how project resources are being used to complete the project objectives. In other words, the people footing the bill and affected by the outcome of the project need some confirmation that things are going the way the project manager has promised.

Performance reporting covers more than just cost and schedule, though these are the most common concerns. Another huge issue is the influence of risks on the project's success. The project manager and the project team must continue to monitor and evaluate risks, including pending risks and their impact on the project's success.

Another major concern with reporting is the level of quality. No one will praise the project manager and the project team for completing the project on time and on budget if the quality of the work is unacceptable. In fact, the project could be declared a failure and cancelled as a result of poor quality, or the project team may be forced to redo the work, business could be lost, or individuals could even be harmed as a result of the poor quality of the project work.

Reviewing Project Performance

The project manager will host performance review meetings to ascertain the progress and level of success the project team is having with the project work. Performance review meetings focus on the work that has been completed and how the work results are living up to the time and cost estimates. In addition, the project manager and the project team will evaluate the project scope to protect it from change and creep. The project manager and the project team will also examine quality and its effect on the project as a whole. Finally, the project manager must lead a discussion on pending or past risks and then determine any new risks, as well as the overall risk likelihood and its potential impact on the project's success.

Analyzing Project Variances

Performance review meetings are not the only tools the project manager uses to assess project performance. Prior to the performance reviews, or spurred by a performance review, the project manager needs to examine the time, scope, quality, and cost variances within the project. The project manager will examine the estimates supplied for the time and cost of activities and compare it to the time and cost actually experienced.

The goals of analyzing project variances include the following:

- Prevent future variances
- Determine the root cause of variances
- Determine if the variances are an anomaly or if the estimates were flawed
- Determine if the variances are within a predetermined acceptable range, such as negative 10 percent or plus 5 percent
- Determine if the variances can be expected on future project work

In addition to examining the time and cost variances, which are the most common, the project manager must examine any scope, resource, and quality variances. A change in the scope can skew time and cost predictions. A variance in

resources, such as the expected performance by a given resource, can alter the project schedule and even the predicted costs of a project. Quality variances may result in rework, lost time, lost monies, and even the rejection of the project product.

Completing Trend Analysis

Picture this: You're a project manager for a long-term project. You'd like to examine how performance has been for the past few years to predict what the upcoming performance will be like. You're doing trend analysis. Trend analysis is an approach that studies trends in past performances in order to predict what upcoming experiences might resemble. It is great for long projects, analysis of team performance, and predicting future activities.

Examining the Results of Performance Reporting

The goal of performance reporting is to share information regarding the project performance with the appropriate stakeholders. Of course, performance reporting is not something done only at the end of the project or after a project phase. Instead, it is done according to a regular schedule, as detailed in the communication plan, or as project conditions warrant. Outputs of performance reporting include such things as:

- **Performance reports**   These are the results and summation of the project performance analysis. The communications management plan will detail the type of report needed based on the conditions within the project, the timing of the communication, and the demands of the project stakeholder.

- **Forecasting**   Will the project end on schedule? Will the project be on budget? How much longer will it take to complete the project? And how much more money will this project need to finish?

- **Change requests**   Performance results may prompt change requests to some area or areas of the project. The change requests should flow into the change control system for consideration and then approval or denial.

- **Recommended corrective actions**   Corrective actions center on bringing future project performance back in alignment with the project plan.

w a t c h

Forecasting project performance can use a time series method, such as earned value management, linear prediction, or the growth curve of the project. Forecasting can also use causal and econometric approaches to predict project performance. The Delphi Technique, scenarios, and forecasts by analogy are all examples of judgmental methods.

INSIDE THE EXAM

Communication is the most important skill a project manager can have. Project managers spend 90 percent of their time communicating. Since the project manager is expected to spend so much time communicating, you can bet she needs a plan to determine what needs to be communicated, to whom, and when. The communications management plan is the comprehensive plan that the project manager and the project team rely on for all communication guidance.

The organizational structure affects the level of communications the project manager can expect. Matrix structures must include the functional managers of the project team from the different units within the organization, whereas a functional organization doesn't require the same level of complexity in reporting.

The basic communication model consists of a sender, a message, a medium, and a receiver. When technology is involved, the project can become more complex: encoders, the medium, and decoders are included. Consider sending a fax: You are the sender, Jane is the recipient, and the message is the information on the page to be faxed. The encoder is your outgoing fax machine, and Jane's fax machine is the decoder. The telephone lines between the fax machines are the medium. Any noise could possibly disrupt the message during transmission.

Management, customers, and other concerned stakeholders will be interested in the performance of the project. The project manager will need to meet their expectations on an established schedule or based on conditions within the project. One of the most common methods for showing performance is through earned value analysis.

Stakeholder management is vital to a project's success. Stakeholders expect the project manager to lead stakeholder management and to include them in the project. And this makes sense—it's their project after all. Issue management is paramount. If a project manager fails to resolve project issues that are important to the stakeholder, the project is likely to be riddled with stakeholder anxiety, conflict, and delays.

CERTIFICATION SUMMARY

Communication is a project manager's most important skill. Project managers have to communicate with management, customers, the project team members, and the rest of the stakeholders involved with the project. The project manager's foundation is communication. Without effective communication, how will work get completed, progress reported, and information dispersed?

Communications planning centers on one question: "Who needs what information—and when do they need it?" Consider all of the different channels for communication on any project. That's many different possibilities for information to be lost, messages to be skewed, and progress to be hindered. The formula for calculating the communication channels is $N(N-1)/2$, where N represents the number of stakeholders. As a general rule, larger projects require more detail—and detail means more planning for communications.

The communications management plan organizes and documents the communication processes, acceptable modalities for types of communication, and the stakeholder expectations for communication. The plan should detail how information is gathered, organized, accessed, and dispersed. The plan should also provide a schedule of expected communication based on a calendar schedule, such as project status meetings. Some communications are prompted by conditions within the project, such as cost variances, schedule variances, or other performance-related issues.

The communication model illustrates the flow of communication from the sender to the receiver. The sender sends the message. The message is then encoded by the encoder and travels over the medium. Once it arrives at its destination, a decoder decodes the message for the receiver. This model is easy to remember if you apply the processes to a telephone call.

Within communicating, there are five characteristics that affect the message.

- **Paralingual** Pitch, tone, and voice inflections
- **Feedback** Sender confirmation of the message by asking questions, requesting a response, or other confirmation signals
- **Active listening** The receiver confirms message receipt
- **Effective listening** The receiver offers confirmation of the message, such as nodding his head, asking questions, or initiating other interactions.
- **Nonverbal** Facial expressions, hand gestures, and body language

KEY TERMS

To pass the PMP exam, you will need to memorize the following terms and their definitions. For maximum value, create your own flashcards based on these definitions and review them daily. The definitions can be found both within this chapter and in the glossary.

active listening   This occurs when the receiver confirms the message is being received by feedback, questions, prompts for clarity, and other signs of having received the message.

communications formula   The formula "N (N – 1) / 2" shows the number of communication channels in a project. N represents the total number of stakeholders.

communications management plan   A plan that documents and organizes the stakeholder needs for communication. This plan covers the communications system, its documentation, the flow of communication, modalities of communication, schedules for communications, information retrieval, and any other stakeholder requirements for communications.

decoder   This is a part of the communications model; it is the inverse of the encoder. If a message is encoded, a decoder translates it back to usable format.

effective listening   The receiver is involved in the listening experience by paying attention to visual clues by the speaker and to paralingual intentions and by asking relevant questions.

encoder   Part of the communications model; the device or technology that packages the message to travel over the medium.

feedback   Sender confirmation of the message by asking questions, requesting a response, or other confirmation signals.

forecasting   An educated estimate of how long the project will take to complete. Can also refer to how much the project may cost to complete.

issue   Any point of contention, debate, or decision that has not yet been made in the project that may affect the project's success.

issue log   A documentation of all identified issues affecting the project. Each issue is assigned an issue owner and an ideal date for resolution, and its status is maintained through the issue log.

medium   Part of the communications model; this is the path the message takes from the sender to the receiver. This is the modality in which the communication travels, and it typically refers to an electronic model, such as e-mail or the telephone.

nonverbal   Approximately 55 percent of oral communication is non-verbal. Facial expressions, hand gestures, and body language contribute to the message.

paralingual   The pitch, tone, and inflections in the sender's voice affect the message being sent.

progress reports   These provide current information on the project work completed to date.

receiver   Part of the communications model: the recipient of the message.

sender   Part of the communications model: the person or group delivering the message to the receiver.

stakeholder analysis   A process that considers and ranks the project stakeholders based on their influence, interests, and expectations of the project.

stakeholder registry   A document that defines each stakeholder, their project requirements, influence on the project, phases of interest, details on the stakeholders contributions, and their contact information for the project.

status reports   These provide current information on the project cost, budget, scope, and other relevant information.

✓ TWO-MINUTE DRILL

Identifying Project Stakeholders

- ❑ Stakeholder identification is a project management process that centers on correctly identifying all of the people, groups, and organizations that are affected by the project's outcome.
- ❑ Stakeholder interests, influence, contributions, and contact information must be documented in the stakeholder registry.
- ❑ A salience model is a stakeholder classification that ranks stakeholders based on their power, urgency, and legitimacy in the project.

Communications Planning

- ❑ Communication centers on who needs what and on when and how you are going to give it to them.
- ❑ Communication requirements are set by stakeholders.
- ❑ Communication planning is accomplished early in the planning process.
- ❑ Communications are linked to the organizational structure of the performing organization.
- ❑ Constraints and assumptions can affect the communications planning.
- ❑ Acknowledgment of a message can be positive or negative. Just because a receiver got the message, doesn't mean she has to agree with it.

Creating the Communications Plan

- ❑ The communications plan provides instructions on how to gather and disseminate project information.
- ❑ It provides instructions on the communications methods, such as hard copies, reports, and e-mail.
- ❑ The communications plan should include a schedule of expected communications, such as reports and meetings.

Preparing for Information Distribution

- ❑ The choice of media is dictated by the urgency and importance of the message to be communicated.

❑ The project manager should be versed in meeting management techniques to effectively run a meeting. Agendas, minutes, and a timetable should be enforced at most meetings.

❑ The project manager should also identify a method to access needed information between regularly scheduled communications for the project stakeholders.

Managing Stakeholder Expectations

❑ Face-to-face meetings are best for resolving issues with stakeholders.

❑ The project manager is responsible for managing project stakeholders.

❑ Issue logs document issues between the stakeholders and the project. When issues are resolved, the issue log should be updated to reflect the resolution.

❑ Stakeholder involvement increases the odds that a project will not veer off track.

Reporting Project Performance

❑ Status reporting provides current information on the project.

❑ Progress reporting provides information on what the team has accomplished—and may include information on what is yet to be accomplished.

❑ Forecasting provides information on how the remainder of the project or phase is expected to go.

❑ Variance analysis examines the reasons why cost, schedule, scope, quality, and other factors may vary from what was planned.

❑ Trend analysis is the study of trends over time to reveal patterns and expectations of future results.

❑ Earned value analysis is a series of formulas that reveal and predict project performance.

❑ Change requests may stem from performance reports.

SELF TEST

1. Of the following, which one is an example of noise?
   A. Fax machine
   B. Ad-hoc conversations
   C. Contractual agreements
   D. Distance

2. You are the project manager of a large technical project. You believe that Jose has received the message but does not agree with it based on his body language. This is known as what?
   A. Acknowledgement
   B. Transmission
   C. Negotiation
   D. Decoder

3. You are the project manager for the LKH Project. Management has requested that you create a document detailing what information will be expected from stakeholders and to whom that information will be disseminated. Management is asking for which one of the following?
   A. The roles and responsibilities matrix
   B. The scope management plan
   C. The communications management plan
   D. The communications worksheet

4. Which of the following will help you, the project manager, complete the needed communications management plan by identifying the stakeholders' communication needs?
   A. Identification of all communication channels
   B. Formal documentation of all communication channels
   C. Formal documentation of all stakeholders
   D. Lessons learned from previous similar projects

5. You are the project manager for the JGI Project. You have 32 stakeholders on this project. How many communication channels do you have?
   A. Depends on the number of project team members
   B. 496
   C. 32
   D. 1

6. You are the project manager for the KLN Project. You had 19 stakeholders on this project and have added 3 team members. How many more communication channels do you have now compared to before?

   A. 171
   B. 231
   C. 60
   D. 1

7. A memo has been sent to you, the project manager, project team members, and the project customers from the project sponsor. In this instance, who is the encoder?

   A. Project sponsor
   B. Project manager
   C. Project team members
   D. Project customers

8. Which one of the following is an example of a project communication constraint?

   A. Ad-hoc conversations
   B. Demands for formal reports
   C. Stakeholder management
   D. Team members in different geographic locales

9. Project managers can present project information in many different ways. Which one of the following is not a method a project manager can use to present project performance?

   A. Histograms
   B. S-curves
   C. Bar charts
   D. RACI charts

10. Of the following, which term describes the pitch and tone of an individual's voice?

    A. Paralingual
    B. Feedback
    C. Effective listening
    D. Active listening

11. You are the project manager of the KMH Project. This project is slated to last eight years. You have just calculated EVM and have a CV of –$3,500, which is outside of the acceptable thresholds for your project. What type of report is needed for management?

    A. Progress report
    B. Forecast report

C. Exception report

D. Trends report

12. You are presenting your project performance to your key stakeholders. Several of the stakeholders are receiving phone calls during your presentation, and this is distracting from your message. This is an example of what?

A. Noise

B. Negative feedback

C. Outside communications

D. Message distracter

13. You are the project manager for the OOK Project. You will be hosting project meetings every week. Of the following, which one is not a valid rule for project meetings?

A. Schedule recurring meetings as soon as possible.

B. Allow project meetings to last as long as needed.

C. Distribute meeting agendas prior to the meeting start.

D. Allow the project team to have input to the agenda.

14. The three basic elements needed for communication in project management include which of the following?

A. Words, sentences, paragraphs

B. Proper grammar, spelling, ideas

C. Verbal, nonverbal, action

D. Sender, receiver, message

15. Which one of the following is a technology factor that may affect project communication?

A. Communications management

B. Management by walking around

C. The project length

D. Variance analysis reporting

16. What percentage of a message is sent through nonverbal communications, such as facial expressions, hand gestures, and body language?

A. More than 50 percent

B. 30 to 40 percent

C. 20 to 30 percent

D. 10 to 20 percent

17. When does lessons-learned identification take place?
    A. At the end of the project
    B. At the end of each project phase
    C. Throughout the project life cycle
    D. Whenever a lesson has been learned

18. Why should a project team complete lessons-learned documentation?
    A. To ensure project closure
    B. To show management what they've accomplished in the project
    C. To show the project stakeholders what they've accomplished in the project
    D. To help future project teams complete their projects more accurately

19. Often in project management you will have to negotiate. Negotiations work best in which environment?
    A. Caution and yielding
    B. Sincerity, honesty, and extreme caution
    C. Mutual respect and admiration
    D. Mutual respect and cooperation

20. You are the project manager for the PMU Project. Your project has 13 members. You have been informed that next week your project will receive the seven additional members you requested. How many channels of communication will you have next week?
    A. 1
    B. 78
    C. 190
    D. 201

21. Performance reporting should generally provide information on all of the following except for which one?
    A. Scope
    B. Schedule
    C. Labor issues
    D. Quality

22. Which one of the following is an output from performance reporting?
    A. Trend analysis
    B. EVM
    C. Variance analysis
    D. Change requests

23. The process of sending information from the project manager to the project team is called what?
- **A.** Functioning
- **B.** Matrixing
- **C.** Blended communications
- **D.** Transmitting

24. George is the project manager of the 7YH Project. In this project, George considers the relationship between himself and the customer to be of utmost importance. Which one of the following is a valid reason for George's belief in this?
- **A.** The customer will complete George's performance evaluation. A poor communication model between George and the customer will affect his project bonus.
- **B.** The customer is not familiar with project management. George must educate the customer about the process.
- **C.** The customer is always right.
- **D.** The communication between the customer and George can convey the project objectives more clearly than can the language in the project contract.

25. Which one of the following means that communications occur?
- **A.** The transfer of knowledge
- **B.** The outputting of knowledge
- **C.** The presence of knowledge
- **D.** The transmission of knowledge

SELF TEST ANSWERS

1. Of the following, which one is an example of noise?
   A. Fax machine
   B. Ad-hoc conversations
   C. Contractual agreements
   D. Distance

   ☑ **D.** Noise is anything that interferes with the transmission and understanding of the message. Distance is an example of noise.
   ☒ **A,** a fax machine, is an example of a decoder. **B** is incorrect; ad-hoc conversations are informal conversations. Contractual agreements, choice **C,** are a type of formal communication.

2. You are the project manager of a large technical project. You believe that Jose has received the message but does not agree with it based on his body language. This is known as what?
   A. Acknowledgement
   B. Transmission
   C. Negotiation
   D. Decoder

   ☑ **A.** Acknowledgement means that Jose has received the message but may not agree with it.
   ☒ **B, C,** and **D** are incorrect. A transmission is the output of the message, negotiation is not relevant to this scenario, and a decoder is the mechanism for decoding the message.

3. You are the project manager for the LKH Project. Management has requested that you create a document detailing what information will be expected from stakeholders and to whom that information will be disseminated. Management is asking for which one of the following?
   A. The roles and responsibilities matrix
   B. The scope management plan
   C. The communications management plan
   D. The communications worksheet

   ☑ **C.** Management is requesting a communications management plan, which details the requirements and expectations for communicating information among the project stakeholders.
   ☒ **A** is incorrect, since a roles and responsibilities matrix depicts who does what and who makes which decisions. **B,** the scope management plan, is also incorrect because this plan explains how changes to the scope may be allowed depending on the circumstances. **D** is not a valid choice for the question.

4. Which of the following will help you, the project manager, complete the needed communications management plan by identifying the stakeholders' communication needs?
   A. Identification of all communication channels
   B. Formal documentation of all communication channels
   C. Formal documentation of all stakeholders
   D. Lessons learned from previous similar projects

   ☑ **D.** Lessons learned and historical information from a previous project are ideal inputs to communications planning.
   ☒ **A, B,** and **C** are incorrect because these choices do not fully answer the question. Lessons learned from previous similar projects is the best tool to identify stakeholders' requirements for communication.

5. You are the project manager for the JGI Project. You have 32 stakeholders on this project. How many communication channels do you have?
   A. Depends on the number of project team members
   B. 496
   C. 32
   D. 1

   ☑ **B.** Using the formula N (N – 1) / 2, where N represents the number of stakeholders, gives us 496 communication channels.
   ☒ **A, C,** and **D** are incorrect. These values do not reflect the number of communication channels on the project.

6. You are the project manager for the KLN Project. You had 19 stakeholders on this project, and have added 3 team members. How many more communication channels do you have now compared to before?
   A. 171
   B. 231
   C. 60
   D. 1

   ☑ **C.** This is a tough question, but typical of the PMP exam. The question asks how many more communication channels exist. You'll have to calculate the new value, which is 231, and then subtract the original value, which is 171, for a total of 60 new channels.

☒ **A** is incorrect. 171 is the original number of communication channels. **B** is incorrect because this value reflects the new number of communication channels. **D** is not a valid choice.

7. A memo has been sent to you, the project manager, project team members, and the project customers from the project sponsor. In this instance, who is the encoder?
   A. Project sponsor
   B. Project manager
   C. Project team members
   D. Project customers

☑ **A.** The project sponsor is the source of the memo, since this is the sender of the message.
☒ **B, C,** and **D** are all recipients of the memo, not the sender, so they cannot be the source of the message.

8. Which one of the following is an example of a project communication constraint?
   A. Ad-hoc conversations
   B. Demands for formal reports
   C. Stakeholder management
   D. Team members in different geographic locales

☑ **D.** Team members that are located physically close together can be a communications constraint, being that it's tougher to communicate when distance between team members exists.
☒ **A, B,** and **C** are all incorrect since these are not project communications constraints.

9. Project managers can present project information in many different ways. Which one of the following is not a method a project manager can use to present project performance?
   A. Histograms
   B. S-curves
   C. Bar charts
   D. RACI charts

☑ **D.** RACI charts do not show project performance, but accountability of the resources involved in the project.
☒ **A, B,** and **C** are incorrect since these choices do present project performance.

10. Of the following, which term describes the pitch and tone of an individual's voice?
    A. Paralingual
    B. Feedback
    C. Effective listening
    D. Active listening

    ☑ **A.** Paralingual is a term used to describe the pitch and tone of one's voice.
    ☒ **B,** feedback, is a request to confirm the information sent in the conversation. **C,** effective listening, is the ability to understand the message through what is said, facial expressions, gestures, tone and pitch, and so on. **D,** active listening, is the process of confirming what is understood and asking for clarification when needed.

11. You are the project manager of the KMH Project. This project is slated to last eight years. You have just calculated EVM and have a CV of –$3,500, which is outside of the acceptable thresholds for your project. What type of report is needed for management?
    A. Progress report
    B. Forecast report
    C. Exception report
    D. Trends report

    ☑ **C.** An exception report is typically completed when variances exceed a given limit.
    ☒ **A** is incorrect. Progress reports describe the progress of the project or phase. **B** is incorrect because this is not a valid answer. **D,** a trends report, is an analysis of project trends over time.

12. You are presenting your project performance to your key stakeholders. Several of the stakeholders are receiving phone calls during your presentation, and this is distracting from your message. This is an example of what?
    A. Noise
    B. Negative feedback
    C. Outside communications
    D. Message distracter

    ☑ **A.** Noise is the correct answer since their phone calls are distracting from your message.
    ☒ **B, C,** and **D** are incorrect, as they do not answer the question.

13. You are the project manager for the OOK Project. You will be hosting project meetings every week. Of the following, which one is not a valid rule for project meetings?
    A. Schedule recurring meetings as soon as possible.
    B. Allow project meetings to last as long as needed.
    C. Distribute meeting agendas prior to the meeting start.
    D. Allow the project team to have input to the agenda.

    ☑ **B.** Project meetings should have a set time limit.
    ☒ **A, C,** and **D** are incorrect answers because these are good attributes of project team meetings.

14. The three basic elements needed for communication in project management include which of the following?
    A. Words, sentences, paragraphs
    B. Proper grammar, spelling, ideas
    C. Verbal, nonverbal, action
    D. Sender, receiver, message

    ☑ **D.** The three parts to communication are sender, receiver, and message.
    ☒ **A, B,** and **C** are all incorrect choices.

15. Which one of the following is a technology factor that may affect project communication?
    A. Communications management
    B. Management by walking around
    C. The project length
    D. Variance analysis reporting

    ☑ **C.** The project duration is the only technology factor that may affect project communication.
    ☒ **A.** Communications management focuses on managing communications, not performance. **B,** management by walking around, is an effective management style, but it does not reflect project performance. **D,** variance analysis, focuses on the root causes of variances within the project, but not solely on the project performance.

16. What percentage of a message is sent through nonverbal communications, such as facial expressions, hand gestures, and body language?
    A. More than 50 percent
    B. 30 to 40 percent

C.   20 to 30 percent

D.   10 to 20 percent

☑   **A.** More than 50 percent of a message is sent through nonverbal communications.

☒   **B, C,** and **D** are incorrect.

17. When does lessons-learned identification take place?

A.   At the end of the project

B.   At the end of each project phase

C.   Throughout the project life cycle

D.   Whenever a lesson has been learned

☑   **C.** Lessons learned takes place throughout the project life cycle, not just at the end of the project or its phases.

☒   **A, B,** and **D** are incorrect choices.

18. Why should a project team complete lessons-learned documentation?

A.   To ensure project closure

B.   To show management what they've accomplished in the project

C.   To show the project stakeholders what they've accomplished in the project

D.   To help future project teams complete their projects more accurately

☑   **D.** Lessons-learned documentation helps future project teams complete their projects with more efficiency and effectiveness.

☒   **A, B,** and **C** are incorrect since each statement does not reflect the intent of lessons-learned documentation: to help future project teams.

19. Often in project management you will have to negotiate. Negotiations work best in which environment?

A.   Caution and yielding

B.   Sincerity, honesty, and extreme caution

C.   Mutual respect and admiration

D.   Mutual respect and cooperation

☑ **D.** Mutual respect and cooperation is the environment needed for fair and balanced negotiations.

☒ **A,** caution and yielding, is not a good environment for negotiations. **B,** while tempting, is not the best choice. **C** is incorrect, since the people involved in negotiations don't necessarily need to admire one another.

20. You are the project manager for the PMU Project. Your project has 13 members. You have been informed that next week your project will receive the seven additional members you requested. How many channels of communication will you have next week?

A. 1
B. 78
C. 190
D. 201

☑ **C.** The project currently has 13 team members, and next week 7 additional team members will come aboard, thus making a total of 20 team members. Using the formula N (N – 1) / 2, where N is the number of identified stakeholders, the communication channels equal 190.

☒ **A, B,** and **D** are all incorrect choices.

21. Performance reporting should generally provide information on all of the following except for which one?

A. Scope
B. Schedule
C. Labor issues
D. Quality

☑ **C.** Labor issues are not part of performance reporting.

☒ **A, B,** and **C** are all part of performance reporting.

22. Which one of the following is an output from performance reporting?

A. Trend analysis
B. EVM
C. Variance analysis
D. Change requests

☑ **D.** Of all the choices, a change request is the only acceptable answer. Incidentally, there are two outputs of performance reporting: change requests and performance reports.

☒ **A,** trend analysis, is the study of project performance results to determine if the project is improving or failing. It is a tool used as part of performance reporting, but it is not an output of performance reporting. **B** and **C** are also tools used in performance reporting, but they are not an output of the process.

23. The process of sending information from the project manager to the project team is called what?
A. Functioning
B. Matrixing
C. Blended communications
D. Transmitting

☑ **D.** When information is sent, it is considered to be transmitted.

☒ **A, B,** and **C** are all incorrect choices.

24. George is the project manager of the 7YH Project. In this project, George considers the relationship between himself and the customer to be of utmost importance. Which one of the following is a valid reason for George's belief in this?
A. The customer will complete George's performance evaluation. A poor communication model between George and the customer will affect his project bonus.
B. The customer is not familiar with project management. George must educate the customer about the process.
C. The customer is always right.
D. The communication between the customer and George can convey the project objectives more clearly than can the language in the project contract.

☑ **D.** George and the customer's relationship can allow clearer communication on the project objectives than what may be expressed in the project contract. The contract should take precedence on any issues, but direct contact is often the best way to achieve clear and concise communication.

☒ **A** is an incorrect choice because the focus is on personal gain rather than the good of the project. **B** is incorrect, since the customer does not necessarily need to be educated about the project management process. **C** is incorrect because the customer is not always right—the contract will take precedence in any disagreements.

25. Which one of the following means that communications occur?

    A.   The transfer of knowledge

    B.   The outputting of knowledge

    C.   The presence of knowledge

    D.   The transmission of knowledge

    ☑   **A.** The transfer of knowledge is evidence that communication has occurred.

    ☒   **B** and **C** do not necessarily mean that knowledge has originated from the source and that is has been transferred to the recipient. **D** is also incorrect because messages are transmitted, but knowledge is transferred.

11

Introducing
Project Risk
Management

R isk is everywhere. From driving a car to parachuting, it's inherent in the activities we choose. Within a project, risks are unplanned events or conditions that can have a positive or negative effect on its success. Not all risks are bad, but almost all are seen as a threat.

The risks that activities bring are an exchange for the benefits we get from accepting that risk. If a person chooses to jump out of a perfectly good airplane for the thrill of the fall, the exhilaration of the parachute opening, and the view of Earth rushing up, there is still a risk that the chute may not open—a risk that thrill seekers are willing to accept.

Project managers, to some extent, are like these thrill seekers. Parachutists complete training, pack their chutes, check and double-check their equipment, and make certain there's an emergency chute for those "just-in-case" scenarios. Project managers—good project managers—take a similar approach.

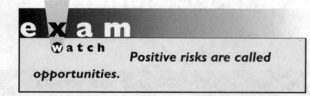

Positive risks are called opportunities.

Risks in a project, should they come to fruition, can mean total project failure, increased costs, and extended project duration, among other things. Risk often has a negative connotation, but like it does for the parachutist, the acceptance of the risk can also offer a reward. For the parachutist, the risk is certain death— but the reward is the thrill of the activity. For project managers, risk can mean failure, but the reward can mean a time or cost savings, as well as other benefits.

Risk management is the process in which the project manager and project team identify project risks, analyze and rank them, and determine what actions, if any, need to be taken to avert these threats. Associated with this process are the costs, time, and quality concerns of the project brought about by the solutions to those risks. In addition, the reactions to risks are analyzed for any secondary risks the solutions may have created.

In this chapter, we'll discuss risk management planning, risk identification, analysis, response planning, and monitoring and controlling the identified risks. For the PMP exam, you'll need a firm grasp on these concepts. You'll be taking a *real* risk if you don't know them well.

Planning for Risk Management

Risk management planning is about making decisions. The project manager, the project team, and other key stakeholders are involved to determine the risk management processes. The risk management processes are related to the scope of the project, the priority of the project within the performing organization, and the impact of the project deliverables. In other words, a simple, low-impact project won't have the same level of risk planning as a high-priority, complex project. It's important to complete risk management planning in order to successfully manage, plan for, analyze, and react to identified risks.

Examining Stakeholder Tolerance

Depending on the project, the conditions, and the potential for loss or reward, stakeholders will have differing tolerances for risk. Stakeholders' risk tolerance may be known at the launch of the project, through written policy statements, or by their actions during the project.

Consider a project to install new medical equipment in a hospital: There's little room for acceptance of errors because life and death are on the line. No shortcuts or quick fixes are allowed. Now, consider a project to create a community garden. Not only are life and death not on the line in the garden project, but the acceptance of risk is different as well.

A person's willingness to accept risk is known as the utility function. The time and money costs required to eliminate the chance of failure is in proportion to the stakeholders' tolerance of risk on the project. The cost of assuring there are no threats must be balanced with the confidence that the project can be completed without extraordinary costs. Figure 11-1 demonstrates the utility function.

The priority of
the project is
relevant to the
risk tolerance.

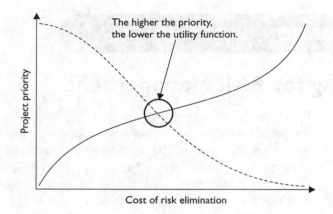

Relying on Risk Management Policies

Organizations often have a predefined approach to risk management. The policies can
define the activities to initiate, plan, and respond to risk. The project manager must
map the project risk management to these policies to conform to the organization's
requirements. Within the confines of the risk management policy, the project
manager must identify any component that can hinder the success of the project. Risk
management policies are considered part of the organizational process assets.

CERTIFICATION OBJECTIVE 11.02

Creating the Risk Management Plan

Through planning meetings, the risk management plan is created. Risk management
plan templates, performing organization policies, and the risk tolerance level of the
stakeholders aid the creation of the risk management plan. Attendees should include:

- The project manager
- Project team leaders
- Key stakeholders
- Personnel specific to risk management
- Any other persons of authority involved or who have input required for the
  risk management processes

The goals of the meeting include defining:

- The project's risk management activities
- The costs of risk elements
- Risk schedule activities
- The assignment of risk responsibilities
- The reliance on templates for risk categories
- Definitions for the level of risk
- The relevant risk probability and impact matrix definitions for the project type

The risk management meetings are iterative processes that guide the identification, ranking, and responses to the identified risks. Risk management meetings will be held throughout the project duration to assess risk, risk responses, and the overall status of risks within the project.

Examining the Risk Management Plan

The risk management plan does not detail the planned responses to individual risks within the project—this is the purpose of the risk response plan. The risk management plan is responsible for determining:

- How risks will be identified
- How quantitative analysis will be completed
- How qualitative analysis will be completed
- How risk response planning will happen
- How risks will be monitored
- How ongoing risk management activities will happen throughout the project life cycle

Methodology

The methodology is concerned with how the risk management processes will take place. The methodology asks the following:

- What tools are available to use for risk management?
- What approaches are acceptable within the performing organization?

■ What data sources can be accessed and used for risk management?

■ Which approach is best for the project type and the phase of the project, and which is most appropriate given the conditions of the project?

■ How much flexibility is available for the project given the conditions, the time frame, and the project budget?

Roles and Responsibilities

The roles and responsibilities identify the groups and individuals who will participate in the leadership and support of each of the risk management activities within the project plan. In some instances, risk management teams outside of the project team may have a more realistic, unbiased approach to the risk identification, impact, and overall risk management needs than the actual project team.

Budgeting

Based on the size, impact, and priority of the project, a budget may need to be established for the project's risk management activities. A project with high priority and no budget allotment for risk management activities may face uncertain times ahead. A realistic dollar amount is needed for risk management activities if the project is to be successful.

Scheduling

The risk management process needs a schedule to determine how often and when risk management activities should happen throughout the project. If risk management happens too late in the project, the project could be delayed because of the time needed to identify, assess, and respond to the risks. A realistic schedule should be developed early in the project to accommodate risks, risk analysis, and risk reaction.

Risk Analysis Scoring

Prior to beginning quantitative and qualitative analysis, a clearly defined scoring system and interpretation of it must be in place. Altering the scoring process during risk analysis—or from analysis to analysis—can skew the seriousness of a risk, its impact, and the effect of the risk on the project. The project manager and the project team must have clearly defined scores that will be applied to the analysis to ensure consistency throughout the project.

Risk Categories

Based on the nature of the work, there should be identified categories of risks within the project. Figure 11-2 is one approach to identifying risk categories by using a risk breakdown structure (RBS). Throughout the project, the risk categories should be revisited to update and reflect the current status of the project. If a previous, similar project's risk management plan is available, the project team may elect to use this plan as a template and tailor the risk categories to the specific project.

Creating Risk Categories

As risks are identified within the project, they should be categorized. Risk categories should be identified before risk identification begins—and should include common risks that are typical in the industry where the project is occurring. Risk categories help organize, rank, and isolate risks within the project. There are four major categories of risks.

- **Technical, quality, or performance risks** Technical risks are associated with new, unproven, or complex technologies being used on the project. Changes to the technology during the project implementation can also be a risk. Quality risks are the levels set for expectations of impractical quality and performance. Changes to industry standards during the project can also be lumped into this category of risks.

- **Project management risks** These risks deal with faults in the management of the project: the unsuccessful allocation of time, resources, and scheduling; unacceptable work results (low-quality work); and lousy project management as a whole.

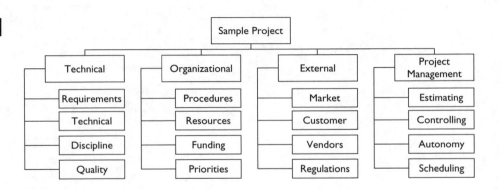

FIGURE 11-2

A risk breakdown structure categorizes project risks.

- **Organizational risks**   The performing organization can contribute to the project's risks through unreasonable cost, time, and scope expectations; poor project prioritization; inadequate funding or the disruption of funding; and competition with other projects for internal resources.
- **External risks**   These risks are outside of the project but directly affect it: legal issues, labor issues, a shift in project priorities, and weather. "Force majeure" risks can be scary and usually call for disaster recovery rather than project management. These are risks caused by earthquakes, tornados, floods, civil unrest, and other disasters.

Using a Risk Management Plan Template

The performing organization may rely on templates for the risk management plan. The template can guide the project manager and the project team through the planning processes, the risk identification, and the values that may trigger additional planning. Hopefully, the organization allows the template to be modified or appended based on the nature of the project. Since most projects resemble other historical projects, the template may need only minor changes to be adapted to the current project.

A risk management plan may grant the project manager decision-making abilities on risks below a certain threshold. Risks above a preset threshold will have to be escalated to a change control board for a determination of their cost and impact on the project's success.

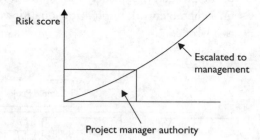

CERTIFICATION OBJECTIVE 11.03

Identifying Risks

After completing the risk management plan, it's time to get to work identifying risks that can hinder the project's success. Risk identification is the process of identifying the risks and then documenting how their presence can affect the project. Risk identification is an iterative process and can be completed by the project manager, the project team, a risk management team, and even SMEs. In some instances, stakeholders and even people outside of the project can complete additional waves of risk identification.

Preparing for Risk Identification

The risk management plan is one of the key inputs to the risk identification process. It describes how the risks will be identified, the requirements for risk analysis, and the overall management of the risk response process. The risk management plan does not include the actual responses to the risks, but rather the approach to the management of the process. In addition to the risk management plan, there are several other inputs to the risk identification process. The risk management plan components that are referenced here specifically include:

- The roles and responsibilities for risk management activities
- The budget for risk management activities
- The schedule for risk management activities
- Categories of risk

Relying on Project Planning

Effective risk identification requires an understanding of why the project exists. The people doing the risk identification have to understand the project's purpose in order to recognize risks that could affect the project. These risk identifiers should understand the customer's objectives, expectations, and intent.

While all areas of project documentation should be referenced for consistency, the specific project plan components referenced here include:

- Risk management plan
- Project documents, including the assumptions log, performance reports, EVM information, and baselines
- Scope baseline
- Duration estimates
- Cost estimates
- Schedule management plan
- Cost management plan
- Stakeholder register
- Quality management plan
- Resource requirements
- Enterprise environmental factors
- Organizational process assets

Identifying the Project Risks

Armed with the inputs to risk identification, the project manager and the project team are prepared to begin identifying risks. Risk identification should be a methodical, planned approach. Should risk identification move in several different directions at once, some risks may be overlooked. A systematic, scientific approach is best.

Reviewing Project Documents

One of the first steps the project team can take is to review the project documentation. The project plan, scope, and other project files should be reviewed. Constraints and assumptions should be reviewed, considered, and analyzed for risks. This structured review takes a broad look at the project plan, the scope, and the activities defined within the project.

Testing the Assumptions

All projects have assumptions. Assumption analysis is the process of examining assumptions to see what risks may stem from false assumptions. Examining assumptions is about finding their validity. For example, consider a project to install a new piece of software on every computer within an organization. The project team has made the assumption that all of the computers within the organization meet the minimum requirements to install the software. If this assumption were wrong, cost increases and schedule delays would occur.

This examination also requires a review of assumptions across the whole project for consistency. For example, consider a project with an assumption that a senior employee will be needed throughout the entire project; the cost estimate, however, has been billed at the rate of a junior employee. All assumptions and their conditions should be recorded in the assumptions log. You'll update this log based on the accuracy of the assumptions and the outcome of assumptions testing.

False assumptions can ruin a project. They can wreck time, cost, and even the quality of a project deliverable. For this reason, assumptions are treated as risks and must be tested and weighed to truncate the possibility of an assumption turning against the project. Assumptions are weighed using two factors.

- **Assumption stability**   How reliable is the information that led to this assumption?
- **Assumption consequence**   What is the effect on the project if this assumption is false?

The answers to these two questions will help the project team deliver the project with more confidence. Should an assumption prove to be false, the weight of the assumption consequence may be low to high—depending on the nature of the assumption.

Brainstorming the Project

Brainstorming is likely the most common approach to risk identification. It's usually completed together as a project team to identify the risks within the project. The risks are identified in broad terms and posted, and then the risks' characteristics are detailed. The identified risks are categorized and will pass through qualitative and quantitative risk analyses later.

A multidisciplinary team, hosted by a project facilitator, can also complete brainstorming. This approach can include subject matter experts, project team members, customers, and other stakeholders who contribute to the risk identification process.

Using the Delphi Technique

The Delphi Technique is an anonymous method to query experts about foreseeable risks within a project, phase, or component of a project. The results of the survey are analyzed by a third party, organized, and then circulated to the experts. There can be several rounds of anonymous discussion with the Delphi Technique—without fear of backlash or offending other participants in the process.

The Delphi Technique is completely anonymous, and the goal is to gain consensus on risks within the project. The anonymous nature of the process ensures that no one expert's advice overtly influences the opinion of another participant.

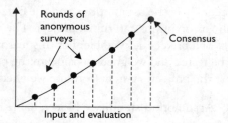

Identifying Risks Through Interviews

Interviewing subject matter experts and project stakeholders is an excellent approach to identifying risks on the current project based on the interviewees' experience. The people responsible for risk identifications share the overall purpose of the project, the project's WBS, and likely the same assumptions as the interviewee.

The interviewee, through questions and discussion, shares his insight on what risks he perceives within the project. The goal of the process is to learn from the expert what risks may be hidden within the project, what risks this person has encountered on similar work, and what insight the person has into the project work.

Analyzing SWOT

SWOT means strengths, weaknesses, opportunities, and threats. SWOT analysis is the process of examining the project from the perspective of each characteristic. For example, a technology project may identify SWOT as:

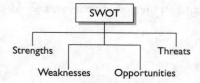

- **Strengths**   The technology to be installed in the project has been installed by other large companies in our industry.
- **Weaknesses**   We have never installed this technology before.
- **Opportunities**   The new technology will allow us to reduce our cycle time for time-to-market on new products. Opportunities are things, conditions, or events that allow an organization to differentiate itself from competitors and improve its standing in the marketplace.
- **Threats**   The time to complete the training and simulation may overlap with product updates, new versions, and external changes to our technology portfolio.

PMP Coach   *You can use SWOT analysis as you prepare to pass your PMP exam. Review your end-of-chapter exam scores to see which chapters you're strong or weak in and which chapters represent your opportunities and threats.*

Utilizing Diagramming Techniques

The project team can utilize several diagramming techniques to identify risks.

- **Ishikawa**   These cause-and-effect diagrams are also called fishbone diagrams. They are great for the root-cause analysis of what factors are causing risks within the project. The goal is to identify and treat the root of the problem, not the symptom.

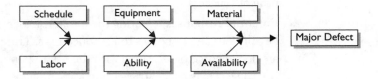

- **Flow charts**   System or process flow charts show the relationship between components and how the overall process works. These are useful for identifying risks between system components.

■ **Influence diagrams** An influence diagram charts out a decision problem. It identifies all of the elements, variables, decisions, and objectives—and how each factor may influence another.

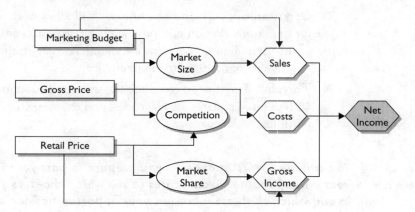

Creating a Risk Register

The risk register is a project plan component that contains all of the information related to the risk management activities. It's updated as risk management activities are conducted to reflect the status, progress, and nature of the project risks. The risk register includes the following:

■ **Risks** Of course, the most obvious output of risk identification is the risk that has been successfully identified. Recall that a risk is an uncertain event or condition that could potentially have a positive or negative effect on the project's success.

■ **Potential responses** During the initial risk identification process, there may be solutions and responses to identified risks. This is fine as long as the responses are documented here. Along with the risk responses, the identification of risk triggers may occur. Triggers are warning signs or symptoms that a risk has occurred or is about to occur. For example, should a vendor fail to complete her portion of the project as scheduled, the project completion may be delayed.

■ **The root causes of risk** Risk identification can identify why risk conditions exist.

■ **Updated risk categories** Risk identification may prompt the project team to identify new categories of risks. These new categories should be documented in the risk register, and if a risk breakdown structure is utilized, it will need to be updated as well.

CERTIFICATION OBJECTIVE 11.04

Using Qualitative Risk Analysis

Qualitative risk "qualifies" the risks that have been identified in the project. Specifically, qualitative risk analysis examines and prioritizes the risks based on their probability of occurring and the impact on the project if they did occur. Qualitative risk analysis is a broad approach to ranking risks by priority, which then guides the risk reaction process.

The end result of qualitative risk analysis (once risks have been identified and prioritized) can lead to more in-depth quantitative risk analysis or move directly into risk response planning. Qualitative is subjective, as it's really a fast human judgment based on experience, a gut feeling, or a best guess about the risk's impact and probability.

See the video Using Quantitative Risk Analysis.

Preparing for Qualitative Risk Analysis

The risk management plan is the key input to qualitative risk analysis. The plan will dictate the process, the methodologies to be used, and the scoring model for identified risks. In addition to the risk management plan, the identified risks from the risk register, obviously, will be needed to perform an analysis. These are the risks that will be scored and ranked based on their probability and impact.

The status of the project will also affect the process of qualitative risk analysis. Early in the project, there may be several risks that have not yet surfaced. Later in the project, new risks may become evident and need to pass through qualitative analysis. The status of the project is linked to the available time needed to analyze and study the risks. There may be more time early in the project, while a looming deadline near the project's end may create a sense of urgency to find a solution for the newly identified risks.

The project type also has some bearing on the process. A project that has never been done before, such as the installation of a new technology, has more uncertainty than a project that has been done repeatedly within an organization. Recurring projects have historical information to rely on, while first-time projects have limited resources to build a risk hypothesis upon.

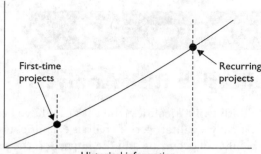

All risks are based upon some belief, proof, and data. The accuracy and source of the data must be evaluated to determine the level of confidence in the identified risks. A hunch that an element is a risk is not as reliable as measured statistics, historical information, or expert knowledge that an element is a risk. The data precision needed is in proportion to the reality of the risk.

Prior to the risk analysis, a predetermined scale of probability and impact must be in place. There are multiple scales a project manager can elect to use, but generally these should be in alignment with the risk management plan. If the performing organization has a risk management model, the scale identified by the performing organization should be used. (We'll discuss the scale values in the next section.)

Finally, the assumptions used in the project must be revisited. During the risk identification process, the project team identified and documented the assumptions used within the project. These assumptions will be evaluated as risks to the project's success.

Completing Qualitative Analysis

Not all risks are worth responding to, while others demand attention. Qualitative analysis is a subjective approach to organizing and prioritizing risks. Through a methodical and logical approach, the identified risks are rated according to probability and potential impact.

The outcome of the ranking determines four things.

- It identifies the risks that require additional analysis through quantitative risk analysis.
- It identifies the risks that may proceed directly to risk response planning.
- It identifies risks that are not critical, project-stopping risks, but that still must be documented.
- It prioritizes risks.

Applying Probability and Impact

The project risks are rated according to their probability and impact. Risk probability is the likelihood that a risk event may happen, while risk impact is the consequence that the result of the event will have on the project objectives. Each risk is measured based on its likelihood and its impact. Two approaches exist to ranking risks.

- Cardinal scales identify the probability and impact on a numerical value from .01 (very low) to 1.0 (certain).
- Ordinal scales identify and rank the risks with common terms, such as very high to very unlikely, or using a RAG Rating (red, amber, green) to signify the risk score.

Creating a Probability-Impact Matrix

Each identified risk is fed into a probability-impact matrix, as seen in Figure 11-3. The matrix maps out the risk, its probability, and its possible impact. The risks with higher probability and impact are a more serious threat to the project objectives than the risks with lower impact and consequences. The risks that are threats to the project require quantitative analysis to determine the root of the risks, the methods to control the risks, and effective risk management. We'll discuss quantitative risk management later in this chapter.

The project is best served when the probability scale and the impact scale are predefined prior to qualitative analysis. For example, the probability scale rates the likelihood of an individual risk happening and can be on a linear scale (.1, .3, .5, .7, .9) or on an ordinal scale. The scale, however, should be defined and agreed upon in the risk management plan. The impact scale, which measures the severity of the risk on the project's objectives, can also be ordinal or cardinal.

FIGURE 11-3

A probability-impact matrix measures the identified risks within the project.

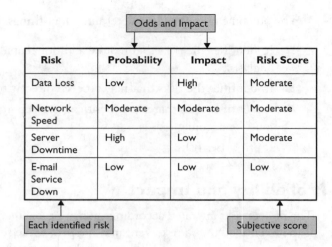

Risk	Probability	Impact	Risk Score
Data Loss	Low	High	Moderate
Network Speed	Moderate	Moderate	Moderate
Server Downtime	High	Low	Moderate
E-mail Service Down	Low	Low	Low

The value of identifying and assigning the scales to use prior to the process of qualitative analysis allows all risks to be ranked by the system and allows for future identified risks to be measured and ranked by the same system. A shift in risk rating methodologies mid-project can cause disagreements in the method of handling the project risks.

A probability-impact matrix multiplies the value for the risk probability by the risk impact for a total risk score. The risk's scores can be cardinal, as seen in Figure 11-4, and then preset values can qualify the risk for a risk response. For example, an identified risk

FIGURE 11-4

The results of a probability-impact matrix create a risk score.

Risk Scores					
Probability					
0.9	0.05	0.09	0.18	0.36	0.72
0.7	0.04	0.07	0.14	0.28	0.56
0.5	0.03	0.05	0.10	0.20	0.40
0.3	0.02	0.03	0.06	0.12	0.24
0.1	0.01	0.01	0.02	0.04	0.08
	0.05	0.10	0.20	0.40	0.80
	Impact				

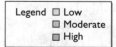

Legend ☐ Low
☐ Moderate
☐ High

in a project is the possibility that the vendor may be late in delivering the hardware. The probability is rated at .9, but the impact of the risk on the project is rated at .10. The risk score is calculated by multiplying the probability times the impact—in this case, resulting in a score of .09.

The scores within the probability-impact matrix can be referenced against the performing organization's policies for risk reaction. Based on the risk score, the performing organization can place the risk in differing categories to guide risk reaction. There are three common categories based on risk score.

- **Red condition**   High risk; these risk scores are high in impact and probability.
- **Amber condition (also called yellow condition)**   These risks are somewhat high in impact and probability.
- **Green condition**   Risks with a green label are generally fairly low in impact, probability, or both.

on the **job**   *Your organization may not have a classification of risks of red, amber, and green—called RAG Rating. Your project risks should map to the methodology your organization uses to identify and classify project risks. If there is no classification of risks, take the initiative and create one for your project. Be certain to document your classification for historical information and include this information in your lessons-learned documentation.*

Relying on Data Precision

One of the toughest parts of qualitative risk analysis is the biased, subjective nature of the process. A project manager and the project team must question the reliability and reality of the data that lead to the ranking of the risks. For example, Susan may have great confidence in herself when it comes to working with new, unproven technologies. Based on this opinion, she petitions for the risk probability of the work to be a very low score.

However, because she has no experience with the technology due to its newness, the probability of the risk of failure is actually very high. The biased opinion that Susan can complete the work with zero defects and problems is slightly skewed because she has never worked with the technology before. Obviously, a low-ranked score on a risk that should be ranked high can have detrimental effects on the project's success.

Data precision ranking takes into consideration the biased nature of the ranking, the accuracy of the data submitted, and the reliability of the biased ranking submitted to examine the risk scores. Data precision ranking is concerned with the following:

- The level of understanding of the project risk
- The available data and information about the identified risk
- The quality of the data and information of the identified risk
- The reliability of the data about the identified risk

Imminent risks are usually considered of higher urgency than distant risks. Consider the risk ranking, the time needed for the risk response, and the conditions that indicate the risk is coming to fruition.

Examining the Results of Qualitative Risk Analysis

Qualitative risk analysis happens throughout the project. As new risks become evident and identified, the project manager should route the risks through the qualitative risk analysis process. The end results of qualitative risk analysis, as shown in the following, are all updated in the risk register:

- **Overall risk ranking of the project**   The overall risk ranking of the project allows the project manager, management, customers, and other interested stakeholders to comprehend the risk, the nature of the risks, and the condition between the risk score and the likelihood of success for a project. The risk score can be compared to other projects to determine project selection, the placement of talent in a project, prioritization, the creation of a benefit/cost ratio, or even the cancellation of a project because it is deemed too risky.
- **Risk categories**   Within the risk register, categories of risks should be created. The idea is that not only will related risks be lumped together, but there may also be some trend identification and root-cause analysis of identified risks. As risks are categorized, it should make it easier to create risk responses as well.

- **Near-term risks** Qualitative analysis should also help the project team identify which risks require immediate or near-term risk responses. Risks that are likely to happen later in the project can be acknowledged, allowing imminent risks to be managed first. Urgent risks can go right to quantitative analysis and risk response planning.

- **The identification of risks requiring additional analysis** The risks categorized as high will likely need additional analysis, such as quantitative analysis. Some risks may demand immediate risk management based on the nature of the risks and the status of the project.

- **Low-priority risk watchlist** Let's face it: Not all risks need additional analysis. However, these low-priority risks should be identified and assigned to a watchlist for periodic monitoring.

- **Trends in qualitative analysis** As the project progresses and risk analysis is repeated, trends in the ranking and analysis of the risk may become apparent. These trends can allow the project manager and other risk experts to respond to the root cause, predict trends to eliminate, or respond to the risks within the project.

CERTIFICATION OBJECTIVE 11.05

Preparing for Quantitative Risk Analysis

Quantitative risk analysis attempts to numerically assess the probability and impact of the identified risks. It also creates an overall risk score for the project. This method is more in-depth than qualitative risk analysis and relies on several different tools to accomplish its goal.

Qualitative risk analysis typically precedes quantitative analysis. All or a portion of the identified risks in qualitative risk analysis can be examined in the quantitative analysis. The performing organization may have policies on the risk scores in qualitative analysis that require the risks to advance to the quantitative analysis. Time and budget constraints may also be factors in the determination of which risks should pass through quantitative analysis. Quantitative analysis is a more time-consuming process and is, therefore, also more expensive. There are several goals of quantitative risk analysis.

- To ascertain the likelihood of reaching project success
- To ascertain the likelihood of reaching a particular project objective
- To determine the risk exposure for the project
- To determine the likely amount of the contingency reserve needed for the project
- To determine the risks with the largest impact on the project
- To determine realistic time, cost, and scope targets

Considering the Inputs for Quantitative Analysis

Based on the time and budget allotments for quantitative analysis, as defined in the risk management plan, the project manager can move into quantitative analysis. There are, however, five inputs to quantitative risk analysis that the project manager should rely on.

- **Risk register**   The risks that have been identified and promoted to quantitative analysis are needed. The project team will also need their ranking and risk categories—all of which are documented in the risk register.
- **Risk management plan**   The risk management plan identifies the risk management methodology, the allotted budget for risk analysis, the schedule, and the risk scoring mechanics—among other attributes.
- **Cost management plan**   The cost management plan is needed for the budgeting of the risk management activities. Risk impacts and the predicted risk reserve can affect the cost estimates and budget for the entire project.
- **Schedule management plan**   The schedule management plan is needed to evaluate the timing of risk events, risk planning, and risk distributions. Network analysis, schedule delays, and project interruptions should be evaluated for risk.
- **Organizational process assets**   Historical information is one of the best inputs for risk analysis, as it is proven information for the project. An examination of the project risks from past experiences can help the project team complete quantitative risk analysis activities.

Interviewing Stakeholders and Experts

Interviews with stakeholders and subject-matter experts can be one of the first tools to quantify the identified risks. These interviews can focus on worst-case, best-case, and most-likely scenarios if the goal of the quantitative analysis is to create a triangular distribution; most quantitative analysis, however, uses continuous probability distributions. Figure 11-5 shows five sample distributions: normal, triangular, uniform, beta, and lognormal.

Continuous probability distribution is an examination of the probability of all possibilities within a given range. For each variable, the probability of a risk event and the corresponding consequence for the event, may vary. In other words, dependent on whether the risk event occurs and how it happens, a reaction to the event may also occur. The distribution of the probabilities and impact include:

- ■ Uniform
- ■ Normal
- ■ Triangular
- ■ Beta
- ■ Lognormal

Applying Sensitivity Analysis

Sensitivity analysis examines each project risk on its own merit. It is an analysis process to determine which risks could affect the project the most. All other risks in the project are set at a baseline value. The individual risk then is examined to see how it may affect the success of the project. The goal of sensitivity analysis is to determine which individual risks have the greatest impact on the project's success and then escalate the risk management processes on these risk events.

FIGURE 11-5

Risk distributions illustrate the likelihood and impact of an event within a project.

Normal

Lognormal

Beta

Triangular

Uniform

Finding the Expected Monetary Value

The expected monetary value of a project or event is based on the probability of outcomes that are uncertain. For example, one risk may cost the project an additional $10,000 if it occurs, but there's only a 20 percent chance of the event occurring. In the simplest form, the expected monetary value of this individual risk is thus $2,000. Project managers can also find the expected monetary value of a decision by creating a decision tree.

Using a Decision Tree

A decision tree is a method to determine which of two or more decisions is the best to make. For example, it can be used to determine buy-versus-build scenarios, lease-or-purchase equations, or whether to use in-house resources rather than outsourcing project work. The decision tree model examines the cost and benefits of each decision's outcomes and weighs the probability of success for each of the decisions.

The purpose of the decision tree is to make a decision, calculate the value of that decision, or determine which decision costs the least. Follow Figure 11-6 through the various steps of the decision tree process.

Completing a Decision Tree

As the project manager of the new GFB Project, you have to decide whether to create a new web application in-house or send the project out to a developer. The developer you would use (if you were to outsource the work) quotes the project cost at $175,000. Based on previous work with this company, you are 85 percent certain they will finish the work on time.

FIGURE 11-6

Decision trees analyze the probability of events and calculate decision values.

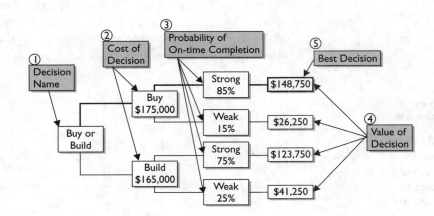

Your in-house development team quotes the cost of the work as $165,000. Again, based on previous experience with your in-house developers, you feel 75 percent certain they can complete the work on time. Now let's apply what we know to a decision tree.

- Buy or build is simply the decision name.
- The cost of the decision if you "buy" the work outside of your company is $175,000. If you build the software in-house, the cost of the decision is $165,000.
- Based on your probability of completion by a given date, you apply the 85 percent certainty to the "strong" finish for the buy branch of the tree. Because you're 85 percent certain, you're also 15 percent uncertain; this value is assigned to the "weak" value on the buy branch. You complete the same process for the build branch of the tree.
- The value of the decision is the percentage of strong and weak applied to each branch of the tree.
- The best decision is based solely on the largest value of all possible decisions identified in the decision tree.

Using a Project Simulation

Project simulations allow the project team to play "what-if" games without affecting any areas of production. The Monte Carlo technique is the most common simulation. This technique got its name from Monte Carlo, Monaco (world-renowned for its slot machines, roulette wheels, and other games of pure chance). Monte Carlo, typically completed through a computer software program, completely simulates a project with values for all possible variables to predict the most likely model.

Examining the Results of Quantitative Risk Analysis

Quantitative risk analysis is completed throughout the project as risks are identified and passed through qualitative analysis, as project conditions change, or on a preset schedule. The end result of quantitative risk analysis should be reflected in the risk register and should include the following:

- **Probabilistic analysis** The risks within the project allow the project manager or other experts to predict the likelihood of the project's success. The project may be altered by the response to certain risks; this response can increase cost and push back the project's completion date.

■ **Probability of costs and schedule objectives**   Based on the identified risks, their impact, and the probability of occurrence, forecasts for the project schedule and the project costs are created. The more negative the risks that occur within a project, the greater the chance of delays and increased costs.

■ **A prioritized list of risks**   This list of quantified risks demonstrates those risks with the highest potential for endangering the project's success. This list includes the risks that have the greatest opportunity for the project. Each risk is identified with its probability and impact.

■ **Trends**   As the project moves towards completion, quantitative risk analysis may be repeated. In each round of analysis, trends in the identified risks may become visible. The trends in the risk can help the project team eliminate the root cause of the risk, reduce their probability, or control their impact.

CERTIFICATION OBJECTIVE 11.06

Planning for Risk Responses

Risk response planning is all about options and actions. It focuses on how to decrease the possibility of risks adversely affecting the project's objectives and on how to increase the likelihood of positive risks that can aid the project. Risk response planning assigns responsibilities to people and groups close to the risk event. Risks will increase or decrease based on the effectiveness of risk response planning.

The responses to identified risks must be in balance with the risk itself. The cost and time invested in a risk must be met with the gains from reducing the risk's impact and probability. In other words, a million-dollar solution for a hundred-dollar problem is unacceptable. The people or individuals who are assigned to the risk must have the authority to react to the project risk as planned. In most cases, several risk responses may be viable for the risk—the best choice for the identified risk must be documented, agreed upon, and then followed through should the risk come to fruition.

Preparing for Risk Response

To successfully prepare for risk response, the project manager, project team, and appropriate stakeholders rely on several inputs—many of which stem from qualitative and quantitative risk analyses. The risk management plan is needed during the risk response planning, but the risk register is also needed to provide the following:

- A list of prioritized risks
- A risk ranking
- A prioritized list of quantified risks
- A probabilistic analysis of the project
- The probability of the project meeting the cost and schedule goals
- The list of potential responses decided upon when risks were first identified
- Any risk owners that have been identified
- A list of risks with common causal factors
- Trends from qualitative and quantitative analyses

Creating Risk Responses

The project team can employ several tools and techniques to respond to risks. Each risk should be evaluated to determine which category of risk response is most appropriate. When a category of risk response has been selected, the response must then be developed, refined, documented, and readied for use, if needed. In addition, secondary responses may be selected for each risk. The purpose of risk response planning is to bring the overall risk of the project down to an acceptable level. In addition, risk response planning must address any risks that have unacceptably high scores.

Avoiding the Negative Risk and Threats

Avoidance is simply avoiding the risk. This can be accomplished in many different ways and generally happens early in the project, when any change will result in fewer consequences than it would later in the project plan. Examples of avoidance include the following:

- Changing the project plan to eliminate the risk
- Clarifying project requirements to avoid discrepancies
- Hiring additional project team members who have experience with the technology that the project deals with
- Using a proven methodology rather than a new approach

Transferring the Negative Risk

Transference is the process of transferring the risk (and the ownership of the risk) to a third party. The risk doesn't disappear; it's just someone else's problem. Transference of a risk usually costs a premium for the third party to own and manage that risk. Common examples of risk transference include:

- Insurance
- Performance bonds
- Warrantees
- Guarantees
- Fixed-price contracts

INSIDE THE EXAM

Risk management planning is the process of determining how risk management should be handled. The stakeholder analysis will reveal their willingness to accept risk—which is also known as their utility function. The performing organization may have standard practices for risk management, risk management templates, or guidance from historical information.

There are two types of risk: business risk, which is a gain or loss from a financial point of view, and pure risks, which only has a downside. Both types of risk must be assessed and managed. Remember, not all risks are bad. The risk impact may have a negative effect on the project, but often a risk may have a positive impact.

Risk identification happens early on in the project to allow time for risk response planning. It also happens throughout the project. The project manager, the project team, customers, and other stakeholders should be involved in the process. There are several methods to risk identification—interviews and the Delphi Technique are two of the most common approaches.

Qualitative analysis qualifies the list of risks in a matrix based on impact and probability. This subjective approach uses common *very low, low, moderate, high,* and *very high* rankings. The risks can be prioritized based on their score.

After qualitative analysis, some risks may be sent through quantitative analysis.

INSIDE THE EXAM

This approach attempts to quantify the risks with hard numbers, values, and data. Quantification of the risk can lead to time and cost contingencies for the project, a prioritization of the risks, and an overall risk score. Monte Carlo simulations are typically associated with quantitative risk analysis.

The three risk responses for negative risks are:

Avoidance   The project plan is altered to avoid the identified risk.

Mitigation   An effort is made to reduce the probability, impact, or both of an identified risk in the project before the risk event occurs.

Transference   The risk is assigned to a third party, usually for a fee. The risk still exists, but the responsibility is deflected to the third party.

The three risk responses for positive risks include:

Exploit   The organization wants to ensure that the identified risk does happen in order to realize the positive impact associated with the risk event.

Share   Sharing is nice. When sharing, the risk ownership is transferred to the organization that can capitalize most on the risk opportunity.

Enhance   To enhance a risk is to attempt to modify its probability of occurrence and/or its impacts on the project in order to realize the most gains from the identified risk.

The two responses for both positive and negative risks are:

Acceptance   The risks are seen as nominal, so they are accepted. Risks, regardless of size, that have no other recourse may also be accepted.

Contingency response   When it's evident that some risks are occurring, or about to occur, a preplanned risk response can be put into play. This is part of the contingency response strategy.

As the project progresses, risk monitoring and control are implemented. Risks are monitored for signs that they may be coming to fruition. The project team and the project manager execute the risk response plan and document the results. Earned value analysis, which is typically used to measure project performance, can also be used to signal impending project risks.

Mitigating the Negative Risk

Mitigating risks is an effort to reduce the probability and/or impact of an identified risk in the project. Mitigation is done—based on the logic—before the risk happens. The cost and time to reduce or eliminate the risk is more cost effective than repairing the damage caused by the risk. The risk event may still happen, but hopefully the cost and impact will be low.

Mitigation plans can be created so that they are implemented should an identified risk cross a given threshold. For example, a manufacturing project may have a mitigation plan to reduce the number of units created per hour should the equipment's temperature cross a given threshold. The reduction is the number of units per hour that it may cost the project in time. In addition, the cost of extra labor to run the equipment longer because the machine is now operating at a slower pace may be attributed to the project. However, should the equipment fail, the project would have to replace the equipment and be delayed for weeks while awaiting repairs.

Examples of mitigation include:

- Adding activities to the project to reduce the risk probability or impact
- Simplifying the processes within the project
- Completing more tests on the project work before implementation
- Developing prototypes, simulations, and limited releases

Managing the Positive Risk and Opportunities

While most risks have a negative connotation, not all risks are bad. There are instances when a risk may create an opportunity that can help the project, other projects, or the organization as a whole. The type of risk and the organization's willingness to accept the risks will dictate the appropriate response.

Exploiting the Positive Risk or Opportunities

When an organization would like to ensure that a positive risk definitely happens, it can exploit the risk. Positive risk exploitation can be realized by adding resources to finish faster than what was originally planned, increasing quality to recognize sales and customer satisfaction, utilizing a better way of completing the project work, or any other method that creates the positive outcomes of the identified risk.

Sharing the Positive Risk

The idea of sharing a positive risk really means sharing a mutually beneficial opportunity between two organizations or projects, or creating a risk-sharing partnership. When a project team can share the positive risk, ownership of the risk is given to the organization that can best capture the benefits from the identified risk.

Enhancing the Positive Risks

This risk response seeks to modify the size of the identified opportunity. The goal is to strengthen the cause of the opportunity to ensure that the risk event does happen. Enhancing a project risk looks for solutions, triggers, or other drives to ensure that the risk does come to fruition so that the rewards of the risk can be realized by the performing organization.

Accepting the Risks

Risk acceptance is the process of simply accepting the risks because no other action is feasible, or the risks are deemed to be of small probability, impact, or both and that a formal response is not warranted. Passive acceptance requires no action; the project team deals with the risks as they happen. Active acceptance entails developing a contingency plan should the risk occur. Acceptance may be used for both positive and negative risks.

A contingency plan is a predefined set of actions the project team will take should certain events occur. Events that trigger the contingency plan should be tracked. A fallback plan is a reaction to a risk that has occurred when the primary response proves to be inadequate.

Most risk acceptance policies rely on a contingency allowance for the project. A contingency allowance is the amount of money the project will likely need in the contingency reserve based on the impact, probability, and expected monetary value of a risk event.

For example, Risk A has a 25 percent chance of happening and has a cost value of –$2,000. The probability times the impact equates to a –$2,000 expected monetary value (Ex$V). Another risk, Risk B, has a 40 percent chance of happening and has a benefit value of $4,000. The Ex$V for Risk B is $1,600. If these were the only risks in the project, an ideal contingency reserve would be $400. This is calculated by adding the positive and negative risk values to predict the amount that the project is likely to be underfunded by if the risks happen. Table 11-1 shows several risks and their Ex$V.

TABLE 11-1	Risk	Probability	Impact: Cost Is Negative; Benefits Are Positive	Ex$V
Contingency Reserve Calculations	A	20%	−$4,000	−$800
	B	45%	$3,000	$1,350
	C	10%	$2,100	$210
	D	65%	−$2,500	−$1,625
			Contingency Reserve Fund	$865

Examining the Results of Risk Response Planning

The major output of risk response planning is the risk register updates. These risk responses are documented in the risk register and guide the reaction to each identified risk. They include the following:

- A description of the risk, what area of the project it may affect, the causes of the risk, and its impact on project objectives
- The identities of the risk owners and their assigned responsibilities
- The outputs of qualitative and quantitative analysis
- Risk strategies and the specific actions necessary to implement those strategies
- Symptoms and warning signs, sometimes called triggers, of each risk event
- A description of the response to each risk, such as avoidance, transference, mitigation, or acceptance
- The actions necessary to implement the responses
- The budget and schedule for risk responses
- The contingency and fallback plans

Working with Residual Risks

The risk response plan also acknowledges any residual risks that may remain after planning, avoidance, transfer, or mitigation. Residual risks are typically minor and have been acknowledged and accepted. Management may elect to add both contingency costs and time to account for the residual risks within the project.

Accounting for Secondary Risks

Secondary risks stem from risk responses. For example, transference may elect to hire a third party to manage an identified risk. A secondary risk caused by the solution is the failure of the third party to complete their assignment as scheduled. Secondary risks must be identified, analyzed, and planned for, just as any another identified risk.

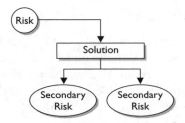

Creating Contracts for Risk Response

When multiple entities are involved in a project, contractual agreements may be necessary to identify the responsible parties for identified risks. The contract may be needed for insurance purposes, customer acceptance, or the acknowledgement of responsibilities between the entities completing the project. Transference is an example of contractual agreements for the responsibility of risks within a project.

on the job

A contingency reserve may also be called a management reserve. Often, a management reserve deals with time, while a contingency reserve deals with dollars. Some organizations lump time and money into the same reserve. You should know what nomenclature your organization uses and what they anticipate the meaning of the reserves to be.

Justifying Risk Reduction

To reduce risk, additional time or monies are typically needed. The process and logic behind the strategies to reduce the risk should be evaluated to determine if the solution is worth the tradeoffs. For example, a risk may be eliminated by adding $7,500 to a project's budget. However, the likelihood of the risk occurring is relatively low. Should the risk happen, it would cost, at a minimum, $8,000 to correct and the project would be delayed by at least two weeks.

The cost of preventing the risk versus the cost of responding to it must be weighed and justified. If the risk is not eliminated with the $7,500 cost and the project moves forward as planned, it has, theoretically, saved $15,500 because the risk did not happen and the response to the risk did not need to happen.

However, if the risk does happen, the project will lose at least $8,000 and be delayed at least two weeks. The cost inherent in the project delay may be more expensive than the solution to the risk. The judgment of solving the risk to reduce the likelihood of delaying the project may be wiser than ignoring the risk and saving the cost by solving the risk problem.

Updating the Project Plan

The risk reactions, contingency plans, and fallback plans should all be documented and incorporated into the project plan—for example, updating the schedule, budget, and WBS to accommodate additional time, money, and activities for risk responses. The responses to the risks may change the original implementation of the project and should be updated to reflect the project plan and intent of the project team, management, and other stakeholders. A failure to update the project plan and the risk register may cause risk reactions to be missed and skew performance measurements.

CERTIFICATION OBJECTIVE 11.07

Implementing Risk Monitoring and Control

Risks must be actively monitored and new risks must be responded to as they are discovered. Risk monitoring and control is the process of monitoring identified risks for signs that they may be occurring, controlling identified risks with the agreed-upon responses, and looking for new risks that may creep into the project. Risk monitoring and control also is concerned with the documentation of the success or failure of risk response plans and keeping records of metrics that signal risks are occurring, fading, or disappearing from the project.

Risk monitoring and control is an active process that requires participation from the project manager, the project team, key stakeholders, and, in particular, risk owners within the project. As the project progresses, risk conditions may change and require new responses, additional planning, or the implementation of a contingency plan.

There are several goals to risk monitoring and control.

- To confirm risk responses are implemented as planned
- To determine if risk responses are effective or if new responses are needed

- To determine the validity of the project assumptions
- To determine if risk exposure has changed, evolved, or declined due to trends in the project progression
- To monitor risk triggers
- To confirm that policies and procedures happen as planned
- To monitor the project for new risks

Preparing for Risk Monitoring and Control

Risk monitoring and control is an active process. The project team and the project manager must rely on several inputs to effectively monitor and control risks, such as:

- **The risk register** The risk register is the central repository for all project risk information. It includes the identified risks, the potential responses, the root causes of risks, and any identified categories of risk.
- **The risk management plan** The risk management plan defines the organization's approach to risk management. It is not the strategy for specific risks within a project, but the overall strategy for risk analysis and planning.
- **Work performance information** The results of project work can inform the project manager and the project team of new and pending risks. In addition, project team members may create reports to monitor or document risks. These reports are known as issue logs, action-items, jeopardy warnings, and escalation notices. Project performance focuses on the balance of the project schedule, costs, and scope. Should the performance of time, cost, or scope suffer, new risks are likely to enter the project.

Completing Risk Monitoring and Control

Risk monitoring and risk control happens throughout the project—it is not a solitary activity that is completed once and never revisited. The project manager and the project team must actively monitor risks, respond with the agreed-upon actions, and scan the horizon for risks that have not been addressed. Risk monitoring and control is a recurring activity that requires input from all project participants. Several tools are available for implementing risk monitoring and control, and they are discussed in the following sections.

Completing Risk Response Audits

A risk response audit examines the planned risk response, how well the planned actions work, and the effectiveness of the risk owner in implementing the risk response. The audits happen throughout the project to measure the effectiveness of mitigating, transferring, and avoiding risks. The risk response audit should measure the effectiveness of the decision and its impact on time and cost.

Completing Periodic Risk Reviews

Project risk should be on the agenda at every project team meeting. The periodic risk review is a regularly scheduled discussion throughout the project to ascertain the level of foreseeable risks, the success of risk responses in the project to date, and a review of pending risks. Based on circumstances within the project, risk rankings and prioritization may fluctuate. Changes to the project scope, team, or conditions may require qualitative and quantitative analyses.

Using Earned Value Analysis

Earned value analysis measures project performance. When project performance is waning, the project is likely missing targeted costs and schedule goals. The results of earned value analysis can signal that risks are happening within the project or that new risks may be developing.

For example, a schedule performance index (SPI) of .93 means the project is off schedule by 7 percent. A risk based on this value could mean that the project team is having difficulty completing the project work as planned. Additional work will continue to be late, the project will finish late, and quality may suffer as the team attempts to rush to complete assigned tasks.

Measuring Technical Performance

Throughout the project, the project team's technical competence with the technology being used in the project should increase. The level of technical achievement should be in proportion to the expected level of technical performance within the project. If the project team is not performing at a level of expected technical expertise, the project may suffer additional risks due to the discrepancy. Technical performance can be measured by the successful completion of activities throughout the project or project phases.

Completing Additional Risk Planning

Most likely, new risks will become evident during the project implementation. The project team, project manager, and key stakeholders who discover the risks should communicate them. The risks must then be acknowledged, documented, analyzed, and planned for. The project team must be encouraged to communicate the discovery of new risks.

on the **Job** *Often, project team members don't want to share discovered risks with the project manager because the presence of a risk can be seen as bad news. The project manager must stress to the project team members that identified risks should be communicated so that the risks can be planned for through avoidance, mitigation, transference, or even acceptance.*

Examining the Results of Risk Monitoring and Control

Risk monitoring and control helps the project become more successful. It measures the planned responses to risks and creates reactions to unplanned risks. The outputs of risk monitoring and control also aim to help the project reach its objectives. There are several outputs of the process.

- **Risk register updates** As the project moves along and the project manager and the project team complete the risk assessments, audits, and risk reviews, they'll need to record their findings in the risk register. This update may include the reevaluation of the risk's impact, probability, and expected monetary value. For those risks that have passed in the project, the risk register should record what actually happened with the risk event and its impact on the project.

- **Organizational process assets updates** The risks from the current project can help other project managers in the future. Therefore, the project manager must work to ensure that the current risks, their anticipated impact, and their actual impact are recorded. The current risk matrix, for example, can become a risk template for other projects in the future. This is true for just about any risk document—from risk responses to the risk breakdown structure, lessons learned, and checklists.

- **Change requests** As workarounds and contingency plans are used, they require changes to the project plan. The changes to the project plan due to the risks are completed through integrated change control. The changes are documented, approved, and incorporated into the project plan. As risks come to fruition, corrective actions are needed to bypass the risk. The two types of corrective actions are workarounds and contingency plans. Corrective actions are actions taken to bring the project back into compliance with the project plan. Preventive actions are steps taken to bring the project back into alignment with the project management plan.

■ **Project management plan updates** Some change requests and risk responses may require updating the project management plan. As risks occur, the responses to those risks should be documented and updated in the risk response plan. Should risk rankings change during the project, the change in ranking, the logic behind the change, and the results of the risk rank change should be documented in the risk response plan. For the risks that do not occur, the risks should be documented and considered closed in the risk response plan.

CERTIFICATION SUMMARY

PMP candidates must have a firm grasp on how to plan for, monitor, and control projects' risks. To effectively handle risks, the project manager needs to begin with risk management planning. A large, complex project will likely have more risks than a smaller project. In any situation, however, risks must be identified and planned for. The performing organization will often have risk management policies that dictate how the risk planning sessions are to be performed and what level of risks call for additional planning.

Some stakeholders—and organizations—will be more tolerant than others of accepting risks.

As risks are identified, the project manager can use the Delphi Technique to build a consensus on which risks have the highest impact on the project. This anonymous approach allows participants to speak freely about the risks, unhindered by the opinions of other stakeholders. The comments on the identified risks are distributed to all of the participants, allowing participants to comment, concur, or dismiss opinions on the identified risks. Through rounds of discussion, a consensus on the risks is reached.

Qualitative risk analysis qualifies identified risks and creates a prioritization of each. Every risk is considered for its impact and likelihood of occurring. Once the risks have passed through qualitative risk analysis, quantitative risk analysis is needed. Quantitative risk analysis assesses the probability and impact of the risks, and it determines a risk score based on further analysis, discussion, expert judgment, simulations, and interviews with stakeholders.

KEY TERMS

If you're serious about passing the PMP exam, memorize the following terms and their definitions. For maximum value, create your own flashcards based on these definitions and review them daily. You can find additional information on these terms in the project glossary.

acceptance   This is a response to a risk event, generally made when the probability of the event and/or its impact is small. It is used when mitigation, transference, and avoidance are not selected.

avoidance   This is one response to a risk event. The risk is avoided by planning a different technique to remove the risk from the project.

brainstorming   The most common approach to risk identification; it is performed by a project team to identify the risks within the project. A multidisciplinary team, hosted by a project facilitator, can also perform brainstorming.

cause-and-effect diagrams   Used for root-cause analysis of what factors are creating the risks within the project. The goal is to identify and treat the root of the problem, not the symptom.

contingency reserve   A time or dollar amount allotted as a response to risk events that may occur within a project.

decision tree analysis   A type of analysis that determines which of two decisions is the best. The decision tree assists in calculating the value of the decision and determining which decision costs the least.

Delphi Technique   A method to query experts anonymously on foreseeable risks within the project, phase, or component of the project. The results of the survey are analyzed and organized, and then circulated to the experts. There can be several rounds of anonymous discussions with the Delphi Technique The goal is to gain consensus on project risks, and the anonymous nature of the process ensures that no one expert's advice overtly influences the opinion of another participant.

enhance   To enhance a risk is to attempt to modify its probability and/or its impacts to realize the most gains from it.

exploit   The organization wants to ensure that the identified risk does happen to realize the positive impact associated with the risk event.

influence diagram   An influence diagram charts out a decision problem. It identifies all of the elements, variables, decisions, and objectives—and how each factor may influence another.

mitigation   Reducing the probability or impact of a risk.

qualitative risk analysis   An examination and prioritization of the risks based on their probability of occurring and the impact on the project if they do occur. Qualitative risk analysis guides the risk reaction process.

quantitative risk analysis   A numerical assessment of the probability and impact of the identified risks. Quantitative risk analysis also creates an overall risk score for the project.

residual risks   Risks that are left over after mitigation, transference, and avoidance. These are generally accepted risks. Management may elect to add contingency costs and time to account for the residual risks within the project.

risk   An unplanned event that can have a positive or negative influence on the project's success.

risk categories   These help organize, rank, and isolate risks within the project.

risk management plan   A subsidiary project plan for determining how risks will be identified, how quantitative and qualitative analyses will be completed, how risk response planning will happen, how risks will be monitored, and how ongoing risk management activities will occur throughout the project life cycle.

risk owners   The individuals or groups responsible for a risk response.

risk register   Documentation of all risk events and their conditions, impact, probability, and overall risk score.

scales of probability and impact   Used in a risk matrix in both qualitative and quantitative risk analyses to score each risk's probability and impact.

secondary risks   Risks that stem from risk responses. For example, the response of transference may call for hiring a third party to manage an identified risk. A secondary risk caused by the solution is the failure of the third party to complete its assignment as scheduled. Secondary risks must be identified, analyzed, and planned for, just like any other identified risk.

sensitivity analysis   This examines each project's risk on its own merit to assess the impact on the project. All other risks in the project are set at a baseline value.

share   Sharing is nice. When sharing, the risk ownership is transferred to the organization that can most capitalize on the risk opportunity.

simulation   This allows the project team to play "what-if" games without affecting any areas of production.

system or process flow charts   These show the relationship between components and how the overall process works. They are useful for identifying risks between system components.

transference   A response to risks in which the responsibility and ownership of the risk are transferred to another party (for example, through insurance).

triggers   Warning signs or symptoms that a risk has occurred or is about to occur (for example, a vendor failing to complete their portion of the project as scheduled).

utility function   A person's willingness to accept risk.

workarounds   Workarounds are unplanned responses to risks that were not identified or expected.

✓ TWO-MINUTE DRILL

Planning for Risk Management

❑ Risk management planning is determining how the risk management activities within the project will take place. It is not the response or identification of risks, but the determination of how to manage project risks.

❑ Risk management planning is accomplished through planning meetings with the project team, management, customers, and other key stakeholders.

❑ A utility function is a person's willingness to accept risks.

❑ The output of risk management planning is the risk management plan.

Creating the Risk Management Plan

❑ Risks are uncertain events that can affect a project's objectives for good or bad.

❑ Risks can be placed into four different categories: technical, quality, or performance risks; project management risks; organizational risks; and external risks.

❑ The risk management plan defines the process to identify, analyze, respond to, and monitor all project risk events.

Identifying Risks

❑ Project records from published information and previous projects can serve as input to risk identification.

❑ The Delphi Technique allows participants to identify risk anonymously without fear of embarrassment. A survey allows results to be shared with all participants for comments on each other's anonymous input. Rounds of surveying and analysis can create consensus on the major project risks.

❑ Triggers are warning signs that a risk is about to happen or has happened.

Using Qualitative Risk Analysis

❑ Qualitative risk analysis is a high-level, fast analysis of the identified project risks.

❑ Risks are evaluated for their impact and likelihood.

❑ Risks can be ranked in an ordinal fashion by using such indicators as very low, low, moderate, high, and very high.

❑ Risks can also be analyzed using a cardinal ranking system of numerical values that are assigned to each risk based on its impact and probability.

❑ An overall project risk ranking can be used to compare the current projects with other projects in the organization.

❑ Risks that have a high score from qualitative analysis can be moved into quantitative analysis for further study.

Preparing for Quantitative Risk Analysis

❑ Risks are assigned an expected monetary value, such as there is a 50 percent likelihood that the risk will occur, causing a $10,000 cost.

❑ Quantitative analysis is an in-depth study of the risk's probability and impact.

❑ Risks and their impact, status, responses, and updates are all recorded in the risk register.

Planning for Risk Responses

❑ Risk response planning focuses on reducing threats and increasing opportunities as a result of risks. Risk thresholds, defined in risk management planning, describe the acceptable level of risk within a company.

❑ Risk owners are the individuals or groups that are responsible for a risk response and that should participate in the risk response planning.

❑ Risk avoidance changes the project plan to avoid the risk (as well as conditions that promote the risk), or it attempts to reduce the risk's impact on the project's success.

❑ Risk transference moves the risk consequence to a third party. The risk doesn't go away, just the responsibility of it. However, ultimately, the performing organization still retains the ultimate accountability and results of the risk event.

❑ Risk mitigation involves actions designed to reduce the likelihood of a risk occurring, the impact of a risk on the project objectives, or both.

❑ Risk acceptance acknowledges that the risk exists but that it isn't worthy of a more in-depth response, or a more in-depth response isn't available for the risk.

❑ Residual risks are risks that remain after avoidance, transference, mitigation, and acceptance. Secondary risks are new risks that arise from a risk response.

❑ To exploit a risk requires that an organization implement measures to ensure that the positive risk definitely happens.

❑ Sharing a risk assigns ownership of the positive risk to an organization that is most likely to utilize the positive risks for the benefit of the project.

❑ To enhance a risk requires that the organization take steps to increase the probability and/or impact of the positive risk.

Implementing Risk Monitoring and Control

❑ Identified risks must be tracked, monitored for warning signs, and documented. The responses to the risks are monitored and documented as successful or less successful than expected.

❑ Issue logs, action-item lists, jeopardy warnings, and escalation notices are all types of communication reports that the project team and risk owners must use to document and track identified risks.

❑ Risk response audits measure the success of the responses and the effectiveness of the cost, scope, and quality values gained or lost by the risk responses.

❑ Earned value analysis can measure project performance, but it can also predict and signal pending risks within the project.

❑ As unexpected risks arise, the project team may elect to use workarounds to diminish the impact and probability of those risks. Workarounds, however, should be documented and incorporated into the project plan and risk response plan as they occur.

SELF TEST

1. When is it appropriate to accept a project risk?

   A. It is never appropriate to accept a project risk.

   B. All risks must be mitigated or transferred.

   C. It is appropriate to accept a risk if the project team has never completed this type of project work before.

   D. If the risk is in balance with the reward.

2. Frances is the project manager of the LKJ Project. Which of the following techniques will she use to create the risk management plan?

   A. Risk tolerance

   B. Status meetings

   C. Planning meetings

   D. Variance meetings

3. Which of the following is not part of a risk management plan?

   A. Roles and responsibilities

   B. Methodology

   C. Technical assessment board compliance

   D. Risk categories

4. You are the project manager of the GHK Project. You and the manufacturer have agreed to substitute the type of plastic used in the product to a slightly thicker grade should there be more than a 7 percent error in production. The thicker plastic will cost more and require the production to slow down, but the errors should diminish. This is an example of which of the following?

   A. Threshold

   B. Tracking

   C. Budgeting

   D. JIT manufacturing

5. An organization's risk tolerance is also known as what?

   A. The utility function

   B. Herzberg's Theory of Motivation

   C. Risk acceptance

   D. The risk-reward ratio

6. A risk trigger is also called which of the following?

    A. A warning sign

    B. A delay

    C. A cost increase

    D. An incremental advancement of risk

7. The customers of the project have requested additions to the project scope. The project manager brings notice that additional risk planning will need to be added to the project schedule. Why?

    A. The risk planning should always be the same amount of time as the activities required by the scope change.

    B. Risk planning should always occur whenever the scope is adjusted.

    C. Risk planning should only occur at the project manager's discretion.

    D. The project manager is incorrect. Risk planning does not need to happen at every change in the project.

8. Which one of the following best describes the risk register?

    A. It documents all of the outcomes of the other risk management processes.

    B. It's a document that contains the initial risk identification entries.

    C. It's a system that tracks all negative risks within a project.

    D. It's part of the project's PMIS for integrated change control

9. _____ include(s) fire, theft, or injury, and offer(s) no chance for gain.

    A. Business risks

    B. Pure risks

    C. Risk acceptance

    D. Life risks

10. Complete this sentence: A project risk is a(n) _____ occurrence that can affect the project for good or bad.

    A. Known

    B. Potential

    C. Uncertain

    D. Known-unknown

11. When should risk identification happen?

    A. As early as possible in the initiation process

    B. As early as possible in the planning process

    C. Throughout the product management life cycle

    D. Throughout the project life cycle

12. You are the project manager of the KLJH Project. This project will last two years and has 30 stakeholders. How often should risk identification take place?

    A. Once at the beginning of the project

    B. Throughout the execution processes

    C. Throughout the project

    D. Once per project phase

13. Which one of the following is an acceptable tool for risk identification?

    A. Decision tree analysis

    B. Decomposition of the project scope

    C. The Delphi Technique

    D. Pareto charting

14. You are the project manager for a project that will create a new and improved website for your company. Currently, your company has more than eight million users around the globe. You would like to poll experts within your organization with a simple, anonymous form asking about any foreseeable risks in the design, structure, and intent of the website. With the collected information, subsequent anonymous polls are submitted to the group of experts. This is an example of _____.

    A. Risk identification

    B. A trigger

    C. An anonymous trigger

    D. The Delphi Technique

15. Which of the following describes SWOT?

    A. An analysis of strengths, weakness, options, and timing

    B. An analysis of strengths, weakness, opportunities, and threats

    C. An elite project team that comes in and fixes project risks and threats

    D. Ratings of 1 to 100

16. Which risk analysis provides the project manager with a risk ranking?

    A. Quantifiable

    B. Qualitative

    C. The utility function

    D. SWOT analysis

17. A table of risks, their probability, their impact, and a number representing the overall risk score is called a _____.

    A. Risk table

    B. Probability and impact matrix

    C. Quantitative matrix

    D. Qualitative matrix

18. You are presented with the following table:

Risk Event	Probability	Impact Cost/Benefit	EMV
1	.20	−4,000	
2	.50	5,000	
3	.45	−300	
4	.22	500	
5	.35	−4,500	

What is the EMV for Risk Event 3?

    A. $135

    B. −$300

    C. $45

    D. −$135

19. You are presented with the following table:

Risk Event	Probability	Impact Cost/Benefit	Ex$V
1	.35	−4,000	
2	.40	50,000	
3	.45	−300,000	
4	.30	50,000	
5	.35	−45,000	

Based on the preceding numbers, what is the amount needed for the contingency fund?

    A. Unknown with this information

    B. 249,000

    C. 117,150

    D. 15,750

20. The water sanitation project manager has determined that the risks associated with handling certain chemicals are too high. He has decided to allow someone else to complete this portion of the project, so he has outsourced the handling and installation of the chemicals and filter equipment to an experienced contractor. This is an example of which of the following?

   A. Avoidance
   B. Acceptance
   C. Mitigation
   D. Transference

21. A project manager and the project team are actively monitoring the pressure gauge on a piece of equipment. Sarah, the engineer, recommends a series of steps to be implemented should the pressure rise above 80 percent. The 80 percent mark represents what?

   A. An upper control limit
   B. The threshold
   C. Mitigation
   D. A workaround

22. You are presented with the following table:

Risk Event	Probability	Impact Cost/Benefit	Ex$V
1	.20	–4,000	
2	.50	5,000	
3	.45	–300	
4	.22	500	
5	.35	–4,500	
6			

   What would Risk 6 be based on the following information: Marty is 60 percent certain that he can get the facility needed for $45,000, which is $7,000 less than what was planned for?

   A. .60, 45,000, 27,000
   B. .60, 52,000, 31,200
   C. .60, 7,000, 4,200
   D. .60, –7,000, –4,200

23. What can a project manager use to determine whether it is better to make or buy a product?

   A. A decision tree analysis
   B. A fishbone model

C. An Ishikawa diagram

D. An ROI analysis

24. Which of the following can determine multiple scenarios, given various risks and the probability of their impact?

A. Decision trees

B. Monte Carlo simulations

C. Pareto charts

D. Gantt charts

25. A project can have many risks with high-risk impact scores but have an overall low risk score. How is this possible?

A. The risk scores are graded on a bell curve.

B. The probability of each risk is low.

C. The impact of each risk is not accounted for until it comes to fruition.

D. The risks are rated high, medium, or low.

SELF TEST ANSWERS

1. When is it appropriate to accept a project risk?
   A. It is never appropriate to accept a project risk.
   B. All risks must be mitigated or transferred.
   C. It is appropriate to accept a risk if the project team has never completed this type of project work before.
   D. If the risk is in balance with the reward.

   ☑ **D.** Risks that are in balance with the reward are appropriate for acceptance.
   ☒ **A, B,** and **C** are all incorrect because these solutions are all false responses to risk management. It certainly is appropriate to accept a project risk in some instances. Consider the weather or the dangerous nature of some project work like construction. You don't have to mitigate or transfer all risks, as some are worth accepting, exploiting, enhancing, or even sharing. Just because a project team has not done a particular type of work before does not equate to accepting risks.

2. Frances is the project manager of the LKJ Project. Which of the following techniques will she use to create the risk management plan?
   A. Risk tolerance
   B. Status meetings
   C. Planning meetings
   D. Variance meetings

   ☑ **C.** Planning meetings are used to create the risk management plan. The project manager, project team leaders, key stakeholders, and other individuals with the power to make decisions regarding risk management attend the meetings.
   ☒ Choices **A, B,** and **D** are incorrect, since these choices do not fully answer the question.

3. Which of the following is not part of a risk management plan?
   A. Roles and responsibilities
   B. Methodology
   C. Technical assessment board compliance
   D. Risk categories

☑ **C.** The technical assessment board may be used as part of the change control system. It is not relevant to risk management planning.

☒ **A** is incorrect. Roles and responsibilities are a part of the risk management plan. **B,** methodology, is part of the risk management plan because it identifies the approaches, tools, and data sources for risk management. **D,** risk categories, is part of the risk management plan.

4. You are the project manager of the GHK Project. You and the manufacturer have agreed to substitute the type of plastic used in the product to a slightly thicker grade should there be more than a 7 percent error in production. The thicker plastic will cost more and require the production to slow down, but the errors should diminish. This is an example of which of the following?

A. Threshold

B. Tracking

C. Budgeting

D. JIT manufacturing

☑ **A.** An error value of 7 percent represents the threshold the project is allowed to operate under. Should the number of errors increase beyond 7 percent, the current plastic will be substituted.

☒ **B** is incorrect, since tracking is the documentation of a process through a system or workflow, or the documentation of events through the process. **C,** budgeting, is also incorrect. **D,** JIT manufacturing, is a scheduling approach to ordering the materials only when they are needed in order to keep inventory costs down.

5. An organization's risk tolerance is also known as what?

A. The utility function

B. Herzberg's Theory of Motivation

C. Risk acceptance

D. The risk-reward ratio

☑ **A.** The utility function describes a person's willingness to tolerate risk.

☒ **B** is incorrect. Herzberg's Theory of Motivation is an HR theory that describes motivating agents for workers. **C** is also incorrect. Risk acceptance describes the action of allowing a risk to exist because it is deemed low in impact, low in probability, or both. **D,** the risk-reward ratio, is incorrect. This describes the potential reward for taking a risk in the project.

6. A risk trigger is also called which of the following?

   A. A warning sign

   B. A delay

   C. A cost increase

   D. An incremental advancement of risk

☑ **A.** Risk triggers can also be known as warning signs. Triggers signal that a risk is about to happen or has happened.

☒ **B, C,** and **D** are all incorrect because these answers do not properly describe a risk trigger.

7. The customers of the project have requested additions to the project scope. The project manager brings notice that additional risk planning will need to be added to the project schedule. Why?

   A. The risk planning should always be the same amount of time as the activities required by the scope change.

   B. Risk planning should always occur whenever the scope is adjusted.

   C. Risk planning should only occur at the project manager's discretion.

   D. The project manager is incorrect. Risk planning does not need to happen at every change in the project.

☑ **B.** When the scope has been changed, the project manager should require risk planning to analyze the additions for risks to the project's success.

☒ **A** is incorrect. The scope changes may not require the same amount of time as the activities needed to complete the project changes. **C** is incorrect because risk planning should not occur at the project manager's discretion. Instead, it should be based on evidence within the project and the policies adopted in the risk management plan. **D** is also incorrect. When changes are added to the project scope, risk planning should occur.

8. Which one of the following best describes the risk register?

   A. It documents all of the outcomes of the other risk management processes.

   B. It's a document that contains the initial risk identification entries.

   C. It's a system that tracks all negative risks within a project.

   D. It's part of the project's PMIS for integrated change control.

☑ **A.** The risk register documents all of the outcomes of the other risk management processes.

☒ Choices **B, C,** and **D** are all incorrect definitions of the risk register.

9. _____ include(s) fire, theft, or injury, and offer(s) no chance for gain.
   A. Business risks
   B. Pure risks
   C. Risk acceptance
   D. Life risks

   ☑ **B.** Pure risks are the risks that could threaten the safety of the individuals on the project.
   ☒ Choice **A** is incorrect because business risks affect the financial gains or loss of a project. **C** and **D** are incorrect, since these terms are not relevant.

10. Complete this sentence: A project risk is a(n) _____ occurrence that can affect the project for good or bad.
   A. Known
   B. Potential
   C. Uncertain
   D. Known-unknown

   ☑ **C.** Risks are not planned—they are left to chance. The accommodation and the reaction to a risk can be planned, but the event itself is not planned. If risks could be planned, Las Vegas would be out of business.
   ☒ **A, B,** and **D** are all incorrect, since these terms do not accurately complete the sentence.

11. When should risk identification happen?
   A. As early as possible in the initiation process
   B. As early as possible in the planning process
   C. Throughout the product management life cycle
   D. Throughout the project life cycle

   ☑ **D.** Risk identification is an iterative process that happens throughout the project life cycle.
   ☒ **A** and **B** are both incorrect because risk identification is not limited to any one process group. **C** is incorrect because risk identification happens, technically, throughout the project management life cycle, which is unique to each project, not the product management life cycle.

12. You are the project manager of the KLJH Project. This project will last two years and has 30 stakeholders. How often should risk identification take place?
   A. Once at the beginning of the project
   B. Throughout the execution processes

C. Throughout the project

D. Once per project phase

☑ **C.** Risk identification happens throughout the project. Recall that planning is iterative—as the project moves towards completion, new risks may surface that call for identification and planned responses.

☒ **A** is incorrect. Risk identification should happen throughout the project, not just at the beginning. **B** is incorrect because risk identification is part of planning. **D** is incorrect because the nature of the project phase may require and reveal more than one opportunity for risk identification.

13. Which one of the following is an acceptable tool for risk identification?

A. Decision tree analysis

B. Decomposition of the project scope

C. The Delphi Technique

D. Pareto charting

☑ **C.** The Delphi Technique, an anonymous risk identification method, is the correct answer.

☒ **A** is incorrect. Decision tree analysis is appropriate for calculating the expected monetary value of a decision, but not for risk identification. **B** is incorrect because the decomposition of the project scope will result in the WBS. **D** is incorrect. Creating a Pareto chart is part of quality control, not of risk identification.

14. You are the project manager for a project that will create a new and improved website for your company. Currently, your company has more than eight million users around the globe. You would like to poll experts within your organization with a simple, anonymous form asking about any foreseeable risks in the design, structure, and intent of the website. With the collected information, subsequent anonymous polls are submitted to the group of experts. This is an example of _____.

A. Risk identification

B. A trigger

C. An anonymous trigger

D. The Delphi Technique

☑ **D.** An anonymous poll allowing experts to freely submit their opinion without fear of backlash is an example of the Delphi Technique.

☒ **A, B,** and **C** are incorrect. These choices do not accurately answer the question.

15. Which of the following describes SWOT?
   A. An analysis of strengths, weakness, options, and timing
   B. An analysis of strengths, weakness, opportunities, and threats
   C. An elite project team that comes in and fixes project risks and threats
   D. Ratings of 1 to 100

☑ **B.** SWOT analysis is part of risk identification and examines the strengths, weakness, opportunities, and threats of the project to make certain all possibilities for risk identification are covered.
☒ **A** is incorrect because SWOT examines all four perspectives. **C** and **D** are incorrect because these ratings are part of quantitative-qualitative risk analysis.

16. Which risk analysis provides the project manager with a risk ranking?
   A. Quantifiable
   B. Qualitative
   C. The utility function
   D. SWOT analysis

☑ **B.** The risk ranking is based on the *very high, high, medium, low,* and *very low* attributes of the identified risks.
☒ **A** is incorrect because it is not relevant to the question. Look again—answer **A** is quantifiable, not quantitative. **C** is incorrect. Utility function describes an organization's tolerance for risk. **D,** SWOT analysis, is part of risk identification.

17. A table of risks, their probability, their impact, and a number representing the overall risk score is called a _____.
   A. Risk table
   B. Probability and impact matrix
   C. Quantitative matrix
   D. Qualitative matrix

☑ **B.** A table of risks, their probability, and their impact equate to a risk score in a risk matrix.
☒ **A** is incorrect, since it does not fully answer the question. **C** and **D** are incorrect because a risk matrix can be used in both quantitative and qualitative risk analyses.

18. You are presented with the following table:

Risk Event	Probability	Impact Cost/Benefit	EMV
1	.20	−4,000	
2	.50	5,000	
3	.45	−300	
4	.22	500	
5	.35	−4,500	

What is the EMV for Risk Event 3?

A. $135

B. −$300

C. $45

D. −$135

☑ **D.** Risk Event 3 has a probability of 45 percent and an impact cost of −$300, which equates to −$135.

☒ **A, B,** and **C** are all wrong because their values are incorrect answers for the formula.

19. You are presented with the following table:

Risk Event	Probability	Impact Cost/Benefit	Ex$V
1	.35	−4,000	
2	.40	50,000	
3	.45	−300,000	
4	.30	50,000	
5	.35	−45,000	

Based on the preceding numbers, what is the amount needed for the contingency fund?

A. Unknown with this information

B. 249,000

C. 117,150

D. 15,750

☑ **C.** The calculated amount for each of the risk events is shown in the following table:

Risk Event	Probability	Impact Cost/Benefit	Ex$V
1	0.35	−4,000	−1,400
2	0.4	50,000	20,000
3	0.45	−300,000	−135,000
4	0.3	50,000	15,000
5	0.35	−45,000	−15,750
			−117,150

☒ **A, B,** and **D** are incorrect answers because they do not reflect the contingency amount needed for the project based on the preceding table.

20. The water sanitation project manager has determined that the risks associated with handling certain chemicals are too high. He has decided to allow someone else to complete this portion of the project, so he has outsourced the handling and installation of the chemicals and filter equipment to an experienced contractor. This is an example of which of the following?
    A. Avoidance
    B. Acceptance
    C. Mitigation
    D. Transference

☑ **D.** Because the risk is not eliminated but transferred to someone else or another entity, it is considered transference.
☒ **A** is incorrect because the risk still exists, but it is handled by another entity. **B** is incorrect because the project manager has not accepted the risk, deciding instead to allow another entity to deal with it. **C** is incorrect. The risk has not been mitigated in the project.

21. A project manager and the project team are actively monitoring the pressure gauge on a piece of equipment. Sarah, the engineer, recommends a series of steps to be implemented should the pressure rise above 80 percent. The 80 percent mark represents what?
    A. An upper control limit
    B. The threshold
    C. Mitigation
    D. A workaround

☑ **B.** The 80 percent mark is a threshold.
☒ **A** is incorrect. An upper control limit is a boundary for quality in a control chart. **C** is incorrect. Mitigation is a planned response should a risk event happen. **D** is also incorrect. A workaround is an action to bypass the risk event.

22. You are presented with the following table:

Risk Event	Probability	Impact Cost/Benefit	Ex$V
1	.20	−4,000	
2	.50	5,000	
3	.45	−300	
4	.22	500	
5	.35	−4,500	
6			

What would Risk 6 be based on the following information: Marty is 60 percent certain that he can get the facility needed for $45,000, which is $7,000 less than what was planned for?

A. .60, 45,000, 27,000
B. .60, 52,000, 31,200
C. .60, 7,000, 4,200
D. .60, −7,000, −4,200

☑ **C.** Marty is 60 percent certain he can save the project $7,000. The $4,200 represents the 60 percent certainty of the savings.
☒ **A, B,** and **D** are all incorrect since these values do not reflect the potential savings of the project.

23. What can a project manager use to determine whether it is better to make or buy a product?
A. A decision tree analysis
B. A fishbone model
C. An Ishikawa diagram
D. An ROI analysis

☑ **A.** A decision tree model can separate the pros and cons of buying versus building.
☒ **B** and **C** are both incorrect. A fishbone diagram and an Ishikawa diagram show cause and effect. **D** is incorrect because ROI analysis does not answer the question as fully as decision tree analysis.

24. Which of the following can determine multiple scenarios, given various risks and the probability of their impact?
    A. Decision trees
    B. Monte Carlo simulations
    C. Pareto charts
    D. Gantt charts

    ☑ **B.** Monte Carlo simulations can reveal multiple scenarios and examine the risks and probability of impact.
    ☒ **A,** decision trees, help guide the decision-making process. **C,** a Pareto chart, helps identify the leading problems in a situation. **D,** Gantt charts, compare the lengths of activities against a calendar in a bar chart format.

25. A project can have many risks with high-risk impact scores but have an overall low risk score. How is this possible?
    A. The risk scores are graded on a bell curve.
    B. The probability of each risk is low.
    C. The impact of each risk is not accounted for until it comes to fruition.
    D. The risks are rated high, medium, or low.

    ☑ **B.** A risk can have a very high impact on the project, but inversely have an extremely low probability score.
    ☒ **A** is incorrect and not relevant to the scenario. **C** is not a true statement. **D** is also incorrect. A model using high, medium, and low versus a numbering system would not alter the overall high- or low-risk score of the project.

12

Introducing Project Procurement Management

Projects routinely require procurements. They need materials, equipment, consultants, training, and many other goods and services. Project procurement management is the process of purchasing the products necessary for meeting the needs of the project scope. It involves planning, acquiring the products or services from sources, choosing a source, administering the contract, and closing out the contract. Procurement management, as far as your PMP exam is considered, focuses on the practices from the point of view of the buyer, not the seller (for example, contractor, subcontractor, vendor, or supplier).

When buying anything from a vendor, the buyer needs a contract, which becomes a key input to many of the processes within the project. The contract, more than anything else, specifies the rules and agreements for the project.

Here's a neat twist: When the seller is completing its obligations to supply a product, PMI treats those obligations as a project itself. In other words, if ABC Electricians were wiring a building for your company, ABC Electricians would be the performing organization completing its own project. Your company becomes the customer of their project—and is, of course, a stakeholder in their project. When the vendor is completing work for a portion of your project, the close contract activities don't wait until the end of the project—they happen as needed.

In the scenarios described in this chapter, the seller will be outside of the performing organization. The buyer will be managing a project and procuring resources from a vendor. However, all of the details in this chapter can be applied to internal work orders, formal agreements, and contracts between organizational units within a single entity.

CERTIFICATION OBJECTIVE 12.01

Planning for Purchases

Procurement planning is the process of identifying which part of the project should be procured from resources outside of the organization. Generally, procurement decisions are made early on in the planning processes. Procurement planning centers on four elements:

- Whether procurement is needed
- What to procure
- How much to procure
- When to procure

When the project manager begins the procurement process, she'll rely on the usual enterprise environmental factors and organizational process assets. For example, the project manager has to consider the marketplace conditions, the availability of the needed items or services in the marketplace, and how the procurement process works within the performing organization. If the project manager's organization has forms, policies, and management guidelines that direct the procurement process, she must follow those established processes.

exam watch

Sellers are also known as contractors, subcontractors, vendors, suppliers, and service providers. Buyers are also known as clients, customers, prime contractors, contractors, acquiring organizations, government agencies, service requestors, or purchases. When faced with procurement questions, identify who is buying and who is selling, and then address the question.

Often, an organization will have resources for managing the procurement process, including contracting and negotiating on behalf of the project. If, however, the performing organization has no such resources for the project manager to rely upon, it is up to the project manager to supply the procurement management resources, including capabilities for negotiating and for obtaining in a fiscally responsible way the right products or services for a fair price on behalf of the performing organization.

Evaluating the Market Conditions

Part of procurement management is to determine what sources are available to provide the needed products or services for the project. An evaluation of the marketplace is needed to determine what products and services are available and from whom and on what terms and conditions they are available.

While in most free market enterprise societies multiple vendors are offering comparable products, there may be times when choices of vendors are limited. The following are three specific terms to know for the PMP exam that you may encounter:

- **Sole source** Only one qualified seller exists in the marketplace.
- **Single source** The performing organization prefers to contract with a specific seller.
- **Oligopoly** There are very few sellers and the actions of one seller will have a direct effect on the other sellers' prices and the overall market condition.

Referring to the Scope Baseline

The project's scope statement, WBS, and WBS dictionary all serve as input to making procurement decisions. Because the project scope baseline defines the project work, and only the required work, to complete the project, it also defines the limitations of the project. Knowing the limits of what the project includes can help the project manager, the contract specialists, and other procurement professionals determine what needs to be purchased and what does not.

The WBS and the WBS dictionary define the details and requirements for acceptance of the project. This information also serves as valuable input regarding what needs to be procured and what does not. The WBS defines what the end result of the project will be. When dealing with vendors to procure a portion of the project, the work to be procured must support the requirements of the project customer.

A statement of work (SOW) may define the work to be accomplished within the project, but it generally does not define the product description as a whole. However, when an entire project is to be procured from a vendor, the SOW and the product description become one and the same. Along with SOW you may need to reference the requirements documentation to ensure the procurement planning process defines exactly what's needed and adheres to any relevant laws, regulations, and standards.

Relying on the Project Management Plan

The project management plan is also needed during the procurement planning processes because it will guide how the project should progress, and each subsidiary plan may need to be referenced for procurement guidelines. For example, the cost management plan, the scope management plan, the quality management plan, and the staffing management plan may all be needed for effective procurement planning.

One of the biggest things to consider during procurement management is the reliance on the risk response transference. Recall that transference is the assignment of a risk to a third party—typically with a fee involved. Insurance and contractors for dangerous work are two common examples of transference. The risk register will help identify the costs associated with the identified risks, and the contractual agreements for transference will be referenced as part of the project costs.

The project management plan also includes the project schedule—something the project manager needs to consider procurement leads, fulfillment time for vendors, and when resources are needed to keep the project moving along. Couple the project schedule with the activity cost estimate and the cost performance baseline, and the project manager can do cash flow forecasting, communicate with management about upcoming expenses, and ensure that vendors are paid on time.

Teaming with Other Organizations

If your organization and another organization partner on an opportunity, it's called a teaming agreement. It's a legally binding venture between two or more organizations to complete a defined set of work or to seize an opportunity, or some other venture that the parties involved couldn't complete necessarily on their own. Teaming agreements end when the venture ends. You might have heard these agreements loosely defined as "coop-etition"—a fun way to describe cooperating with the competition, although teaming doesn't have to be just a partnership with the competition.

Teaming agreements should define in a contract the roles, buyer-and-seller relationships, and how the teaming agreement ends. The parties must all be in agreement with one another as to who does what, communication channels, and how decisions in the partnership will be made.

CERTIFICATION OBJECTIVE 12.02

Completing Procurement Planning

Procurement planning should be done early in the planning processes, with certain exceptions. As needs arise, as project conditions change, or as other circumstances demand, procurement planning may be required throughout the project. Whenever procurement planning happens early in the project, as preferred, or later in the project, as needed, a logical approach to securing the proper resources is necessitated.

Determining to Make or Buy

The decision to make or buy a product is a fundamental aspect of management. Under some conditions, it is more cost-effective to buy—while in others it makes more sense to create an in-house solution. The make-or-buy analysis should be made in the initial scope definition to determine if the entire project should be completed in-house or procured. As the project evolves, additional make-or-buy decisions are needed.

The initial costs of the solution for the in-house or procured product must be considered, but so, too, must the ongoing expenses of the solutions. For example, a company may elect to lease a piece of equipment. The ongoing expenses of leasing the piece of equipment should be weighed against the expected ongoing expenses of purchasing the equipment and the monthly costs to maintain, insure, and manage the equipment.

For example, Figure 12-1 shows the mathematical approach for determining whether it is better to create a software program in-house or buy one from a software company. The in-house solution will cost your company $25,000 to create your own software package and (based on historical information) another $2,500 per month to maintain the software.

The development company has a solution that will cost your company $17,000 to purchase, but the development company requires a maintenance plan for each software program installed, which will cost your company $2,700 per month. The difference between making the software and buying the software is $8,000. The difference between supporting the software the organization has made and allowing the external company to support their software is only $200 per month.

The $200 per month is divided into the difference between creating the software internally and buying the software—which is $8,000 divided by $200—or 40 months. If the software is to be replaced within 40 months, the company should buy the software. If the software will not be replaced within 40 months, it should build the software.

FIGURE 12-1

Make-or-buy formulas are common exam questions.

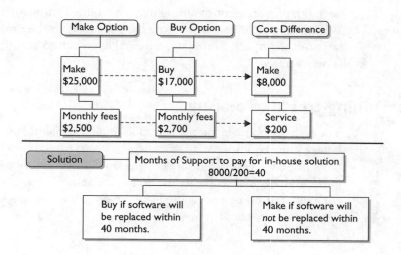

There are multiple reasons why an organization may choose to make or buy. The following are some common examples or reasons for making and buying:

Reasons to Make	Reasons to Buy
Less costly	Less costly
Use in-house skills	In-house skills aren't available or don't exist
Control of work	Small volume of work
Control of intellectual property	More efficient
Learn new skills	Transfer risks
Available staff	Available vendor
Focus on core project work	Allows project team to focus on other work items

Using Expert Judgment

Procurement planning can rely on expert judgment. It may be beneficial to rely on the wisdom of others—those in the performing organization or subject matter experts—to determine the need for procurement. Expert judgment for procurement management planning can come from the following:

- Units or individuals within the performing organization
- Consultants and subject matter experts
- Professional, trade, or technical associations
- Industry groups

PMP Coach *You're at the final knowledge area. Congrats! In my experience teaching PMP Boot Camps, most candidates are worn out by this topic. And they rationalize that since they personally don't handle much of the procurement, they can ease off in this chapter. Wrong! You can expect plenty of questions on procurement on your PMP exam—don't take it easy. You're almost there, but you're not there yet. Keep going—think of how good you'll feel when you're done with this exam.*

Determining the Contract Type

There are multiple types of contracts when it comes to procurement. The project work, the market, and the nature of the purchase determine the contract type.

The following are some general rules that PMP exam candidates, and project managers, should know:

- A contract is a formal agreement between the buyer and the seller. Contracts can be oral or written—though written is preferred.
- The United States and most developed countries back all contracts through the court system.
- Contracts should clearly state all requirements for product acceptance.
- Any changes to the contract must be formally approved, controlled, and documented.
- A contract is not fulfilled until all of the requirements of the contract are met.
- Contracts can be used as a risk mitigation tool, as in transferring the risk. All contracts have some level of risk; depending on the contract type, the risk can be transferred to the seller. If a risk response strategy is to transfer, risks associated with procurement are considered secondary risks and must go through the risk management process.
- There are legal requirements governing contracts. In order for a contract to be valid, it must:
  - Contain an offer
  - Have been accepted
  - Provide for a consideration (payment)
  - Be for a legal purpose
  - Be executed by someone with capacity and authority
  - The terms and conditions of the contract should define breaches, copyrights, intellectual rights, and *force majeure*. *Force majeure* is French for superior force—sometimes called "acts of God." You might know these as tornados, earthquakes, and hurricanes.

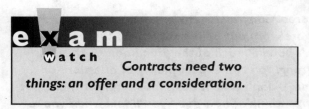

Contracts need two things: an offer and a consideration.

Fixed-Price Contracts

Fixed-price contracts (also known as firm fixed-price and lump-sum contracts) are agreements that define a total price for the product the seller is to provide. These contracts must clearly define the requirements the vendor is to provide. These contracts may also provide incentives for meeting or exceeding contract requirements—such as

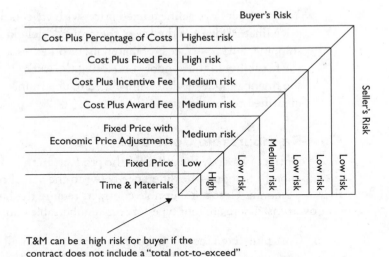

FIGURE 12-2

Fixed-price contracts transfer the risk to the seller.

T&M can be a high risk for buyer if the contract does not include a "total not-to-exceed" clause. Also called an NTE clause.

meeting deadlines—and require the seller to assume the risk of cost overruns, as Figure 12-2 demonstrates. There are three fixed-priced contracts you should know.

- **Firm fixed-price contract** This contract type defines the exact amount for the goods or services provided by the vendor. It's the most common and most preferred contract type for organizations, as the risk for the buyer is relatively low. For the seller, however, the risk is that if their cost of materials, doing business, or completing the work defined in the contract increases, they cannot pass the cost on to the customer. A firm fixed-price contract is also known as a lump-sum contract.

- **Fixed-price incentive fee contract** This contract type is similar to the firm-fixed-price contract in that a lump-sum amount is agreed upon between the buyer and the seller for the work to be performed. However, this contract type allows the contract to include incentives for the project, such as a bonus for completing the project work early, saving costs in the project, or other performance objectives. This contract can also have penalties for the vendor if they're late on the project work or their performance suffers.

- **Fixed price with economic price adjustment contract** This contract type is for long-term projects that may span years to complete the project work.

The contract does define a fixed price, with caveats for special categories of price fluctuation over the life of the project, including inflation, electricity, shipping, labor costs, cost of materials, or other resources that could affect the feasibility of the vendor completing the work. The contract must define the financial indexes that will be used to determine the fluctuation in the identified cost categories.

Cost-Reimbursable Contracts

These contract types pay the seller for the product. In the payment to the seller there is a profit margin—the difference between the actual costs of the product and the sales amount. Cost-reimbursable contracts require the buyer to assume the risk of cost overruns. There are four types of cost-reimbursable contracts.

- **Cost plus fixed fee**   The buyer is responsible for all costs the contracted work incurs plus a predetermined fee for the vendor to manage and complete the contracted work. The fee for the work is usually tied to a percentage of the estimated project costs, but not always. For example, I'll remodel your condo, but you have to pay for all the materials and labor I'll need, which should be close to $80,000. In addition, you'll have to pay me 15 percent of the costs, which will be $12,000. You'll pay the costs as the project progresses and pay my fee based on milestones completed in the project. If I don't finish the project, you don't finish paying me. You do have some risks, though—if I waste materials, you have to buy more and you'll still have to pay my fee for the work.

- **Cost plus incentive fee**   This contract type requires that the buyer pays for all the preapproved costs for materials and labor in the project plus an incentive fee for completing the project early, saving on project costs, managing certain risks, or meeting other performance objectives. The contract will define how the incentives are determined. One popular method attaches dollar amounts to completed milestones and dates. If the vendor delivers the milestones ahead of the promised dates on a consistent basis, the value of the work increases and so will the incentive fee for the vendor. If the contract is based on cost savings for the project and early completions are cost savings, the contract must define how the cost savings are split between the buyer and the seller. Usually, the seller receives 20 percent of the cost savings in what's called an "80/20 split."

- **Cost plus award fee**   This contract requires the buyer to pay for all the project costs and gives the seller an award fee based on the project performance, certain project criteria, or other goals established by the buyer. The award fee can be tied to any factor the buyer determines, and the factor doesn't have to be exact. For example, the buyer can set an award fee of up to $100,000 for a $1,000,000 project based on the technical ingenuity of the project solution, the quality of the work, or the actual cost savings the solution creates for the organization.

- **Cost plus percentage of costs**   This contract type is the absolute pits, and most organizations won't participate with these contracts. In this instance, the buyer has to pay for all of the costs of the materials plus a predetermined percentage for the cost of the materials. The obvious risk is that the vendor can waste materials and the buyer will have to buy new materials and pay the percentage of costs for the materials again. It's easy for the vendor to run up the total project costs just by wasting materials.

on the
!
ⓘ o b

The only time it might be appropriate, and I stress the word might, to use a cost plus percentage of costs contract is when the vendor is working with a highly specialized material and type of work. For example, imagine an artist who's sculpting a marble statue for the lobby of a building or a scientist who's working with a highly complex chemical. The nature of this type of work is so specialized that the artist and the scientist are unlikely to waste materials on purpose just to crank up their project costs. Having said that, I doubt you will see this on the PMP exam. As a general rule, avoid the cost plus percentage of costs contract.

Time and Materials Contracts

Time and materials (T&M) contracts are sometimes called unit price contracts. They are ideal for instances when an organization contracts out a small project for instances when smaller amounts of work within a larger project are to be completed by a vendor. T&M contracts, however, can grow dangerously out of control as more work is assigned to the seller. T&M contracts should have a not-to-exceed clause (NTE clause) to put a ceiling on the procured work. Figure 12-3 is an example of how T&M contracts can pose a risk for the buyer.

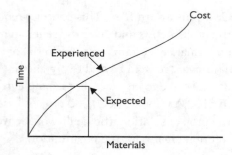

FIGURE 12-3

Time and materials contracts must be kept in check, or costs can skyrocket.

Summary of Contract Types

On the PMP examination, you can expect a few questions on contract types. Familiarize yourself with the following table:

Contract Type	Acronym	Attribute	Risk Issues
Cost plus fixed fee	CPFF	Actual costs plus profit margin for seller	Cost overruns represent risk to the buyer.
Cost plus percentage of cost	CPPC	Actual costs plus profit margin for seller	Cost overruns represent risk to the buyer. This is the most dangerous contract type for the buyer.
Cost plus award fee	CPAF	Actual costs plus an award based on seller-defined objectives for the project	Buyer carries the risk, as the seller is the judge of the contract work and performance.
Cost plus incentive fee	CPIF	Actual costs plus profit margin for seller	Cost overruns represent risk to the buyer.
Fixed-price	FP	Agreed-upon price for contracted product; can include incentives for the seller	Seller assumes risk.
Fixed price with economic price adjustment	FP-EPA	Agreed-upon price for contracted product; can include cost adjustments based on predefined categories of cost	Seller assumes risk.
Firm fixed-price	FFP	Agreed-upon price for contracted product	Seller assumes risk.
Fixed-price incentive fee	FPIF	Agreed-upon price for contracted product; can include incentives for the seller	Seller assumes risk.

Contract Type	Acronym	Attribute	Risk Issues
Time and materials	T&M	Price assigned for the time and materials provided by the seller.	Contracts without "not-to-exceed" clauses can lead to cost overruns.
Unit price		Price assigned for a measurable unit of product or time (for example, $130 for engineer's time on the project)	Risk varies with the product. Time represents the biggest risk if the amount needed is not specified in the contract.

The Procurement Management Plan

Procurement planning is a process that should happen early in the planning processes. The outputs of procurement planning allow the project manager and the project team to proceed with confidence in the procuring of products and services needed to successfully complete the project. If it is determined early in the project that there isn't a need for procurements, then obviously the balance of the procurement processes is not necessary for the project.

This subsidiary project plan documents the decisions made in the procurement planning processes. It specifies how the remaining procurement activities will be managed. The plan details the following:

- How vendors will be selected
- The types of contracts to be used
- The process of independent estimating (also known as should-cost estimates)
- The relationship between the project team and the procurement office within the performing organization (if one exists)
- Planning for the lead time requirements between the vendor and the organizational purchasing processes
- Requirements for performance bonds and insurance requirements for the vendors
- The procurement forms, such as contracts, that the project team is required to use
- How multiple vendors will be managed to supply their contracted product
- The coordination between sellers and the project team and among project activities, project reporting, scheduling, business operations, and other project concerns
- Metrics to be used to determine which vendors qualify for project work and to complete vendor selection

Using the Statement of Work

In the contract statement of work (SOW), the seller fully describes the work to be completed and/or the product to be supplied. The contract SOW becomes part of the contract between the buyer and the seller. The contract SOW is typically created as part of the procurement planning process, and it allows the seller to determine if it can meet the written requirements of the SOW.

Particular industries have different assumptions about what constitutes an SOW. What one industry calls an SOW may be a statement of objectives (SOO) in another. A SOO is a document describing a problem to be solved by the seller. The SOW, what you'll see on the PMP exam, defines the project specifications; requirements for vendor qualification; and details about the project work, location, expected time frame, and similar conditions.

CERTIFICATION OBJECTIVE 12.03

Preparing for Contracting

Contracting planning is the process of preparing to acquire sellers to provide products that the project needs. It's a pretty straightforward business. Three inputs are used for contracting planning.

- **The procurement management plan** This subsidiary plan sets out the methodologies and expectations of procurement within the performing organization.
- **The statement of work** The contract SOW provides detailed information on what the seller will be providing for the performing organization. Recall that this document allows the seller to determine if it can provide the product and meet the requirements of the project team.
- **Other planning outputs** Other details within the project plan, such as the schedules, estimates, constraints, and assumptions, are referenced, since their values may have a direct influence on the contracting process.

Organizing Contracting Materials

Contracting planning relies on the outputs of procurement planning. The procurement management plan will guide the process as the project team has planned, as the performing organization requires, or under the guidance of a procurement office within the performing organization.

Two primary tools are used for contracting planning.

- **Standard forms**   Within the performing organization, there may be many different standardized forms for contracts, descriptions of procurement items, bid documents, and other procurement-related documents.

- **Expert judgment**   Expert judgment may be needed to review and help the project manager select the best source for the procured product.

Creating the Procurement Documents

The primary outputs of contracting planning are the procurement documents. These documents guide the relationship between the buyer and the seller. Communication between the buyer and the seller should always be specific as to the requirements and expectations of the seller. In initial communications, especially when requesting a price or proposal, the buyer should include the SOW, relevant specifications, and, if necessary, any nondisclosure agreements (NDAs). Requests from buyers to sellers should be specific enough to give the seller a clear idea of what the buyer is requesting, but general enough to allow the seller to provide viable alternatives.

The following are some specific terms the project manager—and the PMP candidate—should be familiar with:

Document	Purpose
Bid	From seller to buyer. Price is the determining factor in the decision-making process.
Quotation	From seller to buyer. Price is the determining factor in the decision-making process.
Proposal	From seller to buyer. Other factors—such as skill sets, reputation, and ideas for the project solution—may be used in the decision-making process.
Invitation for bid (IFB)	From buyer to seller. Requests the seller to provide a price for the procured product or service.
Request for quote (RFQ)	From buyer to seller. Requests the seller to provide a price for the procured product or service.
Request for proposal (RFP)	From buyer to seller. Requests the seller to provide a proposal to complete the procured work or to provide the procured product.

Determining the Source Selection Criteria

Another output of contracting planning is the evaluation criteria to determine which source the organization will purchase from. The evaluation criteria is used to rate and score proposals from the sellers. In some instances, such as a bid or quote, the evaluation criterion is focused just on the price the seller offers. In other instances, such as a proposal, the evaluation criteria can be multiple values: experience, references, certifications, and more.

It's essential for the project manager and the project team to create selection criteria that will guide their decision making later in the project. Common questions that should be considered prior to vendor selection include the following:

- Does the vendor understand the project need?
- What is the overall project and/or life-cycle cost?
- What is the vendor's technical capability?
- What is the vendor's management and technical approach to the project work?
- What is their financial capacity to complete the project work?
- Does the vendor qualify in areas that may help in rewarding the contract (such as they're a small business, female-owned, or a disadvantaged small business)?
- What are the proprietary rights and intellectual property rights associated with the project work?
- Will the vendor provide a warranty for the work they complete?

Updating the Contract Statement of Work

The final outputs of contracting planning are updates to the contract statement of work. As the project team creates the requirements from the sellers during invitations for bids, requests for quotes, or requests for proposals, they may discover other needed elements in the SOW. In addition, it is possible the bids, quotes, and proposals may offer alternatives the project team has not considered—and a new SOW is then created.

Changes to the SOW should be updated, documented, and recorded to reflect the logic and reason behind the change.

CERTIFICATION OBJECTIVE 12.04

Completing Procurement Purchasing

Once the contracting planning has been completed, the actual process of contracting can begin. Fortunately, the sellers, not the buyers, perform most of the activity in solicitations—usually at no additional cost to the project. The sellers are busy trying to win the business. There are two inputs to solicitations.

- *Procurement documents* are created in contracting planning. These are the invitations for bid, requests for proposal, and requests for quote documents.

- *Qualified seller lists* are often maintained by performing organizations. These lists of qualified sellers (also preferred sellers or approved sellers) generally have contact information, a history of past experience with the seller, and other pertinent information. In addition to the internal qualified seller list, there are many other resources to determine which sellers may qualify for the proposed work: Internet resources, industry directories, trade associations, and so on.

Procuring Goods and Services

Requesting seller responses is the process of inviting sellers to acquire the business of the performing organization. Three primary tools are needed to complete this process.

- **Bidder conferences**   A bidder conference, also called a contractor conference or vendor conference, is a meeting with prospective sellers to ensure that all sellers have a clear understanding of the product or service to be procured and are equal footing. Bidder conferences allow sellers to query the buyer on the details of the product to help ensure that the seller's proposal is adequate and appropriate for the proposed agreement. At this point of the process, all sellers are considered equal.

- **Advertising** In most circumstances, advertisements inviting bidders are expected. These advertisements can run in newspapers or trade journals specific to the industry of the organization. Some government agencies require advertisements inviting sellers to acquire the project work, attend a bidder conference, or present a proposal for the described work.

- **Developing a qualified sellers list** Many organizations use a qualified sellers list to guide their procurement decisions. The project team may elect to create their own qualified sellers list, use the organization's list, or rely on a third-party qualified sellers list through the Internet or other third-party resources.

on the job
A standard of procurement is that bids and quotes are looking for sellers to provide a price. Proposals are asking the sellers to provide solutions.

Examining the Results of Contracting

The end result of contracting, as expected, is a collection of proposals, bids, and quotations. These documents indicate the sellers' ability and preparedness to complete the project work. The proposals should be in alignment with the stated expectations of the buyer, and they may be presented orally, electronically, or in hard copy format. Of course, the relationship between the buyer and the seller—and the type of information being shared—will determine which modality is the best choice of communication.

Selecting the Seller

Once the sellers have presented their proposals, bids, or quotes (depending on what the buyer requested of them), their documents are examined so that the project manager can select which sellers are the best choice for the project work. In many instances, price may be the predominant factor for choosing a particular seller—but not always. Other factors besides price may also be taken into consideration.

- The cost of an item may not reflect the true cost to the performing organization if the item cannot be delivered in a timely manner. If a seller promises to have a product on site by a specific date and fails to do so, the project can be delayed, costing the organization thousands—or more—in losses.

■ Proposals can be separated into two categories: technical and commercial. The technical category describes the approach and methodology to complete the project work, while the commercial category delves into the price to complete the project work. An evaluation takes into consideration both categories in order to determine the best choice for the project.

■ Critical, high-priority projects may rely on multiple sellers to complete the project work. This redundancy can balance risk, cost, and opportunity among multiple vendors.

Preparing for Source Selection

Source selection weighs and evaluates the proposals, bids, and quotes for the procured portions of the project and then makes a determination as to which seller is the best for the project work. Source selection has three inputs to the decision-making process.

■ **Proposals**   The proposals, bids, and quotations provided by the sellers are key inputs. These are the documents the performing organization will evaluate to determine which seller is the best provider for the project.

■ **Evaluation criteria**   The evaluation criteria, such as referrals, samples of previous work, and references, are considered. The evaluation criteria are evidence of the quality, depth, and experience of work the seller has performed in the past and, hopefully, is capable of performing on the current project. Evaluation criteria are developed in contracting planning and are applied in source selection.

■ **Organizational policies**   The performing organization likely has procurement policies and procedures that the project manager is expected to follow in regard to source selection. The organizational policies should be known before starting the source selection process to avoid any discrepancies, conflicts of interest, or other breaches of policies. For example, some organizations' procurement policies do not allow project managers to accept any gifts beyond $25 in value.

Completing the Seller Selection Process

For the performing organization to finalize the process of seller selection, there must first be eligible sellers. Assuming there is more than one seller that can satisfy the

| FIGURE 12-4 |

Weighting systems remove personal preference from the selection process.

Possible Score	20	20	15	10	10	5	20	100
Value	Experience	Certifications	Level IV Engineers	Security Clearance	Start Date	Waste Removal	Price	Total Score
ABC Constructions	15	20	7	10	10	5	12	79
Allen Builders	12	20	12	10	10	0	10	74
FRJ Construction	18	20	11	0	10	5	18	82
Howe & Who Construction	18	15	5	0	5	5	15	73
Martin & Martin	9	20	13	10	5	0	18	65
Ralph Engineers	15	8	8	0	10	5	17	73

demands of the project, the project manager can rely on several tools and techniques when making a selection.

- **Weighting system**   A weighting system takes out the personal preferences of the decision-maker in the organization to ensure that the best seller is awarded the contract. A weighting system creates a matrix, as seen in Figure 12-4. Weights are assigned to the values of the proposals, and each proposal is scored. Because the weights are determined before reviewing the proposals, the process is guaranteed to be free of personal preferences and bias. The seller with the highest score is awarded the contract.

- **Independent estimates**   These estimates are often referred to as "should-cost" estimates. They are created by the performing organization or outside experts to predict what the cost of the procured product should be. If there is a significant difference between what the organization has predicted and what the sellers have proposed, the statement of work was inadequate or the sellers misunderstood the requirements or the price provided by the seller is too high.

- **Screening system**   A screening system is a method to remove sellers from consideration if they do not meet given conditions. For example, screening could require that sellers must be certified by a specific organization, have prior experience with the project technology, or meet other values. Sellers that don't meet the requirements are removed from the selection process and their proposals are not considered.

- **Contract negotiation**   The performing organization creates an offer, and the seller considers it. The contract negotiation process is an activity to create a fair price for the work the seller is to complete. The performing organization and the seller must be in agreement on the expectations, requirements, authorities, terms, technical and business management approaches, price—and any other pertinent factors covered within, and by, the contract—prior to signing it.

■ **Seller rating systems** How the vendor has performed in the past may guide current and future project procurement decisions. Consider a vendor that has offered poor performance in quality, delivery, and contractual compliance versus a vendor that has scored high marks in quality, delivery, and contract compliance—which should the project manager choose? That's the goal of the seller rating system: to collect and disseminate information on the performance of sellers in order to guide project decisions.

■ **Expert judgment** Often, the project manager and the project team may not be qualified in the discipline the vendor is offering, which the project requires. In these instances, the project manager can rely on expert judgment to help make the best decisions regarding the project's welfare.

■ **Proposal evaluation techniques** There are many different approaches to evaluating vendors' proposals—from weighting systems to screening systems—but all will rely on expert judgment and some sort of evaluation criteria.

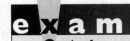

A letter of intent is a letter from the buyer to the seller indicating that the seller will be awarded the contract. *In other words, the buyer intends to do business with the seller.*

Examining the Results of Seller Selection

The one output of seller selection is a contract between the buyer and the seller. A contract is a legally binding agreement between the buyer and the seller in which the seller provides the described product and the seller pays for the product. Contracts are known by many names.

■ Agreement

■ Subcontract

■ Purchase order

■ Memorandum of understanding

Contracts have to be signed by a person with the power to authorize the requirements and payment specified in the contract. This role is called the delegation of procurement authority. Whether this person is the project manager depends on the procurement policies of the performing organization.

In some organizations, all contracts flow through centralized contracting. Centralized contracting requires all contracts for all projects to be approved through a central unit within the performing organization. Other organizations use a decentralized contracting approach, which assigns a contract administrator or contract officer to the project.

CERTIFICATION OBJECTIVE 12.05

Performing Contract Administration

Contract administration is the process of ensuring that the seller lives up to the agreements in the contract. The project manager and the contract administrator must work together to make certain the seller meets its obligations. If the seller does not fulfill its contractual requirements, legal remedies may ultimately be pursued.

Another aspect of contract administration, especially on larger projects with multiple sellers providing various products, is the coordination between the contractors. The project manager or contract officer schedules and confirms the performance of the sellers so that the deliverables, schedule, and performance of a contractor do not infringe or adversely affect the performance of another contractor.

The contract must also include the terms of payment. Typically, the performance and progress of the contractor is directly linked to payments it receives. The project manager must track performance and quality to approve or decline payment as needed. The contract should define the metrics for acceptance to avoid disagreements on performance and to ensure that vendors get paid on time.

Preparing for Contract Administration

The contract and the contract management plan are needed as a guide for effective contract administration. The contract dictates the requirements and expectations of the seller and the buyer. The obligations of both parties should be in alignment with the contract—if not, disagreements, delays, and even work

INSIDE THE EXAM

Project procurement management first begins by determining which facets of the project can best be served through procurement. This decision often focuses on a make-or-buy analysis.

- Is it more cost-effective to make or buy the product or service?
- Is it more time-efficient to make or buy the product or service?
- Are the resources available within the organization to make the product or service?

If the decision has been made to buy the product or service, a statement of work is needed to detail exactly what product or service the organization is buying. The SOW will be given to potential sellers so that they can prepare their offers in alignment with what is needed by the performing organization.

In order to find potential sellers, the performing organization issues an SOW to the sellers, with the appropriate procurement documents. Sellers can be found through a preferred vendor list, advertisements, industry directories, trade organizations, or other methods. The initial communication from the buyer to the seller is a request. Specifically, the seller issues one of the following documents:

- **Request for proposal** Used when there are multiple factors besides price to determine which seller is awarded the contract. The buyer is looking for a solution to a need.
- **Request for quotation** Used when the deciding factor is price.
- **Invitation for bid** Used when the deciding factor is price.

The seller can host a bidder conference to ensure that all sellers have equal opportunity to gain information about the procured work or service and that the information they do get is the same. After the seller conference, the selection process is based on several things.

- Procurement documents from the sellers
- Company policies and procedures
- Screening systems to sift out sellers that do not qualify for the work
- Weighting system to make an unbiased selection of a seller

(Continued)

INSIDE THE EXAM

Once the seller has been selected, the contract is created between the buyer and the seller. This formal, preferably written, agreement between the buyer and the seller defines all requirements of both the buyer and the seller. The seller's requirements specify how and when the work will be completed. The buyer's requirements, on the other hand, specify the terms and conditions that the seller is expected to maintain. The contract may also include information on resolving claims, how changes to the contract are to be made, and who the authorities are within the buyer's organization and the seller's organization.

Contract administration is the process of ensuring that the seller meets the obligations and requirements specified in the contract. If changes arise in the project that affect the contract, there may be additional negotiation for payments based on the added or removed components of the procured work.

At the completion of the contract, the seller and the buyer complete product verification, which is much like administrative closure, to confirm that the seller has met its obligations. Documentation of the procurement experience is created so that the information can be applied to other procurement activities on the current projects and to other projects within the organization.

stoppage can ensue. In addition to the contract, there are three other inputs to contract administration.

- **Performance reports**   Within the contract, the terms for acceptance are defined. Reports on the seller's performance are needed to compare with the requirements of the contracted work.

- **Work results**   The seller's work results must be completed according to the requirements of the contract. As part of project plan execution, the seller must meet the quality standards of the performing organization and expected schedule of completion, and stay within the anticipated costs and the specified range of variance.

- **Change requests**   Change requests can complicate contract administration. The performing organization's change control system must somehow mesh with the seller's change control system. Changes to the project that affect the contracted work require changes to the contract, addendums to the contract, or a new contract for the additional or changed work. In some instances, the seller and the buyer may disagree about the cost of the changes. These differences may be labeled as claims, disputes, or appeals—and may ultimately slow the project's progress if not remedied.

on the *If the seller's performance is unacceptable and a resolution to the problem* **ob** *cannot be found, the performing organization may elect to cancel the contract. This termination of the contract is also handled as a change request within the change control system.*

Completing Contract Administration

The actual process of completing contract administration relies heavily on communication between the project manager, the contract officer, and the seller. The communications plan may have considerations for how and when the communication between the buyer and the seller should take place and what the purpose of the communication should be. There are six primary concerns, in addition to communication, within contract administration.

■ **Contract change control system**   The contract change control system defines the procedures for how the contract may be changed. The process for changing the contract includes the forms; documented communications; tracking; conditions within the project, business, or marketplace that justify the needed changes; dispute resolution procedures; and the procedures for getting the changes approved within the performing organization. The system is part of integrated change control.

■ **Buyer-conducted performance reviews and audits**   As the vendor completes the contracted work, the seller will need to inspect the work for progress; compliance with contract requirements; and adherence to agreed-to time, cost, and quality constraints.

■ **Performance reporting**   Performance reporting is the communication between the project manager and management on how the seller is performing under the guidelines in the contract. This is part of communications and should be documented within the communications management plan.

■ **Payment system**   Sellers like to be paid when they have completed their obligations. How the sellers are paid is controlled by the payment system, which includes interactions between the project manager and the accounts payable department. The performing organization may have strict guidelines for how payment requests are submitted and approved, and how payments are completed. On larger projects, the project management team may have specific procedures for submitting the payment requests.

■ **Claims administration** This is not fun. Claims result from contested changes, such as disagreements about a change that has occurred and who should pay for that change. Though these go by various names—claims, disputes, and appeals—they all mean the same thing: The buyer and the seller are in disagreement over who should pay for the changes to the project work. Resolution may come through negotiation, mediation, or arbitration, as defined by the contract.

■ **Records management system** This is part of the project management information system and is designed to track all contracting documentation. This is essential, since it assists the project manager in managing procurement documents and records, and serves as a point of reference regarding communications and procurement paperwork.

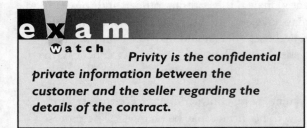

Privity is the confidential private information between the customer and the seller regarding the details of the contract.

Reviewing the Results of Contract Administration

Contract administration calls for communication between the seller and the buyer, between the project manager and the vendor, and among the stakeholders. There must be significant documentation of the agreement that both the buyer and the seller agree to before the procured work begins. Once the procured work, service, or product has been delivered from the seller to the buyer, there must be agreement that the delivery is in alignment with the original agreement.

Correspondence

The performance of the contracted work, the contract obligations, and the procedures of the performing organization generate correspondence between the buyer and the seller. The correspondence often takes the form of warnings, letters of discontent, and project performance reviews from the buyer to the seller. This correspondence can serve as documentation for legal action if disputes arise between the buyer and the seller.

Contract Changes

Both approved and declined changes are documented as to their cost, time, and effect on the project and the procured work. Changes that are approved require updates to the project plan, subsidiary plans, and possibly to other project documentation.

Payment Requests

Within the contract, the terms for payment are specified. The terms for payment may stipulate under what conditions the seller will provide an invoice for the work completed. In addition, the buyer may specify when and how the invoices are paid (for example, "Net 30 days from receipt of the invoice"). If the project is using an external payment system, there will be communication between the buyer and the seller, and between the buyer and the external payment system. If the performing organization is handling its own payment processing, this output would simply be payments.

CERTIFICATION OBJECTIVE 12.06

Performing Contract Closure

Contract closeout is analogous to administrative closure. Its purpose is to confirm that the obligations of the contract were met as expected. The project manager, the customer, key stakeholders, and, in some instances, the seller may finalize product verification together to confirm the contract has been completed.

Contract closeout can also be linked to administrative closure, because it is the process of confirming that the work was finished. In instances where the contract was terminated, contract closeout is reviewed and is considered closed because of the termination. The project records should be updated to reflect the contract closeout and the acceptance of the work or product.

Reviewing Contract Documentation

To successfully close out a contract, the details of the contract need to be reviewed. This review ensures that the product verification is complete and is in accordance with the language and agreement in the contract. The review actually considers more than just the contract; the project manager should review and consider the following:

- Schedules of the procured work
- Contract change requests—approved and declined
- Documentation that the seller has created and provided, if any
- Financial documents, invoices, and payment records
- Results of contractual inspections

Auditing the Procurement Process

The successes and failures within the procurement process of the project are reviewed from the procurement planning stage through contract administration. The intent of the audit is to learn what worked and what didn't during the procurement processes. This knowledge can then be applied to other areas within the current project and to other projects within the performing organization.

Negotiated Settlements

Termination of the contract may not always be because of something the vendor did wrong. The buyer may no longer need the good or service being provided, but the buyer may still be contractually obligated to pay the vendor. The contract overrides everything. When there is a dispute, technically a claim, the contract even directs the claims administration process.

Should the buyer and the seller not be able to work out their differences between themselves, things are escalated. This means the buyer and the seller will participate in alternative dispute resolution—a nice way of saying, "Here come the attorneys!" Alternative dispute resolution includes mediation, arbitration, and even litigation.

Completing Contract Closeout

Once the deliverables have been accepted and the contract has been closed, it's essential to collect all of the contract information and record it in the contract file. A contract file is a complete indexed set of records of the procurement process and is incorporated into the administrative closure process. These records include financial information as well as information on the performance and acceptance of the procured work.

Assuming the procured work is acceptable and meets the requirements of the contract, the contract can be closed. The formal closure of a project comes in a written notice from the contract officer to the seller. The notice informs the seller that its work is acceptable and that the contract is considered closed. The formal closure process may vary according to the size of the project. The requirements for contract closeout should be documented within the contract.

CERTIFICATION SUMMARY

Project procurement management allows a project to ascertain resources, materials, equipment, services, and other components needed to successfully complete the project. It is the process of finding sellers that can supply the needed products or services at a fair rate and that meet the quality, time, and cost expectations of the project. The product description will help the project manager and the vendor determine what the best solution is for the procurement need.

One of the first activities the project manager and the project team complete together before procuring products is to determine the need to buy versus the ability to make the product. A decision tree can help the project manager determine which decision is most cost-effective, reliable, and best for the project. A buy-versus-build analysis can compare the benefits of buying versus selling—including attributes other than just price and time.

Bidder conferences allow the bidders to meet with the project managers and other officials representing the seller to confirm the details of the contract statement of work. Recall that the statement of work is provided to all those vendors that may be creating bids or proposals for the seller. The bidders' conference allows the bidders to obtain any additional information they may need to create a full and complete bid, quote, or proposal. It is part of the contracting process and proceeds to source selection.

PMP candidates—and project managers—must be familiar with the different contract types and when to use each one. Here's a recap of the most common contract types:

- **Cost plus fixed fee**   Details the fixed cost of the contract, which includes a profit margin for the seller.
- **Cost plus percentage of cost**   Has a price for the contracted product or service, but cost overruns are assigned to the buyer.
- **Cost plus award fee**   Requires the buyer to pay for all the project costs and give the seller an award fee based on the project performance, meeting

certain project criteria, or meeting other goals established by the buyer. The award fee can be tied to any factor the buyer determines, and the factor doesn't have
to be exact.

- **Cost plus incentive fee**   The seller determines a price for the product or service, but includes an incentive reward for completing the procured work on time or ahead of schedule.

- **Fixed-price**   A simple fixed price for the contract. This can also include incentives for the seller to complete the project early or ahead of schedule, or for other savings shared between the buyer and the seller.

- **Fixed price with economic price adjustment contracts**   Ideal for long-term projects that may span years to complete the project work. The contract does define a fixed price, with caveats for special categories of price fluctuation.

- **Time and materials**   A price is assigned for the time and materials provided by the seller.

KEY TERMS

To pass the PMP exam, you will need to memorize the following terms and their definitions. For maximum value, create flashcards based on these definitions and review them daily. The definitions can be found within this chapter and in the glossary.

bid   A document from the seller to the buyer. Used when price is the determining factor in the decision-making process.

bidder conference   A meeting with prospective sellers to ensure that all sellers have a clear understanding of the product or service to be procured. Bidder conferences allow sellers to query the buyer on the details of the product to help ensure that the proposal the seller creates is adequate and appropriate for the proposed agreement.

centralized contracting   All contracts for all projects need to be approved through a central contracting unit within the performing organization.

contract   A legal, binding agreement, preferably written, between a buyer and the seller detailing the requirements and obligations of both parties. Must include an offer, an acceptance, and a consideration.

contract administration   The process of ensuring that the buyer and the seller both perform to the specifications within the contract.

contract change control system   Defines the procedures for how contracts may be changed. Includes the paperwork, tracking, conditions, dispute resolution procedures, and procedures for getting the changes approved within the performing organization.

contract closeout   A process for confirming that the obligations of the contract were met as expected. The project manager, the customer, the key stakeholder, and, in some instances, the seller complete the product verification together to confirm the contract has been completed.

contract file   A complete indexed set of records of the procurement process incorporated into the administrative closure process. These records include financial information as well as information on the performance and acceptance of the procured work.

cost plus award fee   This contract requires the buyer to pay for all the project costs and give the seller an award fee based on the project performance, meeting certain project criteria, or meeting other goals established by the buyer. The award fee can be tied to any factor the buyer determines, and the factor doesn't have to be exact.

cost-reimbursable contracts   A contract that pays the seller for the product. In the payment to the seller, there is a profit margin of the difference between the actual costs of the product and the sales amount.

direct costs   Costs incurred by the project in order for it to exist. Examples include equipment needed to complete the project work, salaries of the project team, and other expenses tied directly to the project's existence.

evaluation criteria   Used to rate and score proposals from sellers. In some instances, such as a bid or quote, the evaluation criterion is focused just on the price the seller offers. In other instances, such as a proposal, the evaluation criteria can be multiple values: experience, references, certifications, and more.

fixed price with economic price adjustment contract   A contract for long-term projects that may span years to complete the project work. The contract does define a fixed price, with caveats for special categories of price fluctuation.

fixed-price contracts   Fixed-price contracts are also known as firm-fixed-price and lump-sum contracts. These contracts have a preset price that the vendor is obligated to perform the work for or to provide materials for the agreed-upon price.

force majeure   A powerful and unexpected event, such as a hurricane or other disaster.

invitation for bid   A document from the buyer to the seller. Requests the seller to provide a price for the procured product or service.

letter of intent   Expresses the intent of the buyer to procure products or services from the seller. Not equivalent to a contract.

make-or-buy analysis   Used in determining what part of the project scope to make and what part to purchase.

oligopoly   A market condition where the actions of one competitor affect the actions of all the other competitors.

procurement   The process of a seller soliciting, selecting, and paying for products or services from a buyer.

procurement audits   The successes and failures within the procurement process are reviewed from procurement planning through contract administration. The intent of the audit is to learn from what worked and what did not work during the procurement processes.

procurement management plan   This subsidiary project plan documents the decisions made in the procurement planning processes. It specifies how the remaining procurement activities will be managed.

proposal   A document from the seller to the buyer, responding to a request for proposal or other procurement document.

qualified sellers list   The performing organization may have lists of qualified sellers, preferred sellers, or approved sellers. The qualified sellers list generally has contact information, history of past experience with the seller, and other pertinent information.

quote   A document from the seller to the buyer; used when price is the determining factor in the decision-making process.

request for proposal   A document from the buyer to the seller that asks the seller to provide a proposal for completing the procured work or for providing the procured product.

request for quote   A document from the buyer to the seller asking the seller to provide a price for the procured product or service.

should-cost estimates These estimates are created by the performing organization to predict what the cost of the procured product should be. If there is a significant difference between what the organization has predicted and what the sellers have proposed, the statement of work was inadequate or the sellers have misunderstood the requirements or the price is too high.

single source A specific seller that the performing organization prefers to contract with.

sole source The only qualified seller that exists in the marketplace.

statement of work This fully describes the work to be completed, the product to be supplied, or both. The SOW becomes part of the contract between the buyer and the seller. It is typically created as part of the procurement planning process and is used by the seller to determine whether it can meet the project's requirements.

time and materials A contract type where the seller charges the buyer for the time and materials for the work completed. T&M contracts should have a not-to-exceed clause (NTE) to contain costs.

✓ TWO-MINUTE DRILL

Planning for Purchases

❑ Procurement planning is determining which aspects of the project can best be fulfilled by procuring the specified products or services.

❑ The project scope serves as a key input, as this describes the work, and only the required work, needed to complete the project.

❑ A clearly defined product description is needed in order to successfully procure the product.

❑ Make-or-buy analysis calculates and predicts which is better: for the performing organization to make the product or to hire an entity outside of the organization to make the product.

❑ Some contracts can transfer the risk to the seller, while other contract types require the buyer to retain the risk of cost overruns.

Completing Procurement Planning

❑ The procurement management plan describes the procedures for procuring work or products.

❑ Bids and quotes are needed when the decision is made on price. Proposals are needed when decisions are based on other factors, such as experience, qualifications, and approaches to the project work.

❑ The buyer should provide the seller with an SOW, details on the type of response needed—such as a proposal, quote, or bid, and any information on contractual provisions, such as nondisclosure agreements or a copy of the model contract that the buyer intends to use.

Preparing for Contracting

❑ Contracting is requesting the potential sellers to provide bids, proposals, or quotes to complete the project work or supply the described product.

❑ An organization may retain a qualified sellers list from which the project team is forced to select a vendor. In other instances, the project team can rely on trade associations, industry directories, and other resources to locate qualified sellers.

❑ Advertisements for the procurement needs in newspaper and trade publications can increase the list of sellers the buyer can choose from. Many government entities must publish procurement opportunities.

❏ Bidder conferences allow sellers to meet with the buyer to query the buyer on details of the procurement process. The goal of the bidder conference is to ensure that all prospective sellers have the same information and all of the needed information to complete an accurate bid or proposal.

Completing Procurement Purchasing

❏ Samples of the sellers' previous, related products or services can serve as evaluation criteria.

❏ Contract negotiation focuses on finding a fair and reasonable price for both the buyer and the seller.

❏ Weighting systems are unbiased approaches to determine which seller has the best offer to complete the procured product or service.

❏ Screening systems allow an organization to screen out sellers that do not qualify for the procured product or service.

❏ "Should-cost" estimates are completed by the performing organization to determine if sellers completely understand the requirements of the project work.

Performing Contract Administration

❏ Contract administration ensures the sellers are meeting their contractual obligations.

❏ Change requests may require updates to the contract between the buyer and the seller. Contract change requests are part of the integrated change control system.

❏ The project manager must document and report to the seller and management on how the seller is meeting its contract obligations.

Performing Contract Closure

❏ Contract closeout is similar to administrative closure.

❏ Contract documentation—such as the contract, schedules, relevant documentation, approved contract changes, performance reports, and other pertinent information—is needed to complete contract closeout.

❏ Procurement audits are intended to review, document, and share the successes and failures of the current project's procurement process. The information can be applied to other projects within the organization.

❏ A contract file is created and is included with the project records as part of the historical information of the current project.

SELF TEST

1. Which of the following may be used as a risk mitigation tool?
   A. A vendor proposal
   B. A contract
   C. A quotation
   D. Project requirements

2. A contract cannot have provisions for which one of the following?
   A. A deadline for the completion of the work
   B. Illegal activities
   C. Subcontracting the work
   D. Penalties and fines for disclosure of intellectual rights

3. You are the project manager for the 89A Project. You have created a contract for your customer. The contract must have what two things?
   A. An offer and consideration
   B. Signatures and the stamp of a notary public
   C. The value and worth of the procured item
   D. A start date and an acceptance of the start date

4. The WBS and the WBS dictionary can help a project manager plan for purchases and acquisitions. Which one of the following best describes this process?
   A. The WBS defines the specific contracted work.
   B. The WBS defines the requirements for the specific contracted work.
   C. The WBS defines the specific contracted work, which must support the requirements of the project customer.
   D. Both parties must have and retain their own copy of the WBS.

5. Yolanda has outsourced a portion of the project to a vendor. The vendor has discovered some issues that will influence the cost and schedule of its portion of the project. How must the vendor and Yolanda update the agreement?
   A. As a new contract signed by Yolanda and the vendor
   B. By submitting the change request to the contract change control system
   C. As a memo and SOW signed by Yolanda and the vendor
   D. By submitting the change request to the cost change control system

6. The United States backs all contracts through which of the following?
A. Federal law
B. State law
C. Court system
D. Lawyers

7. Terry is the project manager of the MVB Project. She needs to purchase a piece of equipment for her project. The accounting department has informed Terry she needs a unilateral form of contract. Accounting is referring to which of the following?
A. The SOW
B. A legally binding contract
C. A purchase order
D. An invoice from the vendor

8. Bonnie is the project manager for the HGH Construction Project. She has contracted a portion of the project to the ABC Construction Company and has offered a bonus to ABC if they complete their portion of the work by August 30. This is an example of which one of the following?
A. A project requirement
B. A project incentive
C. A project goal
D. A fixed-price contract

9. You are a project manager for your organization and are progressing through the procurement management processes. Who should receive the procurement document package?
A. Your client
B. Your project sponsor
C. Your accounting/finance department
D. Each seller that will participate in the bidding

10. Privity is what?
A. The relationship between the project manager and a known vendor
B. The relationship between the project manager and an unknown vendor
C. The contractual, confidential information between the customer and vendor
D. The professional information regarding the sale between the customer and vendor

11. Sammy is the project manager of the DSA Project. He is considering proposals and contracts presented by vendors for a portion of the project work. Of the following, which contract is least dangerous to the DSA Project?

A. Cost plus fixed fee

B. Cost plus percentage of cost

C. Cost plus incentive fee

D. Fixed-price

12. Of the following contract types, which one requires the seller to assume the risk of cost overruns?

A. Cost plus fixed fee

B. Cost plus incentive fee

C. Lump-sum

D. Time and materials

13. Benji is the project manager of the PLP Project. He has hired an independent contractor for a portion of the project work. The contractor is billing the project $120 per hour, plus materials. This is an example of which one of the following?

A. Cost plus fixed fee

B. Time and materials

C. Unit price

D. Lump-sum

14. Mary is the project manager of the JHG Project. She has created a contract statement of work (SOW) for a vendor. All of the following should be included in the contract SOW except for which one?

A. The items being purchased

B. The signatures of both parties agreeing to the SOW

C. The expected quality levels

D. A description of the collateral services required

15. You are the project manager for a software development project for an accounting system that will operate over the Internet. Based on your research, you have discovered it will cost you $25,000 to write your own code. Once the code is written, you estimate you'll spend $3,000 per month updating the software with client information, government regulations, and maintenance. A vendor has proposed to write the code for your company and charge a fee based on the number of clients using the program every month. The vendor will charge you $5 per month per user of the web-based accounting system. You will have roughly 1,200 clients using the system each month. However, you'll need an in-house accountant to manage the time and billing of the system, so this will cost you an extra $1,200 per month. How many months can you use the system before it's better to write your own code rather than hire the vendor?

   A. 3 months

   B. 4 months

   C. 6 months

   D. 15 months

16. You are the project manager of a project that will span six years in Columbus, Ohio. You are negotiating with your project customer for considerations for inflation, cost of utilities, and other cost factors that will likely fluctuate over the course of the project. What type of project should your project have?

   A. Cost plus award fee

   B. Fixed price with economic price adjustments

   C. Lump-sum

   D. Fixed-price incentive fee

17. A contract between an organization and a vendor may include a clause that penalizes the vendor if the project is late. The lateness of a project has a monetary penalty. Thus, the penalty should be enforced or waived based on which one of the following?

   A. Whether the project manager could have anticipated the delay

   B. Whether the project manager knew the delay was likely

   C. Whether the delay was because of an unseen risk

   D. Who caused the delay and the reason why

18. A single-source seller means what?

   A. There is only one qualified seller.

   B. There is only one seller the company wants to do business with.

   C. There is a seller that can provide all aspects of the project procurement needs.

   D. There is only one seller in the market.

19. Which one of the following is not a valid evaluation criterion for source selection?

   A. The age of the contact person at the seller

   B. The technical capability of the seller

   C. Financial capacity

   D. Price

20. Henry has sent the ABN Contracting Company a letter of intent. This means which one of the following?

   A. Henry intends to sue the ABN Contracting Company.

   B. Henry intends to buy from the ABN Contracting Company.

    C. Henry intends to bid on a job from the ABN Contracting Company.

    D. Henry intends to fire the ABN Contracting Company.

21. Martha is the project manager of the MNB Project. She wants a vendor to offer her one price to do all of the detailed work. Martha is looking for which type of document?

    A. A request for proposal

    B. A request for information

    C. A proposal

    D. An invitation for bid

22. Which one of the following is true about procurement document packages?

    A. They offer no room for bidders to suggest changes.

    B. They ensure the receipt of complete proposals.

    C. They inform the performing organization why the bid is being created.

    D. The project manager creates and selects the bid.

23. In what process group does source selection happen?

    A. Initiating

    B. Planning

    C. Executing

    D. Closing

24. Within your organization, all project managers are required to document the performance quality ratings, delivery performance, and contractual compliance of each vendor they interact with. This is known as what?

    A. A requirement

    B. A seller rating system

    C. Procurement selection

    D. An incentive contract

25. You are the project manager for a seller, but are managing another company's project as well. Things have gone well on the project, and the work is nearly complete. There is still a significant amount of funds in the project budget. The buyer's representative approaches you and asks that you complete some optional requirements to use up the remaining budget. You should do which one of the following?

    A. Negotiate a change in the contract to take on the additional work.

    B. Complete a contract change for the additional work.

    C. Submit the proposed change through the contract change control system.

    D. Deny the change because it was not in the original contract.

SELF TEST ANSWERS

1. Which of the following may be used as a risk mitigation tool?
   A. A vendor proposal
   B. A contract
   C. A quotation
   D. Project requirements

   ☑ **B.** Contracts can be used as a risk mitigation tool. Procurement of risky activities is known as *transference*—the risk does not disappear, but the responsibility for the risk is transferred to the vendor.
   ☒ **A, C,** and **D** are all incorrect. A vendor proposal, a quotation, and project requirements do nothing to serve as a risk mitigation tool.

2. A contract cannot have provisions for which one of the following?
   A. A deadline for the completion of the work
   B. Illegal activities
   C. Subcontracting the work
   D. Penalties and fines for disclosure of intellectual rights

   ☑ **B.** A contract cannot contain illegal activities.
   ☒ **A** is incorrect, since a contract can stipulate a deadline for the project work. **C** is incorrect, since contracts can specify rules for subcontracting the work. **D** is also incorrect, because a contract can assess a penalty and fines for disclosing intellectual rights and secret information.

3. You are the project manager for the 89A Project. You have created a contract for your customer. The contract must have what two things?
   A. An offer and consideration
   B. Signatures and the stamp of a notary public
   C. The value and worth of the procured item
   D. A start date and an acceptance of the start date

   ☑ **A.** Of all the choices presented, **A** is the best. Contracts have an offer and a consideration.
   ☒ **B** is incorrect because not all contracts demand signatures and notary public involvement. **C** is also incorrect. A contract may not explicitly determine what the value and worth of the procured product or service is. **D** is incorrect as well, because a contract may specify a start date, but the acceptance of the start date is vague and not needed for all contracts.

4. The WBS and the WBS dictionary can help a project manager plan for purchases and acquisitions. Which one of the following best describes this process?
   A. The WBS defines the specific contracted work.
   B. The WBS defines the requirements for the specific contracted work.
   C. The WBS defines the specific contracted work, which must support the requirements of the project customer.
   D. Both parties must have and retain their own copy of the WBS.

   ☑ **C.** The WBS defines the details and requirements for acceptance of the project. This information also serves as valuable input to the process of determining what needs to be procured. The WBS defines what the end result of the project will be. When dealing with vendors to procure a portion of the project, the work to be procured must support the requirements of the project's customer.
   ☒ **A** is incorrect because the WBS defines the project scope as a whole, not just the contracted work, which may be just a portion of the project. **B** is incorrect because the WBS does not define the requirements for the contract work. **D** is also incorrect because the vendor likely will not have a copy of the WBS.

5. Yolanda has outsourced a portion of the project to a vendor. The vendor has discovered some issues that will influence the cost and schedule of its portion of the project. How must the vendor and Yolanda update the agreement?
   A. As a new contract signed by Yolanda and the vendor
   B. By submitting the change request to the contract change control system
   C. As a memo and SOW signed by Yolanda and the vendor
   D. By submitting the change request to the cost change control system

   ☑ **B** is the best answer of all the choices presented. Because the question is asking for the vendor to update the agreement, the change should follow the details of the contract change control system.
   ☒ **A**, while feasible, is not the best answer to the question. A new contract does not update the original agreement and may cause delays since the contract may have to be resubmitted, reapproved, and so on. **C** and **D** are not viable answers.

6. The United States backs all contracts through which of the following?
   A. Federal law
   B. State law

C. Court system

D. Lawyers

☑ **C.** All contracts in the United States are backed by the U.S. court systems.

☒ **A, B,** and **D** are not correct answers.

7. Terry is the project manager of the MVB Project. She needs to purchase a piece of equipment for her project. The accounting department has informed Terry she needs a unilateral form of contract. Accounting is referring to which of the following?

A. The SOW

B. A legally binding contract

C. A purchase order

D. An invoice from the vendor

☑ **C.** A unilateral form of a contract is simply a purchase order.

☒ **A, B,** and **D** are all incorrect choices. An SOW is a statement of work. A legally binding contract does not fully answer the question. **D,** an invoice from the vendor, is not what the purchasing department is requesting.

8. Bonnie is the project manager for the HGH Construction Project. She has contracted a portion of the project to the ABC Construction Company and has offered a bonus to ABC if they complete their portion of the work by August 30. This is an example of which one of the following?

A. A project requirement

B. A project incentive

C. A project goal

D. A fixed-price contract

☑ **B.** A bonus to complete the work by August 30 is an incentive.

☒ **A** is incorrect, since the question does not specify August 30 as a deadline. **C** is incorrect because "project goal" does not fully answer the question. **D** is incorrect because the contract details are not disclosed in this question.

9. You are a project manager for your organization and are progressing through the procurement management processes. Who should receive the procurement document package?

A. Your client

B. Your project sponsor

C. Your accounting/finance department

D. Each seller that will participate in the bidding

☑ **D.** Each vendor that participates in the bidding will need to receive the procurement document package.

☒ **A, B,** and **C** are all incorrect because these parties do not need the procurement document package.

10. Privity is what?

A. The relationship between the project manager and a known vendor

B. The relationship between the project manager and an unknown vendor

C. The contractual, confidential information between the customer and the vendor

D. The professional information regarding the sale between the customer and the vendor

☑ **C.** Privity is a confidential agreement between the buyer and the seller.

☒ **A, B,** and **D** are incorrect choices because they do not fully answer the question.

11. Sammy is the project manager of the DSA Project. He is considering proposals and contracts presented by vendors for a portion of the project work. Of the following, which contract is least dangerous to the DSA Project?

A. Cost plus fixed fee

B. Cost plus percentage of cost

C. Cost plus incentive fee

D. Fixed-price

☑ **D.** A fixed-price contract contains the least amount of risk for a project. The seller assumes all of the risk because cost overruns are the seller's responsibility.

☒ **A, B,** and **C** are incorrect because these contract types carry the risk of cost overruns being assumed by the buyer.

12. Of the following contract types, which one requires the seller to assume the risk of cost overruns?

A. Cost plus fixed fee

B. Cost plus incentive fee

C. Lump-sum

D. Time and materials

☑ **C.** A lump sum is a fixed fee to complete the contract; the seller absorbs any cost overruns. ☒ **A** and **B** are incorrect because these contracts require the seller to carry the risk of cost overruns. **D** is incorrect because time and materials contracts require the buyer to pay for cost overruns on the materials and the time invested in the project work.

13. Benji is the project manager of the PLP Project. He has hired an independent contractor for a portion of the project work. The contractor is billing the project $120 per hour, plus materials. This is an example of which one of the following?
    A. Cost plus fixed fee
    B. Time and materials
    C. Unit price
    D. Lump-sum

☑ **B.** The contractor's rate of $120 per hour plus the cost of the materials is an example of a time and materials contract.
☒ **A** is incorrect because a cost plus fixed fee charges the cost of the materials, plus a fixed fee, for the installation or work to complete the contract. **C** is incorrect because a unit price has a set price for each unit installed on the project. **D** is also incorrect because a lump sum does not break down the time and materials.

14. Mary is the project manager of the JHG Project. She has created a contract statement of work (SOW) for a vendor. All of the following should be included in the contract SOW except for which one?
    A. The items being purchased
    B. The signatures of both parties agreeing to the SOW
    C. The expected quality levels
    D. A description of the collateral services required

☑ **B.** An SOW does not need the signature of both parties agreeing to the SOW—that'll be in the contract.
☒ **A, C,** and **D** are incorrect because these things are generally included in the SOW.

15. You are the project manager for a software development project for an accounting system that will operate over the Internet. Based on your research, you have discovered it will cost you $25,000 to write your own code. Once the code is written, you estimate you'll spend $3,000 per month updating the software with client information, government regulations, and maintenance.

A vendor has proposed to write the code for your company and charge a fee based on the number of clients using the program every month. The vendor will charge you $5 per month per user of the web-based accounting system. You will have roughly 1,200 clients using the system each month. However, you'll need an in-house accountant to manage the time and billing of the system, so this will cost you an extra $1,200 per month. How many months can you use the system before it's better to write your own code rather than hire the vendor?

A.   3 months

B.   4 months

C.   6 months

D.   15 months

☑   **C.** The monies invested in the vendor's solution would have paid for your own code in six months. This is calculated by finding your cash outlay for the two solutions: $25,000 for your own code creation and zero cash outlay for the vendor's solution. The monthly cost to maintain your own code is $3,000. The monthly cost of the vendor's solution is $7,200. Subtract your cost of $3,000 from the vendor's cost of $7,200 and this equals $4,200. Divide this number into the cash outlay of $25,000 to create your own code, and you'll come up with 5.95 months. Of all the choices presented, **C,** six months, is the best choice.

☒   **A, B,** and **D** are all incorrect because they do not answer the question.

16.   You are the project manager of a project that will span six years in Columbus, Ohio. You are negotiating with your project customer for considerations for inflation, cost of utilities, and other cost factors that will likely fluctuate over the course of the project. What type of project should your project have?

A.   Cost plus award fee

B.   Fixed price with economic price adjustments

C.   Lump-sum

D.   Fixed-price incentive fee

☑   **B.** Projects that last for several years often use a fixed price with economic price adjustments for cost categories that are likely to increase over the project duration.

☒   **A, C,** and **D** are all incorrect because these choices do not accommodate fluctuations in the contract price for economic variables such as inflation.

17.   A contract between an organization and a vendor may include a clause that penalizes the vendor if the project is late. The lateness of a project has a monetary penalty. Thus, the penalty should be enforced or waived based on which one of the following?

A. Whether the project manager could have anticipated the delay
B. Whether the project manager knew the delay was likely
C. Whether the delay was because of an unseen risk
D. Who caused the delay and the reason why

☑ **D.** The party that caused the delay is typically the party responsible for it. It would not be acceptable for the project manager to willingly cause a delay and then penalize the contractor because the project was late.

☒ **A, B,** and **C** are all incorrect. **D** is the best answer because it answers the question fully.

18. A single-source seller means what?
    A. There is only one qualified seller.
    B. There is only one seller the company wants to do business with.
    C. There is a seller that can provide all aspects of the project procurement needs.
    D. There is only one seller in the market.

☑ **B.** A single-source seller means there is only one seller the company wants to do business with.

☒ **A** describes a "sole source" seller. **C** is incorrect. There may be multiple sellers that can satisfy the project needs. **D** is also incorrect. Just because there is only one seller in the market does not mean the seller can adequately and fully fill the project needs.

19. Which one of the following is not a valid evaluation criterion for source selection?
    A. The age of the contact person at the seller
    B. The technical capability of the seller
    C. Financial capacity
    D. Price

☑ **A.** The age of the contact at the seller should not influence the source selection. The experience of the person doing the work, however, can.

☒ **B, C,** and **D** are all incorrect because financial capacity and price can be valid evaluation criteria.

20. Henry has sent the ABN Contracting Company a letter of intent. This means which one of the following?
    A. Henry intends to sue the ABN Contracting Company.
    B. Henry intends to buy from the ABN Contracting Company.
    C. Henry intends to bid on a job from the ABN Contracting Company.
    D. Henry intends to fire the ABN Contracting Company.

☑ **B.** Henry intends to buy from the ABN Contracting Company.

☒ **A, C,** and **D** are all incorrect. These choices do not adequately describe the purpose of the letter of intent.

21. Martha is the project manager of the MNB Project. She wants a vendor to offer her one price to do all of the detailed work. Martha is looking for which type of document?

A. A request for proposal
B. A request for information
C. A proposal
D. An invitation for bid

☑ **D.** An IFB is typically a request for a sealed document that lists the seller's firm price to complete the detailed work.

☒ **A** and **B** are both documents from the buyer to the seller requesting information about completing the work. **C** does not list the price to complete the work, but instead offers solutions to the buyer for completing the project needs.

22. Which one of the following is true about procurement document packages?

A. They offer no room for bidders to suggest changes.
B. They ensure the receipt of complete proposals.
C. They inform the performing organization why the bid is being created.
D. The project manager creates and selects the bid.

☑ **B.** Procurement document packages detail the requirements for the work to ensure complete proposals from sellers.

☒ **A** is incorrect. Procurement documents allow input from the seller to suggest alternative ways to complete the project work. **C** is incorrect because informing the performing organization on why the bid is being created is not the purpose of the procurement documents. **D** is not realistic.

23. In what process group does source selection happen?

A. Initiating
B. Planning
C. Executing
D. Closing

☑ **C.** Source selection happens during the execution process group.

☒ **A, B,** and **D** are all incorrect because these process groups do not include source selection.

24. Within your organization, all project managers are required to document the performance quality ratings, delivery performance, and contractual compliance of each vendor they interact with. This is known as what?

A. A requirement
B. A seller rating system
C. Procurement selection
D. An incentive contract

☑ **B.** This scenario describes the seller rating system, which can guide future project managers to choose the best vendor based on past performance.

☒ **A** is incorrect because requirements describe the scope of the project or the procured items. **C** is incorrect because this term is not valid. **D** is incorrect because an incentive contract would define the reward or penalties for adhering or failing to adhere to the contract requirements.

25. You are the project manager for a seller, but are managing another company's project as well. Things have gone well on the project, and the work is nearly complete. There is still a significant amount of funds in the project budget. The buyer's representative approaches you and asks that you complete some optional requirements to use up the remaining budget. You should do which one of the following?

A. Negotiate a change in the contract to take on the additional work.
B. Complete a contract change for the additional work.
C. Submit the proposed change through the contract change control system.
D. Deny the change because it was not in the original contract.

☑ **C.** Any additional work is a change in the project scope. Changes to the project scope should be approved by the mechanisms in the change control system. The stakeholder needs to approve the changes to the project scope.

☒ **A, B,** and **D** are not realistic expectations of the project. These questions could fall into the realm of the PMP Code of Ethics and Professional Conduct. Typically, when a project scope has been fulfilled, the project work is done. The difference in this situation is that the additional tasks are optional requirements for the project scope.

13

The PMI Code
of Ethics and
Professional
Conduct

The PMI Code of Ethics and Professional Conduct is the authoritative guide on how all PMI members should behave. In regard to the PMP exam, this PMI document defines how the PMP should act as a professional and how the PMP should behave with customers and the public in general. Thus, the PMP exam candidate will be tested on his knowledge of the PMI Code of Ethics and Professional Conduct, which is really about ethics, fair business dealing, and doing what's fundamentally correct as a project manager.

The code, six pages in length, covers a broad array of do's and don'ts for PMI members. Essentially, the PMP should always take the high road. There should be no room for misconceptions, errors in judgment, or actions that could be interpreted as conflicts of interest, shady, or just plain wrong.

Whenever the PMP is considering doing something that could be seen as wrong, just remember, "When in doubt, don't." The full PMI Code of Ethics and Professional Conduct is available through PMI's website at www.pmi.org, and you'll have to agree to abide by it when you complete and submit your exam application.

The PMP exam covers more than just the PMI Code of Ethics and Professional Conduct in regard to professional responsibility. Many of these topics have been covered in communications and human resources. The four areas of professional responsibility consist of the following:

- Responsibility
- Respect
- Fairness
- Honesty

CERTIFICATION OBJECTIVE 13.01

Responsibilities to the Profession

The PMP must adhere to a high set of principles, rules, and policies. This includes the organizational rules and policies, the certification process, and the advancement of the profession. On the PMP exam, always choose the answer that best supports the PMP profession and the higher set of principles the PMP is expected to adhere to. PMPs are to only accept and manage projects that they're qualified to manage. And as a PMP you're to aspire to goodness not only in business but also in the project decisions that affect society, public safety, and the environment.

Complying with Rules and Policies

Honesty is expected in all areas regarding the PMP examination process, including:

- Exam applications must be honest and reflect actual education and work experience.
- Test items, questions, answers, and scenarios are not to be shared with other PMP candidates.
- PMP renewal information must reflect an honest assessment of education and experience.
- Continuing education information must be honest and accurate; continuing education reporting must reflect actual courses completed.

The PMP should report violations of the PMI Code of Ethics and Professional Conduct when clear and factual evidence of this exists. Based on the scenario, the reporting may be to PMI, to the performing organization's management, or to the proper law enforcement authorities.

The PMP must disclose to clients and customers scenarios where the PMP may be perceived as having an unfair advantage, a conflict of interest, or where they may profit from conditions within the project. Any appearances of impropriety must be avoided and disclosed.

PMP
Coach   *Be wary of the Internet. It's tempting to scour the Web looking for more insight on the PMP exam, but PMPs are not to share exam question specifics with anyone. Furthermore, just because some clown in Boise says it's a real-live test question doesn't make it a real-live test question. While practice questions are nice, I think you'll be better off to study the facts that this book and the* PMBOK Guide *offer you. Study what you know is accurate, not what might be accurate.*

Applying Honesty to the Profession

The PMP candidate is expected, at all times, to provide honesty in experience documentation, the advertisement of skills, and the performance of services. The PMP must, of course, adhere to and abide by all applicable laws governing the project work. In addition, the ethical standards within the trade or industry should also be adhered to.

on the
Job   *Industry standards are recommendations for how the work and practice should be followed, while regulations are requirements for how the work and practice must be followed. A PMP must know the difference.*

Advancing the Profession

The PMP must respect and recognize the intellectual work and property of others. The PMP can't claim others' work as his own. He must give credit where credit is due. Work, research, and development sources must be documented and acknowledged by the PMP when relying on others' work.

INSIDE THE EXAM

The PMI Code of Ethics and Professional Conduct implies many messages to the project management professional (PMP). The responsibility of the PMP centers on honesty and ethics. The PMP may often find herself in scenarios where she can personally profit through the information within a project. For example, a PMP may discover a project is finishing ahead of schedule—but by finishing early, the PMP's contract will be closed and she'll lose income. The PMP must do what's ethically correct and best for the good of the project and project customer.

On the PMP exam, without breaking this very code, the PMP candidate will face many questions on professional conduct. Always, even if you disagree in theory with the outcome of the scenario, choose the moral high ground. The questions you'll face on the exam are extreme circumstances, but they still test knowledge of this code of ethics.

Part of the PMI Code of Ethics and Professional Conduct deals with customs and laws of foreign countries. The PMP must recognize these laws and customs, and understand how to operate within them. The Sapir-Whorf hypothesis believes an understanding of the local language, its implied meaning, and colloquialisms allow individuals to have a deeper understanding of the people, their values, and actions. The theory suggests a linkage between the language a culture speaks and how that culture operates.

The PMP, when operating in countries other than his home country, should consider the practices and customs of the local country before reacting to conditions and scenarios. What may be considered a conflict of interest in one country may be a common practice in another.

Culture shock is the initial disorientation a person first experiences when visiting a country other than his own. Ethnocentrism happens when individuals measure and compare a foreigner's actions against their own local culture. The locals typically believe their own culture is superior to the foreigner's culture.

Another method of advancing the PMP profession is to distribute the PMI Code of Ethics and Professional Conduct to other PMP candidates. You can get your copy for free at www.pmi.org.

CERTIFICATION OBJECTIVE 13.02

Responsibilities to the Customer and to the Public

The PMP also has a responsibility to the customer of the project and the public. Projects that affect internal customers are expected to meet requirements and standards, and fulfill the business need of the performing organization. Essentially, the PMP is working for the customer.

Projects that serve a community and citizens have a responsibility that's somewhat tied to public service. The PMP is held accountable for the work completed for the public—and for the transactions, quality of work, and ethics enforced in the project.

Enforcing Project Management Truth and Honesty

PMPs must represent themselves and their projects truthfully to the general public. This includes statements made in advertising, press releases, and public forums. When project managers are involved in the creation of estimates, truth is also expected. The PMP must provide accurate estimates on time, cost, services to be provided, and realistic outcomes of the project work.

When a project is assigned to the PMP, the project manager has the responsibility to meet the project scope as expected by the customer. PMPs work for the customer and must strive for customer satisfaction while fulfilling the project objectives. As part of the project implementation, the PMP must keep confidential information confidential. There is an obligation to the customer to maintain privacy, confidentiality, and the nondisclosure of sensitive information.

Project managers should play fair. This means that the project manager should remain impartial, make decisions for the good of the project, provide access to information, and treat stakeholders fairly. In procurement, the project manager should make fair decisions and make opportunities equally available to all qualified providers. The project manager doesn't use favoritism in any area of the project and avoids any kind of prejudice, discrimination, or nepotism.

e x a m
w a t c h

While the project manager must be fair to the project stakeholders, there's also a project management requirement of duty of loyalty. Duty of loyalty is the obligation of the project manager to promote the best interest of *the organization that he's employed by. As a representative of an organization, the project manager protects the best interest of the organization first while maintaining a balance of fairness with those outside the organization.*

Eliminating Inappropriate Actions

A PMP must avoid conflicts of interest and scenarios where conflicts of interest could seem apparent, opportunistic, or questionable to the customer or other stakeholders. In addition, the PMP must not accept any inappropriate gifts, inappropriate payments, or any other compensation for favors, project management work, or influence of a project. The exception to this rule is when the laws or customs of the country where the project is being performed call for gifts to the project manager. However, the PMP should be aware of what gifts are acceptable and appropriate within the country where the project is taking place. Lavish gifts outside of the norm should be refused.

Respecting Others

Project managers are to respect the stakeholders and people they work with. This means that the project manager listens to other people and tries to understand what they're saying. If the project manager doesn't understand, ask questions to fully understand. Part of respecting others is to educate ourselves and understand how other cultures operate to avoid offending someone in that culture.

There's little doubt that in project management there will be conflicts with others. When conflicts are happening, it's up to the project manager to approach that person to seek a resolution to the conflict. Conflict resolution should always be in the best interest of the project, not the project manager. The project manager should always negotiate in good faith, treat others professionally, and respect the property rights of others—even if other people don't treat the project manager this way.

CERTIFICATION SUMMARY

The PMI Code of Ethics and Professional Conduct and the professional conduct of a project manager account for 15 questions on the PMP examination. To answer these questions correctly, the PMP candidate should always take the "ethical high road." The questions concerning ethics, conflict of interest, and personal gain are representative of the types of situations project managers can find themselves in on a regular basis. For the PMP exam—and in daily practice—follow the PMI Code of Ethics and Professional Conduct, and you'll do fine.

A project manager must adhere to the laws she is governed by. This means knowing the difference between optional standards and the required regulations. Next, the project manager must follow the policies of the organization she is employed by. This means if the project manager's company has a policy against a certain condition—no matter how small or innocent it may seem—the policy must be followed first. Finally, the project manager must avoid conflicts of interest and any appearance of impropriety.

When a project manager is completing projects in another country, the project manager must be respectful of the laws, people, culture, and values of the country the work is taking place in. Project managers must not succumb to ethnocentrism— the act of believing their own culture is better than everyone else's culture. The project manager must work to understand the culture, traditions, and expectations of the people she is working with in the foreign countries while still complying with the policies of her organization.

KEY TERMS

To pass the PMP exam, you will need to memorize the following terms and their definitions. For maximum value, create your own flashcards based on these definitions and review them daily. The definitions can be found within this chapter and in the glossary.

confidentiality   A project manager should keep certain aspects of a project confidential; consider contract negotiations, human resource issues, and trade secrets of the organization.

conflict of interest   A situation where the project manager could influence a decision for personal gain.

culture shock   The initial reaction a person experiences when in a foreign environment.

ethics   Describes the personal, cultural, and organizational interpretation of right and wrong; project managers are to operate ethically and fairly.

ethnocentrism   Happens when individuals measure and compare a foreigner's actions against their own local culture. The locals typically believe their own culture is superior to the foreigner's culture.

inappropriate compensation   The project manager is to avoid inappropriate compensation, such as bribes. The project manager is to act in the best interest of the project and the organization.

PMI Code of Ethics and Professional Conduct   A PMI document that defines the expectations of its members to act responsibly, respectfully, fairly, and honestly in their leadership of projects and programs.

Sapir-Whorf hypothesis   A theory that suggest there's a linkage between the language a person (or culture) speaks and how that person or culture behaves in the world.

✓ TWO-MINUTE DRILL

Responsibilities to the Profession

- ❏ PMP candidates and professionals must provide accurate and truthful information in all aspects of PMP certification.
- ❏ PMP exam questions and scenarios should not be shared with other PMP candidates.
- ❏ Violations of the PMI Code of Ethics and Professional Conduct should be reported to the proper parties.
- ❏ PMPs must acknowledge and recognize others' work, intellectual property, and development.

Responsibilities to the Customer and to the Public

- ❏ PMPs must comply with all laws, regulations, and ethics in regard to project management practices.
- ❏ PMPs must provide accurate and truthful information to the public and customers when estimating costs, services, and the realistic outcomes of project work.
- ❏ PMPs must keep confidential information confidential.
- ❏ PMPs must avoid conflicts of interest and disclose any perceivable incidences.
- ❏ PMPs must not accept inappropriate compensation or gifts for their project management work.

SELF TEST

1. You are the project manager of the JKN Project. The project customer has requested that you inflate your cost estimates by 25 percent. He reports that his management always reduces the cost of the estimates, so this is the only method to get the monies needed to complete the project. Which of the following is the best response to this situation?

   A. Do as the customer asked to ensure the project requirements can be met by adding the increase as a contingency reserve.

   B. Do as the customer asked to ensure the project requirements can be met by adding the increase across each task.

   C. Do as the customer asked by creating an estimate for the customer's management and another for the actual project implementation.

   D. Complete an accurate estimate of the project. In addition, create a risk assessment on why the project budget would be inadequate.

2. You are the project manager for the BNH Project. This project takes place in a different country than where you are from. The project leader from this country presents a team of workers that are only from his family. You should do which one of the following?

   A. Reject the team leader's recommendations and assemble your own project team.

   B. Review the résumé and qualifications of the proposed project team leader before approving the team.

   C. Determine if the country's traditions include hiring from the immediate family before hiring from outside the family.

   D. Replace the project leader with an impartial project leader.

3. You are about to begin negotiations on a new project that is to take place in another country. Which of the following should be your guide on what business practices are allowed and discouraged?

   A. The project charter

   B. The project plan

   C. Company policies and procedures

   D. The PMI Code of Ethics and Professional Conduct

4. One of your project team members reports that he sold pieces of equipment because he needed the money to pay for his daughter's school tuition. He says he has paid back the money by working overtime without reporting the hours worked so that his theft remains private. What should you do?

   A. Fire the project team member.

   B. Report the team member to his manager.

C. Suggest that the team member report his action to human resources.

D. Tell the team member you're disappointed in what he did, and advise him not to do something like this again.

5. You are the project manager of the SUN Project. Your organization is a functional environment, and you do not get along well with the functional manager leading the project. You are in disagreement with the manager on how the project should proceed, the timings of the activities, the suggested schedule, and the expected quality of the work. The manager has requested that you get to work on several of the activities on the critical path even though you and she have not solved the issues concerning the project. Which of the following should you do?

A. Go to senior management and voice your concerns.

B. Complete the activities as requested.

C. Ask to be taken off the project.

D. Refuse to begin activities on the project until the issues are resolved.

6. PMI has contacted you regarding an ethics violation of a PMP candidate. The question is in regard to a friend who said he worked as project manager under your guidance. You know this is not true, but to save a friendship, you avoid talking with PMI. This is a violation of which of the following?

A. The PMI Code to cooperate on ethics violations investigations

B. The PMI Code to report accurate information

C. The PMI Code to report any PMP violations

D. The law concerning ethical practices

7. You are the project manager for the Log Cabin Project. One of your vendors is completing a large portion of the project. You have heard a rumor that the vendor is losing many of its workers due to labor issues. In light of this information, what should you do?

A. Stop work with the vendor until the labor issues are resolved.

B. Communicate with the vendor in regard to the rumor.

C. Look to secure another vendor to replace the current vendor.

D. Negotiate with the labor union to secure the workers on your project.

8. You are the project manager for the PMH Project. Three vendors have submitted cost estimates for the project. One of the estimates is significantly higher than similar project work in the past. In this scenario, you should do which of the following?

A. Ask the other vendors about the higher estimate from the third vendor.

B. Use the cost estimates from the historical information.

   C. Take the high cost to the vendor to discuss the discrepancy before reviewing the issue with the other vendors.

   D. Ask the vendor that supplied the high estimate for information on how the estimate was prepared.

9. You are the project manager of the LKH Project. This project must be completed within six months, but after two months, the schedule has begun to slip. As of now, the project is one week behind schedule. Based on your findings, you believe you can make some corrective actions and recover the lost time over the next month to get the project back on schedule for its completion date. Management, however, requires weekly status reports on cost and schedule. Which of the following should you do?

   A. Report that the project is one week behind schedule, but will finish on schedule based on cited corrective actions.

   B. Report that the project is on schedule and will finish on schedule.

   C. Report that the project is off schedule by a few days, but will finish on schedule.

   D. Report that the project is running late.

10. As a contracted project manager, you have been assigned a project with a budget of 1.5 million U.S. dollars. The project is scheduled to last seven months, but your most recent EVM report shows that the project will finish ahead of schedule by nearly six weeks. If this happens, you will lose $175,000 in billable time. What should you do?

   A. Bill for the entire 1.5 million dollars since this was the approved budget.

   B. Bill for the 1.5 million dollars by adding additional work at the end of the project.

   C. Report to the customer the project status and completion date.

   D. Report to the customer the project status and completion date, and ask if they'd like to add any additional features to account for the monies not spent.

11. You are the project manager of the PMH Project. You have been contracted to design the placement of several pieces of manufacturing equipment. You have completed the project scope and are ready to pass the work over to the installer. The installer begins to schedule you to help with the installation of the manufacturing equipment. You should:

   A. Help the installer place the equipment according to the design documents

   B. Help the installer place the equipment as the customer sees fit

   C. Refuse to help the installer since the project scope has been completed

   D. Help the installer place the equipment, but insist that the quality control be governed by your design specifications

12. You are the project manager of the 12BA Project. You have completed the project according to the design documents and have met the project scope. The customer agrees that the design document requirements have been met; however, the customer is not pleased with the project deliverables and is demanding additional adjustments be made to complete the project. What is the best way to continue?

    A. Complete the work as the customer has requested.

    B. Complete the work at 1.5 times the billable rate.

    C. Do nothing. The project scope is completed.

    D. Do nothing. Management from the performing organization and the customer's organization will need to determine why the project failed before adding work.

13. You are the project manager of the AAA Project. Due to the nature of the project, much of the work will require overtime between Christmas and New Year's Day. Many of the project team members, however, have requested vacation during that week. What is the best way to continue?

    A. Refuse all vacation requests and require all team members to work.

    B. Only allow vacation requests for those team members who are not needed during that week.

    C. Divide tasks equally among the team members so each works the same amount of time.

    D. Allow team members to volunteer for the overtime work.

14. You are a project manager for your organization. Your project is to install several devices for one of your company's clients. The client has requested that you complete a few small tasks that are not in the project scope. To maintain the relationship with the client, you oblige her request and complete the work without informing your company. This is an example of:

    A. Effective expert judgment

    B. A violation of ethics

    C. Contract change control

    D. Integrated change control

15. You are completing a project for a customer in another country. One of the customs in this country is to honor the project manager of a successful project with a gift. Your company, however, does not allow project managers to accept gifts worth more than 50 dollars from any entity. At the completion of the project, the customer presents you with a new car in a public ceremony. Which of the following should you do?

    A. Accept the car since it is a custom of the country. To refuse it would be an insult to your hosts.

    B. Refuse to accept the car since it would result in a conflict with your organization to accept it.

    C. Accept the car and then return it to the customer in private.

    D. Accept the car and then donate the car to a charity in the customer's name.

16. You have a project team member who is sabotaging your project because he does not agree with it. Which of the following should you do?

A. Fire the project team member.

B. Present the problem to management.

C. Present the problem to management with a solution to remove the team member from the project.

D. Present the problem to management with a demand to fire the project team member.

17. You are the project manager of a project in Asia. You discover that the project leader has hired family members for several lucrative contracts on the project. What should you consider?

A. Cultural issues

B. Ethical issues

C. Organizational issues

D. Political issues

18. Of the following, which one achieves customer satisfaction?

A. Completing the project requirements

B. Maintaining the project cost

C. Maintaining the project schedule

D. Completing the project with the defined quality metrics

19. A PMP has been assigned to manage a project in a foreign country. The disorientation the PMP will likely experience as he gets acclimated to the country is known as:

A. The Sapir-Whorf hypothesis

B. Time dimension

C. Ethnocentrism

D. Culture shock

20. You are the project manager for an information technology project. It has come to your attention that a technical problem has stopped the project work. How should the project manager proceed?

A. Measure the project performance to date and account for the cost of the technical problem.

B. Rebaseline the project performance to account for the technical problem.

C. Work with the project team to develop alternative solutions to the technical problem.

D. Outsource the technical problem to a vendor.

21. A PMP has been assigned to manage a project in a foreign country. What should be done to ensure that the project's success is not hindered by the fact that the project manager is working in a foreign country?

    A. Teach the project manager about the customs and laws of the foreign country.

    B. Find a project manager that is from that country.

    C. Assign the project manager a guide to the foreign country.

    D. Allow the project manager to travel home on weekends.

22. Your company does not allow project managers to accept gifts of any kind from vendors. A friend who you have known for years now works for a vendor that your company may be doing business with. Your friend from the vendor asks you to lunch to discuss an upcoming project, and you accept. When the check arrives at the lunch table, your friend insists on paying. You should:

    A. Allow the friend to buy because you've been friends for years

    B. Allow the friend to buy because lunch isn't really a gift

    C. Don't allow the friend to buy because your company does not allow any gifts from vendors

    D. Insist that you purchase your friend's lunch and your friend buys yours

23. You are a project manager on a construction project. Your project needs an experienced mason to repair and restore an old chimney that the customer wants to keep as part of the project. Your brother, as it happens, is an expert at restoring historical chimneys, and you award the work to him. This is an example of:

    A. Networking

    B. A conflict of interest

    C. Poor procurement

    D. Acceptable practice, because your brother is an expert

24. While studying for your PMP exam, you are invited to participate in a study group. At your first meeting, another attendee announces that he has "real, live questions" from the PMP exam. What should you do?

    A. Examine the questions.

    B. Report the study group to PMI.

    C. Leave the study group.

    D. Ask where the person got the questions so you can report the testing center to PMI.

25. You are a project manager within an organization that completes technical projects for other entities. You have plans to leave your company within the next month to launch your own consulting business, which will compete with your current employer. Your company is currently working on a large proposal for a government contract that your new company could also benefit from. What should you do?

A. Resign from your current job and bid against your employer to get the contract.

B. Decline to participate due to a conflict of interest.

C. Help your employer prepare the proposal.

D. Inform your employer that you will be leaving their company within a month and it would be inappropriate for you to work on the current proposal.

SELF TEST ANSWERS

1. You are the project manager of the JKN Project. The project customer has requested that you inflate your cost estimates by 25 percent. He reports that his management always reduces the cost of the estimates, so this is the only method to get the monies needed to complete the project. Which of the following is the best response to this situation?

A. Do as the customer asked to ensure the project requirements can be met by adding the increase as a contingency reserve.

B. Do as the customer asked to ensure the project requirements can be met by adding the increase across each task.

C. Do as the customer asked by creating an estimate for the customer's management and another for the actual project implementation.

D. Complete an accurate estimate of the project. In addition, create a risk assessment on why the project budget would be inadequate.

☑ **D.** It would be inappropriate to bloat the project costs by 25 percent. A risk assessment describing how the project may fail if the budget is not accurate is most appropriate.

☒ **A, B,** and **C** are all incorrect, since these choices are ethically wrong. The PMP should always provide honest estimates of the project work.

2. You are the project manager for the BNH Project. This project takes place in a different country than where you are from. The project leader from this country presents a team of workers that are only from his family. You should do which one of the following?

A. Reject the team leader's recommendations and assemble your own project team.

B. Review the résumé and qualifications of the proposed project team leader before approving the team.

C. Determine if the country's traditions include hiring from the immediate family before hiring from outside the family.

D. Replace the project leader with an impartial project leader.

☑ **C.** You should first confirm what the local practices and customs call for in regard to hiring family members before others.

☒ **A** and **D** are incorrect since they do not consider the qualifications of the project team leader and the project team. In addition, they do not take into account local customs. **B** is incorrect as well; although it does ponder the qualifications of the project team leader, it does not consider the local customs. The project team leader's ability is not called into question—it is the family members.

3. You are about to begin negotiations on a new project that is to take place in another country. Which of the following should be your guide on what business practices are allowed and discouraged?

   A. The project charter
   B. The project plan
   C. Company policies and procedures
   D. The PMI Code of Ethics and Professional Conduct

   ☑ **C.** The company policies and procedures should guide the project manager regarding the decision he makes in the foreign country.
   ☒ **A** and **B** are incorrect since these documents are essential but usually do not reference allowed business practices. **D** is also incorrect. While the PMP Code of Ethics and Professional Conduct harbors crucial information, the company's policies and procedures are more specific to the project work and requirements.

4. One of your project team members reports that he sold pieces of equipment because he needed the money to pay for his daughter's school tuition. He says he has paid back the money by working overtime without reporting the hours worked so that his theft remains private. What should you do?

   A. Fire the project team member.
   B. Report the team member to his manager.
   C. Suggest that the team member report his action to human resources.
   D. Tell the team member you're disappointed in what he did, and advise him not to do something like this again.

   ☑ **B.** This situation calls for the project team member to be reported to his manager for disciplinary action.
   ☒ **A** is inappropriate because the project manager may not have the authority to fire the project team member. **C** is inappropriate because the project manager must take action to bring the situation to management's attention. **D** is also inappropriate because no formal discipline actions are taken to address the problem.

5. You are the project manager of the SUN Project. Your organization is a functional environment, and you do not get along well with the functional manager leading the project. You are in disagreement with the manager on how the project should proceed, the timings of the activities, the suggested schedule, and the expected quality of the work. The manager has requested that you get to work on several of the activities on the critical path even though you and she have not solved the issues concerning the project. Which of the following should you do?

A. Go to senior management and voice your concerns.

B. Complete the activities as requested.

C. Ask to be taken off the project.

D. Refuse to begin activities on the project until the issues are resolved.

☑ **B.** The project manager must respect the delegation of the functional manager.

☒ **A, C,** and **D** are all inappropriate actions since they do not complete the assigned work the functional manager has delegated to the project manager.

6. PMI has contacted you regarding an ethics violation of a PMP candidate. The question is in regard to a friend who said he worked as project manager under your guidance. You know this is not true, but to save a friendship, you avoid talking with PMI. This is a violation of which of the following?

A. The PMI Code to cooperate on ethics violations investigations

B. The PMI Code to report accurate information

C. The PMI Code to report any PMP violations

D. The law concerning ethical practices

☑ **A.** By avoiding the conversation with PMI in regard to the ethics violation of a friend, you are, yourself, violating the PMI Code of Ethics and Professional Conduct.

☒ **B, C,** and **D** are incorrect answers since they do not fully answer the question.

7. You are the project manager for the Log Cabin Project. One of your vendors is completing a large portion of the project. You have heard a rumor that the vendor is losing many of its workers due to labor issues. In light of this information, what should you do?

A. Stop work with the vendor until the labor issues are resolved.

B. Communicate with the vendor in regard to the rumor.

C. Look to secure another vendor to replace the current vendor.

D. Negotiate with the labor union to secure the workers on your project.

☑ **B.** The project manager should confront the problem by talking with the vendor about the rumor.

☒ **A** is incorrect and would delay the project and possibly cause future problems. **C** is incorrect and may violate the contract between the buyer and the seller. **D** is also incorrect—the agreement is between the vendor and the performing organization, not the labor union.

8. You are the project manager for the PMH Project. Three vendors have submitted cost estimates for the project. One of the estimates is significantly higher than similar project work in the past. In this scenario, you should do which of the following?

   A. Ask the other vendors about the higher estimate from the third vendor.

   B. Use the cost estimates from the historical information.

   C. Take the high cost to the vendor to discuss the discrepancy before reviewing the issue with the other vendors.

   D. Ask the vendor that supplied the high estimate for information on how the estimate was prepared.

   ☑ **D.** Most likely, the vendor did not understand the project work to be procured, so the estimate is skewed. A clear statement of work is needed for the vendors to provide accurate estimates.

   ☒ **A, B,** and **C** are all inappropriate actions since they discuss another vendor's estimate. This information should be kept confidential between the buyer and the seller. In some government projects, the winning bid may be required to be released.

9. You are the project manager of the LKH Project. This project must be completed within six months, but after two months, the schedule has begun to slip. As of now, the project is one week behind schedule. Based on your findings, you believe you can make some corrective actions and recover the lost time over the next month to get the project back on schedule for its completion date. Management, however, requires weekly status reports on cost and schedule. Which of the following should you do?

   A. Report that the project is one week behind schedule, but will finish on schedule based on cited corrective actions.

   B. Report that the project is on schedule and will finish on schedule.

   C. Report that the project is off schedule by a few days, but will finish on schedule.

   D. Report that the project is running late.

   ☑ **A.** The project manager should report an honest assessment of the project with actions on how he plans to correct the problem.

   ☒ **B** is incorrect because it does not provide an honest answer to management. **C** is also incorrect because it does not provide an honest answer to management. **D** is incorrect because it does not provide a solution to the problem.

10. As a contracted project manager, you have been assigned a project with a budget of 1.5 million U.S. dollars. The project is scheduled to last seven months, but your most recent EVM report shows that the project will finish ahead of schedule by nearly six weeks. If this happens, you will lose $175,000 in billable time. What should you do?

A. Bill for the entire 1.5 million dollars since this was the approved budget.

B. Bill for the 1.5 million dollars by adding additional work at the end of the project.

C. Report to the customer the project status and completion date.

D. Report to the customer the project status and completion date, and ask if they'd like to add any additional features to account for the monies not spent.

☑ **C.** An honest and accurate assessment of the project work is always required.

☒ **A** and **B** are incorrect because these actions do not reflect an honest assessment of the work. **D** is incorrect because it offers gold plating and recommends additional changes that were not part of the original project scope. In addition, because this is a contracted relationship, the additional work may not be covered within the original project contract and may result in legal issues.

11. You are the project manager of the PMH Project. You have been contracted to design the placement of several pieces of manufacturing equipment. You have completed the project scope and are ready to pass the work over to the installer. The installer begins to schedule you to help with the installation of the manufacturing equipment. You should:

A. Help the installer place the equipment according to the design documents

B. Help the installer place the equipment as the customer sees fit

C. Refuse to help the installer since the project scope has been completed

D. Help the installer place the equipment, but insist that the quality control be governed by your design specifications

☑ **C.** When the project scope is completed, the contract is fulfilled and the project is done. Any new work items should be sent through the proper channels within an organization to create a new project or work order. In this instance, the contract change control system should be used or a new contract should be created.

☒ **A, B,** and **D** are incorrect because these choices are outside of the scope and have not been covered in the contract.

12. You are the project manager of the 12BA Project. You have completed the project according to the design documents and have met the project scope. The customer agrees that the design document requirements have been met; however, the customer is not pleased with the project deliverables and is demanding additional adjustments be made to complete the project. What is the best way to continue?

A. Complete the work as the customer has requested.

B. Complete the work at 1.5 times the billable rate.

C. Do nothing. The project scope is completed.

D. Do nothing. Management from the performing organization and the customer's organization will need to determine why the project failed before adding work.

☑ **C.** When the project scope has been completed, the project is completed. Any additional work, without a contract change or new contract, would be dishonest and would betray the customer or the project manager's company.

☒ **A** and **B** are both incorrect. Additional work is not covered in the current contract. **D** is incorrect because the project did not fail—the deliverables met the requirements of the project scope and the design document.

13. You are the project manager of the AAA Project. Due to the nature of the project, much of the work will require overtime between Christmas and New Year's Day. Many of the project team members, however, have requested vacation during that week. What is the best way to continue?

A. Refuse all vacation requests and require all team members to work.

B. Only allow vacation requests for those team members who are not needed during that week.

C. Divide tasks equally among the team members so each works the same amount of time.

D. Allow team members to volunteer for the overtime work.

☑ **D** is the best choice for this scenario because it allows the project team to be self-led and is sensitive to the needs of the project team.

☒ **A, B,** and **C** are all autocratic responses to the problem, and while the results may seem fair, **D** is the best choice.

14. You are a project manager for your organization. Your project is to install several devices for one of your company's clients. The client has requested that you complete a few small tasks that are not in the project scope. To maintain the relationship with the client, you oblige her request and complete the work without informing your company. This is an example of:

A. Effective expert judgment

B. A violation of ethics

C. Contract change control

D. Integrated change control

☑ **B.** When the project manager completes activities outside of the contract and does not inform the performing organization, it is essentially the same as stealing. The PMP must be held accountable for all the time invested in a project.

☒ **A** is incorrect. This is not expert judgment. **C** is incorrect because the contract has not been changed or attempted to be changed. **D** is also incorrect. The changes the project manager completed for the customer were not sent through any change control system, but were completed without documentation or reporting.

15. You are completing a project for a customer in another country. One of the customs in this country is to honor the project manager of a successful project with a gift. Your company, however, does not allow project managers to accept gifts worth more than 50 dollars from any entity. At the completion of the project, the customer presents you with a new car in a public ceremony. Which of the following should you do?

A. Accept the car since it is a custom of the country. To refuse it would be an insult to your hosts.

B. Refuse to accept the car since it would result in a conflict with your organization to accept it.

C. Accept the car and then return it to the customer in private.

D. Accept the car and then donate the car to a charity in the customer's name.

☑ **B** is the best answer. Although this solution may seem extreme, it is the best answer because to accept the car in public would give the impression that the project manager has defied company policy. In addition, accepting the car would appear to be a conflict of interest for the project manager.

☒ **A, C,** and **D** are all incorrect. Accepting the car, even with the intention of returning it or donating it to charity, would be in conflict with the company's policies regarding the acceptance of gifts.

16. You have a project team member who is sabotaging your project because he does not agree with it. Which of the following should you do?

A. Fire the project team member.

B. Present the problem to management.

C. Present the problem to management with a solution to remove the team member from the project.

D. Present the problem to management with a demand to fire the project team member.

☑ **C.** The project team member who is causing the problems should be presented to management with a solution to remove the project team member from the project. Remember, whenever the project manager must present a problem to management, he should also present a solution to the problem.

☒ **A** is incorrect because it likely is not the project manager's role to fire the project team member. **B** is incorrect because it does not address a solution to the problem. Never go to management with a problem unless a proposed solution is also presented. **D** is incorrect because the project manager's focus should be on the success of the project. By recommending that the project team member be removed from the project, the problem is solved from the project manager's point of view. Management, however, may come to the decision on their own accord to dismiss the individual from the company altogether. In addition, a recommendation from the project manager to fire someone may be outside the boundary of the human resource procedure for employee termination.

17. You are the project manager of a project in Asia. You discover that the project leader has hired family members for several lucrative contracts on the project. What should you consider?

A. Cultural issues

B. Ethical issues

C. Organizational issues

D. Political issues

☑ **A.** The project manager should first determine what the country's customs and culture call for when hiring relatives. It may be a preferred practice in the country to work with qualified relatives first before hiring other individuals to complete the project work.

☒ **B, C,** and **D** are not the best choices in this scenario. They may be followed up by first examining the cultural issues within the country.

18. Of the following, which one achieves customer satisfaction?

A. Completing the project requirements

B. Maintaining the project cost

C. Maintaining the project schedule

D. Completing the project with the defined quality metrics

☑ **A.** The largest factor when it comes to customer satisfaction is the ability to complete the project requirements.

☒ **B, C,** and **D** are incorrect because achieving these factors, while good, is not as complete as achieving the project requirements, which may include the cost, schedule, and quality expectations.

19. A PMP has been assigned to manage a project in a foreign country. The disorientation the PMP will likely experience as he gets acclimated to the country is known as:

    A. The Sapir-Whorf hypothesis
    B. Time dimension
    C. Ethnocentrism
    D. Culture shock

    ☑ **D.** Culture shock is the typical disorientation a person feels when visiting a foreign country.
    ☒ **A** is incorrect. The Sapir-Whorf hypothesis states that an individual can understand a culture by understanding its language. **B** is incorrect. Time dimension is the local culture's general practice for respecting time and punctuality. **C** is also incorrect. Ethnocentrism is the belief by individuals that their own culture is the best and that all other cultures should be measured against it.

20. You are the project manager for an information technology project. It has come to your attention that a technical problem has stopped the project work. How should the project manager proceed?

    A. Measure the project performance to date and account for the cost of the technical problem.
    B. Rebaseline the project performance to account for the technical problem.
    C. Work with the project team to develop alternative solutions to the technical problem.
    D. Outsource the technical problem to a vendor.

    ☑ **C.** When problems arise that stop project tasks, the project manager should work with the team to uncover viable alternative solutions.
    ☒ **A** and **B** do nothing to find a solution to the problem, so they are incorrect. **D** is incorrect because the solution for the problem has not necessarily been addressed. The end result of **C**, to find an alternative solution, may be **D**, but outsourcing the problem to a vendor should not be the first choice in this scenario.

21. A PMP has been assigned to manage a project in a foreign country. What should be done to ensure that the project's success is not hindered by the fact that the project manager is working in a foreign country?

    A. Teach the project manager about the customs and laws of the foreign country.
    B. Find a project manager that is from that country.
    C. Assign the project manager a guide to the foreign country.
    D. Allow the project manager to travel home on weekends.

☑ **A.** Training the project manager on the laws and customs of the foreign country is the best choice to ensure the project's success is not jeopardized.

☒ **B, C,** and **D** may all work, but they are not the best option, considering that the project manager has already been selected and needs to be educated about the foreign country's customs. **D** is incorrect because the travel option does not take into consideration the customs of the foreign country.

22. Your company does not allow project managers to accept gifts of any kind from vendors. A friend who you have known for years now works for a vendor that your company may be doing business with. Your friend from the vendor asks you to lunch to discuss an upcoming project, and you accept. When the check arrives at the lunch table, your friend insists on paying. You should:

A. Allow the friend to buy because you've been friends for years

B. Allow the friend to buy because lunch isn't really a gift

C. Don't allow the friend to buy because your company does not allow any gifts from vendors

D. Insist that you purchase your friend's lunch and your friend buys yours

☑ **C** is the best choice. Although you have been friends for years, the friend is now working with a vendor, and it would be inappropriate for the friend to purchase lunch. This would clearly be a violation of your company's policies because you and your friend are discussing an upcoming project.

☒ **A, B,** and **D** are all incorrect because you would be allowing your friend to purchase your lunch, and this is against company policies.

23. You are a project manager on a construction project. Your project needs an experienced mason to repair and restore an old chimney that the customer wants to keep as part of the project. Your brother, as it happens, is an expert at restoring historical chimneys, and you award the work to him. This is an example of:

A. Networking

B. A conflict of interest

C. Poor procurement

D. Acceptable practice, because your brother is an expert

☑ **B.** This is a conflict of interest—or may appear to be a conflict of interest to others on the project. There are several things the project manager can do in this scenario: excuse himself from the decision because of the relationship with the brother, create a weighted scoring model, allow several vendors to participate, and so on.

☒ **A, C,** and **D** are all incorrect, because these choices do not address the potential for the conflict of interest.

24. While studying for your PMP exam, you are invited to participate in a study group. At your first meeting, another attendee announces that he has "real, live questions" from the PMP exam. What should you do?

A. Examine the questions.

B. Report the study group to PMI.

C. Leave the study group.

D. Ask where the person got the questions so you can report the testing center to PMI.

☑ **C** is the best choice. You should not participate in the study group.

☒ **A** is incorrect, as it clearly violates the PMI Code of Ethics and Professional Conduct. **B** and **D** are not good choices because there isn't any clear evidence that the questions are genuine. The questions may have been purchased through a website or other entity—not necessarily through a testing center.

25. You are a project manager within an organization that completes technical projects for other entities. You have plans to leave your company within the next month to launch your own consulting business, which will compete with your current employer. Your company is currently working on a large proposal for a government contract that your new company could also benefit from. What should you do?

A. Resign from your current job and bid against your employer to get the contract.

B. Decline to participate due to a conflict of interest.

C. Help your employer prepare the proposal.

D. Inform your employer that you will be leaving their company within a month and it would be inappropriate for you to work on the current proposal.

☑ **D.** Of the choices presented, this is the best answer. You should inform your employer of your intent to leave the organization and work on similar projects to avoid a conflict of interest.

☒ **A** is incorrect because you would have a conflict of interest, information gained about your current employer's proposal (such as price and methods), and other advantages that would be ethically wrong. **B** is incorrect because there is no rationale behind what the conflict of interest may be. **C** is incorrect because a conflict of interest exists by preparing the proposal for your future competition.

Part III

Appendices

A

About the CD

The CD-ROM included with this book comes complete with MasterExam, an electronic version of the book, and Session #1 of LearnKey's Online Training. The software is easy to install on any Windows 2000/XP/Vista computer and must be installed to access the MasterExam feature. You may, however, browse the electronic book and the PMP video training directly from the CD without installation. To register for LearnKey's Online Training or the bonus MasterExam, simply click the Bonus MasterExam link on the main launch page and follow the directions to the free online registration.

System Requirements

Software requires Windows 2000 or higher, Internet Explorer 6.0 or above, and 20 MB of hard disk space for full installation. The Electronic book requires Adobe Reader. To access the Online Training from LearnKey, you must have Windows Media Player 9 or higher and Adobe Flash Player 9 or higher.

LearnKey Online Training

The LearnKey Online Training link will allow you to access online training from Osborne.OnlineExpert.com. The first session of this course is provided at no charge. Additional sessions for this course and other courses may be purchased directly from www.LearnKey.com or by calling 800-865-0165.

The first time that you click the LearnKey Online Training link, you will be required to complete a free online registration. Follow the instructions for a first-time user. Please make sure to use a valid e-mail address.

Installing and Running MasterExam

If your computer CD-ROM drive is configured to auto run, the CD-ROM will automatically start up upon inserting the disc. From the opening screen you may install MasterExam by clicking the MasterExam link. This will begin the installation process and create a program group named LearnKey. To run MasterExam, use Start | All Programs | LearnKey | MasterExam. If the auto run feature does not launch your CD, browse to the CD and click on the LaunchTraining.exe icon.

MasterExam

MasterExam provides you with a simulation of the actual exam. The number of questions, the type of questions, and the time allowed are intended to be an accurate representation of the exam environment. You have the option to take an open book exam, including hints, references, and answers; a closed book exam; or the timed MasterExam simulation.

When you launch MasterExam, a digital clock display will appear in the bottom-right corner of your screen. The clock will continue to count down to zero unless you choose to end the exam before the time expires. There are three exams included on the CD:

- A 200-question PMP-specific practice exam
- A 200-question bonus online PMP-specific practice exam
- A 200 question practice exam just on the project management processes

PMP Video Training

PMP video training clips on the CD provide detailed examples of key certification objectives in audio video format direct from the author of the book. These clips walk you step-by-step through various certification objectives. You can access the clips directly from the video's table of contents by clicking the videos link on the main launch page.

The PMP video training clips are recorded and produced using Adobe Flash. You can download the most recent Adobe Flash player free of charge from www.adobe.com.

Electronic Book

The entire contents of the Study Guide are provided in PDF. Adobe Reader has been included on the CD.

Help

A help file is provided through the help button on the main page in the lower-left corner. Individual help features are also available through MasterExam and LearnKey's Online Training.

Removing Installation(s)

MasterExam is installed to your hard drive. For best results removing programs, use the Start | All Programs | LearnKey | Uninstall option to remove MasterExam.

Technical Support

For questions regarding the content of the electronic book, MasterExam, or PMP video training, please visit www.mhprofessional.com or e-mail customer.service@mcgraw-hill.com. For customers outside the 50 United States, e-mail international_cs@mcgraw-hill.com.

LearnKey Technical Support

For technical problems with the software (installation, operation, removing installations), and for questions regarding LearnKey Online Training content, please visit www.learnkey.com, e-mail techsupport@learnkey.com, or call toll free at 1-800-482-8244.

B

Critical Exam
Information

Exam candidates want to pass their PMP exam on the first attempt. Why bother sitting for an exam if you know you're not prepared? In this appendix, you'll find the details that you must know to pass the exam. These facts won't be everything you need to know to pass the PMP exam—but you can bet you won't pass the exam if you do not know the critical information in this appendix.

Exam Test-Passing Tips

For starters, don't think of this process as preparing to take an exam, but think of it as "preparing to pass an exam." Anyone can prepare to take an exam: just show up. Preparing to pass the PMP exam requires project management experience, diligence, and a commitment to study.

Days Before the Exam

In the days leading up to your scheduled exam, here are some basics you should do to prepare yourself for success:

- **Get some moderate exercise**   Find time to go for a jog, lift weights, take a swim, or do whatever workout routine works best for you.
- **Eat smart and healthy**   If you eat healthy food, you'll feel good—and feel better about yourself. Be certain to drink plenty of water, and don't overdo the caffeine.
- **Get your sleep**   A well-rested brain is a sharp brain. You don't want to sit for your exam feeling tired, sluggish, and worn-out.
- **Time your study sessions**   Don't overdo your study sessions—long, crash study sessions aren't that profitable. In addition, try to study at the same time every day at the time your exam is scheduled.

Practice the Testing Process

If you could take one page of notes into the exam, what information would you like on this one-page document? Of course you absolutely cannot take any notes or reference materials into the exam area. However, if you can create and memorize one sheet of notes, you absolutely may re-create this once you're seated in the exam area.

Practice creating a reference sheet so you can immediately, and legally, re-create this document once your exam has begun. You'll be supplied with several sheets of blank paper and a couple of pencils. Once your exam process begins, re-create your reference sheet. The following are key pieces of information you'd be wise to include on your reference sheet (you'll find all of this key information in this appendix):

- Activities within each process group
- Estimating formulas
- Communication formula
- Normal distribution values
- Earned value management formulas
- Project management theories

Testing Tips

The questions on the PMP exam are fairly direct and not too verbose, but they may offer a few red herrings. For example, you may face questions that state, "All of the following are correct options expect for which one?" The question wants you to find the incorrect option, or the option that would not be appropriate for the scenario described. Be sure to understand what the question is asking for. It's easy to focus on the scenario presented in a question and then see a suitable option for that scenario in the answer. The trouble is that if the question is asking you to identify an option that is not suitable, you just missed the question. Carefully read the question to understand what is expected for an answer.

Here's a tip that can work with many of the questions: Identify what the question wants for an answer and then look for an option that doesn't belong with the other possible answers. In other words, find the answer that doesn't fit with the other three options. Find the "odd man out." Here's an example:
EVM is used during the _____.

    A. Controlling phase

    B. Executing phase

    C. Closing phase

    D. Entire project

Notice how options A, B, and C are exclusive? If you choose A, the controlling phase, it implies that EVM is not used anywhere else in the project. The odd man out here is D, the entire project; it's considered the "odd" choice because it, by itself, is not an actual process group. Of course, this tip won't work with every question—but it's handy to keep in mind.

For some answer choices, it may seem like two of the four options are both possible correct answers. However, because you may only choose one answer, you must discern which answer is the best choice. Within the question, there will usually be some hint describing the progress of the project, the requirements of the stakeholders, or some other clue that can help you determine which answer is the best for the question.

Answer Every Question—Once

The PMP exam has 200 questions—of which 175 are "real questions"—you don't have to answer every question correctly, just enough to pass. In other words, don't waste three of your four hours laboring over one question—the hard questions are worth just as much as the easy ones. And you know, I'm sure, that you never leave any question blank—even if you don't know the answer to the question. A blank question is the same as a wrong answer. As you move through the exam and you find questions that stump you, use the "mark question" option in the exam software, choose an answer you suspect may be correct, and then move on. When you have answered all of the questions, you are given the option to review your marked answers.

Some questions in the exam may prompt your memory to come up with answers to questions you have marked for review. However, resist the temptation to review those questions you've already answered with confidence and haven't marked. More often than not, your first instinct is the correct choice. When you completed the exams at the end of each chapter, did you change correct answers to wrong answers? If you did in practice, you'll do it on the actual exam.

Use the Process of Elimination

When you're stumped on a question, use the process of elimination. For each question, there'll be four choices. On your scratch paper, write down "ABCD." If you can safely rule out "A," cross it out of the ABCD you've written on your paper. Now focus on which of the other answers won't work. If you determine that "C" won't work, cross it off your list. Now you've got a 50-50 chance of finding the correct choice.

If you cannot determine which answer is best, "B" or "D" in this instance, here's the best approach:

1. Choose an answer in the exam (no blank answers, remember?).
2. Mark the question in the exam software for later review.

3. Circle the "ABCD" on your scratch paper, jot any relevant notes, and then record the question number next to the notes.

4. During the review, or from a later question, you may realize which choice is the better of the two answers. Return to the question and confirm that the best answer is selected.

Everything You Must Know

As promised, this section covers all of the information you must know going into the exam. It's highly recommended that you create a method to recall this information. Here goes.

The 42 Project Management Processes

Table B-1 lists the 42 project management processes you should be familiar with. I've ordered them here according to knowledge area and the corresponding chapter in this book.

TABLE B-1   Project Management Processes

Knowledge Area	Number of Processes	Processes	Chapter
Project Integration Management	6	Develop project charter Develop project management plan Direct and manage project execution Monitor and control the project work Perform integrated change control Close project or phase	4
Project Scope Management	5	Collect requirements Define scope Create WBS Verify scope Control scope	5

(Continued)

TABLE B-1 Project Management Processes (*Continued*)

Knowledge Area	Number of Processes	Processes	Chapter
Project Time Management	6	Define activities Sequence activities Estimate activity resources Estimate activity durations Develop schedule Control schedule	6
Project Cost Management	3	Estimate costs Determine budget Control costs	7
Project Quality Management	3	Plan quality Perform quality assurance Perform quality control	8
Project HR Management	4	Develop human resources plan Acquire project team Develop project team Manage project team	9
Project Communications Management	5	Identify stakeholders Plan communications Distribute information Manage stakeholder expectations Report performance	10
Project Risk Management	6	Plan risk management Identify risks Perform qualitative risk analysis Perform quantitative risk analysis Plan risk responses Monitor and control risks	11
Project Procurement Management	4	Plan procurements Conduct procurements Administer procurements Close procurements	12

Magic PMP Formulas

The following shows the major formulas you should know for the exam.

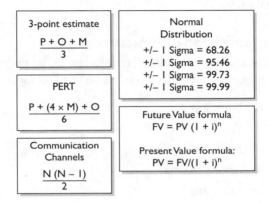

3-point estimate
$\dfrac{P + O + M}{3}$

PERT
$\dfrac{P + (4 \times M) + O}{6}$

Communication Channels
$\dfrac{N(N-1)}{2}$

Normal Distribution
+/– 1 Sigma = 68.26
+/– 1 Sigma = 95.46
+/– 1 Sigma = 99.73
+/– 1 Sigma = 99.99

Future Value formula
$FV = PV (1 + i)^n$
Present Value formula:
$PV = FV/(1 + i)^n$

Earned Value Management Formulas

Table B-2 shows the EVM formulas you should know for the exam.

TABLE B-2

Project Management Earned Value Management Formulas

Name	Formula	Sample Mnemonic Device
Planned Value	PV = % complete where the project should be	Please
Earned Value	EV = % complete × BAC	Eat
Cost Variance	CV = EV – AC	Carl's
Schedule Variance	SV = EV – PV	Sugar
Cost Performance Index	CPI = EV / AC	Candy
Schedule Performance Index	SPI = EV / PV	S (This and the following two spell "SEE")
Estimate at Completion	EAC = BAC / CPI	E
Estimate to Complete	ETC = EAC – AC	E
To-complete performance index (BAC)	(BAC – EV) / (BAC – AC)	The
To-complete performance index (EAC)	(BAC – EV) / (EAC – AC)	Taffy
Variance at Completion	VAC = BAC – EAC	Violin

Quick PMP Facts

This section has some quick facts you should know at a glance. Hold on, this moves pretty fast.

Organizational Structures

Organizational structures are relevant to the project manager's authority. A project manager has authority from weakest to highest in the following order:

- Functional
- Weak matrix
- Balanced matrix
- Strong matrix
- Projectized

WBS Facts

The work breakdown structure is the big picture of the project deliverables: It is not the activities that will create the project, but the components the project will create. The WBS helps the project team and the project manager create accurate cost and time estimates. The WBS also helps the project team and the project manager create an accurate activity list. The WBS is an input to five planning processes.

- Cost estimating
- Cost budgeting
- Resource planning
- Risk management planning
- Activity definition

Project Scope Facts

Projects are temporary endeavors to create a unique product. They are selected by one of two methods.

- **Benefit measurement methods**   These include scoring models, cost-benefit ratios, and economic models.
- **Constrained optimization**   These include mathematical models based on linear, integer, and dynamic programming. (This probably won't be on the PMP exam as a viable answer.)

The project scope defines all of the required work, and only the required work, to complete the project. Scope management is the process of ensuring that the project work is within scope and protecting the project from scope creep. The scope statement, along with the WBS and WBS dictionary, is the baseline for all future project decisions. There are two types of scope.

- **Product scope**   Defines the attributes of the product or service the project is creating
- **Project scope**   Defines the required work of the project to create the product

Scope verification is the process completed at the end of each phase and of each project to confirm that the project has met the requirements. It leads to formal acceptance of the project deliverable.

Project Time Facts

Time can be a project constraint. Effective time management is the scheduling and sequencing of activities in the best order to ensure that the project completes successfully and in a reasonable amount of time. These are some key terms for time management.

- **Lag**   Waiting between activities
- **Lead**   Activities come closer together and even overlap
- **Free float**   The amount of time an activity can be delayed without delaying the next scheduled activity's start date
- **Total float**   The amount of time an activity can be delayed without delaying the project's finish date
- **Float**   Sometimes called *slack*—a perfectly acceptable synonym
- **Duration**   May be abbreviated as "du." For example, du = 8d means the duration is eight days.

There are three types of dependencies between activities.

- **Mandatory**   This hard logic requires a specific sequence between activities.
- **Discretionary**   This soft logic prefers a sequence between activities.
- **External**   Due to conditions outside of the project, such as those created by vendors, the sequence must happen in a given order.

Project Cost Facts

There are several methods of providing project estimates.

- **Bottom-up** Project costs start at zero, each component in the WBS is estimated for costs, and then the "grand total" is calculated. This is the longest method to complete, but provides the most accurate estimate.
- **Analogous** Project costs are based on a similar project. This is a form of expert judgment, but it is also a top-down estimating approach, so it is less accurate than a bottom-up estimate.
- **Parametric Modeling** Price is based on cost per unit; examples include cost per metric ton, cost per yard, and cost per hour.

There are four types of costs attributed to a project.

- **Variable costs** The costs are dependent on other variables. For example, the cost of a food-catered event depends on how many people register to attend the event.
- **Fixed costs** The cost remains constant throughout the project. For example, a rented piece of equipment has the same fee each month, even if it is used more in some months than in others.
- **Direct costs** The cost is directly attributed to an individual project and cannot be shared with other projects (for example, airfare to attend project meetings, hotel expenses, and leased equipment that is used only on the current project).
- **Indirect costs** These are the costs of doing business; examples include rent, phone, and utilities.

Quality Management Facts

The cost of quality is the money spent investing in training, in meeting requirements for safety and other laws and regulations, and in taking steps to ensure quality acceptance. The cost of nonconformance is the cost associated with rework, downtime, lost sales, and waste of materials.

Some common quality management charts and methods include the following:

- *Ishikawa diagrams* (also called *fishbone diagrams*) are used to find causes and effects that contribute to a problem.

- *Flow charts* show the relationship between components and the flow of a process through a system.

- *Pareto diagrams* identify project problems and their frequencies. These are based on the 80/20 rule: 80 percent of project problems stem from 20 percent of the work.

- *Control charts* plot out the result of samplings to determine if projects are "in control" or "out of control."

- *Kaizen technologies* comprise approaches to make small improvements in an effort to reduce costs and achieve consistency.

- *Just-in-time* ordering reduces the cost of inventory, but requires additional quality because materials would not be readily available if mistakes occur.

Human Resource Facts

There are several human resource theories the PMP candidate should be familiar with on the PMP exam. They are the following:

- **Maslow's Hierarchy of Needs**   There are five layers of needs for all humans: physiological, safety, social (such as love and friendship), self-esteem, and the crowning jewel, self-actualization.

- **McClelland's Theory of Needs**   Needs are developed by the person's life experiences, and may shift over time. Of the three needs that drive people—power, affiliation, and achievement—one of these is the most prominent. McClelland developed the Thematic Apperception Test to determine what needs are driving individuals.

- **Herzberg's Theory of Motivation**   There are two catalysts for workers: hygiene agents and motivating agents.

  - **Hygiene agents**   These do nothing to motivate, but their absence demotivates workers. Hygiene agents are the expectations all workers have: job security, a paycheck, clean and safe working conditions, a sense of belonging, civil working relationships, and other basic attributes associated with employment.

  - **Motivating agents**   These are the elements that motivate people to excel. They include responsibility, appreciation of work, recognition, opportunity to excel, education, and other opportunities associated with work other than just financial rewards.

- **McGregor's Theory of X and Y**   This theory states that "X" people are lazy, don't want to work, and need to be micromanaged and that "Y" people are self-led, motivated, and can accomplish things on their own.
- **Ouchi's Theory Z**   This theory holds that workers are motivated by a sense of commitment, opportunity, and advancement. Workers will work if they are challenged and motivated. Think participative management.
- **Expectancy Theory**   People will behave based on what they expect as a result of their behavior. In other words, people will work in relation to the expected reward of the work.

Communication Facts

Communicating is the most important skill for the project manager. With that in mind, here are some key facts on communication:

- Communication channels formula: $N(N-1)/2$. N represents the number of stakeholders. For example, if you have 10 stakeholders, the formula would read $10(10-1)/2$ for 45 communication channels. Pay special attention to questions wanting to know how many additional communication channels you have based on added stakeholders. For example, if you have 25 stakeholders on your project and have recently added 5 team members, how many additional communication channels do you now have? You'll have to calculate the original number of communication channels, $25(25-1)/2 = 300$; then calculate the new number with the added team members, $30(30-1)/2 = 435$; and finally, subtract the difference between the two: $435 - 300 = 135$, the number of additional communication channels.
- Fifty-five percent of communication is nonverbal.
- Effective listening is the ability to watch the speaker's body language, interpret paralingual clues, and decipher facial expressions. Following the message, effective listening has the listener asking questions to achieve clarity and offering feedback.
- Active listening requires receivers of the message to offer clues, such as nodding to indicate they are listening. It also requires receivers to repeat the message, ask questions, and continue the discussion if clarification is needed.
- Communication can be hindered by trendy phrases, jargon, and extremely pessimistic comments. In addition, other communication barriers include noise, hostility, cultural differences, and technical interruptions.

Risk Management Facts

Risks are unplanned events that can have positive or negative effects on the projects. Most risks are seen as threats to the project's success—but not all risks are bad. For example, there is a 20 percent probability that the project will realize a discount in shipping, which will save the project $15,000. If this risk happens, the project will save money; if the risk doesn't happen, the project will have to spend the $15,000. Risks should be identified as early as possible in the planning process. A person's willingness to accept risk is the utility function (also called the utility theory). The Delphi Technique can be used to build consensus on project risks.

The only output of risk planning is the risk management plan. There are two broad types of risks.

- **Business risk**   The loss of time and finances (where a downside and upside exist)
- **Pure risk**   The loss of life, injury, and theft (where only a downside exists)

Risks can be responded to in one of seven methods.

- **Avoidance**   Avoid the risk by planning a different technique to remove the risk from the project.
- **Mitigation**   Reduce the probability or impact of the risk.
- **Acceptance**   The risk's probability or impact may be small enough that the risk can be accepted.
- **Transference**   The risk is not eliminated, but the responsibility and ownership of the risk is transferred to another party (for example, through insurance).
- **Exploit**   The organization wants to ensure that the identified risk does happen to realize the positive impact associated with the risk event.
- **Share**   Sharing is nice. When sharing, the risk ownership is transferred to the organization that can most capitalize on the risk opportunity.
- **Enhance**   To enhance a risk is to attempt to modify its probability and/or its impacts to realize the most gains from the identified risk.

Risk management also includes the monitoring and controlling of risk characteristics, new risks, and the results of risk responses. Terms that are unique to risk management are:

- **Contingency funds**   Monies reserved for risk events.
- **Secondary risks**   A risk that comes into a project as a direct result of another risk response.

- **Risk triggers**   A condition, event, or warning signs of a risk event that causes a risk reaction.
- **Residual risks**   Risks that remain after a risk response. These are usually small and are accepted by the project team.

Procurement Facts

A contract statement of work (SOW) is provided to the potential sellers so they can create accurate bids, quotes, and proposals for the buyer. A bidders' conference may be held so sellers can query the buyer on the product or service to be procured.

A contract is a formal agreement, preferably written, between a buyer and a seller. On the PMP exam, procurement questions are usually from the buyer's point of view. All requirements the seller is to complete should be clearly written in the contract. Requirements of both parties must be met, or legal proceedings may follow. Table B-3 sums up all the contract types you should know for your exam.

You should also know that *a purchase order* is a unilateral form of contract and that a *letter of intent* is not a contract, but shows the intent of the buyer to purchase from a specific seller.

TABLE B-3	Contract Type	Acronym	Attribute	Risk Issues
Project Management Contract Types	Cost Plus Fixed Fee	CPFF	Actual costs plus profit margin for seller	Cost overruns represent risk to the buyer.
	Cost Plus Percentage of Cost	CPPC	Actual costs plus profit margin for seller	Cost overruns represent risk to the buyer. This is the most dangerous contract type for the buyer.
	Cost Plus Award Fee	CPAF	Actual costs plus an award based on seller-defined objectives for the project	Buyer carries the risk, as the seller is the judge of the contract work and performance.
	Cost Plus Incentive Fee	CPIF	Actual costs plus profit margin for seller	Cost overruns represent risk to the buyer.
	Fixed-Price	FP	Agreed price for contracted product; can include incentives for the seller	Seller assumes risk.
	Fixed Price with Economic Price Adjustment Contracts	FP-EPA	Agreed-upon price for contracted product; can include cost adjustments based on predefined categories of cost	Seller assumes risk.
	Firm Fixed-Price	FFP	Agreed-upon price for contracted product	Seller assumes risk.
	Fixed-Price Incentive Fee	FPIF	Agreed-upon price for contracted product; can include incentives for the seller	Seller assumes risk.
	Time and Materials	T&M	Price assigned for the time and materials provided by the seller.	Contracts without "not-to-exceed" clauses can lead to cost overruns.
	Unit Price		Price assigned for a measurable unit of product or time (for example, $130 for engineer's time on the project)	Risk varies with the product. Time represents the biggest risk if the amount needed is not specified in the contract.

Glossary

360-degree appraisal   A performance review completed by a person's peers, managers, and subordinates. It's called a 360-degree appraisal because it's a circle of reviews by people at different levels of an organization.

acceptance   This is a response to a risk event, generally made when the probability of the event and/or impact are small. It is used when mitigation, transference, or avoidance are not selected.

active listening   This occurs when the receiver confirms the message is being received by feedback, questions, prompts for clarity, and other signs of having received the message.

activity attributes   Activities with special conditions, requirements, risks, and other conditions should be documented.

activity cost estimates   The cost of resources, including materials, services, and, when warranted, labor should be estimated.

activity list   A listing of all of the project activities required to complete each project phase or the entire project. This list is an input to the project network diagram.

activity on node   A network diagramming approach that places the activities on a node in the project network diagram.

activity sequencing   The process of mapping the project activities in the order in which the work should be completed.

actual costs   The amount of funds the project has spent to date. The difference between actual costs and the earned value will reveal the cost variance.

adjourning   The final stage of team development; once the project is done, the team moves on to other assignments, either as a unit or the project team is disbanded and individual team members go on to other work.

affinity diagram   Clusters like ideas together and allows for decomposition of ideas to compare and contrast project requirements.

analogous estimating   This relies on historical information to predict estimates for current projects. Analogous estimating is also known as top-down estimating, and is a form of expert judgment.

application areas   The areas of discipline that a project may center upon. Consider technology, law, sales, marketing, and construction, among many others.

assumption log   A document that clearly identifies and tracks assumptions that are made in the project. All assumptions need to be tested for their validity, and the outcome of the test should be recorded.

autocratic   The project manager makes all of the decisions.

avoidance   This is one response to a risk event. The risk is avoided by planning a different technique to remove the risk from the project.

benchmarking   A process of using prior projects within or external to the performing organization to compare and set quality standards for processes and results.

benefit measurement methods   Project selection methods that compare the benefits of projects to determine which project the organization should invest its funds in.

benefit/cost analysis   The process of determining the pros and cons of any project, process, product, or activity.

benefit/cost ratios   Shows the proportion of benefits to costs; for example, 4:1 would equate to four benefits and just one cost.

bid   A document from the seller to the buyer. Used when price is the determining factor in the decision-making process.

bidder conference   A meeting with prospective sellers to ensure that all sellers have a clear understanding of the product or service to be procured. Bidder conferences allow sellers to query the buyer on the details of the product to help ensure that the proposal the seller creates is adequate and appropriate for the proposed agreement.

bottom-up estimating   A technique where an estimate for each component in the WBS is developed and then totaled for an overall project budget. This is the longest method to complete, but it provides the most accurate estimate.

brainstorming   The most common approach to risk identification; it is performed by a project team to identify the risks within the project. A multidisciplinary team, hosted by a project facilitator, can also perform brainstorming.

budget at completion   The predicted budget for the project; what the project should cost when it is completed. Budget at completion represents 100 percent of the planned value for the project's completion.

cause-and-effect diagrams   Used for root-cause analysis of what factors are creating the risks within the project. The goal is to identify and treat the root of the problem, not the symptom.

centralized contracting   All contracts for all projects need to be approved through a central contracting unit within the performing organization.

change control board   A group of decision makers that reviews proposed project changes.

change control system   A predefined set of activities, forms, and procedures to entertain project change requests.

change log   As changes to the project time, cost, or scope enter the project, they should be recorded in the change log for future reference.

change management plan   When changes are approved for a project, including time, cost, scope, or contract, there needs to be a plan on how the project team will manage these new changes within the project.

chart of accounts   A coding system used by the performing organization's accounting system to account for the project work.

checklists   A listing of activities that workers check to ensure the work has been completed consistently; used in quality control.

closing   The fifth of five project management process groups. It contains the processes responsible for closing a project, a project phase, or the procurement relationships.

coercive power   The project manager uses fear and threats to manage the project team.

collective bargaining agreements   These are contractual agreements initiated by employee groups, unions, or other labor organizations; they may act as a constraint on the project.

communications formula   The formula "N (N – 1)/2" shows the number of communication channels in a project. N represents the total number of stakeholders.

communications management plan   A plan that documents and organizes the stakeholder needs for communication. This plan covers the communications system, its documentation, the flow of communication, modalities of communication, schedules for communications, information retrieval, and any other stakeholder requirements for communications.

composite structure   An organizational structure that uses a blend of the functional, matrix, or projectized organization to operate and manage projects.

compromising   A conflict resolution method; this approach requires both parties to give up something. The decision ultimately made is a blend of both sides of the argument. Because neither party completely wins, it is considered a lose-lose solution.

confidentiality   A project manager should keep certain aspects of a project confidential; consider contract negotiations, human resource issues, and trade secrets of the organization.

configuration management   The control and documentation of the project's product features and functions.

conflict of interest   A situation where the project manager could influence a decision for personal gain.

constrained optimization methods   Complex mathematical models to determine the likelihood of a project's success in order to determine if the organization should invest its funds in the project.

constraints   Anything that limits the project manager's options; for example, time, cost, and scope are always project constraints.

contingency reserve   A time or dollar amount allotted as a response to risk events that may occur within a project.

continuous process improvement   A goal of quality assurance to improve the project's processes and deliverables; meshes with the project's process improvement plan.

contract   A legally binding agreement, preferably written, between a buyer and a seller detailing the requirements and obligations of both parties. Must include an offer, an acceptance, and a consideration.

contract administration   The process of ensuring that the buyer and the seller both perform to the specifications within the contract.

contract change control system   Defines the procedures for how contracts may be changed. Includes the paperwork, tracking, conditions, dispute resolution procedures, and the procedures for getting the changes approved within the performing organization.

contract closeout   A process for confirming that the obligations of the contract were met as expected. The project manager, the customer, the key stakeholder, and, in some instances, the seller complete the product verification together to confirm that the contract has been completed.

contract file   A complete indexed set of records of the procurement process incorporated into the administrative closure process. These records include financial information as well as information on the performance and acceptance of the procured work.

control charts   These illustrate the performance of a project over time. They map the results of inspections against a chart. Control charts are typically used in projects or operations that have repetitive activities, such as manufacturing, test series, or help desk functions. Upper and lower control limits indicate if values are within control or out of control.

cost baseline   This shows what the project is expected to spend. It's usually shown in an S-curve and allows the project manager and management to predict when the project will be spending monies and over what duration. The purpose of the cost baseline is to measure and predict project performance.

cost budgeting   A process of assigning a cost to an individual work package. This process shows costs over time. The cost budget results in an S-curve that becomes the cost baseline for the project.

cost change control   This is part of the integrated change control system and documents the procedures to request, approve, and incorporate changes to project costs.

cost control   An active process to control causes of cost change, document cost changes, and monitor cost fluctuations within the project. When changes occur, the cost baseline must be updated.

cost estimating   The process of calculating the costs, by category, of the identified resources to complete the project work.

cost management plan   Explains how variances to the costs of the project will be managed. The plan may be based on a range of acceptable variances and the expected response to variances over a given threshold.

cost of conformance   The cost of completing the project work to satisfy the project scope and the expected level of quality. Examples include training, safety measures, and quality management activities. Also known as the cost of quality.

cost of nonconformance   The cost of not completing the project with quality; includes wasted time for corrective actions, rework, and wasted materials. Could also mean loss of business, loss of sales, or lawsuits. Also known as the cost of poor quality.

cost performance index   The process of calculating the costs, by category, of the identified resources to complete the project work.

cost plus award fee   This contract requires the buyer to pay for all the project costs and give the seller an award fee based on the project performance, meeting certain project criteria, or other goals established by the buyer. The award fee can be tied to any factor the buyer determines, and the factor doesn't have to be exact.

cost-reimbursable contracts   A contract that pays the seller for the product. In the payment to the seller, there is a profit margin, which is the difference between the actual cost of the product and the sales amount.

cost variance   The difference between the earned value and the actual costs.

crashing   A duration compression technique that adds project resources to the project in an effort to reduce the amount of time allotted for effort-driven activities.

critical chain method   A network diagramming approach that considers the availability of project resources and the project's promised end date to determine the critical path(s) in the project.

critical path method   A network diagramming approach that identifies the project activities that cannot be delayed or the project completion date will be late.

cultural norm   The accepted practices, culture, ideas, vision, and nature of an organization.

culture shock   The initial reaction a person experiences when in a foreign environment.

decision tree analysis   A type of analysis that determines which of two decisions is the best. The decision tree assists in calculating the value of the decision and determining which decision costs the least.

decoder   This is a part of the communications model; it is the inverse of the encoder. If a message is encoded, a decoder translates it back to usable format.

decomposition   The breakdown of the project scope statement into the project's work breakdown structure. The smallest item of the project's decomposition into the WBS is called the work package.

deliverable   A thing that a project creates; projects generally create many deliverables as part of the project work.

Delphi Technique   A method to query experts anonymously on foreseeable risks within the project, phase, or component of the project. The results of the survey are analyzed and organized and then circulated to the experts. There can be several rounds of anonymous discussions with the Delphi Technique. The goal is to gain consensus on project risks, and the anonymous nature of the process ensures that no one expert's advice overtly influences the opinion of another participant.

democratic   The project team is involved in the decision-making process.

design of experiments   This relies on statistical "what-if" scenarios to determine which variables within a project will result in the best outcome; it can also be used to eliminate a defect. The design of experiments approach is most often used on the product of the project, rather than on the project itself.

dictatorship   A group decision-making process where the person with the most power forces the decision even though the rest of the group may oppose the decision.

direct costs   Costs incurred by the project in order for it to exist. Examples include equipment needed to complete the project work, salaries of the project team, and other expenses tied directly to the project's existence.

discretionary dependencies   The order of the project activities do not have to be completed in a particular order, so they can be done in the order of the project manager's or the project team's discretion.

duration estimate   The prediction of how long the project work will take to complete.

earned value   The value of the work that has been completed and the budget for that work: EV = % complete × BAC.

earned value management   Earned value management integrates scope, schedule, and cost to give an objective, scalable, point-in-time assessment of the project. EVM calculates the performance of the project and compares current performance against plan. EVM can also be a harbinger of things to come. Results early in the project can predict the likelihood of the project's success or failure.

effective listening   The receiver is involved in the listening experience by paying attention to visual clues by the speaker and to paralingual intentions and by asking relevant questions.

encoder   Part of the communications model; the device or technology that packages the message to travel over the medium.

enhance   To enhance a risk is to attempt to modify its probability and/or its impacts to realize the most gains from the identified risk.

estimate at completion   A hypothesis of what the total cost of the project will be. Before the project begins, the project manager completes an estimate for the project deliverables based on the WBS. As the project progresses, there will likely be some variances between what the cost estimate was and what the actual cost is. The EAC is calculated to predict what the new estimate at completion will be.

estimate to complete   Represents how much more money is needed to complete the project work: ETC = EAC – AC.

estimating publications   Typically, a commercial reference to help the project estimator confirm and predict the accuracy of estimates. If a project manager elects to use one of these commercial databases, the estimate should include a pointer to this document for future reference and verification.

ethics   Describes the personal, cultural, and organizational interpretation of right and wrong; project managers are to operate ethically and fairly.

ethnocentrism   Happens when individuals measure and compare a foreigner's actions against their own local culture. The locals typically believe their own culture is superior to the foreigner's culture.

evaluation criteria   Used to rate and score proposals from sellers. In some instances, such as a bid or quote, the evaluation criterion is focused just on the price the seller offers. In other instances, such as a proposal, the evaluation criteria can be multiple values: experience, references, certifications, and more.

exceptional   The project manager only pays attention to the top 10 percent and the bottom 10 percent of the project team performers.

executing   The project management process group that carries out the project management plan to create the project deliverables.

Expectancy Theory   People will behave on the basis of what they expect as a result of their behavior. In other words, people will work in relationship to the expected reward of the work.

expert power   A type of power where the authority of the project manager comes from experience with the area that the project focuses on.

exploit   The organization wants to ensure that the identified risk does happen to realize the positive impact associated with the risk event.

facilitated workshop   A collection of stakeholders from around the organization that come together to analyze, discuss, and determine the project requirements.

fast tracking   A schedule compression technique that allows phases to overlap in order to compress the schedule and finish the job faster. Fast tracking does increase project risk.

feedback   Sender confirmation of the message by asking questions, requesting a response, or providing other confirmation signals.

finish-to-finish   A relationship between project activities where the predecessor activities must finish before successor activities may finish.

finish-to-start   A relationship between project activities where the predecessor activities must finish before the successor activities may start; this is the most common network diagramming relationship type.

fixed costs   Costs that remain the same throughout the project.

fixed price with economic price adjustment contracts   A contract for long-term projects that may span years to complete the project work. The contract defines a fixed price, with caveats for special categories of price fluctuation.

fixed-price contracts   Fixed-price contracts are also known as firm fixed-price and lump-sum contracts. These contracts have a preset price that the vendor is obligated to perform the work for or to provide materials for the agreed-upon price.

float   A generic term to describe the amount of time an activity may be delayed without delaying any successor activities' start date.

flow chart   A chart that illustrates how the parts of a system occur in sequence.

FNET   A project constraint that requires an activity to finish no earlier than a specific date.

focus group   A conversation of stakeholders led by a moderator to elicit project requirements.

force majeure   A powerful and unexpected event, such as a hurricane or other disaster.

forcing   A conflict resolution method where one person dominates or forces their point of view or solution to a conflict.

forecast   An educated estimate of how long the project will take to complete. Can also refer to how much the project may cost to complete.

formal power   The type of power where the project manager has been assigned by senior management to be in charge of the project.

forming   The initial stage of team development; the project team meets and learns about their roles and responsibilities on the project.

fragnet   A portion of the project that is usually contracted to a vendor to complete, yet the project work is still represented in the project network diagram.

function analysis   Related to value engineering, this allows team input to the problem, institutes a search for a logical solution, and tests the functions of the product so the results can be graphed.

functional managers   The managers of the permanent staff in each organizational department, line of business, or function such as sales, finance, and technology. Project managers and functional managers interact on project decisions that affect functions, projects, and operations.

functional structure   An organization that groups staff according to their expertise. Entities that have a clear division regarding business units and their associated responsibility. Project managers in functional organizations have little power and report to the functional managers. The project team exists within one department.

future value   A formula to predict the current amount of funds into a future amount of funds. The formula is: future value = present value$(1 + i)^n$, where i is the value of return and n is the number of time periods.

halo effect   When one attribute of a person influences a decision.

hard logic   The project activities must be completed in a particular order; this is also known as mandatory dependencies.

Herzberg's Theory of Motivation   Posits that there are two catalysts for workers: hygiene agents and motivating agents. Hygiene agents do nothing to motivate, but their absence demotivates workers. Hygiene agents are the expectations all workers have: job security, paychecks, clean and safe working conditions, a sense of belonging, civil working relationships, and other basic attributes associated with employment. Motivating agents are components such as reward, recognition, promotion, and other values that encourage individuals to succeed.

histogram   A bar chart; a Pareto diagram is an example of a histogram.

historical information   Any information created in the past that can help the current project succeed.

human resource plan   Defines the management of the project human resources, timing of use, and enterprise environmental factors the project manager must adhere to in the organization.

inappropriate compensation   The project manager is to avoid compensation, such as bribes. The project manager is to act in the best interest of the project and the organization.

indirect costs   These costs can be shared across multiple projects that use the same resources—such as for a training room or piece of equipment.

influence diagram   An influence diagram charts out a decision problem. It identifies all of the elements, variables, decisions, and objectives—and how each factor may influence another.

initiating   The start and authorization of the project; the project manager is identified, the project is authorized through the charter, and the stakeholders are identified.

internal rate of return   A benefit measurement formula to calculate when the present value of the cash inflow equals the project's original investment.

interviews   A requirements elicitation process to collect requirements from the project stakeholders.

invitation for bid   A document from the buyer to the seller. Requests the seller to provide a price for the procured product or service.

Iron Triangle   A term used to describe the three constraints of every project: time, cost, and scope. The sides of the Iron Triangle must be kept in balance, or the quality of the project will suffer.

ISO 9000   An international standard that helps organizations follow their own quality procedures. ISO 9000 is not a quality system, but a method of following procedures created by an organization.

issue   Any point of contention, debate, or decision that has not yet been made in the project that may affect the project's success.

issue log   Issues are decisions that are usually in disagreement among two or more parties. Issues are recorded in the issue log along with an issue owner designation, an issue date for resolution, and the eventual outcome of the issue.

iterative relationships of project phases   Ideal for projects like research. The next phase of the project is not planned until the current phase of the project is underway. The direction of the project can change based on the current work in the project, market conditions, or as more information is discovered.

kill point   An opportunity to halt the project based on project performance in the previous phase. Kill points typically come at the end of a project phase and are also known as phase gates.

knowledge areas   There are nine knowledge areas within project management; each knowledge area is a specific portion of the project, and all nine project management knowledge areas are interrelated.

lag   Time added to a project activity to delay its start time; lag time is considered positive time, and it is sometimes called waiting time.

laissez faire   The project manager has a hands-off policy and the team is entirely self-led regarding the decision-making process.

lead   Time added to activity to allow its start time to begin earlier than scheduled; lead time is negative time, as it moves the activities closer to the project's start date.

lessons learned   Ongoing collection of documentation about what has and has not worked in the project; the project manager and the project team participate in lessons-learned creation.

letter of intent   Expresses the intent of the buyer to procure products or services from the seller. Not the equivalent to a contract.

majority   A group decision-making process where a vote is offered and the majority wins.

make-or-buy analysis   Used in determining what part of the project scope to make and what part to purchase.

management by projects   An organization that uses projects to move the company forward is using the management by projects approach. These project-centric entities could manage any level of their work as a project.

mandatory dependencies   Project activities must happen in a particular order due to the nature of the work; also known as hard logic.

Maslow's Hierarchy of Needs   A theory that states that there are five layers of needs for all humans: physiological, safety, social, esteem, and the crowning jewel, self-actualization.

matrix structure   An organization that groups staff by function but openly shares resources on project teams throughout the organization. Project managers in a matrix structure share the power with functional management. There are three types of matrix structures—weak, balanced, and strong—to describe the amount of authority for the project manager.

McClelland's Theory of Needs   People have three needs: achievement, affiliation, and power. One of the needs drives the person's actions.

McGregor's Theory of X and Y   This theory states that "X" people are lazy, don't want to work, and need to be micromanaged. "Y" people are self-led, motivated, and strive to accomplish.

medium   Part of the communications model; this is the path the message takes from the sender to the receiver. This modality in which the communication travels typically refers to an electronic model, such as e-mail or the telephone.

mind mapping   A visual representation of like and opposing ideas, thoughts, and project requirements.

mitigation   Reducing the probability or impact of a risk.

monitoring and controlling   The project management process group responsible for ensuring that the project execution is completed according to the project management plan and expectations.

Monte Carlo analysis   A what-if scenario to determine how scenarios may work out given any number of variables. The process doesn't actually create a specific answer, but a range of possible answers. When Monte Carlo is applied to a schedule, it can present, for example, the optimistic completion date, the pessimistic completion date, and the most likely completion date for each activity in the project.

murder board   A group of decision makers that may determine to "kill" a proposed project before it is officially launched based on the board's findings on the likelihood of the project's success.

net present value   A benefit measurement formula that provides a precise measurement of the present value of each year the project generates a return on investment.

network template   A network diagram based on previous similar projects that is adapted for the current project work.

nominal group technique   A group creativity technique that follows the brainstorming model but ranks each brainstorm idea.

nonverbal   Approximately 55 percent of oral communication is nonverbal. Facial expressions, hand gestures, and body language contribute to the message.

norming   Project team members go about getting the project work, begin to rely on one another, and generally complete their project assignments.

observation   A requirements elicitation process where the observer shadows a person to understand how they complete a process. Observers may be a participant observer or an invisible observer.

oligopoly   A market condition where the actions of one competitor affect the actions of all the other competitors.

operational definitions   The quantifiable terms and values used to measure a process, activity, or work result. Operational definitions are also known as metrics.

operations   The ongoing work of the business. Operations are a generic way to describe the activities that support the core functions of a business entity.

operations management   Operation managers deal directly with the income-generating products or services the company provides. Projects often affect the core business, so these managers are stakeholders in the project.

organizational breakdown structure   Though these charts are similar to the WBS, the breakdown is by department, units, or team.

organizational charts   These show how an organization, such as a company or large project team, is ordered, the reporting structures, and the flow of information.

Ouchi's Theory Z   This theory posits that workers are motivated by a sense of commitment, opportunity, and advancement. Workers will work if they are challenged and motivated.

overlapping relationship of phases   Allows project phases to overlap to compress the project duration. This is also known as fast tracking.

paralingual   The pitch, tone, and inflections in the sender's voice affect the message being sent.

parametric estimating   Ideal for projects with repetitive work where a parameter, such as five hours per unit, is used to estimate the project duration.

parametric modeling   A mathematical model based on known parameters to predict the cost of a project. The parameters in the model can vary based on the type of work being done. A parameter can be cost per cubic yard, cost per unit, and so on.

Pareto diagram   A Pareto diagram is related to Pareto's Law: 80 percent of the problems come from 20 percent of the issues (this is also known as the "80/20 rule"). A Pareto diagram illustrates problems by assigned cause, from smallest to largest.

Parkinson's Law   Work expands to fill the amount of time allotted to it.

payback period   The duration of time it takes a project to earn back the original investment.

performance reports   These formal reports define how the project is performing on time, cost, scope, quality, and any other relevant information.

performing   If a project team can reach the performing stage of team development, the team members trust one another and work well together, and issues and problems get resolved quickly and effectively.

planned value   The worth of the work that should be completed by a specific time in the project schedule.

planning   The iterative process group where the intention of the project is determined and documented in the project management plan.

plurality   A group decision-making process approach that allows the biggest section of a group to win even if a majority doesn't exist.

PMBOK Guide   The abbreviated definition for PMI's *A Guide to the Project Management Body of Knowledge*.

PMI Code of Ethics and Professional Conduct   A PMI document that defines the expectations of its members to act responsibly, respectfully, fairly, and honestly in their leadership of projects and programs.

PMIS   A project management information system is typically a software system, such as Microsoft Project, used to assist the project manager in managing the project.

PMP   Your goal. A PMP is certified by the Project Management Institute as a Project Management Professional.

portfolio management review board   A collection of organizational decision makers, usually executives, that reviews proposed projects and programs for their value and return on investment for the organization.

precedence diagramming method   The most common method of arranging the project work visually. The PDM puts the activities in boxes, called nodes, and connects the boxes with arrows. The arrows represent the relationships and the dependencies of the work packages.

present value   A benefit measurement formula to determine what a future amount of funds is worth today. The formula is Present Value = Future Value $/ (1 + i)^n$, where i is the value of return and n is the number of time periods.

problem solving   The ability to determine the best solution for a problem in a quick and efficient manner.

process adjustments   When quality is lacking, process adjustments are needed for immediate corrective actions or for future preventive actions to ensure that quality improves. Process adjustments may qualify for a change request and be funneled through the change control system as part of integration management.

process improvement plan   Identifies methods to track and eliminate waste and non-value-added activities.

procurement   The process of a seller soliciting, selecting, and paying for products or services from a buyer.

procurement audits   The successes and failures within the procurement process are reviewed from procurement planning through contract administration. The intent of the audit is to learn from what worked and what did not work during the procurement processes.

procurement documents   All of the documents for purchasing, such as requests for quotes, invitations to bid, and requests for proposal, and the responses are stored as part of the project documentation.

procurement management plan   Describes the procurement process from solicitation to source selection. The plan may also include the requirements for selection as set by the organization.

product life cycle   The unique life, duration, and support of the thing a project creates. Product life cycles are separate from the project life cycle.

product scope   The attributes and characteristics of the deliverables the project is creating.

program manager   Coordinates the efforts of multiple projects working together in the program. Programs are comprised of projects, so it makes sense that the program manager would be a stakeholder in each of the projects within the program, right?

programs   A collection of projects working in unison to realize benefits that could not be achieved by managing each project independently of one another.

progress reports   These provide current information on the project work completed to date.

progressive elaboration   The process of starting with a large idea and, through incremental analysis, actions, and planning, the idea becomes more specific. Progressive elaboration is the generally accepted planning process for project management, wherein the project management team starts broad and works towards a specific, detailed plan.

project   An undertaking outside of normal operations to create a unique product, service, condition, or result. Projects are temporary, while operations are ongoing.

project baselines   There are three baselines in a project that are used to measure project performance: cost, schedule, and scope.

project calendar   A calendar that defines the working times for the project. For example, a project may require the project team to work nights and weekends so as not to disturb the ongoing operations of the organization during working hours. In addition, the project calendar accounts for holidays, working hours, and work shifts the project will cover.

project charter   A document that authorizes the project, defines the high-level requirements, identifies the project manager and the project sponsor, and provides initial information about the project.

project communications management   One of the nine project management knowledge areas; it is the planning and management of communication among project stakeholders. (See Chapter 10.)

project cost management   One of the nine project management knowledge areas; it is the estimating, budgeting, and controlling of the project expenses. (See Chapter 7.)

project customer/end user   The person or group that will use the project deliverable. In some instances, a project may have many different customers.

project funding requirements   In larger projects, this document identifies the timeline of when capital is required for the project to move forward. This document defines the amount of funds a project needs in order to reach its objectives and when the project funds are needed.

project governance   Defines the rules for a project. It's up to the project manager to enforce the project governance to ensure the project's ability to reach its objectives. The project management plan defines the project governance and how the project manager, the project team, and the organization will all follow the rules and policies within the project.

project human resource management   One of the nine project management knowledge areas; projects are completed by people, and the project manager generally oversees the management of the human resources on the project team. (See Chapter 9.)

project integration management   One of the nine project management knowledge areas; this knowledge area coordinates the activities and completeness of the other eight knowledge areas. (See Chapter 4.)

project life cycle   Unique to each project and comprised of phases of work. Project life cycles typically create a milestone and allow subsequent phases to begin.

project management The management of the projects within an organization. It is the initiation, planning, executing, monitoring and controlling, and closing of the temporary endeavor of the project.

Project management integration A project management knowledge area that coordinates all of the effort of the project's initiation, planning, executing, monitoring and controlling, and closing.

project management office (PMO) Organizes and manages control over all projects within an organization. PMOs may also be known as a program management office, project office, or simply the program office. Coordinates all aspects, methodology, and nomenclature for project processes, templates, software, and resource assignment.

project management team People on the project team who are involved with managing the project.

project manager The person accountable for managing the project; guides the team through the project phases to completion.

project plan A comprehensive document comprised of several subsidiary plans that communicates the intent and direction of the project.

project portfolio management A management process to select the projects that should be invested in. Specifically, it is the selection process based on the need, profitability, and affordability of the proposed projects.

project procurement management One of the nine project management knowledge areas; this knowledge area oversees the purchasing and contract administration for a project. (See Chapter 12.)

project quality management One of the nine project management knowledge areas; this knowledge area defines quality assurance, quality control, and the quality policy for the project. (See Chapter 8.)

project risk management A project management knowledge area that creates the risk management plan, performs qualitative and quantitative risk analysis, plans risk responses, and monitors and controls the project risks.

project scope management A project management knowledge area responsible for collecting project requirements, defining the project scope, creating the WBS, performing scope verification, and controlling the project scope. The project scope statement includes the product scope description, product acceptance criteria, project deliverables, project exclusions, project assumptions, and project constraints.

project sponsor Authorizes the project. This person or group ensures that the project manager has the necessary resources, including monies, to get the work done. The project sponsor is someone within the performing organization who has the power to authorize and sanction the project work, and is ultimately accountable for the project's success.

project team The collection of individuals that will work together to ensure the success of the project. The project manager works with the project team to guide, schedule, and oversee the project work. The project team completes the project work.

project time management A project management knowledge area that defines the project activities, sequences project work, estimates resources and activity durations, and develops the project schedule. This knowledge area is also responsible for controlling the project schedule.

projectized structure Group of employees, collocated or not, by activities on a particular project. The project manager in a projectized structure may have complete, or very close to complete, power over the project team.

proposal A document from the seller to the buyer, responding to a request for proposal or other procurement documents. Proposals are an exposé on ideas, suggestions, recommendations, and solutions to an opportunity provided by a vendor for a seller. Proposals include a price for the work and document how the vendor would provide the service to the buyer.

prototype A mockup of the project deliverable to confirm, adapt, or develop the project requirements.

qualified sellers list The performing organization may have lists of qualified sellers, preferred sellers, or approved sellers. The qualified sellers list generally has contact information, history of past experience with the sellers, and other pertinent information.

qualitative risk analysis   An examination and prioritization of the risks based on their probability of occurring and the impact on the project if they do occur. Qualitative risk analysis guides the risk reaction process.

quality assurance   An executing process to ensure that the project is adhering to the quality expectations of the project customer and organization. QA is a prevention-driven process to perform the project work with quality to avoid errors, waste, and delays.

quality audits   A quality audit is a process to confirm that the quality processes are performing correctly on the current project. The quality audit determines how to make things better for the project and other projects within the organization. Quality audits measure the project's ability to maintain the expected level of quality.

quality control   A process in which the work results are monitored to see if they meet relevant quality standards.

quality function   A philosophy and a practice to fully understand customer needs—both spoken and implied—without gold-plating the project deliverables.

quality management plan   This document describes how the project manager and the project team will fulfill the quality policy. In an ISO 9000 environment, the quality management plan is referred to as the "project quality system."

quality policy   The formal policy an organization follows to achieve a preset standard of quality. The project team should either adapt the quality policy of the organization to guide the project implementation or create its own policy if one does not exist within the performing organization.

quantitative risk analysis   A numerical assessment of the probability and impact of the identified risks. Quantitative risk analysis also creates an overall risk score for the project.

quote   A document from the seller to the buyer; used when price is the determining factor in the decision-making process.

RACI chart   A chart designates each team member against each project activity as either Responsible, Accountable, Consult, or Inform (RACI). A RACI chart is technically a type of responsibility assignment matrix chart.

receiver   Part of the communications model; the recipient of the message.

referent power   Power that is present when the project team is attracted to, or wants to work on the project or with, the project manager. Referent power also exists when the project manager references another, more powerful person, such as the CEO.

request for proposal   A document from the buyer to the seller that asks the seller to provide a proposal for completing the procured work or for providing the procured product.

request for quote   A document from the buyer to the seller asking the seller to provide a price for the procured product or service.

requirements documentation   A clearly defined explanation of the project requirements. The requirements must be measurable, complete, accurate, and signed off by the project stakeholders.

requirements management plan   Defines how requirements will be managed throughout the phases of the project. This plan also defines how any changes to the requirements will be allowed, documented, and tracked through project execution.

requirements traceability matrix   A table that identifies all of the project requirements, when the requirements are due, when the requirements are created, and any other pertinent information about the requirements.

residual risks   Risks that are left over after mitigation, transference, and avoidance. These are generally accepted risks. Management may elect to add contingency costs and time to account for the residual risks within the project.

resource breakdown structure   This type of chart breaks down the project by types of resources utilized on it no matter where the resource is being utilized in the project.

resource calendar   The resource calendar shows when resources, such as project team members, consultants, and SMEs, are available to work on the project. It takes into account vacations, other commitments within the organization, restrictions on contracted work, overtime issues, and so on.

resource histogram   A bar chart reflecting when individual employees, groups, or communities are involved in a project. Often used by management to see when employees are most or least active in a project.

resource-leveling heuristics   A method to flatten the schedule when resources are overallocated or allocated unevenly. Resource leveling can be applied in different methods to accomplish different goals. One of the most common methods is to ensure that workers are not overextended on activities.

resource requirements   The identification of what resources are needed to complete the project work as a supporting document for planning. This includes people, materials, equipment, facilities, and services.

responsibility   The person who decides what will happen in a particular area of a project.

responsibility assignment matrix   A chart type designating the roles and responsibilities of the project team.

reward power   The project manager's authority to reward the project team.

risk   An uncertain event that can have a positive or negative influence on the project's success. It can affect the project costs, project schedule, and often both. All risks and their status should be recorded in the risk register.

risk categories   These help organize, rank, and isolate risks within the project.

risk management plan   A subsidiary project plan for determining how risks will be identified, how quantitative and qualitative analysis will be completed, how risk response planning will happen, how risks will be monitored, and how ongoing risk management activities will occur throughout the project life cycle.

risk owners   The individuals or groups responsible for a risk response.

risk register   A risk is an uncertain event or condition that can have a positive or negative effect on the project. All risks, regardless of their probability or impact, are recorded in the issue log and their status is kept current.

role   Who does what types of activities in a project.

roles and responsibilities   Maps project roles to responsibilities within the project; roles are positions on the project team, and responsibilities are project activities.

run chart   Similar to a control chart, a run chart tracks trends over time and displays those trends in a graph with each plotted data mapped to a specific date.

Sapir-Whorf hypothesis   A theory that suggest there's a linkage between the language a person (or culture) speaks and how that person or culture behaves in the world.

scales of probability and impact   Used in a risk matrix in both qualitative and quantitative risk analyses to score each risk's probability and impact.

scatter diagram   Tracks the relationship between two or more variables to determine if one variable affects the other. It allows the project team, quality control team, or project manager to make adjustments to improve the overall results of the project.

schedule control   Part of integrated change management, schedule control is concerned with three processes: the project manager confirms that any schedule changes are agreed upon; the project manager examines the work results and project conditions to know if the schedule has changed; and the project manager manages the actual change in the schedule.

schedule management plan   A subsidiary plan of the overall project plan. It is used to control changes to the schedule. A formal schedule management plan has procedures that control how changes to the project plan can be proposed, accounted for, and then implemented. Identifies circumstances that may change the project schedule, such as the completion of project phases or the reliance on other projects and outside resources.

schedule performance index   This reveals the efficiency of work. The closer the quotient is to 1, the better: $SPI = EV / PV$.

schedule variance   The difference between the planned work and the earned work.

scope baseline   Comprised of the project scope statement, the work breakdown structure, and the WBS dictionary.

scope management plan   Explains how the project scope will be managed and how scope changes will be factored into the project plan. Based on the conditions of the project, the project work, and the confidence of the project scope, the scope management plan should also define the likelihood of changes to the scope, how often the scope may change, and how much the scope can change.

scope verification   An inspection-driven process led by the project customer to determine the exactness of the project deliverables. Scope verification is a process that leads to customer acceptance of the project deliverables.

scoring models   A project selection method that assigns categories and corresponding values to measure a project's worthiness of investment.

secondary risks   Risks that stem from risk responses. For example, the response of transference may call for hiring a third party to manage an identified risk. A secondary risk caused by the solution is the failure of the third party to complete its assignment as scheduled. Secondary risks must be identified, analyzed, and planned for, just as any identified risk is.

sellers and business partners   Vendors, contractors, and business partners that help projects achieve their objectives. These business partners can affect the project's success and are considered stakeholders in the project.

sellers list   A listing of the vendors an organization does business with. You might know this document as a preferred vendors list in your company.

sender   Part of the communications model; the person or group delivering the message to the receiver.

sensitivity analysis   This examines each project risk on its own merit to assess its impact on the project. Each risk is analyzed independently to see what its impact on the project may be, while all other risks in the project are set at a baseline value.

sequential relationship of phases   Each phase of a project relies on the completion of the phase before it can begin.

share   Sharing is nice. When sharing, the risk ownership is transferred to the organization that can most capitalize on the risk opportunity.

should-cost estimates   These estimates are created by the performing organization to predict what the cost of the procured product should be. If there is a significant difference between what the organization has predicted and what the sellers have proposed, either the statement of work was inadequate or the sellers have misunderstood the requirements.

simulation   This allows the project team to play "what-if" games without affecting any areas of production.

single source   A specific seller that the performing organization prefers to contract with.

smoothing   A conflict resolution method that "smoothes" out the conflict by minimizing the perceived size of the problem. It is a temporary solution, but it can calm team relations and reduce boisterousness of discussions. Smoothing may be acceptable when time is of the essence or any of the proposed solutions would work.

SNET   A project constraint that demands that a project activity start no earlier than a specific date.

soft logic   The preferred order of activities. Project managers should use these relationships at their "discretion" and document the logic behind making soft logic decisions. Discretionary dependencies allow activities to happen in a preferred order because of best practices, conditions unique to the project work, or external events; also known as discretionary dependencies.

sole source   The only qualified seller that exists in the marketplace.

source selection criteria   A predefined listing of the criteria to determine how a vendor will be selected—for example, cost, experience, certifications, and the like.

staffing management plan   This subsidiary plan documents how project team members will be brought on to the project and excused from it. This plan is contained in the human resources plan.

stakeholder analysis   A process that considers and ranks the project stakeholders based on their influence, interests, and expectations of the project.

stakeholder registry   A document defining each stakeholder, their project requirements, influence on the project, phases of interest, details on the stakeholders' contributions, and their contact information for the project.

start-to-finish   A relationship structure that requires an activity to start so that a successor activity may finish; it is unusual and is rarely used.

start-to-start   A relationship structure that requires a task to start before a successor task activity may start. This relationship allows both activities to happen in tandem.

statement of work   This fully describes the work to be completed, the product to be supplied, or both. The SOW becomes part of the contract between the buyer and the seller. The SOW is typically created as part of the procurement planning process and is used by the seller to determine whether it can meet the project's requirements.

statistical sampling   A process of choosing a percentage of results at random for inspection. Statistical sampling can reduce the costs of quality control.

status reports   These provide current information on the project cost, budget, scope, and other items of relevance.

storming   The second stage of team development; the project team struggles for project positions, leadership, and project direction.

subprojects   A subproject exists under a parent project but follows its own schedule to completion. Subprojects may be outsourced, assigned to other project managers, or managed by the parent project manager but with a different project team.

supporting detail for estimates   The project manager should document how time and cost estimates were created.

system or process flow charts   These show the relationship between components and how the overall process works. They are useful for identifying risks between system components.

systems engineering   Focuses on satisfying the customers' needs, cost requirements, and quality demands through the design and creation of the product. There is an entire science devoted to systems engineering in various industries.

teaming agreement   A contractual agreement that defines the roles, responsibilities, considerations, and partnerships of two or more organizations that work together in a project. It's not unlike a partnership or subcontractor relationship.

three-point estimate   An estimate that uses optimistic, most likely, and pessimistic values to determine the cost or duration of a project component.

time and materials   A contract type where the seller charges the buyer for the time and materials for the work completed. T&M contracts should have a not-to-exceed clause (NTE) to contain costs.

to-complete performance index   An earned value management formula that can forecast the likelihood of a project to achieve its goals based on what's currently happening in the project.

top-down estimating   A technique that bases the current project's estimate on the total of a similar project. A percentage of the similar project's total cost may be added to or subtracted from the total, depending on the size of the current project.

transference   A response to risks in which the responsibility and ownership of the risk is transferred to another party (for example, through insurance).

trend analysis   Trend analysis is taking past results to predict future performance.

triggers   Warning signs or symptoms that a risk has occurred or is about to occur (for example, a vendor failing to complete its portion of the project as scheduled).

Triple Constraints of Project Management   Describes the required balance of time, cost, and scope for a project. The Triple Constraints of Project Management is also defined by the Iron Triangle of Project Management.

unanimity   A group decision-making process where all participants are in agreement.

utility function   A person's willingness to accept risk.

value analysis   Similar to value engineering, this focuses on the cost/quality ratio of the product. Value analysis focuses on the expected quality against the acceptable cost.

value engineering   Deals with reducing costs and increasing profits, all while improving quality. Its focus is on solving problems, realizing opportunities, and maintaining quality improvement.

variable costs   Costs that vary depending on the conditions within the project.

variance   The time or cost difference between what was planned and what was actually experienced.

virtual teams   Project teams that are not collocated and may rarely, if ever, meet face-to-face with other project team members. The virtual team relies on e-mail, video, and telephone conferences to communicate on the project.

voice of the customer   The initial collection of customer requirements that serves as part of the quality function deployment in a facilitated workshop.

war room   A centralized office or locale for the project manager and the project team to work on the project. It can house information on the project, including documentation and support materials. It allows the project team to work in close proximity.

withdrawal   A conflict resolution method that is used when the issue is not important or the project manager is outranked. The project manager pushes the issue aside for later resolution. It can also be used as a method for cooling down. The conflict is not resolved, and it is considered a yield-lose solution.

work breakdown structure   A decomposition of the project scope statement into work packages. The WBS is an input to seven project management processes: developing the project management plan, defining the project activities, estimating the project costs, determining the project budget, planning the project quality, identifying the project risks, and planning the project procurement needs.

work breakdown structure dictionary   A companion to the WBS, this document defines all of the characteristics of each element of the WBS.

work breakdown structure templates   Based on historical information, this is a WBS from a past project that has been adapted to the current project.

work performance information   The current status of the project work; includes the results of activities, corrective and preventive action status, forecasts for activity completion, and other relevant information.

work performance measurements   These are predefined metrics for measuring project performance, such as cost variances, schedule variances, and estimate to complete.

workarounds   Workarounds are unplanned responses to risks that were not identified or that were accepted.

INDEX

E

F